Effective Crime Reduction Strategies

International Perspectives

T0383753

International Police Executive Symposium Co-Publications

Dilip K. Das, *Founding President-IPES*

PUBLISHED

Global Trafficking in Women and Children
By Obi N.I. Ebbe and Dilip K. Das, ISBN: 978-1-4200-5943-4

Contemporary Issues in Law Enforcement and Policing
By Andrew Millie and Dilip K. Das, ISBN: 978-1-4200-7215-0

Trends in Policing: Interviews with Police Leaders Across the Globe, Volume Two
By Dilip K. Das and Otwin Marenin, ISBN: 978-1-4200-7520-5

Criminal Abuse of Women and Children: An International Perspective
By Obi N.I. Ebbe and Dilip K. Das, ISBN: 978-1-4200-8803-8

Urbanization, Policing, and Security: Global Perspectives
By Gary Cordner, AnnMarie Cordner and Dilip K. Das, ISBN: 978-1-4200-8557-0

Global Environment of Policing
By Dilip K. Das, Darren Palmer, and Michael M. Berlin, ISBN: 978-1-4200-6590-9

Trends in Policing: Interviews with Police Leaders Across the Globe, Volume Three
By Otwin Marenin and Dilip K. Das, ISBN: 978-1-4398-1924-1

Police Without Borders: The Fading Distinction between Local and Global
By Cliff Roberson, Dilip K. Das, and Jennie K. Singer, ISBN: 978-1-4398-0501-5

Effective Crime Reduction Strategies: International Perspectives
By James F. Albrecht and Dilip K. Das, ISBN: 978-1-4200-7838-1

FORTHCOMING

Policing Neoliberal Societies
By Allison Wakefield, Bankole Cole, and Dilip K. Das, ISBN: 978-1-4398-4135-8

Terrorism, Counterterrorism, and Internal Wars: Examining International Political Violence
By Austin Turk, Dilip K. Das, and James Ross, ISBN: 978-1-4398-2104-6

Strategies and Responses to Crime: Thinking Locally, Acting Globally
By Melchor de Guzman, Aieteo Mintie Das, and Dilip K. Das, ISBN: 978-1-4200-7669-1

Justices of the World: Their Views, Opinions and Perspectives
By Chandrika M. Kelso and Dilip K. Das, ISBN: 978-1-4200-9978-2

Cross Cultural Profiles of Policing
By Dilip K. Das, Osman Dolu, and Bonnie Mihalka, ISBN: 978-1-4200-7014-9

*ENHANCING LAW ENFORCEMENT PROFESSIONALISM,
EFFECTIVENESS AND LEADERSHIP IN THE 21ST CENTURY*

Effective
Crime
Reduction
Strategies

International Perspectives

Edited by
James Albrecht and Dilip K. Das

International Police Executive Symposium
Co-Publication

CRC Press is an imprint of the
Taylor & Francis Group, an **informa** business

CRC Press
Taylor & Francis Group
6000 Broken Sound Parkway NW, Suite 300
Boca Raton, FL 33487-2742

First issued in paperback 2019

ISBN-13: 978-1-4200-7838-1 (hbk)
ISBN-13: 978-0-367-86533-7 (pbk)

Library of Congress Cataloging-in-Publication Data

Effective crime reduction strategies : international perspectives / edited by James F. Albrecht,
  Dilip K. Das.
      p. cm.
      Summary: "Police worldwide are finding it increasingly difficult to prevent crime and maintain public safety and a sense of security while dealing with decreasing budgets and personnel. The exchange of effective crime fighting principles and proven best practices is crucial to helping them succeed. Drawn from the proceedings at the 2005 IPES meeting in the Czech Republic on effective crime prevention, this book addresses the impact of terrorism and transnational crime on law enforcement in the U.S. and Europe, the effects of democratic reforms on policing, and the positive influence of the unionization of police forces. It also reviews counterterrorism, border control, transnational criminality, measurement of police effectiveness, and the investigation of juvenile crimes."-- Provided by publisher.
      Includes bibliographical references and index.
      ISBN 978-1-4200-7838-1 (hardback)
      1. Crime prevention--Congresses. 2. Transnational crime--Prevention--Congresses. 3. Terrorism--Prevention--Congresses. I. Albrecht, James F. II. Das, Dilip K., 1941-

HV7431.E245 2010
364.4--dc22   2010031212

Visit the Taylor & Francis Web site at
http://www.taylorandfrancis.com

and the CRC Press Web site at
http://www.crcpress.com

This book is dedicated to my parents, James and Christa Albrecht, who ensured that I knew the difference between right and wrong and who recognized the benefits of a university education.

The book is also dedicated to police officers across the world that have made the ultimate sacrifice in the pursuit of justice and democracy, including the 66 heroes who perished at my side while at the World Trade Center on September 11, 2001.

James F. Albrecht

This book is dedicated to my wife, Dr. Ana Mijovic-Das, MD, and daughter, Mintie, who have both been supportive and patient as I have pursued my professional projects.

Dilip K. Das

Table of Contents

Part VI
SIGNIFICANT ISSUES FACING TWENTY-FIRST CENTURY LAW ENFORCEMENT

Foreword

The comparative approach to learning is generally felt to be of a higher cognitive level and to provide the opportunity to "search for order." A comparative view of foreign justice systems therefore provides an opportunity for students to better assess and put into perspective the role and functions of their own justice system, and it allows us to look for the common properties of these systems. Furthermore, any study of a venue's policing system will also, by extension, permit one to study that venue's human rights position; each government uses its police system to enforce its rule of law—however democratic or autocratic it might be.

As one who has instructed upper-division comparative criminal justice system courses for many years, and conducted national surveys concerning such courses (subsequently publishing the findings in the *Journal of Criminal Justice Education*), I am very enthusiastic about the publication of this most needed book—and, frankly, cannot wait to obtain my copy and put it to good use in my comparative criminal justice course offerings.

Crime is an international problem, and human rights an international concern. There has come to pass a globalization of life, in general, and of crime, in particular. Crime easily transcends national borders; the fruits of those crimes are likewise dispatched with ease across geographical boundaries, to be laundered and used for the furtherance of criminal enterprises. Crime and social justice issues are clearly transcontinental, and thus it is very important to understand the structure and function of international policing systems.

This book examines most, if not all, of the prevailing social issues that encircle and engulf our world, and I am particularly struck by the breadth, depth, and contemporaneous nature of the chapters contained herein. Those chapters include, but are not limited to, crime prevention, information systems and technology, trafficking of human beings, policing reform, community policing of crime and disorder, crime in the schools, HIV and AIDS in Africa, intelligence-led policing, the rule of law, ethical dilemmas, and the promoting of accountability, policing terrorism, and crimes involving juvenile victims.

Additionally, the book is divided nicely into six disparate parts; doing so serves to organize the contents very appropriately and conveniently for the reader. It is doubtful that one could find two individuals who are better suited to serve as coeditors for an international policing tour de force such as this, and I am proud to say I have been professionally associated with both "Jimmy" Albrecht and Dilip Das for more than 15 years. They are widely traveled, and each possesses an enviable level of academic and police practitioner/administrative experience.

Jimmy Albrecht is a 20-year veteran of the New York City Police Department, retiring as captain and possessing two bachelor's and numerous master's degrees in fields in which he studied international affairs and criminal justice. He is also highly experienced as an academician, having received a prestigious Fulbright Fellowship, instructed at the National Police College of Finland, and lectured in China, Taiwan, Russia, Germany, Austria, Sweden, Norway, Estonia, Finland, Italy, Kosovo, Macedonia, and Canada. He serves as a consultant to the United Nations, the European Union, and the U.S. government.

Dr. Das has also traveled extensively as an international police researcher, and is connected globally in academia. He served as a chief executive officer in the Indian Police Service, and is the founding president of the International Police Executive Symposium and the founding editor of *Police Practice and Research: An International Journal.* He has also authored, edited, and coedited more than 30 books and numerous articles and is a long-standing human rights consultant to the United Nations.

In sum, while other books may look at international policing systems and focus on their history, forms of government, or responses to different forms of crime, and/or only examine policing in a handful of venues, none that I am aware of fills the gap, as this one does, in looking at international policing in terms of crime problems and issues against a backdrop of professionalism, effectiveness, and leadership. I wholeheartedly recommend this book to your own "must-read" list, whether a faculty member, criminal justice practitioner, or an aspiring student of the field.

Ken Peak
University of Nevada
Reno, Nevada

Preface

This book consists of thoroughly revised, fully updated, and meticulously edited papers that were presented at the *Thirteenth Annual Meeting of International Police Executive Symposium*, IPES, www.IPES.info, in Prague, the Czech Republic. A few papers that were considered for publication in *Police Practice and Research: An International Journal* (PPR), the official journal of the IPES, have also been included in this book because, during the peer-review process, these were found to be more suitable as book chapters. Moreover, the topics of these papers were compatible with the theme of the IPES Prague book.

As always, Carolyn Spence, acquisition editor, CRC Press/Taylor & Francis Group, has been of enormous help, and a source of inspiration, motivation, and guidance in the preparation of this book. It is always a pleasure to work with the production staff of CRC Press. We offer heartfelt thanks to all of them.

The book would not have been possible without the generous help and magnificent support of the Police Academy of the Czech Republic in hosting the *Thirteenth IPES Annual Meeting*. Our thanks are due in abundant measure to the administration and the faculty members of the academy.

Finally, I would like to thank all the contributors for their wonderful efforts. Special mention to my most able and outstanding coeditor, James Albrecht, for his tireless efforts to make this book a reality, and to Dr. Ken Peak for writing the foreword to this book.

Dilip K. Das
International Police Executive Symposium

Editors

James F. Albrecht is presently serving in the joint United States and European Union Rule of Law Mission (EULEX) in Kosovo (former Yugoslavia) as the police chief in charge of all critical criminal investigations. Chief Albrecht had previously been assigned to the United Nations Police in Kosovo as an intelligence analyst and United States liaison to the European Union Police. Albrecht is also a 20-year veteran of the New York Police Department (NYPD). He retired as the commanding officer of NYPD Transit Bureau District 20, responsible for the supervision and prevention of crime in the subway and rapid transit system. He was a first responder and FEMA incident commander at the September 11, 2001 terrorist attack on the World Trade Center and the November 12, 2001 commercial airliner accident in Queens, New York City. He received two bachelor's degrees in biology and German language and culture from New York University, New York, in 1983; a master's degree in criminal justice from the State University of New York at Albany, New York, in 1990; a master's degree in human physiology from the City University of New York (CUNY) at Queens College in 1992; and a master's degree in history from the City University of New York at Queens College in 2006. He also completed extensive doctoral studies in criminal justice at both Sam Houston State University in Texas and John Jay College of Criminal Justice (CUNY). Albrecht served as a professor and graduate coordinator of the Criminal Justice Leadership Masters Degree Program at St. John's University in New York City from 2004 through 2007. He received a prestigious Fulbright Fellowship in 1998 and worked as a professor at the National Police College of Finland.

Dilip K. Das joined the Indian Police Service, an elite national service with a glorious tradition, after obtaining his master's degree in English literature. Following 14 years in law enforcement service as a police executive including his promotion to chief of police, he moved to the United States where he received another master's degree in criminal justice as well as a doctorate in the same discipline. Founding president of the International Police Executive Symposium (IPES) and founding editor of *Police Practice and Research: An International Journal*, Dr. Das has authored, edited, and coedited more than 30 books and numerous articles. He has traveled extensively throughout the world in comparative police research, as a visiting professor in various universities, for organizing annual conferences of the IPES, and as a human rights consultant to the United Nations. Dr. Das has received several faculty excellence awards and was a distinguished faculty lecturer.

Contributors

James F. Albrecht
New York City Police Department (ret.)
New York, New York

A. Oyesoji Aremu
Department of Guidance and Counselling
University of Ibadan
Ibadan, Nigeria

Christiaan Bezuidenhout
Department of Social Work and
    Criminology
University of Pretoria
Pretoria, South Africa

Norman Conti
Sociology Department
Duquesne University
Pittsburgh, Pennsylvania

Ronald G. DeLord
Combined Law Enforcement Associations
    of Texas
Austin, Texas

Christopher Devery
New South Wales Police Force
Golburn, New South Wales, Australia

Maximilian Edelbacher
Vienna University of Economics
Vienna, Austria

Siva Ganesh
Institute of Fundamental Sciences
Massey University
Palmerston North, New Zealand

Rune Glomseth
Norway Police University
Oslo, Norway

Petter Gottschalk
Department of Leadership and
    Organizational Management
Norwegian School of Management
Oslo, Norway

David Griffin
Canadian Police Association
Ottawa, Ontario, Canada

Belinda L. Guadagno
School of Psychology
Deakin University
Burwood, Victoria, Australia

Robert D. Hanser
Department of Criminal Justice
University of Louisiana at Monroe
Monroe, Louisiana

Dee Wood Harper, Jr.
Department of Criminal Justice
Loyola University
New Orleans, Louisiana

Garth den Heyer
Security, Counter Terrorism and
    Emergency Planning
New Zealand Police
Wellington, New Zealand

Saima Husain
AWAZ–Voices Against Violence Unit
South Asian Network
Artesia, California

Tülin Günşen İçli
Department of Sociology
Hacettepe University
Ankara, Turkey

A.A. Jones
Department of Guidance and Counselling
University of Ibadan
Ibadan, Nigeria

Larry Karson
Department of Criminal Justice
University of Houston–Downtown
Houston, Texas

Attapol Kuanliang
Department of Criminal Justice
University of Louisiana at Monroe
Monroe, Louisiana

Bruno Meini
Faculty of Education
University of L'Aquila
L'Aquila, Italy

Adrianus Meliala
Department of Criminology
University of Indonesia
Depok, Indonesia

Jean Louis Messing
Office of National Security, Northwest
   Region
Bamenda, Cameroon

Scott Mire
Criminal Justice Department
University of Louisiana at Lafayette
Lafayette, Louisiana

Margaret Mitchell
Faculty of Criminology
Edith Cowan University
Perth, Australia

Zsolt Molnar
Crime Prevention Academy
Budapest, Hungary

Gwen Moity Nolan
New Orleans Police Department
New Orleans, Louisiana

James J. Nolan, III
Division of Sociology and Anthropology
West Virginia University
Morgantown, West Virginia

Greg O'Connor
New Zealand Police Association
Wellington, New Zealand

Willard M. Oliver
College of Criminal Justice
Sam Houston State University
Huntsville, Texas

Michelle Owen
Department of Criminal Justice and Legal
   Studies
University of West Florida
Pensacola, Florida

Rick Parent
School of Criminology
Simon Fraser University
Burnaby, British Columbia, Canada

Seong min Park
Criminal Justice and Legal Assistant
   Studies
The University of Tennessee at Chattanooga
Chattanooga, Tennessee

Martine B. Powell
School of Psychology
Deakin University
Burwood, Victoria, Australia

Sebastián Sal
Sal & Morchio, Attorneys at Law
Buenos Aires, Argentina

Cheryl Swanson
Department of Criminal Justice and Legal
   Studies
University of West Florida
Pensacola, Florida

Lindsay K. Wight
Grand Valley State University
Grand Rapids, Michigan

Abbey Witbooi
Police and Prisons Civil Rights Union
Johannesburg, South Africa

Kam C. Wong
Department of Criminal Justice
Xavier University
Cincinnati, Ohio

Introduction

As the world moved quietly into the twenty-first century, the role of technology in the quest to reduce and prevent crime was made obvious as crime mapping and "hot-spot" deployment replaced community policing as the primary crime-fighting initiative. Along with other factors, such as demographic shifts and economic stability, strategic deployment of law enforcement personnel has led to dramatic reductions in crime rate, not only in the United States, but also in other democracies. However, less than two years into the new millennium, society was faced with a larger dilemma as the atrocious terrorist attacks in the United States on September 11, 2001, brought a new priority to the attention of police administrators and government leaders across the globe. Subsequent attacks in Spain, Bali, Russia, and London made it clear that terrorism perpetrated by international subversive fanatical groups would sway both attention and funding from traditional law enforcement to domestic security issues and critical incident response. Complicating these initiatives is that legislative efforts to thwart future attacks and enhance investigative endeavors by law enforcement and military personnel have come under recurring scrutiny. Regardless of these events, the predominant responsibilities of police executives across the globe remain the prevention of crime and the maintenance of public safety and sense of security, often with decreased budgets and diminishing personnel.

In an effort to address these issues, the International Police Executive Symposium (IPES) coordinates annual international conferences to evaluate critical issues and recommend practical solutions to law enforcement executives deployed across the globe. One of these conferences was hosted by the government of the Czech Republic in late 2005. Every IPES summit witnesses the assembly of recognized police executives and acknowledged criminal justice academics from all ends of the world in an attempt to guide the law enforcement profession more effectively into the new millennium. It has been acknowledged that international terrorism and transnational organized crime have compounded and complicated the traditional law enforcement mission, and only a global cooperative response will have a notable and effective outcome.

This IPES conference in 2005 was attended by over 100 renowned criminal justice and law enforcement professionals dedicated to the accomplishment of this important objective—continued reduction in crime by engaging in both local and global response. Over 60 comprehensive presentations were made with accompanying distribution of detailed reports to all participants for potential incorporation into their respective regional policing practices. While intelligence-led policing has resulted in diminished crime, it is believed that this exchange of effective crime-fighting principles and tried and proven best practices (and, additionally, the evaluation of failed efforts) will enhance contemporary law enforcement endeavors and educate academics and students to better comprehend the challenges faced by today's policing leaders.

A number of central themes were developed during the IPES conference and have become the core issues addressed in this book titled *Effective Crime Reduction Strategies: International Perspectives*. These predominant topics include

Part I: Critical Issues in European Law Enforcement

Part II: Contemporary Concerns: Policing in the United States and Canada

Part III: Paradigm Shifts: Policing as Democracy Evolves

Part IV: Revising Traditional Law Enforcement in Asia to Meet Contemporary Demands

Part V: The Positive Influence of Unionization on Police Professionalism

Part VI: Significant Issues Facing Twenty-First Century Law Enforcement

Of the dozens of papers available for this book, only 28 were selected as those that would provide the reader with the most detailed and relevant insight into the concerns of contemporary law enforcement executives from both a local and an international perspective, and guide them effectively into the twenty-first century. All chapters have been revised to highlight contemporary literature, research, and data. Please take the time to peruse the Table of Contents and note the significant and current nature of the authors' works.

In Part I, Critical Issues in European Law Enforcement, the authors have portrayed their thorough analysis of efforts to improve police services in Hungary, Austria, and Norway as ideological perspectives have evolved, and the quest to stabilize crime, disorder, terrorist threats, and transnational influences within the European Union has been addressed. Each nation highlighted has been forced to revise their policies and organizational structures to meet the demands of developing events and political pressures.

In Part II, Contemporary Concerns: Policing in the United States and Canada, analyses of the impact of international terrorism and transnational crime on the law enforcement and investigatory practices in North America have been conducted by renowned academics who have been provided considerable insight into these issues by police administrators affected by these significant global justice concerns. The most critical issues facing today's law enforcement executives are addressed in detail.

In Part III, Paradigm Shifts: Policing as Democracy Evolves, the authors have undertaken an evaluation of revised law enforcement and justice endeavors that have transpired across the globe with specific examples involving South Africa, Brazil, Argentina, Nigeria, and Cameroon, as recent efforts to institute democratic reforms have been undertaken. These successes (and failures) will be of utmost interest to government officials, justice administrators, and academics across the globe who are undertaking or have been considering similar political, ideological, and administrative reformations to ensure that a proper and contemporary democracy can develop.

In Part IV, Revising Traditional Law Enforcement in Asia to Meet Contemporary Demands, noted academics and ranking law enforcement practitioners in New Zealand, Turkey, Indonesia, and Thailand attempt to apply the contemporary issues of counterterrorism, cultural ideology, and transnational criminal influence to the traditional nature of policing in the eastern regions of the world, thereby providing the reader with a frontline perspective into these modern law enforcement concerns, and the revisions to practices, policies, and resource allocation that have resulted.

In Part V, The Positive Influence of Unionization on Police Professionalism, respected practitioners and scholars have evaluated the progress attained within law enforcement agencies once unions were formed and police associations were permitted influence on management decision-making and policy development. The traditional belief was that unions would hamper progress; yet examples from the United States, Canada, New Zealand, and South Africa will reveal that professionalism actually was enhanced by union participation and input.

In Part VI, Significant Issues Facing Twenty-First Century Law Enforcement, the predominant and contemporary concerns of law enforcement executives that involve counterterrorism, border and transnational criminality, the measurement of police effectiveness, and the investigation of juvenile crime by law enforcement investigators are addressed by noted scholars. The threat of international terrorism and transnational crime, the public perception of the measurement of law enforcement agency efficacy, and victimological investigation of child abuse are clearly matters that confront police administrators in the twenty-first century.

This book has been designed to address the contemporary needs of law enforcement leaders and the interests of criminal justice scholars across the globe by providing insight into critical topics at the core of regional and transnational crime reduction endeavors, and efforts to improve the professionalism, integrity, and effectiveness of criminal justice and policing agencies across the world. It clearly addresses a plethora of policing and justice issues ranging from traditional crime fighting, counterterrorism, leadership, measurement of agency efficacy, transnational organized crime eradication, homeland security, integrity control, respect for democratic ideals, and enhanced effectiveness and efficiency in an era of budgetary restraints.

Critical Issues
in European Law
Enforcement

I

Global Law Enforcement and the Cosmopolitan Police Response: The Role of Situational Policing in Transnational Crime Prevention—An Example from Hungary

1

NORMAN CONTI, JAMES J. NOLAN, III,
AND ZSOLT MOLNAR

Contents

Evaluating the Hungarian Crime Prevention Academy

A Hungarian public safety initiative known as the Crime Prevention Academy has been created from the perspective of the theoretical model for situational policing (Nolan et al. 2004). The Hungarian CPA has published its own evaluation and documentation on its efforts (Ministry of Justice 2003,

MoI Regional Crime Prevention Academy 2004, 2005). These documents will be analyzed from a modified version of the grounded theory perspective (Glasner and Strauss 1967, Charmaz 1983).* They were originally coded for emerging themes, strategies, and functions. When connections to the situational model of policing began to emerge, the documents were once more reviewed in order to determine how the empirical example and the theoretical model fit together. Eventually, it is apparent that a number of key elements of the model were operating within the organization's central documents.

Additional data were provided by the director of the institution. His first-hand experience with the CPA and understanding of the situational model of policing were invaluable in determining the ways in which the two either fit or do not mesh together. Furthermore, any bias has been mitigated by two factors. First, the data come primarily in the form of official documents that exist as public record, so it is the documents that are really the subject of the analysis rather than the continued activities of the CPA. This methodological specificity points to a need for future research dealing with what exactly the CPA is doing, how they are going about it, and what effect it is having upon the groups and individuals working with and through it—not to mention transnational crime. Second, the analysis was mainly conducted by those with no vested interest whatsoever in the organization, and this allowed for a check and a double check of objectivity.

Social Crime Prevention

The CPA is a training regime designed in the spirit of what is referred to as social crime prevention. Social crime prevention is a model of public safety that shares a great many commonalities with situational policing. Social crime prevention maintains the fundamental presupposition that public safety cannot be achieved through the methods of traditional law enforcement. While social crime prevention does utilize the criminal justice system, it also relies heavily on a wide range of other institutional actors to play equal, if not more important, roles. From this perspective, the general phenomenon of crime is recognized as a social product that must be addressed through a strategy that is fully integrated within the larger social structure. The architects of this strategy imagine it as a social field comprised of professionals and civilians, which is organized and supported by the state. The practical dynamics of social crime prevention are modeled below in Figure 1.1.

Within this diagram, it is apparent that the criminal justice system is connected to and functioning in conjunction with various other social sectors.

---

* Generally, the grounded theory perspective is utilized for the quantitative analysis of ethnographic field notes. However, for this project we have substituted an official summary of the CPA's activity in place of observational data.

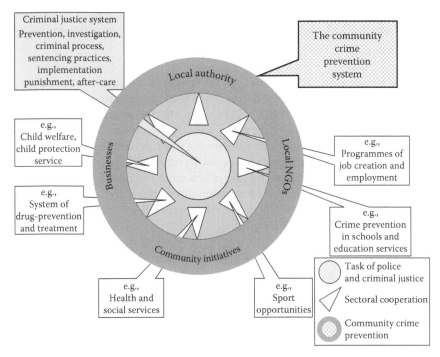

Figure 1.1 Social crime prevention subsystems (From Ministry of Justice, *The National Strategy for Social Crime Prevention*. Budapest, Hungary, 2003, p. 42).

The criminal justice system holds a position at the core of the model, but the larger community is fully involved through close cooperation between state institutions, local authorities, and civic organizations. Proponents of this strategy explain that a system of social crime prevention will not function unless local and wider communities assume their share of responsibility for public safety (Hungarian Ministry of Justice 2003, p. 43). Active cooperation between local authorities, civic organizations, churches, businesses, as well as other economic interests, individuals, and communities is particularly important to the operation of this strategy. From this perspective, individuals and organizations are responsible for taking action in order to assure that the community's self-defense mechanisms are operating at maximum capacity. The necessary goal of this cooperation is to reduce the causes, opportunities, and risks of becoming a victim of crime.

The Goal of Community Policing

The model of social crime prevention (or community crime prevention as it is sometimes called) exists as a holistic approach for dealing with chronic, long-term public safety problems. It is social control conceived within a sociological imagination and it inspires us to question the method, function, and goal of community policing in the United States and elsewhere. In the foreword to Wesley Skogan's book, *Community Policing: Can it Work?*, Jeremy Travis writes about the promise of community policing:

> The police will solve problems, not just respond to calls for service. The police will develop constructive new partnerships with the community, not serve as occupying forces. The police will be more effective at reducing and preventing crime. The morale of the police will improve as they see the fruits of their labor. Police organizations will become more decentralized, hierarchical structures will be flattened, and specialists imprisoned in outdated chains of command will be replaced by generalists more responsive to a changing world. Police will help organized communities so they can help themselves. Public trust in the police will increase as stereotypes dissolve and understanding is enhanced. (Skogan, 2004, p. x)

Above, Skogan offers a clear and concise summary of how community policing was supposed to be different from, and better than, the traditional law enforcement model of policing. However, nowhere in this list of "big ideas" about community policing is it made clear what it is that the police are actually supposed to *accomplish*. This omission is a central problem in the evaluation of actual or proposed policing strategies; there does not seem to be a clearly defined goal—or a desired end state—from which to make this evaluation. The problem becomes particularly evident when one is asked a question such as "Does community policing work?" (Skogan 2004). This question is somewhat loaded because it seems to contain the hidden question "What do the police do when they do community policing?" There are quite a number of evaluation studies that ask the question "Does community policing work?," and then go on to answer the question by looking at what the police do. "Do they hold community meetings?," "Are they engaged in problem-solving activities?," and "Do they patrol on foot or on bikes to make them more accessible to the public?" (Roth et al. 2004). The answers to these questions tend to focus more on what the police *do* instead of what they *accomplish*.

In answering his own question "Can community policing work?," Skogan (2004) suggests that if it were adopted by police agencies perhaps it would "increase the legitimacy of the police in the eyes of the public, and it may help [the police] target problems that are of priority concern to the community" (Skogan, p. xxxi). Are these really the goals of policing: legitimacy in the eyes of the community and better targeting of problems? Or instead, is the goal simply the lowering of area crime rates as suggested by Roth et al. (2004)? Or perhaps the goal is to enhance the quality of neighborhood life as suggested by Reisig and Parks (2004), who claim that when the police reduce incivilities in neighborhoods, the other forms of social control, private (family and friends) and parochial (neighbors and neighborhood associations), are better able to function, and order is maintained. Or, maybe the goal of community policing is solving community problems as suggested by Eck (2004), who argues that the police organization, its processes, and whether communities get involved at all are less important than the problems themselves, which should remain the focus of the police and criminologists alike.

A *desirable end state* for policing must be delineated. Most importantly, this end state must be one that can be used as a guide for selecting policing tactics and situations, and to evaluate the effectiveness of existing strategies. One model is grounded in a situationalist perspective, i.e., the local situation should dictate whether the police focus on law enforcement, problem-solving, or dealing with neighborhood incivilities as they work locally to prevent crimes globally.

Situational Policing

The concept of situational policing involves building neighborhood-specific policing strategies that move beyond simple considerations of the type and rate of crime in an area (Nolan et al. 2004). While these basic crime statistics may always play a key role in the police function, the situational model argues that public safety could be better served if the police would also factor in group-level social processes. This model suggests the construction and implementation of policing strategies focus on the social psychological characteristics of a neighborhood as a whole in addition to crime rates. The goal of this model is to cultivate more organic defense mechanisms within neighborhoods in order to prevent disorder from reaching a point where police response is the only viable option.

The idea for situational policing comes out of the recent body of work on neighborhood-level collective efficacy and crime rates (Sampson and Raudenbush 1997). Sampson and Raudenbush (1997) define collective efficacy as "cohesion among residents combined with shared expectations for social control of public space." In this definition, the neighborhood is conceptualized with a strong emphasis on sense of community. A collectively efficacious neighborhood is more like a fully functional group than an aggregate of isolated individuals who all happen to live in the same geographic area. An efficacious environment is one where people play roles in the life of the community rather than in an alienated social context. In their research on 196 Chicago neighborhoods, Sampson and Raudenbush discovered that the degree of collective efficacy present within a locality was the single most significant predictor of disorder and crime.

These findings present a substantial challenge to the "broken windows" thesis (Wilson and Kelling 1982) and its longstanding place within policing. For almost 30 years, a great deal of work within American policing has been based on the idea that a serious violent crime is the result of neighborhood disorder (Wilson and Kelling 1982, Goldstein 1990, Kelling and Coles 1996). This notion stems from Wilson and Kelling's (1982) observation that disorder, of both the physical and social varieties, illustrates fear and apathy among the neighbors.* As a result of being afraid or having given up, the residents fail to take an active role in the informal social control of their environment.

Sampson and Raudenbush argue that while Wilson and Kelling provide a useful starting point, the conception of disorder as a precursor to crime is inherently flawed. They point out that disorder, in any of the forms mentioned above, actually *is* crime or is at least evidence of a crime, albeit a crime at the lower end of the seriousness continuum. From this perspective, Wilson and Kelling's argument becomes "crime or evidence thereof causes crime." While the existence of a behavior or phenomenon at one point is frequently predictive of its later repetition, noting this phenomenon does not address its root causes. Sampson and Raudenbush improve upon what we have learned from Wilson and Kelling by demonstrating that it is a lack of collective efficacy from which the broken windows as well as the more serious crimes arise.

In the situational model of policing, Nolan et al. (2004) use Sampson and Raudenbush's work on collective efficacy to make the argument that neighborhoods share many characteristics of small groups, and that it is appropriate, therefore, to apply what has been learned over the years about small group dynamics and development to the local "neighborhood." For example, the group-level phenomenon we are calling collective efficacy, has been present in the literature on small groups for many years. Only recently, however, has this concept been applied to neighborhoods (Sampson and Raudenbush 1997). This is the starting point for the situational policing model, i.e., that neighborhoods can be studied and understood in the same way small groups are studied and understood.

It is strongly believed that it would be more helpful to understand collective efficacy from a developmental perspective than simply as existing or not existing, or existing on a continuum from high to low. Conceived of in this way (as high or low collective efficacy) hides the fact that neighborhoods develop through stages, and that high levels of collective efficacy represent a developmental process that has worked optimally, but that low levels of collective efficacy indicate that neighborhoods must be at early stages of development and are either dependent on the police to control their public space or in conflict with the police (and others) because this expectation is not being met to the satisfaction of the residents. Based on research in group

---

* The authors give such examples as litter, graffiti, abandoned cars, vacant buildings, and discarded drug paraphernalia as evidence of physical disorder while they present the observation of vagrants, prostitutes, the obviously intoxicated, and apparent gangs as evidence of social disorder.

development, it is suggested that all groups (neighborhoods included) pass through, regress to, or get stuck in one of three stages: (1) dependence, (2) conflict, or (3) interdependence.

In Stage 1, the group is dependent on a leader (i.e., the police) for direction; the members share the assumption that the leader is competent and able to provide effective guidance. In Stage 2, the group experiences conflict. This conflict is likely to occur over incongruent assumptions about the goal of the group, the roles of the members, or whether the leader is able to meet the unrealistic expectations of the membership. In Stage 3, the group has successfully resolved its conflicts and its members work together interdependently toward their agreed-upon goals. Normal group development occurs this way, sequentially through the first two stages and into the third where the members work together most effectively. However, this process is dynamic and at any time a group may regress to or get stuck in one of the first two stages, which limits the efficacy of the group. To make this clearer, consider how this developmental sequence might play out in a neighborhood that is dealing with crime and disorder.

Stage 1: Dependence (on the Police)

In Stage 1, community members want the police to solve problems related to public order and the police are willing, and sometimes able, to do so. At this stage, the police are viewed as competent and are respected by most residents. As long as the police are able to address most of the problems of community disorder, the residents will likely remain satisfied with their services and continue to *depend* on them. In this stage, the police may view the neighborhood as unable or unwilling to care for itself. They may see themselves as having a mandate to protect the community. If the police are not able to meet the neighborhood expectations, they move to the next stage of development—conflict.

Stage 2: Conflict (with the Police and among the Residents)

In situations where the police are unable to solve community problems through enforcement or to effectively keep the neighborhood safe, residents become dissatisfied and frustrated. They still see the police as having the primary responsibility for maintaining order in the neighborhood and keeping them safe, but they believe the police are just not doing a very good job. Individual residents might decide to take action on their own because the police are viewed as ineffective, and the neighborhood has yet to develop the structures, processes, and trusting relationships that would inspire collective action. The dissatisfaction and frustration that exist in the community may result in complaints against the police. While defending themselves, the police may consider new and innovative programs, such as high-visibility foot or bike patrols, in order to appease the residents and to try to regain their confidence. At this point, the police may feel vulnerable since they are asked to meet unrealistic expectations with very limited resources.

In order to move out of Stage 2 in the desired direction toward interdependence (i.e., collective efficacy), both the police and the community must give up the notion that they alone can protect the neighborhood against public disorder. Both the police and the neighborhood residents must come to recognize the importance of collective action and informal social controls in restoring and maintaining order in the neighborhood before the neighborhood can move toward Stage 3. This point is critical, for the neighborhood as a whole cannot develop out of the conflict stage toward the interdependence stage until there is a shared acceptance of this reality. Indications by the police that they will work harder or deploy more officers to the location serve only to move the neighborhood back to Stage 1, Dependence, instead of in the preferred direction toward Stage 3, Interdependence.

Stage 3: Interdependence

Once the community and the police come to recognize their mutual responsibilities in restoring order and neighborhood safety, members begin to develop the social networks and processes needed to make this happen. The police at this point may play a less prominent and less directive role in the maintenance of public order. As they continue to work together interdependently, the police and neighbors will likely develop stronger and more trusting relationships. In this final stage of neighborhood development, strong, trusting community networks exist in order to maintain control over neighborhood order and safety. The police work with the community as needed to deal with situations that are beyond the scope and capability of residents (see Figure 1.2).

Conceiving of crime/disorder and neighborhood development along horizontal and vertical axes gives rise to four neighborhood types: (1) strong, (2)

| Stage 1 | Stage 2 | Stage 3 |
| Dependence | Conflict | Interdependence |

- Stage (1) *Dependence*—Residents rely on the police to solve problems of public order.

- Stage (2) *Conflict*—Residents are in conflict with the police because they perceive them as being ineffective in maintaining public order.

- Stage (3) *Interdependence*—Residents rely on each other to ensure enforcement of community values/norms/laws.

Figure 1.2 Stages of neighborhood development.

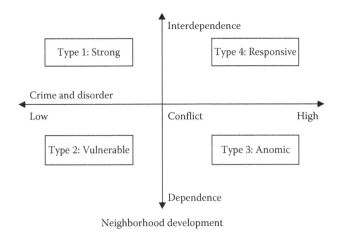

Figure 1.3 Neighborhood types.

vulnerable, (3) anomic, and (4) responsive (see Figure 1.3). Matching appropriate policing strategies to each developmental stage (along the vertical axis) and each neighborhood type (see Figure 1.3) would be most appropriate. In the first stage of neighborhood development, one would find a dependent neighborhood where the residents rely solely on police intervention for their community's well-being. As long as the police are able to satisfy the expectations of the residents, they have no need to develop into a more efficacious collective. Neighborhoods in this stage of development may have either low or high crime rates depending upon other variables. Nolan et al. categorize a neighborhood with low collective efficacy and low crime rates as vulnerable, while a neighborhood with low collective efficacy and high crime rate as anomic.* The distinction between the two is that while both are weak neighborhoods, the problem of crime has not seriously threatened the vulnerable neighborhood. If crime and disorder were to develop into something more than infrequent anomalies within the control of the police, the residents within the vulnerable neighborhood would quickly become dissatisfied with their guardians. Residents living in the anomic context most likely already have a history of this kind of resentment. As the negative sentiment grows, the neighborhood moves into the second stage of development, i.e., conflict.

The second stage is one of conflict and dissatisfaction with the police for not providing the residents with the type of neighborhood protection they

---

* In Figure 1.3 Nolan et al. recommend strategies of "substituting and selling" in vulnerable neighborhoods and "securing and organizing" in anomic neighborhoods (Nolan et al. 2004, p. 112). Within the vulnerable neighborhood, where crime is not an issue, the community's efficacy may need to be built around other local issues. For the anomic neighborhood, since crime is already out of control, the police must employ the best of their traditional tactics in order to clear some space for the community to begin coalescing as a group.

desire. In this stage, community frustration is likely to result in some kind of action, even if that collective action is little more than the expression of hostility toward the police for failing to keep the neighborhood safe. This action can then push the neighborhood further along the development continuum to a state of greater collective efficacy (i.e., some type of community mobilization, such as a neighborhood watch) or it can lead to a regression back to a state of dependence. A slip back into dependence may result from actions taken by the police in order to appease the community. In this instance, the police are likely to be responding to political pressure to "clean up" a neighborhood with the implementation of a zero-tolerance policy that will at least present an acceptable image of their efforts to ensure public safety for the community. Whether or not this policy will actually be effective is of less political consequence than if it is able to ameliorate community dissatisfaction with the police. At this point, public safety is relegated to a largely theatrical endeavor (Manning 1978).

The other direction that a neighborhood can take from this "conflict" position is toward interdependence. An interdependent community is one in which both the police and the citizens recognize their role in public safety. In this environment, police do not have to overdramatize their efforts because the members of the community are beginning to form a more cohesive social unit. While the work of policing will not necessarily be reduced by this occurrence, it can be better directed. As the neighbors develop mechanisms for informal social control, police effort can be used for the problems requiring more formal solutions.*

The ideal social environment is what Nolan et al. refer to as the strong neighborhood. In a strong neighborhood group, interdependence (and collective efficacy) is high and crime is low. A strong neighborhood is by all definitions a safe neighborhood since it has low levels of crime and is able to prevent serious public disorder through informal social control. In this strong neighborhood, all the police have to do to promote collective efficacy is to "support and recognize" community mobilization organic to the locality (see Figure 1.4). This police effort involves ensuring maximum participation within community life by augmenting indigenous efforts at organization with police resources and honoring residents who have played particularly important roles in the neighborhood's social life.

In order to maximize public safety within the situational model of policing, a reduction in crime and an increase in neighborhood level efficacy must

---

* In Figure 1.3 Nolan et al. call for a policing style of "systems planning and response" in responsive neighborhoods. In this environment, many of the community's problems extend beyond the range of the police as well as the citizens. In order to effect positive social change, other agencies and organizations must be included within the dialogue. The authors suggest engaging social services, education, local advocacy groups, and urban planners among others. It is up to these various groups to work together in establishing a vision and making it a reality.

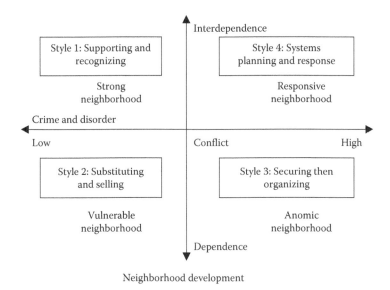

Figure 1.4 Policing styles.

be mutual occurrences. In this conception of effective policing, the goal of public safety is transformed from a task to be completed into a process to be facilitated. Since relevant neighborhood conditions are fluid, policing must be thought of as a type of stewardship where the service provided aids in pushing neighborhoods in the direction of community strength. To better understand this distinction, traditional policing might be symbolized as conventional western medicine with specialized aptitude in dealing with extreme and emergency situations that are beyond the capabilities of the layperson. Situational policing can alternatively be thought of as a more integrative approach that uses all of the conventional law enforcement techniques as well as methods derived from other traditions and places the neighborhood at the center of its own healing experience. It is a perspective that is analogous to a physician who might initially employ something like acupuncture or its equivalent with the hope of cultivating more natural healing and defense mechanisms in order to allow the patient to take responsibility for his or her own health and well-being. The challenge and value of this perspective is in understanding how, when, and to what end these various techniques should be employed.

Nolan et al. lay out an example of this strategy in Figure 1.5. Starting in the lower right-hand quadrant, representing the anomic neighborhood, a sequence of policing styles that explain their potential effect upon the community is exhibited. Initially, since crime is high, efficacy is low, and this neighborhood is dependent on the police to solve its problems of crime and disorder, the police are left with few options beyond the traditional

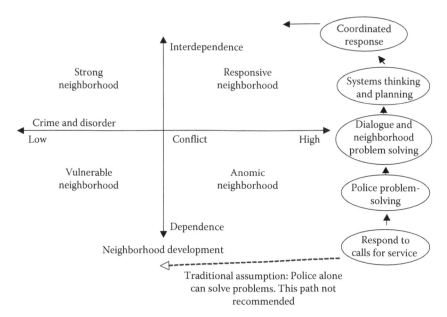

Figure 1.5 Situational policing in motion.

approaches of responding to calls for service and implementing conventional crime-prevention techniques via law enforcement. However, this must be acknowledged as only an initial triage. Both the police as well as the citizens have to understand that a strong (i.e., safe) neighborhood cannot be enforced into existence. Moreover, if the police are able to make an initial impact on crime with the standard methods, the citizens can easily fall back into complacency with the assumption that their community's problems are best left to the authorities. In this event, the neighborhood remains "vulnerable" despite a temporary reduction in crime.

Nolan et al. go on to explain that after an initial stage of increased law enforcement activities, the focus might shift to something on the order of problem-oriented policing (Goldstein 1990), where the root causes of the service calls are identified and eliminated. Within the model, it is essential that this problem-solving entail a dialogue between the police and the citizens that are willing to play leadership roles in strengthening relationships within the community. Working in community-based collaborative problem-solving connects the police and citizens through common projects where relationships are forged and a local civic discourse can evolve. While these relationships grow, all parties will have to begin to accept the reality that no police force is capable of keeping any neighborhood truly safe or secure. As this understanding is achieved, the neighborhood moves into the responsive quadrant of the diagram. Once the transition to responsive neighborhood is underway, the community can organize adapted methods of systems thinking and planning for neighborhoods with regard to issues of crime and disorder (Weisbord 1987, 1992, Weisbord and Janoff 1995, Emery and Purser 1996, Parenti 2000). Responsive neighborhoods are ready to work with individuals and groups that have a stake in the long-term safety of the community, i.e., those represented in Figure 1.1.

The Hungarian Crime Prevention Academy

Following the above explanation of the theoretical model of situational polic-ing, an empirical discussion of how many of its key elements are captured in the CPA can begin. The CPA is a training institution that was established by the Hungarian Ministry of Interior in response to the security demands of European citizens following the September 11, 2001 terrorist attacks. It receives additional support from various Central-Eastern European and the Balkan nations and follows a set of guidelines for community crime prevention put forth by the UN Office on Drugs and Crime, the European Union's Crime Prevention Network, the Council of Europe, the International Organization for Migration, and the National Crime Prevention Board and Committee.

Founded in response to political pressure, the CPA's establishment may seem like a macrolevel version of what one would expect in a vulnerable neighborhood at the initial introduction of crime and disorder; a state of conflict develops as a result of global events and a threatened regional com-munity demands security from its sworn protectors. While these may have been the circumstances of its inception, the more important question is whether institutional response builds or breaks collective efficacy. The subse-quent analysis of the CPA's objectives, structures, and activities is a prelimi-nary attempt to answer this question.

Objectives of the Hungarian Crime Prevention Academy

Formally, the CPA was founded in order to respond to the emerging chal-lenges of transnational crime and to cultivate prevention strategies that are viable within as well as across national boundaries. It builds a "methodologi-cal recommendation system" from the perspective of social crime preven-tion, and then disseminates it to all interested parties. At the settlement level, local authorities, in cooperation with civilian organizations, use this recom-mendation system to develop crime prevention strategies and to plan their implementation. In this crosspollination, local authorities and community groups work together with a transnational organization, in acknowledgment of state level directives, in order to develop broadly based policies for ensur-ing public safety.

A very important part of this mission is facilitating cooperation between local law enforcement agencies and the communities they serve in order to cultivate a common vision of crime prevention that is both specifically indigenous and globally informed. A commitment to society, as well as a plan to work with both police agencies and civilians is observed as an encouraging statement within the institutional mission. What is found encouraging is an implicit acknowledgment that if policing, by itself, cannot ensure safety at the local level, it is unlikely that even the most upscaled and advanced version of it can really provide security for a nation or region, much less the world. Understanding the value of cooperation in this way denotes an evolution out of the traditional law enforcement model.

The essential anticrime objective of the CPA is to contribute to the development of a universal anticrime policy for preventing people from becoming either criminal offenders or victims of crime. Its more general objective is to "promote the appearance of a crime prevention attitude in the daily activity and way of thinking of state organisations, local authorities, civilian organisations, businesses and private individuals" (Minister of the Interior Regional Crime Prevention Academy 2004). This general objective recognizes the significance of a "way of thinking" on the part of both individuals and organizations, and thus understands public safety as a shared responsibility between all stakeholders. An ethos of collective obligation is evidence of congruence between the CPA and the situational model of policing. However, the fact that the phrase "promoting an appearance of" is used in the statement of objectives in regard to the "attitude" in question, clouds the discussion. Promoting the appearance of a crime prevention attitude and actually maintaining that attitude are, as a matter of course, two completely separate activities, and this distinction calls to mind the earlier discussion of policing as theatrics. Still, there is enough of an explicit description of how the CPA functions within the specific content of its objectives, that the notion of *things being other than they appear* may initially be set to the side as perhaps little more than a semantic artifact rather that a peek into the organization's backstage agenda.

The CPA is a decentralized institution that seeks to provide equal service to both rural settlements and urban centers. It operates on a principle of regional organization where the courses that constitute its core curriculum are offered in a region according to local demands. Moreover, they tailor the training to focus on themes of relevance within the region and in specialized sections for the local authorities as well as those working in education, child and youth protection, and law enforcement. To accomplish its goal of equivalent service despite geography or population density, the CPA employs a national network of trainers as an essential part of their staff. The network is diverse and dependent upon the integration of academics and practitioners working individually or through organizations to teach the courses that constitute the academy's curriculum.

One of the CPA's special objectives is to create and manage a single international and national crime prevention training and further training (i.e., train-the-trainer), and the international harmonization of this activity. This objective includes the CPA's basic educational mandate as well as a dissemination strategy and administrative role. The academy is designed to function as a hub where initial waves of trainees are socialized into its perspective and method, and then sent out into their native milieus to implement the vision. Additionally, they may be further trained in order to take the role of instructor in order to further expand the program. The CPA refers to this as the "multiplying effect" of their training and information dissemination. Multiplying effect refers to a contagion strategy by which the CPA's establishment of a national trainer network is perpetually augmented by the later organization of professional and methodological instruction for individuals interested in bringing the CPA's program to their home environment. A "train-the-trainer" model such as this maximizes the institution's potential for recruitment and socialization therefore deepening its potential social impact.

Another objective is to ensure that the largest circle of people interested in crime prevention acquire the latest relevant knowledge. Specifically, this second objective of including and educating the fullest spectrum of institutions and individuals in the activity of crime prevention is very interesting in relation to the aforementioned recommendations for community building and socialization within the situational model of policing. Since the core of the anticrime policy objective is to prevent people from becoming either victims or offenders, one can imagine a significant amount of grassroots level work that may be undertaken by civilians. The task is so vast that it cannot be commented on in brief, other than to note that it involves a monumental degree of community mobilization and the CPA's first specific objective of "training-the-trainer" may serve as an essential element for providing the requisite labor.

Structure of the Hungarian Crime Prevention Academy

The activities of the CPA revolve around a set of basic principles that include complexity, a multidisciplinary approach, partnership, socialization, the principle of being international and EU compatible, structuredness, and openness. The principle of complexity involves embracing a variety of techniques including general information seeking, training, and scientific research. Complexity is tied to a multidisciplinary approach that acknowledges that criminology is not the only field that is useful in understanding crime and criminality. In this regard, the CPA is expressing a willingness to utilize the methods of any field with the potential to contribute to improving public safety. Including the full range of social sciences as well as criminology in order to gain and use as much knowledge about crime and its prevention is the great hope of this multidisciplinary approach.

The multidisciplinary approach is part of an underlying ethos that recognizes the importance of the crucial link between theory and practice that is carried further by the principle of "structuredness." Structuredness requires the organization to conduct ongoing original research projects on the methods and topics of crime prevention that are included within its curriculum. The CPA explains this as teaching what they do research on and doing research on what they teach. Additionally, the academy seeks to present its curriculum as a training system in the tradition of the Hungarian Police College as well as in other educational institutions.

Of particular interest is the principle of socialization. It is explained as follows: "the activities within the Academy shall be structured in a way to try to break away from the traditional police-centred crime prevention philosophy, creating an approach involving the entire society" (MoI Regional Crime Prevention Academy 2004, 2005). This structure is built on the working philosophy that the local communities must create their own crime prevention strategies by thinking together, assigning a role/place in the structure, and a task in the course of implementation to all state organs dealing with crime prevention, the local authorities, and civilian organizations. By involving as wide a range of the local community as possible, the academy is fulfilling an important requirement of situational policing. Local and regional recruitment are fed by an openness principle via the invitation for "anybody at any time [to] get involved in the activity of the academy, provided s/he accepts and observes the working principles, legal regulations and the standards of professional integrity" (Minister of the Interior Regional Crime Prevention Academy 2004, p. 6).

The preceding principles are tied to a mandate of partnership with "all international, foreign and national organizations, civilian groupings and persons who play a role in crime prevention" (Ministry of the Interior Regional Crime Prevention Academy 2004, p. 5). The principle of internationalism and EU compatibility lays down some specific regulations for how international partnerships will be carried out in its demand that "the crime prevention activities of the Academy shall be in accordance with the decisions, recommendations of the UN and the Council of the European Union, and also with the resolution that defines the necessity of creating a community crime prevention organizational system and common methods" (Ministry of the Interior Regional Crime Prevention Academy 2004, p. 5). Through this principle, the CPA recognizes community as well as national interests of those they partner with and gives space to each.

Activities at the Hungarian Crime Prevention Academy

The CPA's National Training Program begins with an education in the theory and practice of social crime prevention. In this module, the academy addresses the origin, the legal framework, and the regulations of social crime prevention. Additionally, they explicate the organizational system responsible for social crime prevention with an emphasis on operation, scope of activities, and competencies. The recommended participants in this training include local authority deputies, experts, councillors, delegates of the public security committee of the local authority, the public security councillor or "rapporteur," the representative of the police force, pedagogues, medical doctors, representatives of the civil guard, representatives of the public security foundation, representatives of the public maintenance inspectorate, managers of private security companies, managers of social institutions or retirement homes or their delegates, other persons, and organizations showing an interest in local crime prevention.

An essential part of the training involves participants familiarizing themselves with one another's perspective on the topic they seek to address. Once all the individual perspectives are understood, they can then begin to identify their priorities and lay the foundation of a local crime prevention program and action plan.

An important element of the CPA is an international training program with the objective of providing comprehensive knowledge and improving skills in combating and preventing transnational crime. The training program consists of three components: theoretical foundation training, methodological training, and training supporting the practical application of knowledge (thematic training). The theoretical foundation training is particularly interesting in regard to our current discussion because it mandates a familiarity with the formal mechanisms of crime prevention within a nation state, as well as an understanding of the public safety roles available to other groups interested in crime prevention. These groups include local authorities, community organizations, cultural, and other civilian associations. In addition to all of this, basic community outreach trainees are also expected to be aware of the variables that affect individual attitudes toward crime prevention. Working in this fashion, with these kinds of civilian groups, is in accord with the CPA's principle of socialization and demonstrates a commitment to the kind of community integration that we find essential to effective crime prevention.

As part of the methodological training, there is an emphasis on cooperation and creativity within, as well as between, groups. This emphasis is a reiteration of the CPA's basic philosophy that local communities should develop their own crime prevention strategies. From this perspective, all stakeholders share a responsibility to "think together" in the design and implementation of a public safety structure. Roles are to be assigned to state and national institutions, local authorities, and civilian groups that facilitate maximal community involvement.

The CPA explains that their "direct aim is to support the cooperation of all those who are concerned or interested in public safety, in order to be able to create together a local crime prevention strategy and action plan." Their motto is "*joint creation–joint implementation*" and the training methodology pushes all concerned parties to take ownership of their program. Viewing the program as their own serves to include the larger community into the crime prevention strategy. A philosophy such as this is in sharp contrast to the ownership of crime and its prevention by law enforcement officials and agents who view the public as a passive audience and a public that sees crime prevention as the duty of their sworn protectors. The CPA summarizes its goal very concisely in the following:

> We hope that as a consequence of personal relationships and common experiences, the communication, contacts and cooperation between the parties will improve. The participants will be able to use the common experiences acquired during the training. They will be able to share their experiences with their colleagues as a means of cooperation. The atmosphere of the training guarantees that the established personal relationships remain sincere and long-lasting. The crime prevention strategy, the concrete form of cooperation and contacting and the sharing of tasks will also be discussed.

The target group includes the law enforcement officials of Albania, Bosnia-Herzegovina, Bulgaria, Croatia, the Czech Republic, Estonia, Latvia, Lithuania, Macedonia, Moldova, Poland, Romania, Serbia-Montenegro, Slovakia, Slovenia, Ukraine, and Hungary. While focusing on the law enforcement officials within these nations, the CPA is temporarily excluding the wider citizenries. While it can be strongly argued, in the situational model of policing, that a full integration of police with community is the best route to promote public safety, this model also begins with efforts aimed at the hearts and minds of the police organizations prior to implementing progressive neighborhood strategies (Conti and Nolan 2005). Putting the public on hold while conveying a larger vision to the law enforcement officials is not quite ideal but it is still an appropriate way to carry out the organizational mission. This is a reasonable technique because the location of initial efforts are potentially far less important than the eventual radius of the model's spread and development.

Global Law Enforcement and a Transnational Police Response

Since this analysis of the CPA, and its relationship to situational policing, exists as part of a larger project addressing the "challenges to policing which have arisen from changing security contexts in an era of globalization," some attention to the larger sociological theme is warranted. Specifically, it would be interesting to place some emphasis on "glocalization." The understanding of how the CPA functions in a globalized context owes much to Roudometof's (2005) theoretical analysis of transnationalism, cosmopolitanism, and "glocalization." While transnationalism is commonly understood to be the various activities and relations—including crime (Beck 2000)—taking place across national boundaries, and cosmopolitanism is easily recognized as an intellectual and aesthetic appreciation of, or openness to, global culture on the level of an ethical or moral value (Hannerz 1990), "glocalization" is substantially more esoteric.

Robertson (1994) first brought the terms glocality and glocalization into the sociological vernacular in order to capture the interplay of both the global and the local in the everyday lives of ordinary people. Glocalization, or internal globalization as it is sometimes described (Beck 2000), is the operation of transnationalism at the local level (i.e., the constant exposure of large numbers of locally situated individuals to a cultural multiplicity via encounters with foreign nationals, the media, and multinational corporations, such as McDonalds). Glocalization is a twin process of macro-localization and micro-globalization. Khondker explains this dialectic as follows:

> macro-localization involves expanding the boundaries of locality as well as making some ideas, practices, [and] institutions global... [while] micro-globalization involves incorporating certain global processes into a local setting. (2004, p. 4).

Roudometof goes on to explain that glocalization is the process of creating arenas for transnational interactions by providing material and nonmaterial infrastructure for human interaction across national boundaries. Beck (2000) refers to this infrastructure as a transnational social space and it includes international telephone calls, faxes, emails, satellite communication, conferences, and organizations. As interactions are formalized over time and space, power relations develop and transnational social fields evolve. The individuals operating and interacting upon these fields, in turn, constitute a transnational social network.

The mission of the CPA entails the creation of a national, as well as a transnational social space where "all interested parties" can come together and begin to address the issue of crime. In doing this, the CPA is taking part in the glocalization of public safety. Even though much of its behavior is regionally concentrated, its larger connection to the EU and interest in transnational crime carry it beyond all local boundaries. The essential glocal element of its function is the cultivation of methodological recommendation systems to be utilized at the settlement level. These systems are globally informed and locally implemented. Social crime prevention appears to be a preferential theoretical standpoint to anything accepted as part of the traditional law enforcement model, and the CPA is its progressive application in practice. Roudometof's description of the distinction between local and cosmopolitan is helpful in understanding the place of the CPA in the global context. He explains that cosmopolitans actively engage as much of the broader world culture as possible while locals seek to escape it. Within the CPA, individuals and organizations utilize a cosmopolitan strategy in order to ensure safety within their local communities.

Summary and Conclusions

The terrorist attacks in the United States on September 11, 2001 have forced law enforcement and other government officials, along with social scientists, to rethink the role of the police in our society, especially in relation to crime prevention. This is not to say that the role of the police has really ever been a settled issue. For the past 25 years, there has been an internal struggle in many police agencies regarding whether or not the primary role of the police is law enforcement, i.e., what has come to be known as the "traditional approach" to policing, or problem-solving and community relations, also known as the "community policing" approach. One factor complicating this debate is the lack of a clear and agreed-upon goal for the police, i.e., what is it that the police are trying to *accomplish*? In recent years, international crimes, including terrorism, have added a level of complexity to this debate. Contemporary sociological research has found that neighborhood-level collective efficacy prevents crime. The reverse is sometimes clearer: lack of collective efficacy at the neighborhood level predicts high crime rates, and that the police will be overwhelmed with calls for service. Situational policing is a conceptual framework that clearly identifies the goal of policing and provides a road map to get there. It is an integrative approach that suggests different policing strategies at different times and under a variety of different conditions. Since they are grounded in the social crime prevention perspective, the CPA's policies are consistent with the objectives of situational policing. The CPA prepares local and regional groups (including citizens, police, and many other stakeholders) to think and respond interdependently to crime and disorder. The impact of this local interdependence provides both a model for dealing with global crime problems (macro-localization) and for local areas to effectively prevent and respond to transnational crimes such as terrorism (micro-localization).

References

Beck, U. 2000. The cosmopolitan perspective: Sociology in the second age of modernity. *British Journal of Sociology*, 51:79–105.

Charmaz, K. 1983. The grounded theory method: An explication and interpretation. In *Contemporary Field Research: A Collection of Readings*, ed. R. M. Emerson. Prospect Heights, IL: Waveland Press.

Conti, N. and J. J. Nolan III. 2005. Policing the platonic cave: Ethics and efficacy in police training. *Policing and Society*, 15:166–186.

Eck, J. E. 2004. Why don't problems get solved? In *Community Policing: Can It Work?*, ed. W. Skogan. Belmont, CA: Wadsworth/Thomson Learning.

Emery, M. and R. E. Purser. 1996. *The Search Conference: A Powerful Method for Planning Organizational Change and Community Action*. San Francisco, CA: Josey-Bass.

Glasner, B. G. and A. L. Strauss. 1967. *The Discovery of Grounded Theory: Strategies for Qualitative Research*. Chicago, IL: Aldine.

Goldstein, H. 1990. *Problem-Oriented Policing*. New York: McGraw-Hill.

Hannerz, U. 1990. Cosmopolitans and locals in world culture. In *Global Culture: Nationalism, Globalization, and Modernity*, ed. Mike Featherstone, pp. 237–253. London, U.K.: Routledge.

Kelling, G. L. and C. M. Coles 1996. *Fixing Broken Windows: Restoring Order and Reducing Crime in Our Communities*. New York: Free Press.

Khondker, H. H. 2004. Glocalization as globalization: Evolution of a sociological concept. *Bangladesh e-Journal of Sociology*, 1(2):1–9.

Manning, P. K. 1978. The police mandate: strategies and appearances. In *Policing: A View from the Street*, eds. Manning, P. K. and J. Van Maanen. New York: Random House.

Ministry of Justice. 2003. *The National Strategy for Social Crime Prevention*. Budapest, Hungary.

MoI Regional Crime Prevention Academy. 2004. *Summary of the Activity of the MoI Crime Prevention Academy*. Nagykovácsi, Hungary.

MoI Regional Crime Prevention Academy. 2005. The European frameworks of police and criminal cooperation. *International Training Programme for the Course*. Nagykovácsi, Hungary.

Nolan, J. J., N. Conti, and J. McDevitt. 2004. Situational policing: Neighborhood development and crime control. *Policing & Society*, 14:99–117.

Parenti, C. 2000. *Lockdown America: Police and Prisons in the Age of Crisis*. New York: Verso.

Reisig, M. D. and R. B. Parks. 2004. Community policing and the quality of life. In *Community Policing: Can It Work?*, ed. W. Skogan. Belmont, CA: Wadsworth/Thomson Learning.

Robertson, R. 1994. Globalization or glocalization? *The Journal of International Communication*, 1:33–51.

Roth, J. A., J. Roehl, and C. C. Johnson. 2004. Trends in community policing, in transnationalism, cosmopolitanism and glocalization. *Current Sociology*, 53:113–135.

Sampson, R. J. and S. W. Raudenbush. 1997. Neighborhoods and violent crime: A multilevel study of collective efficacy. *Science*, 227:918–924.

Skogan, W. 2004. *Community Policing: Can It Work?* Belmont, CA: Wadsworth/ Thomson Learning.

Weisbord, M. 1987. *Productive Workplaces: Organizing and Managing for Dignity, Meaning, and Community*. San Francisco, CA: Jossey-Bass.

Weisbord, M. 1992. *Discovering Common Ground*. San Francisco, CA: Berrett-Koehler.

Weisbord, M. and S. Janoff. 1995. *Future Search*. San Francisco, CA: Berrett-Koehler.

Wilson, J. Q. and G. L. Kelling. 1982. Broken windows: Police and neighborhood safety. *The Atlantic Monthly*, 249:29–38.

The Impact of Information Systems and Technology on Police Investigative Effectiveness in Norway

2

PETTER GOTTSCHALK AND RUNE GLOMSETH

Contents

Introduction

Investigation is the police activity concerned with (1) the apprehension of criminals by the gathering of evidence leading to their arrest and (2) the collection and presentation of evidence and testimony for the purpose of obtaining convictions. Investigations are normally divided into two major areas of activity: (1) the preliminary investigation normally carried out by officers in the uniform patrol division and (2) the follow-up investigation normally carried out by officers formally trained in investigative techniques, often part of a detective bureau (Thibault et al., 1998).

The performance of police investigation units is subject to considerable variability. One potential explanation for such variation is the extent to which detectives have access to information technology and electronic information sources. IT performance research has previously examined the organizational performance impacts of information technology

(Brynjolfsson and Hitt, 1996; Melville et al., 2004). The value configuration of the value shop to describe and measure organizational performance can be applied (Stabell and Fjelstad, 1998). The value shop consists of the five primary activities: problem understanding, solutions to problems, decisions on actions, implementation of actions, and evaluation of actions in an interactive, problem-solving cycle. Police investigation work can also be defined as value shop activities.

Police Investigations

Knowledge work in police investigations is based on a variety of information sources such as incident reports, crime scene investigator reports, witness statements, suspect statements, tip lines, crime scene photographs and drawings, fingerprints, DNA, physical evidence (e.g., ballistics, tool marks, and blood spatters), informants, and property tracking (Fraser, 2004).

Information from witnesses is typically assigned great importance in criminal investigations. The important role of witness reports has spurred a great deal of research investigating witnesses' memories for criminal events. As an example, the aim of the research conducted by Fahsing et al. (2004) was to provide reliable documentation on the nature of offender descriptions provided by witnesses to actual crimes and to conduct indirect tests of some of the established notions within witness psychology.

In doing so, some complexities underlying the witnesses' psychological processes were revealed. An archival study was conducted using 250 offender descriptions by witnesses of armed bank robberies. The accuracy of the descriptions was gauged against authentic video documentation of the witnessed crimes. In general, witnesses provided accurate descriptions of the offenders but reported few identifying details. Multiple regression analyses revealed that the witnesses' role (bank tellers vs. customers), the type of weapon used, and the number of perpetrators involved were moderately predictive of the quality of offender descriptions. However, several of the observed relationships were conditional on whether descriptions of basic attributes (e.g., height, age, and build) or more detailed features were considered. Hence, the authors concluded that verifying all aspects of witness descriptions is crucial when studying memories for actual crimes.

As an example, the investigation of economic crime is an intriguing subject. The complexity of the crime challenges the investigators, while the richness of the investigation process challenges the researcher. Economic criminality efficiently exploits the loopholes of the legislation and the new opportunities provided by the changes in the operational environment. Economic crime is an increasingly planned, professional activity, the forms of which constantly change (Puonti, 2004).

Information Systems

Luen and Al-Hawamdeh (2001) find that the amount of information that police officers come into contact with in the course of their work is astounding. This and the vast knowledge that police officers need in order to perform their normal duties suggest the need for police officers to be proficient knowledge workers, being able to access, assimilate and use knowledge effectively to discharge their duties.

As we trace the evolution of computing technologies in business, we can observe their changing level of organizational impact. The first level of impact was at the point work got done and transactions (e.g., orders, deposits, and reservations) took place. The inflexible, centralized mainframe allowed for little more than massive number crunching, commonly known as electronic *data* processing. Organizations became data heavy at the bottom and data management systems were used to keep the data in check. Later, the management *information* systems were used to aggregate data into useful information reports, often prescheduled, for the control level of the organization—people who were making sure that organizational resources like personnel, money, and physical goods were being deployed efficiently. As information technology (IT) and information systems (IS) started to facilitate data and information overflow, and corporate attention became a scarce resource, the concept of *knowledge* emerged as a particularly high-value form of information (Grover and Davenport, 2001).

Related to the new changes in computer technology is the transformation that has occurred in report writing and recordkeeping. Every police activity or crime incident demands a report on some kind of form. The majority of police patrol reports written before 1975 were handwritten. Today, officers can write reports on small notebook computers located in the front seat of the patrol unit; discs are handed in at the end of the shift for hard copy needs. Cursor keys and spell-check functions in these report programs are useful timesaving features (Thibault, 1998).

An example of an officer-to-technology system is the Major Incident Policy Document designed by the British Home Office (2005). This document is maintained whenever a Major Incident Room using the British HOLMES policing information system is in operation (HOLMES is named after the famous detective Sherlock Holmes in the United Kingdom). Decisions, which should be recorded, are those that affect the practical or administrative features of the enquiry, and each entry has clearly to show the reasoning for the decision. When the HOLMES system is used, the senior investigating officer (SIO) directs which policy decisions are recorded on the system.

The basic information entered into HOLMES is location of incident, data and time of incident, victim(s), senior investigating officer, and the date enquiry commenced. During the enquiry, which has been run on the HOLMES system, a closing report is prepared and registered as another document linked to a category of the closing report. The report will contain the following information: introduction, scene, the victim, and miscellaneous.

Four examples of IT in police work can be examined. These systems have functionality that typically covers more than one stage in the stages of knowledge management technology model. Therefore, these examples of policing systems suggest that the stages are overlapping. However, as we shall see at the functional and user level, stage perspectives might determine system perceptions.

The first example is COPLINK described by Chen et al. (2002, 2003); the second is geocomputation described by Ashby and Longley (2005); the third is SPIKE described by *ComputerWeekly* (2002); and the fourth and final example is closed-circuit television described by Surette (2005).

COPLINK Connect is an application for information and knowledge sharing in law enforcement. The system uses a three-tiered architecture. The user accesses the system through a Web browser. The middle tier connects the user interface and the backend databases and implements the work logic. COPLINK Detect is targeted for detectives and crime analysts. The system shares the same incident record information as the Connect module and utilizes the database indexes it generates. However, the Detect system has a completely redesigned user interface, and employs a new set of intelligence analysis tools to meet its user needs.

Much of crime analysis is concerned with creating associations or linkages among various aspects of a crime. COPLINK Detect uses a technique called concept space to identify such associations from existing crime data automatically. In general, a concept space is a network of terms and weighted associations within an underlying information space. COPLINK Detect uses statistical techniques such as co-occurrence analysis and clustering functions to weight relationships between all possible pairs of concepts.

In COPLINK Detect, detailed criminal case reports are the underlying information space, and concepts are meaningful terms occurring in each case. These case reports contain both structured (e.g., database fields for incidents containing the case number, names of people involved, address and date) and unstructured data (narratives written by officers commenting on an incident, e.g., witness A said he saw suspect A run away in a white truck).

Several field user studies have been conducted to evaluate the COPLINK system. For example, a group of 52 law-enforcement personnel from the Tucson Police Department representing a number of different job classifications and backgrounds were recruited to participate in a study to evaluate COPLINK Connect. Both interview-data and survey-data analyses support a conclusion that use of the application provided performance superior to using the legacy police records management system. In addition to the statistical data, these findings were supported by qualitative data collected from participant interviews (Chen et al., 2003).

The other application to be presented here is concerned with geocomputation for geodemographics. Geodemographic profiles of the characteristics of individuals and small areas potentially offer significant breakthroughs in clarifying local policing needs in the same way they have become an integral part of many commercial and marketing ventures. Geodemographic systems were one of the first emergent applications areas of what is now known as geocomputation.

Ashby and Longley (2005) conducted a case study of the Devon and Cornwall Constabulary. They found that geodemographic analyses of local policing environments, crime profiles, and police performance provided a significantly increased level of community intelligence for police use. This was further enhanced by the use of penetration ranking reports where neighborhood types were ranked by standardized crime rates, and cumulative percentage of the crime was compared with the corresponding population at risk.

SPIKE (Surrey Police Information and Knowledge Environment) is an information management system. Surrey Police in the United Kingdom recognized that it needed to transform itself into a virtual organization if it wanted to continue to deliver its unique community-based policing service under the pressure to become more efficient. Only a drastic improvement in productivity and reduced costs would allow their style of policing to survive. The solution was SPIKE, which enables real-time knowledge sharing and has become a catalyst for a quantum change in the organization's structure and the method by which it delivers its services (*ComputerWeekly*, 2002).

To be a truly useful utility, the Surrey Police had to decide what information had to go into it in the first place. Conceptual work was done to develop information architecture. Staff had to be able to create and access information using a consistent method and interface. Moreover, the criteria for access— ensuring that only those personnel with a right to know can access what it is they are authorized to know, and no more—had to be both preset and nonintrusive. All the issues of security levels and clearance were worked out up front.

In the end, the system had to prove itself on the street. Like most people with real jobs to do, police officers tend to regard a heavy burden of administrative paperwork as an unnecessary evil. Since the information utility is only as valuable as the information it contains, convincing officers that taking the time to input that information in the first place can be a challenge. Only when they experience the fruits of that input, by way of receiving the output they need to ease and speed up their real jobs, will it be accepted. Key to the value to be got out of SPIKE is making it possible for officers to have mobile information and access. Increasingly, information is most useful when it is delivered on the beat (*ComputerWeekly*, 2002).

A final interesting example of IT in police work is closed-circuit television (CCTV). The second generation of CCTV is called the thinking eye, since the main difference between first- and second-generation surveillance is the change from a dumb camera that needs a human eye to evaluate its images to a computer-linked camera system that evaluates its own video images.

Value Shop Performance

For a long time, Porter's (1985) value chain was the only value configuration known to managers. Stabell and Fjeldstad (1998) have identified two alternative value configurations. A value shop schedules activities and applies resources in a fashion that is dimensioned and appropriate to solve a specific problem, while a value chain performs a fixed set of activities that enables it to produce a standard product in large numbers. Examples of value shops are professional service firms, as found in medicine, architecture, engineering, and law. A value network links clients or customers who are or wish to be interdependent. Examples of value networks are telephone companies, retail banks, and insurance companies.

It can be argued that the police investigation process has the value configuration of a value shop, similar to law firms (Gottschalk, 2006). The value shop is an organization that creates value by solving unique problems. Knowledge is the most important resource. A value shop is characterized by five primary activities: problem finding and acquisition, problem solving, choice, execution, and control and evaluation, as illustrated in Figure 2.1.

As can be seen in Figure 2.1, these five activities are interlocking and while they follow a logical sequence, much like the management of any project, the difference from a knowledge management perspective is the way in

Figure 2.1 Police investigation as value shop activities.

which knowledge is used as a resource to create value in terms of results for the organization. Hence, the logic of the five interlocking value shop activities in this example is of a police organization and how it engages in its core business of conducting reactive and proactive investigations.

Also, noted on Figure 2.1 is how in practice these five sequential activities tend to overlap and link back to earlier activities, especially in relation to activity 5 (control and evaluation) in police organizations when the need for control and command structures are a daily necessity because of the legal obligations that police authority entails. Hence, the diagram on Figure 2.1 is meant to illustrate the reiterative and cyclical nature of these five primary activities for managing the knowledge collected during and applied to a specific police investigation in a value shop manner.

These five primary activities of the value shop in relation to a police investigation unit can be outlined as follows:

1. *Problem definition and information acquisition.* This involves working with parties to determine the exact nature of the crime and hence how it will be defined. For example, a physical assault in a domestic violence situation depending on how the responding officers choose and/or perceive to define it can be either upgraded to the status of grievous bodily harm to the female spouse victim or it may be downgraded to a less serious common, garden variety assault where a bit of rough handing took place toward the spouse. This concept of making crime, a term used on how detectives choose to make incidents into a crime or not, is highly apt here and is why this first activity has been changed from the original problem finding term used in the business management realm to a problem definition process here in relation to police work. Moreover, this first investigative activity involves deciding on the overall investigative approach for the case not only in terms of information acquisition but also as indicated on Figure 2.1 in undertaking the key task, usually by a SIO in a serious or major incident, of forming an appropriate investigative team to handle the case.

2. *Problem solving approaches.* This involves the actual generation of ideas and action plans for the investigation. As such, it is a key process for it sets the direction and tone of the investigation and is very much influenced by the composition of the members of the investigative team. For example, the experience level of investigators and their preferred investigative thinking style might be a critical success factor in this second primary activity of the value shop.

3. *Solution choice.* This represents the decision of choosing between alternatives. While the least important primary activity of the value shop in terms of time and effort, it might be the most important in

terms of value. In this case, trying to ensure as far as is possible that what is decided on to do is the best option to follow to get an effective investigative result. A successful solution choice is dependent on two requirements. First, alternative investigation steps were identified in the problem solving approaches activity. It is important to think in terms of alternatives. Otherwise, no choices can be made. Next, criteria for decision-making have to be known and applied to the specific investigation.

4. *Solution execution.* As the name implies, this represents communicating, organizing, investigating, and implementing decisions. This is an equally important process or phase in an investigation as it involves sorting out from the mass of information coming into the incident room about a case and directing the lines of enquiry as well as establishing the criteria used to eliminate a possible suspect from further scrutiny in the investigation. A miscalculation here can stall or even ruin the whole investigation.

5. *Control and evaluation.* This involves monitoring activities and the measurement of how well the solution solved the original problem or met the original need. This is where the command and control chain of authority comes into play for police organizations and where the determination of the quality and quantity of the evidence is made as to whether or not to charge and prosecute an identified offender in a court of law.

The value shop approach is very much in line with the investigative process as defined by Smith and Flanagan (2000). The process begins with an initial crime scene assessment where sources of potential evidence are identified. The information derived from the process then has to be evaluated in order to gauge its relevance to the investigation. During the next stage, the information is interpreted to develop inferences and initial hypotheses. This material can then be developed by the SIO into appropriate and feasible lines of enquiry. The SIO will then have to prioritize actions, and to identify any additional information that may be required to test that scenario. As more information is collected, this is then fed back into the process until the objectives of the investigation are achieved. Providing a suspect is identified and charged, the investigation then enters the post-charge stage, where case papers are compiled for the prosecution. Subsequently, the court process will begin.

Research Models

Two research models have been applied to this research. The first model investigates the extent to which the IS used in police investigations

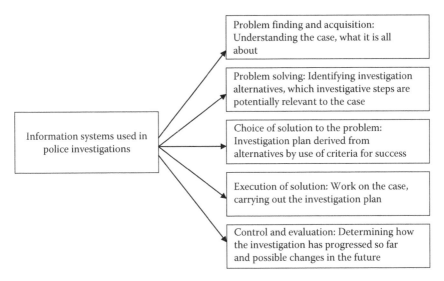

Figure 2.2 First research model linking average systems use to performance in value shop.

influence the performance. Performance in police investigations is represented by the five primary activities in the value shop, as illustrated in Figure 2.2.

The second research model investigates the extent to which each information system used in police investigations influences the performance. Performance in police investigations is represented by the average of the five primary activities in the value shop, as illustrated in Figure 2.3.

In the first research model, the average use of all IS is applied to predict the extent of investigation performance in each value shop activity. In the second research model, all individual IS are applied to predict the extent of average investigation performance for all value shop activities. In addition, variations of these research models are possible. For example, it is possible to define a research model predicting the extent of performance in one value shop activity based on all individual IS.

Research Methodology

To measure both dependent and independent constructs, a survey instrument was developed. The questionnaire was e-mailed to SIOs in charge of criminal investigations in Norway. A total of 101 questionnaires were returned. Among the respondents, 40% had more than ten years of experience as SIOs. The average age was 46 years; 89% were male and 11% were female officers.

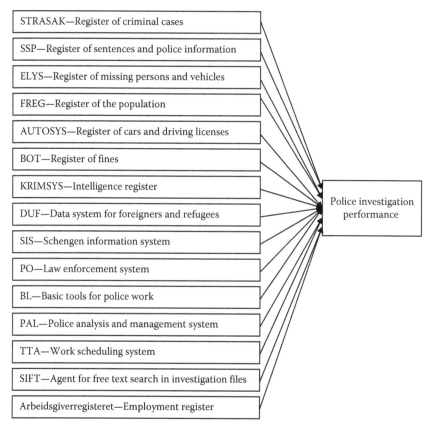

Figure 2.3 Second research model linking systems to overall performance in value shop.

The dependent variables were all measured on multiple item scales as listed in Table 2.1. All five scales have acceptable reliability in terms of Cronbach's alpha (Hair et al., 1995). Out of the five primary activities in the value shop, problem finding and solving achieve the highest scores (5.0), while control and evaluation achieves the lowest score (4.0) on a scale from 1 (not clever) to 7 (very clever).

The independent variables are listed in Table 2.2. Each represents one specific system that is used by police officers in criminal investigations. Taken together, they represent a multiple item scale for the use of IS with an acceptable reliability of .938.

Research Results

The first research model was tested using correlation analysis. If significant correlation was found between the performance in a value shop activity and

Table 2.1 Multiple Item Scales for the Dependent Variables

Police Investigation Performance in the Value Shop	Average	Alpha
Understanding the case, what it is all about: Problem finding and acquisition	5.0	.934
Channel the case to the right investigator	5.1	
Assess initial case information and other relevant information	5.2	
Collect additional historical information	4.3	
Evaluate whether there is suspicion of a criminal offence	5.5	
Assess the police task in the case	5.4	
Inform parties and stakeholders of the case	4.6	
Identifying investigation alternatives, which investigative steps are potentially relevant to the case: Problem solving	5.0	.956
Determine the purpose of the investigation	5.1	
Assess the extent to which there is experience from similar cases	5.0	
Discuss with colleagues what potential investigation schemes are appropriate	4.9	
Assess the seriousness of the criminal offence	5.1	
Find methods for investigative steps	5.0	
Plan for alternative investigative steps	4.6	
Investigation plan derived from alternatives by use of criteria for success: Choice of solution to the problem	4.8	.942
Identify criteria for choice of investigation program	4.6	
Discuss with colleagues which investigation program is the best	4.8	
Check routines and guidelines for police work	4.4	
Check resources for investigative actions	4.7	
Find a qualified investigation leader	4.8	
Determine what the police must do in the case	5.2	
Work on the case, carrying out the investigation plan: Execution of solution	4.8	.915
Collect information from files	4.6	
Collect information from persons	5.0	
Secure leads	4.9	
Interrogate potential suspect(s)	5.4	
Interrogate potential witness(es)	5.3	
Inform involved persons (such as relatives) about the future	4.3	
Determining how the investigation has progressed so far and possible changes in the future: Control and evaluation	4.0	.926
Evaluate the quality of police work in the case	4.1	
Evaluate the quality of legal work in the case	4.0	
Involve in the evaluation everyone who has participated in the investigation	3.7	
Assess how the investigation of the case was managed	3.7	
Control the use of resources in the case	4.0	
Learn from the case	4.6	
Average overall performance in the value shop	4.7	.965

Note: Scale from 1 = not clever to 7 = very clever in carrying out investigation tasks in the police unit/department/group/section/team.

Table 2.2   Information Systems' Use as Independent Variables

	Average	Alpha
Use of IS in police investigations	4.6	.938
STRASAK—Register of criminal cases	6.0	
SSP—Register of sentences and police information	5.5	
ELYS—Register of missing persons and vehicles	4.9	
FREG—Register of the population	5.8	
AUTOSYS—Register of cars and driving licenses	5.5	
BOT—Register of fines	4.3	
KRIMSYS—Intelligence register	4.1	
DUF—Data system for foreigners and refugees	3.6	
SIS—Schengen information system	3.5	
PO—Law enforcement system	5.3	
BL—Basic tools for policing	6.2	
PAL—Police analysis and management system	3.8	
TTA—Work scheduling system	3.6	
SIFT—Agent for free text search in investigation files	2.9	
Arbeidsgiverregisteret—Employment register	3.6	

Note: Scale from 1 = little extent to 7 = great extent.

the extent of system use, then the hypothesis is supported. Correlation coefficients are listed in Table 2.3.

Table 2.3 documents that all five research hypotheses in the research model are supported in this research, as all correlation coefficients are statistically significant.

The second research model was tested by applying multiple regression analysis to the collected data. The dependent variable is a combination of all five value-shop activities, as this combination achieved an acceptable reliability of .965 as listed in Table 2.1. The regression model achieved an adjusted R-square of .756, which means that more than three quarter of the variation in police investigation performance can be explained by the use of these systems. The regression model is statistically significant

Table 2.3   Correlation Coefficients for System Use with Investigation Phases

Police Investigation Phases	Systems
Understanding the criminal case	.755**
Identifying alternative investigation approaches	.780**
Selecting best investigation approach	.820**
Carrying out the investigation	.793**
Determining the performance of the investigation	.687**

**$p < .01$.

Table 2.4   Significance of Independent Variables in the Regression Analysis

Use of IS in Police Investigations	Relational Coefficient	Value t-Statistic	Significance t-Statistic
STRASAK—Register of criminal cases	.026	.150	.881
SSP—Register of sentences and police information	.226	1.907	.060
ELYS—Register of missing persons and vehicles	−.274	−2.605	.011
FREG—Register of the population	.110	.876	.384
AUTOSYS—Register of cars and driving licenses	.000	.001	1.000
BOT—Register of fines	−.022	−.285	.777
KRIMSYS—Intelligence register	.128	1.305	.196
DUF—Data system for foreigners and refugees	.089	.743	.460
SIS—Schengen information system	−.010	−.087	.931
PO—Law enforcement system	.088	.958	.341
BL—Basic tools for policing	.427	3.622	.001
PAL—Police analysis and management system	.089	1.243	.218
TTA—Work scheduling system	.026	.387	.700
SIFT—Agent for free text search in investigation files	.137	1.691	.095
Arbeidsgiverregisteret—Employment register	.141	1.968	.053

($p < .01$). The significance of each independent variable can be explored in Table 2.4.

The statistical results in Table 2.4 show that one hypothesis is supported at the significance level of $p < .01$, while another hypothesis is supported at the significance level of $p < .05$. The first supported hypothesis is that the increased use of basic tools for policing (BL) will improve police investigation performance. The second supported hypothesis is that the more the register of missing persons and vehicles (ELYS) is used, the better police investigation performance is achieved.

While Table 2.3 in the total systems model suggests that the hypotheses are all true, in the individual systems model in Table 2.4, only two systems are significant. This result implies that while the systems as a package are all significant, when broken down into individual systems, only two of them represent the statistical significance found.

When the five dependent measures of value shop activities were cross-correlated with the complete set of system utilization independent variables, some insight was revealed into the efficacy of different systems for different value shop activities. For most activities there was no change compared to the average value shop. However, for the implementation of investigation in activity 3, also SIFT turned out to be a significant system. SIFT enables investigators to search freely in all kinds of documents and databases for words and numbers.

Discussion

Ultimately, the basic tools for policing (BL) and register of missing persons and vehicles (ELYS) were the only individual IS significantly influencing police investigations in terms of overall value shop performance.

BL stands for basic solutions (in Norwegian, "basisløsninger"). In Norway, it is a case handling system for all parts of the police. The system has continuously been revised and improved. It is a tool for police officers' and administrative staff's work on criminal cases. When used properly, the system improves the efficiency of case handling, enhances quality and guarantees basic justice. The system is built so that both detectives and prosecutors can do almost all their work on a case within the system. The user manual for the system is considered to be good and readily understandable.

BL has several standard forms to be filled in by detectives and prosecutors in criminal investigations. The system keeps and provides an overview of case status, officers working on the case, investigation steps, and deadlines. Within the system are formalities and standard procedures, rulebook and other support for casework. When BL was implemented, the ambition was to improve the utilization of policing resources as well as make the investigation process more effective. BL is also designed to help improve the utilization and reuse of information that is registered electronically in the system for all kinds of policing work, so that the information may be used in police intelligence and in other cases than the original case causing the information to be collected and registered.

BL belongs to the category of IS labeled end-user-tools. Such tools have been found to be extremely useful in policing in general (Gottschalk, 2006). The SIO with his or her team has a tool to collect, organize, structure, and present electronic information. Hence, it is not surprising that BL turned out to be a significant system predicting the extent of investigation performance.

ELYS stands for searching register (in Norwegian "etterlysningsregister"). The system is a database with all missing and wanted persons, vehicles, boats, and boat engines. In addition to persons who are nationally wanted for criminal offences, all other wanted individuals are as well registered in this database. Persons who are missing or wanted from abroad, which is reported by Interpol, either for arrest or for information about current location, are also registered in ELYS. The system is available to police officers and persons who have a documented need.

ELYS is a decentralized system, so that each police district in Norway enter and retrieve information from the system. The Central Bureau of Investigations in Oslo enters Interpol messages into the system. ELYS belongs to the category of IS labeled officer-to-information systems. Such systems provide access to information resources for a police investigation (Gottschalk, 2006). Again, it is not surprising that ELYS turned out to be a significant system predicting the extent of investigation performance since most investigations involve the search for persons and/or vehicles.

The model for stages of growth in IS supporting knowledge work in police investigations is illustrated in Figure 2.4. While BL is officer-to-technology in terms of an end-user-tool, ELYS is officer-to-information in terms of what-they-know. The stages-of-growth model developed by Gottschalk (2006) enables the classification of IS into different stages.

Based on the stages of growth model, it can now be discussed why all the other IS available to Norwegian detectives were not significant predictors of performance in police investigations. Almost all of the systems belong to stage 3: STRASAK, SSP, FREG, AUTOSYS, BOT, KRIMSYS, and the Norwegian Work Registry (In Norwegian, "Arbeidsgiverregisteret"). Only one such system was significant in this research: ELYS. A potential explanation is that ELYS seems to be the database with a purpose most closely related to police investigations.

Among the remaining systems, there are DUF for special cases involving foreigners, SIS for special cases involving more than one European country, PO for general policing, PAL for all kinds of police analysis, TTA for

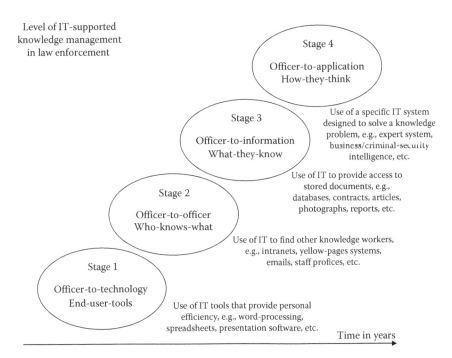

Level of IT-supported knowledge management in law enforcement

Stage 4
Officer-to-application
How-they-think

Stage 3
Officer-to-information
What-they-know

Use of a specific IT system designed to solve a knowledge problem, e.g., expert system, business/criminal-security intelligence, etc.

Stage 2
Officer-to-officer
Who-knows-what

Use of IT to provide access to stored documents, e.g., databases, contracts, articles, photographs, reports, etc.

Stage 1
Officer-to-technology
End-user-tools

Use of IT to find other knowledge workers, e.g., intranets, yellow-pages systems, emails, staff profices, etc.

Use of IT tools that provide personal efficiency, e.g., word-processing, spreadsheets, presentation software, etc.

Time in years

Figure 2.4 The knowledge management systems stage model.

scheduling of police resources, and the electronic text search engine SIFT. None of them are specifically designed for police investigations. Rather, most of them have either another primary purpose or a much more general purpose than investigation support.

Conclusion

The activities and work carried out by police forces are increasingly in the areas of crime prevention as well as incident management, investigation, and community policing. An empirical analysis of criminal investigations within the Norwegian police force has drawn some interesting conclusions and clearly warrants the attention of those involved in criminal investigation. What was overwhelmingly revealed is that the performance of crime investigations was linked to the extent of IS used to support investigative work. Specifically, it was discovered that IS improves the performance of all investigative processes defined as value shop activities.

Furthermore, out of 14 common systems used by the Norwegian police force, only 2 systems had a significant impact on investigation performance. The features of these IS that give them enhanced utility in criminal investigations seem to be that they either represent an end-user-tool in terms of officer-to-technology or what-they-know system in terms of officer-to-information. The latter system category is a database with information about missing and wanted persons and vehicles that are central to most police investigations. Utilization of these or similar databases while conducting criminal investigations can enhance the effectiveness and efficiency of policing efforts.

References

Ashby, D.I. and Longley, P.A. 2005. Geocomputation, geodemographics and resource allocation for local policing. *Transactions in GIS*, 9(1): 53–72.
Brynjolfsson, E. and Hitt, L. 1996. Paradox lost? Firm-level evidence on the returns to information systems spending. *Management Science*, 42(4): 541–558.
Chen, H., Schroeder, J., Hauck, R.V., Ridgeway, L., Atabakhsh, H., Gupta, H., Boarman, C., Rasmussen, K., and Clements, A.W. 2002. COPLINK Connect: Information and knowledge management for law enforcement. *Decision Support Systems*, 34: 271–285.
Chen, H., Zheng, D., Atabakhsh, H., Wyzga, W., and Schroeder, J. 2003. COPLINK Managing law enforcement data and knowledge. *Communications of the ACM*, 46(1): 28–34.
ComputerWeekly. 2002. Knowledge management: Surrey Police. *ComputerWeekly*, February 28, 2002.
Fahsing, I., Ask, K., and Granhag, P.A. 2004. The man behind the mask: Accuracy and predictors of eyewitness offender descriptions. *Journal of Applied Psychology*, 89(4): 722–729.

Fraser, C. 2004. Strategic information systems for policing. *Police Executive Research Forum*. Connecticut Avenue, Washington, DC.

Gottschalk, P. 2006. *Knowledge Management Systems in Law Enforcement: Technologies and Techniques*. Hershey, PA: Idea Group Publishing.

Grover, V. and Davenport, T.H. 2001. General perspectives on knowledge management: Fostering a research agenda. *Journal of Management Information Systems*, 18(1): 5–21.

Hair, J.F., Anderson, R.E., Tatham, R.L., and Black, W.C. 1995. *Multivariate Data Analysis with Readings*, 4th edn. Englewood Cliffs, NJ: Prentice-Hall.

Home Office. 2005. *Guidance on Statutory Performance Indicators for Policing 205/2006*. Police Standards Unit, Home Office of the UK Government, www.policereform.gov.uk. http://www.google.no/search?source=igandhl=noandrlz =1G1GGLQ_NONO307andq=Home±Office±2005.±Guidance±on±statutory ±performance±indicators±for±policing±205%2F2006.±Police±Standards±Un it%2C±Home±Office±of±the±UK±Government%2C±www.policereform.gov. uk.andbtnG=Google-s%C3%B8kandmeta=lr%3Dandaq=-1andoq=

Luen, T.W. and Al-Hawamdeh, S. 2001. Knowledge management in the public sector: Principles and practices in police work. *Journal of Information Science*, 27(5): 311–318.

Melville, N., Kraemer, K., and Gurbaxani, V. 2004. Information technology and organizational performance: An integrative model of IT business value. *MIS Quarterly*, 28(2): 283–322.

Porter, M.L. 1985. *Competitive Strategy*. New York: The Free Press.

Puonti, A. 2004. Tools for collaboration: Using and designing tools in inter-organizational economic-crime investigation. *Mind, Culture, and Activity*, 11(2): 133–152.

Smith, N. and Flanagan, C. 2000. *The Effective Detective Identifying the Skills of an Effective SIO*. London, U.K.: British Home Office.

Stabell, C.B. and Fjeldstad, Ø.D. 1998. Configuring value for competitive advantage: On chains, shops, and networks. *Strategic Management Journal*, 19: 413–437.

Surette, R. 2005. The thinking eye: Pros and cons of second generation CCTV surveillance systems. *Policing: An International Journal of Police Strategies and Management*, 28(1): 152–173.

Thibault, E.A., Lynch, L.M., and McBride, R.B. 1998. *Proactive Police Management*. 4th edn. Upper Saddle River, NJ: Prentice Hall.

Challenges of Policing in the New Millennium: Reform of the Austrian Police Structure

3

MAXIMILIAN EDELBACHER

Contents

Introduction: Enlargement of the European Union

Europe is a continent with a very long and old history. Approximately 40 countries are home to 700 million inhabitants. The largest countries are Germany, France, Italy, Poland, Spain, Sweden, Turkey, the United Kingdom, and Russia. Twenty-seven countries are now members of the European Union. Since the fall of the "Iron Curtain" in 1989, the biggest migration since 1945 has been taking place. The European Union now has approximately 450 million inhabitants. Over the next few years, the European Community will be taking on between 300,000 and 600,000 immigrants every year, including 250,000 from the former Eastern Bloc. Between 1980 and 1992, approximately 15 million foreigners settled in the European Community; 45% of them came from Africa, Asia, Latin America, and Turkey. A 1993 survey by the United Nations showed that approximately 20 million eastern Europeans had planned to immigrate to the European Community. For many people in the East, the target countries in the European Community are Germany and Austria. According to Russian estimates, 1.5–2 million citizens are ready to emigrate for economic reasons. An additional 5–6 million are "considering" emigration. These large demographic challenges also have an impact on organized crime [1].

New Economic Development

Global economic development has changed the economy in Europe as well. Geographically, Europe seems to be not just one continent, it also seems to be one market. Some international companies are sometimes much more powerful than the smaller countries. They think and act in a market-oriented manner. For example, if production facilities are cheaper in Eastern countries, these companies change the location of their factories. This significantly influences the police deployment of a country. For example, discussions in Germany show just how powerful car producers are: Mercedes and Volkswagen put a lot of pressure on their employees and on the German government.

Trafficking in Human Beings

A lot has changed in Europe since 1988. The communist regimes in Eastern Europe have collapsed, the successor states have lifted their travel restrictions, and the Iron Curtain has fallen. Although there has been an ongoing process of democratization in the successor countries, there are still a lot of difficulties to be overcome. Thus, the general situation of the former Eastern Bloc countries is characterized by the challenge to the community, such as mass unemployment, collapse of companies, and a decrease in performance and welfare. In addition, there are many problems associated with the adoption of European standards. Many international conferences examining the topic of security have highlighted that the most important problems and fears of people today and in the future are related to

- Terrorism
- Crime
- Migrant tendency to violence
- Drugs
- Corruption
- Human rights violation

Since the Republic of Austria has become a member of the European Union and is participating in the four freedoms (freedom of service, freedom of goods trafficking, freedom of capital, and freedom of residence), they must fulfill the standards of Schengen and Maastricht. The following list of priorities has been set up by the Treaty of Schengen, 1985 and 1992, to achieve the aim of a safe Europe [2]:

- Common asylum politics
- The protection of the external borders of neighboring countries
- Common immigration policies
- A common fight against drug dealing
- A common fight against international fraud
- Judicial cooperation in civil matters

- Judicial cooperation in criminal matters
- Cooperation in customs enforcement
- Police cooperation against terrorism, illegal drug trafficking, and serious forms of international crime

Effects on Crime

The newest member countries of the European Union are now in the same position as Austria was in 1995. The following changes can be foreseen:

- High proportion of imported crime due to high mobility of criminals
- Higher proportion of immigrants among the criminal population
- An increase in the types of organized crime
- An increase in violent crime and terrorist-related activities

Movement of the People

The prognosis of the United Nations is that, in the year 2010, approximately 5 billion people will live under rather poor conditions and 1.5 billion people will be rather well-off. Young people especially, driven by the information that life is much better in America and Europe, will try to leave their countries and move to the richer continents. These movements from East to West and South to North are accelerated by the globalization of the world economy. As mentioned earlier, the biggest migration since 1945 has been taking place since the fall of the Iron Curtain in 1989. The predominant reasons for the ever-increasing migration involve

- No noticeable improvement of the economic situation in home countries
- The wish for better social living conditions
- Political instability and fear of the future
- More crimes of violence (cold-blooded criminals commit murders, robberies, and blackmail without regard to the victims in order to satisfy their greed for money)
- The increasing destruction of the environment and the resultant restriction of living space
- Political tensions (e.g., civil wars)
- Violation of human rights by totalitarian and dictatorial regimes
- The population explosion in the developing countries (in the year 2010, approximately 1.36 billion people will be living in developed areas in comparison to approximately 6 billion people in underdeveloped ones)

The analysis of migration movement during the second half of the 1990s confirms the stabilization in legal immigration inflows, and a decline in immigration to certain countries. Although Germany receives the highest number of foreigners in absolute terms in Europe, it is Luxembourg and Switzerland where the influx of foreigners is the most significant.

There are two geographic areas in Central and Eastern Europe as well as East and South East Asia that exemplify the regionalization and globalization of migration movements. This is characterized by the diversity of the nationalities involved and the growing importance of flows between neighboring countries. Asia has seen the highest rate of economic growth of any region over the last decade, which has been accompanied by an increase in international migration.

In Central and Eastern Europe, the determining factors behind population movements are the recent political and economic changes as well as social and ethnic tensions. The regionalization and globalization of migration flows necessitates the implementation of effective measures and initiatives in the area of international cooperation to control flows of migration.

Ethnic Minorities

Hand in hand with the movement of the people, other problems concerning ethnic minorities arise. As a lot of ethnic minorities are settling down in Europe, there is a tendency by the home population not to accept these foreigners. Some young members of our society see foreigners as a threat to their jobs. One reason for this might be that unemployment rates among the young are increasing in all European countries. As a consequence, xenophobia has become a serious problem these days. The danger of extremism was best illustrated by the letter-bomb attacks that worried Austria in the 1990s and by the attacks against homes of foreign migrants in Germany. Chinese, Vietnamese, Black Africans, people from Russia, Poland, Turkey, or former Yugoslavia are not accepted very cordially anymore. Besides this fact, there are lots of problems that have to do with the increasing rate of crime committed by these minorities.

Terrorism

Since September 11, 2001, the world has changed dramatically. Terrorism became the number one threat for neo-capitalism, especially in North America. The United Nations Office on Drugs and Crime hosted a

Symposium at the Vienna International Centre in June 2002 on the topic "Combating International Terrorism." The Symposium was attended by more than 100 nations, 10 intergovernmental organizations, 6 nongovernmental organizations, high-level representatives of the Secretariat of the United Nations, and individuals from the UN member states serving as panelists.

For many, September 11, 2001, was seen as a wake-up call. "In a few minutes the international community realized that a small group of well-organized people could bring the daily life of civil society to a halt," commented Antonio Maria Costa, the chief of the United Nations, in Vienna. As the threat to global peace and security from terrorism has become more manifest, the resolve of the international community to take effective concerted action to counter it has increased correspondingly. From this perspective, terrorism prevention requires an open-ended, long-term process entailing total commitment toward this end from European Union member states and others in the United Nations (Ali Sarwar Naqvi, ambassador, permanent representative of Pakistan to the UN).

The outstanding primary dilemma, the consensual definition of terrorism, has been instrumental in creating difficulties in tackling terrorism and all its manifestations on a global level, as all countries have their own individual definitions based on national circumstances. The existing United Nations instruments are all regional instruments criminalizing certain behaviors in specific locations. The definition of terrorism is restricted to the framework and scope of each individual instrument. None of these is comprehensive or all-inclusive. Therefore, states feel that the ambiguity of interpretation can be used against them. Until "terrorism" is defined properly, with internationally agreed qualifications, the reluctance toward implementation of one international counter-terrorism strategy will continue.

The Federal Bureau of Investigation in the United States, for example, defines terrorism as "the unlawful use of force or violence against persons or property to intimidate or coerce a government, the civilian population, or any segment thereof, in furtherance of political or social objectives;" which can involve "domestic or international terrorism depending on the origin, base, and objectives of the terrorist organization" [3].

Corruption

Corruption has existed ever since antiquity as one of the worst and, at the same time, most widespread forms of behavior that is detrimental to the administration of public affairs when indulged in by public officials and elected representatives. In the last 100 years, it has come to encompass behavior within the purely private domain.

Definition of Corruption [4]

Corruption is like a prism with many surfaces. The draft United Nations Convention against Corruption contained the following provisions in Article 1:

> Each Contracting State undertakes to make the following acts punishable by appropriate criminal penalties under its national law:
>
> 1. The offering, promising, or giving of any payment, or other advantage by any natural person, on his own behalf or on behalf of any enterprise or any person whether juridical or natural, to or for the benefit of a public official as undue consideration for performing or refraining from the performance of his duties in connection with an international commercial transaction.
> 2. The soliciting, demanding, accepting or receiving, directly or indirectly, by a public official of any payment, gift or other advantage, as undue consideration for performing or refraining from the performance of his duties in connection with an international commercial transaction.

The Council of the OECD, in the Recommendation on Bribery in International Business Transactions in May 1994, adopted the following definition:

> Bribery can involve the direct or indirect offer or provision of any undue pecuniary or other advantage to or for a foreign public official, in violation of the official's legal duties, in order to obtain or retain business.

Corruption is a "regular, repetitive, integral part" of the operation of political systems. Corruption pervades every level of government and the economy. Corruption cases are wrongful acts on the part of public holders, involving misuse of their office. Political corruption is a cooperative form of unsanctioned, usually condemned policy to apply influence for some type of significant personal gain, in which the reward (or bribe) could be economic, social, political, or even ideological remuneration. Potential targets of corruption mainly involve influencing:

- Political parties
- Elections and candidates
- Business leaders (construction industry, banks, etc.)
- Bureaucrats
- Journalists

The typical "modus operandi" of corruption could include bribery, bid fixing, kickbacks, trading in influence, financing of political parties, and slanted media coverage. Transparency International reported the following figures with respect to corruption in 2004 (index range from 1 = high corruption to 10 = low corruption).

1. Finland 9.7%
2. New Zealand 9.6%
3. Denmark and Iceland 9.5%

Countries reportedly with the highest levels of corruption:

- Nigeria
- Bolivia
- Columbia
- Russia
- Pakistan
- Mexico
- Indonesia
- India
- Venezuela
- Vietnam
- Argentina
- China
- The Philippines
- Thailand
- Turkey
- Romania

Organized Crime

Corruption is a tool used to establish and support organized crime. This means that organized crime is not possible without corruption. For centuries, organized crime was not a topic openly discussed throughout Europe. Although the phenomena of organized crime existed in Italy, represented by the legendary Italian Mafia, there was also influence felt in the other parts of Europe. Even in Middle Europe, organized forms of crime existed for a long time before it became an open challenge. Until the late 1970s, the existence of organized crime was denied by government officials within nearly all the European countries. Interest in organized crime was highlighted by reports from the United States and their fight against such mysterious figures as Al Capone and by reports about the brutality used by the Italian Mafia. In the last 40 years, crime has approximately doubled in Europe. It should be noted that it is rather complicated to make precise comparisons of crime in European countries, because of the differences in legal definitions and statistics. Not only has the quantity of crime become a challenge for public security agencies, but the more notable issue is the enhanced fear of the quality of violent crime that is exhibited by organized crime groups. "Organized Crime is like cancer: it cannot be openly seen, but it grows and can soon endanger the whole society (body). It grows slowly but continuously and when the symptoms come out—it is almost too late to react. Fighting organized crime is therefore extremely difficult and sometimes it seems useless. It is like fighting a tornado, a hurricane or the great floods." Another important point of view is that controlling the development of organized crime is related to the extent of how far a democratic police organization has been established. Organized crime might be controlled if nepotism and favoritism can be eliminated. A study conducted in Turkey shows that nepotism and favoritism, the primary factors of corruption, are dangerous for those involved in the field of policing. Influence by politicians, media, and pressure groups such as human right organizations affect police work negatively. Today, organized crime is the number one challenge in Europe. Additionally, it is difficult to estimate the extent of organized crime in Europe.

Since 1989, after the Iron Curtain fell, an enormous change has taken place in Europe. The general economic, social, and political conditions are the bases for the development of organized crime structures. If these conditions worsen, organized criminal groups can settle in and often take over (including politics and legitimate business). The history of the "Italian Mafia," and now the expansion of the "Russian Mafia," are proof of this theory. Like terrorism, defining organized crime has also become an issue. In Europe, there is no single definition that has been accepted by all European nations. Therefore, definitions of organized crime used by Interpol, the German Bureau of Criminal Investigation ("Bundeskriminalamt"), and the Federal Bureau of Investigation in the United States are commonly used in Europe.

The United Nations Convention against Transnational Organized Crime

The United Nations Convention against Transnational Organized Crime was adopted by the General Assembly in its resolution 55/25 of November 2000. The purpose of this convention was to promote cooperation to prevent and combat transnational organized crime more effectively [5].

Article 2 of this resolution defines the use of terms:

(a) "Organized criminal groups" shall mean a structured group of three or more persons, existing for a period of time and acting in concert with the aim of committing one or more serious crimes or offenses established in accordance with this Convention, in order to obtain, directly or indirectly, a financial or other material benefit.

(b) "Serious crime" shall mean conduct constituting an offense punishable by a maximum deprivation of liberty of at least 4 years or a more serious penalty.

(c) "Structured group" shall mean a group that is not randomly formed for the immediate commission of an offense and that does not need to have formally defined roles for its members, continuity of its membership or a developed structure.

(d) "Property" shall mean assets of every kind, whether corporeal or incorporeal, movable or immovable, tangible or intangible, and legal documents or instruments evidencing title to, or interest in, such assets.

(e) "Proceeds of crime" shall mean any property derived from or obtained, directly or indirectly, through the commission of an offense.

(f) "Freezing" or "seizure" shall mean temporarily prohibiting the transfer, conversion, disposition or movement of property or temporarily assuming custody or control of property on the basis of an order issued by a court or other competent authority.

(g) "Confiscation," which includes forfeiture where applicable, shall mean the permanent deprivation of property by order of a court or other competent authority.

(h) "Predicate offense" shall mean any offense as a result of which proceeds have been generated that may become the subject of an offense as defined in article 6 of this Convention.

Other pertinent definitions clarified in this resolution also include

Article 5—Criminalization of participation in an organized criminal group—each (member state) shall adopt such legislation and other measures as may be necessary to establish as criminal offenses, when committed intentionally.

Articles 6 and 7 refer to the criminalization of the laundering of proceeds of crime and the measures to combat money laundering.

Articles 8 and 9 refer to the criminalization of corruption and define measures against corruption.

Article 10 refers to the liability of legal persons.

Interpol defines organized crime as

"Organized crime comprises systematically prepared and planned committing of serious criminal acts with the view to gain financial profits and powers and which were committed in a longer, undefined period of time by more than three accomplices united in hierarchy and job division organized criminal association in which the methods of violence, various types of intimidation, corruption and other influences are used, with the view to secure the development of criminal activities." By this definition, organized crime consists of using violence or corruption to achieve profitable goals.

Interpol outlines that the following elements are symptomatic of organized crime groups:

- The existence of a criminal association or group
- A criminal activity is carried out in an entrepreneurial way
- The basic goal of the group is to achieve profit with illegal activities
- The group uses violence or corruption to achieve its goals

Within the Netherlands, criminal intelligence units (CIUs) deal with organized crime in a way that differs from the traditional forms of tackling serious crime [6]. Their crime analysts complete a structured questionnaire on every active criminal group. A criminal group has been defined as the cooperation among two or more people who are involved in crimes that, in view of their impact or their frequency or the organized framework within which they are committed, represent a serious violation of the legal order. The questionnaires that were completed were processed at the national Criminal Intelligence Division (Central Recherche Informateinest, CRI). In their analysis of the results, a number of characteristics were used as selection criteria, in order to establish the organizational degree of criminal groups. The following main criteria, particularly the first eight, were applied:

Mandatory criteria:

1. Collaboration of three or more people
2. Criminal activity for a prolonged or indefinite period of time
3. Groups suspected or convicted of committing serious criminal offenses
4. Activity with the objective of pursuing profit and/or power

Optional criteria:

5. Having a specific task or role for each participant
6. Using some form of internal discipline and control
7. Using violence or other means suitable for intimidation
8. Exerting influence on politics, the media, public administration, law enforcement, the administration of justice, or the economy by corruption or any other means
9. Using commercial or business-like structures
10. Engaging in money laundering
11. Operating at an international level

In the analysis of the data, the degree of organization of a criminal group is determined simply by counting the number of characteristics that match the CRI criteria. The greater the number of characteristics present, the higher is the degree of criminal organization. The designation "organized" is given to groups that complied with six or more of the first eight main criteria. This specified formula (at least six out of the first eight characteristics) takes into account both the diversity of organized crime and the fact that the police in the early stages of the investigation process usually do not have complete knowledge of all features.

What is now clear is that all definitions highlight one important mandatory ingredient: organized crime is greed-driven. From a practical perspective, transnational and cross-border threats of terrorism and organized crime are the main challenges facing law enforcement today.

Facts about the Republic of Austria

Covering an area of 84,000 km², Austria is a relatively small country situated in the lower central region of Europe. Of its 8 million inhabitants, 750,000 are foreigners [7]. Austria's capital Vienna, situated in the Eastern part of the country, has a population of 1.6 million inhabitants.

The Austrian Political Structure

Austria is a democratic republic and, since January 1995, a member of the European Union. Since 1945 and even as far back as 1919, Austria has been a democracy. After the end of the Second World War, Austria was occupied by the Allied forces. In 1955, Austria became a free republic. Today, four political parties are active: the People's Party and the Freedom Party are conservative parties; the opposition coalition includes the Social-Democratic Party and the Green Party [8].

The Austrian Constitution and Policing

After the breakdown of the Austrian-Hungarian monarchy, the Austrian Federal Constitution, established in 1920 by Kelsen, was essentially modified by a Constitutional Amendment in 1929. Therefore, today the Constitution is a federal one. Austria consists of nine federal provinces ("Bundesländer"). Jurisdictions are divided between the federal government and the nine provinces or states. The villages and local communities form a third force. The main principles of the Constitution are the separation of powers and protection of human rights. Legislation, administration, and the judiciary are separated from each other [9].

- Legislation
- Administration
- Jurisdiction

Police and security institutions are bound to the administration and the judiciary. The justice system is based on the foundation of investigating the material truth.

The History of Policing

"Over centuries, the legal development in Europe's democracies has reflected the field of tension between the claim of the state regarding the maintenance of public law and order and the fundamental right of the individual to personal freedom as well as compliance with Human Rights. Constitutional laws change in accordance with political and social conditions. But one of the most important tasks of a democratic state governed by the rule of law is the adoption of administrative and police laws to political and social changes." A glance at the Austrian legal history shows the development toward the rule of law in police law [9]. The concept of police developed from the tensions between the medieval corporative order which allowed the execution of power, but only a minimum of changes, developed into the "ius politiae" relating to the sovereignty, which was a comprehensive right that governed the organization in all aspects of life at the discretion of the sovereignty (see: Marsilius von Padua, the defender of peace, first published in 1324). As a consequence, "administration" in the absolutistic police state was mainly "political" (police) administration. It was understood as the execution of laws for the maintenance and the promotion of the general welfare (see: Antoniolli, administrative law). In the era of absolutism, police power was practically unrestricted. It was used for implementing the claim of the sovereignty to exercise the monarchical power. The Enlightenment and political liberalism confronted the "ius politiae" as "general title for all sorts of things" with another police concept. The opinion that the warding off of dangers should be the most important and unique task of the police gained acceptance during the nineteenth century. Thus, the concept of an "absolutistic welfare police" changed to "security police." This organized power that takes over the fight against dangers is the police. In the constitutional era, the legal independence of police power gradually turned into a legally regularized power in such a way that admissible police interventions, as well as the way such interventions were carried out (the employed means), were increasingly regulated by the legal provisions. The beginnings of a police law date back to 1849 (Imperial patent dated March 4, 1849, official gazette no. 151), which standardized certain fundamental rights of the citizen and, thus, provided limits for police interventions. The 1860s brought important legal steps toward the determination of police activities in accordance with the rule of law:

- The law of 27.10.1862, official gazette no. 87, regarding the protection of personal freedom

- The law of 27.10.1862, official gazette no. 88, regarding the protection of the domestic rights
- The Basic State Law of 21.12.1967, official gazette no. 142, regarding the general rights of citizens

When founding the First Republic, the federalists and centralists disagreed as to whether the police power was to be assigned to the Federal Government or to the provinces. Finally, the federal constitution (art. 10, para 1, fig. 7; Federal Constitutional Law) stated that the general security police should be exclusively assigned to the Federal Government (legislation and execution—maintenance of public law and order). During the German occupation (March 1938 to April 1945), the Austrian administrative organization and, thus, the existent municipal and rural police organizations were dissolved. The Prussian-German scheme was introduced instead. Police matters were transferred to the governors of the Reich (Austria was divided into seven "Reichsgaue").

Austria's Old Security Structure [9]

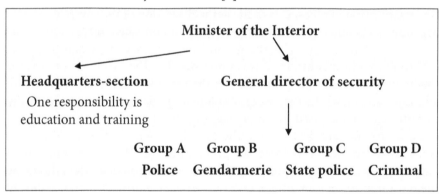

Investigation

The Former Federal Police [10]

The federal police were organized into corps, assigned to each one of the 14 federal police directorates. The Federal Police Directorate of Vienna, e.g., is divided into the Headquarters ("Presidia") Division (bureau for organization, control, and internal revision; bureau for questions of law and data protection; bureau for budget, logistics, and infrastructure; staff department; bureau for information and public relations), the Provincial Department for the Protection of the Constitution and Fight against Terrorism, the Criminal Department, Vienna (criminal investigators' inspectorate; criminal direction 1—for severe and white-collar crimes; criminal direction 2 with 5 commissariats; criminal direction 3—criminal investigation, records, and criminal advisory service), the Administrative Police Department (immigrant and aliens police; administrative bureau; bureau for club, association, and assembly matters and press law affairs; bureau for penal records; police department at the Public Prosecutors Office of Vienna), the Security and Traffic Police Department (traffic office; police prison; the 14 police regional headquarters), and the Inspectorate-General for Public Security. These police officers traditionally wore green uniforms and applied law enforcement to the large cities and urban regions of Austria.

The Former Gendarmerie [10]

The Gendarmes operated in rural areas and in towns that had no contingent of federal police, acting under the direction and on behalf of the District Administration Authorities. Thus, the Gendarmerie was responsible for the security of approximately 70% of the Austrian population. It was organized into eight provincial command units, which formed part of the Provincial Public Security Directorates. In addition, each provincial headquarters had special departments for certain tasks: staff department, criminal department, technology department, organization department, economic department, traffic department. In the former organizational chart, below the provincial headquarters were the district Gendarmerie headquarters corresponding to the District Administration Authorities, 86 in number, and then the village Gendarmerie posts. There were previously a total of 825 Gendarmerie posts. A post may have had from 3 to as many as 30 Gendarmes, but most had about 10. Border posts were served by Border Gendarmes and Alpine posts by Gendarmerie Alpinists and guides.

Until recently, Gendarmerie and federal police directorates had their own mobile commando units (tactical emergency units). Now (since 2002) there are unified commando groups named "Echo Cobra," stationed in Wiener Neustadt, Graz, Linz, and Innsbruck, with branch offices in Krumpendorf (Carinthia), Feldkirch-Gisingen (Vorarlberg), and in the city of Salzburg. These units consist of approximately 336 officers.

In 2002, the Gendarmerie had a total of 13,472 officers, and approximately 5% of them were women. The federal police were 9670 officers strong, with 11% of them being female. The Bureau for Criminal Investigation consisted of 2324 plainclothes officers, and 6% of them were women. The headquarters of the federal police employed 2818 officers; 75% of them were women. Prior to the national police reform, there was 1 member of the federal police for the 233 residents in the cities it patrolled, and there was 1 Gendarme for the 386 inhabitants in the areas subject to its supervision. In summary, the police-civilian ratio in Austria in 2002 was 1 officer for every 315 inhabitants, which is in line with some other comparable countries. As Austria is such a "well-policed" country, private security services are of minor importance (the private security guard to civilian ratio is 1:1,231), although there have been partial privatizations of some public security services in the course of the last years.

Policing before the Reform

The 1789 Declaration of Human and Civic Rights in Austria already contained security as a postulated human right. Today, the state has taken over the monopoly of legitimate physical power, with the promise to establish an elemental (physical) security for all her citizens. Therefore, any individual resistance is excluded as long as the sovereignty of the state succeeds in establishing individual physical security and guarantees general peace. In the mind of many people, the state has developed into a monster bound only by its own laws. Because of its monopoly, the state thus has the task to fight alone against criminality, terrorism, and illegal violence.

Developments over the last few decades have shown that the security monopoly of the state does not any longer guarantee the security the individual expects from the state bodies. Municipal and rural police have been increasingly overstrained. There are several reasons for this development. The opening of the borders to the Eastern countries in 1989, the development toward violence, the increasing drug problem, and the increase in organized criminality bring about fear and a declining efficiency of the executive authority. After the reestablishment of the Austrian Republic in April 1945, the beginnings of legislation were characterized by transitional provisions. Reference is made in this context to art. II § 4 of the Constitutional Transitory Law, which, in certain cases, offered the possibility of the security police issuing orders on its own. This provisional legislation was superseded by the Constitutional Law, BGBl. no. 565/1991, which constitutes the basis for the Security Police Law, BGBl. no. 566/1991. Already in 1929 there were good prospects to pass a federal law regarding the competencies of the authority in the field of the general security police. In 1969, the government presented a bill for a federal law regarding the competencies of the police. In 1991, it was followed by another government bill, which passed the National Council after its revision on October 3, 1991 [9].

The Security Police Law

Since May 1993, a new legal basis exists for the security executive forces within Austria. The Security Police Act dealt for the first time in a comprehensive way with the organization, structure, and jurisdiction of the security executive forces. The Minister of the Interior is the highest responsible person for the security executive forces. Before the reform, the Department of the Interior was staffed with 32,000 employees, out of which approximately 15,000 were police members and approximately 15,000 were members of the Gendarmerie. The rest of the staff was in administration. In the 14 largest Austrian cities, security matters were handled by federal police agencies. Approximately 2.8 million people live in these urban areas.

Vienna houses the largest police headquarters in Austria. More than 9000 staff members are employed there, out of which 5800 belong to the Security Police Service and approximately 820 belong to the Criminal Investigation Service. In rural areas, comprising approximately 5.2 million people, security lay in the hands of the Gendarmerie. In each of the Austrian provinces, the security director was the highest authority in security matters. Vienna is the national capital, with its own general of police who was, at the same time, the provincial security director.

The Austrian Police Law consists of six parts [11]:

- Structure of the authority
- Tasks of the authority
- Competencies of the police
- Data protection provisions
- Penal provisions
- Legal protection provisions

The core of this law includes the second and the third parts, which define the tasks of the general security police and the competencies required for their fulfillment. The police may intervene in the rights of persons only if

- Such a measure is provided for in the Security Police Law
- No other means are suitable to fulfill the task
- The relationship between cause and expected success is maintained

Warding off dangers, general obligation to provide help, and prevention instead of repression are the fundamental objectives of the Security Police Law.

Advantages and Disadvantages of the Old Security Structure

Before the reform, both the federal police and the Gendarmerie were well-established factors in public security. Citizens knew their local police officers and the location of their patrol stations. The police and Gendarmerie were organized in such a way that officers were responsible for their specific regions. Only special units were organized at the central level. Because this system existed for many decades, people knew where to go to ask for police support.

In Austria, and especially in Vienna, law enforcement organizations were divided into too many regions. Because of the very large number of stations, the forces of the Gendarmerie and the police were not staffed sufficiently to work effectively within their respective regions. Many of these stations could not operate productively because only one or two officers worked day and night shifts at the station. The reduction in the number of police stations and Gendarmerie stations has now become an important issue.

The New Austrian Security Structure [10]

The Austrian Police was and still is headed by the Federal Ministry of the Interior. As previously outlined, they were divided into (1) the federal police, (2) the federal Gendarmerie, (3) the state police, and (4) the criminal police. The police operated in Vienna and 13 of the larger cities: Schwechat, St. Pölten, Wiener Neustadt (all Lower Austria), Linz, Steyr, Wels (all Upper Austria), Salzburg (provincial capital), Innsbruck (Tyrol), Eisenstadt (Burgenland), Graz, Leoben (both Styria), Klagenfurt, Villach (both Carinthia). The police in each of these cities was headed by a chief. The Gendarmes operated in rural areas and in towns without a contingent of federal police or local police, acting at the lowest instance as organs on behalf of the district administration authorities. Thus, the Gendarmerie, which in contrast to the federal police directorates did not have authoritative power, was responsible for the security of approximately 70% of the Austrian population. It was organized into eight provincial command units, which formed part of the Provincial Public Security Directorates.

Provincial Command Structure		
Public security/law enforcement	Traffic enforcement	Criminal investigation
Police inspections in the different regions		
Operative law enforcement agents		

The Political Change in Austria

In the year 2000, the elections in Austria brought a major political change. Conservative parties took over political power in the nation. Former government regimes had always spent more money than the national income. This deficit spending has now been stopped by the new government. The new government was under pressure due to the European Union goals to reduce the budget deficit and to implement strategies of "new public management." Each of the federal ministries was directed to reduce the number of their employees by approximately 10%.

Goals: Reduction of Costs and Personnel

The primary goal of the new government was the reduction of costs and personnel. The Federal Chancellor immediately declared that the first step of the new government was to reduce the level of personnel by approximately 10%. In line with this objective, the budget of every ministry was cut by 10%. Consequently, the consolidation of the budget followed. Immediately, a series of changes started. Many of these reforms directly affected police personnel nationally.

Centralization Shall Bring More Efficiency

It was decided that the only way these goals could be reached was to move toward a strong centralized police structure. In the Ministry of the Interior, a lot of stations of the Gendarmerie in the rural areas were closed. This was not so easy to do in the cities, but the reduction of personnel had commenced. Hundreds of police officers retired and the number of officers in the police force was reduced dramatically.

New Centralized Organizations

To check and balance the efficiency of the system, new central organizations were set up. This centralization aimed to bring a better overview of overall resources and flexibility to react to problems. The idea was to centralize all intelligence and specialized units and equipment to realize more efficiency and effectiveness.

New Crime Fighting Tools

To bring about and to support efficiency, new crime fighting tools were implemented. In the last 10 years, every police agency has attempted to change its strategies from reactive to proactive responses to police problems.

To recognize these major issues, new tools, especially computer technology and software, were used to accumulate quick and better information and to learn what was going on in an area or region. These strategic and operational analysis tools helped the law enforcement agencies to use their capacities more efficiently and effectively.

Implementation of a New Leadership

It has long been a tradition in Austria that any reform or changes are normally implemented smoothly. However, with this reform, many former police leaders were unexpectedly reassigned, often to lower responsibilities. A new leadership team took over the power positions and was responsible for commencing the stark reforms of the Ministry of the Interior. The new leadership was advised by external consultants. Some police leaders were not impressed by these advisors, as many had no practical law enforcement experience, nor did they seek the advice of veteran police leaders.

Reforming the Ministry of the Interior

This reform started with changes in the police command leadership and in the administrative offices of the Ministry of the Interior. Personnel were reduced and the police organizational structure was comprehensively revised. However, it is alleged that new leaders were chosen due to their political affiliation and not their abilities. Some former police executives even referred to this reform as being "brutal."

	Minister of the Interior		
Section I	**Section II**	**Section III**	**Section IV**
	Commander of provinces		
	Commanders of regions	**Commanders of cities**	
	Police stations (inspections)		

The Reform of Policing in Vienna

The Minister of the Interior immediately started to revise its own organization and thereafter created the National Criminal Bureau of Investigation for Austria ("Bundeskriminalamt"), similar to the German model. Because of the events of September 11, 2001, the structure of the uniformed police factions throughout Austria were also completely reorganized. The reform goals of the Austrian government were officially declared [12]:

- More safety and security for people
- Increasing the satisfaction of agency employees

The project of reforming the police agencies in Vienna commenced in 2001. This initiative served as a future model for further reform activities throughout Austria. Out of 33,000 employees in the Ministry of the Interior, approximately 10,000 worked in Vienna. The reform of the police in Vienna reduced the number of officers by approximately 1000. The uniformed police were separated from the criminal investigators and were dramatically centralized. Before the reform, Vienna had 23 police centers, equivalent to the 23 districts of the city of Vienna. Uniformed and undercover police were deployed together.

After the reform took place, there were only 14 police stations in which the uniformed police were deployed and six locations where criminal investigators were based. Nationally, there were approximately 100 police stations, but they have been reduced to approximately 50 police stations across the country.

Combining the Austrian Police with the Gendarmerie

After the elections in 2002, a new government was formed. Still, the conservative powers were the leading ones and the Minister of the Interior continued the reformation of law enforcement agencies. In 2003, under the "Team 04," a reform of the whole law enforcement structure in Austria commenced. Ultimately, the new goal of this reform was to unify the Gendarmerie, the police, and customs officials. The main goals are [13]

- Creating a new law enforcement mechanism capable of dealing with the challenges of the twenty-first century
- Centralization and unification of the Gendarmerie, the police, and customs officials
- More efficiency and effectiveness

The new structures were implemented on July 1, 2005. The historical differentiation between the police and the Gendarmerie was abolished.

Law Enforcement and Administration

The reform changed the structure and organization of Austrian law enforcement, but did not deal with the structural framework of the Austrian

Constitution. The consequence was that after the reform that started in July 2005, a "fight" started involving who and what belongs to the national administrative power and who and what belongs to the law enforcement agencies. The dilemma, which existed before the reform started, continued. The goal of the reform was to avoid a double structure. The reform ended up with a double structure just as the one that had existed before.

Examining Some Potential Problems with the Austrian Police Reform

In June 2001, the U.S. Department of Justice Office of Justice Programs published the book *Democratizing the Police Abroad: What to Do and How to Do It*, written by David Bayley, internationally recognized professor and expert of modern democratic policing. The purpose of the report was to create a roster of what is known about how to reform police forces so as to support the development of democracy and the rule of law. It was set up as an overview of what observers and participants have learned about the process of changing police organizations. According to Bayley, the conditions for democratic policing include [14]:

> Police must give top operational priority to servicing the needs of individual citizens and private groups, because police are the most visible manifestation of governmental authority;
> Police must be accountable to the law rather than to the government;
> Police must protect human rights, especially those that are required for the sort of unfettered political activity that is the hallmark of democracy; and
> Police should be transparent in their activities.

In addition, David Bayley [15] described the following 17 core lessons that have been learned about changing the standard operating practices of police forces in developed democracies:

1. Any reform program must be based on a clearly articulated understanding of the connections between the objectives to be achieved and the actions proposed.
2. Sustained and committed leadership by top management, especially the most senior executive, is required to produce any important organizational change.
3. The key to changing any aspect of policing is management—that is, the way in which the members of a police organization are brought to do what policies call for.

4. Police behavior cannot be changed by formal reorganization within the police or by restructuring on a national basis.
5. Material resources may support desired changes, but they are rarely essential and never sufficient to bring them about.
6. Significant reform requires widespread acceptance across ranks and assignments in a police department.
7. When pilot projects are undertaken, they must have committed leadership and personnel who are not continually pulled away for other purposes.
8. Police officers will not change their behavior unless they perceive it to be in their personal interest to do so.
9. Reformers both inside and outside police organizations should be careful not to denigrate the motivation, knowledge, or skill of the people whose behavior they are trying to change.
10. Program evaluations that emphasize outputs rather than outcomes as a measure of success inhibit organizational creativity.
11. Reform requires that new programs be monitored so that midcourse changes can be made. At the same time, burdensome evaluation can discourage reform.
12. Change is more likely to occur when new resources are made available rather than when existing ones are redistributed.
13. If the incidence of crime and disorder is thought to be unacceptable or increasing, police reform will be inhibited.
14. Increasing contacts between police personnel and respectable, non-criminal members of the public is an important way of encouraging the development of an accountable, service-oriented police organization.
15. Issuing clear statements of the organizational policy accompanied by appropriate positive and negative sanctions is a powerful way to change the behavior of police officers, even in situations of high stress and urgency.
16. Reform is more likely to occur if police officials are connected to professional networks of progressive police leaders (regional, national, international).
17. Labor organizations within the police must be included in the development and planning of any reform program.

Legal Restrictions Imposed by the Austrian Constitution

As previously noted, the reform of the police organization did not properly match the framework of the constitution. Initially, it was hoped that the Austrian Convent, dealing with the change and reform of the constitution would change the framework in line with the reform undertaken within law enforcement. However, this did not happen. Nevertheless, the reform of the law enforcement continued, and the combination of the police and Gendarmerie was the main goal. The primary problem was, and still is, that the Gendarmerie is legally just a body of law enforcement without administrative authority. The "imperium" of the government is represented by the Polizeidirektionen (Police headquarters). However, since July 2005, a military body, the National Police, was created, not respecting the old constitutional issue of administrative power. The government must still deal with this dilemma. The question is who is in charge: the legal advisers or the leading officers of the new National Police.

Militarization of Law Enforcement

The reformers, the members of "Team 04," were primarily high-ranking officers from the Gendarmerie. The outcome was apparent from the onset. They created a paramilitary system, as they were acclimated to within the Gendarmerie. The Gendarmerie and the police were unified in Austria, but some believe that basically what was sold as new is the old model of the Gendarmerie with the new name of National Police ("Bundespolizei"). Structure, organization, ranks, and training features remain strictly militarized. The new paramilitary mechanism could not deal with the police's legal advisors, so their roles remain unclear.

The New Penal Code

In 2008, the new Penal Code took effect in Austria. This new Penal Code defines the new roles of judges, prosecutors, and law enforcement agencies. In addition, offenders and suspects now have stronger rights of defense. The prosecutor is now the "new boss" in the criminal investigation team. What does this mean for the police organization? It means that the prosecutor now coordinates the investigation and, in practical terms, will change the police to a judicial police, similar to other national models.

Centralization or Decentralization?

This question is an ongoing academic and practical one. The new challenges of the twenty-first century emphasize terrorism, corruption, and organized crime. Does this mean that the only answer to these problems is centralization? No one has yet analyzed the security market in Austria. The main question revolves around understanding the security problems. Is it terrorism or is it organized crime? How great are these dangers and what are the main problems identified by the citizenry? What is the best way to solve these problems in the interest of the victims? In the simplest understanding of the front-line police officer, approximately 80% of the problems and issues faced by patrol personnel seem to be regionally oriented. Would a centralized structure therefore be the most effective and efficient?

What Do People Expect of Police Work?

Historically, it had been the tradition in Europe that the police served the monarch or the state leaders. In Austria, in 1991 the new role of policing was written down in the Security Police Law. The new role of the police is to serve the community. In reality, we are far away from this model. Centralization and militarization are not the best answers to the expectations of the people. The police cannot fulfill the expectation of managing the problems of society at large or the residents of a region that they are responsible for.

Did the Austrian Reform Follow David Bayley's Recommendations?

A comparison of the main goals of police reform outlined by Bayley with the police reforms implemented in Austria leads to the conclusion that very little was achieved by these reformers:

1. Do police serve the needs of the citizens? Not really. Since the start of the reform, police executives care much more about their own problems than about the needs of the people.
2. Are the police accountable to the law rather than to the government? This is partially fulfilled. Nonetheless, laws are very important and must continue to be respected, but the political influence of the government is increasing.
3. Do the police respect human rights? To overcome the threat of terrorism, there arises the fear that the respect of human rights will decline in the future.
4. Are the police transparent? Because of the tendency to centralism, the transparency of police activities is decreasing.

If one compares the 17 core lessons that have to be learned about changing the standard operating practices of police forces in developed democracies (as outlined by Bayley), again little has been acknowledged. Senior police executives were not involved; police behavior has not basically changed;

enhanced material resources were not invested; widespread acceptance was not solicited across ranks; motivation, knowledge, and skill were not required; a revised monitoring procedure was not implemented; new personnel resources were not invested; when the reform commenced, crime was on a dramatic increase; the communities were not integrated into the reform process; professional networking was excluded; and labor organizations were not really involved in the reform procedure.

What Was Missed by the Reform?

The reform missed the integration of the knowledge, skills, and experience of senior police administrators, and was mainly coordinated by a team of Gendarmerie executives, without any experience of the problems of big-city policing. The reform was driven by political pressure and opportunism by a small number of young, relatively inexperienced officers who had the political chance to receive promotion due to political support and favoritism. Ultimately, one could easily conclude that the main goal was not to obtain the best policing model for the people, but rather the main objective was to implement a reform based on political influence while reducing costs and personnel.

Future Expectations of Law Enforcement

Because terrorism creates so much fear around the world, this centralized, militarized model of policing is sold as the best response to address this issue. In former times, America declared war on drugs. Now it has declared war on terrorism and argues that the war is necessary to defend democratic goals. Fighting for freedom at the same time that individual and human rights of the citizens are reduced has become the apparent outcome.

Critics to the Reform in Austria

When discussing the issues of community and policing, it was clear from the beginning that the reformation efforts involving the police in Austria were "running in the wrong direction." Instead of improving the partnership between the community and the police, the reform measures suffer extensively from the restrictions and reductions of personnel and budgetary support. The second goal, to improve the satisfaction of the justice employees, has failed completely. Police officers now appear to be unmotivated; agency efficiency and effectiveness may have declined; and the international reputation of the police in Austria has waned. In 2000, Austria was the second safest country in Europe, and Vienna was the safest city in Europe. Because of the overall failures of the political reform, this position has been lost.

What Are the Failures of the Security Policy of the Government? [16]

Generally the political, sociological, and economical conditions and environment in Europe and Austria were not favorable for starting a reform of policing at the time it was decided to do so.

The reform was started when crime was increasing dramatically (in Austria, from approximately 500,000 to more than 640,000 offenses annually); and the clearance rate decreased from 51% to 39%. Consequently, Austria is not one of the safest countries any more in Europe, and Vienna is no longer the safest city in Europe (crime increased from more than 150,000 to up to 240,000 offenses annually). That means that Austria and Vienna do not offer, as decades before, attractions for economic investment and for tourism.

Austria is a border country between the rather well-off countries and the poorer part of Eastern Europe. In the year 2004, the European Union was enlarged and some of the former Eastern Bloc countries became new member countries. Although these new members have boosted their economies, there are still enormous problems with the standards of security and crime. It was foreseeable that problems with crime will continue. If people from the new economically challenged European Union member countries can come easily to Central Europe, the crime rate will continue at high levels. The question therefore remains: why did Austria reduce public security forces at a time when the framework conditions were worsening?

There is little research conducted within Austria that examines public perception of the security market. However, a basic study was done in 1991 by Dr. Hanak of the Institute of Crime and Sociology, which showed that 80% of the security problems are regional and only about 20% are centrally oriented.

The Austrian police reform is based primarily on a centralistic model of policing. The consequence is that the community and the citizens of Vienna and Austria are neglected by the services of the revised law enforcement agencies. Community leaders have expressed open criticism that police officers are not seen on the street. The objective security situation is reportedly worsening, and the subjective security situation of citizens shows a tendency of increasing feelings of insecurity. Crime is on the increase, fewer crimes are solved, the number of officers has been reduced, and, as a result, streets and homes have become less secure. More and more people have become victims of robbery and theft. Citizens can no longer easily find police officers on patrol, have to wait at the police stations to report crimes, and as a result they are no longer served properly when criminal events happen. Contrary to prior efforts to specifically serve the public in their respective neighborhoods, the centralization of criminal investigation units has caused the manpower to "balloon" like in the new Bundeskriminalamt (National Bureau of Investigation for Austria), where there are now double the number of central investigators and administrative staff, but the service has decreased, as evinced by declining clearance rates.

The main goals that should have been addressed by police reforms were neglected. The international trend of policing shows a tendency to create higher standards of professionalism, training, and scientific background. The former government wanted to open a new police academy with enhanced education, on the level of a university. The new government stopped this project immediately and reduced the budget for training, education, and research dramatically. The proposal for creating better infrastructure for cooperation between universities (as research platforms) and practitioners was not accepted. Additionally, a gap emerged, especially in the development of forensic investigation and technology, which will be dangerous for the future standards of professional policing in Austria.

Today, forensic institutions in the poorer neighboring countries have a higher standard of technology than the former famous Vienna School of Criminology. In the field of international cooperation, Austrian law enforcement has steadily lost its reputation. Instead of creating an atmosphere of bureaucratic autonomy as delineated in Max Weber's model, politicians have interfered excessively in police matters and may have damaged the traditional system of professional knowledge and expertise. Because of this political influence, Austria's police leaders have been selected by and are strongly dependent upon their "political masters" and have limited chances to continue operational decision-making to any sufficient degree of independence. History has taught us that police institutions have become specialized and segregated from other state administrations such as the military for a reason. However, as a result of these police reforms, there has been a tendency to revert to militarism, and the political masters have supported this trend by emphasizing the threat of terrorism.

Conclusion

Each Austrian police officer is proud when entering the headquarters of Interpol in Lyon, France, and finding there the statue of Dr. Schober, the former chancellor of Austria and former president of the Police in Vienna. Although the political conditions in those days were much worse than they are today, he pushed the Austrian police to a high international reputation. One can conclude that the present situation has pushed Austrian law enforcement to diminished standards. Austria may continue to lose international reputation and acknowledgment.

Much worse than this possible outcome is the potential dimension of the loss of public confidence in the policing mechanism within Austria. For many years, people trusted the police, expressed confidence in them, and reported crime cases. The basic communication lines between the people and the police were alive. Because of the enormous restriction measures and the tendency toward privatized security, a two-class society may be created by the government. If you can afford it, you will have safety and security; if you cannot afford private security, you will not be secured enough by public security agencies.

The new threat of terrorism was one of the official motivations used to commence the reform of the law enforcement agencies in Austria. However, new legal and procedural restrictions may endanger the democratic society in Austria. It is time to recognize that political influence and interference may ultimately lead to the failure of the rule of law mechanism, and, at the least, a loss of public confidence in the police and employee satisfaction will result in diminished efficiency and effectiveness.

References

1. Council of Europe, Organized crime situation report, 2002, Strasbourg, France.
2. N. Madoka, Organized crime: A world perspective, in *Third International Police Executive Symposium*, Kanagawa University, Yokohama, Japan, 1996, Edelbacher Max, Organized Crime in Austria, pages 313 ff.
3. D.K. Das and P. Kratcosci, Victimization of terrorism, paper for the Vienna United Nations Conference on Crime, 2000.
4. S. Rick, D.K. Das, and H.J. Albrecht, *Policing Corruption, International Perspectives*, Lexington Books, Lanham, MD, 2005.
5. *United Nations Convention against Transnational Organized Crime and the Protocols Thereto*, United Nations, New York, 2002.
6. Council of Europe, *Octopus Progamme*, Combating Organized Crime Council of Europe Publishing, Strasbourg, France, 2004.
7. Austrian Federal Press Service, *Austria Facts and Figures 2004*, pp. 6–8, 2004.
8. Austrian Federal Press Service, *Austria Facts and Figures 2004*, p. 22, 2004.
9. E. Max and F. Peter, Public order in Austria, in D.K. Das and A.Y. Jiao (eds.), *Public Order: A Global Perspective*, Prentice Hall, Upper Saddle River, NJ, 2005.
10. G. Norden and M. Edelbacher, The challenges of policing democracies, the case of Austria, in D.K. Das and Otwin Morenin (eds.), *The Challenges of Policing Democracies: A World Perspective*, Gorden and Breach Publishers, Amsterdam, the Netherlands, 2000.
11. Security Police Law of Austria, enacted May 1, 1993.
12. Strasser Ernst, Former Minister of the Interior of Austria, Statement, January 2003, published in the Vienna daily news papers.
13. Austrian Ministry of the Interior, *Goals of the Reform Team 4*, 2001, published in the News Letter of the Ministry of the Interior.
14. D.H. Bayley, Democratizing the police abroad: What to do and how to do it, U.S. Department of Justice, Office of Justice Programs, National Institute of Justice, Issues in International Crime, Washington, DC, p. 3, pp. 13–15, June 2001.

15. D.H. Bayley, Democratizing the police abroad: What to do and how to do it, U.S. Department of Justice, Office of Justice Programs, National Institute of Justice, Issues in International Crime, Washington, DC, pp. 35–50, June 2001.
16. Edelbacher, Punctuation of failures in security policy, June 2003, Draft Proposal for the Socialist Democratic Party.

Contemporary Concerns: Policing in the United States and Canada

II

Legislation and Guidelines Addressing the Trafficking of Human Beings in the United States of America

4

LINDSAY K. WIGHT

Contents

Introduction

The issue of human trafficking has gained a significant amount of attention from governments across the globe over the previous decade. In recent years, as more information is becoming known about the much-hidden organized criminal enterprise, new legislation and guidelines are being developed to address the apprehension and punishments of persons who are committing these atrocious crimes against other human beings. The United States, which is listed currently as a primary destination country for traffickers, has taken significant steps in recent years to address the trafficking epidemic, both domestically and abroad, and to act as a catalyst for other nations to do the same. Legislation and guidelines that have so far been implemented and followed in the United States will be delineated. One has to acknowledge the absolute international dimension of a crime such as trafficking, and recognize some of the international frameworks that affect the issue in the United States. Much work is still to be done, but the groundwork has been laid and actions applied by law enforcement agencies.

The trafficking of persons in the United States is an epidemic of significant proportions, which is only continuing to grow as time passes. The United States has been documented as having served as a *source* country (a nation recorded as having had its citizens trafficked to other nations) as well as a *transit* country (a nation that has been recorded as having citizens of other nations trafficked through there en route to another destination). However, the nation is best known for its status as a *destination* country, or the final arrival place for trafficked persons who often are brought through multiple countries beforehand.

In 2003, the U.S. government presented its estimates of trafficking both domestically and abroad. The figures presented were near a total of an estimated 1 million people as being trafficked across international borders each year throughout the world. Out of this, it was estimated that somewhere in the range of 18,000–20,000 were being trafficked specifically into the United States for purposes ranging from involuntary servitude to domestic labor to sexual exploitation and prostitution. The Central Intelligence Agency (CIA) and many nongovernmental organizations, however, estimate that these initial forecasts of trafficking count in the high ten thousands. The numbers presented in the 2003 Trafficking in Persons Report are actually significantly higher (U.S. Department of State, 2003).

Of important domestic concern is that men, women, and children are trafficked internally, within the confines of American borders. Trafficking itself is a very hidden criminal operation and some nongovernmental organizations consider this number to be significantly higher as all of them are not recorded. In 2004, the Justice Department opened 120 investigations and began 51 prosecutions. Going by these figures, less than 1% of the trafficking cases are going through investigation each year. As well, investigation does not automatically equal prosecution. These are startling figures that should send shivers down the spines of both the citizens and government in the United States. Oftentimes, trafficking goes on in both urban and suburban as well as even rural communities in the midst of unsuspecting citizens and local officials who do not even realize that this epidemic exists, and is right in their own backyard. This situation must be addressed and is of high immediate importance.

One of the reasons that trafficking perpetrators get away with these heinous and often vicious crimes is that, as a product of their crime, "they have the financial resources to hire attorneys, post bail, and engage the system" (Florida State University Center for the Advancement of Human Rights, 2003, p. 21). The trafficking of human beings worldwide is a multibillion dollar industry. The U.S. judicial system is not specifically designed to safeguard against all powers controlled by the wealthy elite. Of course, until recent decades, crime and wealth were not as strongly associated with one another as crime and poverty have been. The "birth" per se of white-collar crime in the United States and abroad has led to a situation where scholars, researchers, activists, and governments are having to reevaluate measures to effectively combat these types of crime and the threats to security that they pose.

Logistics also have a key role in the difficulty faced by law enforcement and the criminal justice system in identifying and investigating these occurrences. The scope of human trafficking is vast and not entirely measurable at this point in time due to lack of qualitative research. However, researchers do know that most nations experience some form of trafficking—just some more than others. Eastern Europe, for example, has high rates of women and children trafficked for sexual exploitation. "If you go to other parts of Eastern Europe, there is such a flow of women leaving the country, that you can actually see the reduction in numbers of young women who are in society" (Tomiuc, 2003, p. 2).

The international scope of trafficking in person epidemic makes it difficult for different national governments and law enforcement agencies to effectively coordinate their efforts to address the problem. There are many reasons for this lack of coordination, but the important one is the fact that when considerations are given to something on a *global* scale, they almost automatically involve opposing cultural norms and opinions that come into play, which can greatly affect defining the problem in the first place. For instance, is prostitution an illegal activity? What is the universal definition of a child? These are types of questions that must be addressed before governments can properly coordinate their efforts because their answers are sure to differ depending on what area of the world is being addressed. "Traffickers often transport victims from their home communities to unfamiliar destinations, including foreign countries away from family and friends, religious institutions, and other sources of protection and support, leaving the victims defenseless and vulnerable" (Office on Violence Against Women, 2000, p. 1).

Since no culture can accurately be described as right or wrong, per se, when in comparison to another, one of the best global documents to guide the combat of human trafficking worldwide is the Universal Declaration of Human Rights. The declaration was adopted by the United Nations in December of 1948 in efforts to combat slavery worldwide and uphold the importance of human dignity in maintaining human rights for all people and it has been used by many governments and organizations in efforts to combat human rights violations on numerous occasions since its inception (United Nations, 1998). This document, however, is not universal law and there are no immediate, severe sanctions for criminals who directly deviate from the guidelines, unless another criminal act that they commit in the process is legally punishable by preestablished laws.

As such, many nations have formulated their own legislation to address the issue of trafficking within their own borders. Most of this legislation is still relatively new. The United States is perhaps the current frontrunner in the development and implementation of trafficking legislation, despite the problem still being as widespread as it currently is. There are presently several grants being given out by various U.S. government offices and outside agencies to fund different trafficking initiatives, such as the formation of task forces to combat the problem, both within the United States and abroad. The government under the Bush Administration has identified trafficking, specifically for the purposes of commercial sexual exploitation—which is the main purpose for the modern human slave trade—as a serious problem and a grave violation of human rights. Yet, the trafficking of persons does not only produce crimes that are costing lives. "Trafficking is linked to international crime syndicates that peddle drugs, guns and false documents, as well as people. Trafficking is a global public health threat that helps spread HIV/ AIDS and other terrible diseases. And trafficking is a global security threat, because the profits from trafficking finance still more crime and violence" (Powell, 2004, p. 2).

It is obvious that this epidemic needs to be addressed. Globalization is only adding to the already existing problem. Some of the effects of globalization, such as borders opening in the European Union, migration growing worldwide, and rise in demand for cheap labor, ensure that the rates of human trafficking increase as well. The rates will continue to rise until legislation is in place, and police are able to, under federal, state, *and* local laws, efficiently apprehend suspects of trafficking in the United States and globally. If these measures are not put into effect in the near future, the modern-day slave trade is going to grow far more out of hand than it already has become.

The United States has established several different laws independently to combat human trafficking. Perhaps the main document that guides the United States on how it addresses the trafficking dilemma is the Thirteenth Amendment of the Constitution. The Thirteenth Amendment that governs U.S. policy on slavery and involuntary servitude states that, "Neither slavery nor involuntary servitude, except as a punishment for crime whereof the party shall have been duly convicted, shall exist within the United States, or any place subject to their jurisdiction" (U.S. Senate, 1996, p. 1). This Constitutional Amendment has served as the primary basis for future legislation that has come into action. No legislation written after this Constitutional Amendment has been allowed to conflict with its basic principles.

Human beings who are not citizens of America, unfortunately, are not guaranteed some of the Constitutional rights listed in other parts of the United States governing doctrine. For instance, while foreign nationals do have the right to an attorney in the court of law, they do not have the right for an attorney at government expenditure. This is extremely problematic in that, due to the very nature of most human trafficking cases, in most cases victims do not have financial resources to support themselves and are placed at the mercy of the trafficker once they reach the destination country. As well, Fourth Amendment rights are not written in the Constitution as mandatory for noncitizens of the United States, and thus, evidence that has been seized illegally is still permissible to be used against the victim, and not the trafficker if he or she is a U.S. citizen. Nor do trafficking victims from outside the

United States have any Fifth Amendment rights to remain silent and protect themselves against self-incrimination. This seems to be an unjust division of protections.

Beyond the Constitution, most of the legislation governing trafficking in the United States has been drafted and adopted in more recent years. The Trafficking Victims Protection Act of 2000 was created by U.S. government to establish harsh penalties for perpetrators of trafficking. It has also allocated nearly $1 billion for antitrafficking efforts. Congress states in the Act, "The purposes of this division are to combat trafficking in persons, a contemporary manifestation of slavery, whose victims are predominantly women and children, to ensure just and effective punishment of traffickers and to protect their victims" (Office on Violence Against Women, 2000, p. 1).

One interesting aspect the Trafficking Victims Protection Act has changed is the scope of what person(s) involved in the crime can now be officially considered a perpetrator of the crime and accordingly be held responsible for their participation and involvement. Particular emphasis was given to brothel-type operations that account for a large percentage of crimes against the trafficked person. Under this policy, the following people can be held criminally liable for their actions involved with any human trafficking: recruiters, anyone who obtained documents or arranged travel, anyone who assisted with travel, anyone who worked in a brothel, landlords, drivers, guards, assistants who brought meals, accountants, and managers (Hughes, 2003, p. 3). Previously, under U.S. law, there was no legal ramifications established to properly convict involvement from many of the previous people listed and they had to be charged under laws for other crimes that often did not give them a punishment that could be considered to be fitting for the criminal acts they committed.

The Trafficking Victims Protection Act also requires the Department of State to annually conduct a systematic study of nations across the globe to continually assess and acknowledge which countries are making appropriate efforts to combat human trafficking, and which ones are not. This report is entitled the Trafficking in Persons Report. The report involved countries of origin, transit, and/or destination for significant numbers of victims and categorically labels each country in any one tier of a three-tiered classification labeling system, with countries placed in a "Watch List" whose "governments do not fully comply with the Act's minimum standards but are making significant efforts to bring themselves into compliance with those standards, and:

a. The absolute number of victims of severe forms of trafficking is very significant or is significantly increasing; or
b. There is a failure to provide evidence of increasing efforts to combat severe forms of trafficking in persons from the previous year; or

c. The determination that a country is making significant efforts to bring itself into compliance with minimum standards was based on commitments by the country to take additional future steps over the next year" (U.S. Department of State, 2004, p. 17).

The *Trafficking in Persons Protocol* was introduced by the United States in collaboration with Argentina. This, however, is an international protocol that applies to both the United States and numerous countries outside of its borders. The protocol was proposed in 1999 and adopted in 2003. It was designed to help criminalize trafficking offenses in different countries and to help create plans for how different nations can aid victims of these heinous crimes. Also in 2003, the United States adopted the Trafficking Victims Protection Reauthorization Act. This important piece of legislation was adopted in an effort to amend the initial 2000 Act. It was an important legislation that put the subcategorical tier of the "Special Watch List" officially onto the Trafficking Report, and increased the stated need for investigation, conviction, and sentencing of trafficking rings and criminals associated in the trafficking process.

In a Statement of Administrative Policy, the White House publicly affirmed the Reauthorization Act and approved the improvements it made to original Act, including "facilitating the prosecution of the crime of sex trafficking through jurisdictional improvements to Federal criminal law, authorizing programs to increase public awareness of this problem, and facilitating family reunification with minors who are trafficking victims" (White House, 2003, p. 1).

The most recent newly established legislation to be passed in the United States regarding the combat of trafficking in persons was the Prosecutorial Remedies and Other Tools to end the Exploitation of Children Today Act that was adopted in the Spring of 2003. Otherwise known as the PROTECT Act, this policy tool was passed by Congress to serve as a new tool in handing out severe punishment to perpetrators who prey on children. This Act specifically targets crimes of sex tourism, the element of sex trafficking that is global. It is the act of people traveling abroad with specific intention to engage in sexual acts with natives from a foreign country. Where prostitution is illegal, citizens from such countries will often travel to places where prostitution is legal or to places that are commonly known for having large underground prostitution networks or brothels.

Unfortunately, children happen to be the prostitutes of choice for many criminal sexual tourists because of them having lower chances of being carriers of the HIV/AIDS virus or other sexually transmitted diseases. Children are seen as more *pure* than their adult counterparts and are thus preyed on more commonly. What the PROTECT Act enables federal law enforcement to do is to bring charges against sexual predators from the United States who engage in sex tourist crimes, even if they occur outside the U.S. borders. This is a gigantic step in establishing legislation that can more efficiently combat human trafficking in a world with so many geographical and cultural borders. "The Act serves as a historic milestone for protecting children while severely punishing those who victimize young people" (Patt, 2005, p. 1).

There is still an incredible amount to be done. The steps that have been taken by the United States are significant and a breakthrough in many aspects; they are the first baby steps in the global fight against the trafficking of human beings. Secretary of State Colin Powell stated in 2004 that, "Up to 18,000 cases a year afflict our own country despite the redoubling of our efforts under the PROTECT Act. And we are not satisfied with our progress abroad, because trafficking is linked to other problems of the gravest concern" (Powell, 2004, p. 2). There must be continual efforts made to not only develop policy on human trafficking, but on providing law enforcement and courts with the resources to implement these policy directives.

One way in which the U.S. government is preparing for future actions regarding the formation of legislation and policy, as well as implementation procedures, is through the delegation of grant money to fund different research projects regarding human trafficking–related issues. Task forces focusing on the trafficking in persons domestically seem to be one of the main uses of the money so far. In 2003, the U.S. Department of Justice awarded more than $7.6 million in grants—of which $450,000 went to the District of Columbia—to enable state and local law enforcement to fight human trafficking by creating task forces to aid in the identification of human trafficking cases. Task forces, such as the one in the District of Columbia, are a good way to start collaborative efforts between local, state, and federal law enforcement agencies because they offer the opportunity to address the human trafficking issue at a regional level. Since the varying demographics can differ what approaches are most appropriate and efficient in various cities, task forces allow regions to put specific focus on the needs of their given area versus trying to formulate answers in response to an epidemic of such massive proportions that their efforts may not have as much impact.

Each Protocol, Act, and Amendment stated up to this point has had an important role in the U.S. effort to combat trafficking. However, all of the previously cited forms of legislation and policy do not make up the entirety of such legal tools that govern the United States in its efforts to resolve this worldwide epidemic. As a member of the United Nation, the United States, as with all other member states, has the option of ratifying different treaties, conventions, and protocols underwritten by the United Nations. However, whether the United States chooses to adopt certain pieces of this type of legislation or not, they still often, if only indirectly, have a bearing on the United States. This is because, in the countries to which they are adopted, they have an effect on the trafficking epidemic locally. Trafficking, however, is an international phenomenon, and thus, will always have a bearing on destination countries, of which the United States currently is one.

There are certain international documents and conventions that play a significant role in determining the actions of the U.S. government in addressing trafficking issues, particularly when it must implement specific guidelines that has a direct effect on the other nations involved. Primarily, these treaties and conventions are drafted and adopted by the United Nations, but include some other documents specifically pertinent to other nations or cultures. Such legislation includes, but is not limited to the following:

- The Berlin Treaty (1885)
- International Convention for the Suppression of the "White Slave Traffic" (1910)
- Geneva Declaration on the Rights of the Child (1924)
- Slavery, Servitude, Forced Labour and Similar Institutions and Practices Convention (1926)
- Forced Labor Convention (1930)
- Convention Concerning Forced or Compulsory Labour (1932)
- Commission on the Status of Women (1946)
- Universal Declaration of Human Rights (1948)
- Convention for the Suppression of the Traffic in Persons and of the Exploitation of the Prostitution of Others (1951)
- Protocol Amending the 1926 Slavery Convention (1953)
- [European] Convention for the Protection of Human Rights and Fundamental Freedoms (1953)
- Protocols (14) to the 1953 Convention for the Protection of Human Rights and Fundamental Freedoms (1954–2005)
- Supplementary Convention on the Abolition of Slavery, the Slave Trade, and Institutions and Practices Similar to Slavery (1957)
- Declaration of the Rights of the Child (1959)
- Abolition of Forced Labour Convention (1959)
- International Covenant on Economic, Social and Cultural Rights (1966)
- Convention on the Elimination of All Forms of Discrimination Against Women (1979)
- Convention Against Torture and Other Cruel, Inhumane or Degrading Treatment or Punishment (1984)
- African [Banjul] Charter on Human and Peoples' Rights (1986)
- European Convention for the Prevention of Torture and Inhumane or Degrading Treatment or Punishment (1989)
- International Convention on Rights of All Migrant Workers and Members of their Families (1990)

- Convention on the Rights of the Child (1990)
- Cairo Declaration on Human Rights in Islam (1990)
- Additional Protocol to the 1978 American Convention on Human Rights in the Area of Economic, Social and Cultural Rights (1992)
- American Convention on Human Rights (1992)
- Declaration of the Elimination of Violence Against Women (1993)
- Inter-American Convention on International Traffic in Minors (1994)
- The Special Rapporteur on Violence Against Women (1994)
- Inter-American Convention on the Prevention, Punishment, and Eradication of Violence Against Women (1995)
- The Resolution for the Protection of Human Rights in the Context of Human Immunodeficiency Virus (HIV) and Acquired Immunodeficiency Syndrome (AIDS) (1997)
- African Charter on the Rights and Welfare of the Child (1999)
- Convention Against Transnational Organized Crime (2000)
- Convention Concerning the Prohibition and Immediate Action for the Elimination of the Worst Forms of Child Labour (2000)
- Charter of Fundamental Rights of the European Union (2000)
- Protocol to Prevent, Suppress and Punish Trafficking in Persons, Especially Women and Children (2003)
- WHO Ethical and Safety Recommendations for Interviewing Trafficked Women (2003)

University of Minnesota Human Rights Library, 2005

As one can easily discern, the battle to uphold human rights is a vast one. There is practically no place in the entire world that has not been directly affected. As both media and technology have advanced, so have the tools that criminals commonly use to commit these atrocious acts. Yet, in other ways, more light has now been shed on the international epidemic through media campaigns in many nations across the globe. Human trafficking advocates are fighting to ensure that the media does not lose sight of this epidemic as much of it did in the case of the genocide in Rwanda and during other instances of horrible crimes against humanity as a whole, as well as on numerous individual levels.

In 2004, during a United Nations address, President George W. Bush made a statement that has become rather well known in the battle against human trafficking worldwide. "There's a special evil in the abuse and exploitation of the most innocent and vulnerable. The victims of sex trade see little of life before they see the worst of life—an underground of brutality and lonely fear. Those who create these victims and profit from their suffering must be severely punished. Those who patronize this industry debase themselves and deepen the misery of others. And governments that tolerate this trade are tolerating a form of slavery. The trade in human beings for any purpose must not be allowed to thrive in our time" (Bush, 2004). It is now the time that police agencies, government, and NGOs must work together to find an effective solution to the trafficking epidemic. They must also find effective measure to coordinate efforts with social services to provide rehabilitation and resources to victims of this criminal by-product of globalization.

This is a harsh reality of the world today, but it is one that all citizens, regardless of race, creed, sex, age, religion, gender, nationality, or culture, share amongst one another. It is a criminal web intricately interwoven between nations and cultures with conflicting values and definition of these criminal actions, in order for the crime of human trafficking to flourish. It is the responsibility of each nation and its citizens, as human beings defending themselves against the viciousness of self-destruction, to move forward in the development of legislation and policy to address the issue of human trafficking domestically and abroad. As well, it is the responsibility of nations to provide law enforcement, prosecutors, and court system with the knowledge, training, and resources to be able to effectively combat the crime of human trafficking that has soared as a result of changes globalization has brought to the world in the twenty-first century.

Police need to be trained to properly identify trafficked persons and actions that are indicative of this type of crime. Many large departments are beginning to be trained or at least made aware of the issue and types of activities to be watched, but some smaller cities do not yet have the resources or manpower to address the issue. However, trafficking rings are being busted in cities of all sizes across the United States. Oftentimes, a victim is not recognized by the police as having been trafficked until the investigation is already underway. This is because of the nature of the crime. Many times, a trafficked person is brought to the attention of police simply because of the criminal act they are engaging in, such as prostitution. They are initially arrested for that particular crime, but then are later found to have actually been victimized. It is at this point that law enforcement can recommend them to any social service agencies for rehabilitation. Unfortunately, programs for victims of trafficking in social services are also few and far between.

It is of great importance that state and local governments place a great emphasis on trying to combat human trafficking as the federal government does, primarily because federal laws cannot be applied to individual cases. So far, only five states have adopted any legislation at a level below federally to be applied in cases of human trafficking. This is simply unacceptable and must serve as a red flag to this nation's citizens that reform is drastically needed.

Attempting to effectively handle something as large, serious, and widespread as human trafficking with the local and state laws that are currently in place seems as absurd as trying to heat a home with a matchstick or attempting to trim an entire lawn with a pair of scissors. All of the laws and policies can be in force, but it also requires the law enforcement agencies working on the ground to be properly made aware of what the laws are, what activities to be watched, and how enforcement should be applied. Appropriate tools, resources, and training must be provided for all parties involved in addressing the situation. It is time to pull together and save men, women, and children from the grave amounts of physical, sexual, mental, and emotional abuse they are subjected to in our surroundings or otherwise they would simply continue unabated.

References

Anonymous (2004). U.S. wants local help in human trafficking [Electronic version]. *Organized Crime Digest*, 25(9), 7–8 from ProQuest (689509661).

Bush, G. W. (2004). Speech at the United Nations General Assembly.

Florida State University Center for the Advancement of Human Rights (2003). *Florida Responds to Human Trafficking: Introduction to Human Trafficking, Background and Overview*. Tallahassee, FL: Florida State University. Retrieved February 28, 2005 from http://www.cahr.fsu.edu/J%20-%20Chapter%201.pdf

Hughes, D. (2003). *Hiding in Plain Sight: A Practical Guide to Identifying Victims of Trafficking in the U.S.* Retrieved March 26, 2005 from: http://www.acf.dhhs.gov/trafficking/resources/plain_site.html

Office on Violence Against Women (2000). *Focus on: Trafficking Victims Protection Act of 2000*. Washington, DC: United States Department of Justice. Retrieved January 24, 2005 from http://www.ojp.usdoj.gov/vawo/laws/vawo2000/stitle_a.htm#purposes

Patt, M. (2003). *Human Trafficking & Modern-Day Slavery: The United States of America (USA)*. Retrieved February 28, 2005 from http://www.gvnet.com/humantrafficking/USA.htm

Powell, C. (2004). *Our Trafficking Signal. Stop!* Moscow: United States Embassy. Retrieved January 24, 2005 from http://moscow.usembassy.gov/embassy/oped.php?record_id=10

U.S. Department of State (2003). *Victims of Trafficking and Violence Protection Act of 2000: Trafficking in Persons Report, June 2003*. Washington, DC: U.S. Department of State.

U.S. Department of State (2004). *2004 Trafficking in Persons Report: Introduction*. Washington, DC: Office to Monitor and Combat Trafficking in Persons. Retrieved February 28, 2005 from http://www.state.gov/g/tip/rls/tiprpt/2004/34021.htm

United Nations (1998). *Universal Declaration of Human Rights, 1948*. New York: United Nations. Retrieved January 24, 2005 from http://www.un.org/Overview/rights.html

United States Senate (1996). *The Constitution of the United States of America: Thirteenth Amendment – Slavery and Involuntary Servitude*. Washington, DC: United States Senate. Retrieved January 24, 2005 from http://www.gpoaccess.gov/constitution/html/amdt13.html

University of Minnesota Human Rights Library (2005). *International Human Rights Instruments.* Minneapolis, MN: University of Minnesota. Retrieved April 1, 2005 from http://www1.umn.edu/hjumanrts/instree/ainstls1.htm

White House (2003). *Statement of Administration Policy: H.R. 2620: Trafficking Victims Protection Reauthorization Act.* Washington, DC: Executive Office of the President. Retrieved February 28, 2005 from http://www.whitehouse.gov/omb/legislative/sap/108-1/hr2620sap-h.pdf

Three Decades of Policing Reform in the New York City Police Department

5

JAMES F. ALBRECHT

Contents

Over the last three decades, the New York City Police Department (NYCPD) has been exposed to reforms, often dramatic, to agency policy. A number of factors may influence a jurisdiction to promote and institute procedural change. Some of the more common grounds for agency reform are the following:

- New federal or local government administration
- New agency leadership
- New organizational philosophy
- Sensational event
- Media and public pressure
- Court decree
- Budgetary constraints

While this list is clearly not all inclusive, it is apparent that many of these issues may be interrelated. As an example, a sensational event reported or emphasized by the media may lead to the election of an opposing political party. Newly elected politicians routinely appoint a new police department head, who is in line with their political agenda and goals. A new agency philosophy may be developed, or recommended budgetary constraints may force the policing agency to institute new deployment strategies.

In New York City, as in most American cities, the most likely basis for policy reform is a change in governmental administration. With each newly elected president, governor, mayor, or county executive, a routine review of policy and procedure is undertaken. Each new elected official likely has run on a platform promoting change, and a personal goal for most politicians is to eventually leave office with a positive legacy.

Since the early 1980s, the NYCPD has experienced four major revisions to agency operational policy. Of course, the tragedy of September 11, 2001 is the most recent event that has resulted in drastic changes to law enforcement practices both nationally and internationally. However, returning to the rampant and violent crime rate of the 1980s, the NYCPD had continued its predominantly reactive police response, which had little impact on crime reduction efforts. In 1990, the public, expressing a need for change, elected a new mayor who emphasized tighter bonds with the community and an enhanced police presence. The public actually supported an increase in taxes to support the hiring of more police officers. The result was a dramatic increase in the number of uniformed patrol personnel and the institutionalization of community policing as the agency's official philosophy (NYCPD, 1990). The increase in police resources lead to the stabilization in crime rate, and the community policing ideology did improve citizen satisfaction of the police in New York City. It was not until a conservative candidate, Rudy Giuliani, was elected mayor in 1994 that a major revision in policing strategy took place. With the assistance of new Police Commissioner William Bratton, a corporate management mindset was incorporated into agency practices, with crime analysis, strategic deployment, and a "zero tolerance" strict enforcement ideology becoming the mainstays of organizational practices (New York City Police Department, 1994). According to Bratton, the source of this concept was the "broken windows" proposal raised by Wilson and Kelling (1982). The resultant and impressive reduction in violent and serious crime added support for this policy reform. Unfortunately, one drawback to this success was the reduction on the emphasis on neighborhood cooperation, as resources have been redeployed from community policing functions to proactive initiatives (Albrecht, 2005).

This policy reform, however, which received national and international accolades for its success in crime reduction, led to a severe reduction in support for the NYCPD in 1997 when a major police brutality incident drew widespread attention. In the Borough of Brooklyn in August 1997 in the early morning hours, as a crowd was leaving a dance club that was closing for the night, a large group of Haitian immigrants began fighting with each other. When NYCPD's 70th Precinct personnel responded to the call for assistance, they themselves were turned upon by members of the intoxicated crowd. When further police officers arrived and the crowd was finally separated, one of the original combatants, Abner Louima, punched a uniformed police officer in the face without provocation. That officer placed the individual under arrest. What happened next was clearly bizarre and difficult to comprehend. Later the same day, the suspect made the sensational allegation that the officer that had arrested him had brutally and sexually attacked him in the police station bathroom. The Haitian and African American communities immediately staged large-scale demonstrations. The media grasped the allegation as the major headline for months, relying mainly on the sensationalized claim by certain African American leaders that this single isolated incident was an indication that police brutality against minorities in New York City was widespread. Almost 2 years later in the summer of 1999, the suspect pleaded guilty to this unbelievable crime, but that in itself did not rectify the damage done to community confidence in the police.

This brutal attack clearly initiated a sense of mistrust in the NYCPD, which promptly responded with an internal strategy to counter these claims and improve community satisfaction in the agency. Within weeks of the incident, in direct response to the 70th Precinct police brutality case, the NYCPD released a new strategy aimed at improving the professional image of the police by emphasizing increased courtesy and respect to the public, criminal suspects and NYCPD supervisors and peers. A copy of the report, entitled "Courtesy Professionalism Respect" (NYCPD, 1997), was distributed to each of the 41,000 police officers and 9,000 civilian employees of the NYCPD. The ultimate goal of this strategy, nicknamed "CPR," was to breathe new life into police–community relations and improve the performance of agency personnel.

The CPR report emphasized positive interaction with the public and noted that if "crime levels decline, but members of the community are reluctant to approach police for fear of a negative encounter, then the police have not met their obligations to the public" (NYCPD, 1997). The document continued that "negative perceptions of police behavior toward the public" may emanate "not only from incidents of actual misconduct, but also from situations where proper police actions were mistakenly viewed by the public as inappropriate" (NYCPD, 1997). This is a clear reference to the media's continuous sensationalizing of controversial police actions and their practice of reporting contradictory information from somewhat or clearly unreliable or questionable sources, which in itself has repeatedly caused community unrest and, on occasion, rioting within the confines of New York City.

In addition, the NYCPD undertook considerable effort to improve the image of the police. New initiatives have been instituted to enhance the quality of newly hired police officers. The applicant screening process has been revised to emphasize the "screening in" of candidates with desirable characteristics, rather than the "screening out" of unqualified candidates. In addition, efforts have been made to recruit most candidates from the pool of New York City residents, not from the surrounding suburbs. Many sociologists believe that persons who reside outside of major American cities may not appreciate the diversity and comprehend the cultural differences in the various communities in the neighboring metropolis. New York City residents now receive extra points toward the final score on hiring and promotional exams, and increased effort has been made to conduct recruitment drives at colleges and schools in predominantly minority neighborhoods. Educational requirements for newly hired police officers have also been increased from a high school diploma to 2 years of college education or 2 years of military service (NYCPD, 1997).

In addition to attending mandatory community meetings with representatives from the respective neighborhoods that they serve, all police officers have obtained and will continue to receive both ethical and cultural awareness training, and now have the opportunity to obtain language instruction to overcome barriers and better communicate with neighborhood residents.

The NYCPD now has six separate performance monitoring programs that are designed to proactively identify and track police officers who present disciplinary problems, appear to use excessive force, or have personal difficulties that may impact their job performance. This computerized early warning system applies numerical points to incidents that occur within a police officer's career. When a police officer obtains a target number of points, the individual is called into police headquarters and is interviewed by a peer counselor who apprises the officer of the situation and the negative impact it may have on his or her career aspirations. If the negative conduct fails to improve, then the officer concerned is assigned to a nonpatrol function, thereby limiting his interaction with the general public. In addition, precinct and unit commanders are advised of the "special monitoring" status of personnel within their command and must then reevaluate the progress of these individual officers over an extended time frame (NYCPD, 1997).

The most important aspect of the CPR initiative is the regularly scheduled community meeting attended by police commanders in each of New York City's neighborhoods that allows an open dialogue between the public and the police. In addition, many highly successful programs have been instituted that involve community youth in sporting and other positive activities, where police officers can interact directly with the juvenile population in an informal and friendly environment (NYCPD, 1997).

While some minority leaders and the media have contended that the new "zero tolerance" philosophy would create a "police state" in minority communities, and that there would be an overwhelming increase in negative interactions with the police, Civilian Complaint Report statistics clearly indicate that the opposite is true. From 1997, when the CPR initiative was fully institutionalized, through the turn of the millennium, the number of civilian complaints filed against the NYCPD had decreased by −17% and the number of excessive force complaints had declined by −28% (NYC Civilian

Complaint Review Board, 2002).* This impressive reduction occurred at the same time that the complement of police officers in the NYCPD increased by approximately 12,000, which reflects a +40% increase in police personnel through 2001.

Of the approximately 35,000 police officers presently in the NYCPD, there are over 500 investigators assigned to the Internal Affairs Bureau, which is responsible for thoroughly investigating allegations of corruption and police misconduct. With the dramatic increase in police resources in recent years, there has been a notable decrease in the number of corruption complaints filed against NYCPD employees. In the period between 1997 and 2001, these complaints had declined approximately −33% and carry on a trend that commenced in 1994 (NYCPD Internal Affairs Bureau, 2002). Fortunately, this trend continues through 2009 (NYCPD Internal Affairs Bureau, 2010).

In proactive fashion, Internal Affairs Bureau investigators routinely conduct integrity tests either randomly or involving targeted police personnel. These tests evaluate a police officer's reaction to found currency or narcotics and ensure that legal and police department procedural guidelines are complied with. From 1997 through 2001, only one police officer has failed a random integrity test and approximately 40 police employees have failed targeted tests. Individuals failing an integrity test are subsequently arrested and suspended and all efforts are made to terminate them from their employment with the NYCPD (NYCPD Internal Affairs Bureau, 2002).

All police officers are administered tests for illegal drug usage. These urine and hair sample tests are administered to all newly hired police candidates, to all promoted and newly transferred personnel, to officers suspected of using drugs illegally based on allegations and observation, and to all police personnel on a random basis. In 1998, 16 and in 1999, 25 police officers failed the illegal drug examinations and were subsequently and automatically fired from the NYCPD. The numbers of drug test failures continues to decline (NYCPD Internal Affairs Bureau, 2002).

While the media and certain minority leaders would have one believe that NYCPD officials, having implemented the new "zero tolerance" philosophy, have created a racially biased "police state" promoting a "cowboy" and

---

* However, the New York City Civilian Complaint Review Board now permits the filing of complaints against NYCPD personnel online. In addition, complaints against NYCPD personnel can be filed via telephone through the new 311 system designed for non emergency inquiries in New York City. Since these complaints are not preliminarily screened to ensure that the reported complaints fall within the official civilian complaint guidelines, which involve allegations of abuse of authority, excessive force, improper language or the use of ethnic slurs, the number of reports filed at the CCRB has increased exponentially (NYC Civilian Complaint Review Board, 2008). However, the number of substantiated complaints involving NYCPD officers has actually declined over the same time period.

abusive environment, the opposite is actually true. In 1990, at the peak of the rising crime rate, there were 41 fatal shootings by NYCPD personnel, which declined to 30 in 1994, when the "zero tolerance" philosophy was initially instituted. In 1999, there were 11 fatal shootings, a −75% reduction since 1990 and a −65% drop since 1994. In addition, the number of shooting incidents involving NYCPD officers has decreased over −50% since 1994, and the number of bullets shot by NYCPD personnel has decreased more than −45% over the same time frame (NYCPD Firearms and Tactics Section, 2005). These dramatic reductions occurred as the firearms carried by NYCPD officers were upgraded from the six shot revolver to the 16 shot 9MM handgun. To better appreciate these statistics, one must recall that the number of sworn officers in the NYCPD increased almost +40% over the same period. When compared to other metropolitan police departments in the United States, the NYCPD is actually one of the most restrained law enforcement agencies in America. Even more importantly, as the streets of New York City have become safer for the public, they have also become safer for NYCPD officers. From 1999 through early 2003, no member of the NYCPD was killed by gunfire.

Not only has the 1994 reorganization of the NYCPD and the institutionalization of the zero tolerance philosophy resulted in the dramatic −80% reduction in serious crime in New York City through 2009, but all indications are that the NYCPD has evolved into a highly professional police agency.

From 1994, the sworn officer complement of the NYCPD had increased by approximately 12,000 police officers (or about +40%) through 2001, yet the number of civilian complaints filed against the police, fatal police shootings, police shooting incidents, police brutality complaints, and corruption and misconduct allegations made against the NYCPD have all drastically declined. It appears, therefore, that the negative perspective of the police that the media and certain minority leaders have often portrayed is inaccurate and that the opposite is actually true. The stereotyping of NYCPD personnel as being brutal, abusive and racist is not based on fact or reality, but on isolated incidents or fabricated allegations, and it often appears that the media is merely relying on the sensationalism created by opportunistic minority leaders to sell more newspapers and obtain more television advertisement revenue.

It is clear that agency reform may be triggered by one or more factors, some of which are planned and some which are dictated by unforeseen events. The NYCPD reacted to political change in both 1990 and 1994. In both cases, the NYCPD, under new political and internal executive guidance, instituted major organizational philosophical reforms that were both effective and impressive. The move to community policing and enhanced uniformed neighborhood presence from 1990 through 1993 led to a stabilization in crime rate and a stronger relationship with the public. In 1994, the shift to a more conservative and proactive strategy with corporate styled productivity goals (i.e., increased enforcement and reduced crime) revolutionized metropolitan policing in the United States and in other nations, as violence and serious crime thereafter plummeted. These planned reforms were the result of political and leadership change.

Often the need for reform is the result of an unpredictable event, as was the case with the 1997 police brutality event in Brooklyn that brought shame on the police department and caused extreme community unrest. The NYCPD launched a major policy initiative to ensure that all personnel are proactively screened in an effort to remove potentially abusive and problematic employees from regular contact with the public. In addition, these individuals were identified for enhanced direct and external supervision. All personnel were reminded that corruption and abuse would not be tolerated and would be harshly handled. Other agency endeavors were put into place to increase cultural awareness and improve interaction with the public and criminal clientele. It appears that the result of the CPR policy was a decline in the recognized negative indicators used to measure police performance, namely, substantiated citizen complaints against the police, substantiated police brutality allegations, and reports of police corruption and serious misconduct.

Probably the clearest example of an unforeseen and sensational event that promoted immediate law enforcement deployment and policy reform were the tragic events of September 11, 2001. Terrorism on American soil was not totally a new phenomenon. The 1993 attack on the World Trade Center in New York City by Muslim fundamentalists undoubtedly revealed that international terrorist attacks on the United States homeland were possible. However, the peaceful nature of the American lifestyle left most believing that a recurrence was improbable. The surprise suicide attack on the World Trade Center in 2001 left New York City dealing with an overwhelming number of tasks: a long-term rescue and recovery effort, a 6 week firefighting battle, the investigation of one of the largest crime scenes in history, and the need to deploy all available resources (including personnel from outside agencies) to counter a future terrorist strike.

More than 5 years later, the drain on resources that this event has created has not abated. In addition, the excessive costs of counterterrorism have dramatically affected the funds available for the NYCPD's traditional responsibility, crime deterrence, and reduction. This has lead to jurisdictional budgetary constraints on police department funding. In an effort to reduce agency costs, the size of police academy classes has been drastically reduced. The Mayor's directive is that police managers must now engage in "smarter policing" and therefore "do more with less." In reality, although the responsibilities of the organization have increased, the budget and complement available to accomplish these tasks have been reduced. The new policy mindset is therefore to anticipate and promote more effectiveness, effort, and dedication from each individual employee. The predominant issue for NYCPD commanders has therefore become the development of motivational mechanisms to incite police personnel to increase individual productivity.

The current mayor of New York City has taken a business or corporate approach and directed that a rational "machine" model would improve the efficiency and effectiveness of the police department. In essence, each officer or "machine" is expected to increase his or her effort and productivity merely by requesting or dictating that this be done. One would believe that this strategy would not prove to be effective in a civil service environment. Surprisingly, this tactic has proven to be successful in that crime continues to decline, albeit at a slower rate than in the late 1990s, and enforcement efforts (i.e., arrests and the issuance of traffic tickets and quality of life court summonses) have increased noticeably. This truly is an astonishing accomplishment since the complement of available patrol personnel has declined almost over −20% since the tragedy of 2001. However, there is a clear shortcoming to this directive. Government and agency management have failed to recognize the physiological strain that this productivity pace may have placed on NYCPD personnel. Few have recovered from the physical and emotional fatigue of the unforeseen sacrifices made necessary by the 2001 event. To endorse further exhaustion by mandating overtime assignments in an effort to maintain necessary manpower levels has resulted in drastic reductions in workplace morale. This then promotes retirement-eligible personnel to discontinue their employment, which thus necessitates additional overtime, which promotes more agency exile. It appears that the cycle will continue, and additional policy reform will be needed to achieve desired police department goals. The alternative would be a rising crime rate, which could have negative (and financial) repercussions on New York City.

Above are a number of examples of the motivating influences for agency policy reform as it related to the NYCPD over the last three decades. These illustrations from New York City compare to the policy cycle outlined in the *Australian Policy Handbook*. The three predominant stages of policy development involve ideation, realization, and evaluation (Bridges and Davis, 2000). When the concept of ideation or issue identification is applied to the above examples from the NYCPD, one can see that the motivating influence for policy reform mainly results from political factors. A political candidate may design his political campaign by promoting philosophical change in government practices. This may involve the emphasis on a shift from liberal to conservative, or conservative to liberal ideology. The jurisdictional executive, whether it be a national president, governor, mayor, or local councilperson, will have to incorporate the party philosophy into all or at least a majority of the agencies under his guidance. In order to promote agency reform, the executive must assemble a number of appropriate experts to evaluate each agency's practices to determine if they are in line with the political agenda. Traditionally this executive compiled his team of reformers after election. However, the recent trend in the political realm has seen the involvement of a noted expert in the election campaigning process, who supports the candidate in his election endeavor. If successful, this individual, as a reward, is appointed as an agency head or top level manager in the relevant public service organization. This "expert" would then be responsible for instituting the political ideology into the policy reform effort. As is the case in New York City, an expert who is "outsider" to the agency is routinely selected in order to ensure loyalty to the new political regime. Both internal and external professionals would be selected to evaluate present policy and recommend appropriate change. Policy analysis can be clearly influenced by a number of factors, including political influence, budgeting concerns, organization (or union) resistance and feedback from practitioners that indicates that some suggested reform may not be feasible. As the *Australian Policy Handbook* indicates, the "interaction between coalitions of interests, policy brokers and political institutions produces a policy community that discusses ideas and develops a shared understanding of the problem" (Bridges and Davis, p. 26). Due to these influences, the ensuing policy reform may be the result of concessions made by competing interests. However, the most dramatic changes outlined above, such as the agency wide institutionalization of community policing in 1990 and the implementation of the strategic "zero tolerance" deployment concept in 1994, which met much internal resistance, actually created immense organizational reform, and in fact, created a revised agency ideology. Both of these initiatives achieved the desired positive effect on crime rate in New York City. However, the "realization" phase, which involved planning and implementation for these major reforms, was costly in both the financial and training sense. The "evaluation" stage was quite easy, at least in the eye of the mayor, police department leadership and the public, as the targeted crime reduction was attained and could be easily measured.

However, one could argue, as some have, that the proactive or "aggressive" style of policing in New York City that has caused the dramatic decline in crime rate, has also fostered abusive or "aggressive" conduct by police personnel. This is highlighted by the above mentioned police brutality scandal that occurred in Brooklyn's 70th Precinct. As a direct result, the NYCPD was quickly forced to institute agency wide reforms in an effort to prevent or deter similar events from happening in the future. Although promptly instituted, these reforms appear to have resulted in the desired effect. Ideation and realization, in this case, were incorporated at an unbelievably quick rate.

Another obvious example of a single event that dramatically induced agency wide reform was the need for immediate response to the terrorist attack on September 11, 2001. Fortunately each local police station had previously designed a disaster plan for events in their own region. Unsurprisingly, these basic plans assisted police station and regional commanders in mobilizing personnel to an unforeseen major disaster, and at the same time allow the NYCPD to deploy personnel immediately in a citywide defensive counterterrorism response. In this case, ideation and realization of a challenge of this magnitude could not have been predicted. More importantly, failure of this policy reform is not an option, as the measuring ("evaluation") device would be a future terrorist attack.

The above clearly provides credence to the belief that policy reform can be a monumental task. At times, the planning and implementation stage may be short-lived. However, when planning is properly, comprehensively, and practically addressed, the results may be positive, as they have been in New York City.

References

Albrecht, J. (2005) Community policing in the USA: What does the future hold? Paper presented at the *Annual Conference of Criminal Justice Sciences Annual Conference*. Chicago, IL.

Bridges, P. and G. Davis (2000) *A Policy Cycle in Australian Policy Handbook* (2nd edn.). Allen and Unwin: Sydney, Australia.

New York City Civilian Complaint Review Board (2002) NYC civilian complaint review board annual report 2001.

New York City Civilian Complaint Review Board (2008) NYC civilian complaint review board annual report 2007.

New York City Police Department (1990) NYCPD staffing needs plan.

New York City Police Department (1994) The COMPSTAT process.

New York City Police Department (1997) Courtesy, professionalism, respect.

New York City Police Department (1994–1999) Police department: City of New York public information division media advisory (Daily press bulletins).

New York City Police Department (2002) NYCPD internal affairs bureau annual report 2001.

New York City Police Department (2005) NYCPD firearm and tactics section: Firearms discharge and assault annual report 2004.

New York City Police Department (2010) NYCPD internal affairs bureau annual report 2009.

Wilson, J. Q. and G. L. Kelling (1982) Broken windows: The police and neighborhood safety. *Atlantic Quarterly* 256: 29–38.

Examining Community Policing Implementation in the United States

6

KAM C. WONG

Contents

Introduction

The concept of community policing (COP) is so intuitively appealing that there is little open opposition to the philosophy. Yet, transforming this philosophy into a working program within police departments has been irregular, with internal organizational change moving at a slower pace than policing practices in communities. A number of studies have investigated the factors that influence the survival and acceptance of the COP concept for a number of populations, including the police themselves. A specific research project examined the stability of acceptance of COP over time in Racine, Wisconsin. Attitudinal differences among the population of officers in the Racine Police Department (RPD) were examined, to first assess how police officers' attitudes varied on the basis of demographics—age, years of service, rank, years of school completed, marital status, and gender. Using these demographic makers, attitudinal change over time between program onset and full implementation allows further analysis.

Police opinions of COP have been centrist, at best. Yet, few studies have examined police opinions over time and have used qualitative information to augment quantitative findings. While study outcomes support an overall neutral assessment of COP on the part of officers, differences in opinion by rank underscore the tensions present in the department on the basis of power differentials. These outcomes support research that has suggested that officers of low rank are most resistant to COP. Yet, comments from officers may lead one to ask how departments might change to involve the patrol and investigators in departmental decision-making. Discussion of quantitative and qualitative findings moves beyond description to questioning the organizational structure of departments and offer alternatives to current practice. Ultimately, it could be suggested that the dissolution of the COP unit that has drawn resources from traditional policing and movement toward a departmental policy of COP. To accomplish this with a buy-in from all officers is impossible. COP does not require uniformity and thus can accommodate a diverse department. How this is possible is the challenge of departments and future studies.

Literature Review

The challenges of implementing COP have been daunting, with senior command often ill-prepared to tackle resistance within departments, torn by competing public interests, and unprepared to lead departments toward organizational change (Williams and Sloan, 1990; Wolford, 1994; Skogan et al., 1999). Two strong predictors of officer satisfaction with COP have been job satisfaction and perceived organizational changes within departments (Hayeslip and Cordner, 1987; Greene and Taylor, 1988; Wycoff, 1988; Greene, 1989; Lurigio and Rosenbaum, 1994; Skogan and Hartnett, 1997) with some interest in the decentralization of command structures (Weisburd et al., 1988, 1989). Enlarging the police role, modifying the organizational structure of the department, improving relationships with supervisors, and increasing the responsibility of the community in crime prevention have corresponded to increases in officers' reported job satisfaction (Wycoff and Skogan, 1992; Lurigio and Rosenbaum, 1994; Skogan and Hartnett, 1997).

In their research in Illinois, Rosenbaum et al. (1994) measured whether officers in the Joliet and Aurora police departments saw improvement in the meaningfulness of their jobs, using a variety of work indicators as well as attitudes about COP, and problem solving knowledge to predict job satisfaction. They found that at the onset of the program, there were some positive changes concentrated in the neighborhood-oriented policing unit with favorable attitudes reported regarding COP and problem-solving capabilities. Moreover, after two years, these favorable attitudes spread across the whole department with all officers showing gains in their overall knowledge of COP.

Despite these encouraging outcomes, absence of change in job satisfaction is often the norm regarding evaluations of COP. Thus, results from the Rosenbaum et al. research failed to support predictions that officers would have a bigger role in management decision-making, have greater satisfaction interacting with supervisors, and have greater support among management for problem-solving activities. Joliet fared somewhat better than Aurora because the Joliet police department's organizational structure was less centralized than in Aurora. In Joliet, participatory management was encouraged and paper process was not paramount as it was in Aurora. On the other hand, Joliet kept the COP unit relatively isolated from the rest of the department, while Aurora did not (Wilkinson and Rosenbaum, 1994). The bureaucratic structure of these two departments suggests that a formalized bureaucracy can act to slow down progress in COP and that COP units should be a department-wide initiative (Rosenbaum and Wilkinson, 2004).

In a larger study conducted with the Chicago Police Department (CPD), Lurigio and Skogan (1994) examined officers' views regarding the Chicago Alternative Policing Strategy. They found that officers were concerned about their autonomy and their workload in the face of changed administrative policies in the department and that in general, officers were ambivalent about COP. Officers reported they found satisfaction in working with others, but had low mean scores on receiving feedback from their supervisors and being able to identify the completion of one job and the start of another. Rank and age were significant predictors of attitudes toward COP with higher-ranking and older officers more optimistic about the future of COP than patrol officers and officers younger than 50.

Other research involving the CPD indicates that most officers desire job autonomy, challenging assignments, and jobs that offer the potential for creativity and imagination. Despite these wishes, less than half the officers surveyed by Skogan and Hartnett (1997) felt they were committed to their current assignments and many officers who were assigned to COP roles were reluctant to adopt the activities associated with this program, e.g., patrolling neighborhoods on foot or helping with family disputes. High-ranking officers, women, officers of color, and young officers were more supportive of COP than were patrol officers, men, white officers, and older officers. The deepest demographic divisions were along racial and ethnic lines.

Adams et al. (2002) studied six mid-size law enforcement agencies in North Carolina. They found that length of time on the force was related to negative ratings of job satisfaction. While officers trained in COP felt capable of working with residents, less than half reported they had the ability to solve residents' problems, develop solutions to these problems, or evaluate how effective their solutions were.

Wilson and Bennett (1994) found little change in officer attitudes over time across three districts in Louisville, Kentucky. Similar to other studies, police officers reported a predominantly neutral stance toward COP. Officers reported communication problems with special units in the department, but were moderately satisfied with their jobs, and generally satisfied with their supervisors.

Community Policing in Racine

Racine, Wisconsin is located on Lake Michigan, 25 miles south of Milwaukee and 65 miles north of Chicago. The city of Racine covers just over 15 square miles, and had a population of 84,298 people in 1990, 2 years before the first COP substation was established (U.S. Bureau of the Census, 1992). Racine is an industrial community, home to 300 firms, the most notable of which is S. C. Johnson Wax and Company, producer of chemicals for home and industry.

Racine's police department is the third largest in the state, ranking behind Milwaukee and Madison, respectively. Racine is one of only 435 municipal police agencies in the United States with 100 or more full-time sworn officers (Maguire, 1997). The COP movement in Racine was a response to gang and crime problems that increased in the late 1980s and early 1990s. In 1991, the city of Racine reported a higher violent crime rate (1018.8 per 100,000 population) than the city of Milwaukee (979.2 per 100,000 population). In 1993, the RPD established two community-based offices in areas with high crime rates. One field station is adjacent to a local park where drug trafficking and gang activity was widespread. There are four field stations throughout high crime areas of the city.

There have been no new hiring of officers in the department for COP, but officers are eligible to apply as "neighborhood officers" after 18 months tenure in the department. Each field office has a "neighborhood officer" and a traffic investigator; an eight-man gang unit operates from three of the locations. Sanitarians (city health inspectors), state probation and parole agents, and civic groups utilize the substations as a base of operations on a part-time basis.

COP officers' duties are community intensive in that they are responsible for attending Neighborhood Watch and Crime Stoppers meetings, are required to have a presence in the schools, and be available to children and families throughout the day. COP officers are expected to patrol their neighborhoods in foot, rather than in squad cars.

In 1997, as part of the COP initiative, the RPD instituted the Gang Diversion Program and the School Patrol Program, which assigned off-duty officers to various schools to address issues of truancy, drinking, and smoking. At the same time these programs were established, four supervisory positions were eliminated and two patrol and five investigative officers were reassigned to police substations in an effort to decentralize the department (Polizin, July 14, 1998).

COP officers have responded favorably to the local press and signs of positive community engagement between police and the public are palpable. While these activities are highly publicized, what remains veiled are police opinions of COP and their perspectives on departmental efforts to transform the organizational structure of the department in accordance with this philosophy.

Methodology

The instrument construction, a 40-item survey instrument, was preceded by demographic inquiries regarding age, years of service on the RPD, rank, years of schooling, marital status, and gender. Officers were asked to rate their agreement with each statement on a scale of 1–5 with 1 indicating strong disagreement, 3 being 'Not Sure,' and 5 indicating strong agreement (Hagen, 1993). Twenty-one statements were worded positively and 19 were worded negatively. Scoring was reversed on the negative items producing positive measures of attitudes toward COP for all items. A total of 12 responses to statements were missing from Wave 1, with six respondents neglecting to answer from 1 to 4 of the 40 statements. A total of 16 responses to statements were missing from Wave 2, with nine respondents neglecting to answer from 1–7 of the 40 statements. The average of the available information for each item was used to create one of six attitudinal subcomponents. A blank section of the survey was available for open-ended comments from officers.

The dependent variable for this study is the respondent's attitude toward community policing. *Attitude* is defined as the extent to which an officer expresses support for COP and problem-solving activities.

There are six attitudinal subcomponents of the COP model examined in the questionnaire. These subcomponents form the basis for the six predicted subscales:

1. *Organizational structure*: five statements.
   Defined as the extent to which an officer expresses support for a decentralized, less authoritarian police department than the traditional model.

2. *Community policing substations*: seven statements.
   Defined as the extent to which an officer expresses support for the four police substations located in the high crime areas of Racine.
3. *Relationship between supervisors and subordinates*: five statements.
   Defined as the extent to which supervisors and subordinates are supportive of each other. This includes the attitudes of management (front-line supervisors and above) and rank and file toward each other, as well as the attitude of front-line supervisors and shift/unit commanders (captains and lieutenants) toward each other.
4. *Community policing concepts*: nine statements.
   Defined as the extent to which an officer supports some of the under-lying concepts or philosophy of COP, including but not limited to: foot patrols, becoming more involved in community problems of a noncriminal nature, and getting to know the neighborhood and neighbors better.
5. *Community policing unit*: six statements.
   Defined as the extent to which an officer expresses support for the COP unit. The unit, consisting of nine officers, staffs the five substations and is primarily responsible for overseeing the progression and success of the COP program.
6. *Specific community policing programs*: eight statements.
   Defined as the extent to which an officer expresses support for specific programs designed to enhance COP. This program involves all available sworn personnel from the chief down changing their hours of work at least one night a month during the spring and summer months to supplement foot patrols in high-crime areas.

Scale Reliability

The extent to which individual survey items within each COP attitudinal grouping were internally consistent was measured by the Chronbach's alpha coefficient (Morgan and Griego, 1998). Four statements from the survey were not internally consistent with other scale items in the construct and were removed from further analysis. Five of the six scales have high inter-item reliability across both Waves of the study, while the scale representing opinions about the organizational structure of the department has moderate inter-item reliability.

Data Collection

Within Wave 1 of the data collection, all officers within the RPD ($N = 209$) were asked to participate in the survey through a letter from the Chief of Police that was stapled to their paychecks one week prior to survey dissemination.

The first administration of the survey took place at roll call on Wednesday, February 19, 1997. The general consensus among command staff was that allowing the respondents to complete the survey at the beginning of their shift on duty time would produce a greater response rate than having them complete surveys before roll call on their own time.

Surveys were administered with a cover letter from the Chief of Police stapled to the front of the survey. The letter instructed officers to place completed surveys in one of two boxes, one placed in the patrol roll call room and the second placed in the detective roll call room. A postage paid envelope addressed to the University of Wisconsin-Parkside and an index card were distributed with the surveys. Each survey was assigned a unique identification number that matched a number on the index card that accompanied it. The card contained a space for the respondent's mother's maiden name and the respondent's last social security number (SSN) digit.

Most respondents completed the survey within 15 min and placed them in one of the two aforementioned boxes. Some respondents chose to mail their questionnaires directly to the university in the postage-paid envelope provided.

Wave 2 of the survey was distributed at roll call on Thursday, September 24, 1998, about 19 months after Wave 1. The lapse between waves was designed to leave enough time for officers to become familiar with COP procedures and form or change opinions regarding this new initiative. The survey distributed at Wave 2 was the same survey that was distributed at Wave 1 and survey administration mirrored that of the Wave 1.

The study population is all sworn officers of the RPD. The unit of analysis was each officer. There were 209 officers in the department for both waves of data collection.* There are nine sworn officers assigned specifically to the COP unit. The D.A.R.E., crime prevention, and "officer friendly" officers are technically not part of the COP unit.

One hundred sixty-seven officers completed the survey at Wave 1. The card giving the respondent's mother's maiden name and the last digit of the respondent's SSN accompanied most, but not all of the completed surveys. During the time that intervened between surveys, an interview in the [Racine] Journal Times with the third author revealed this person to be the Assistant City Attorney and former legal counsel for the RPD. In addition, the article discussed some of the controversy surrounding items in the survey. Specifically, officers took issue with one statement that described COP as a "cushy" job and officers felt that items, in general, were worded in a negative manner. In addition, officers were suspicious as to why they had to provide their mothers' maiden names and last digit of a SSN if the survey was truly

---

* Eleven newly hired officers replaced eleven officers who left the department after the Wave 1 survey.

anonymous. These factors influenced the response rate for the second wave of the survey. By Wave 2, only 92 completed surveys were returned, a response rate of 45%, as opposed to a Wave 1 response rate of 80%. These sample outcomes are similar to findings by Wilson and Bennett (1994), which indicate that officers exhibit skepticism about stated confidentiality of research and sometimes refuse to provide information that would aid researchers in matching surveys over time.

After the completion of Wave 2, we matched surveys across waves on the basis of matched identification numbers obtained from index cards. Some officers completed both waves of the survey ($N = 69$), while many completed Wave 1, but not Wave 2 ($N = 98$) and others completed Wave 2, but not Wave 1 ($N = 23$).

Results: Demographic Description

Forty percent of the sample at Wave 1 was between 24 and 35 years old, but only 26% was between these ages at Wave 2. The mean age of officers at Wave 1 was 38 and the mean age of officers at Wave 2 was 40. On average, officers reported 13.66 years of service at Wave 1 ($N = 163$) and 16 years of service at Wave 2 ($N = 89$). About 44% of officers had 10 or fewer years of service at Wave 1 and 32% of officers had 10 or fewer years of service at Wave 2. It should be noted that a substantial part of this difference is being attributed to aging from Wave 1 to Wave 2 (19 months) as the turnover rate in the department is very small (less than 5%). One hundred sixty-four officers at Wave 1 and 90 officers at Wave 2 reported their rank. Fifty-eight percent of respondents at Wave 1 and 47% of respondents at Wave 2 were patrol officers. Three percent at Wave 1 and 4% at Wave 2 were traffic investigators and about 16% at both waves were investigators. Twelve percent of the sample at Wave 1 and 19% of the sample at Wave 2 held the rank of sergeant. The remaining officers in the sample, i.e., 8.4% at Wave 1 and 12% at Wave 2, consisted of lieutenants, captains, the Inspector of Police, Assistant Chief of Police, and Chief of Police. The ranks of officers were dummy coded to create four distinct groups. Patrol officers and sergeants remained separate categories. All investigators were grouped together and personnel ranked as lieutenant or higher were defined as one group representing senior command staff.

The mean number of years of education reported by officers for both waves was about 15 years. There is a split in the department with about half the force having less than a college degree and the other half earning a college degree or higher. This is consistent across waves of the study. Three-fourths of respondents were married at Wave 1 and 80% were married at Wave 2. Ninety-five percent of respondents at Wave 1 were men as were 91% at Wave 2.

Comparison of the demographic distributions between waves suggests that officers who dropped from the survey between waves were patrol officers who were young and had fewer years of service compared to their peers. To verify this, two sets of t-tests were calculated for each demographic predictor. One set of t-tests compared differences for Wave 1 between officers who responded to the survey at both waves ($N = 69$; Wave 1) and officers who dropped out of the study after Wave 1 ($N = 98$). The second set of t-tests compared differences at Wave 2 between officers who responded to the survey at both waves ($N = 69$; Wave 2) and those who were added to the study at Wave 2 ($N = 23$).

Significantly more patrol officers dropped from the study after Wave 1 than remained. There were no significant differences on other demographic indicators across t-test comparisons. Researchers often consider failure to participate in surveys over time a common problem of data collection and discount the impact of missing data from our analyses. Yet, the decision not to participate in a research study and the result of this nonparticipation provided valuable information that can aid in data interpretation. Indeed, the loss of significant numbers of patrol officers from this study is considered an important part of the data that has impacted its outcomes.

Attitudes toward Community Policing

Within Wave 1 of this study, mean attitudes toward COP on the six concepts range from 2.68 to 3.52 indicating that police officers, overall, do not have extreme views regarding COP. On average, officers are in favor of COP concepts ($\bar{x} = 3.44$), favor COP programs ($\bar{x} = 3.24$) and favor a flattened organizational structure ($\bar{x} = 3.52$). Over 80% (81.4%) of officers were supportive or very supportive of COP concepts in general, with mean scores of over 3.5 obtained for statements that supported foot patrols in neighborhoods, officer involvement in the community, and permanent community assignments. Fewer, but still a majority (68%) agreed that COP programs, such as Neighborhood Watch, the bicycle patrol, neighborhood sweeps, and National Night Out were effective. With regard to responses supporting a flattened organizational structure in the department, 83% agreed or strongly agreed that the department could reduce the number of front-line officers and that officers should have more input in department operations. Yet, respondents were divided on how much supervision officers need and if the department has too many shift and unit commanders on the force.

Officers are neutral regarding their approval of police substations in the community ($\bar{x} = 3.08$) and slightly disapprove of the COP unit ($\bar{x} = 2.68$). Just over 60% of officers (61.7%) agreed or strongly agreed that the presence of substations in the community is good but only about one-third (37%) indicated approval for the COP unit.

Officers' assessment of the relationship between supervisors and subordinates is slightly below average ($\bar{x} = 2.84$), with less than half (48%) of officers reporting good or very good communication between officers and shift and unit commanders.

Within Wave 2, a t-test comparison between waves indicates that there were no significant mean differences over time for five of the six COP concepts. However, the mean approval rating supporting a flattened organizational structure decreased between Wave 1 and Wave 2. Examination of mean differences between the specific statements that make up this construct indicates that by Wave 2, there was less support among respondents for eliminating shift and unit command in the department.

Inter-Correlations among Dependent Constructs

An inter-correlation of the six constructs for Wave 1 indicates a strong to moderate, positive relationship among five of the constructs: favorable attitudes toward COP concepts, support of COP programs, support for locating substations outside the central office, support for the COP unit, and reporting that relationships between supervisors and subordinates are good are all positively related. In contrast, attitudes of respondents who favor a flattened organizational structure in the department are negatively correlated with support for all other constructs. Thus, those who favor more autonomy and less supervision in the department do not support COP concepts and programs, do not support the COP unit, nor favor locating substations outside the central office. Moreover, those who support a flattened organizational structure in the department also report that relationships between supervisors and subordinates are strained. These trends do not change across waves of the study.

Mean attitudes on the six constructs toward COP for the 69 officers who responded to both waves of the study were compared and found no significant differences in their attitudes toward COP over time. Thus, officers who participated in both waves of the study did not change their attitudes toward COP.

A second comparison noted the Wave 1 responses of the 69 officers who participated in both waves of the study with the Wave 1 responses of the 98 officers who dropped out of the study at Wave 2. Findings revealed that officers who dropped from the study after Wave 1 were more supportive of a flattened organizational structure than officers who stayed in the study. This supports the earlier supposition that officers who dropped out of the study, i.e., primarily patrol officers, were supportive of having more input in department operations and having fewer shift and unit command in the department. There were no other differences in mean attitudes toward COP between these two groups. Finally, another comparison revealed that the

Wave 2 responses of the 69 officers who participated in both Waves of the study with the Wave 2 responses of the 23 officers who did not participate in Wave 1. There were no statistically significant differences on COP constructs between the 23 officers who were added to the study at Wave 2 and those who responded to both waves of the study.

Mean differences between officers who participated in both waves of the study and those who dropped from the study, i.e., patrol officers who tended to have fewer years of service and are young; indicate that patrol officers are those who seek more autonomy and input in decision making. When this outcome is interpreted in light of correlations among dependent measures, one can conceivably predict that patrol officers are most likely to support organizational change in the department and are also resentful of COP, in general, disapproving of the COP unit, and report strained relationships between themselves and their supervisors.

Predicting Support for Community Policing

In order to examine the stability of subject attitudes toward the various subscales, a series of one-way analysis of variances were conducted for rank and attitude for time one and time two measures for those subjects who had completed both schedules.

The attitudes toward COP were relatively stable with significant relationships for attitudes toward the use of substations and attitudes toward the COP unit itself. For substations, attitudes tended to improve for all ranks except for traffic officers. For attitudes toward the COP units, attitudes increased except for patrol officers.

The basic patterns remained for all subscales. Generally speaking, supervisors have more positive attitudes than line officers and investigators for all subscales except for organizational structure when the pattern reverses. While the changes for attitudes toward substations and COP units are significant, the general pattern remains essentially the same.

Comments from Officers

At Wave 1, one-third (32%) of respondents provided comments and at Wave 2, 37% provided comments. Officers' comments underscore statistical outcomes, with the patrol and investigators more negative in their evaluations than sergeants and senior command. Officers' comments focused on COP as a philosophy, the COP unit specifically, substations in the community, relationships between low-ranking officers and their supervisors, and the survey instrument.

Community Policing Philosophy

There seem to be two factions in the department, one that believes that COP is not "real police work" and a second that supports the concept. One investigator comments, "Law enforcement's role is not to address the ills of society but rather to respond to crime and arrest the perpetrators of such. There is a distinct line between social service providers and law enforcement officers and I think the leaders in our department forgot the lessons taught in basic criminal justice classes." Another patrol officer states that COP is an excellent philosophy, but that people are reluctant to change, suggesting that while the concept is supported, the organization of the department and deployment of staff remains as before. Another stated, "Breaking paradigms in police work is going to be a long, hard battle."

Community Policing Unit and Substations

Overwhelmingly, police officers are opposed to having a separate COP unit in the department. A patrol officer comments that, "Community policing should be a department wide concept. It should not be a select group of officers." Part of the problem with having a COP unit is the lack of communication between members of the unit and the rest of the department. Some patrol officers feel that they are uninformed about what the COP unit actually does. "The department as a whole needs to be better educated about community policing and there needs to be better communication between COP officers and patrol officers...Many people have a negative attitude about COP because they don't know what it is."

It is noted that the COP unit was established at the expense of other programming. Specifically, the RPD had lost a crime analysis officer, a fingerprinting examiner and cross-training officers for investigative work—all so that COP positions could be filled. Thus, by Wave 2 of the study, resentment for this unit was high. Moreover, the relative isolation of COP officers in the community substations brought into question the activities of these officers. "...(A)s long as they keep throwing money into these programs, you will have COP and all the politics that go with it. But the Department can sure start to take care of the patrol division a lot better...." One officer accused the COP unit of "hiding" in the substations, saying they need to be seen, "even if they are sitting in a lawn chair in the front yard."

The few responses from sergeants were less caustic than those of patrol or investigators, yet continued to state the ills of having one COP unit. "Current attention to one specialized unit and the purchase of equipment and training for such few people, causes patrol officers and investigators to feel like second-class personnel." Of the five senior command officers who provided comments, two praised the philosophy of COP, with one stating, "The astounding positive results of the officers in community policing are a credit to this philosophy."

Communication among Ranks

There were consistent comments regarding the withholding of information by senior command. One respondent blames the breakdown in communication between command staff and patrol on sergeants who "…tells the chief what he wants to hear, because they also are clueless." On the other hand, sergeants placed the burden of this on their supervisors indicating that top administration need to explain COP and its implementation and need to provide officers with problem-solving and team-building skills. "What good is the information if change is not introduced to better educate this department…The street officer is still the primary respondent to all problems and received little support or backing from the top." One patrol officer suggests, "Top administration should effectively communicate with everyone what is up, what is new, what is changing to keep everyone involved."

Problems with the Survey

Finally, officers are critical of this survey. Some were skeptical as to whether respondents' identities were truly anonymous, while others felt statements were difficult to answer accurately and were dependent upon officer experience and service on the force. One investigator states, "Another survey, but as usual nothing changes to improve the overall working conditions for the officers working the street. ANOTHER JOKE!"

Two officers commented on their neutral responses to the survey statements. One officer felt he or she was uninformed, while a second stated, "Please don't confuse not caring with lack of knowledge. Our opinion is not important…Please quit wasting our time filling in these useless surveys which you only do for grant money." Statements such as these lead us to question early research findings that suggest that officers are neutral on COP. Indeed, rather than neutral responses, officers may indicate a general apathy and negativity toward the program by simply circling the "not sure" or "neutral" response.

COP is believed by many to be a political decision that is mostly show. Resentment of this program is focused on senior command staff that is viewed as succumbing to the pressures of grant monies and public opinion to establish a program that is a "dog and pony" show. Moreover, this seems to have been accomplished without the buy-in of rank and file officers.

Discussion

While overall attitudes favoring COP in the RPD did not change over time, differences in approval for the initiative by rank indicate the very people who are counted on to make it succeed do not support this program. Rank stratifies the department, signifying responsibilities and privileges that correspond to the various positions. COP, as a philosophy, challenges this stratification structure. It is understandable that senior command, while supporting COP, in general, are reluctant to give up decision-making power in the department. It is also understandable that patrol officers and investigators, who are delegated to carry this out, want the independence of decision-making that goes along with this new philosophy. What is damaging in the case of the RPD is the implementation of some aspects of COP, without the apparent approval from the top for the patrol to make independent decisions. Add to this system, privileges for a select group of patrol officers, the COP unit, and divisions on the basis of resources and ideology are created within ranks as well as across them.

Focus must be placed on the diversity in perspective in departments that attempts to consolidate COP into a unified policy. How can one study variations in perspectives within ranks with the goal of understanding, accommodation, and perhaps change? Which are the subcultures within the department that distinguish officers on the basis of attitudinal sets? A future study could examine the diverse "types" within departments on the basis of opinion and experience to learn about attitudinal differences among officers regarding COP with the goal of understanding diverse perspectives and accommodating programming on the basis of various levels of support, talents, and motivations.

Secondly, it is important for departments to step back and assess their commitment to COP. Can participatory management be viewed as favorable and can dissention among ranks be tolerated and incorporated into a dialog for change? With a view of COP through a qualitative lens and an examination of the culture within ranks, future questions asked of future survey officers must change. Ultimately, the optimism for COP programs has waned, particularly since the tragedy of September 11, 2001. The steady and continuous decline in serious and violent crime nationally has also contributed to a lack of government concern for law enforcement and COP initiatives have become the common victims.

References

Adams, E. R., William, R. M., Thomas, A. 2002. Implementing community-oriented policing: Organizational change and street officer attitudes. *Crime and Delinquency* 48, 399–430.

Greene, J. R. 1989. Police officer job satisfaction and community perceptions: Implications for community-oriented policing. *Crime and Delinquency* 26, 168–183.

Greene, J. R. and Taylor, R. 1988. Community-based policing and foot patrol: Issues of theory and evaluation. In J. Greene and S. Mastrofski (Eds.), *Community Policing: Rhetoric or Reality* (pp. 195–224). New York: Praeger.

Hayeslip, D. and Cordner, G. 1987. The effects of community printed patrol on police officer attitudes. *American Journal of Police* 1, 95–119.

Lewis, S. 1998. Police officers' perspectives on community policing: The Racine, Wisconsin experience. Master's thesis, University of Alabama, Department of Criminal Justice, Tuscaloosa, AL.

Lurigio, J. A. and Rosenbaum, D. P. 1994. The impact of community policing on police personnel. In D. P. Rosenbaum (Ed.), *The Challenge of Community Policing: Testing the Promises* (pp. 147–163). Thousand Oaks, CA: Sage.

Lurigio, J. A. and Skogan, W. 1994. Winning the hearts and minds of police officers: An assessment of staff perceptions of community policing in Chicago. *Crime and Delinquency* 4, 335.

Maguire, E. R. 1997. Structural change in large municipal police organizations during the community policing era. *Justice Quarterly* 14, 547–576.

Morgan, G. A. and Griego, O. V. 1998. *Easy Use and Interpretation of SPSS for Windows.* Mahwah, NJ: Lawrence Erlbaum Associates.

Polizin, R. July 14, 1998. Personal communication to Chief Leslie Sharrock, Waukesha Police Department, Waukesha, WI.

Rosenbaum, D. P. and Wilkinson, D. L. 2004. Can police adapt? Tracking the effects of organizational reform over six years. In W. G. Skogan (Ed.), *Community Policing (Can it work)?* (pp. 79–108). Belmont, CA: Wadsworth.

Rosenbaum, D. P. and Yeh, S., Wilkinson, D. 1994. Impact of community policing on police personnel: A quasi-experimental test. *Crime and Delinquency* 40, 331.

Skogan, W. G. and Hartnett, S. M. 1997. *Community Policing: Chicago Style.* New York: Oxford University Press.

Skogan, W. G., Hartnett, S., DuBois, J., Comey, J. T., Kaiser, M., and Lovig, J. H. 1999. *On the Beat.* Boulder, CO: Westview Press.

U.S. Bureau of the Census. 1992. *Census of Population and Housing: Summary Social, Economic, and Housing Characteristics of Wisconsin* (1990 edn.). Washington, DC: U.S. Government Printing Office.

Weisburd, D., McElroy, J., and Hardyman, P. 1988. Challenges to supervision in community policing: Observation on a pilot project. *American Journal of Police* 7, 29–59.

Weisburd, D., McElroy, J., and Hardyman, P. 1989. Maintaining control in community-oriented policing. In D. Kenney (Ed.), *Police and Policing: Contemporary Issues.* New York: Praeger.

Wilkinson, D. L. and Rosenbaum, D. P. 1994. The effects of organizational structure on community policing: A comparison of two cities. In Rosenbaum, D. P. (Ed.), *The Challenge of Community Policing: Testing the Promises.* Thousand Oaks, CA: Sage.

Williams, J. and Sloan, R. 1990. Turning concept into practice: The Aurora, Colorado story. East Lansing, MI: Michigan State University, National Center for Community Policing.

Wilson, G. B. and Bennett, F. S. 1994. Officers' response to community policing: Variations on a theme. *Community Policing* 40, 354.

Wolford, J. 1994. Conflict and controversy: Can the chief fill the void? *The Police Chief* 61, 52, 54.

Wycoff, M. A. 1988. The benefits of community policing: Evidence and conjecture. In J. R. Greene and S. D. Mastrofski (Eds.), *Community Policing: Rhetoric or Reality* (pp. 103–120). New York: Praeger.

Wycoff, M. A. and Skogan, W. 1992. Quality policing in Madison: An evaluation of its implementation and impact. Final Technical Report. Washington, DC: National Institute of Justice.

The Recruitment and Retention of Law Enforcement Personnel in the United States

7

DEE WOOD HARPER, JR. AND GWEN MOITY NOLAN

Contents

Introduction

Police departments nationwide spend money on continuing education, tuition reimbursement, and educational salary incentives. The funding for these incentives usually comes from agency budgets, police foundation grants, or scholarships. The central issue is return on investment. The cost of recruiting, hiring, and training is becoming more expensive and with the growth in federal law enforcement agencies since September 11, 2001, retaining qualified police personnel is even more difficult.

Local law enforcement agencies across the country have reported soaring attrition rates and erosion of police personnel at a most critical time. Several attrition factors and how they affect the stability of individual police departments must be examined. The challenge for law enforcement agencies is to invest in a long-term plan to identify and recruit personnel that in all likelihood will be effective and will persist in the job. Some aspects that will be examined include policies and salary incentives as they affect the recruitment and retention of officers.

Recruitment and retention issues vary from department to department and city to city. Many departments report a lack of proper representation of members of minority groups and also properly qualified candidates (Koper, 2004). Why are police departments having problems recruiting good quality officers and retaining them? Experience and observations on by front line and ranking officers lead to the following reasons officers leave the department for other local departments, the federal government, and/or the private sector:

- Low, noncompetitive salaries
- Family circumstances
- Poor quality of life
- Lack of advancement opportunities and/or not meeting the requirements for advancement
- Extremely high work load, stress, burnout, and poor job satisfaction
- Lack of support from city, public, department, and/or rank
- Residency requirements
- "reality shock" leading to early attrition, e.g., "policing is not what I thought it would be"
- The "frustration factor," including the criminal justice system as a whole, i.e., lack of tools needed to perform the job efficiently and effectively, as well as the district attorney's failure to prosecute cases and/or the "slap on the hand" punishments given by judges

Eventually, these factors add up and take a toll on an officer's perspective. The officer begins to think, "Is it worth it?" and "Why am I doing this?" This is where departments need to act. This is the tipping point in an officer's decision to stay or leave.

Incentives can be a valuable recruiting tool and for this reason, the type of incentives offered is important. If departments offer the correct incentives, officers will think more seriously about what they are giving up and weigh their options before leaving the agency. The incentives offered make a difference in who will stay or who will go. The incentives can attract the type of candidates the department seeks. It is likely that police departments offering educational incentive pay and a higher salary will experience less in the way of recruitment and retention issues.

Literature Review

As early as the 1900s, the push for "professionalization" in law enforcement was well underway. August Vollmer, the acknowledged Berkeley

California police chief from 1905 to 1932, is credited with beginning the professionalization movement. He advocated for higher education for police officers and sought to raise personnel standards and define policing as a profession (Bell, 1979).

The president's 1967 *Task Force Report: Police* emphasized the need for higher education. "The importance of advanced education was perceived to be a function of the complexity of performing police tasks. The ultimate goal was to have all enforcement personnel possess a baccalaureate degree" (Baker, 1995, p. 41). While the movement has progressed slowly over the past 40 years, it is firmly established that professionalization is the goal of modern policing and higher education is one of the main pathways to achieving a truly professional police force (Rodriguez, 1995).

In spite of the positive arguments there has also been strong resistance to educational requirements beyond high school graduation or equivalent for hire and promotions, as well as questioning the value of college-educated officers within police agencies particularly among the "old timers" and those without a college education. They argue that there is no direct evidence linking higher education to better police officers. Others argue the recruitment issue. Some administrators feel many "good cops" will be eliminated from the candidate pool because they do not possess higher education.

Still others in the community fear the requirement will reduce the number of minority group representatives in the candidate pool and eventually skew the racial composition of the police force to the point of not reflecting community demographics. Finally, and realistically, are the financial costs. Agencies are concerned that tight budgets will not support the higher salaries college-educated officers will expect.

To add to the dilemma, many officers feel the college education requirement for promotion is unfair. The department's education policy has changed from what it was when they were hired. Departments that now require officers to possess college hours or a degree, in a sense, have changed the rules in the middle of the game. This creates a situation where an otherwise excellent veteran police officer becomes ineligible for promotion because she/he does not meet the education requirements. In this context, departments are, in a sense, telling veteran officers that their tenure and job experience is not worthy of consideration for promotion (Hawley, 1998).

The Rise and Fall of College Education Programs

The Law Enforcement Education Program (LEEP), a federal program of the Law Enforcement Assistance Administrations (LEAA), was created by the Omnibus Crime Control and Safe Streets Act of 1968. In the 1970s, the LEAA paid for officers to attend college. The LEEP program was extremely beneficial for law enforcement. According to Flick (1994), prior to LEEP only 20% of law enforcement possessed a college education and when the program ended, 65% had attended college and 25% finished with a 4-year degree. An important aspect of the LEEP program was that officers who accepted the grant agreed to remain employed in the department for which they worked for a period of at least 2 years following completion of the study period. While the program was successful, it lacked political support and was discontinued. Some of the officers who were products of the LEEP program are the officers who run today's departments.

No other organization has pushed for police professionalization like the Commission on Accreditation for Law Enforcement Agencies (CALEA). In order for a law enforcement agency to become CALEA certified, it must comply with 436 standards (Baker, 1995). The CALEA standards include departments encouraging all officers to obtain a college education.

More recently, communities and enforcement agencies have felt the need to fund tuition reimbursements as a recruitment incentive. Also, the Police Corps program, which is funded by the federal government, is an attempt to produce a new breed of college-educated officers. This is an excellent program for individuals who are truly interested in a career in law enforcement. However, law enforcement looses when individuals use the program to obtain a free degree and then leave law enforcement for other careers.

The Police Association for College Education (PACE) is an organization of college-educated police officers working to upgrade personnel, improve performance, and enhance the status of police. "The mission of the Police Association for College Education (PACE) is to advance the quality of police agencies and services through police officers, by encouraging and facilitating a minimum education level of a four-year college degree for officers" (PACE Web site, 2004).

The Pros and Cons of College-Educated Officers

There has been much debate on the effects of higher education and law enforcement officers' job performance. The results are inconsistent and conflicting (Truxillo et al., 1998). Nevertheless, officers possessing higher education are sought after. The modern police officer has enormous responsibilities managing the different circumstances they encounter everyday. Police officers have become counselors, referees, teachers, problem-solvers; they need to know the ever-changing laws and must possess the foresight to see the consequences of their decisions (Davis, 1983).

According to CALEA standards, officers who receive a broad general education have a thorough understanding of society and have learned to communicate more effectively. A college education provides a competitive edge in police promotional examinations because, generally, study skills learned in college carry over to the occupational context (Whetstone, 2000).

Polk and Armstrong (2001) conducted a study of the relationship of education with career paths and promotions. Their findings revealed, "Education is one of the top two factors in attaining higher rank and in shortening the length of time to promotion or favorable transfer. The level of current education best predicted the level of rank in the large agencies." Furthermore, the study found that as education increased, the amount of time spent in an assignment decreased. The results also support those who believe the attainment of such education should be rewarded when possible.

Educational Requirements and Department Incentives Trends

Incentives range from take-home vehicles to Police Officer Placement Solution (POPS), a Phoenix, Arizona police department program that places officers in homes. Additional incentives offered to officers include flexible hours, day care programs for their children, uniform allowance, hazard pay, shift pay, longevity pay, college education pay, and college tuition assistance programs.

In 1988, the Police Executive Research Forum (PERF) conducted a study focusing on the progress of the education movement. Approximately 250,000 officers were surveyed. The study found, "the state of police education is good" (Carter and Sapp, 1992, p. 3). The study also revealed from 1968 to 1988, there was steady growth of educational levels and several departments had increased the educational level requirements for employment and/or promotion.

Carter and Sapp (1992) pointed out that "(i)n 1967, the average educational level of officers was 12.3 years, barely more than a high school diploma" (p. 4). In the 1988 study, the average college level was 13.6 years. Carter and Sapp (1992) states, "this increase in educational levels is notably fast" (p. 4).

The PERF study also found that

- Fourteen percent of departments had a formal college requirement for employment.
- The number of college credits required for employment ranged from only 15 semester hours to a baccalaureate degree, with most departments requiring an average of 60 semester hours.
- A notable number of police chiefs indicated that they believed a graduate degree should be required for officers in command ranks.
- To be eligible for promotion, 8% of the departments required some college beyond their entry-level requirements, while 5% wanted a college degree.

In 1995, Stephen A. Baker conducted a CALEA study focusing on the effects of law enforcement accreditation on officer selection, promotions, and education. The study surveyed 150 departments, both accredited and nonaccredited, selected from lists arranged by size. Baker (1996, p. 104) asked, "Do accredited and unaccredited agencies differ in the incentives offered to support higher education?" Baker found that tuition reimbursement was the most commonly used incentive (76% accredited and 67% nonaccredited agencies). The second most commonly used incentive was incentive pay (57% accredited and 50% nonaccredited agencies). Promotional qualifications ranked third, with 36% of accredited agencies and 28% nonaccredited agencies. Overall, the study found accredited agencies offer officers more incentives than nonaccredited agencies (Baker, 1996). However, the study also found 75.7% of departments already had educational incentives in place prior to CALEA certification. Furthermore, Baker found 90% of accredited agencies recruited college graduates versus 70% of nonaccredited agencies. Pay incentives were the second most used method by accredited and nonaccredited agencies. Very few agencies required two- or four-year degrees as an educational requirement for employment (Baker, 1996).

To see the impact of higher education on promotion, Baker also asked accredited and nonaccredited agencies if education was beneficial for promotion. The survey asked departments if education was a requirement used in promotions. It was revealed that most agencies indicated education was important (70% of accredited and 78% nonaccredited) and require higher education for promotions (Baker, 1995).

A survey, by Reeves (2000), under the auspices of the U.S. Department of Justice included information from individual state and local agencies with 100 or more officers and collected data from 501 municipal police departments, 222 sheriffs' offices, 32 county police departments, and the 49 primary State police departments. According to the data, "nearly all police departments (98%) local police departments had an education requirement for new officer recruits. Fifteen percent of departments had some type of higher education requirement for new officers. Six percent of departments required some college, eight percent required a two-year college degree, and only one percent required a four-year degree." The results revealed, "nationwide, 38 percent of local police departments, employing 58 percent of all officers, offered tuition reimbursement to officers. An estimated 30 percent of departments offered education incentives pay to qualifying officers" (Reeves, 2000, p. 8).

In 2002, Reeves and Hickman compiled data for the Bureau of Justice Statistics Special Report. The data were gathered from 62 local police departments serving cities with a population of 250,000 or more during the years 1990–2000. The findings revealed that "(d)epartments requiring new officers to have at least some college rose from 19 percent to 37 percent, and the percent requiring a 2-year or 4-year degree grew from 6 percent to 14 percent" (Reeves and Hickman, 2002, p. 1). In addition, the percentage of departments requiring a four-year degree for new officers rose from 1.6% in 1990 to 4.8% in 2000. Furthermore, the percentage of departments requiring a two-year degree for employment increased from 4.8% in 1990 to 9.7% in 2000. The percent of nondegree college requirements increased from 12.9% in 1990 to 22.6%. "Overall, about twice as many departments had some type of college education requirement for new officers in 2000 (37.1%) as did in 1990 (19.3%)" (Reeves and Hickman, 2002, p. 3).

The Present Study

In an effort to determine how far the professionalization movement has progressed, an assessment was attempted to link minimum educational requirements and promotional requirements with higher education. Additional variables, such as the department's accreditation status and tuition and salary incentives, were also examined. Ultimately, the goal is to understand the effects educational policies have on law enforcement agencies' ability to recruit and retain higher-educated officers.

The following factors influence recruitment and retention rates, as well as police turnover and help predict the length of time an officer stays with the agency:

- Agency educational requirements for hiring
- Agency educational level requirements for promotion to the rank of sergeant, lieutenant, and captain
- Starting base salary
- Educational incentives (extra salary/bonuses)
- College education assistance plan (tuition reimbursement/free college)
- Agency accreditation status
- Department size (number of sworn officers in the department)

Data Collection Instrument

In June 2004, a survey was conducted of the 200 largest police departments nationwide. The list of departments was retrieved from the Web site, www. policepay.net. The Web site gathers information from departments nationwide, compares the total compensation, and ranks agencies using a scientific method (for additional information, see Appendix #1). Departments are ranked using two charts—chart one ranked the departments using the adjusted cost of living and the second chart is not adjusted for the cost of living. For this study, the 200 departments were chosen from the cost of living list. (The department's salary information was retrieved from http://www.theblueline.com/salary1.html. The Web site was updated in May 2004. The CALEA accreditation listed was gathered from http://www.calea.org/agcysearch/searchagcy2.cfm).

The following information from the 200 largest departments was gathered:

- Educational requirements for entry level positions and promotion
- Whether or not the departments offered salary and tuition incentives
- Whether these agencies were experiencing recruitment and retention issues

Visiting the departments' Web sites was the first method for gathering this information. This method was limited due to the fact that many departments did not list all information and some departments did not have Web sites. The remaining departments were then contacted via telephone or e-mail. This analysis is based on responses from 195 police agencies that responded. The following research questions will be examined:

1. What are the minimum educational requirements to be hired?
2. What, if any, are the educational requirements for promotion to the ranks of sergeant, lieutenant, and captain?
3. Does the department offer tuition reimbursement or provide tuition assistance?
4. Does the department offer salary incentives for higher education?
5. Is the department experiencing recruitment problems?
6. Is the department experiencing retention problems?

In addition to these specific questions, we interviewed recruiters and/or department human resources personnel. The information gathered from these interviews included why the department was/was not experiencing personnel issues and what actions the departments could take or had taken to resolve these issues. The survey results are based on the departments' *written* hiring and promotional requirement policies.

Data Gathered and Analysis

Base salary for new sworn officer: Offering a competitive salary is an important variable not only in retention, but in recruitment as well. (The department's

salary information was retrieved from http://www.theblueline.com/salary1.
html, when information on the department Web sites was unavailable.)

Minimum educational requirements for hire: Many agencies only require
applicants to possess a high school diploma (HSD) or general education
development (GED). Some less than 60 h, associates degree or 60 h, bache-
lors degree or 120 h. A few departments do not require college education for
hire, but a certain amount of college education is required before a specified
amount of time in service has passed.

Educational requirements for promotion: Some agencies are raising the
educational requirements for promotion to a ranking officer, from sergeant
to chief of police. Only the requirements for the sergeant, lieutenant, and
captain positions were tracked. An additional coding category was added to
account for departments requiring some college education plus time on the
job or time in a certain position.

Educational salary incentives: Departments are offering officers educational salary incentives that include yearly bonuses and/or additional
monthly bonuses.

Tuition assistance plan: Departments are offering officers tuition reimbursement or reduced tuition rates at participating institutions of higher
learning. The police departments' recruiters and/or personnel staff were also
asked if the departments were experiencing recruitment and/or retention
problems.

Recruitment issues: Departments were asked if they were having problems recruiting officers.

Retention issues: Departments were also asked if they were having problems retaining new officers (less than 5 years with the department) and if any
of those officers were leaving their departments to defect to other agencies
with better pay and/or better benefits.

The findings revealed that 100% of the 195 departments surveyed required
a new officer to possess a minimum of an HSD or GED for employment.

Table 7.1 presents department educational hiring requirements. In all,
195 departments were available for the hiring requirement analysis; 69.2% of
the departments require only an HSD or a GED.

Table 7.2 presents the hiring requirements and the departments' accreditation status. Of the 59 accredited departments, 43 require only an HSD or
GED for hire.

The analysis of the above data suggests that an agency's accreditation
status does not play a role in educational polices. CALEA encourages departments to require higher education for employment. These findings propose
that accredited agencies are not following through with CALEA recommendations. This could be for several reasons. First, the process of accreditation is extremely time consuming and expensive. Nonaccredited agencies
may encourage higher education by following through with educational

Table 7.1   Hiring Requirements

	Frequency	Valid Percent
High school diploma or GED	135	69.2
GED + college hours	5	2.6
Less than 60 college hours	11	5.6
AA or 60 h	16	8.2
BA or 120 h	6	3.1
HSD/GED ± SC and/or military or lateral	18	9.2
None—some college required after hired	4	2.1
Total	195	100.0
System	5	
Total	200	

Table 7.2   Number of Accredited versus Nonaccredited Departments CALEA Accreditation

	Accredited	Nonaccredited	Total
High school diploma or GED	43	92	135
GED + some college (SC)	1	4	5
Less than 60 college hours	2	9	11
AA or 60 h	5	11	16
BA or 120 h	3	3	6
HSD/GED ± SC and/or military or lateral	4	14	18
None—some college required after hired	1	3	4
Total	200	136	195

incentives and minimum hiring requirements, but cannot afford to become accredited. Second, some agencies have suggested that officers possessing higher education become "bored" with the job, leading to frustration and eventually resignation. Third, a department's higher education employment policy may cause a shrinking candidate pool. This negative effect is the most common explanation for lowering education requirements for employment.

Table 7.3 presents the education requirements for hire and the department's educational salary incentive. In all, data from 184 departments was analyzed. It is a welcoming sign to note that 66.8% of departments offer a salary incentive for college-educated officers. In the case of departments requiring a bachelor degree or 120 h for hire, three of the agencies do not provide additional salary. It is promising to see 65.1% of departments only requiring an HSD or GED and 100% of departments requiring a GED plus SC are promoting higher education and backing up their commitment to the officers by offering this incentive.

Table 7.3   Education Requirements for Hire and Educational Salary Incentives

Education Salary Incentive	Yes	No	Total
High school diploma or GED	82	44	126
GED+SC	5	0	5
Less than 60 college hours	7	3	10
AA or 60h	8	7	15
BA or 120h	3	3	6
HSD/GED±SC and/or military or lateral	15	3	18
None—some college required after hired	3	1	4
Total	123	61	184

Table 7.4   Education Requirements for Hire and College Tuition Assistance Plan Incentive

Tuition Assistance	Yes	No	Total
High school diploma or GED	104	23	127
GED+SC	3	2	5
Less than 60 college hours	8	2	10
AA or 60h	13	3	16
BA or 120h	6	0	6
HSD/GED±SC and/or military or lateral	11	7	18
None—some college required after hired	4	0	4
Total	149	37	186

Table 7.4 represents the educational requirements for hire and their college assistance plan. In all, data was collected from 186 departments. Eighty-one percent of the departments requiring only an HSD or GED offered a college assistance plan. This indicates that these departments are assisting and encouraging their officers to pursue a college education. Furthermore, as expected, 100% of the departments requiring college education after hire also offer the college education plan.

As an officer rises through the ranks, educational requirements are raised. Table 7.5 illustrates how departments' higher education expectations as a prerequisite for promotion change by increased rank. While some departments do not have a written policy in place, many department recruiters stated that their departments believed in the value of higher education and gave officers extra points on promotional exams or extra consideration over those without higher education.

Table 7.5 represents the educational requirements for hire and the educational requirements for promotion in rank. Data from 158 departments were gathered. Seventy-seven out of 107 departments that require only an

Table 7.5   Educational Promotional Requirements by Rank

Requirements	Sergeant	Lieutenant	Captain	Total
High school diploma or GED	77	62	55	194
GED + college hours	4	4	3	44
Less than 60 college hours	6	6	5	17
More than 60 college hours	0	0	0	0
AA or 60h	4	3	3	10
BA or 120h	2	2	1	5
MA	0	0	8	8
HSD/GED ± SC and/or military or lateral	7	7	7	21
None—some college required after hired	1	1	0	2
Total	101	85	82	268

HSD or GED for hire do not require any college education for promotion to sergeant. Only 11 departments require a BA or 120 college hours. Furthermore, a total of 30 out of the 107 departments require some college education or a degree.

For promotion to the rank of lieutenant, data from 150 departments were analyzed. Sixty-two departments require no college education for promotion to lieutenant. However, 35 departments require a four-year degree or 120h for promotion to lieutenant; this is up from 11 for the rank of Sergeant.

For promotion to captain, eight departments require a Master's Degree and 53 require a BA or 120h. Of the 105 departments that require no college education for hire, 50 of those require some college education for captain's positions. This is an indication that departments expect officers to return to school after they have been hired.

Of the 185 departments surveyed, 66% offered educational pay incentives and 75% offered tuition assistance plans. This indicates that departments are backing up their demands for officers to possess higher education. Only 18% of the departments did not offer the tuition assistance plan. One reason for this may be that these departments require college education in order to be hired. Table 7.6 regresses salary and education incentives on retention.

Table 7.6 represents the correlation between departments offering educational incentive pay along with higher salary and its relationship with retention issues. As seen in Table 7.6, the negative correlation between education incentive pay and the lack of retention issues is significant. Starting salary is of course highly correlated with retention. This model explains variation in retention problems. Departments with high starting salaries and education incentive pay have fewer retention issues. Moreover, these findings suggest educational salary incentives may be more effective in retaining officers than tuition assistance plans.

Table 7.6   Salary and Education Incentives and Retention

Model		Unstandardized Coefficients		Standardized Coefficients		
		B	Std. Error	Beta	t	Sig.
1	(Constant)	1.303	0.255		5.110	0.000
	education_	−0.182	0.086	−0.212	−2.112	0.038
	salary	1.947E−05	0.000	0.341	3.399	0.001

[a] Dependent variable: retention.

Discussion

Having more college-educated officers on the force will require greater monetary commitment to cover the education salary incentives and tuition costs. Several department recruiters advised that their departments did offer tuition reimbursement, but have discontinued the program due to budget constraints. Only a few departments discontinued the policy requiring college credits to be hired. These departments suggested that the policy contributed to the shrinking recruitment pool. One agency discontinued the minimum college education requirements for employees, but noted that most of the community and applicants were veterans or members of the military. This agency believed military experience could be substituted for the higher education requirement.

In this study, 53% of departments offer both salary and tuition incentives. It is clear that these two incentives compliment one another and there are benefits for departments using this combination to improve recruitment and reduce attrition. Recruits who are hired by departments offering salary incentives for college education are able to reap the benefits of being recognized for their efforts and can use the extra money to pay off student loans. Furthermore, those officers seeking a higher education can see their efforts rewarded in benefits they receive such as acquiring a free college education or reduced tuition and salary incentives. Moreover, when departments discontinue their tuition incentives, the agencies lose out. They lose the "hiring incentives," such as the officers' ability to improve themselves and the department.

Departments that do not offer salary incentives are losing out as well. Many officers who are college educated leave in order to transfer to better-paying departments or to the federal government. Studies show that officers who are neither rewarded for their hard work nor recognized for their efforts often become frustrated and leave for other jobs.

This finding is supported by a 2002 Florida Study conducted by the Florida Police Chiefs Association (FPCA), which focused on recruitment and retention issues. The study identified six factors contributing to high attrition rates: "economy, changing demographics of the workforce, 'Gen-Xers,' upgraded educational requirements, uncompetitive salaries and benefits, and negative public perceptions" (FPCA, 2002, p. 3). Moreover, recruiting and training a new officer is expensive and time consuming. New Orleans Police Department (NOPD) (2004) estimates it costs an average of $44,665 to recruit and train a new officer.

Vest (2001) lists negative consequences of attrition such as increased overtime pay, which drains the agency's budget, but stresses that the most problematic consequence is that of young, inexperienced officers leaving the department.

It is also very difficult to replace veteran officers. Whatever their reasons for leaving, whether they are taking advantage of early retirement or leaving for other agencies, their knowledge and experience cannot be replaced. As a result, agencies are left with very few veteran officers to train the new recruits.

There are also problems with offering a tuition reimbursement. This type of education policy can hurt an agency by unintentionally encouraging some of their brighter officers to defect. In a number of agencies, "defectors" take advantage of the educational tuition incentives and after they have a degree in hand, they leave departments for higher salaries. Therefore, offering competitive salaries linked with educational incentives is not only important in retention, but in recruitment as well. The present trend indicates that officers are willing to relocate and defect to better-paying agencies. NOPD (2004) study revealed "75% of officers responded that pay and benefits would be a very likely reason they would consider leaving the NOPD" (p. 32). Many respondents felt that this undermined the integrity of the promotional process and affected negatively officer and departmental morale. It was felt that when promotional standards and procedures change to accommodate the less educated and less qualified, officers do not see the department as playing by the rules. Therefore, it is extremely important for departments to have set promotional standard and procedure, and not regress.

Conclusion

August Vollmer recognized the value of education in law enforcement more than 100 years ago and the same values still exist. If the law enforcement field wants to be treated and regarded as a true profession, then personnel must be paid as professionals. Departments are faced with the problem of sacrificing quality officers for quantity, and as a result, some have lowered their standards. Departments need to set clear goals for promotions and clarify all educational policies. Previous studies indicate educational requirements have increased for promotion and employment. The above findings suggest that departments without retention issues have higher salaries and educational salary incentives. Every time an officer leaves or defects, the agency loses money and invaluable police experience. In the end, departments will pay one way or another. Agencies need to do everything possible to become and stay competitive.

References

Baker, S. A. (1995). *Effects of Law Enforcement Accreditation: Officer Selection, Promotion, and Education.* Westport, CT: Praeger Publishers.

Bell, D. J. (1979). The police role and higher education. *Journal of Police Science and Administration, 7,* 467–475.

Carter, D. L and Sapp, A. D. (1992, January). College education and policing: Coming of age. *FBI Law Enforcement Bulletin, 61*(1), 8.

Carter, D. L. and Sapp, A. D. (1988). Higher education as a bona fide occupational qualification (BFOQ) for police: A blueprint. *American Journal of Police, 7*(2), 1–27.

Davis, P. L. (1983). Toward a philosophy of law enforcement education. *Police Chief, 50,* 48–49.

Hawley, T. J. (1998). The collegiate shield: Was the movement purely academic? *Police Quarterly, 1*(3), 35–59.

Flick, B. C. (1994, January). College-educated officers: A proven benefit. *Law & Order, 42*(1), 324.

Florida Chiefs of Police Study (FPCA). (2002). The Florida Police Chiefs Association recommendation presentation. Recruiting and retention recommendations committee. Tallahassee, FL.

Koper, C. (2004, July). *Hiring and Keeping Police Officers,* Washington, DC: U.S. Department of Justice, National Institute of Justice, NCJ 202289.

New Orleans Police Department (NOPD). (2004, January). Understanding the recruitment and retention need and challenges of the New Orleans police department. Recruitment and retention study. University of New Orleans, New Orleans, LA.

Police Association for College Education (PACE). Retrieved from the World Wide Web on July 10, 2004. http://www.police-association.org/pace1/main.aspx?dbID=DB_Mission320

Reeves, B. (2004). *Law Enforcement and Management and Administrative Statistics, 2000: Data for Individual State and Local Agencies with 100 or More Officers.* Washington DC: U.S. Department of Justice, Bureau of Justice Statistics, April 2004, NCJ 203350.

Reeves, B. and Hickman, M. (2002, May). *Police Departments in Large Cities, 1990–2000.* Washington DC: U.S. Department of Justice, Bureau of Justice Statistics, NCJ 175703.

Rodriguez, M. (1995). Increasing the importance of higher education in police human resource development programs. *CJ: The Americas, 8*(2), 6–9.

Truxillo, D. M., Bennett, S. R., and Collins, M. L. (1998). College education and police job performance: A ten-year study. *Public Personnel Management, 27*(2), 269–280.

Whetstone, T. S. (2000). Getting stripes: Educational achievement and study strategies used by sergeant. *American Journal of Criminal Justice: AJCJ 24*(2), 247–257.

Vest, G. (2001, November). Closing the recruitment gap. *FBI Law Enforcement Bulletin, 70*(11), 13–18.

Building Bridges to Reduce Adolescent Crime and Disorder in American Schools: Integrating Restorative Justice with the School Resource Officer Model

CHERYL SWANSON AND MICHELLE OWEN

Contents

Introduction

School safety could be possibly enhanced by integrating restorative justice principles and practices into the school resource officer (SRO) model. In its solicitation for a national assessment of SRO programs in the United States, the National Institute of Justice (NIJ) recognized the training of students in conflict resolution and restorative justice as one of numerous versions of SRO programs (NIJ, 1999). However, when the assessment was complete, restorative justice was not identified as a major component of any of the established or relatively new SRO programs surveyed in its national sample (Finn and McDevitt, 2005). Furthermore, the National Association of School Resource Officers (NASRO), which offers training to its 15,000 members, does not highlight restorative justice among its workshop offerings (NASRO, 2005b). Nor are its university/educational partners affiliated with restorative justice education. This suggests that restorative justice is largely a footnote within the SRO community. Given its mission, could the SRO community benefit through the more explicit development of a restorative justice focus? To address this question, it is necessary to (1) evaluate the restorative approach to school safety, (2) review and analyze the mission statement of the NASRO and other related literature on SRO programs, (3) examine literature on the use of restorative models in schools, (4) peruse literature where police have worked closely with schools in promoting restorative justice, and (5) finally make recommendations concerning the advantages and disadvantages of integrating restorative principles and practices more systematically within SRO programs.

A Note on the Restorative Philosophy

Restorative justice can be described as an alternative to the retributive model of justice that prevails in our current system (Zehr, 1995). While restorative justice principles and practices have been introduced primarily into criminal justice and juvenile justice practice, over the last several years there has been an increased interest in public school applications.

Restorative justice can be defined as a response to conflict, misbehavior, and crime that makes things as right as possible for all those impacted by the incident (Claassen, 2002, p. 19). Rather than being rule based and punishment driven, the restorative justice model focuses on taking responsibility for repairing the harm done by the offending action. It is an inclusive problem-solving approach that is victim centered, requires offender accountability, and encourages community responsibility for victim and offender reintegration. In *The Little Book of Restorative Justice*, Zehr (2002) provides one of the most parsimonious descriptions of the concepts on which restorative justice is based, noting that "…[it] requires at a minimum, that we address victim harms and needs, hold offenders accountable to put right those harms, and involve victims, offenders, and communities in the process" (2002, p. 25). The restorative model contrasts with retributive justice which prevails in most justice systems throughout the world. Retributive justice views crime as lawbreaking, involves establishing guilt when the law is broken, and assigns punishment to those who have been found guilty by rule of law (Zehr, 2002, p. 81). In addition to just deserts, other goals of punishment-based justice systems include deterrence and incapacitation.

The central goal for implementing restorative practices in the schools is the same as the goal underlying punishment-based models—to produce safe schools. Punishment-based models in schools include but are not limited to zero tolerance policies, suspensions, expulsions, mandatory study hall, and other disciplinary practices. The restorative model focuses on developing a sense of "connectedness" and community responsibility within a school to promote safety. Thorsborne (2000, p. 4) notes that "restorative justice in the school setting views misconduct, not as school rule breaking, and therefore a violation of the institution, but as a violation against people and relationships in the school and wider school community." The typical law enforcement approach in a school context focuses on respect for the law, violations of the law, consequences for breaking the law, and punishing those who have violated the law. In contrast, the restorative approach focuses on behavior that causes crime, the harmful consequences of that behavior for victim(s) and community, a process for healing the harm done, and a plan for improving the future (Amstutz and Mullet, 2005).

The restorative model is attractive to those concerned with school safety because of its relational component. A national longitudinal study of adolescent health in 127 schools found that school environments that promote a sense of community have lower levels of deviant behavior and violence (McNeely et al., 2002). Theoretically, restorative justice strengthens community by holding those who cause harm accountable and engaging the community in processes of accountability, support, and healing (Wachtel and McCold, 2001). In the school setting, restorative justice relies extensively on informal social control, while retributive justice is based on hierarchical authority models (Braithwaite, 1989).

One problem area where a restorative solution has attracted attention is school bullying. Through encounter, respectful dialogue, and support, restorative practices have the potential to help transform the denial, shame, and anger experienced in the victim/bully relationship to accountability, healing, and a sense of belonging (Morrison, 2005, p. 34). More traditional rule-based punitive processes are associated with further alienation that can contribute to deviant behavior (Braithwaite, 1989). As Riese (2003, p. 4) notes, responding to the victim is central, but "everyone, including the bully, belongs to the community and needs our support."

In the school context, best practice suggests that restorative justice involves a continuum of responses. At the primary level, all students are trained to develop social and emotional competencies that support respect, peaceful conflict resolution, and mutual support (Morrison, 2005, p. 37). This level equates with preventive action.

The secondary and tertiary levels target individuals or groups in a more reactive mode and draw other members of the school and larger community. Peer mediation and problem-solving methods might be utilized at the secondary level, while the tertiary level might require even more participation including members of the school community, family members, and other professionals (Morrison, 2005, p. 37). Hopkins (2004) has identified a wider range of responses based on restorative justice. Her whole-school approach includes restorative inquiry, restorative discussion, mediation, victim/ offender mediation, community conferences, problem-solving circles, restorative conferences, and family group conferences as a range of responses (see also, McCold and Wachtel, 1997).

This brief introduction to restorative justice and its application in schools provides a backdrop against which to examine restorative applications to the SRO model.

The School Resource Officer Model

Should the integration of the restorative philosophy with the SRO model be more strongly encouraged to promote safer schools? This can be answered by examining literature on SRO programs, along with the mission statement of the NASRO. Of particular interest is the extent to which the philosophies and working practices of the restorative and SRO models offer challenges and opportunities.

Involvement of the police in schools is not a new phenomenon, but the role has changed over time. Until the 1950s, police officers were primarily involved with picking up truants, teaching bicycle and traffic safety, and manning crosswalks during the opening and closing of schools. The role of police in schools changed substantially in most Western countries from the 1960s to the 1990s due to changes in attitudes toward aggression and violence in schools, dramatic incidents of violence in schools involving weapons and mass shootings, drug use, gang involvement, technological challenges brought about by issues of sexual exploitation and pornography on the Internet, and the recognized connection between truancy and crime (Shaw, 1999).

The institutionalization of police–school linkages is primarily found in Western democracies. Shaw notes that in developing nations such as Africa and Latin America, corruption, violence, and low levels of police professionalism make comparisons with European countries, the United States, Canada, Australia, and New Zealand difficult (2004, p. 6). One exception is South Africa where communities, police, and schools have formed alliances to reduce school violence (Shaw, 1999, p. 24). With this in mind, the focus of this writing is on western democracies in general, and specifically the SRO model developed in the United States.

Shaw (1999) identifies three models of police involvement in schools: school-based police officers, police officers as teachers, and comprehensive police–school liaison programs. While elements of each model may coexist, the model of officers as teachers, for example, implies that teaching is the *only* involvement of officers in the schools. An example is programs where the only role of law enforcement is the teaching of Drug Abuse Resistance Education (DARE program) in school settings.

This study focuses on school-based resource officers, with a particular focus on the SRO model developed in the United States. The comprehensive police–school liaison model which includes linkages with a variety of social service agencies involved with at-risk students may be more effective in implementing restorative-based programs. However, at the present time, the best-known and longest-surviving model is the SRO model, which was established in the 1950s and adopted with variations by countries such as Canada, Australia, and Great Britain (Shaw, 1999, p. 9). In England, police officers dedicated to schools are referred to as school liaison officers. Their role has paralleled that of the SRO model in the United States with an emphasis on law enforcement, counseling, and teaching. A new school officer program, the Safer School Partnership (SSP) program, which began in 2002, targets high-risk areas and schools and places greater emphasis on a prevention and welfare approach to offending. School-based policing in the Netherlands and Queensland, Australia, is relatively new and similar to the SRO model but without teaching responsibilities (Shaw, 1999).

The NASRO, based in the United States, has over 15,000 members. The SRO model is recognized in Part Q of Title I of the Omnibus Crime Control and Safe Streets Act, and since 1999 the Office of Community Oriented Policing Services (COPS) has funded more than 1500 SROs in more than 700 jurisdictions in the United States (NIJ, 1999, pp. 1–2). While COPS has encouraged collaborative community-based practices for SROs that more closely resemble the comprehensive police–school liaison model, the program recognizes that SRO programs take on many forms from the collaborative comprehensive to more traditional policing models (NIJ, 1999, p. 1).

The term *school resource officer* is attributed to a Miami, Florida, police chief who coined the phrase in the early 1960s (Cawthon, 2002). SRO programs expanded significantly in the 1990s, with an increase in support for the concept of community policing. In 1999, President Clinton was successful in getting legislation passed through Congress that amended the Omnibus Crime Control and Safe Streets Act to provide funding to encourage law enforcement–school district partnerships. President Clinton's initiative focused on hiring new police officers to work with the school community in a variety of ways including counseling and the mediation of conflicts (Cawthon, 2002).

NASRO's mission statement identifies the SRO program as "...a collaborative effort by certified law enforcement officers, educators, students, parents, and the community to offer law related educational programs in the schools in an effort to reduce crime, drug abuse, violence, and provide a safe school environment" (NASRO, 2005a). Building trust and rapport between police and the school community is emphasized as the primary way to achieve the overall goal of school safety (Finn and McDevitt, 2005, p. 17; Mulqueen, 1999).

NASRO-sponsored training is wide ranging, including workshops in interviewing and interrogating, alcohol-drug curriculums, civil liability, gangs, crisis management, after-school programs, bullying, youth suicide, and terrorism safeguards (NASRO, 2005b). While SRO programs have a preventive community policing orientation, some programs emphasize on law enforcement functions.

NASRO has adopted what is referred to as a triad model to school policing, which includes the role of (1) the law enforcement officer, (2) the counselor, and (3) the classroom instructor. While teaching content may vary, a major theme of SRO programs is the development of more responsible attitudes toward breaking the law (Shaw, 1999, p. 9). A 2001 NASRO survey showed that the work of the majority of respondents fit the model (Trump, 2001). A subsequent survey showed that respondents identified the role they spent the most time on while working as an SRO was 41% law enforcement officer, 46% counselor/mentor, and 13% instructor/teacher (Trump, 2002). Ninety-one percent of the SROs reported that at least half of their job consisted of preventative duties and only 7% said that their emphasis was on enforcement and investigation duties. The most recent national survey of SRO programs found a slightly larger proportion of weekly hours (20) spent on law enforcement in comparison to other activities including advising and mentoring (10 h), teaching (5 h), and other activities (6–7 h) (Finn and McDevitt, 2005, p. 4). It was noted that different SRO programs vary a great deal in terms of the percentage of time devoted to the three major activities designated in the SRO model. In one large site, administrators indicated that they were as much interested in mentoring and teaching roles as they were in providing security (Finn and McDevitt, 2005, p. 22). In another large site, the amount of time spent on various activities shifted according to what was going on in the school so that in the beginning of the SRO program a fairly large percentage of time was spent on law enforcement but 5 years later 10% of the time was spent on this role.

NASRO surveys show that members identify with the importance of building trust between SROs and stakeholders in the schools, particularly students. Furthermore, students' perceptions of SROs do increase positively as their contacts with SROs increase (Finn and McDevitt, 2005, p. 42; Jackson, 2002). The most recent national assessment of SRO programs found that a larger percentage of students who have a positive view of the SRO report are feeling safe in school and are more comfortable reporting crime. The authors of the report concluded, "…perhaps the most important and easily modifiable variable… is creating a positive opinion of the SRO among the student body. The results suggest that it is important to determine the best method for SROs to create a positive image" (Finn and McDevitt, 2005, p. 42). Interestingly, students who have experienced some type of victimization, either in school or out of school, are less likely to feel safe in the school locations (Finn and McDevitt, 2005, p. 41).

Survey findings also suggest that key stakeholders often *do not understand the role* of the SRO in the school community (Cawthon, 2002). In one study, school principles and SROs saw their roles differently, with principles emphasizing safety primarily through SRO presence, and SROs viewing their roles much more broadly than security focused deterrence (Lambert and McGinty, 2002). Cawthon's (2002) research in a Florida school district found a recurrence of themes pointing to the importance of effective communication between SROs and their constituents with respect to role and function. The national assessment of SROs discovered that a major lesson learned was the importance of defining specific roles and responsibilities. The report noted that when this is not done, "problems are often rampant" and lead to role confusion and conflict with school administrators about SRO responsibilities (Finn and McDevitt, 2005, p. 43).

Of particular importance was the need to more specifically define "what it means for SROs to engage in law enforcement" (Finn and McDevitt, 2005, p. 44). In collaborating with school administrators and teachers, the national assessment found "a fundamental difference in the law enforcement culture and the school culture in terms of goals, strategies, and methods" (Finn and McDevitt, 2005, p. 45). Of particular concern were conflicts over "who is in charge" and who should decide whether the student should be arrested or referred to an alternative process.

The national assessment also noted role conflict resulting from the SRO model in terms of maintaining authority as law enforcers while at the same time improving relationships with students (Finn and McDevitt, 2005, p. 46). The power imbalance that exists between police and young people in street encounters or in school detracts from the trust-building process identified as being a key component of SRO effectiveness (Jackson, 2002). Teaching and, particularly, counseling help familiarize officers with students, but some officers feel that while they have built positive relationships in the counselor role, they are exposed to the criticism and even civil liability, with respect to practicing psychology without a license (Finn and McDevitt, 2005, p. 46).

Very few evaluation studies of SRO programs have been conducted with sufficient design and statistical rigor to draw conclusions on their effectiveness in terms of outcome measures. In one southern district, Johnson (1999) found serious offenses in high schools and middle schools decreased substantially within 1 year after the SRO program was implemented. However, most studies focus on perceptions of teachers, administrators, and students, rather than objective measures of change. For example, Chen et al. (1999)

surveyed members of the school community in a suburban Kansas school district. Respondents believed their SRO program created a safe learning environment, but that it did not change students' behavior. Interestingly, teachers, administrators, and SROs showed a significantly stronger belief in the effectiveness of the SRO program than did the students. The need for more diversified topics related to youth problems in SRO training was noted in another evaluation (Cawthon, 2002). It their national assessment of SROs, Finn and McDevitt note that "the vast majority of responding schools expressed considerable satisfaction with their programs" (2005, p. 4). Still, "most programs fail to collect important process and outcome evaluation data," and compared to smaller schools, those surveyed in large schools were much less likely to attribute changes in fear of crime and trust in police to SRO programs (Finn and McDevitt, 2005, p. 4, 17).

There is also a perception that numerous kinds of activities contribute to safe schools. For example, in one large school district, it was concluded that SROs prevent crime through their presence, tips from students about impending problems, and informally mediating disputes among students (Finn and McDevitt, 2005, p. 24). Clearly, the range of activities of the SRO has expanded over time, and the latest national survey found that many SROs are responsible for activities *for which they have very little training* (Finn and McDevitt, 2005, p. 4). Indeed, among 19 schools that the national survey evaluated in depth, few officers had any SRO training before they entered the job, and many learned by a "sink-or-swim" approach (Finn and McDevitt, 2005, p. 44).

Summary of SRO Programs

The SRO programs are well established in the United States and have been adopted in other countries. They enjoy a great deal of support among their constituents and have the flexibility to adapt to the varying needs of the communities they serve. The primary goal of SRO programs is to keep schools safe. A secondary goal emphasizes improving relationships between law enforcement and young people. While many programs focus on traditional law enforcement, SRO programs see themselves as part of a community policing approach which is more proactive and preventive. The teaching and counseling components of the tripartite model are more conducive to prevention, with teaching tending to focus on respect for the law and the consequences of violating the law.

While perceptions of the effectiveness of SRO programs is highly positive, there is very little evidence that SROs improve school safety or improve relationships between the police and juveniles. The SRO model by itself is not based on a well-developed model of prevention theory or research (Shaw, 1999, p. 10). While the tripartite model contributes to community responsiveness, it can also contribute to confusion and conflict particularly among administrators, teachers, and SROs with respect to what their role should actually be and how this role fits into the school culture and the overall objective of building safe schools. Reconciling the role of law enforcement with the need to build trust between police and young people also poses a challenge.

While the SRO model is very popular, particularly in the United States, its popularity is not matched with the evaluation data on process or outcome measures. Furthermore, while the program has a framework (law enforcement, teaching, and counseling), it does not enjoy a well-articulated theoretical framework that links its practices to safer schools.

Restorative Models in the School Setting: The Theoretical Perspective

Those who have linked restorative justice with school safety underscore the importance of grounding restorative practice in theory that supports safe communities. Morrison (2005, p. 29) notes that two theories, procedural justice and reintegrative shaming, are relevant to the analysis of restorative justice in schools.

Based on the concept of procedural justice, Tyler (1990) explains why people comply with the law. While deterrence theory works in some situations, punishment and fear of punishment are less effective in bringing about compliance than "relational criteria" that give people feedback about the quality of their relationships with authorities and organizations. These criteria include evaluations of whether or not the individual is treated with respect, perceptions of the trustworthiness of authorities, perceptions of the neutrality of the decision-making process, and opportunities for the individual to participate in the outcome. Empirical research supports the relationship between perceptions of fairness and compliance in keeping mediation agreements and relationships with the police among others (Tyler, 1990).

Braithwaite's (1989) theory of reintegrative shaming also provides theoretical support for the restorative justice approach. Braithwaite argues that when one's misbehavior is held to account by people that matter, the offender is more likely to "take on" responsibility for his or her actions and to experience true remorse (and shame). Taken together with the community's responsibility for holding the offender to account, healing the harm done, distinguishing the act from the actor, and welcoming the accountable offender back into the community, this process provides an alternative model to formal regulation (Braithwaite, 2002). Braithwaite's theory is grounded in both criminology theories and empirical findings (Braithwaite, 1989). A national longitudinal study of adolescent health in 127 schools found that school environments that promote a sense of community are less violent and provide support for approaches that have strong relational and community-oriented components (McNeely et al., 2002).

Wachtel and McCold's (2001) social discipline window (Figure 8.1) illustrates reintegrative shaming in a more concrete fashion. The restorative approach in this context is high on control *and* support. The punitive model, widespread in Western culture, is high on control but low on support contributing to problems associated with labeling, alienation, and future misbehavior (Braithwaite, 1989). The advantage of the restorative process is that it separates the act—which is the target of social disapproval—from the individual who committed the offending behavior. Thus, the boundary is still in place in terms of recognizing the injustice of an act and holding the individual accountable for the act (Marshall et al., 2002). An example of restorative language in a case of vandalism would be, "that was a thoughtless act that costs time and money to repair, and makes students feel less comfortable and safe, I am surprised you would engage in such an act" (Wilson and Braithwaite, 1977).

The therapeutic functions of talking and storytelling explained by Nathanson (1992) through affect theory and Pranis (2005) through circle processes help understand the potential of restorative justice. Expressing negative emotions in structured restorative processes provides an opportunity for transforming these emotions to positive ones, reducing alienation, and promoting healing (McDonald and Moore, 2001, p. 130). Pranis (2005, pp. 9, 71–73) notes the positive function of circles for community building, particularly in schools, as well as the ability of the circle to safely address and process negative emotions.

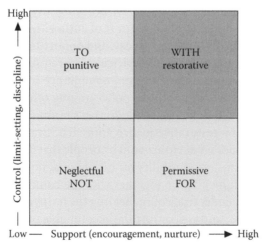

Figure 8.1 Social discipline window. (From Wachtel, T. and McCold, P., *Restorative justice in everyday life*, in Strang, H. and Braithwaite, J. (Eds.) *Restorative Justice and Civil Society*, Cambridge University Press, Cambridge, U.K., 2001, pp. 114–129.)

Finally, restorative approaches fit well with international trends to promote school safety. A report of the International Centre from the Prevention of Crime identifies the following directions:

- Framing the issues less as school violence and more as school safety.
- Linking school safety to the needs of victims and victimizers and to healthy behaviors.
- A change in emphasis from a reactive and punitive focus on perpetrators of school violence to proactive approaches.
- A shift from physical situation prevention of school inclusion to comprehensive approaches using a range of policies and programs.
- These include not only programs geared to individual problem students, but to the school population as a whole to ensure that teacher needs, family and community links are viewed as incorporated parts of their personal communities.
- The involvement of young people themselves in the assessment of problems and project design (Shaw, 1999, p. 19).

Restorative Justice in the School Setting: In Practice

The introduction of restorative justice in schools has occurred in a number of Western nations. There is some concern over the appropriateness of the word "justice" in school settings. As a result, some practitioners prefer the term "restorative discipline" (Amstutz and Mullet, 2005; Claassen, 1993). One of the conditions that exist in school settings is the lack of a clearly identifiable victim. Instead, more common is the existence of two or more parties in conflict who have perpetuated harm on one another over time (Edgar et al., 2002; McDonald and Moore, 2001, p. 139). Furthermore, some of the incidences that restorative justice addresses in schools, such as bullying, do not fit the definition of a crime. Thus, restorative philosophy addresses these kinds of events. The philosophy in this context remains the same, however, with its intent to address, heal, and prevent further harm.

Some restorative justice initiatives do not include law enforcement agencies. Others directly involve the police, although when police are involved, their participation more closely fits the comprehensive school liaison program model. Evaluations of restorative justice programs in schools are similar to those that have been conducted on SRO programs in that they often rely on perceptions of safety rather than being tied to objective measures of safety and security. Given the theoretical bases of restorative justice, measures of perceptions that are grounded in how the restorative process is designed to work—for example, the linkages between perceptions of fairness, community support, and pro social behavior—are relevant from an evaluation standpoint.

The National Restorative Justice in Schools Program in England has recently been evaluated to determine the impact of restorative justice conferences and other restorative approaches in 20 secondary and 6 primary schools. What distinguishes conferences from mediations is that other parties are invited to attend. Their role is to give voice to the aggrieved, make sure that the full consequences of the event are made clear to the perpetrator, and provide support to both parties. About 92% of conferences resulted in successful agreements among parties, only 4% of agreements were broken, 89% of pupils who participated in conferences were satisfied with the outcome, and 93% reported that the process was fair and that justice had been done (YJB, 2004, pp. 31–31). The National Restorative Justice in Schools Program includes law enforcement as partners, but only 8% of the conferences evaluated were conducted by police facilitators. One police officer/restorative justice facilitator who was interviewed noted, "Amazingly, kids tell the truth. The process allows them to be respected. People take their turns, they have their say... they feel listened to. The aren't talked down to... they can say what they feel" (YJB, 2004, p. 36).

Whole-school findings were less dramatic. Baseline and follow-up pupil surveys were conducted in program and nonprogram schools focusing on bullying, which was targeted by the program. Program school students showed greater increases in the perception that the schools were doing a better job in preventing bullying, but differences with nonprogram schools in terms of attitudes and level of victimization were not statistically significant (YJB, 2004, p. 37). While bullying actually increased in some program schools, it increased at a much lower rate than in nonprogram schools. Furthermore, there were statistically significant reductions in both bullying and verbal threats in the Lambeth schools where restorative justice had been more successfully implemented (YJB, 2004, p. 40). There was not a consistent pattern for the implementation of restorative justice and school expulsions, although the data on expulsions did suggest the merits of categorizing restorative programs into those that have been more fully implemented and those that have been poorly implemented (YJB, 2004, p. 46).

The use of restorative community conferences was first introduced into schools in Queensland, Australia, in 1994, and two evaluations were published in 1996 and 1998 involving 119 schools. The first study showed highly positive outcomes for satisfaction of participants, recidivism, compliance with agreements, perceptions of safety by victims, perceptions of closer relationships with conferencing participants, school administrator beliefs that conferencing reinforced school values, and perceptions of participating family members of the process and the school (Educational Queensland, 1998 as reported in Cameron and Thorsborne, 2001). However, the 1998 study showed that while conferencing was a very effective strategy, a significant number of cases were not being referred to conference, primarily because of perceptions about the "attitudes" of the offenders (Department of Education, 1998 as reported in Cameron and Thorsborne, 2001). Cameron and Thorsborne analyze these seemingly contradictory findings, noting that "...while schools generally become more positive towards a restorative approach, they still favor a traditional approach for students with a 'bad attitude'" (Cameron and Thorsborne, 2001, p. 183). Cameron and Thorsborne (2001, pp. 184–185) contrast the control paradigm embedded in school policy and culture as a major obstacle to change, and contrast Australian culture and practice with that in Japan where values, beliefs, and norms provide greater support for relational thinking.

Addressing the same issue on implementation in Australia, Morrison (2001) notes that while teachers agreed that bullying behavior could be effectively addressed through restorative practices, reported bullying as well as suspensions were increasing. After surveying teachers, Morrison (2001, pp. 206–207) concluded that while teachers supported restorative practices and found them to be compatible with their own views on education and behavioral change, they perceived parents as favoring more punitive approaches. Follow-up interviews with a sample of parents showed this not to be the case. Another evaluation involving juvenile offenders in nonschool settings found that, parents whose children participated in restorative conferences had higher levels of satisfaction and perception of fairness than the parents of children in a control group who used the juvenile court system (McCold and Wachtel, 1998, p. 72). The findings suggest that while the restorative philosophy is very compatible with educational theory and with teachers and parents themselves, the traditional control paradigm is strongly embedded in belief systems in Western nations.

The Safer Saner Schools program has introduced pilot programs in 30–40 schools mostly in Pennsylvania, New York, New Jersey, and Michigan, as well as Canada, Hungary, the Netherlands, the United Kingdom, the Netherlands, South Africa, and Australia. Selected schools in other states such as Indiana, Minnesota, Wisconsin, Florida, and Colorado have also introduced restorative practices.

Preliminary data from Palisades High School in southeastern Pennsylvania showed decreases in disciplinary referrals to the student office, administrative detentions, detentions assigned by teachers, incidents of disruptive behavior, and out-of-school suspensions (Mirsky, 2003, p. 2). The program was subsequently introduced in Palisades Middle School where decreases in disciplinary referrals as well as incidents in fighting were realized (Mirsky, 2003, p. 4). Springfield Township High School in the suburbs of Philadelphia also introduced the Safer Saner Schools Program and found substantial decreases in incidents of inappropriate behavior, disrespect to teachers, and classroom disruption (Mirsky, 2003, p. 6). However, while these initial data are encouraging, they do not provide for sufficient rigorous design and statistical treatment to conclude that there is a causal relationship between the program and school outcomes.

One of the most rigorous research designs to date on the implementation of restorative justice was completed for a treatment program for adjudicated delinquents in the CSF Buxmont schools in southeastern Pennsylvania. Although the program was not implemented in a traditional school setting, the findings are noteworthy because they involve school-aged youth, and the program was evaluated using a research design with statistical controls. Findings showed significant improvements in attitude and behavioral measures of the delinquents and a reduction in offending after completing the program (McCold, 2002). A subsequent study with a new cohort as well as an extended evaluation period for the original cohort showed that prolonged exposure to a restorative setting reduced the recidivism rates of misbehaving and at-risk youth (McCold, 2004).

Summary of Restorative Justice in Schools

The restorative justice model provides a comprehensive, holistic, and well-integrated model for managing conflict and reducing crime and misbehavior. The restorative approach is supported by empirically tested theories based on psychology, sociology, and criminology. Furthermore, the approach is compatible with behavioral theories in the education field.

As is the case with SRO programs, few school-based restorative programs have been tested using a rigorous evaluation design. Findings show a high degree of participant satisfaction with the restorative method and are based on those who have actually participated in restorative processes. Some research points to successes with respect to behavior change and repeat offending. As is the case with SRO model, restorative justice programs have faced implementation problems. While participants do not see apparent conflicts between the restorative model and school culture, at a deeper level, authority-based punishment-driven approaches are often viewed as the safe "fall-back" position.

Police Involvement in Restorative Justice in Nonschool and School Settings

Police involvement with restorative practices originated in a nonschool setting in the New South Wales city of Wagga Wagga in 1991 (Daly and Hayes, 2001). Police introduced restorative conferencing to the administrative procedure of cautioning juveniles. Replacing a stern warning or lecture from the police officer in charge, restorative cautioning and restorative conferences were held in the local police department, facilitated by an officer in the community policing unit, and designed to both shame and reintegrate (support) the offending juvenile with the assistance of family or community members.

While there are a number of police restorative-led conferencing programs used throughout the world, the Wagga Wagga model developed in New South Wales, Australia, has had the most influence (Young, 2001, p. 195). It is based on Braithwaite's theory of reintegrative shaming and uses a script to conform conferencing to best practice. Three programs embracing this model have been subject to evaluation—one in Bethlehem, Pennsylvania, another in Canberra, Australia, and a third involving the Thames Valley Police in three counties in England. All three programs found high levels of satisfaction and perception of fairness on the part of participants. The Canberra reintegrative shaming experiments found that young offenders who attended police-led conferences were less likely to state they would reoffend than those who went through traditional court proceedings. Interestingly, for young offenders, the average court case took 13 min, while the average conference took 71 min (Sherman and Strang, 1997).

A key concern has been whether there is a conflict between police culture, which could lead to dominance and control on the part of the police facilitator, and the restorative philosophy, which emphasizes empowering the parties to a conflict as well as giving victims and offenders an opportunity to express their views and reach mutually agreeable settlements (Young, 2001, p. 205). The possibility that police will take a punitive and less than impartial role with respect to the offender has also been voiced. Further concern has been expressed about issues of fairness should an incidence of police misbehavior come to light during a conference. Focusing on the general need for accountability in restorative justice, Roche (2003, p. 137) argues that conferences should not be led by police officers nor should they be convened in police stations less the appearance of independence be compromised. On the other hand, O'Connell (2000), who has conducted training for police officers in both school and nonschool settings, cites a number of advantages of using police officers as conference facilitators, including skills in managing difficult situations, ability to maintain a clear conference focus, and a sense of formality.

Young (2001) has been involved in a review of Thames Valley Police participation in restorative practices and has compared his findings with those in Canberra and Bethlehem. The Canberra study was not designed to focus on police behavior, although observations of conferences did not raise any red flags about the appropriateness of law enforcement performance in the role of facilitator (Sherman and Strang, 1997 as reported in Young, 2001, p. 202). In the Bethlehem study, there were observed incidences of police lecturing and domination, but these problems were reduced substantially after the officer facilitators received feedback about their behavior in light of the restorative philosophy (McCold and Wachtel, 1998, p. 37). Interestingly, the evaluation of the Bethlehem restorative policing experiment found that officers who knew about conferencing or participated in conferencing showed significant increases in their perception of community cooperation and a significant decrease in the crime control view of policing (McCold and Wachtel, 1998, p. 56).

Young's (2001) study focused more specifically on police practices and found more subtle indicators of sources of police dominance such as bringing the case file to the conference and referring to it during conference proceedings, and asking questions that seemed more investigative than facilitative. When the number of words contributed to the conference proceedings was counted, there were cases where police domination was evident, although there was a great deal of variation by case, and in the case that was the most one-sided, domination involved a social worker (Young, 2001, pp. 206–213).

In contrast with Roche (2003), Young concludes that the popularity of police-led restorative practices, the perception of participants that police-led practices contribute to legitimacy, and the reported fairness on the part of conference participants need to be weighed against problems that could arise from aspects of police culture that contribute to authoritarian control (2001, pp. 222–223). These potential problems can be checked through training and evaluation, and this requires a sufficient number of nonprofessional participants to be present at conferences.

Restorative justice programs in schools that involve police as partners in what Shaw describes as a comprehensive police liaison program were included in the "National Evaluation of the Restorative Justice in Schools Programme" (YJB, 2004). Graham Robb, a former head teacher of Drayton School in Oxfordshire, England, worked in partnership with the Thames Valley Police, Youth Justice Board teams, and a restorative justice trainer/consultant between 1999 and 2004 to improve the quality of relationships in a school that had received the designation of "Special Measures," which meant it was lacking in leadership, achieving, teaching, and learning (Robb, 2005, p. 102). While Robb observes that there were implementation failures, there were also stunning success stories for individual pupils and staff. He notes that:

> As head of a school in challenging circumstances, it would have been easy to adopt a punitive policy towards children displaying challenging behavior. This would have led to exclusions from school, further corrosion of relationships between the school and the community, and an increased chance of excluded young people engaging in crime and anti-social behavior (Robb, 2005, p. 103).

The Annual Youth Crime Survey conducted in Great Britain showed that students expelled from school are more than twice as likely to commit offenses than those who remain in school (MORI, 2004). Support for this concept was expressed by two police officers who were part of the restorative justice school programming reviewed by the Youth Justice Board.

One police officer noted:

> Keeping kids in school is a major protective factor. When they are excluded, they are more likely to cause trouble in the community and they end up in the criminal justice system. Restorative justice is a key approach to achieve this (YJB, 2004, p. 48).

Another officer commented:

> Restorative justice keeps kids in schools and lets you continually challenge their behavior. It also challenges parents to work with the school for the benefit of their child. Exclusion just makes things look less visible, as if the problem's gone away until such time that a crime has been reported (YJB, 2004, p. 48).

At Draydon, police participated in training and development work involving a variety of restorative approaches ranging from informal inquiry and problem solving through the full conference. Robb (2005, p. 103) emphasized the importance of placing police officers in schools *and* deploying restorative justice as the primary strategy to prevent crime. He concurred with the Youth Justice Board evaluation that police should be among a range of conference facilitators and are especially helpful in serious cases (Robb, 2005, p. 108). Additional feedback from the Youth Justice Board report was provided by a head teacher and a police officer:

> There is no substitute for having a police officer running the conference. It sends a clear message that if the young person doesn't take the opportunities on offer to change, they will be seeing a lot more of the police, maybe in a different role. (YJB, 2004, p. 54)—Head teacher, secondary school

While this particular head teacher took more of a deterrent than a restorative approach, a reaction from a police officer was much more restorative in tone.

> "I think it gives us a great opportunity for young people to get to work with us so they can get to see us as human beings—as people—not just the law. I think it's building relationships between the police and young people, breaking down barriers, preconceptions…" (YJB, 2004, p. 54)—Police Officer

Sir Charles Pollard, Chief Constable of the Thames Valley Police in England, has been a leader in introducing restorative interventions for young people. Pollard explains the usefulness of the restorative approach from a police practice perspective:

> One of the main options for the police has always been strict law enforcement. for officers faced with minor disorder and nuisance, the only viable alternative

was to exercise their discretion and use negotiation and persuasion to solve the problem. This highlights a curious paradox: these informal skills are used much more often and usually with greater impact than law enforcement, yet police training has always been about how to access and use the mechanics of the *formal* criminal justice system. (Pollard, 2001, pp. 165–166)

The more mundane nature of school conflict was empirically verified in a project supported by the NIJ in the Charlotte-Mecklenburg County School District (Kenney and Watson, 1999). The Charlotte School Safety Program used a problem-solving approach to school safety, incorporating a student–teacher–police partnership. In a series of problem-solving exercises attend by representatives of all three groups in the partnership, the group concluded that while gangs, drugs, and guns in school receive the most attention, most conflicts identified during the project were part of everyday school interactions including long lines in the lunchroom that led to campus disorder as a result of service delivery problems (Kenney and Watson, 1999, p. 10). These findings were supported by Charlotte Police Department records which reported that of a total of 1409 events in the year prior to the implementation of the project, most were for order maintenance problems which "contribute to a sense of an unsafe environment" (Kenney and Watson, 1999, p. 2).

In addition, many youth problems stem from interpersonal conflict whether they are with family, friends, teachers, administrator, and others. When these conflicts occur, if is often not clear which party or parties are at fault. Thus, the retributive model that assigns guilt and deals out punishment may be less appropriate than a restorative approach that uses dialogue to explore the nature of the problem and works toward its solution. A survey of SROs in middle and high schools in the Okaloosa County (Florida) School District, indicated that SROs favor punitive approaches, they are receptive to conflict resolution and restorative principles. However, without training and an organizing framework, it is difficult to bring these ideas to fruition (Owen, 2003).

In addition to providing new approaches to working with juveniles, Pollard notes that the restorative approach is important to assist the police in moving more toward a problem-oriented, community style of policing (2001, p. 167). While the community policing approach has been encouraged at the national, state, and local levels, police may have difficulty defining what constitutes their respective communities and effectively involving community members with their work.

Putting It All Together: Problems and Opportunities

Strengths and Weaknesses of SRO Programs

The possibility of more fully integrating the restorative justice philosophy into the SRO model has now been evaluated in detail. To assess the possible pitfalls and the potential for doing so, the SRO model has additionally been examined from the perspective of its mission and operating framework as well as assessments of its application. The philosophy of restorative justice and literature on its application to schools has been reviewed as well. Finally, relevant literature on police involvement in restorative practices has been discussed.

A major challenge is posed by differences in philosophies underlying the two models. The training of SROs is rooted in a retributive philosophy. Police officers are embodiments of the law and are viewed as authority figures. Those who practice restorative justice cast themselves in nonprofessional roles as facilitators of a process. The retributive model on which the entire criminal justice system is based focuses on lawbreaking, assignment of guilt, and punishment. The restorative model focuses on harm that results from misbehavior and crime, repairing that harm, and making plans for the future. However, there are more bridges between the SRO model and the restorative model than might be suggested by their different approaches to offending and misbehavior.

First, while grounded in law enforcement, the SRO model fits squarely in the tradition of community policing. Community policing focuses on building relationships between community and law enforcement, with the recognition that these relationships have the potential to contribute to safer communities. Effective community policing requires trust, participation, respect, and empowerment. The SRO mission statement reflects the community policing approach through its partnership status with relevant stakeholders including teachers, students, and the community. The question then becomes whether the SRO triad of law enforcement, education, and counseling is the best design for a community policing approach.

It has been documented that the SRO model is extremely popular in the school community. The triad approach is flexible and allows officers to adapt to the needs of a particular school environment. On the other hand, while popular, like the DARE program, there is no evidence that the SRO program is effective nor is the SRO framework a product of a single theoretical approach that links its activities to crime prevention and safety (Brown and Kreft, 1998). Police presence in the schools to prevent crime is closely associated with the traditional law enforcement function, while practices that bring the student in closer contact with the SRO, such as teaching and counseling, are more closely aligned with community policing.

Evaluations of SRO programs suggest that the SRO model can contribute to role confusion and role conflict. Expectations of SROs by teachers and administrators can be very different than those of the SROs. Furthermore, over time, the SROs have been given greater and more varied responsibilities in the schools with commensurate training lagging behind. Thus, while there is strong support for the SRO model, there is not a solid integrated theory behind it that can guide the direction of the SRO or show the SRO how what he or she is doing can be improved upon.

Integrating a Restorative Component

The literature review suggests a number of possibilities for strengthening SRO programs using the restorative approach. These include methods for better realizing the community policing philosophy, providing a more coherent philosophy for meeting SRO objectives, role clarification, training, and moving SRO programs closer to approaches that fit with international trends.

There is a gap between theory and practice that often occurs in community policing (McCold, 1998, p. 13). Evaluations of SRO programs show the need for involving stakeholders including administrators, teachers, and students with their work. Indeed, programs that do not do this are less likely to be successful. The restorative philosophy requires community involvement and provides models for bringing stakeholders together. Furthermore, one strength of restorative justice is that it provides some practical working concepts of community. It is often difficult to define community or bring about community participation, when one defines community solely in terms of place. Restorative justice practitioners have suggested defining community from the perspective of the "event" or as a "community of care." In other words, those who have been affected by the event or care about people affected by the event (McCold and Wachtel, 1997). Presently, the SRO approaches community policing through trust building. Students who positively interact with SROs are more likely to trust them and hopefully feel more comfortable reporting crimes. While this is a good strategy, the restorative approach gives SROs a framework and additional tools to broaden community involvement in problem solving and developing relationships that build trust. Figure 8.2 depicts relationships between community policing, the SRO model, and restorative justice.

Second, restorative justice, particularly as it has been applied to school discipline, provides a coherent philosophy for school safety which is not

Figure 8.2 Interrelationships between community-based programs, SRO programs, and restorative justice.

incompatible with the retributive approach. Retribution seeks accountability and vindication through punishment. Restorative justice seeks accountability and vindication by addressing the victims' harms and needs, encouraging the offender to take responsibility, repairing the harm, and supporting parties to the conflict in making plans for a more positive future (Zehr, 2002, p. 59). Both theory and empirical studies point to the effectiveness of using high levels of control and support in response to misbehavior and crime. Those police officers who have been involved with restorative justice understand the process, evaluate it positively, and are less likely to focus on control to the exclusion of support.

The contribution that restorative justice can make to a reduction in role conflict stems from the restorative philosophy which provides mechanisms for realizing social control as well as building trust and supportive relationships. Qualitative research suggests that when restorative processes are implemented correctly, the presence of the law enforcement officer adds legitimacy to them. Provided that the officer understands the restorative approach, he or she can provide useful information to both parties and can serve as a community member speaking to the consequences of the misbehavior. In this role, the officer is not an "outside authority" but rather a member of the community itself, holding those responsible for misbehavior accountable but also providing support. Furthermore, when cooperation cannot be obtained from the offending student, restorative justice practice acknowledges that it may be necessary to fall back on traditional authority, sanctioning the invocation of the law enforcement role (Claassen, 2002).

Fourth, evaluation of SRO programs suggests that officers are being asked to take on more diverse functions, many for which they feel they have little or no training. A range of informal to formal restorative practices can be linked to activities encompassed in the SRO triad particularly with respect to counseling. For example, affective statements, affective questions, and affective small impromptu conferences can enhance the counseling role. Restorative justice trainings and certification are available which would give the police officer effective tools for dealing with negative emotions that do not violate professional ethics. Training in affective statements and questions are also helpful in moving the officer away from the role of aggressive interrogator, which does not contribute to building trust and conflicts with the school culture. Providing officers with training to lead formal conferences, particularly for serious, controversial cases, gives the officer the tools to better bridge the law enforcement and community policing roles.

Finally, NASRO does an excellent job providing trainings that reflect popular concerns such as Internet crime, drug use, gang membership, bullying, and the like. However, more comprehensive approaches are evidenced in trends in school safety. These include responding to the needs of victims and victimizers, using proactive rather than reactive approaches, and using inclusive processes that involve student, teachers, administrators, parents, and other members of the community. The literature review speaks to the strength of restorative justice both in philosophy and practice in responding to these trends.

Summary and Conclusions

SRO programs and restorative justice share the common goal of creating safer schools. Restorative approaches are not a panacea for creating safer schools nor are they easy to implement on a whole-school basis. However, a more modest objective, that of more effectively introducing the restorative philosophy to SROs through teaching, training, and pilot projects, is merited given this review.

SRO programs are highly decentralized, and the SRO model provides for responding to the needs of their respective schools. However, research suggests that what SROs are doing could be improved upon, particularly with respect to expanding their tool kit in a complex, primarily noncriminal environment. The restorative justice community could do more in terms of establishing links with the SRO national organization, building bridges through education partnerships between NASRO and numerous restorative justice training centers. Administrative heads of law enforcement agencies with SRO programs may wish to directly participate in restorative justice training/education partnerships as well. Finally, funding agencies could be encouraged to provide support for the development of these relationships, creating pilot projects, and providing for their evaluation in terms of impact on building trust, establishing community connections, promoting community participation, and producing safer school environments.

References

Amstutz, L. and Mullet, J. (2005). *The Little Book of Restorative Discipline for Schools: Teaching Responsibility: Creating Caring Climates*. Intercourse, PA: Good Books.

Braithwaite, J. (1989). *Crime, Shame, and Reintegration*. New York: Cambridge University Press.

Braithwaite, J. (2002). *Restorative Justice and Responsive Regulation*. Oxford: Oxford University Press.

Brown, J.H. and Kreft, I.G. (1998). Zero effects of drug prevention programs: Issues and solutions. *Evaluation Review*. 22(1): 3–14.

Cameron, L. and Thorsborne, M. (2001). Restorative justice and school discipline: Mutually exclusive? In Heather, S. and Braithwaite, J. (Eds.) *Restorative Justice and Civil Society*, pp. 180–194. Cambridge, U.K.: Cambridge University Press.

Cawthon, C.E. (2002). Ratings of school resource officer program in a northwest Florida school district by students, teachers, administrators, and school resource officer. A dissertation submitted to the Division of Diversity Studies and Applied Research, College of Professional Studies, the University of West Florida, Pensacola, FL.

Chen, S., Chang, K., and Tombs, B. (1999). An evaluation of a school resource officer program in Kansas. Topeka, KS: Kansas Criminal Justice Coordinating Council.

Claassen, R. (1993). An introduction to discipline that restores. *Conciliation Quarterly Newsletter.* 12(2): 1–3.

Claassen, R. (2002). An introduction to discipline that restores (DTR). Retrieved August 19, 2005, from http://peace.fresno.edu/ocs/rjfrmae 0201.pdf

Claassen, R., Tilkes, C., Kader, P., and Noll, D.E. (2001). *Restorative Justice: A Framework for Fresno.* Fresno, CA: Center for Peace Making and Conflict Studies.

Daly, K. and Hayes, H. (2001). Restorative justice and conferencing in Australia. Trends and issues in crime and criminology. No. 186. Australian Institute of Criminology, Canberra, Australia.

Edgar, K., Bitel, M., Thurlow, J., and Bowen, G. (2002). The evaluation of the Lambeth Restorative Justice conference pilot project in schools. Youth Justice Board website www.youth-justce-board.gov.uk.

Education Queensland (1998). 1997 pilot of community accountability conferencing report, unpublished paper, Education Queensland, Brisbane.

Finn, P. and McDevitt, J. (2005). National assessment of school resource officer programs: Final project report. Abt Associates, Cambridge, MA.

Hopkins, B. (2004). *Just Schools: A Whole-School Approach to Restorative Justice.* London, U.K.: Jessica Kingsley Publishers.

Jackson, A. (2002). Police-school resource officers' and students' perceptions of the police and offending. *Policing: An International Journal of Police Strategy and Management.* 25(3): 731–650.

Johnson, I.M. (1999). School violence. The effectiveness of a school resource officer program in a southern city. *Journal of Criminal Justice.* 27(2): 173–192.

Kenny, D.J. and Watson, S. (1999). *Crime in the Schools. Reducing Conflict with Student Problem Solving.* Washington, DC: National Institute of Justice.

Lambert, R.D. and McGinty, D. (2002). Law enforcement officers in schools: Setting priorities. *Journal of Educational Administration.* 40(3): 257–273.

Marshall, P., Shaw, G., and Freeman, E. (2002, August). Restorative practices: Implications for educational institutions. From a session presented at the *Third International Conference on Conferencing, Circles and other Restorative Practices,* Minneapolis, MN.

McCold, P. (1998, November). Police-facilitated restorative conferencing: What the data show. Paper presented at *the Second Annual International Conference on Restorative Justice for Juveniles, Florida Atlantic University and the International Network for Research on Restorative Justice for Juveniles,* Fort Lauderdale, FL.

McCold, P. (2002, November). Evaluation of a restorative milieu: CSF Buxmont School/Day Treatment Center. Paper presented at *the Annual Meeting of the American Society of Criminology,* Chicago, IL.

McCold, P. (2004, November). Evaluation of a restorative milieu: Replication and extension for 2001–2003 discharges. Paper presented at *the Annual Meeting of the American Society of Criminology,* Nashville, TN.

McCold, P. and Wachtel, B. (1997, June). Community is not a place: A new look at community justice initiatives. Paper presented to *the International Conference on Justice without Violence: Views from Peacemaking Criminology and Restorative Justice*, Albany, NY.

McDonald, J. and Moore, D. (2001). Community conferencing as a special case of conflict transformation. In Strang, H. and Braithwaite, J. (Eds.) *Restorative Justice and Civil Society*, pp. 195–210. Cambridge, U.K.: Cambridge University Press.

McNeely, C.A., Nonnemaker, J.M., and Blum, R.W. (2002). Connectedness: Evidence from the national longitudinal study of adolescent health. *Journal of School Health*. 72(4): 138–146.

Mirsky, L. (2003). Safer saner schools. Transforming school culture with restorative practice. Retrieved February 27, 2005, from http://www.iirp.org/library/sspilots.html

MORI. (2004). *Annual Youth Crime Survey*. London, U.K.: Youth Justice Board.

Morrison, B. (2001). The school system: Developing its capacity in the regulation of civil society. In Strang, H. and Braithwaite, J. (Eds.) *Restorative Justice and Civil Society*, pp. 195–210. Cambridge, U.K.: Cambridge University Press.

Morrison, B. (2005). Restorative justice in schools. In Elliott, E. and Gordon, R.M. (Eds.) *New Directions in Restorative Justice*, pp. 26–52. Portland, OR: Willan.

Mulqueen, P. (1999). School resource officers: More than security guards. *American School and University*. 71(11): SS17.

Nathanson, D.L. (1992). *Shame and Pride: Affect, Sex, and the Birth of Self*, New York: W.W. Norton.

National Association of School Resource Officers (NASRO). (2005a). About NASRO. Retrieved August 18, 2005, from http://nasro.org/about_nasro.asp

National Association of School Resource Officers (NASRO). (2005b). Conference. Retrieved February 17, 2005 from http://www.nasro.org/conference.asp

National Institute of Justice (NIJ). (1999). A national assessment of school resource officer programs. U.S. Department of Justice, Washington, DC.

O'Connell, T. (2000). Restorative justice for police: Foundations of change. Paper presented at *the United Nations Crime Congress, Ancillary Meeting on Implementing Restorative Justice in the International Context*. Vienna, Austria, April 20–27.

Owen, M. (2003). *School resource officers addressing conflicts in Okaloosa County*. Department of Criminal Justice and Legal Studies, The University of West Florida, Pensacola, FL, Unpublished.

Pollard, C. (2001). If your only tool is a hammer, all your problems will look like nails. In Strang, H. and Braithwaite, J. (Eds.) *Restorative Justice and Civil Society*, pp. 130–143. Cambridge, U.K.: Cambridge University Press.

Pranis, K. (2005). *The Little Book of Circle Processes: A New/Old Approach to Peacemaking*. Intercourse, PA: Good Books.

Riese, J. (2003). Anti-bullying program aims to shift culture in schools: Is this restorative justice in action? *VOMA Connections*. 13: 3.

Robb, G. (2005, November). Restorative approaches in schools: A perspective from England. Paper from, the next step: Developing restorative communities, presented at *the IIRP's Seventh International Conference on Conferencing, Circles, and other Restorative Practices*, Manchester, England, U.K.

Roche, D. (2003). *Accountability in Restorative Justice*. Oxford: Oxford University Press.

Shaw, M. (1999, February). Police, schools and crime prevention: A preliminary review of current practices. Unpublished report. International Centre for the Prevention of Crime, Montreal, Canada.

Sherman, L. and Strang, H. (1997). The right kind of shame for crime prevention. RISE working paper, Australian Institute of Criminology, Canberra, Australia.

Thorsborne, M. (2000). APAPDC Online: Conference 2000. Retrieved February 17, 2005 from http://www.apapdc.edu.au/archive/ASPA/conference2000/papers/art_2_13.htm

Trump, K.S. (2001). NASRO school resource officer survey. Unpublished report. National School Safety and Security Services, Cleveland, OH, October 5.

Trump, K.S. (2002). NASRO school resource officer survey. Unpublished report. National School Safety and Security Services, Cleveland, OH, September 25.

Tyler, T. (1990). *Why People Obey the Law*. New Haven, CT: Yale University Press.

Wachtel, T. and McCold, P. (2001). Restorative justice in everyday life. In Strang, H. and Braithwaite, J. (Eds.) *Restorative Justice and Civil Society*, pp. 114–129. Cambridge, U.K.: Cambridge University Press.

Wilson, P. and Braithwaite, J. (1977). School truancy and delinquency. In Wilson, P.R. (Ed.). *Delinquency in Australia: A Critical Appraisal*. St. Lucia, Queensland, Australia: University of Queensland Press.

Young, R. (2001). Just cops doing 'shameful' business? Police-led restorative justice and the lessons of research. In Morris, A. and Maxwell, G. (Eds.) *Restorative Justice for Juveniles: Conferences, Mediations and Circles*, pp. 195–226. Portland, OR: Hart.

Youth Justice Board for England and Wales (YJB). (2004). National evaluation of restorative justice in schools programme. Retrieved August 8, 2005 from www.youth-justice-board.gov.uk/Publications/Downloads/RJ%20in%20schools.pdf

Zehr, H. (1995). *Changing Lenses*, 3rd edn. Scottsdale, PA: Herald Press.

Zehr, H. (2002). *The Little Book of Restorative Justice*. Intercourse, PA: Good Books.

Suicide-by-Cop: Adding Stress to an Already Stressed Profession

RICK PARENT

Contents

Introduction

Many researchers have attempted to examine the underlying reasons for the police use of deadly force in North America, and numerous questions have been asked about the phenomenon of victim-precipitated homicide, also known as "suicide-by-cop." This concept will be examined in relation to the police use of deadly force in North America and other democratic countries. During victim-precipitated incidents that are specific to suicide-by-cop, an individual will engage in a suicide mission by threatening the life of a police officer or innocent bystander. The provoking individual typically forces the situation until the police officer has no other option but to use deadly force.

The physiological, psychological, physical, and emotional impact that has affected many of the police officers who have taken the life of another, or who have faced a lethal threat during the course of their duties, have also to be considered. These individuals have experienced a life-threatening event that often extends beyond the officer to their family and close friends.

Ultimately, a strong recommendation can be made that operational police personnel be made aware of the dynamics associated with victim-precipitated homicide, with a particular emphasis on the phenomenon of suicide-by-cop. Police training should also give serious consideration to establishing rigorous training in relation to dealing with irrational individuals who are vulnerable owing to factors that may include suicidal ideation, psychosis, emotional upheaval, and the influence of alcohol or other intoxicating or disorienting substances.

Police Use of Deadly Force: International Comparisons

A precarious relationship exists between democratic societies and the police agencies that have been created for the purpose of maintaining law and social order. In an attempt to maintain law and order, police officers must routinely use force in their day-to-day contact with the public. Police have at their disposal the capacity to act as judge, jury, and executioner, if need be. Force that is legitimately and properly applied serves as an essential ingredient in maintaining an ordered society.

However, the decision to use deadly force is of such significance that, if at any time a death results, the appropriateness of the action will always be questioned. Police use of lethal force can only be justified in those few situations in which no other reasonable option is available. When an officer is issued a firearm, the expectation is that it will only be used in very limited circumstances. The vast majority of police officers within the United States and Canada will complete their entire careers without having to shoot or utilize potentially deadly force. Generally, officers who discharge a firearm or utilize other potentially deadly force are attempting to immediately incapacitate a perceived threat. In those rare instances when deadly force is used, the decision-making by the officer is often complex, multifaceted, and instantaneous (Matulia, 1985).

It is within this setting that approximately 400 individuals are shot and killed by U.S. law enforcement personnel each year (U.S. Department of Justice, 2004; Uniform Crime Reports (UCR), 2004). In the neighboring nation of Canada, there have been 118 fatal police shootings between 1999 and 2008, approximately 12 per year.

In Australia, 41 deaths were attributed to gunshot wounds inflicted by police personnel from January 1, 1990 through to June 30, 1997 (Australian Institute of Criminology (AIC), 1998). In New Zealand, there have been approximately 20 fatal police shootings in the past 60 years. The vast majority of these shootings have occurred since the mid-1970s (New Zealand Police, 2002).

In Europe, the United Kingdom recorded 23 incidents involving the discharge of a firearm by police in England and Wales during the period between 1991 and 1993. In seven of these incidents, an individual was killed (Police Scientific Development Branch (PSDB), 1996). A more recent review of police shootings in England and Wales during the period between 1998 and 2001 indicates that 24 incidents occurred. Eleven of these firearm incidents were fatal. In the nearby Netherlands, 67 fatal police shootings were recorded from 1978 through to 1999. During this same period, a total of 288 individuals were wounded by police (Timmer, 2005).

The Risk to Police Personnel

Added to these figures are numerous documented incidents where law enforcement personnel in the United States and Canada have faced a potentially lethal threat, but the death of a suspect *did not* occur. This category includes those incidents in which a police officer utilized potentially deadly force by discharging his or her firearm, but death did not result. In these instances, the suspect either survived his or her wounds or, in other instances, the police missed, so the suspect was not shot (Keram et al., 2000).

Finally, it must be emphasized that there are also countless incidents of lethal threats to law enforcement personnel that are resolved each year *without the discharge of a firearm*. During these instances, the officers utilized alternate tactics or less lethal compliance tools such as pepper spray or Taser guns to subdue the individual who was posing a lethal threat. Often, this method of resolution has occurred with an increased risk to the police officer. This increased risk to police officers has at times resulted in their deaths. Owing to the very nature of their day-to-day duties, operational police personnel routinely face the real possibility of being assaulted or murdered.

On average, approximately 60 police officers are feloniously killed in the line of duty each year within the United States. In addition, approximately 80 police officers will be killed accidentally each year in the United States owing to mishaps such as automobile and aircraft accidents (Bureau of Justice Statistics (BJS), 2008; Officer Down Memorial Page (ODMP), 2009). In Canada, during the period from 1980 through to 2000, assailants murdered a total of 47 police officers, reflecting a rate of approximately 2 police murders per year. In addition to these willful killings, approximately 7 police officers will die each year accidentally in the line of duty (Officer Down Memorial Page (ODMP), 2009).

Theoretical Perspectives

In the United States, researchers have attempted to explain the underlying reasons for extreme violence, including police use of deadly force. In their attempts, researchers have derived a number of theoretical perspectives, each providing a viewpoint that must be considered within the unique circumstances of individual lethal force incidents. Wolfgang and Ferracuti's (1967) "subculture of violence" is one of the most cited theories of violence. These authors present the concept that there exist in different communities "subculture(s) with a cluster of values that support and encourage the overt use of force in interpersonal relations and group interactions."

Geller and Scott (1992) state that the structural theory asserts the significance of "broad-scale" societal forces such as lack of opportunity, institutional racism, persistent poverty, demographic transitions, and population density; these combine to determine both homicide rates and to influence the police use of deadly force. It is argued that these factors serve to facilitate violent crime within a community, thereby influencing the propensity for police use of deadly force.

The interactional theory focuses upon the character of relationships that escalate into homicide. Police use of force is seen as resulting from the interaction process itself. The act of the participant precipitates the acts of the police officer. This may result in an escalation of conflict that culminates in deadly force being utilized. In his 1982 study, Luckenbill states that the most severe form of violence, murder, takes a sequential form. In his analysis of 70 murder cases, it was noted that in every case, the killing was a culmination of an interchange between the offender and the "target" (victim).

The transaction of violence would occur in a sequential form. The "target" would act in a manner that the offender deemed to be offensive. In response, the offender would typically retaliate with a verbal or physical challenge. These events would establish a "working agreement" favoring the use of violence. A battle would then ensue, typically leaving the target dead or dying (Luckenbill, 1977).

In applying Luckenbill's theory to police use of deadly force, the police officer would typically take on the role of the target. A police officer unknowingly attending the scene of an in-progress crime, or attempting to intervene in a violent situation, is typically perceived as the "offensive individual" by threatening the goal of the perpetrator.

As this interaction commences, it becomes apparent to both the target (police officer) and the offender (suspect) that each individual favors *opposing outcomes*. The police officer, if allowed to fulfill his or her role, will not only terminate the offender's progress toward his or her goal, but will also hold the offender accountable for his or her actions. In most instances, this accountability will occur in a court of law, with consequences that may include punishment and the possibility of imprisonment.

It is within this context that the offender retaliates with the use of violence or with the threat of violence. The offender sees the option of surrender or compliance as being an unsuitable means of settling the confrontation (Luckenbill, 1977).

The offender's actions (or inaction) will ultimately determine what level of force is required by the police officer. Should the offender choose to display a real, or perceived, potentially lethal threat toward the officer or another individual, then it is likely that police personnel will respond with their firearms or other appropriate levels of force.

Reactions to Violence

Violence by police is also said to be situational in nature. In each particular situation, there is a unique set of dynamics that include personality, stress, and danger. Parent (1996) significantly emphasizes that, in some instances, the police officer is forced to react within seconds, and there is little that the involved officers could have done differently to alter the nature of their encounter.

Individual officers who have been involved in shootings have detailed how the often split-second incident appeared to unfold in "slow motion," with their only focus being upon the actions of the assailant. In most cases, police officers responded to the perceived threat in an "automatic" manner, based upon their repeated training in dealing with life-threatening situations. In the vast majority of cases, a potentially violent encounter will develop into a deadly violent situation in just a matter of seconds.

An essential factor in controlling this iatrogenic situation is the obligation of the individual police officer to check for specific factors as they approach the scene of a potentially violent encounter. The mere presence of a police officer may serve to intensify and escalate the situation into which they are entering. Researchers have noted that a key factor in increasing the amount of time available to an officer is the training in violence reduction (Parent, 1996; Justice Institute of British Columbia (JIBC), 2009). This would include such matters as deciding upon how and when to enter a situation and what precautions to take, including developing a habit of checking in-progress crime scenes for the purpose of identifying dangers, options, and bystanders (Geller and Scott, 1992; Justice Institute of British Columbia (JIBC), 2009). The rapid timing and physiological effects that occur during violent encounters tend to indicate that there are few, if any, alternatives to deadly force.

It is important to recognize that an officer engaged in a potentially lethal encounter will experience a variety of perceptual alterations. Tunnel vision may occur, which, in effect, nullifies the officer's peripheral vision. The officer may require this vision in order to see other dangers, identify other alternatives to deadly force, or to become aware of the presence of innocent bystanders (Klinger, 2001).

Researchers have cited "time distortions" and "increased auditory and visual acuity" among other physiological effects of high-stress confrontations. These physiological changes, collectively known as the "general adaptive syndrome," are intrinsic within human beings, acting as a survival mechanism (Murray and Zentner, 1975). In conjunction with the general adaptive syndrome, the "alarm stage" is an instantaneous, short-term, life-preserving, and total sympathetic nervous-system response that occurs when a person consciously or unconsciously perceives a danger-inducing stressor. Stress is a physical and emotional state that is always present in a person, but is intensified when an environmental change or threat occurs to which the individual must respond. An individual's survival depends upon constant negotiation between environmental demands and the person's own adaptive capacities (Murray and Zentner, 1975; Klinger, 2001).

In a modern society, the police are continually occupied with the threat of violence in their day-to-day activities. Skolnick (1966) stated that in reaction, police officers develop a "perceptual shorthand" to identify certain kinds of people as "symbolic assailants." These symbolic assailants are individuals who use specific gestures, language, and attire that the officer has come to recognize as a prelude to violence. This may also apply to symbolic settings, which the officer has come to recognize as having the potential for danger (Justice Institute of British Columbia (JIBC, 2009).

The physiological and psychological changes that occur in police officers under stress serve as important factors in an officer's decision to deploy deadly force. Physical and social settings—including dark or poorly-lit places, high-crime and high-violence areas, angry or upset people, and non-supportive social structures—also serve to heighten anxiety. While these factors affect all individuals, police officers are likely to experience even higher levels of anxiety, as they often have little choice as to whether to enter a dangerous situation (Klinger, 2001; Sheehan and Warren, 2001).

Victimology and Suicide-by-Cop

Researchers have also attempted to explain police use of deadly force by examining the role of the victim. Marvin Wolfgang (1958) notes that victim-precipitated homicides are those instances in which the victim is a direct, positive precipitator in his or her own death. It is the victim who is the first to resort to physical violence in the interaction process, and not the subsequent slayer.

Wolfgang verified much of this phenomenon through sociological analysis in his hypothesis that an individual may commit an unorthodox form of suicide by provoking another person to slay him or her. In his research, Wolfgang noted that victim-precipitated homicides represented 26% of a total of 588 homicides studied in Philadelphia (Wolfgang, 1958:345). Within this framework, anecdotal research also revealed the phenomenon of suicide-by-cop (Geberth, 1993; Van Zandt, 1993).

During victim-precipitated incidents that are specific to suicide-by-cop, an individual will engage in a suicide mission by threatening the life of a police officer or an innocent bystander. The provoking individual typically *forces* the situation until the police officer has no other option but to use deadly force. In these instances, despite its name, victim-precipitated homicide is, in essence, a form of suicide (Lord, 2004; Homant, 2000).

Suicide has been defined as "death resulting directly or indirectly from a positive or negative act of the victim himself, which he knows will produce this result" (Durkheim, 1897/1951:44). Thus, by virtue of this definition, suicide becomes an intentional act and is goal-directed behavior. It is noteworthy that the characteristics associated with an individual predisposed to victim-precipitated homicide are also generally defined within the category of suicidal behavior.

In some instances, the suicidal behavior appears as an instrumental goal; in other instances, it is more expressive. Instrumental goals of suicidal behavior may include avoidance of consequences such as reconciliation of a failed love relationship or incarceration. In contrast, expressive goals may include venting hopelessness or rage about an individual's life or proving an emotional point. These motivations are usually present in any given incident of suicide-by-cop. There are also three common "meta" or ultimate goals, at least one of which is present in every suicide-by-cop situation: suicide, homicide-suicide, or attention or "cry for help" (Mohandie and Meloy, 2000:384).

Mohandie and Meloy (2000) state that instrumental behavior typifies individuals who are

- Attempting to escape or avoid the consequences or criminal or shameful actions
- Utilizing a forced confrontation with police to reconcile a failed relationship
- Intending to avoid the exclusion clauses of life insurance policies
- Rationalizing that while it may be morally wrong to commit suicide, being killed resolves the spiritual problem of suicide
- Seeking what they believe to be a very effective means of accomplishing death

In contrast, expressive behavior typifies individuals that are communicating:

- Hopelessness, depression, and desperation
- Statements pertaining to their perceived identification as a victim
- Their need to save face by dying or being forcibly overwhelmed rather than surrendering
- Their intense power needs

- Rage and revenge
- Their need to draw attention to an important personal issue

Schneidman (1981) identifies the main elements of *high lethality suicide* as being the desire to die; a direct and conscious role in bringing about one's own death; and the fact that death results primarily due to the deceased's actions. In addition, specific psychological characteristics associated with suicide include a general sense of depression, hopelessness, and low self-esteem on the part of the deceased. Often, these characteristics are overtly displayed by actions such as self-inflicted wounds, statements of suicide, or the desire to die.

Foote (1998) adds that victim-precipitated homicide is really made up of several dimensions that include risk-taking, aggressiveness, and intentionality. It is within this framework that the concept of suicide-by-cop emerges. During victim-precipitated incidents, these factors culminate with a risk-taking person aggressively and intentionally engaging in *perceived life-threatening behavior*, typically resulting in a police officer or another individual taking their life (Homant, 2000; Lord, 2004).

Geller and Scott's (1992) analysis of this phenomenon revealed that these cases are usually difficult to discover, as there is little or no documentation of the victim's intent. Unfortunately, the actions of the victim have led to his or her demise, without the benefit of a post-shooting explanation for his or her behavior. Police investigators have equally confounded this situation by failing to examine, in detail, the *root causes* of the victim's behavior. All too often, the police shooting has been explained as a "crazy person who came at the officer with a knife or a gun." It is only within the last decade that police and conflict-management trainers have begun to examine and make reference to the phenomenon of victim-precipitated homicide as a cause of police shootings (Parent, 1996, 2004; Lord, 2004).

In the United States and Canada, recent research surrounding the police use of deadly force has identified the frequency and degree of victim-precipitated acts that have constituted lethal threats against police officers. The characteristics associated with victim-precipitated homicide, or suicide-by-cop, appear to be a significant factor in approximately one-third of police shooting cases that have occurred within North America.

Several empirical studies of the phenomenon colloquially known as suicide-by-cop have been published in academic journals in recent times (Parent, 1996; Hutson et al., 1998; Parent and Verdun-Jones, 1998; Wilson et al., 1998; Homant and Kennedy, 2000; Lord, 2004; Parent, 2004; Kennedy et al., 1998). This phenomenon has also been cited in international studies of police shootings in nations that include England, Wales, and Australia (Police Scientific Development Branch (PSDB), 1996; Australian Institute of

Criminology (AIC), 1998) and in academic papers that have been presented at various academic annual meetings that include the Academy of Criminal Justice Sciences and the American Academy of Psychiatry and the Law (Lord, 2004; Keram et al., 2000).

More recently, Mohandie et al. (2009) found that 36% of a sample of 707 officer-involved shootings revealed characteristics of a suicide-by-cop case. Suicide-by-cop subjects were armed with weapons during 80% ($n = 205$) of the incidents, and 19% feigned or simulated weapon possession. The authors of the study note that suicide-by-cop cases were more likely to result in the death or injury of the subjects than other shooting cases involving officers. It is noteworthy that 51% ($n = 131$) of the suicide-by-cop subjects were killed during the encounter with police.

Also noteworthy is that in some instances, research findings have revealed that the victim caused or contributed to the lethal threat of a police officer by intentionally provoking the officer to use deadly force or potential deadly force, resulting in the death or wounding of the individual. In these cases, the individual's statements and actions clearly illustrate their intent to commit suicide (Lord, 2004; Parent, 2004).

In other cases, the individual did not make a suicidal statement. In these cases, the conclusion is drawn that the individual was suicidal, based upon his or her actions and irrational behavior. The actions and behavior documented within these cases is consistent with the behavior and characteristics associated with suicide (Parent, 1996; Lord, 2004). Also significant is the fact that, in several cases, the perpetrator of a lethal threat had a documented history of mental illness and/or suicidal tendencies. In addition, documentation in several of the cases indicates that the victim had a high blood-alcohol reading at the time of his or her death. Often, alcohol, substance abuse, and mental illness were added to the complex picture of suicidal tendencies and irrational behavior (Lord, 2004; Parent, 2004).

Researchers have noted that suicide prevention techniques and alternatives to lethal weapons must be made available to police officers, if these situations are to be minimized. However, persons who are strongly predisposed to taking their own lives may resort to extreme methods in an attempt to carry out their goal. It is well known through television, movies, and literature that police officers are trained and will deploy deadly force, with some degree of certainty, upon being confronted by a life-threatening situation. As a result, an individual predisposed to suicide may confront the police with a knife or other weapon, advancing upon and *forcing* the officer to utilize lethal force. An extreme individual may confront the police with a loaded firearm and even discharge their weapon at the police, in the hope of being killed. These situations would provide few, if any, options for the attending officers except to respond with deadly force.

Why Suicide-by-Cop?

Durkheim (1897/1951) believed that *cohesion* (integration of societal forces) reduced suicidal activity within a community, while *anomie* (social disorganization) promoted it. In today's contemporary society, sociocultural factors facilitating suicide include a general state of societal demoralization or fragmentation, permissive social attitudes toward suicide, and even media attention to celebrity suicides. Additional facilitating factors include social isolation from a supportive network, suicide of role models or peers (television and films icons), unemployment, and an environment that facilitates suicide, such as the availability of firearms. In this regard, the government and the media share a key role in shaping public attitudes and in facilitating public education. Committing suicide by "traditional methods" that include jumping from a high structure, crashing a speeding vehicle into a stationary object, or by a self-inflicted wound requires a decision and commitment on the part of the victim. In victim-precipitated homicides that are born out of suicide, the difficult decision to end one's life is made by someone else. Van Zandt (1993), Homant and Kennedy (2000), and Homant et al. (2000) note that suicidal individuals specifically single out the police, as they are the only community agency equipped with firearms and the training to react to potentially life-threatening situations with accurate and deadly force. Van Zandt adds that in most instances the police are only a phone call away.

In addition, the stigma and social taboos associated with suicide can be *absolved* upon being terminated by an *external mechanism* such as the police. As agents of the state, the police officer truly represents a faceless means of ending one's life in a somewhat dignified manner (Van Zandt, 1993; Homant and Kennedy, 2000; Homant et al., 2000). This argument is supported by the psychoanalytical explanation of homicide as it relates to suicide and the drive for self-punishment. Wolfgang and Ferraculti (1967) illustrate that in the past there have been data that have supported the "murder as indirect suicide" thesis. A case in point is the epidemic of indirect suicides that took place in Norway and Denmark in the seventeenth and eighteenth centuries. Depressed individuals committed murder, presumably so that they would be put to death. These individuals would not commit suicide as their religious beliefs precluded the taking of their own life. These authors note that the occurrences of murder were so frequent that a special law was passed excluding those individuals from the death penalty. The intent of the legislators was to stop this particular type of homicide (Wolfgang and Ferraculti, 1967:206).

Lord (2000) and Homant and Kennedy (2000) further this position by stating that the police can symbolically represent the social conscience to certain individuals. Lord notes that, at times, suicidal individuals feel guilty about things that are real or imagined. Police officers traditionally and symbolically represent law and order within society. A guilt-ridden, suicidal individual may enter into an interaction with the police in an attempt to seek punishment that may include death.

In other instances, the suicidal individual may not have the determination to end his or her own life. In these cases, the suicidal individual cannot "pull the trigger" to end his or her own life and, therefore, must seek assistance in fulfilling this goal. Geberth (1993) cites instances in which an apparently armed individual has confronted the police and was killed. The subsequent police investigation revealed that the assailant knowingly confronted the police with an unloaded or inoperable weapon. Geberth cites two cases to illustrate his point.

Case A

The fatal shooting of a 17-year-old male occurred on December 23, 1992 when the police had attempted to stop the youth for series of traffic violations. A vehicle pursuit developed when the youth failed to stop for the police, which eventually ended when the subject's car drove onto a front yard of a residence. As the police approached the youth he reached for a gun in the back seat of his car. In response, the officers twice order the subject to drop the weapon. Upon hearing the commands the youth stated "You'll have to kill me" and then turned and pointed the gun at the police.

The police officers responded to the youth's action by firing four shots. As the youth was being handcuffed he stated 'Please kill me, please kill me.' A check of his weapon revealed that his gun had not been loaded. Further investigation into the incident revealed that the youth was upset with his girlfriend and had told his grandmother that he was going to kill himself or someone else. Relatives confirmed that the youth had been "acting and talking crazy" and that he had made statements that he was going to kill himself.

Case B

On October 08, 1990 a 40-year-old male was shot and killed by an off duty police officer, working part-time as a uniformed security officer. The subject had entered a closed restaurant brandishing a handgun. Upon seeing the uniformed officer he pointed his gun at him. The officer responded by drawing his firearm and subsequently killing the subject. It was later learned that the subject's gun was unloaded.

Further investigation into the incident revealed that the subject had a lengthy criminal history and had recently returned to drug use. He had stated to friends that if he didn't get out of town he felt that he was going to die in a police shooting. He had also told one acquaintance that he was contemplating suicide. Witnesses to the shooting noted that the subject was seen peering into the restaurant ten minutes before entering. The restaurant was well known to the public as always having a uniformed and armed security officer within the premise. It appeared that the subject had calculated the events that had unfolded.

Geberth adds that suicidal individuals may use hostage-taking incidents to bring about their demise. In these situations, the suicidal person will create a confrontational negotiation posture with the police. They will often announce their intention to die or make biblical references, particularly to the Book of Revelations and the resurrection. In addition, these individuals may set a deadline for their own death, or begin talking about people who are dead as if they are still alive. In following this course of action, the individual accomplishes his or her own self-destruction while going out in a "blaze of glory."

Foote (1998) notes that, in some instances, the act of suicide is pre-planned with the assailant engaging in a *calculated intentional act* of life-threatening behavior ultimately resulting in a victim-precipitated homicide. In other instances, the act of suicide is *impulsive*, with suicidal motivation occurring *only after* police involvement in a given situation (Foote, 1998; Homant and Kennedy, 2000). For example, at the conclusion of a police pursuit, an individual may suddenly decide that it is better to die at the hands of the police than to face a public trial with the possibility of a lengthy prison term.

The Police as Victims

The research and findings surrounding suicide-by-cop incidents suggest that the so-called victim must share some of the responsibility in police shootings that are victim-precipitated. The shooting incident may not have occurred except for the precipitated actions of the deceased. In many instances, police officers are "baited" into situations that are escalated by the participant, in an attempt to have the police officer take his or her life (Parent, 1996; Homant, 2000; Lord, 2004).

In other instances, police officers did not use their firearms and placed themselves at substantial risk of death or serious injury during a particular incident. In the vast majority of these cases, the police officers would have been justified in using potential or deadly force, but did not do so for a variety of reasons (Parent, 1996, 2004).

During his study of homicides in Philadelphia, Marvin Wolfgang (1958) noted that within contemporary society the survivor of a homicide incident is typically viewed in a negative fashion. The victim, regardless of his or her precipitated role, is typically viewed in a more favorable light. In an attempt to explain the social conscience that is associated with a homicide, Wolfgang writes:

> In many cases the victim has most of the major characteristics of an offender; in some cases two potential offenders come together in a homicide situation and it is probably only chance which results in one becoming a victim and the other an offender. At any rate, connotations of a victim as a weak and

passive individual, seeking to withdraw from an assaultive situation, and of an offender as a brutal, strong, and overly aggressive person seeking out his victim, are not always correct. Societal attitudes are generally positive towards the victim and negative towards the offender, who is often feared as a violent and dangerous threat to others. (Marvin Wolfgang, 1958:265)

Carolyn Block (1992) examined the phenomenon of victim-precipitation criminal incidents by codifying the empirical observation that violence attracts violence. In her analysis, Block states that the concept of victim precipitation can lead to the trap of blaming the victim (suspect) for the resulting act of violence. In avoiding the blame-the-victim trap, she states that researchers may fall into another trap—that of blaming the "wicked offender" (the police officer) for the violent and sometimes deadly outcome. Block argues that in order to avoid either of these traps, a more general approach must be taken in explaining the interaction of the victim and the offender during a violent situation.

Block adds that, when examining victim-precipitated incidents, the entire spectrum of epidemiological risk must be taken into account, including the risk of a particular type of individual being killed by a particular type of offender (police officer). In essence, police shootings must recognize that the participation of the suspect and the police officer cannot be understood independently of each other; they both must be seen in light of the total situation.

Critical-Incident Stress: The Personal Impact

As has been illustrated, there is a need for police to be aware of the dynamics associated with a police shooting and the tragic consequences that occur to both the deceased and the surviving officer. Often, the police officer and his or her family are left alone to understand and come to terms with a police shooting incident that may include a controversial death.

Interviews with police officers who had been involved in a fatal shooting have revealed the personal impact that the event has had on their lives and their families (Klinger, 2001; Parent, 1996, 2004). Without exception, all of the officers involved in a fatal shooting indicated that they had, to some degree, been subject to the physiological, psychological, physical, and emotional factors associated with critical incident stress.

The most commonly cited physiological factors experienced by these officers included perception of time, visual, and auditory distortions. As the incident unfolded, individual officers noted that their deadly-force encounter appeared to occur in slow motion. Often, their vision was focused upon the perceived threat, with minimal awareness of the events taking place around them. Finally, when shots were fired, they were generally heard as muffled sounds, even though the officers were not wearing ear-protection devices (Parent, 1996).

> We stopped the car and got out. A couple of seconds later a shot rang out. My focus was on the threat. I fired three rounds off at the silhouette and hit the target, one fatal at the head. It was like a scene in a bad movie. It all happened in slow motion. I just knew I got him… it all happened in less than ten seconds. "X" (my partner) was lucky not to be killed.

In addition to perception distortions, the majority of these police officers stated that they experienced a loss of fine motor coordination upon conclusion of their deadly encounter. Typically, their hands would begin to shake or their legs would go into uncontrollable spasms. After the fatal shooting incident concluded, the majority of officers interviewed stated that they faced a wide variety of psychological and physical effects associated with critical incident stress. The physical effects included a loss of appetite, sleeping pattern changes, and a marked decrease in their sex drive, resulting in an absence of sexual relations with their spouse or partner. One officer stated:

> Your mind says "You can't cope with this." Sleep? I'd wake up every night for several months. I would never re-live the incident but my mind would focus on the incident.

The psychological effects reported included depression, guilt, nightmares, flashbacks, and a heightened sense of danger and fear. One of the officers related the flashbacks as a "video going on in your head that you can't control; it just keeps playing the video over and over and over again and you've got no control to turn it off." Another officer reported an overwhelming and uncontrollable emotional state that caused him to suddenly weep and cry for days on end (Parent, 1996).

In some instances, the factors associated with critical incident stress are further intensified when the shooting incident is a suicide-by-cop. In these particular cases, the officer is faced with the additional impact of killing an individual who is, in essence, seeking help from the police in doing something that he or she could not do—the taking of his or her own life. For some officers, this situation results in the additional impact of feelings that include anger and confusion for "being set up," manipulated, and tricked into using deadly force.

> I was angry; there was no reason for him to kill me. He was gonna shoot me, he would have killed me. If anything, I waited too long (before I shot and killed him). I was lucky.

In other instances, the officer felt responsible for the surviving members of the deceased, as the officer had taken away the life of their loved one. In this regard, one officer stated:

No matter what I think about this guy and what he did, I can't help but feel responsible to his mother and father. I know that every Christmas, for the rest of their lives, it will never be the same for them because of me. I took away their son's life, and they will never have Christmas with him again. It will never be the same for them. No matter what you think, he is still a person.

Another officer who was involved in a suicide-by-cop shooting incident added:

From the decent people, I got a lot of support. Generally supportive and understanding. However... some, the shit heads, they're critical. Sure he was a shit-head, a 99 percent shit head and I shouldn't feel sorry (re: shooting him) but... it's that one percent of him... it's tough for me to not think of him as a person.

The media frequently intensified this situation, and this was cited by most of the police officers as one of the greatest sources of stress immediately after their fatal shooting incidents. This was a consequence of the continual coverage that surrounds many of the fatal shooting incidents. Particularly painful was the speculation and supposition by many journalists who were impatient regarding the release of the official police investigation.

These journalists often produce media articles that are written in a negative or distorted manner regarding the actions of the shooting officer or the police agency. Issues such as racism, inadequate training, or improper police procedure were often cited as explanations for the shooting incident, particularly during suicide-by-cop incidents where the deceased was later found to have an inoperable or imaginary weapon (Parent, 1996, 2004; Geberth, 1994).

These officers stated that the negative slant portrayed in many of the media articles served to further intensify their emotional and psychological state in regards to the fatal shooting incident.

The media; I've never had a problem with what we did. We're the good guys and out here to help the public and did a good thing; what we're suppose to do; and now we're getting fucked. I couldn't watch the television or read the papers; [they were] obvious examples of distortion.

One of the police officers related to the event as to the "death of a child," an event in his life that he described as painful and sad, something that he wished had never happened, something that he has obviously tried to put behind him. When the officer was interviewed, he produced a file containing more than 50 separate newsprint articles surrounding his fatal suicide-by-cop shooting incident (Parent, 1996).

The police officer's mother had followed the shooting incident through the local print media. She had clipped and saved all of the print articles that were related to her son's fatal shooting incident. In conjunction with the 50-plus newsprint articles, the officer kept a "scrapbook" regarding the legal, union, and departmental correspondence that were related specifically to his shooting incident. The officer stated that he has never been able to bring himself to read most of the print articles within the file. Many of the articles that were first published, initially after the shooting, indicate inappropriate action by the officer. Some of these headlines are as follows:

> "Relatives Want Police Charged In Shooting," "Were Four Bullets The Only Answer?" "Police Procedures Deficient," "Mayor Queries Police Policy," "Police Training Called Flawed," "Slain Man's Mother Asks For Probe," "Police Stay Silent Until Inquiry Done."

However, months later, when a public inquest into the shooting was held and independent evidence presented, the police were exonerated for their actions. During the public inquest, the media coverage was less frequent and inflammatory, but continued to be sensational in nature. Some of these newsprint headlines include:

> "Said 'Stay Back,' Then He Died," "I Would Have Shot Him Too," "Cops Off Hook In Fatal Shooting," "Officer Sorry, But Says Forced To Shoot."

Only upon the conclusion of this public disclosure of evidence were many of the officers able to get on with life and leave the tragedy of the shooting incident behind them. Even years after the fatal shooting incident had taken place, all of the officers reported that they considered it a significant event in their life, one that they will never forget. In this regard, one police officer stated:

> This guy is not gonna fuck-up my life forever. It's completely up to me whether I cope with this and get on with life. I'm sure I drank too much several times. I think about it every day.

Post-Shooting Effects and Deadly Force

In the months and years since their fatal shooting incidents occurred, many of the police officers interviewed reported a variety of personal life changes, attributing these changes to their fatal shooting. Several of the police officers who were involved in a fatal shooting reported marital or relationship breakdowns shortly after the incident. Often, these individuals stated that their relationship with their significant other was "o.k." prior to the shooting. However, when faced with the pressures and stresses that accompanied a fatal shooting, the relationship often crumbled. One officer stated, "I went through two marriages after the shooting incident." Another officer reported, "My marriage ended within a year or two after the shooting. I became distant from my wife, and I didn't talk about the shooting incident with her."

However, there was an equal number of police officers who spoke highly of their spouses or significant others, intimate relationships that served to support the police officer during a time of personal crisis. Often, these established relationships were strengthened as a result of the shooting incident. One officer in a smaller agency stated:

> The Chief said to me, "You should leave town because I'm gonna release your name." So the wife and I took off in a car and drove 4 hours away to a cabin and stayed there. We were there for a week. It gave me time to be with my wife, as a sounding board, with what happened. It took about a year for all of it to blow over.

Unfortunately, several of the officers stated that their spouses, significant others, or their children suffered as a result of their shooting incident. The police officer's fatal shooting frequently became a "family crisis." One officer stated, "My wife needed help [psychological] after what happened to me."

Finally, in a small number of instances, individual officers had suffered post-traumatic stress to such a degree that they required extensive counseling and a lengthy time away from the work site. For these individuals, their personal goal was to come to terms with an incident that has had a profound impact upon their lives, an incident that they will never forget. One officer described the impact of the suicide-by-cop shooting by stating:

> I really look forward to retiring. I've got nine years to go. My wife has noted a change in me. I've noted a change in me. If I had known the shooting incident was gonna happen, I would have taken a sick day. I wish it would never had happened.

In summary, the complexities of a suicide-by-cop incident emphasize the physiological, psychological, physical, and emotional consequences that have affected many of the police officers that have taken the life of another during the course of their duties. Traditionally, police use of deadly force has placed the police officer on the defensive, regardless of how justified the officer's actions may have been. The notion of a "license to kill" and a "shield to hide behind" have created a social stigma that frequently surfaces with a police shooting. These officers are frequently exonerated in a public forum for their actions but, unfortunately, many have paid a personal price for the life that has been taken.

Discussion

It remains unclear why some individuals confront police with a lethal or perceived lethal threat. However, research findings of various studies indicate that suicidal ideation and the phenomenon of suicide-by-cop are significant factors in the lethal threats that law enforcement personnel within North America face. Individuals predisposed to suicide have, in many instances, confronted armed police in an attempt to escalate the situation in which they have placed themselves.

In other instances, alcohol, substance abuse, mental disorder, and suicidal tendencies were added to a complex picture of irrational behavior. Individuals acting in a bizarre or irrational manner have confronted armed police with either inferior or imaginary weaponry, resulting in their death. These victims have often precipitated their own demise.

Regardless of the subject's motivation or mind-set, it remains that these individuals chose to pose a perceived lethal threat to law enforcement personnel. In this regard, the so-called victims must share some of the responsibility during a police shooting, as it is their actions that often precipitate the final outcome. An outcome that tragically has resulted in a "lose–lose situation," often having negative consequences for the victims, their family, the police agency, and the police officer involved.

The findings of this research underscore the need for a greater degree of emphasis to be placed upon the training of both police recruits and in-service personnel in relation to those verbal and tactical skills associated with suicide intervention and dealing with the mentally ill. In addition to this training, police personnel must be made aware of the dynamics associated with victim-precipitated homicide, with a particular emphasis on the phenomenon of suicide-by-cop. Police officers require training that will allow them to identify suicidal and psychotic cues when confronting an individual who is violent and dangerous. By identifying these cues, the police officer may be able to assess which use-of-force option is appropriate for the circumstances at hand.

Police training must additionally emphasize the importance of information gathering prior to police personnel attending a call for service. Call-takers and dispatch personnel within police agencies must be aware of the dynamics associated with a victim-precipitated police shooting. It is essential that call-takers and dispatch personnel solicit pertinent information from members of the public who summon the police. Dispatch personnel must then relay this information to the attending police units, prior to their arrival, to allow for a planned police response.

Finally, there is also a need to understand and identify the systematic differences in subjects' motivations that result in a police shooting. By identifying these differences, police personnel will be better equipped in responding to incidents of a potential lethal threat. Future research regarding the police use of deadly force and the role of individuals rendered vulnerable due to their emotional, mental, and physical state will hopefully provide additional insight and solutions to a complex social problem.

References

Australian Institute of Criminology (1998) Police shootings 1990–9. No. 89, *Trends and Issues in Crime and Criminal Justice*. Canberra, Australia.

Block, C. R. and Block, R. (1992) Beyond Wolfgang: An agenda for homicide research in the 1990s. *The Journal of Criminal Justice*, 14, 31–70.

Bureau of Justice Statistics (2008) *Sourcebook of Criminal Justice Statistics—2008*. U.S. Department of Justice, Washington, DC.

Durkheim, E. (1951) *Suicide: A Study in Sociology* (trans. J.A. Spaulding and G. Simpson). Free Press, New York. (originally published, 1897.)

Foote, W. E. (1998) Victim-precipitated homicide. In *Lethal Violence: A Sourcebook on Fatal Domestic, Acquaintance and Stranger Violence* (H. Hall ed.). CRC Press, New York.

Geberth, V. J. (1993, July) Suicide-by-cop: Inviting death from the hands of a police officer. *Law and Order*, 41, 105–109.

Geberth, V. J. (1994, January) The racial component in suicide-by-cop incidents: Public perception confused. *Law and Order*, 42, 318–319.

Geller, W. A. and Scott, M. S. (1992) *Deadly Force: What We Know: A Practitioners Desk Reference on Police-Involved Shootings*. Police Executive Research Forum, Washington, DC.

Homant, R. J. and Kennedy, D. B. (2000) Suicide by police: A proposed typology of law enforcement officer assisted suicide. *Policing: An International Journal of Police Strategies and Management*, 23, 339–355.

Homant, R. J., Kennedy, D. B., and Hupp, R. T. (2000) Real and perceived danger in police officer assisted suicide. *Journal of Criminal Justice*, 28(1), 43–52.

Hutson, H. R., Anglin, D., Yarbrough, J., Hardaway, K., Russell, M., Strote, J., Canter, M., and Blum, B. (1998) Suicide-by-cop. *Annals of Emergency Medicine*, 32, 665–669.

Justice Institute of British Columbia (JIBC) (2009) *Recruit Training Manual. Block I and Block III*. New Westminster, BC.

Kennedy, D. B., Homant, R. J., and Hupp, R. T. (1998, August) Suicide-by-cop. *FBI Law Enforcement Bulletin*, 67, 21–27.

Keram, E., Farrell, B., Perrou, B., and Parent, R. (2000) Suicide-by-cop: Incident management and litigation in Canada and the United States, Paper presented at *Annual Meeting of American Academy of Psychiatry and the Law*.

Klinger, D. (2001) *Police Responses to Officer-Involved Shootings*. U.S. Department of Justice, St. Louis, MO.

Lord, V. (2004) *Suicide-by-Cop—Inducing Officers to Shoot: Practical Directions for Recognition, Resolution and Recovery*. Looseleaf, Flushing, NY.

Luckenbill, D. F. (1977) Criminal homicide as a situated transaction, *Social Problems*, 25, 176–186.

Matulia, K. J. (1985) *A Balance of Forces: Model Deadly Force Policy and Procedure* (2nd edn.). International Association of Chiefs of Police, Gaithersburg, MD.

Mohandie, K. and Meloy, J. R. (2000) Clinical and forensic indicators of "Suicide-by-cop". *Journal of Forensic Sciences*, 45, 384–389.

Mohandie, K., Meloy, J. R., and Collins, P. I. (2009) Suicide-by-cop among officer-involved shooting cases. *Journal of Forensic Sciences*, 54(2), 456–462.

Murray, R. and Zentner, J. (1975) *Nursing Concepts for Health Promotion*. Prentice-Hall, Toronto, Ontario.

New Zealand Police (2002) Fatal police shooting incidents 1941–2001. New Zealand Police National Headquarters Document. Wellington, New Zealand.

Officer Down Memorial Page (2010) http://www.odmp.org

Parent, R. (1996) Aspects of police use of deadly force in British Columbia: The phenomenon of victim-precipitated homicide. Simon Fraser University, Burnaby, BC, Master's thesis.

Parent, R. (2004) Aspects of police use of deadly force in North America: The phenomenon of victim-precipitated homicide. Simon Fraser University, Burnaby, BC, Doctorial thesis.

Parent, R. B. and Verdun-Jones, S. (1998) Victim-precipitated homicide: Police use of deadly force in British Columbia, *Policing: An International Journal of Police Strategies and Management*, 21, 432–448.

Police Scientific Development Branch (1996) A review of the discharge of firearms by police in England and Wales 1991–1993. Joint Standing Committee on the Police Use of Firearms, St. Albans, U.K.

Schneidman, E. S. (1981) The psychological autopsy. Suicide and life threatening behavior. *The American Association of Suicidology*, 11(4), 325–340.

Sheehan, D. and Warren, J. (2001) From critical incident stress to police suicide: Prevention through mandatory academy and on-the-job training programs. *Suicide and Law Enforcement*. U.S. Department of Justice, FBI, Washington, DC.

Skolnick, J. (1966) *Justice without Trial: Law Enforcement in a Democratic Society*. Wiley & Sons, Inc., New York.

Timmer, J. S. (2005) *Politiegeweld: geweldgebruik van en tegen de politie in Nederland*. Kluwer Publishers, Amsterdam, Holland.

Uniform Crime Reports (2004) *Crime in the United States*. Federal Bureau of Investigation, U. S. Department of Justice, Washington, DC.

U.S. Department of Justice (2004) *Local Police Departments, 2000*. Office of Justice Programs, Bureau of Justice Statistics, Washington, DC.

Van Zandt, C. R. (1993, July) Suicide-by-cop. *The Police Chief*, 60, 24–30.

Wolfgang, M. E. (1958) *Patterns in Criminal Homicide*. University of Pennsylvania Press, Philadelphia, PA.

Wolfgang, M. E. and Ferracuti, F. (1967) *The Subculture of Violence: Towards an Integrated Theory in Criminology*. Tavistock, New York.

Paradigm Shifts: Policing as Democracy Evolves

Changes in the Police of Argentina as Democracy Progresses

10

SEBASTIÁN SAL

Contents

Introduction

During the last century, the Argentine Republic suffered many changes in its political map, changing from democratic governments to dictatorial ones from 1930 to 1983. These kinds of changes have affected the peoples' human rights and the scope of police activities. There have also been significant changes that the Argentinean Police Department has suffered since 1983. In that year, the last dictatorial government switched to a democratic one. As a result, there have been limits on the functions that the police officials in Argentina may now carry out without committing violations to citizen and human rights.

Changes in the Argentinean Police Force

There are different changes that can be made in order to modify a police organization. However, much depends on the kind of country and on the historical events and practices. A "police reform may connote something different: depolitization (e.g., in postcommunist Eastern Europe), decentralization (e.g., in postwar Germany), increased responsiveness to ethnic concerns (e.g., in Los Angeles or Bosnia), or better oversight systems (e.g., in New York City). But in Latin America and the Caribbean, demilitarizing public security—ending the extraordinary military control over and nature of policing—is correctly viewed as a first step in the ability of elected civilian officials to exercise political power" (Call, 1998). The Argentine case is a mix between depolitization and demilitarization of the police power.

Changes were made rather slowly in the Argentinean Police Department. One has to keep in mind that every country that suffered a dictatorial government had a very strong and tough police, in order to help the dictatorial governments control the people. That is why trying to change the Police Department and its functions in these kinds of countries is similar to a very acute and difficult surgery. At the beginning of most fledgling democratic governments, certain crimes related with this new kind of "freedom"—for example drug consumption and prostitution—normally increase.

Therefore, the new government and the police in Argentina had to deal with a novel and different problem. Argentina was a drug free country until 1983. Since then, drug consumption has been increasing day by day. Today illicit drugs are a major problem in Argentina. For example, on February 2005, 60 kg of cocaine was found at the airport of Barajas, Madrid in Spain. The drugs, which had been placed in two suitcases, came from Buenos Aires, Argentina. The luggage was found abandoned in the luggage room. The suitcases were labeled as "diplomatic" with the address of the Argentine Embassy. That would clearly lead one to believe that Argentina is not only a drug consumer country but also an exporting one.

According to Argentinean government statistics, there was more cocaine seized in the first three quarters of 2004 than in the entire 2003 calendar year. In addition to Argentine traffickers, there is evidence that Colombian drug traffickers have greatly increased their presence in all aspects of the Argentinean drug trade. In 2004, there was an increase in domestic cocaine production, using coca as base imported from Bolivia. In November 2004, the Federal Police seized 32.5 kg of cocaine from a Colombian-run cocaine laboratory in the Buenos Aires area.* Nowadays, the huge problem in Argentina involves synthetics drugs (e.g., ecstasy and amphetamines) that are produced in the Buenos Aires province and exported to Europe.

To fight this problem, the government started with the most basic thing—education. A seminar in toxicology for Argentinean police officers was presented on February 14, 1984. In addition, the Argentinean government improved the exchange of information with the Drug Enforcement Administration (DEA) of the United States. In this way, some police officers were sent to Glynco, Georgia, in the United States in order to take part in a seminar related to recognizing and arresting drug dealers. A new department was created in the Argentinean police institution. It was called "División Drogas Peligrosas" (Dangerous Drugs Division). Since then, the interchange

---

* http://www.state.gov/g/inl/rls/nrcrpt/2005/vol1/html/42363.htm

of information between American and Argentinean Police Departments has increased each year.

Cooperation between the U.S. government and Argentine authorities, both federal and provincial, continued to be excellent. During 2004, the U.S. government assistance supplied a wealth of equipment and training programs for Argentine law enforcement personnel. Examples of these U.S.-funded programs in 2004 include two law enforcement tactical training courses provided by DEA; a money laundering course sponsored by the Department of Homeland Security (ICE); an airport narcotics interdiction course sponsored by DEA/INL; and a prevention seminar by Public Affairs Section (PAS) and the U.S. Department of State. The U.S. DEA and INL also sponsored several American law enforcement professionals to participate in regional training programs.

Illicit drug legislation in Argentina was also amended. Drug crimes were declared federal crimes. This decision now permits Federal Police to investigate drug crimes all over the country. As a result, Federal Police may ask for help from and answer requests for assistance from the provincial police authorities.

Many more positive developments have occurred. In 1998, a witness protection program for key witnesses in drug-related prosecutions was created. In 1997, the United States and Argentina signed a new extradition treaty, which entered into force in June 2000. In 1990, Argentina and the United States signed a mutual legal assistance treaty that entered into force in 1993. This supports Argentina's participation in the 1988 UN Drug Convention.

The Argentinean government had to strongly address the illicit drugs trade. After an incredible long discussion, the Argentinean Congress approved the Money Laundering Law in the 2000.* Before this, Argentina did not have any legislation against Money Laundering. Other new economic crimes involving smuggling and drug trading were committed. Tax evasion and suspicious bank transactions have increased dramatically in Argentina since 1983. The government created a new law (23771, modified later by other laws) in which tax evasion was prosecuted with tough punishments. With the increased use of technology, computer related crimes have also appeared.

An important event happened in July 1984. The Argentine Republic signed the Human Rights American Agreement, commonly known as the "Pacto de San Jose de Costa Rica." This landmark action initiated the major initiative in respecting human rights in Argentina, thereby mandating that police officers undertake extensive training and participating in seminars

---

* Argentine Law 25.246 "Lavado de Activos de origen delictivo." In the year 2008, a new law was passed by the Congress, allowing the introduction of money from abroad, without any state control. It seems that money laundering is not more a crime in Argentina.

related to human rights issues. The goal of the Argentinean administration was and continues to be an effort to train police officers to develop a new moral consciousness. This movement has had a great impact in the people of the country as well as in the police officers since this Human Right Agreement was included in the National Constitution in 1995.

In September 1985, a new law was passed by the Congress, i.e., Law # 23.098, which created an office that provides permanent service and information related to *habeas corpus* matters. What this means is that police officers must always be available in order to assist judges to find quick solutions to any requirement or request made by lawyers or common people in missing-persons cases.

Police procedural rules were gradually but extensively amended. Before the new legislation, police officers were allowed to stop and arrest people and detain them for 24h in order to identify them. They could keep this people in their precincts if they failed to show proper identification document, after a police request, or if someone was seen acting with "suspicious behavior."* This law was clearly related with dictatorial governments.

A very important legal revision occurred in 1994 when Article 5.1 of the Organizational Police Law was changed. Presently, police officers can only stop and detain people for identification for no longer than 6h. However, it continues to be legal for police officers to request an identification document from people on the street, and they are then free to leave once this is done.†

Many judges, including those of the Argentinean Supreme Court, have ruled that many Police Organizational Laws are against the National

---

* The "suspicious behavior" is not an objective question. People could be stopped for identification, because police functions include the prevention of crimes. The "stop for ID" must be done with prudence and fairness. See, "Dell Aquila (1991). "La detención de una persona con fines identificatorios, al resultar "sospechosa" su conducta al personal policial, aunque no se explicite la situación objetiva que llevo a tal estado de sospecha, no es inválida, pues dentro de las facultades legalmente acordadas a la policía de prevención y represión, se encuentra la de demorar a las personas a fin de indentificarlas, siempre que esta facultad sea ejercida dentro de un marco de prudencia y razonabilidad, respetando las garantías constitucionales protegidas." Vázquez Acuña (en disidencia), Giudice Bravo y Ragucci (h) (National High Court Judges).

† If it is not an abuse of police officers' duties, they can stop people in the street for identification. Sometimes the abuse depends on how long are you stopped. See M.M. et al. (1985). "Debe revocarse la sentencia apelada y absolver a los procesados del delito de privación ilegítima de la libertad, por cuanto ninguna ilicitud configura la actitud de los procesados al interceptar en la vía publica a los sospechosos, interrogarlos y exigirles la exhibición de sus documentos identificatorios, sin que sea válido cuestionar el procedimiento por su extensión temporal mientras este no resulta a ojos vista totalmente desproporcionada e importe, por si sola, un lado abuso funcional; situación que no se da en autos por que los jóvenes fueron prontamente autorizados a circular." Valdovinos, Campos, Escobar. (High Court Judges).

Constitution. Ultimately, in March 1998, the Police Organizational Law was declared illegal and was no longer valid, and a new Cohabitation Code was enacted in Buenos Aires City. Argentina is a Federal State and each province has its own proper procedural rules. On the contrary, Federal Criminal Code is applied all over the country.

New rules were created by the Argentinean police related to misdemeanor offences and subsequent arrest procedures. The following rights were established for criminals after being arrested: (1) the criminal is allowed to make a phone call to whoever they may want in order to let that person know that they are under arrest and provide their location; (2) the suspect must be informed that they can remain silent, and that their silence does not create any criminal presumption against them; (3) the arrestee must be informed of the crime that they have been charged with before answering any questions asked by police officers; (4) the suspect must be informed of all the proof that the police have against them; (5) the arrestee will be "invited" to make a statement with the possibility of refusing to speak and be advised that this would not create any negative consequence on them; and finally (6) once a resolution has been made, they may appeal it. It is important to note that for serious offenses, i.e., felonies, police officers are not allowed to take any statements from the suspect, nor from the witnesses. Only the judge with jurisdiction in this kind of crime can assume these responsibilities. If police arrest someone because they are suspected of committing a serious crime, they have to provide the opportunity for immediate intervention to the proper judge. As a result, any statement made by criminals in the presence of police officers is not valid as a confession.* Nevertheless, if the criminal does make a statement in the presence of police officers, they are responsible to inform the respective judge involved. Judges are able to use the criminals' statements in order to obtain evidence,[†] but not as a confession.

---

* Police Officers are allowed to take statement to criminals only in misdemeanors. As I mentioned supra, for serious offenses, police could not take statements, and the criminal's enunciation could not be taken as a confession. See Fed. (1989). "Si bien el inc.1 del art. 316 del C.P.M.P. establece que los dichos efectuados ante la autoridad de prevención carecerán de valor probatorio y no podrán ser utilizados en la causa, parece claro que esa restricción esta referida a los efectos legales de la de la confesión—como reza la primera parte del artículo citado—y que debe ser vinculada a la prohibición de cualquier cláusula que torne obligatoria la autoincriminación." Costa, Rodríguez Basavilbaso—Cortelezzi. (Federal High Court Judges).

† In this way, the Judges of the National High Court, # 4 ruled the case "Aisemberg Oscar." "Si bien nuestro Código de Procedimiento en Materia Penal impide acordar valor probatorio a la declaración espontanea para ser invocada per se, ello no la convierte en un acto contra la ley ni nulifica su contenido que puede muy bien ser aprovechado de existir pistas e investigaciones que la policía esta obligada a seguir, logrando en muchas oportunidades establecer sucesos ilícitos." Campos, Escobar, Valdovino (Judges) (1990).

Traffic control is another field that highlights the changes that have occurred in the police department. Some police functions have been delegated to private corporations since 1986. For example, a private company is in charge of the surveillance of the transit of the City of Buenos Aires. This company is authorized to charge fines to the citizens of Buenos Aires City if they commit any traffic violations. This turns out to be a very profitable arrangement for the police department, because 50% of the income from the tickets that the private company collects goes to the Police Department.

The amount of police training has also been increased. In September 1984, a new postgraduate course commenced in the University of Buenos Aires related to Legal Chemical Tests. New study plans were introduced into the Federal Police School. Many credits in the fields of criminal law and social science are required in order to get the police degree. In January 1995, an agreement was signed between the police department and the University Of Morón, in order to permit police officers to take part in seminars in the School of Law and Engineering of that University. In addition, many seminars were presented related to counterterrorism tactics. Reflecting the changes in the Argentinean police, the United Nations peacekeeping program sent some police officers to the policing mission in Slovenia.

The Argentinean police have also improved the personal standards of their officers. Since 1996, psychological tests have been mandatory for police officers that take part in high-risk procedures. Moreover, in 1996 a new internal norm was dictated by the police department; no one can be promoted to chief constable if they do not have 22 years of service in the Police Department and possess a college degree. In August 1997, by resolution number 1431, the National Department of Culture and Education created a new university statute for the Argentinean Federal Police. The statute rules the admission process in order to achieve the Law Degree in the Federal Police College.

Although high standards of entry into newly reformed police agencies are generally important for the effectiveness and reputation of those organizations, relaxing such standards to ensure representation of important political, religious, gender, or ethnic groups into the police force may be worthwhile, if such groups would otherwise be excluded or severely underrepresented in police forces (Call, 1998).

New plans are being implemented in order to create new schools inside the Police Department. These plans consist of creating Schools of Biological Science, Business, Engineering in Telecommunications, and postgraduates degrees as Bank, Hotel and Tourism, Ecology, and Transit Safety.

Some cities have developed the community police concept in order to help and control the police activity. Many NGOs collaborate with this new project, e.g., the Jewish Mutual Association in Argentina (AMIA) and the United Nations Development Program (UNDP).

For example, in the city of Rosario, Province of Santa Fe, the UNDP is sponsoring a new initiative for local improvement, where learning about human rights and applying human rights are seen as a way of positively influencing life in the community. This initiative considers that the relationships between the police and the population are an essential part of this approach. Known as the "Human Rights Cities Program," it is implemented in cooperation with PDHRE (the People's Movement for Human Rights Education) that first came up with and developed the concept of the human rights city program. PDHRE and INSGENAR (the Gender, Law and Development Institute) chose Rosario as the first Human Rights City in Argentina in July 1997.

Rosario is a large, industrial city with a lively cultural and civic life. Nevertheless, the crime rate has continued to rise and the number of police-involved shootings were quite high. The citizens of Rosario called some police officers "trigger-happy" because they claim that they prefer to shoot first and ask questions later. The police of Rosario had formerly received only four months of training, none of which included human rights. There was virtually no ongoing training or opportunity to enhance one's skills or advance professionally. Salary was low and corruption was common. Most of any budget increases resulted in purchasing more vehicles, weapons, and communication equipment, rather than being used to develop the intellectual capital and skills of the police officers.

By 1997, some local leaders felt that the time had come in order to try to work with the police in a constructive way. The head of the Police Academy, located in Rosario, also supported the change. Meetings were held and the proponents decided to try to implement a new human rights training course at the Academy, focusing on the new recruits, the future police.

The actual training took the form of seminars, with joint presentations by Police School faculty and civilian experts. The issues were sensitive and feelings still raw, so these proved to be wise decisions.

The first seminar discussed the right to a life free from violence with a focus on domestic violence, and the right to live in a healthy environment. The methodology involved plenty of participation and interaction—something new for the police cadets.

The domestic violence module included a role-play with the police cadets playing the role of the victim, which allowed them to see directly how the police treat the victim. The police were encouraged to express their views of the training, the issues, and to critique the entire process—something never done before at the Police Academy.

The organizations involved in the police initiative in Rosario have reached several conclusions after the seminars.* In Buenos Aires City, we are able to find a similar situation. Usually the city is under control of the Federal Police. The Federal Police depends on the Ministry of Internal Affairs, and the Ministry is part of the executive power. In other words, the National Government is in charge of the Federal Police and the security of the city of Buenos Aires.

Nevertheless, the Government of the city of Buenos Aires started a plan in order to have its own police force. In this way, they created the "Communitarian Police." The Communitarian Police was a project of the former Minister of Justice, Gustavo Beliz.[†]

---

* Conclusions stated that; (a) the process of the police inclusion in the project Rosario, Human Rights City was complex, and its development required a group of people and institutions with a clear understanding of the need to educate the police in human rights; (b) an important lesson learned from this process and to be taken into account for future activities was that the process of negotiation, management, and organization of the courses/seminars was as fundamental as the seminars themselves; (c) it was also important to count on the support and sponsorship of prestigious agencies and institutions, such as the European Union, which helped motivate both the police and the provincial government to participate; (d) many police officers learned that human rights are not something "bad," belonging to the "enemy" who had always criticized them, but that they themselves, since they were persons, were entitled to human rights that must be respected; and that an increase in the police budget alone was not necessary to respect human rights; (e) the human rights organizations learned about how difficult and challenging police work is and that police officers themselves suffer from discrimination and abuse in some cases; (f) the NGOs were pleasantly surprised to learn that, contrary to their expectations, the police cadets were always open to discuss the issues, showed great interest, and demanded further training; (g) the human security approach made it clear that the reasons for crime and insecurity arise from social and economic problems related to poverty and discrimination; (h) there are certain indicators that have allowed the Human Rights Cities project to assess the impact of the work thus far; (i) human rights is now an official part of the Police Cadets' School syllabus; (j) a Human rights course is now included in the regular four-month training given to low-ranking cadets; (k) there is a greater openness within the police force to discuss and receive further training on issues like domestic violence, prostitution, general human rights, and public security; (l) according to some unofficial statistics, the incidence of police abuse and mistreatment appears to have declined following these trainings/workshops; (m) in some cases of sexual violence, the authorities themselves reported the involvement of their subordinates; (n) generally, the police have changed their behavior in the cases of domestic or sexual violence, even within their institution. In the past, this was an issue, which tended to be concealed and silenced. Police have created a special unit addressing sexual violence against women; (o) other human rights organizations have lowered their resistance to talk with the police and participate in their training; and (p) the creation of the Internal Affairs Division, has led to a review of over 3,600 cases of police corruption and "trigger-happy" officers. The Director is a strong supporter of human rights (O'Neill, 2004).

† Palermo Online Newspaper (2004) Beliz anunció la Creación de la Policía Comunitaria de la Ciudad. (2004) Este lunes, el ministro de Justicia de la Nación, Gustavo Beliz, anunció el Plan Nacional de Justicia y Seguridad, compuesto por decretos y proyectos de ley con los que se intentará atacar la inseguridad en todo el país. En la Ciudad de Buenos Aires, se impulsará la creación de la policía comunitaria que incorporará, en los próximos tres años, 1.500 efectivos nuevos. También se promueve la transferencia de competencias penales a la Justicia Contravencional porteña y la apertura de fiscalías en todos los barrios. http://www.palermonline.com.ar/noticias/nota234_beliz.htm

At the beginning, the number of communitarian officers was 500, and the idea was to increase this number until it reached 1500 members during the following years. The Chief of the Government of the Police of Buenos Aires said, "…for the first time the city of Buenos Aires will finance 500 new agents of the Federal Police. This is within the agreement signed among the National government, the ministry of Justice and the City, because it is necessary to have greater police presence in the street. It is a decisive element in order to reduce and to contain the crime. In many cases, the police did not count with the appropriated elements. We [the city] have acquired them, as well as vehicles so that the police could perform better its functions…."*

The agents of the new Communitarian Police are not working in any police station, but in the green parks, conflicting zones of transit, and other public places. The Communitarian Police depends on the Metropolitan Security Office and Technical Committee of Citizen Security, whose work consists in analyzing, coordinating, and orchestrating citizen security programs.

This committee is integrated by members of the National and the City Government as well as by the Federal Police Department.[†] This indicates that the National Government still has some kind of control over these new police agents.

Besides, the Government of the city of Buenos Aires created a new kind of police force called the *La Guardia Urbana* (the Urban Guard). This police force is exclusively under the control of the city of Buenos Aires. The Federal Police Department and the National Government have no part in it.

La Guardia Urbana is an unarmed civil corps. It is formed with 100 members—it will increase to 600 members in the future with 30 trucks and bicycles. This corps is not a "parallel police," and does not replace the functions established for the Federal Police. *La Guardia Urbana* works in cooperation with other security forces, the Fire Department, the Civil Defence Department, and the Federal Police and the Wealth Department of the City (SAME).

---

* "Por primera vez en la ciudad de Buenos Aires se financiarán a 500 agentes nuevos de la Policía Federal, esto es en el marco de un acuerdo con el gobierno Nacional, con el ministerio de Justicia, porque es necesario tener mayor presencia policial, es un elemento decisivo, se ha comprobado, para bajar y contener el delito. En muchos casos, la policía no contaba con elementos y nosotros los hemos adquirido, así como vehículos para que la policía tuviera facilidad para desempeñar sus funciones." http://www.buenosaires.gov.ar/areas/seguridad_justicia/seguridad_urbana/noticias/

† Los agentes de la nueva Policía Comunitaria no trabajarán en comisarías, sino en los parques, plazas, espacios verdes, zonas conflictivas de tránsito y otros lugares públicos que resulten de la ejecución del Plan de Prevención del Delito. También serán auxiliares de los funcionarios del Gobierno de la Ciudad, del Poder Judicial y del Ministerio Público.

The main role of the *Guardia Urbana* is the prevention of crimes, specifically misdemeanors. For example, the *Guardia Urbana* agents are in charge of preventing any damages to public places (squares, monuments), to protect and aid tourist—many of the agents are bilinguals—to help school students in the street, and to organize the car traffic in rush hours.*

What is, however, highly interesting is that the residents of Buenos Aires routinely report that they have not seen any of these agents in the street. If the *Guardia Urbana* agents are not in the tourist and downtown areas, then where are they? Buenos Aires citizens are very angry about this situation. Many of them think that "this is more of the same"—that these new agents will be corrupt. Many think that this is a demagogic decision, a politic propaganda. In fact, no one trusts or believes in this new corps.

In the end, none of the above solutions had functioned well. In fact, the *Guardia Urbana* was dissolved and it appears that the Police Community Project never truly materialized.

In 2008, an important law was passed by the government of Buenos Aires city creating the Police of Buenos Aires City. The recruitment for this new agency has started, and it is expected to be fully functional in three years (2011).

What about the Province of Buenos Aires? It is believed that the Province of Buenos Aires has the most corrupt police force in Argentina and is one of the places in which a huge percentage of the nation's crimes occur. An emblematic case, called the Blumberg case, which involved a kidnapping followed by a murder, drew public and political attention to the police role in crime fighting. Juan Carlos Blumberg, father of the murdered Axel Blumberg, proposed to apply the model of community policing in New York City to the neighborhoods of the Buenos Aires province. He had drawn this idea after

---

* Palermo Online Newspaper, 2005. Cuales son sus Funciones? Su presencia debe fortalecer la política de seguridad y reducir los índices de conflictividad urbanos. Actúa en todo el territorio de la Ciudad durante 24 horas todos los días del año. La Guardia Urbana se ocupa de detectar situaciones de riesgo y emergencia en la vía pública, brindando ayuda hasta tanto acudan los medios de respuesta específica, por ejemplo ante un accidente o un incendio. Contribuye a la seguridad pública. Controla los espacios verdes –para evitar peleas o daños a monumentos, al césped, etc., los corredores turísticos—hay guardias urbanos bilingües para orientar a los extranjeros—y las inmediaciones de establecimientos educativos. Están presentes en los quince Senderos Seguros de la Ciudad. Colabora con el ordenamiento del tránsito. Cumple funciones educativas y preventivas y promueve el cumplimiento de las normas viales—control de alcoholemia, del casco o del cinturón de seguridad. Está autorizada a labrar actas. Aplica técnicas de mediación y resolución alternativas ante conflictos comunitarios. Participa en las estrategias de prevención comunitaria desarrolladas por el Plan de Prevención del Delito. Promueve el cese de las conductas que configuren faltas ya que podrá labrar actas y efectuar decomisos en bares y restaurantes que ocupen el espacio público fuera de la normativa. Colabora en los operativos de verificación y control, verificando el cumplimiento efectivo de las clausuras. http://www.palermonline.com.ar/noticias002/nota163_guardia.htm

meeting with Carlos Medina, director of the "Manhattan Institute," created specifically for conducting research on policing.[*]

This proposal is similar to city or county police departments in the United States or the *Policía Municipal* in Spain. It is also similar to the "Communitarian Police" and the *Guardia Urbana* in Buenos Aires city. In Buenos Aires Province, some neighborhood security forums began to work in order to collaborate with the provincial police power. Some recommendations made by this forum include: (a) organize informal meeting with institutions and citizens in each neighborhood to review security matters and other subjects, of local interest, in order to accompany dissemination campaigns with concrete actions; (b) complete zonal analysis by neighborhoods including needs and resources, based on crime maps in order to design prevention projects in conjunction with the authorities and NGOs; (c) promote the responsible participation, granting transparency through audits and performance control; (d) ensure the genuine participation of the community in their claims, leaving aside political opportunism and self-promotion; (e) facilitate citizens' access to denouncements informing them of their rights and guarantees and accompanying the denouncing neighbor in the claim; (f) strengthen relations between NGOs, minority organizations, justice, and penitentiary service, to create a web of assistance to prisoners; (g) consolidate mutual cooperation with municipal governments and local police, in order to secure credibility on institutions to promote community participation; (h) collaborate with police stations in order to activate operational actions and speed in responses to prisoners on their social requirements, casual and jurisdictional; and (i) control and cooperate in maintaining satisfactory prisons for the social recovery of prisoners.[†]

The Rosario Project, the communitarian police, the Guardia Urbana, and the proposals for the Buenos Aires Province have the same idea: to bring the police closer to common people, to create confidence between the police officers and the individuals, to teach police officers to respect human rights, and to fight crimes from different perspectives.

Limits for Police Activity

Where is the limit on the human rights on criminal suspects? When exactly do the police violate them? For example, can the police beat or shoot a kidnapper who has hostages? In which situations may the police apply deadly

[*] The mission of the Inter-American Policy Exchange at the Manhattan Institute is to foster increased contact, collaboration, and cooperation among institutions and individuals in the Americas that will result in benefits for both hemispheres. http://www.manhattan-institute.org/

[†] http://www.partnersglobal.org/case_studies/Supp%20Materials/Argentina-publicsafety-recomm.html

force upon criminals? It is hard to apply common sense to these situations. As everybody knows "common sense is the less common of the senses."

Sometimes, we have heard "The police is badly trained and under paid, and they're not respected... Instead of enforcing the law, they're raising the level of violence in this society."* Clearly, sometimes this is true.

Criminals, without doubt, have the same rights as everybody else. The difference is that they put themselves in a risky situation and do not respect the human rights of the rest of the population—the law abiding. One can find similar situations in countries that passed laws against terrorist crimes, laws that affect civil rights.†

The contrast between the police and criminals should be this one: Police respect human rights, criminals do not. If the Police do not respect human rights, there are no differences between cops and criminals. However, some might think that if the police respect human rights, then the criminals have an advantage.

---

* "Cops say it's a kinder, safer bullet, but it certainly isn't gentler. The new expanding hollow-point bullets city cops will be getting soon don't ricochet and are less likely to hit innocent bystanders in a street shootout. What the bullets do is expand and slow to a stop when they hit flesh or bone with the hollowed-out tip filling instantly with human tissue and blood. Civil Rights advocates have long criticized them for their brutal power and activist Al Sharpton complains city cops will be carrying out 'on the street death penalties.' Cops say the first delivery of the new bullets—to replace the old full metal jacket ones—is expected any day." Tuesday March 4th 7:08 AM EST New Bullets To Be Issued To Police By Newsradio 88 Staff. http://ny.yahoo.com/external/wcbs_radio/stories/8574772853.html

† House Reauthorizes USA Patriot Act. Reuters. Published: July 22, 2005. The House of Representatives, ignoring protests from civil liberties groups, renewed the USA Patriot Act on Thursday mostly along party lines, to make permanent the government's unprecedented powers to investigate suspected terrorists. Sixteen provisions of the 2001 law, hastily enacted in response to the Sept. 11 attacks on New York and Washington, are due to expire at the end of this year unless renewed by Congress. President Bush, who has repeatedly called on lawmakers to make the entire law permanent, commended lawmakers for approving the measure. "The Patriot Act is a key part of our efforts to combat terrorism and protect the American people, and the Congress needs to send me a bill soon that renews the act without weakening our ability to fight terror," the president said in statement. The House reauthorized the act by 257–171 with several changes designed to increase judicial and political oversight of some of its most controversial provisions.... The original act allowed expanded surveillance of terror suspects and gave the government the ability to go to a secret court to seize the personal records of suspects from bookstores, libraries, businesses, hospitals and other organizations—the so-called "library clause." House Republicans agreed last week that this clause—perhaps the most contentious—and another allowing so-called roving wiretaps, which permits the government to eavesdrop on suspects as they switch from phone to phone, would be renewed for only 10 years instead of being made permanent. The Senate judiciary committee voted unanimously to recommend its own version of the act on Thursday, which included only four-year renewals of these two clauses. The full Senate is expected to take its bill up in the fall. The House also passed an amendment requiring the director of the FBI to personally approve all requests for library or bookstore records and a number of other amendments designed to add civil liberty safeguards to the bill.

Conclusion

Across the world, the police are often conveyed, at least by the media, in a negative fashion. News reports routinely highlight police abuses (rather than note the heroic and positive actions of law enforcement). However, the police are clearly needed in every society. Not only necessary, police are essential. No social order could be kept if the police were not there. "Homo homini lupus" as Thomas Hobbes said in *Leviathan*.

In South America, many police officers are badly trained and under paid. This is the first step that has to be changed. If society is trying to improve the moral strength of the police and if the goal is to get the best men and women for that institution, the governments will have to pay for this. Nobody can expect high integrity, dedication and commitment, and properly trained and educated police professionals without paying a proper salary. Competent personnel need to survive, both financially and also in their highly risky environment. It is the public's duty to promote and to encourage the hiring of the best people. Once hired, these men and women must be presented with proficient and realistic training and education. Finally, there must be some social control of police, and this includes media and public scrutiny and the development of agencies that can objectively investigate allegations of police abuse and corruption. The goal is to make the police the respectful institution that we expect them to be.

References

Call, C. Police reform, human rights and democratization in post-conflict settings: Lessons from El Salvador. Department of Political Science, Stanford University, Stanford, CA, 1998. http://idbdocs.iadb.org/wsdocs/getdocument.aspx?docnum=362102

Cámara Nacional en lo Criminal, Sala IV. M.M. et al. *Boletín de Jurisprudencia*, 1, p. 59. 1985.

Cámara Nacional en lo Criminal, Sala IV. Campos, Escobar, Valdovino, *Boletín de Jurisprudencia*, 2. 1990.

Cámara Nacional en lo Criminal, Sala II. S.G. Dell Aquila, *Boletín de Jurisprudencia*, 3, 1991.

Cámara Nacional en lo Criminal y Corr. Fed. Sala I. Loiacono, Domingo s/ infr. Arts. 293 3er. Párrafo y 189 bis del Código Penal, *Boletín de Jurisprudencia*, p. 286, 1989.

O'Neill, W.G. Police reform and human rights, 2004. http://www.pogar.org/publications/other/undp/hr/PoliceReform-04e.pdf

Severe Challenges Continue in Policing Brazil during the Twenty-First Century

11

SAIMA HUSAIN AND JAMES F. ALBRECHT

Contents

Introduction

In most cases, when examining informal communities, the police are considered formal actors within the criminal justice apparatus. However, across the globe, some law enforcement agencies have come under scrutiny in this role due to allegations of corruption and abuse. In Brazil, the police continue to be criticized for their participation in both the formal and informal communities as they engage in their traditional and formal occupations as peace maintainers and law enforcers, yet engage in such informal practices as bribe receivers and "death squad" members. One of the contributing factors to the acceptance and the abundance of the use of force by police personnel in Brazil has been the military nature of academy training. This is due to the strong role that the military has played throughout Brazil's history. This phenomenon can be explained by reviewing the national history of Brazil and the concurrent legal and justice practices that resulted from significant historic events. The involvement of the Brazilian police in the informal community is exemplified by their participation in the police "death squads" in the poor urban "*favelas*" (shantytowns). Efforts have been made over the last decade to improve police professionalism and strengthen their relationship with the public. In 1999, the Proper Police Station Program (*Programa Delegacia Legal*) was created in order to augment the productivity and quality of the service of the Civil Police, the investigatory police, in

Rio de Janeiro, Brazil. This program signified the largest and most expensive shift of the Rio de Janeiro civil police, its mentality, and procedures since the changes made at the beginning of the twentieth century. Yet 6 years after its creation, only half of the police stations within the state of Rio de Janeiro have been incorporated into the program. So even when Brazil attempts a major change to the policing field, there appears to be no continuity to any acknowledged successes and lessons learned.

The History of Brazil

In order to better understand the military mentality of the Brazilian government and its law enforcement ideology, one must consider the turn of events throughout the nation's history. In 1500, Portuguese explorers landed in the area of South America that is now referred to as Brazil. Colonists quickly arrived to cultivate brazil trees and sugar plants, and to export these products. Over two centuries, Portugal fought off the French, the Dutch, the Spaniards, and others to maintain their monopoly over this productive and vast empire. With the advent of the industrial revolution at the start of the nineteenth century, the Portuguese crown opted to advance the economy of the colony by cooperating with Great Britain, one of the world leaders in the industrialization movement. In 1815, Brazil became a kingdom, but the Portuguese Prince Pedro declared independence in 1822 and Brazil became its own empire (Burns, 1980, pp. 541–546). One of Emperor Pedro's first tasks was the promulgation of a national constitution in 1824. It was overwhelmingly accepted by most municipalities. This constitution called for the establishment of four branches, specifically the executive, the legislative, the judicial, and the moderating, which would maintain the harmony and equilibrium of the nation and her twenty provinces (Burns, 1980, pp. 164–166). As democratic as this system did sound, the fact that the emperor maintained the task of monitoring and regulating the government administrations, both nationally and locally, allowed him to preserve his control of most political resolutions. The emperor was considered "inviolable and sacred" and "not subject to any accountability" (Barman, 1988, p. 125), and had been transformed into the "supreme inspector" and "keeper of the nation's honor and conscious" (Evanson, 1969, pp. 32–34). However, as controversial as the power of the emperor was often considered, the longevity of the document (through the end of the monarchy in 1889) is evidence of the constitution's efficacy and acceptance. However, protest over imperial control did frequently lead to violence and rebellion, but the emperor continued his reign.

    Experiments with federalism and a one-regent system, consequential to revisions to the constitution in 1834, resulted in a return to the ascension of Pedro II to the Brazilian throne in 1840. In 1850, efforts began to abolish slavery, which eventually took hold entirely in 1888. But the repercussions were dramatic as the military dethroned the emperor, and the Republic of Brazil was founded a year later in 1889 (Burns, 1980, p. 286). The militarization of the Brazilian government (and its law enforcement arm) had begun.

By instituting a quasi-military republican rule, the new government was able to form and develop with little bloodshed. Under the rule of the army commander Deodoro, the new republic first separated the church and the state, and then moved on to preparing a new constitution, using the American and Argentina models for support. The goal was to develop a liberal, democratic nation based on capitalistic success. Based on American constitutional philosophy, popular elections became the norm, and provinces (states) were granted considerable power, including the maintenance of a provincial militia. However, while a republic existed facially, the reality was that a military dictatorship had evolved, evinced by Deodoro's abolishment of the congress in 1891. The Brazilian navy incited rebellion, and in the ensuing chaos, politicians from Sao Paulo forced a presidential election, which had been required by constitutional decree. In 1894, Brazil experienced her first civilian president (Burns, 1980, pp. 285–290). In 1910, an army marshal once again won the presidential election, which returned the emphasis on military dominance to Brazilian politics. The national armies were used to quell regional disturbances (Burns, 1980, pp. 342–344). This once again reiterated the importance to the federal government of maintaining a strong control over the military. The use of force was the preferred option to maintain order. "Order above law" had become the government's political philosophy (Burns, 1980, p. 388).

The rule of the Brazilian dictator and President Vargas started as a result of a military junta in 1930. His titles included chief of the provisional government (1930–1934), congressionally elected president (1934–1937), dictator of the "Estado Novo" (1937–1945), and finally president by popular election (1951–1954) (Burns, 1980, p. 398). In 1954, much to the shock of Brazilians, the domineering Vargas committed suicide. Following his death, it was actually a military coup (the Constitutional Military Movement) that ensured that the democratically elected officials Kubitschek and Goulart took their presidential positions in 1956. The military had thus acted to maintain democracy (Burns, 1980, 447). Under Kubitschek's rule, industrialization, productivity, modernization, and economic growth were emphasized (Burns, 1980, 457). The flux of people from the countryside to the urban centers quickly increased, and overpopulation in large cities developed into a major unmanageable problem.

An equally significant issue rose as military coup became the norm to gain government control. The threat or use of force became a political option to rule the nation. Coups in 1964, 1968, and 1969 reinforced the importance of the military in Brazilian politics. Even when elections did occur through

1980, military leaders were often triumphant (Burns, 1980, p. 546). Given the history of Brazil, it is not surprising, then, that militaristic ideology continues to be influential in the development of national and local policy, law, and justice practices.

History of Justice Administration in Brazil (1822 through the New Millennium)

After achieving political independence from Portugal in 1822, Brazil placed most of the responsibility for preventing and punishing crime in the hands of the judiciary. Reformed in 1827 to the British "Justice of the Peace" model, the development of the "Criminal Code of the Empire" in 1830 and the "Code of Criminal Procedure" in 1831 formalized the criminal justice process, however leaving all aspects of the justice system in the hands of judicial officials (Holloway, 2001, pp. 734–735). At the same time, locally, provincial assemblies, attempting to improve order maintenance and social control (policing) at the regional level, often contravened the national legal codes of 1830 and 1832 and discounted the role of the national guard (i.e., the military) in local law enforcement, thereby creating friction between federal and provincial government executives and assemblies (Barman, 1988, p. 187). This division of the National Guard units at the provincial level led to the occasional triumph of local aspiring politicians when rebelling against the national administration (Barman, 1988, p. 232).

A minor national reform in 1841 divided the tasks of law enforcement and judicial mediation, but little was done to ensure an appropriate separation of powers as only judges could be selected as provincial (state) police chiefs (Holloway, 2001, pp. 734–737; Holloway, 1993). These police leaders had been granted a monopoly of the justice system, and the same official would routinely be responsible for apprehending, charging, trying, and judging the same subject (Evanson, 1969, p. 70). Efforts at liberal reform were recommended by the Radical Party in 1869 by the abolition of the National Guard (a rudimentary form of a military police) and the election of regional police commanders and magistrates (Evanson, 1969, p. 108), but the loyalty of the Liberal Party to Emperor Pedro precluded most of their recommendations from getting properly implemented. Through the end of the nineteenth century, the emperors continued to be concerned with the "questao militar," i.e., ensuring the loyalty of their strong military commanders who could have easily threatened an overthrow of the imperial regime. The National Guard, loyal to the emperor, had maintained a balance with the national militia and calmed the civil–military tensions present through most of the century (Evanson, 1969, pp. 318–320). However, this balance was abruptly ended in 1889 when the emperor was dethroned by the army and the Republic of

Brazil was established (Burns, 1980, p. 544). The influence of the military in everyday life and politics in Brazil had begun.

Law Enforcement in Brazil

As soon as the concept of law enforcement developed in 1809 in Brazil, the main objectives of the police (the "watchmen") were to contain slave revolts, punish insurrection, and capture fugitives (Hinton, 2005, p. 81). The police were therefore in place, for the most part, to maintain the political control of the elitist class. It should be highlighted that Brazil was the last country in the western world to end slavery, which continued until 1888 (Hinton, 2005, p. 81). Control of the underclass, namely the Afro-Brazilians, often involving torture, corporal and capital punishment, had become the norm. This trend continued into the twentieth century, even with the never ending incidents of military coups (in 1930, 1945, 1954, 1955, and finally throughout the 1960s), which brought an end to different eras of social "democracy" (Hinton, 2005, p. 81). With the military routinely in control of government officiating throughout most of the last century, provincial police agencies were placed under the control of the national army. It does not come as a surprise then that after the dictatorship epoch ended in the mid-1980s, the newly elected government, in its new constitution, maintained this practice and directed that all law enforcement functions would be conducted by the "Military Police" at the provincial (state) level (da Silva, 2000, p. 127). Little revision in training occurred as both the National Army and the Military Police received similar instruction, i.e., force was taught as an appropriate means to gain compliance from society's delinquents and law breakers (da Silva, 2000, p. 125). Holding true to this mandate, police use of force and violence became a common practice. Further complicating the issue is the federal government's use of the army to enforce the law when the military and municipal police have staged job actions and strikes (Anonymous, Brazil Report, 2004a), and in instances when law enforcement personnel are outnumbered or outmaneuvered by informal actors.

The Brazilian *Favelas*

With industrialization fueled migration to the urban centers becoming a widespread concern from the 1950s onward, overpopulation developed into a major problem. The local infrastructure could not properly handle this influx from the countryside to Brazil's largest cities. Hope for employment routinely ended in unfulfilled enthusiasm.

This move involved predominantly lower class, rural migrants overwhelming the large metropolises Sao Paulo and Rio de Janeiro. (In Rio de

Janeiro alone, it is estimated that over one million people live in more than 600 *favelas*.) In lieu of traveling hours from distant suburbs, many laborers opted to move to the cities, finding that high costs precluded the comfort of an apartment. Many decided to avoid a lengthy bus commute and moved to the hillside shacks surrounding the city. Consisting of a collection of simple sheds made of wood, cardboard, scrap metal, or other available material perched on steep slopes, these "*favelas*" or "*invasoes*" had no infrastructure, no running water, no legal source of electricity, no formal shopping opportunities, and no educational opportunities for the unfortunate juvenile residents. With little government influence or supervision, these *favelas* relied mainly on informal opportunities to survive. This lower class community developed its own subculture rife with criminality and vice (Wagley, 1971, pp. 105–111). The informal and isolated nature of these communities has presented the government with a quagmire, as the police are often hesitant to enter these areas without a show of force.* It would not take much to delineate that the crime rate, both nationally and locally, is drastically underreported. Informal order control within the *favelas* does not come to the attention of the media or the government administration unless extremely violent and sensational. Criminals are therefore left to keeping other criminals "in line."

Police Death Squads

Keeping in line with the militaristic mandate of using or threatening force to accomplish the mission, police violence became the common practice, particularly in the "*favelas*," the poor, minority, crime-infested urban shantytowns within major cities. In one case in Rio de Janeiro in 1994, 21 civilians were killed during a police raid of a *favela* (Anonymous, *The Economist*, 1994). It has been estimated that in the city of Sao Paulo alone, police have killed over 12,000 people since 1980 with a high of 1470 police homicides in 1992 (Caldeira, 2002, p. 235). Deadly force continues to be an option for contemporary police agencies in large Brazilian cities. In 1997, the police of Sao Paulo killed over 400 civilians in both 1997 and 1998 (Anonymous, *The Economist*, 1994) and this number increased to over 800 and 700 in 2000 and 2001, respectively (Caldeira, 2002, p. 245). During the same 2 years, the police of Rio de Janeiro were responsible for the killing of an average of 60 civilians each month. Nationally, the killing of civilians by police has accounted for approximately 25% of all homicides on average during the last

---

* Author James F. Albrecht was invited by the police of Rio de Janeiro in February 2004 to view the condition of the local *favelas* there via helicopter. They relayed their repeated experiences of armed conflict; and noted that they rarely entered these "neighborhoods." Even the police helicopters flying overhead were also faced with adversarial gunfire. These "independent" regions were therefore left to maintain order and control on their own informal terms, usually by violence and threats.

decade (Chevigny, 1995, p. 87; Chevigny, 2003, p. 78). In addition, torture is reportedly a routine tool utilized when police conduct investigations and interrogations (Anonymous, *The Economist*, 1994). What also demands more attention is the racially disparate impact of police use of lethal force. While black people account for only 5% of the population in Sao Paulo, they compromise 54% of all those killed by the police there (Caldeira, 2002, p. 246) and the residents of the *favelas* are consistently the intended targets. To clarify these statistics further, the profile of the typical victim of police violence is male, 15–29 years of age, poor, black, and a resident of a *favela* or some other poor enclave (Paes-Machado and Noronha, 2002, p. 72). To further complicate the situation was the widespread substantiated statistic that revealed that poor, male blacks and mulattos were the most likely candidates to participate in violent street crime (Paes-Machado and Levenstein, 2004, p. 9).

On the other hand, the reality is that many police officers continue to be killed in the line of duty, and the response is that many police view the community, particularly those in poor, crime-ridden neighborhoods, as "the enemy" (Brown, 2000). Vigilantism and contracted private security, often involving former and active police personnel and hired thugs and killers, have become part of mercantile practices to ensure the safety of merchants and their customers (Paes-Machado and Noronha, 2002, p. 66). In addition, although an informal practice, promotion and pay increases often resulted from these "acts of bravery" (Anonymous, Human Rights Watch, 2005, p. 1), which served to formalize the abusive conduct as being a viable aspect of law enforcement. It should be emphasized that these police "death squads" do not officially exist within the two police departments (Paes-Machado and Noronha, 2002, p. 66). Further support for these abusive practices can be interpreted by the lack of prosecution of police personnel identified in deadly force incidents (Anonymous, Human Rights Watch, p. 4). Even after the approval of the Torture Code in 1997 to deter police abuse, no convictions were recorded through the end of the last millennium (Hinton, 2005, p. 90). Judicial indifference appears to promote these informal practices (Brinks, 2003, p. 1). Many recent surveys have also revealed that the middle and upper classes of Brazil also endorse these practices, even though they often believe that police personnel are connected to organized crime (Chevigny, 1995, p. 88). However, those in the lower classes, mainly Afro-Brazilians, also claimed that they were more likely to suffer discrimination at the hands of the police (Mitchell and Wood, 1999, p. 1001).

Improving the Police of Brazil

Brazil now finds itself under a microscope as international and human rights agencies continue to criticize these state-sponsored violations of human dignity. Efforts have been made with international assistance to reform the police function to reflect a more democratic model. Improved training sponsored by respected police and human rights agencies from North America and Europe are now promoting enhanced contact between the police and the community (Brown, 2000). The International Red Cross has recently been called upon to revise law enforcement training to integrate human rights into the mandatory military and state police curricula (Lino, 2004, p. 129). In addition, contemporary initiatives have been undertaken to promote a "unified public security system," with the "community policing" ideology as the basis for this $125 million effort (Anonymous, *The Economist*, 2004b). The office of the ombudsman has also been created to investigate allegations of police abuse at the provincial and national levels (Brown, 2000).

It does appear, however, that the informal criminal justice system in Brazil may be resisting this attempt, as history and public support seem to agree that unsanctioned police practices continue to be part of long-standing Brazilian tradition and custom.

The Informal Community within Brazil

The informal community is a staple, but threatening, aspect of Brazilian society, and is an undercurrent of social and economic life. The informal economy interacts with three different forms of formal order: the financial/economic order (the formal economy), the social order (national and city politics), and the criminal justice system. The financial order concerns the economic effects of the informal economy (e.g., tax evasion and low wages). The social order involves regulation of zoning, environmental control, health, safety and employment, among other matters. The criminal justice system is in place to address illegal activity and maintain public order. Ultimately all are intertwined, but the justice system has been designed to ensure the stability of all aspects of the social organization (Shapland, 2004, pp. 1–8). The major difficulty to this expectation is when the justice system reneges on its responsibilities. When bribery, corruption, and abuse become common or even expected practices, then the integrity of the criminal justice system comes into question.

Analyzing the History of Law Enforcement in Brazil

It is clear that the country of Brazil has a long and proud history. However, since her independence in the early 1800s, the military has played a predominant role in order maintenance and in ensuring government control. So dominant and powerful has been the army throughout the nation's history, that military coup and "democratic" autocracy had become common events through the end of the twentieth century.

The influence of military ideology and tactics in government policies is most visible in contemporary law enforcement practices. Since use of force is stressed in the academy setting to establish and to preserve order, it is not surprising that lethal actions are advocated and utilized in the field. Compounding the situation has been the settlement of the poor shantytown *favelas* in the suburbs of the nation's largest cities. With little opportunity in the formal arena, the residents of the *favelas* have resorted to informal practices, i.e., crime, vice, and other illegal actions, to survive. In order to counter the actions of the most violent inhabitants of these *favelas*, both the military and the state (civil) policing agencies often engage in corrupt, brutal, and fatal responses to maintain an atmosphere of control. The actors most visibly responsible for the *formal* maintenance of the peace and the law have therefore turned to *informal* practices to accomplish their tasks. The law enforcers have thus routinely become violent law breakers to achieve their mission.

While this conduct should be scrutinized and punished, both government and civilians tolerate (and at times reward) these illegal actions. The police in Brazil have therefore become participants in both the formal and informal sectors. The international community has had to get involved in order to attempt to rectify this misbalance of justice. Efforts have to be made to implement social changes in poor communities, particularly the *favelas*, and to improve opportunities in the formal market. In addition, police training has to be revised to reflect democratic ideals, community participation, and to institute an atmosphere of transparency. Traditional practices and policies must therefore be revised to reflect contemporary and international expectations.

An Attempt at Professional Improvement

In 1999, the then state governor, Anthony Garotinho, created the Proper Police Station Program (*Programa Delegacia Legal*) in order to augment the productivity and quality of the service of the Civil Police in the state of Rio de Janeiro. The Proper Police Station Program uses continuous training for law enforcement officials, modern station surroundings, access to technology, and a restructuring of the process of police work in order to make the civil police more professional, accessible, and better able to attend to the population.* This program signifies the largest and most expensive shift in the *fluminense*† civil police, its mentality, and procedures since the changes made during the beginning of the twentieth century.‡ Over the past 6 years,

---

* In this way extending the philosophy of community policing to the civil, investigative police.
† Native or inhabitant of the state of Rio de Janeiro.
‡ Interview with the State Secretary of Public Security, Marcelo Itagiba, November 27, 2004. Interview with the President of the Institute of Public Security, Ana Paula Miranda, November 3, 2004. Interview with *Delegado* Walter Barros, creator of the Proper Police Station Program and coordinator of the Executive Group, November 12, 2004.

more than 223 million Brazilian reais (R$), approximately US$89,655,448, have been invested in constructing and converting 84 proper police stations across the state of Rio de Janeiro, supplying them with the technological equipment required, constructing eleven custodial homes in which to house criminal suspects, and employing the needed technical and administrative staff, a move that has created over a thousand jobs in the area of public security.*

In order to ensure the success of the program, Garotinho created the Executive Group (*Grupo Executivo*) to manage the Proper Police Station Program. This is a body of civil police officers and civilians charged with overseeing the day-to-day functioning of the program, making the expertise of the creators accessible to the numerous police stations around the state where this program has been implemented, offering technical backup, and ensuring that the program goals are realized.[†] Although it is referred to as a monotonous body under the command of the civil police chief and the State Secretary of Public Security, the Executive Group employs civil police officers of different ranks, computer technicians, psychologists, social scientists, and management personnel who are committed to monitoring the cases registered within each station, offering advice, developing programs to better serve the needs of the police officers and to protect the data available on the Proper Police Station Program system, and conducting research on crime and violence in Rio de Janeiro.

The first station to be converted, the 5th DP (*Delegacia Policial*— Police Station) near the downtown business district was inaugurated in March 1999. Six years later, there are 84 proper police stations in the state of Rio de Janeiro, seventeen more are in the process of being converted, and subsequent governor Rosina Garotinho has promised to continue with what her husband began.[‡] She intends to convert all 159 police stations in the state into proper police stations by the end of her term in office in 2006.[§]

---

* http://www.delegacialegal.rj.gov.br/. Interview with Maria Isabel Marmello, Representative of the Executive Group, December 8, 2004.

† Interview with *Delegado* Walter Barros, creator of the Proper Police Station Program and coordinator of the Executive Group, November 12, 2004.

‡ When the governor in charge of implementing the program, Anthony Garotinho, resigned from his post in 2001 to run for president of the republic. He was replaced by Benedita da Silva from a different political party (PT) and although she did not inaugurate any new Proper Police Stations she did not abandon the program either. In 2003, da Silva was replaced as governor by the PMDB's candidate for governor, Garotinho's wife, Rosina Matheus Garotinho. After her husband lost the election for president she promptly named him the State Secretary of Public Security and they continued inaugurating new Proper Police Stations.

§ *Police Newsletter*, Number 20, February 2005.

Major Changes to These Police Stations

The goals of the Proper Police Station Program was to improve the productivity and quality of the service offered by the civil police in Rio de Janeiro, by training them to be more professional, to focus more on the various methods of investigation, and to successfully resolve more cases, thereby increasing the population's trust in the capacity of this police organization.* The creators of the program aimed to reestablish the image of the police and to diminish the distrust and fear that kept the population from entering the police stations. As part of the program, the existing police stations in the state of Rio de Janeiro were to be reformed on two levels, resulting in a structural and cultural change.

In comparison, conventional police stations in Rio de Janeiro, and in much of Brazil, are so run-down and outdated that they are referred to as "illegal" by law enforcement officers. Officers assigned to both conventional and reformed police stations complained about the uncomfortable working conditions and difficulties encountered while working at the conventional police stations and welcomed the structural and technological changes involved in the Proper Police Station Program.

> The conditions in a conventional station, or should I say illegal station, are really very different. Often there is no electricity and water, and sometimes the phones do not even work. I do not know how any police work gets done there. It is a very unpleasant experience. (Inspector, 21st DP).
>
> There are many problems with conventional stations that need to be changed. We refer to them as illegal stations because the name really fits. It is difficult to work due to the lack of resources but the most serious problem is the presence of the criminal suspects. Their presence makes the station smelly, noisy, and chaotic, and makes everyone tense. (Shift Chief, Police Station for the Repression of Organized Crime—DRACO).
>
> Our main disadvantage is that we do not have access to information and technology. We do not have computers nor are we connected to other stations via a network. There are piles of paper like this everywhere in the station, it is difficult to be organized, and even the smallest tasks take a very long time. (Inspector, 4th DP).

The difference between the converted and the conventional police stations is obvious. Take for example the 4th DP that is housed within Rio de Janeiro's central station—a hub of bus, train, and pedestrian activity in the heart of downtown Rio. Despite its central location, the 4th police station has yet to be converted into a proper police station. Upon entering the station, one

---

* Trust that has been jeopardized by years of inefficiency and the widespread use of torture both during the years of military dictatorship and after the return to democracy. For more information see Huggins et al. (2002); Archdiocese of São Paulo (1986).

comes face to face with a civil police officer, often dressed unprofessionally sitting behind a typewriter. If a person wants to ask for directions, enquire about a shelter or another social assistance program, or register a crime, he or she will have to wait in line for this police officer. If a person decides to register a crime in a police report (*Bulletim* or *Registro de Occurência—BO*), he or she will have to stand in front of the reception desk and describe the sequence of events in front of everyone while the civil police officer types. The complainant would receive one of the five copies of the police report and another copy would be filed at the station for future reference. Since there are no computers at conventional police stations like the 4th DP, the paperwork would be added to the already full room of case files. If a suspect is arrested in a case, he or she will be brought in through the same reception area where the victim waits to register the crime. He would be locked up along with the rest of the suspects and convicts in the building perhaps for the entirety of his sentence contributing to the noise and tension in the air of the station. The conventional police stations are not air-conditioned nor are there telephones or water fountains available for the citizens to use. Despite the state of most of the conventional police stations, there is always one room that is an exception: the office of the station chief (*delegado(a) titular*), a civil police officer with a law degree who is responsible for all the shifts and employees within a station. The office of the station chief in conventional police stations has an air conditioner, a computer, comfortable chairs and couches, a television, and bookshelves filled with books. The hierarchy within the civil police is clearly visible in this situation.

In contrast, the nearby 5th DP, which is the pilot and model station for the Proper Police Station Program, is rather inviting. There are a few plants and places to sit outside the station. The transparent glass entrance door allows the employees and their actions to be completely visible both to citizens seeking assistance and those passing by. This decreases the mystery surrounding police actions and makes law enforcement officials more accessible to the population. The 5th DP is well-lit, air-conditioned, and its bathrooms, telephones, and water fountain are accessible to everyone. These seemingly small changes seem to lead to a big difference in that the more vulnerable members of the homeless population, who used to fear the police, have begun spending the night next to the station where they know they will be safe and can have access to toilets and water. Civil police officers working in a proper police station are required to wear jeans or trousers with dress shirts and ties to work in order to give them a more professional image. The station chiefs (*delegado(a) titular*) and shift chiefs (*delegado(a)s*) set the example by wearing suits.

Upon approaching the reception desk in a proper police station, one is greeted by a social assistant or an intern. The social assistant is a civilian employee with a degree and work experience in the field of social science, psychology, social work, or communication. The interns* are university students within the same fields who volunteer at the stations for a 6-month period. Although the social attendants cannot dispense legal advice since they are not law enforcement officers and do not have legal training, they are able to help the population in a variety of other ways depending on the type of assistance needed. In the case of lost documentation, the social attendants register the types and numbers of the lost documents into the Proper Police Station Program system and the individual seeking assistance receive a form stating that his or her documents have been lost and giving him or her permission to request for another copy of the documents to be issued. In the case of a legal, but not criminal, matter, the social attendants search for an agency or a lawyer that could better assist the client. In the case of individuals requiring social assistance, the social attendants refer the client to various agencies and programs specializing in the matter. Lastly, in the case of a crime, the victim's and/or witness' details are entered into the Proper Police Station Program system and then the case is passed on to a law enforcement official who will enquire about the details of the incident, and take the statement of all the parties concerned in order to fill out a police report and register the crime. Along with the process of registering a crime and beginning an investigation, which is conducted by civil police officers, the social attendants are also able to offer social support to victims of certain violent crimes. This support is available for all victims if they ask for it, but for victims of sexual abuse, rape, domestic violence, and attempted murder, the social attendants always take the victim(s) to a private room to discuss the incident and the various possibilities the victim(s) have.[†]

Daily Functioning of a Proper Police Station

The changes brought about by the implementation of the Proper Police Station Program encompass various aspects of the physical structure of the station, the division and assignment of work among employees, the day-to-day realities of police work, the officers' manner of behaving and working, and the supervision and control of individual officers. The essential characteristics of the Proper Police Station Program that have been implemented in the converted stations throughout Rio de Janeiro State, and have set them apart from the conventional police stations, are as follows:

Culture

The primary difference is the importance and continuity of training. Before civil police officers can begin working within a proper police station, they

---

* Here on in, social assistants and interns will be jointly referred to as social attendants.
† For example, access to psychological counseling or safe houses.

are required to attend initial training sessions* about the idea behind the program, the importance of investigation, investigation methods, the Brazilian penal procedural code, human rights, equality, notions of psychology, computers and the software used, and firearms training, including others.[†] After the successful completion of this course, the officers are entitled to an increase of R$500 (US$200) in their monthly salary as long as they continue their training by logging in at least 12 h of training per month within the police station, at the police academy, or via Internet distance learning. This is the first time there has been such an emphasis on studying and training within the civil police in Rio de Janeiro.

In addition, as mentioned above, in a proper police station, a citizen's initial interaction is not with a law enforcement official but with social attendants who work the reception desk. The social attendants are trained to attend to the population, direct people who do not wish to report a crime to other relevant agencies, and pass on the crimes to be registered to the police officers. Removing the police officers from the reception desk allows them to focus on registering and investigating crimes, and delegates the responsibility of attending to the population's social needs to those trained for the job. In order to keep police officers involved in their own activities, administrative matters, maintenance, the stock of needed materials, and the functioning of equipment is also managed by a nonlaw enforcement official. This civilian office manager is basically charged with matters relating to the day-to-day functioning of the station.

Police officers working in the proper police stations are individually responsible for investigating each of the crimes that they register regardless of the type of crime. In the conventional police stations, the chief of the station assigns which police officer will investigate which case. Often one officer is made responsible for similar cases, which increases the officer's risk of becoming involved in crime and corruption and also prevents the officers from learning different methods of investigation. This is not the case in the proper police stations. With the assistance of computer programs that form part of the Proper Police Station Program, the station chief and the shift chiefs are better able to coordinate investigations and closely supervise each law enforcement officer.

Structure

Furthermore, the proper police stations have a more welcoming environment and better access to technology. The proper police stations are equipped with

---

* These sessions are in addition to the 6 month training period attended by all civil police officers.
[†] Interview with *Delegado* Walter Barros, creator of the Proper Police Station Program and coordinator of the Executive Group, November 12, 2004. Interview with *Delegado* Gilberto da Cruz Ribeiro, then-*delegado titular* of the 5th DP, November 28, 2003.

glass entry doors, air-conditioning, an open layout, new furniture, bright lighting, clean and functioning bathrooms, public telephones, and a water fountain, thereby making the stations modern, functional, and more accessible, providing comfort to the citizens, and better working conditions for the law enforcement officers. The noisy, old typewriters used in the conventional police stations have been replaced by computers, printers, scanners, digital cameras, Internet, intranet, links to other proper police stations via a network, and access to other data banks, new cars, and better firearms.

In the proper police stations, a back door is provided through which criminal suspects arrested red-handed are brought in so as to avoid contact with the victim(s) and/or witness(es) who are waiting in the reception area of the station in order to register the crime. During this process of registering a crime, the suspect is digitally photographed, and his or her image is loaded onto the computer and into the Proper Police Station Program network. The suspect is fingerprinted in the old-fashioned way but digital fingerprinting will soon be introduced in the proper police stations. In cases where no suspect is arrested, victims who saw their attacker are given the opportunity to browse the digital photographs available on the network. Suspects can be searched for on the basis of age, sex, race, height and weight, distinguishing physical characteristics, address, location of the crime, modus operandi, known accomplices, aliases etc.

Arrested suspects can be identified by victim(s) and/or witness(es) in an identification room that has two entrances and is divided by a one-way mirror. During their time within a proper police station, suspects are housed in custodial rooms. There are two such rooms in each proper police station, one for the male suspects and one for the female. The rooms are 4 m², have an open toilet for the suspect's use, and a window through which the suspect can converse with his or her lawyer, and be provided with food. The suspects are only housed in these rooms temporarily, usually about 3–4 h but always less than 24 h, before they are transferred to a custodial house. By eliminating the longer-term holding cells within the police stations, the creators of the Proper Police Station Program have improved the environment of the police stations, reduced the stress experienced by the police officers, reduced the opportunity to abuse prisoners, and eliminated activities such as feeding, guarding, and transporting prisoners that interfere with the civil police officer's primary tasks of registering and investigating crimes. In addition to this, the governor has opened 11 custodial houses around the state to which over six thousand suspects, awaiting trial, have been transferred. Five more custodial houses are being constructed and more penitentiary guards are being hired in order to incorporate the suspects being sent over by the proper police stations.

In addition, each proper police station includes an auditorium equipped with chairs, a dry-erase board, and a television and video set that may be used for training sessions, meetings between a particular shift and their respective shift chief, and debates with the community concerning public security. The proper police stations are also equipped with a wheelchair accessible ramp, handicap bathrooms, and telephones to make the police stations accessible to the handicapped population. Each civil police officer has access to the same software, follows a uniform procedure of entering the needed information, this information is secure, may be accessed by the police officer at a later date, and becomes part of the statistics about the station and reported crimes in Rio de Janeiro accessible by the Executive Group and other proper police stations. Finally, each converted station is connected to the central database and is therefore able to access information about crimes that occurred within the jurisdiction of other proper police stations.

Police Station Layout

Although the proper police stations have an open plan, with the offices of the station chief and the shift chief being the only ones with doors, they are divided into various sections. The reception desk, also known as the social assistance desk, is immediately in front of the entrance doors. The other sections of the proper police station are the preliminary investigation area, which is composed of the desks immediately behind the reception desk where police officers initially register a crime in the form of a police report. The desks of the complementary investigation area are placed further back in the proper police station, or on a separate floor. They are usually occupied by police officers continuing their investigation, reviewing the case, receiving witness, and writing reports. The other sections of a proper police station include the complementary investigation group (GIC—*Grupo Investigação Complementar*), the operational support section (SESOP—*Setor Apoio Operacional*), the police intelligence section (SIP—*Setor Inteligência Policial*), and the employee's area. These sections occupy different locations in the layout of the various proper police stations. The complementary investigation group is a section occupied by a group of officers, usually assigned on the basis of their seniority, skills, or experience who investigate the most serious crimes registered within a police station. They function much like a special case squad. The operational support section is manned by civil police officers responsible for administrative matters relating to investigations and operations. The police intelligence section is often located in the back of the proper police station, which is only accessible to employees. This is where the custodial rooms are located, where the suspects are bought in to be searched, fingerprinted, photographed, and detained. The computers in this section are connected to the Internet and can also be used to access all existing databases on crimes and criminal suspects. Each converted police station also includes a personal area for the law enforcement officials and other employees. This area comprises of a kitchen equipped with a fridge, a water cooler, a microwave, a coffee maker, and a small television, individual lockers for the employees' personal items, toilets and showers, and a male and female dorm room with bunk beds for the officers to rest on during the night shift.

The Reality of the Proper Police Station Program in Different Neighborhoods

In theory, the Proper Police Station Program remains the same regardless of which neighborhood it is implemented in. According to one senior civil police official, the program is implemented in the same manner around the state of Rio de Janeiro and is provided with the same resources, and although the chief of each station has discretion on how to use the resources, technology, and intelligence available to deal with the problems and crimes specific to the area under his or her jurisdiction, the program itself remains equal.*

The 5th DP was the first station to be inaugurated within the Proper Police Station Program in March 1999. It is housed next to the Executive Group, and around the corner from civil police headquarters in the central, historical district of Lapa/Lavradio. A large portion of Rio de Janeiro's downtown business district falls within the jurisdiction of the 5th DP. The 5th DP is seen as the model of what the Proper Police Station Program can accomplish for several reasons. Its central location, proximity to two key organizations responsible for the successful implementation of the program, its status as the station that started it all, and the fact that many of the civil police officers that work there are highly experienced and also serve as professors at the civil police academy are all contributing factors. It has been profiled in the police journal, a monthly newsletter released by the office of the State Secretary of Public Security, as an example for all other proper police stations to follow.† As the 5th DP was the first police station to be converted as part of the Proper Police Station Program, and since it was highly regarded by most senior civil police officials,‡ it is an appropriate location to observe how the theory of the Proper Police Station Program is put into action.

Conversations with civil police officers made it obvious that there was more to the Proper Police Station Program than what was observed at the 5th DP.

> The 5th is the 5th, there is no other place like it. (Station Chief, 5th DP).

> The 5th was the first (to be converted), it is a model, an example, but it is also an anomaly. (Inspector, 5th DP).

---

* Interview with *Delegado* André Carlos da Silva, Assistant Chief of the Civil Police, November 5, 2004.
† 5th DP, an example, *Police Newsletter*, Number 16, October 2004.
‡ Allowing for easier access to the station.

Analysis and research in two more proper police stations within the city of Rio de Janeiro was conducted. The 13th DP in Ipanema, an upper-class, residential neighborhood in the south zone (*zona sul*) and the 21st DP in Bonsucesso, a working class, residential neighborhood in the north zone (*zona norte*) were evaluated.

The 13th DP was inaugurated in December 2001. In the past 4 years, it has gone from being a dark building that instilled fear in passersby to a point of reference for community residents. The 13th DP has jurisdiction over part of the famous Copacabana beachfront neighborhood, and part of the less internationally renowned, yet more exclusive Ipanema beachfront neighborhood. Ipanema is characterized by high-rise apartments, beachfront restaurants, chic shops, and cafes. The majority of neighborhoods in the city of Rio de Janeiro are not clearly divided on the basis of economic status and it is common to see expensive high-rise residential complexes next to shantytowns (*favelas*). The Copacabana and Ipanema neighborhoods are no different. There are a couple of *favelas* (shantytowns) within the jurisdiction of the 13th DP, but it is nothing compared to the jurisdiction of the 21st DP.

The 21st DP was inaugurated in April 2001 in a poor, violent neighborhood. The police station is immediately surrounded by 43 shantytowns (*favelas*), and has over seventy *favelas* within its jurisdiction, some of which are considered the most violent and dangerous in the city.* But there is more to Bonsucesso than just the *favelas*; it is a regular residential neighborhood with a thriving commercial center, and is home to several universities. There are poorer neighborhoods in Rio de Janeiro than Bonsucesso, especially in the less-developed west zone (*zona oeste*). Many regional law enforcement officials believe that the jurisdiction of the 21st DP and the greater north zone is considered to be where real police work takes place. To quote some Brazilian police:

> You should conduct your research at the police station in Bonsucesso. This is nothing. That is the location where real police work takes place. You will observe many differences there. Even the police officers will be different. (Detective, 5th DP).

> The 21st DP, now that's the site of real, tough police work. They say it is like hell on earth. (Civil Police Official, Executive Group).

The differences in these police stations ranged from the demeanor of the law enforcement officials towards the population, what the law enforcement

---

* In Rio de Janeiro, and several other Brazilian cities, hillside shantytowns, or *favelas*, have come under the control of armed gangs. These gangs take advantage of the gaps left by the state in providing for the population of these shantytowns and the difficulty the police experience in navigating the narrow, steep streets to sell illegal drugs from strategic points within the shantytowns. For more, see Dowdney (2003).

officials considered to be their main purpose, the type of supervision offered by the station chiefs, and the amount and kinds of crimes commonly registered and investigated at the station.

Police Station Visits

Visits to these police stations revealed some interesting points. Normally, all law enforcement officials assigned to a proper police station are expected to wear a dress shirt and a tie to work. This rule was put into place in order to make them appear more presentable and professional looking.* Yet, while the station chiefs of each of the three stations wore suits, the rest of the law enforcement officials did not always follow suit. The shift chiefs and the officers at the 5th DP all wore shirts and ties, though not always happily. Some officers complained that instead of spending the extra R$500 they earned working at the proper police stations on their families, they had to spend part of it on clothes for work which they considered to be a waste. Despite their discomfort and their resistance to change, the law enforcement officials assigned to the 5th DP maintained their professional ensemble until the end of their shift or the end of the day[†] when shirts began to be untucked and ties began to be loosened. This was not the case in the 13th and 21st DPs. Most officers in the 13th DP wore jeans and t-shirts to work. Some of them began the day in dress shirts and ties but the shirts soon became untucked, the ties discarded and the buttons opened and the officers began looking just like those in conventional stations. At the 21st DP, not even the shift chiefs were professionally dressed (unless they were expecting a visitor or had an important meeting to attend) so there was not much of an example for the other law enforcement officials to follow. The typical attire at the 21st DP was t-shirt, jeans, and sneakers, though some officers continued to stick to the traditional button-down, shirts open to the chest look that is common among the civil police.

Communication Skills

Another immediately observable difference between the three proper police stations researched is the way in which law enforcement officials communicate with the citizens. At the 5th DP, all the desks were occupied by police

---

* Before the implementation of the Proper Police Station Program, civil police officers were able to wear whatever they wanted. This usually meant that they wore jeans and t-shirts or half-sleeved, button-down shirts open to the mid-chest region.

† When I began my research in October 2003, police officers in Rio de Janeiro were working 12 h shifts from 8 a.m. to 8 p.m. or from 8 p.m. to 8 a.m. In February 2004, the State Secretary of Public Security decided to reintroduce the 24 h shift that had been in place before, stating that this gave the officers more time in which to fight crime. The officers then began to work from 8 a.m. on 1 day until 8 a.m. on the following day, and then they had 3 days off.

officers attending to the population. This does not mean that every case was handled immediately; in fact, there was often a long waiting line (for work-load, see section 5.5.5), but the officers made sure to attend to each citizen as soon as they completed registering the previous case. The officers went to lunch alone or in pairs and made sure to stagger their breaks* instead of leaving the station at the same time so that there were always officers in the station registering and investigating cases and the process did not come to a standstill.† At the 5th DP, victims, witnesses, and citizens seeking assis-tance were always treated with respect. This does not mean that every case was taken seriously and registered in a police report. Instead, every citizen was attended to as soon as possible, his or her statement and concerns were listened to, the civil police officer then explained the situation to him or her patiently, and dispensed the relevant advice.‡ At the 13th DP, usually only one of the three preliminary investigation desks was occupied by a civil police officer. If the case being registered by this police officer was compli-cated and required an extensive amount of time, then this created a backlog at the attendance desk. Yet, this backlog was not attended to by other officers resulting in a line of unsatisfied citizens. This was a cause for concern for the social attendants working at the 13th DP.

The social attendance coordinator at the Executive Group conducted fre-quent meetings with the social attendants of each proper police station to discuss problems encountered, to offer advice, to reinforce the regulations, and to make sure the social attendance operates up to the standard expected. In several meetings with the social attendants of the 13th DP, the social attendance coordinator emphasized the importance of attending well to the citizens, especially as members of the Executive Group and their friends resided in and around the jurisdiction of the 13th DP. The social attendants were advised to take care as it was not always obvious who in this upper-class area had contacts at the Executive Group and who did not, and it was important not to allow them the opportunity to give a bad report about the service offered at the 13th DP. According to a social assistant at the 13th DP, this put them in an awkward position as they promptly attended to the citi-zens, but if the citizens wished to register a crime, they had to wait for the

---

* The law enforcement officers informed each other and the social attendants before they went to lunch or left the station for any other reason.
† With exception of the GIC who went to lunch as a unit, usually with the station chief.
‡ With the exception of one inspector who was often very vocal about not registering crimes committed under the jurisdiction of other stations as it drastically increased the workload of the 5th DP. According to him, 13% of the 5th DP's workload was created by cases outside its jurisdiction. Though this concern is understandable and needs to be voiced, it sometimes took the form of yelling at already distressed victims. The station that has jurisdiction over a particular area can change from one end of a street to another yet this information is not common, public knowledge. So people often report crimes to the "wrong" police stations.

law enforcement officials. While the social attendants informed the police officers when there was a long line forming, or when someone was waiting to meet them, and they tried to reassure the waiting citizens, they did not think it was their place to tell the officers what to do. So they would inform them, but then it was up to the police officers to do what they wanted to do with the information. This structure puts the social attendants in a tough position as they are the primary point of interaction with the population and often bear the criticisms of the population who are unsatisfied with the slowness of the registration process, yet the attendants do not have the power to change it.

This feeling was echoed by the social attendants at the 21st DP where the law enforcement officers did not seem keen on interacting with, and attending to, the population. Yet, since rich and connected people do not live in the area covered by the 21st DP, the social attendants there were not frequently visited and advised by the social attendant coordinator. It was a common sight to see only one or two civil police officers registering crimes at the 21st DP even though it has a high intake rate. Some of the officers at the 21st DP preferred to investigate crimes and attend to their paperwork during the day instead of attending to citizens. Of course, crimes need to be investigated as well, but this can also be done at night when there is much less movement within the station. According to a social attendant:

> They have all morning and all night to do their paperwork and receive testimonies about past crimes. Why do they need to set aside the afternoon to do this? The afternoon is always the busiest time of the day. They do it on purpose so they do not have to attend to the population. They do not want to attend. (Social attendant, 21st DP).*

Other officers came and went as they pleased; attending to chores, catching up with their friends, etc., with little regard for the timing of their shift. The officers at the 21st DP did not stagger their breaks so attendance often came to a standstill during the lunch hours. There were a few officers (always the same ones in each shift) who dutifully attended to the population, were respectful and thorough. On the other hand, there were officers that attended to the population but did not take this part of their job seriously or treat the citizens with respect. Regardless of whether they were dealing with a victim, a witness, or a perpetrator, these officers took it upon themselves to chastise the individual for creating more work for them. One of these officers regularly asked the citizens why they were bothering to register a particular crime. And then answered the question himself by stating they were

---

* To avoid this problem, the station chief of the 5th DP designated set hours during which the officers under his command attended to the population, conducted investigations, and took part in external operations.

probably registering the crime "because it is a free service offered by the state and since they did not have anything better to do that day they decided to go bother the police."

Program Analysis

The above statement goes against the purpose of the Proper Police Station Program to make the police more professional, accessible, productive, and to revive the population's faith in civil police officers and the organization as a whole. But it does shed light on the mentality of some civil police officers. It is clear from the above example that some civil police officers do not consider attending to citizens their main priority. But then what is their highest priority? What do civil police officers consider to be the most important aspect of their job? The answer can be divided into four categories*: fighting crime, putting an end to drug trafficking, investigating crime, and maintaining the status quo.

Fighting Crime

Civil police officers considered fighting crime and catching the "bad" guys the most important aspect of their job. This obviously involves a variety of different activities but during the fieldwork periods, this was inevitably linked to Operation Maximum Pressure (*Operação Pressão Maxima*).[†] The goal of the operation, which included civil, military, and federal police officers from various battalions and stations, was to crack down on criminal gangs especially those involved in the trafficking of arms and drugs. The pursuit of this goal concerned gathering intelligence on the activities of criminal groups, forming informed strategies, intensifying police presence in shantytowns and other "no-go" locations considered to be the haven of criminal elements, conducting planned insurrections to serve warrants, and searching for known criminals. This operation was originally intended to last for only 30 days (with the possibility of an extension). Almost 2 years later, it is still going strong and involves so many police officers that it is no longer seen as a special operation, but rather a standard operating procedure. Civil police officers at three proper police stations were involved in this operation, which often kept them out of the station as they patrolled the streets and asserted police presence in certain areas in cooperation with the military and federal police forces. These officers were extremely proud of the people they helped to arrest and the drugs and arms they confiscated. They believed their actions would help the police win the war against crime; that if they waited

---

* Based on interviews with civil police officers at the 5th, 13th, and 21st districtual police stations.

[†] It was launched on November 7, 2003 as the second phase of Operation Suffocate (*Operação Asfixia*), which was later, renamed Security and Peace (*Segurança e Paz*).

long enough and inflicted enough casualties the criminal elements would give up the fight.

Ending Drug Trafficking

Some civil police officers, especially those at the 21st DP considered decreasing and eventually putting an end to the drug trade their primary purpose, despite the costs. The "war against drugs and drug gangs" mentality is much more prevalent among the military police who frequently confront the "soldiers" of the drug gangs on their patrols (Dowdney, 2003). But it is also pervasive within the civil police especially in some areas, such as the 21st DP, which are surrounded by drug-gang controlled shantytowns. This mentality translates into frequent raids of homes and businesses within the shantytowns in search of a suspect for arrest or questioning or simply patrolling particular areas looking for drug-related activities. While the specialized GIC at the 5th DP used their skills, experience, and the technology available to them to solve crimes and arrest suspects using the minimum amount of force,* members of the GIC at the 21st DP were consistently in the streets asserting their power. At the 21st DP, a minimum of four GIC officers went on patrol together, sometimes in plain clothes but mostly in gear similar to the specialized unit of the civil police, CORE (*Coordenadoria de Recursos Especiais*). This typically includes black jeans or trousers, with black t-shirts, a baseball hat, wraparound sunglasses, bulletproof vests, thigh straps for pistols, and submachine guns.

Investigating Crime

A third priority highlighted by civil police officers was investigating crime as the predominant focus of their jobs. According to these police officers, investigation is what set them apart from the military police officers who patrolled the streets. They seemed to think patrolling was below them and were not in favor of the Operation Maximum Pressure that required all police officers to be present on the streets of Rio de Janeiro. In the words of one civil police officer:

> I don't mind going out onto the streets to arrest someone after conducting an investigation but I do not understand why we are often sent out to patrol at night. I prefer to spend the night-time hours investigating but the chief always approaches us in the middle of the night, tells us to stop our work, put away the files, and go out on patrol. We drive around the streets for hours like idiots when we should be investigating. No one is motivated to do anything during those operations. It is the job of the military police to patrol the streets. If they

---

* The GIC at the 5th DP had conducted over 130 arrests without firing a single bullet. *Police Newsletter*, Number 16, October 2004.

do not have enough military police officers then they should begin another application process and train more officers. Just let the civil police do their job otherwise investigations will not take place and crimes will not be solved. (Inspector, 5th DP).

Maintaining the Status Quo

Finally, some civil police officers believed that their main function was to protect one group in society from another. This outlook was common at the 13th DP in Ipanema. The Proper Police Station Program's goals to make the police more accessible to everyone and to offer better service to the population regardless of gender, race, or social class are compromised by the mentality of some police officers and public security programs, such as Secure Tourism (*Turismo Seguro*).* The implementation of this program, as far as police actions were concerned, involved patrolling the streets in search of homeless people, especially youths. Once they were located, they were brought into the police stations in regular police cars or in buses borrowed from the military police, even if there was no evidence against them.† These people could not be arrested simply for being homeless, but day after day they were handcuffed and bought into the police stations, searched, and locked up while their background was being investigated. In the few instances where it was discovered that there was an outstanding warrant for the arrest of one of these people, they were arrested, and processed in the manner described above. In the majority of the cases though, the people had clean records and, therefore, had to be let go. In this case, they were given a letter signed by the social attendants directing them to a shelter. The youths were driven to the shelters by military police officers but the adults were expected to make their own way. Often, these shelters were quite a distance from the police station and even if they wanted to go, the homeless people did not have enough money for their bus fare to the shelter. According to news reports, 80% of those that were escorted to, or went on their own, to the shelter were back on the streets within 24 h making the enterprise a waste of time and effort (O Globo, 2004).

This homeless eradication program was implemented in the 13th DP in the heart of Rio de Janeiro's tourist district, but it was short lived due to much

---

* The program was implemented on October 17, 2004 after some highly publicized attacks on tourists on Rio's beaches and after several reports were published stating that attacks against tourists in Rio de Janeiro had tripled in the past 10 years. The attacks were blamed on the homeless population especially homeless children and adolescents who are often seen together in Rio's south zone.

† Adults were taken to the police station that had jurisdiction over the area where they were located while minors were taken to the Police Station for the Protection of Children and Adolescents (DPCA—*Delegacia de Proteção à Criança e ao Adolescente*) according to Law number 8.069: *Estatuto da Criança e do Adolescente e dá outras providências*.

negative publicity. Large numbers of homeless people were brought into the station, reportedly were handled roughly, and then locked up for a few hours simply because they were poor and the upper class residents and visitors in the neighborhood were afraid of them.

Personal Commitment or Bias?

One inspector was more intent than the others to clean up the streets and protect the upper classes from crime and criminal elements. This inspector believed that every homeless person he brought in was a wanted criminal. In one particular case, he believed the man was wanted for assault and trafficking in the states of Rio de Janeiro and Minas Gerais. This officer proceeded to comment very loudly, that in the paperwork, the occupation of this individual should be listed as "*vagabundo*" (bum, tramp, vagrant) and that the suspect's day had finally come because he (the inspector) was going to make sure he was jailed for a very long time. Upon further investigation though, it was discovered that it was a case of mistaken identity and the homeless man was actually innocent. The dejected officer then left it to the social attendants to give the homeless man information about a shelter where he could stay and release him.

It is easy to conclude that what civil police officers consider to be their main duty can affect the way they view their work and, therefore, the way in which they interact with the population. A civil police officer's belief is further influenced by the station chief, the Executive Group, and finally the policies of the State Secretary of Public Security.

Some Pressures from Above

Pressure from the Executive Group and the changes in the policies of the State Secretary of Public Security affect the behavior of civil police officers within the framework of the Proper Police Station Program.

The Role of the Police Station Chief

There is one station chief (*delegado(a) titular*) assigned to each police station. Since they are present in the stations on a daily basis, they work regular business hours* instead of 24h shifts like the civil police officers and shift chiefs (*delegado(a)*). The station chief oversees all registrations, coordinates all investigations, and external operations, supervises all the officers in the station, can implement additional regulations (as long as they do not contradict the civil police code or the Proper Police Station Program guidelines), and is ultimately responsible for the officers under his or her command and the functioning of his or her station.

---

* Most station chiefs come into the station at 10 a.m. and work until 7–8 p.m., with a 1h lunch break.

Although the civil police is a less hierarchical organization than the militarized police, the station chiefs still command the respect of the officers working underneath them.* Regardless of their experience or years of service, civil police officers must possess a law degree and pass a public exam (*concurso*) in order to become a shift chief and supervise other civil police officers.† The public exam for shift chief is an open one so that means a civilian with no operational experience could pass the exam and become a shift chief. There are three classes of shift chiefs. After passing the public exam, one can become a shift chief of the third class and to become a station chief one must be a shift chief of the first class. Even though candidates become shift chiefs based on their merit, they are assigned and reassigned to locations based on favoritism, clientalism, and some strategic planning on behalf of the civil police chief and the State Secretary of Public Security.‡

The role of the station chiefs within the proper police stations is important especially since representatives of the Executive Group cannot always be present and the station chief is the only form of daily (top down) supervision of civil police officers that is available. Not only do station chiefs have the ultimate say in what is acceptable police behavior, but they are also answerable to the Executive Group, to the civil police headquarters, and to the State Secretary of Public Security for the actions of the law enforcement officers under their command and the accomplishments of the station as a whole. The demeanor of the station chief can have quite an effect on the station as a whole. The chief assigned to the 5th DP was another factor that set the 5th apart from the other proper police stations in Rio de Janeiro. For example, station chief "GCR" is considered by many in the office of the State Secretary of Public Security and the civil police headquarters to be the best police chief in Rio de Janeiro. Until December 2004, when he was assigned to head a specialized police station, Division for the Robbery and Theft of Automobiles (DRFA—*Divisão de Roubos e Furtos de Automóveis*), Chief GCR§ had won numerous prizes for the 5th DP by being involved in all the activity within

---

* In general, higher ranking civil police officers eat and socialize with lower ranking civil police officers and occasionally ask for their opinion and input on policing matters whereas higher ranking military police officers are trained in a separate academy, take their meals in a separate mess hall, do not usually socialize with the lower ranks and tend to issue orders without consulting those who have to carry out the orders. For more information see Muniz, Jacqueline.

† Not all shift chiefs work within the police stations, some are assigned to administrative functions within the civil police headquarters and the civil police academy.

‡ The chief of the civil police and the general commander of the military police are appointed by the governor. As political appointees, they have no job stability and can change at any time. This means that station chiefs and commanders of battalions can also be changed at any time.

§ In Brazil, anyone with a university degree is referred to as a Dr., and attaching this prefix to their first name is the most common way to refer to shift and station chiefs.

the station, making sure the law enforcement officers under his command always dressed and behaved professionally, encouraging the use of new technologies, and holding frequent meetings with the law enforcement officers to stress the importance of being attentive to the population, conducting thorough investigations, and efficient police work.* After bringing the 5th DP up to a high standard, he was transferred to the DRFA so that he could use his organizational and management skills to make the investigation of car theft and robberies in the state of Rio de Janeiro more efficient.† When Chief GCR moved to the DRFA, he took with him what he described as his "men of confidence." The group of men he had trained, whom he could trust, and who he wanted working with him when he took over the large 200 law enforcement officer strong DRFA, included all but a few of the officers and shift chiefs from the 5th DP.

It was immediately obvious that not all station chiefs were as involved and hands-on as Chief GCR. The layout of the 13th DP in Ipanema meant that the station chief there was on a different floor from the main areas of the station. This created a distance between him and the law enforcement officers assigned to the 13th DP, and it was easy to see that he did not have the same rapport with his officers that was observable between the station chief and the officers at the 5th DP. At the 21st DP, the office of the station chief was directly across from where the registration and investigation of crimes took place. By leaving his door open and making frequent rounds of the station, this station chief remained connected with the officers under his command and their activities. Yet, due to his other commitments he was frequently away from the station and none of the other employees seemed to know where he was. During both his presence and his absence, this chief delegated most direct supervisory activities to the chiefs for each shift. The 21st DP chief frequently held meetings with these shift commanders, yet meetings were not held with the rest of the employees in order to motivate them and bring them up to par.‡

Unequal Workloads

The last factor that set these three proper police stations apart from each other was the difference in the workload that they dealt with. The amount of cases and the intensity of crimes commonly registered at each police station

* The importance of the presence of a station chief, such as Dr. Gilberto was highlighted when he was away on holiday. Under the temporary chief, Dr. Barbara, the police officers at the 5th DP began working slower and talking among themselves more than attending to the population.
† Since his transfer, the DRFA has also been included into the Proper Police Station Program.
‡ With the exception of the GIC officers who met frequently with Torres, the head of their unit.

varied considerably, and affected the feel of the station and the demeanor of the officers. In the period from September to November 2004, the most frequently registered crime at the 5th DP was street robbery (of a pedestrian on the street). This accounted for 8.2% of the cases registered while cell phone theft was the next most common crime accounting for 7.7% of all registered cases.* At the 13th DP, during the same period, the most frequent registration was that of people turning in their gun(s).[†] Even though this is not a crime, it accounted for 10.3% of the cases registered. Threats were at the number two spot accounting for 6.2% of all the registrations.[‡] Car theft was the most common case registered at the 21st DP.[§] It accounted for 13.7% of all the cases and the recuperation of stolen cars accounted for the second most frequent registration at 12.5%.[¶]

The three proper police stations researched differed due to the types of crimes that were commonly registered at them and the length of the registration process for different crimes (complicated crimes with large amounts of evidence or many witnesses take longer to register). On top of this, the three stations have different rates of registration. This difference is easily observable on an average day. While the 13th DP has a rather relaxed pace of registration, the 5th and 21st DPs are usually very crowded and there is usually a long line of people waiting to register their cases. The law enforcement officers that work there jokingly refer to the 5th DP as the 5th from hell ("5° de inferno") because of the amount of cases they have to deal with and the high standards they have to keep to because of the pressure from their station chief and their proximity to the Executive Group and civil police headquarters. At the 21st DP, it is not immediately obvious whether the long lines are caused by higher rates of incidents and registrations or by the slower pace of the officers. Yet, data gathered from the Executive Group system

---

* 1891 cases were registered at the 5th DP between September and November 2004.
[†] As part of the antigun legislation and a disarmament campaign created following the efforts of the prominent NGO VivaRio. The legislation makes it incredibly difficult to purchase guns legally and provides cash rewards (the amount differs based on the type of gun) to citizens and police officers who turn in guns. The disarmament program really caught on, especially in areas such as Copacabana and Ipanema, that has a large elderly population with old guns, and the federal government ended up giving out many more rewards than they initially anticipated.
[‡] 931 cases were registered at the 13th DP between September and November 2004.
[§] When asked what was the most common crime registered at the 21st DP, law enforcement officers, social attendants, and senior civil police officials both at the 21st DP and elsewhere answered that it was homicide and physical assault. Yet, this was not the case. In fact, homicide did not even appear in the top 10 most-commonly registered cases. This interesting contradiction may be explained by the fact that people have a certain image of the 21st DP because of the area over which it exercises its jurisdiction—a dangerous, shantytown-filled area. Or by the fact that a homicide is likely to make more of an impact on people's minds than a robbery and, therefore, is more likely to be remembered.
[¶] 2967 cases were registered at the 21st DP between September and November 2004.

Table 11.1   Number of Cases Registered and Processed

Police Station	# of Cases Registered	# of Cases Processed	% Processed	# of Officers[a]	Registrations per Officer	Processes per Officer
5th police station	1891	1767	93.44	33	57.3	53.5
13th police station	931	788	84.6	19	49	41.5
21st police station	2967	2490	83.9	42	70.6	58.6

Note: Comparisons cannot be made with the workload of the conventional police stations as no such data is kept.

[a] Number of law enforcement officers involved in the registration and investigation of cases, not the total number of officers assigned to a particular station.

for the 3-month period from September to November 2004 makes it clear that the three police stations experience different rates of registrations (see Table 11.1). Even though the busier stations have more working officers, they still register more cases per officer than the quieter stations. The percentage of registered cases that were processed (the amount of registered cases that are investigated and processed) is lower for the 13th and the 21st DPs than for the 5th DP.

As has been demonstrated above, though the three stations where in-depth research was conducted were all part of the Proper Police Station Program and had many things in common, such as physical structure and the process of registering a crime, there were also several fundamental differences between them. Differences ranged from the way law enforcement officers dressed, the way they communicated with and acted around the population, what they considered to be the most important aspect of their jobs, the amount of supervision exercised by the station chiefs, the types of incidences most commonly registered, and the amount of cases registered. These differences meant that each station had a different atmosphere and an internal culture. Though the researched stations were chosen because of the neighborhoods over which they had jurisdiction, the everyday realities of the stations ran deeper than simply a matter of location.

Brief Evaluation of Each Highlighted Police Station

The first police station to be converted, the 5th, is situated in the central business district. With its status as the first proper police station, and due to its location next to the Executive Group and around the corner from civil police headquarters, the 5th DP is viewed as the model station, an example for others to follow. Crime; theft during the day and physical assaults at night, is a frequent occurrence in the jurisdiction of the 5th DP. Despite their own workload and often having to pull up the slack of surrounding conventional stations, the 5th DP has managed to maintain the standards that are expected of it. This was due in large part to the presence of a competent and involved station chief who closely supervised and motivated his equally competent staff who viewed solving crimes as a priority. With the transfer of the chief and the majority of the staff, it remains to be seen whether the 5th DP can maintain its high standards.

The 13th DP is located in a privileged beachfront neighborhood that has a high concentration of people, but not of crimes. Yet, it is in this station that the least amount of progress seems to have been made. Instead of attending well to everyone, the officers at the 13th often ignored poorer, darker citizens, or attended to the seemingly better-off citizens first. Due to the high fear of crime in this area and the policies of the State Secretary of Public Security, policing at the 13th DP involved focusing on and being suspicious of the poverty-ridden, homeless population. The 13th DP has a higher standard to maintain as some citizens living within its jurisdictions are members of, or have connections with the Executive Group and senior civil police officials, yet the station chief is not connected enough with his officers in order to motivate them to increase the standard of the work performed and the services offered by the 13th DP.

The 21st DP is located in a troubled neighborhood, surrounded by shantytowns occupied by drug gangs. The crime rate in the area of the 21st DP is high and so is the number of cases registered at the station. In order to deal with the heavy workload, the 21st DP also employs more officers than the other proper police stations, yet the number of cases per officer remains high. The workload is also not evenly distributed. Despite the fact that the station and shift chiefs are present and accessible, a majority of the officers at the 21st DP do not attend to the population and register cases. The officers do not necessarily lack motivation because, although they are slow in attending to the population, they can spring to action if an external operation needs to be performed.* It is apparent at the 21st DP that the office of the State Secretary of Public Security and civil police headquarters are not concerned with attending to the population in all neighborhoods. Areas like that under the jurisdiction of the 21st DP are important because they are the front line in the war against drugs and drug gangs. The importance of winning this war has been internalized by officers to the detriment of the rest of the population.

---

* The officers and chiefs at the 21st DP would often have to spring to action to respond to a call of distress in their jurisdiction that came over the civil police radio.

Police Officer Perspectives of the Proper Police Station Program*

Since its creation, the civil police of the state of Rio de Janeiro has not undergone such an extensive shift as it has experienced under the Proper Police Station Program. Half of the stations and civil police officers within the state have been included in the program and this number is constantly increasing. Most of the officers involved in the program choose to be part of it because it entails better working conditions and an extra R$500 (US$200) per month on top of their monthly salary, although not all of them welcome the professionalism and increased contact with the population that come along with it. The police stations differ on many different levels but the law enforcement officers that work within them also differ in terms of their opinion of the Proper Police Station Program and what it means for them as civil police officers. Whereas some officers thought the program was an important change, others believed it was only the first of many steps that needed to be taken to improve the quality of their lives and the effectiveness of their work. While many officers made it clear that they loved their jobs, others cited the numerous negative aspects associated with their chosen profession especially the instances which overwhelmed them.

Overall, the majority of police officers involved in the Proper Police Station Program were positive about the program and the change it brought for them as civil police officers. They cited the improved surroundings in the police stations, the increased resources provided to them that made it easier for them to do their work, and which also contributed to their self-esteem and pride in their work.

> The Proper Police Station Program is the best thing to happen to the police. It provides us (the officers) with a better environment and offers better services to the population. They provide us with a nice office, better surroundings, a personal place to put our things, and technological advances to help us with our work. (Inspector, 5th DP).

> We work in much better surroundings, and we have all learnt to be proficient on the computer. I have never worked on a computer before but now I can do the same things as the young people, as much as my children. It feels good. We often receive visitors here at the station from other police forces but also from all around the world and they really admire the changes. I feel proud to work here. (Detective, 5th DP).

> I like the Proper Police Stations much more than the conventional ones. The working conditions are good, the surroundings are better, and the desks and chairs are not falling apart like they do at the conventional stations. (Inspector, 13th DP).

---

* Based on the author's interviews with law enforcement officials at the 5th, 13th, and 21st Proper Police Stations.

> I think the Proper Police Stations are a good change, they offer a better, more comfortable atmosphere. The police officers and the space is more open so the population feels at ease when entering. We dress more professionally and are better organized. I believe we have really benefited from the computers and the system – this way if you make a mistake you can always go back and change it. (Inspector, 21st DP).

This positive outlook stretched to much more than just the surroundings and the technological advances that accompany the Proper Police Station Program. Other civil police officers cited changes that they viewed as positive supplements to the program.

> In the program there is no hierarchy except for the chief. All inspectors are essentially equal except for their experience which is immediately observable. The program has helped to break down the hierarchy within the civil police and involve us in the decision making process. (Inspector, 21st DP).

> The set up of the program necessitates cooperation between officers. In the conventional stations we each had our own cases, we kept them to ourselves, there was no dialogue but now we work together, we help each other, and share the information through the database. (Inspector, 5th DP).

The Proper Police Station Program did not only receive positive reviews from the law enforcement officers interviewed. In fact, numerous officers who praised the program also cited its deficiencies. The station chief of the 5th DP, which is known as the model of the program, himself insisted that despite its fame, the 5th still had a lot to accomplish. The shortcoming all the interviewees agreed upon was the lack of investment made in the human capital of policing: the officers themselves.

> The government is investing in machines and infrastructure but not in the individuals that use them. This job requires a lot of mental work. The government needs to invest in us (the officers) as well, to make our lives and circumstances better so we can do our jobs better. (Inspector, 5th DP).

> There are two negative points about the program: low salaries and a lack of career opportunities. To progress to the next rank as a civil police officer, I have to take a state exam: there is no other way to be promoted. But I do not have time to take classes and prepare for the exam, nor do I have money to give the exam. I work hard yet I cannot rise in the ranks. But some rich kid who is supported by his parents can study and pass the exam and become my boss without a single day of practical experience. That is just not right. (Inspector, 13th DP).

> The program is certainly a good start but other things must be changed as well to really make an impact on policing and public security. For one thing, the state also needs to invest in the police officers so they can give their best. But our salaries are low and we have to obtain 2nd (or 3rd) jobs in order to provide

for our families. We work hard and risk our lives every day, in the end we might live well but we never have time for our families. (Inspector, 21st DP).

It is the police officers who solve crimes, right? Yet the state does not invest in us and the population does not trust us. We constantly have to prove that we are not criminals. (Inspector, 5th DP).

Not all the criticism revolved around lack of investment in the officers. The other shortcomings of the program as voiced by the officers were

The program is very good in theory but we sometimes run into problems in practice. Changing the traditions of the civil police and the nature of investigations is not as easy as it seems. But eventually we will progress and improve more. (Station Chief, 5th DP).

These forms on the computer are really troublesome. There are so many forms, you cannot memorize them all. They require so much detail, and you cannot just skip over a section because the computer does not let you. You have to do everything in just the right way otherwise you get stuck and it will not let you progress to the next page. It is very complicated, I preferred the old typewriters, they were easy. (Inspector, 21st DP).

I didn't know anything about attending to the public when I first started working here. In the specialized station where I used to work we were less preoccupied with things. We were used to working on our own investigations, in our own time. But it is different now with the contact with the public and people constantly being on my head. It does not stop all day long. (Inspector, 5th DP).

Despite the deficiencies of the program and the frustrations the police officers felt because of it, there was a large group of interviewees who spoke very passionately about their jobs.

There are some people who join the police simply for a stable paycheck; they often ignore a crime in progress or people in need because they are not 'on duty' at that time. But I love my job, I am committed to helping others and getting rid of the bad guy. (Inspector, 5th DP).

I love my job. I believe you have to. It is not always easy, the job is hard, you see a lot of disturbing crimes and they stay with you. They take a toll on you mentally. But I love what I do. People think only doctors save lives but police officers save lives too. (Inspector, 21st DP).

I love being a police officer though I am hoping to work and study more and hopefully get promoted. For me working as an inspector is a rite of passage, it is not my final destination though I want to continue to work within the civil police. (Inspector, 5th DP).

For many police officers, their job came laden with several negative aspects as well.

Due to a few immoral people, the entire police force has a bad reputation. People call us criminals but then these are the same people that come to us for help when something goes wrong. (Inspector, 13th DP).

As police officers we often have to partake in operations where we arrest or shoot someone. Like this one time we conducted an operation in a shanty-town and shot a drug trafficker. The population was very angry with us because the man had given monetary assistance to the community and its children. The community did not care that this guy was a criminal because he supported them. As police officers we often have to do such things but it does not make us very popular. (Inspector, 21st DP).

We are unable to provide for our families on our police salaries so everyone has a second job. I work as a security guard. So I put in a twenty-four hour shift here in the station and then I work another eight hours as a security guard. I earn enough now so my family can live peacefully but I never get to see them because I am always working. It is a very tough job, you see horrible crimes, encounter criminals, sometimes you get shot at, it is difficult. But they do not provide psychological assistance for us. Your friends are your psychologists. Often you go home and your children want to play with you but you just cannot. You cannot. Your family doesn't understand, they don't know what you have been through. That is why many officers turn to drugs or alcohol, to forget, but some end up being aggressive and abusing their families. The same families they worked so hard to provide for. I have seen many families fall apart this way (Inspector, 5th DP).

The low pay, long hours, heavy workload, and lack of organizational or societal support cited leads to the law enforcement officers feeling overwhelmed. Some of them stated that they simply could not solve every small problem that people brought to them, that they often found it hard to place people with the right help, and to equally fulfill their two roles. For example, the officers were expected to dress professionally for their duty within the stations and attend to the population, yet they were often interrupted in their attendance and investigation duties in order to partake in an external operation, something that was not advisable for them to do in their professional dress. Not only did they find solving every problem difficult, but some officers stayed on the alert and believed they had to protect themselves from the population and also from their colleagues within the organization. They often conveyed that they could "trust no one" and routinely took their official stamp with them everywhere for the fear that someone would use it and create trouble for them.

Although the Proper Police Station Program has many positive aspects and is received by many police officers as a welcome change that has improved the conditions of their job and the efficiency of their investigations, the program has yet not managed to improve all aspects of a civil police officer's life and work. The program offers better attendance to the population, provides the police officers a more agreeable office environment in which the furniture is not on its last legs, allows them to work together as equals and to use technological advances to help them in their investigations. Unfortunately, the officers continue to be paid low salaries that require them to obtain another job in order to support their families, continue to work long hours and be exposed to dangerous environments, and have heavy caseloads without receiving any encouragement from the state or the people. The Proper Police Station Program is certainly a start but it will need to alter other aspects of police work before it can truly function at its optimum potential.

Noticeable Impediments

New programmatic policies, such as the Proper Police Station Program, that aim to improve a police force and its interactions with the population cannot exist without considering the existing police subculture and historical trends. Policy makers must realize that new initiatives are being implemented into an existent organization with its own specific ideology, made up of individuals with their own characteristic way of doing their job, and within a society with its own peculiar demands and expectations. Any new program is, therefore, influenced by several individual, organizational, and societal factors that either facilitate or impede its implementation.

The Proper Police Station Program as it has been implemented in Rio de Janeiro includes certain factors and policies that inherently facilitate its chances of being realized successfully.

The Executive Group

The first of these factors is the existence of the Executive Group. This body, created exclusively to oversee the day-to-day functioning of the program, makes the expertise of the creators accessible to the numerous police stations around the state where this program has been implemented, coordinates the activities of the various proper police stations, offers technical backup, supervises the employees (police and civilians) of the stations in order to maintain the standards expected of the proper police stations, and ensures that the program goals are achieved. The employees of the Executive Group are committed to monitoring the cases registered within each station, to offering advice, to developing programs to better serve the needs of the police officers, to protecting the data available on the Proper Police Station Program system, and to conducting research on crime and violence in Rio de Janeiro. Their entire reason for being is to coordinate the Proper Police Station Program and to ensure its success. Therefore, the Executive Group is not only a part of the Proper Police Station Program, but also a facilitator of it as its very existence increases the program's chances of achieving its goals.

The Proper Police Station Program Computer Network

Another factor that facilitates the implementation of the Proper Police Station Program is the computerized network that forms part of the program. Requiring the civil police officers to work on computers and save all case files with information on the type, scene, and details of crime, along with the details on the victims, witnesses, and perpetrators increases the transparency of police work and investigations, and also allows for greater supervision of the police officers. Cases previously registered can later be accessed by the chiefs, the officer who registered the crime, the police officers investigating a case with a similar modus operandi, or by the same perpetrator and social attendants in instances when, for example, the victim has misplaced his or her copy of the police report. Although the cases can be viewed by several parties thereby making the work of police officers transparent, they cannot be changed or altered in anyway without the permission of a shift chief.* This policy was created to counter police corruption and to decrease the ability of civil police officers to alter statements and the description of the case to suit them or the needs of the investigation. As this example demonstrates, the Proper Police Station Program's computerized network and the policies that accompany it have allowed for transparency and supervision to increase hand in hand, both within stations and between the stations and the Executive Group. Using the computer network, the station and shift chiefs are able to closely oversee the officers working under their authority. This includes, among other things, having access to the number of cases registered by an officer, their details, the follow up on the cases (if there was any), and the time spent on each of these activities. If used properly, the supervisory system allows station and shift chiefs to catch and to discipline chronic mistakes, laziness, inefficiency, rule breaking, and criminal activity. But as was highlighted above, not all chiefs use this system to its full potential.

Individual Responsibility for Cases

Another factor that facilitates this program by making corruption and involvement in criminal activity increasingly difficult is the policy that puts an end to the hierarchy among inspectors and makes each one responsible for his cases from start to finish. Initially, civil police officers were only assigned to certain duties, such as registration or investigation, and some only investigated certain crimes. This created divisions between police officers, kept them from working together on cases, and prevented them from accepting full responsibility for their cases. It also increased a civil police

---

* Even then, only the supervising chief of the particular shift that the registering police officer belongs to.

officer's chances of partaking in criminal activity or being corrupt because there were some officers who only dealt with drug-related crimes, and others who only dealt with robberies and had no one overseeing their conduct. The policy inherent in the Proper Police Station Program does not guarantee the complete eradication of corruption, but it does make it much more difficult for police officers to indulge in this and other criminal behavior in secret.

Removal of Holding Cells from the Police Stations

An additional factor that acts as a facilitator of the Proper Police Station Program is the removal of the holding cells from within the police stations. The fact that criminal suspects are no longer housed within the stations allows the police officers to focus on their primary task, which is to register and investigate cases. Equally importantly, it decreases the possibility of civil police officers engaging in the torture or the abuse of the suspects as they are only under their control for a very short period of time. The open layout of the proper police stations also diminishes the likelihood of physical abuse as there is very little space where the officers could hide and beat a suspect.

Continuation of State Government

The final factor that facilitated the implementation of the Proper Police Station Program is the continuity of the majority political party (i.e., the PMDB) that implemented the program. This has guaranteed the program a fixed amount of certainty and continuance. There is a tendency in Brazil, and other Latin American countries, for a new government to scrap the policies and programs implemented by the preceding government. Even if the programs and policies seem to be working, they are disposed of as unnecessary or ineffective and replaced by new programs created and promoted by the current government. As this takes place with each successive change of government, implemented programs do not have a chance to succeed or yield their long-term effects. This is not the case with the Proper Police Station Program. Although the Proper Police Station Program is currently benefiting from the continuation of the state government, it is by its very nature a very difficult program to get rid of altogether. Unlike most programs implemented in Rio de Janeiro, the Proper Police Station Program involves the investment of large sums of money. Entire buildings have been converted and machinery has been bought. Even if a future government chooses not to inaugurate any more proper police stations, stops offering extra training to the civil police officers, or fires all the social attendants, there are some parts of the program that will remain. The Proper Police Station Program has brought with it some positive changes that cannot be reversed.

Noted Impediments

Just as there are factors that facilitate the successful implementation of the Proper Police Station Program, there are also factors that have impeded its implementation.

Low Salary and the Risks of the Job

One of the greater impediments to the program, as stressed above by the police officers interviewed, is the low salary given to civil police officers and their frustration with it. Civil police inspectors in Rio de Janeiro receive between R$1200 (US$500) and R$1800 (US$750) per month.* This amount, which includes the additional R$500 (US$200) received for participation in the Proper Police Station Program, is not enough to raise a family on. Civil police officers are currently very frustrated because they believe the monetary compensation they receive for their job as police officers does not justify the risks they take in doing their job. According to an inspector with 17 years of experience:

> We are paid low salaries. I do not think the salary is worth the risk, it is a very dangerous job. When I initially joined the civil police seventeen years ago it was not so bad. We did not have face-to-face interactions with the drug traffickers and when we did they were not as well-armed as they are now. It is different now. (Inspector, 5th DP).

In addition to this, health insurance is not included in a civil police officer's salary; therefore, they have to pay for it themselves. Most police officers choose to buy coverage for their children, and if there is money left over, they insure themselves but not all of them can afford it and then they remain uninsured.

Secondary Employment

In order to provide for their families and to offer them some sort of long-term financial security, civil police officers also work second or third jobs (and their families work too). It used to be illegal for police officers (both civil and military) to hold second jobs (known as *bicos*), but the state recently legalized them stating that since it was unable to meet the police officers' monetary demands, they would be allowed to earn a supplementary income elsewhere.† Making the *bicos* legal or illegal does not make a difference as

---

* In Brazil, police salaries vary by state with the police forces in the poorer northern states being the lowest paid, and those in Brasilia, the Federal District, being the highest paid.
† This could also be the reason for the state's support of 24 h shifts for police officers as it gives them more uninterrupted time to devote to their second and third jobs in the 3 days they are free between shifts.

they are a normal, accepted part of the police. Having police officers working several jobs is justified by senior police officials and society at large because "it is better that they earn an honest living through their jobs than partake in corruption and extortion" (Garotinho et al., 2000). Most police officers have second jobs as private security guards (at firms that are usually owned by higher-ranking police officers), though those with more experience teach courses at the police academies or offer private tuition to prepare those who wish to sit for the state exam to become a police officer. The obvious consequence of police officers who also work elsewhere is that it is hard to gauge where an officer's loyalty lies. Will the officer be loyal to the police organization (and by extension the state), the private firm that employs him or her and often pays more than the state, or the individual he or she has been hired to protect? But there are other consequences as well, such as police officers consistently being tired, feeling frustrated because they are always working and never getting to spend time with their family and friends, which as some of the officers revealed above, can lead to a host of other problems.

Heavy Workload

Another impediment to the Proper Police Station Program is the extremely heavy caseload most officers are exposed to. Although the caseload differs by station and the neighborhood over which it has jurisdiction, the amount of cases registered in Rio de Janeiro is very high. In order to investigate and solve each of these cases, the current number of civil police officers would have to work more hours than exist in a day. Since they simply cannot do that, especially on a low salary and with the demands of their other jobs, many police officers cut corners, conduct sloppy investigations, and simply chose to ignore certain cases. This also leads to police officers who do not think about individual cases. They know they cannot possibly help every individual victim; they begin to think general and believe they will be able to apprehend criminals once all the pieces of data they collect come together in the computer system.

Internal Opposition to Change

Another impediment that has existed for some time within the civil police organization, but is also directed towards the Proper Police Station Program is the internal police opposition to change. As is common in many organizations, while some police officers support modernization and change, others view it as unnecessary or even as a threat to themselves or to the values that they hold dear. Within the civil police, there are those who oppose the Proper Police Station Program because they believe the civil police do not need to be reformed and improved or because they do not agree that this program is the way to go about reforming the organization. Some officers feel that this program puts them under attack by expecting them to change many aspects of their own appearance, behavior, and method of doing their job without contributing to a broader change within the criminal justice system and society at large. They do not agree with the proposed improvements to their wardrobe, refuse to wear button-down shirts and ties and continue to dress as they always have. Other officers do not give importance to the increased contact with, and attending to the population that the program calls for, and if not motivated by their supervisors, refuse to attend to the population or only choose to register the simple cases that do not put too much of a demand on their time. Some officers oppose the program because it places full responsibility of a case with them and decreases opportunities to indulge in corruption and violence that may diminish the "efficiency" of their police work or lessen their personal gain. Many of these officers are also aware of the trend in Brazilian politics for policies and programs to change from one government to the next. They believe that governments and their policies will come and go; they will not stick around for long, whereas the police organization itself will be around for a long time. Therefore, they do not see any point in altering themselves.

Conflict with Other Programs, Policies, and Operations
Another organizational factor that obstructs the successful implementation of the Proper Police Station Program is its conflict with other programs or operations carried out by the police under the orders of the State Secretary of Public Security. Whereas internal police opposition to change is a some-what informal resistance to the program, conflicting programs are usually planned out and involve the cooperation of other groups and forces as well. This is not to suggest that the conflicting programs are created explicitly to cause the Proper Police Station Program to fail, but rather that programs with different, often incompatible goals and methods are launched at the same time by the same organization. This can occur either due to a lack of coordination between two departments of the same organization or due to the belief that the two programs will not affect each other and can exist at the same time.

These other programs are clearly obstructions to the success of the Proper Police Station Program. Operation Maximum Pressure, for example, which is so widespread and has lasted so long that it has become standard operating procedure, involves heavily armed police officers intensifying their presence in the shantytowns, raiding homes, and searching for suspected drug traffickers. This operation's repressive tint goes against the aim of the Proper Police Station Program, i.e., to reestablish the image of the police and to diminish the distrust and fear that kept the population from entering the stations. It is understandable that heavily armed officers raiding homes and terrorizing entire communities would not help to reduce the population's mistrust and fear of the police. One could conclude that the only way that

Operation Maximum Pressure and the Proper Police Station Program would not be incompatible with each other is if they were intended for two different sets of citizens. Is the Proper Police Station Program meant to appease the upper and middle class citizens while going hand in hand with Operation Maximum Pressure, which represses lower and working class ones? Another way in which the two conflict with each other is that civil police officers registering and investigating crimes are frequently pulled away from their desks to patrol the streets or partake in an operation, thereby sacrificing the quality of investigation and police productivity in terms of cases resolved, called for in the Proper Police Station Program, for the sake of increased police presence on the street.

Societal Fear of Crime

A final but crucial factor is society's demand for tougher policies on crime and the expectation of a faster resolution of cases. As a result of the growing feeling of insecurity that is further heightened by the media, these demands and expectations hinder strategies, such as the Proper Police Station Program, from succeeding. The citizens of Rio de Janeiro often cite fear of crime and the government's inability to do anything to curb crime as their number one concern (Mesquito Neto, 2002; Rotker 2000). This fear of crime is not entirely imagined. The city of Rio de Janeiro does have much higher rates of crime than other parts of the world, countries in Latin America, and even states in Brazil, yet the rates are not evenly distributed; the probability of being a victim of a crime is higher for some sections of the population that others.

So although crime and violence are widespread in Rio de Janeiro, and a considerable number of people in the city have been victimized by crime, the general fear of crime is still much greater than the actual incidences of crime. The fear of crime and frustration with the police for not making the city safer is amplified by the constant stream of media coverage of crime and the support of repressive policies. Recent studies have shown that violent crime has been on the rise in Rio de Janeiro since the 1980s but has leveled out since 1995; yet, the crime and violence that currently exists in the state, specifically in the city, is characterized as a "new crime wave" (Cano, 1998). But what crime wave? The misrepresentation of facts in the nightly news programs and by right-wing talk show hosts give people the wrong idea about the reality in Rio de Janeiro. It also does not give strategies like the Proper Police Station Program a chance for future success as they are frequently presented in the media as being ineffective against crime.

Final Perspective

Perhaps, as it is described here, the essence of the Proper Police Station Program is not anything new by western standards, but it is a breakthrough for the civil police as far as Brazil and the fascinating city of Rio de Janeiro is concerned. Not since the beginning of the twentieth century has there been such a concrete, comprehensive plan to professionalize the civil police, and never has so much been invested into the realization of the plan. In the past 6 years, more than R$223 million (US$89,655,448) has been invested in the Proper Police Station Program. This investment has been channeled towards training officers, hiring and training social assistants, renovating existing police stations, furnishing them with new furniture, computers, and other technology, and linking them to a centralized network. These changes have been put into place in order to improve the productivity and quality of the police service, thereby increasing the population's trust in the capacity of the civil police organization.

The Proper Police Station Program aims at improving several aspects of police work. One of the most drastic changes brought about by the program is the improvement of the working conditions and the physical space of the police stations. The proper police stations are a far cry from the conventional stations that are dark, dirty, hot, lacking in resources, with dilapidated equipment, and the presence of long-term holding cells for suspects and convicts. The program also involves hiring social attendants to give the police stations a more friendly face and to offer numerous other services to the population than just the registration of crimes. Law enforcement officers are offered a monthly monetary bonus for partaking in the program, and for the first time in the state of Rio de Janeiro, there is a profound concentration on training the officers with an in-depth focus on conducting investigations above anything else. On the basis of these initiatives, many of these concepts have already been implemented in other Brazilian states that wish to professionalize their state civil police forces with the help of this program.

Yet, the Proper Police Station Program has not even been implemented to its full potential in the state where it was created. Over the past 6 years, only half of the police stations within the state of Rio de Janeiro have been incorporated into the program. It remains to be seen whether the state government will be successful in incorporating the remaining seventy-five stations into the program by 2006. Having some conventional and some converted stations in the same state, city, and even neighborhoods creates an immense amount of confusion among the population and discontent among the law enforcement officials who do not all have access to the same service, resources, and technology.

Even within those stations that have been modernized, the Proper Police Station Program has not been incorporated in its entirety. Some rules and changes have been adopted yet not internalized whereas others have been ignored. The reality of the Proper Police Station Program is different in each neighborhood, in each station, because the extent to which the program is implemented in each neighborhood is different. Observations of, and interviews with, the law enforcement officers who work within the proper police stations revealed that their experience of the program differed considerably depending, among other things, on the location where they were employed, the availability of the chief they worked under, and the work load they were exposed to. In general, the police officers were optimistic about the changes accompanying the Proper Police Station Program, such as improved working conditions, technological advances, and an increased focus on investigations. The program has increased the interaction between civil police officers and the population and, to a certain extent, made a positive impact on the civil police officers' lives. Yet, there are several factors that keep the police officers and the population from embracing this program wholeheartedly, without reservations. In order to fully professionalize the civil police, the changes introduced by the Proper Police Station Program need to be internalized and other programs need to be commenced along with it to target those aspects of policing and the criminal justice system that are not targeted by this program.

Conclusion

The police and justice system in Brazil have been deeply affected by their proud culture and history. The long tradition of a paramilitary police organization and related subcultural ideology have hampered the potential progress of the police. However, the investments made in the Proper Police Station Program have moved many of the police stations into the twenty-first century. The key will be government and institutional commitment and continuity.

References

Anonymous, Crime, law and disorder in Brazil, A disease of society, *The Economist* November 5, 1994, from Lexis-Nexis, October 19, 2005.

Anonymous, Brazil: Human rights developments, Human Rights Watch World Report 1999, from www.hrw.org (October 19, 2005).

Anonymous, Army called out to police two more states, Brazil Report, June 29, 2004a, from Lexis-Nexis, October 19, 2005.

Anonymous, The battle for safer streets, *The Economist*, 372(8395): 35–36, 2004b, from EBSCO, October19, 2005.

Anonymous, Secretaria da Segurança Pública do Estado do Rio de Janeiro, Numero 20, Fevereiro 2005.

Archdiocese of São Paulo, *Torture in Brazil: A Shocking Report on the Pervasive Use of Torture by Brazilian Military Governments, 1964–1979*. University of Texas Press, Austin, TX, 1986.

Barman, R., *Brazil: The Forging of a Nation, 1798–1852*. Stanford University Press, Stanford, CA, 1988.

Brinks, D. M., Informal institutions and the rule of law: The judicial response to state killings in Buenos Aires and Sao Paulo in the 1990s, *Comparative Politics*, 36(1): 1–19, 2003.

Brown, E., Reaching out to build a better police force: Brazil is getting lesson in 'democratic policing' from Canada, *The Ottawa Citizen*, January 31, 2000, from Lexis-Nexis, October 19, 2005.

Burns, E. B., *A History of Brazil*, 2nd edn. Columbia University Press, New York, 1980.

Caldeira, T., The paradox of police violence in democratic Brazil, *Ethnography* 3(3): 235–63, 2002.

Cano, I., *Análise Territorial da Violência no Rio de Janeiro*. Instituto de Estudos da Religião, Rio de Janeiro, Brazil, 1998.

Chevigny, P., *Edge of the Knife*: *Police Violence in the Americas*. The New Press, New York, 1995.

Chevigny, P., The populism of fear: Politics of crime in the Americas, *Punishment and Society* 5(1): 77–96, 2003.

da Silva, J., The Favelados in Rio de Janeiro, Brazil, *Policing and Society* 10(1): 121–130, 2000.

Dowdney, L., Children of the drug trade: A case study of children in organized armed violence in Rio de Janeiro. 7Letras, Rio de Janeiro, 2003.

Evanson, P., *The Liberal Party and Reform in Brazil, 1860–1889*. University Microfilms, Inc., Ann Arbor, MI, 1969.

Garotinho, A., Magalhães, L. R., and da Silva, J., *Política Pública Para a Segurança, Justiça e Cidadania. Plano Estadual*. Governo do Estado do Rio de Janeiro, Rio de Janeiro, Brazil, 2000.

Hinton, M. S., The distant reality: Democratic policing in Argentina and Brazil, *Criminal Justice* 5(1): 75–100, 2005.

Holloway, T., *Policing Rio de Janeiro*: *Repression and Resistance in a 19th Century City*. Stanford University Press, Stanford, CA, 1993.

Holloway, T., The Brazilian 'judicial police' in Florianopolis, Santa Catarina, 1841–1871, *Journal of Social History* 20: 733–756, 2001.

Huggins, M., Haritos-Fatouros, M., and Zimbardo, P., *Violence Workers: Police Torturers and Murderers Reconstruct Brazilian Atrocities*. University of California Press, Berkley, CA, 2002.

Lino, P. R., Police education and training in a global society: A Brazilian overview, *Police Practice and Research* 5(2): 125–136, 2004.

Mesquito Neto, P., Crime, violence, and democracy in Latin America. Presented at the *Integration in the Americas Conference*, University of New Mexico, Albuquerque, April 2, 2002, http://laii.unm.edu/conference/mesquita.php

Mitchell, M. and Wood, C., Ironies of citizenship: Skin color, police brutality, and the challenge to democracy in Brazil, *Social Forces* 77(3): 1001–1020, 1999.

Paes, V. F., Os Desafios da Reforma: Uma Análise de Novas e Velhas Prácticas da Polícia Judiciária do Estado do Rio de Janeiro. Universidade Estadual do Norte Fluminense Centro de Ciências do Homen, Ciências Socias. Campos dos Goytacazes. Fevereiro 2004 (thesis).

Paes-Machado, E. and Levenstein, C., I'm sorry but this is Brazil: Armed robbery on the buses in Brazilian cities, *The British Journal of Criminology* 44(1): 1–14, 2004.

Paes-Machado, E. and Noronha, C., Policing the Brazilian poor: Resistance to the acceptance of police brutality in urban popular classes, *International Criminal Justice Review* 12(1): 53–76, 2002.

Rohter, L., Amnesty report finds use of torture is common in Brazil, *The New York Times*, October 19, 2001, from Lexis-Nexis, October 19, 2005.

Rotker, S., *Citizens of Fear: Urban Violence in Latin America*. Rutgers University Press, New Brunswick, NJ, 2000.

Shapland, J., *The Informal Economy: Threat and Opportunity in the City*. Max Planck Institute, Freiburg, Germany, 2004.

Viva Rio, Rio Sem Armas, Viva Rio, www.vivario.org.br and www.disarme.org. Last visited on August 2, 2005.

Wagley, C., *An Introduction to Brazil*. Columbia University Press, New York, 1971.

HIV and AIDS: Implications for Law Enforcement and Public Safety in South Africa

12

BRUNO MEINI

Contents

Introduction

There are clear links between HIV/AIDS, law, public safety, and policing in South Africa, where we find the world's highest number of HIV/AIDS victims. One of the consequences of AIDS for South Africa will be an increase in the proportion of adolescents and young adults relative to the general population. This larger youthful population could result in more delinquent behaviors (Schönteich 2003: 1). Simultaneously, the epidemic will impact a rising number of police officers who will not be able to respond to crime in an efficient manner and contribute to create an unsafe environment for many citizens. This situation is now an emergency that calls for the attention of the South African government and more so the police authorities.

AIDS, Orphans, and Deviant Tendencies

The HIV/AIDS epidemic has modified the demographic structure of Southern Africa (Heuveline 2004). The most devastating effect is the creation of a generation of orphans* (UNICEF 2003). At the end of 2003, the AIDS epidemic has left behind an estimated 15 million orphans. About 80% of these live in sub-Saharan Africa. This orphan population will increase in the next decade, especially in Southern Africa,† as HIV-positive parents become ill and die from AIDS (although a massive increase in the availability of anti-retroviral therapy could bring the projected figures down to some extent) (UNAIDS et al. 2004: 3; Makubalo et al. 2003). The burgeoning orphan population is not only traumatized by the loss of parents (whose physical deterioration they may often have witnessed), but they will also be deprived of the necessary control and crucial parental guidance through progressive life-stages of identity, autonomy, and socialization into adulthood. Moreover, most of them are often compelled to leave school because the traditional African safety net, the extended family, will probably not be able to pay school fees and they may have to look after their siblings. This may mean that orphaned children constitute a social group of disenfranchised young people who will grow up without education or any parental guidance and protection. In these pressured circumstances, these children are at high risk of turning to crime to survive (Schönteich 2002: 30). Dr. Schönteich, senior researcher with the *Institute for Security Studies* in Pretoria, said

> In the next 5–10 years many South African children will grow up without parental guidance and support because of HIV/AIDS. This situation will fuel the phenomenon of the AIDS deviant orphans, poor and uneducated minors engaged in criminal activities. The main challenge for these children is to be able to get out of a vicious circle, but it is not easy because, on the one hand, the unemployment rate is quite high and, on the other hand, social services are not efficient in South Africa.‡

The absence of a father figure early in the lives of young males tends to increase later delinquency (Gabel 1992). Moreover, such an absence may affect a boy's ability to develop self-control:

> The secure attachment or emotional investment process (a father figure provides) facilitates the child's ability to develop and demonstrate both empathy and self-control. By extension, an insecure attachment will lead to lower levels of empathy and self-control, and to an increase in violent behaviour" (Katz 1999).

---

* UNAIDS defines as orphans children who before the age of 18 have lost either one or both parents to AIDS.
† The largest increases will be in countries with the highest HIV rates, such as Botswana, Lesotho, and Swaziland, where the national adult prevalence exceeds 30% (Whiteside and Sunter 2000).
‡ Opinion collected during an interview on March 18, 2003.

The erosion of strong kinship ties, the lack of father figures for children, and the disintegration of family has characterized the Southern African region for decades. It is not clear whether the dynamics surrounding orphans represent a "special risk" or whether the potential impact lies simply in the scale of the epidemic. The relationship between orphans and crime is an area in which more empirical studies are required (Pharaoh and Schönteich 2003: 11). However, given that there will be some 5 million AIDS orphans in Southern Africa by 2010, it is conceivable that the region will experience a significant increase in violent interpersonal crimes such as murder, rape, and assault; violent property crimes such as robbery, mugging, and burglary; and violent crime against property such as malicious injury to property (Schönteich 2001: 7). McCrindle K., a social worker of the *Child Welfare Society* in South Africa, argues on AIDS orphans issue:

> It is obvious that an increasing number of children orphaned by AIDS will have no role models in the future and they will grow without sound values. It will be a logic consequence to resort to crime to survive.*

In Southern African states, the median survival with HIV/AIDS is estimated to be around 10 years. In these countries, the majority of HIV infections occur between 15 and 25 years for women, and between 20 and 30 years for men. Thus, many men aged 30–40 years will die over the next decade or so as a result of HIV/AIDS, leading to an overrepresentation of young men between 15 and 29 years (UNAIDS/WHO 2005: 20–25). The criminological theory suggests that demographic change caused by AIDS may be a significant contributor to an increase in the levels of crime and violence in the region. For example, in a decade's time, every fourth South African will be aged between 15 and 24 years—an age group where people's propensity to commit crime is at its highest level (Schönteich 1999: 34). A South African Department of Health publication, which looks at the impact of AIDS in South Africa, predicts that children orphaned because of AIDS could be at risk to engage in delinquent behavior:

> As [orphaned] children under stress grow up without adequate parenting and support, they are at greater risk of developing antisocial behaviour and of being less productive members of society (Kinghorn and Steinberg 2000).

Infected Inmates and Risk of Recidivism

According to the South African National HIV Survey in 2005, HIV/AIDS seroprevalence for adults and young people (from 15 to 49 years old) in the

---

* Opinion collected during an interview on March 10, 2003.

general population in South Africa in 2005 was estimated at 16.2% (Shisana et al. 2005). In South Africa, HIV "flourishes most in areas that are burdened by unemployment, homelessness, welfare dependency, prostitution, crime, a high school drop-out rate, and social unrest" (Whiteside and Wood 1996). The impact of joblessness, illiteracy, and a general environment of lawlessness, all commonly considered contributing factors toward criminal behaviors, has also been studied as a factor in HIV infection. The poor are more likely to become migrant laborers or commercial sex workers as a survival strategy. HIV prevalence is also connected to levels of social cohesion. Unstable and unsafe social areas where family violence, high rate of crime and substance abuse, substandard housing, and overcrowded, unsanitary living conditions, and unemployment can also fuel AIDS epidemic. In marginalized communities, most people have low levels of HIV/AIDS knowledge and awareness; they do not have access to health care and are thus more likely to suffer from untreated sexually transmitted infection (STIs), which increases the probability of HIV transmission (UNAIDS 2000: 7–8).

The South African Department of Correctional Services (DCS) includes statistics on HIV/AIDS infection in the prisons in its annual report. These statistics reflect only the reported cases from the health services of each prison and are not considered reliable. The DCS statistics underestimate the extent of HIV infection because reporting is inconsistent and often AIDS-related deaths are recorded only as TB or pneumonia (Goyer 2003: 25).

The spread of communicable disease and declining health conditions in South African prisons are mainly linked to overcrowding. When prisons cells are overcrowded, water and other supplies are depleted at a faster rate. Toilets, showers, and washing facilities are often not in proper working condition. When toilets are blocked or not running, and inmates are forced to live and eat in an unhealthy environment, diseases are likely to spread (Sekhonyane 2005: 2).

The people who are likely to be incarcerated are also those who are more likely to be HIV positive. The socioeconomic factors that significantly contribute to the prevalence of HIV-positive people within a specific population group are very similar to those issues that lead to criminal activity and incarceration. Poverty is a defining characteristic of both prisoner and HIV-positive populations alike (Goyer 2003: 12). Prisoners are primarily young and black men from impoverished communities already hardest hit by HIV/AIDS. Much of their behavior prior to incarceration is high risk for contracting HIV and is likely to continue upon their release. Conditions in South African prisons also contribute to increased HIV prevalence due to gang violence, unprotected homosexual activity, sharing needles, use of contaminated objects for tattooing, poor nutrition, and inadequate health care. If the issues are not addressed, the consequences will be dire, not only for the prison population, but for the broader society into which prisoners are released upon completion of their sentences (Goyer 2002: 24).

There exists only one instance of independent research regarding HIV prevalence in South African prisons. The Goyer's research was done in Midlands Medical B, a prison in the province of Kwazulu-Natal, an area with a very high infection rate among the general population. The report was banned from publication by the DCS because it was believed to be "too explosive." Among Goyer's observation were that

- At Westville Medium B prison, communal cells originally intended for 18 are "crammed" with 50 people who spend 18 h a day in close proximity to each other with no ventilation or air circulation, increasing the risk of TB (often associated with AIDS), which is affecting the prison population at an alarming rate.
- Gang-related sex is so far-reaching that it is inescapable. A social worker at Westville B said that while many prisoners and prison guards will not admit or discuss it, homosexual intercourse and rape are "rife." (Lawyers for Human Rights estimate that 65% of inmates participate in homosexual activity.)
- Tattooing is a part of the extremely powerful gang structure within the prisons. Because everyone's clothing is standard issue, identifying tattoos become the medium for communicating who belongs to which gang. This practice is against the regulations in prison, so a prisoner is not likely to seek medical attention for an infected wound resulting from a tattoo.
- Prisoners with money or influence can "acquire" a prisoner as a passive sexual partner without that person having a choice.
- Restricted access to adequate nutrition. More than one member of staff at Westville said smuggling and theft in the prison kitchen was the primary cause for the lack of decent meals.
- The management strategy for HIV/AIDS in prison of the DCS was poorly communicated to the staff and not uniformly implemented.

In the fight to contain the spread of AIDS in the outside community, the research document recommends that prisons should be ideal processing centers for information, education, counseling, and testing. Emphasis should be given to prison health care, and prison hospitals should run as a public facility and not be the responsibility of DCS. Condoms and lubricants to lessen the risk of transmission should be provided discreetly (Clarke 2003).

The WHO advocated early release of those prisoners with advanced stages of AIDS. The motivation is to allow a person to die in dignity, either in their home or with their family, rather than forcing them to die isolated and alone in prison. In the WHO Guidelines on HIV infection and AIDS in Prison, Section L.51 states

> If compatible with considerations of security and judicial procedures, prisoners with advanced AIDS should be granted compassionate early release, as far as possible, in order to facilitate contact with their families and friends and to allow them to face death with dignity and in freedom (WHO 1993).

On October 11, 2005, Inspecting Judge for Prisons Johannes Fagan told a parliamentary select committee on security and constitutional affairs that deaths from natural causes, including HIV/AIDS, in South African prisons have surged more than 700% in the past 9 years. Although enthusiastic about prison improvements resulting from the recent remission of sentences for approximately 30,000 prisoners, Fagan called for changes in the handling of terminally ill prisoners in the country's overcrowded prisons.

South African law allows for a terminally ill prisoner to be placed on medical parole with conditions. In 2004, only 4.5% of terminally ill prisoners were placed on medical parole, compared to 23% in 1996. Fagan pointed out that the minimum sentencing regime requiring prisoners to serve 80% of their sentences before being eligible for parole "is simple wrong" noting that under normal circumstances prisoners were eligible for parole after serving half their sentences (Hartlej 2005).

Prior to the AIDS epidemic, prisons normally maintained a program of early release for the relatively rare occurrence of prisoners who were terminally ill. Today, this policy desperately needs to be updated to accommodate the increasing number of prisoners who are dying of AIDS while incarcerated. This trend is likely to increase as the epidemic escalates, leaving large numbers of orphans in its wake.

The bulk of the increase in the prison population is made up of prisoners awaiting trial, which means that an increasing number of unsentenced prisoners are also dying before their release. Whether sentenced or not, reintegration is not likely for anyone who has endured the brutalization and violence that is endemic in South African prisons. Recidivism rates, or the likelihood that a prisoner will reoffend upon release, are estimated to be as high as 94% in South Africa. Rehabilitation cannot take place without first providing prisoners with conditions of detention that are consistent with human dignity. This includes addressing concerns about health, which both worsen, and are worsened by, the impact of HIV/AIDS (Goyer 2002: 25–26).

AIDS, Police, and Public Safety

HIV/AIDS on an epidemic scale can detrimentally affect the capacity of government institutions. AIDS can decimate the number of public servants and elected officials with serious consequences on the process of political institutionalization that young democracies need in order to develop a strong and effective state which enforces a system of rules. A shrinking proportion of competent officials will have been at their positions long enough to develop the specialized skills, expertise, and professionalism needed to do their work. This situation represents a great pressure on the governmental structure that can eventually cause a collapse in the state capacity to respond to social and political issues (Mattes 2003: 6–7).

One of the most affected sectors is the police, and the high incidence of infection, illness, and death place a serious danger on peace and safety of Southern Africa. The South Africa Police Service risks becoming a completely ineffective institution, unable to carry out its duties (Allen 2003: 1):

- Prevent and investigate crime.
- Maintain public order.
- Protect and secure South Africans and their property.
- Uphold and enforce the law [Government Communication and Information System (GCIS) 2004: 452].

The same Constitution of the Republic of South Africa lists in an official way the four "objects" of the South African Police Service (SAPS):

> to prevent, combat, and investigate crime, to maintain public order, to protect and secure the inhabitants of the Republic and their property, and to uphold and enforce the law (Constitution of the Republic of South Africa 1996).

Southern Africa risks becoming a continent on the verge of lawlessness. Until AIDS is brought under control and the epidemic is also addressed as a serious endangerment to the future of the police force, the criminal element risks ravaging African society (Allen 2003: 2). In fact, the police who are entrusted with the responsibility of enforcing and maintaining law and order have now become themselves victims of the epidemic ailment.

It is widely argued that members of the uniformed services, including police, are at particular risk of contracting HIV. In 1998, UNAIDS pointed out that in peacetime sexually transmitted disease (STDs), including HIV/AIDS, infection rates among armed forces are generally two to five times higher than in comparable civilian populations. In time of conflict, the difference can be 50 times higher or more (UNAIDS 1998: 3). According to UNAIDS

> Uniformed services, including defence and civil defence forces, are a highly vulnerable group to sexually transmitted infections (STIs) mainly due to their work environment, mobility, age and other facilitating factors that expose them to higher risk of HIV infection. Simultaneously, uniformed services

also offer a unique opportunity for HIV awareness and training with a large 'captive audience' in a disciplined and highly organized setting. At the same time, uniformed services, including armed forces and police, are often perceived as role models in their society. Among male population groups studied, military and police generally report higher levels of HIV/AIDS infection than the national average in many countries (UNAIDS 2003: 1).

Supporting this assumption, a disproportionate number of police personnel tend to be more sexually active, personnel often operate in a dangerous environment that encourages risk-taking and machismo, staff are posted away from home, and personnel enjoy status and relative wealth compared to the communities in which they live and work—all of which increase opportunities for sex with multiple partners (Foreman 2002: 7–19). Most of them are in a high-risk age group for HIV infection—the sexually active 25- to 35-year age group. Relatively low levels of testosterone and peer pressure among this age group boosts aggression and the willingness to take risk. These traits are further enhanced by the paramilitary culture that still pervades some sections of the SAPS—such as the public order units, dog units, crime prevention units, and the flying squad—which encourages aggressiveness, virility, and risk-taking as important characteristics of effective "crime fighting." Outside of work, these attitudes can lead to risky sexual behavior such as purchased sex and sex without condoms (Schönteich 2003: 3). In South Africa, this may be abetted by the fact that police forces, particularly those stationed in rural areas, and military personnel usually have more income at their disposal than the local population around them. This gives them the financial means to purchase sex on an ongoing basis, which is facilitated by the fact that the two groups, due to the nature of their work, frequently interact with large numbers of sex workers. It can also happen that military forces use rape as weapon of war as well. During times of conflict, rape is abetted by high levels of alcohol and drug abuse by soldiers far removed—both physically and psychologically—from the commonly accepted social norms (Fleshman 2001: 16). This phenomenon can fuel the spreading of HIV/AIDS. The South African government and the SAPS have been persuaded to implement a strong intervention to mitigate the most adverse consequences of HIV/AIDS. Initiatives such as multiskill training courses for both new recruits and existing personnel, proper record-keeping to archive the police service's institutional memory, and outsourcing of some labor-intensive police functions can be effective tools (Fleshman 2001: 6).

Uniform personnel, as compared to the civilian population, have a higher rate of infection for STDs worldwide. HIV and other STDs threaten the uniform populations' ability to perform important functions. There is a critical need to find effective ways to lower risky behavior. South African police conform to many of these trends. Behavior change based on acquiring knowledge and learned skills, along with individual risk assessment, are an effective method for reducing risky behaviors (Stutterheim 2000: 1).

The technical nature of police work creates certain vulnerabilities. A great deal of experience, skills, and personal information could be lost because of staff with HIV/AIDS retiring from service or dying and because these skills would take years to replace. The police depend on staff with specialist skills, such as detectives, personnel involved in judicial processes and liaison, handwriting experts, and other technical staff, who require specialized (often foreign) training and are hard to replace. A number of organizational factors could be negatively impacted by the epidemic. These include a tendency toward hierarchy that prevents sharing of information and teamwork, the provision of generous funeral benefits, and lenient sick and compassionate leave policies that are financially costly and make it difficult to replace staff (Institute for Security Studies (ISS) and Malawi Institute for Management 2003: 11).

In South Africa, one out of every seven police officials will have HIV/AIDS by 2015 in a country where more cops will be needed to deal with crime that could escalate because of the pandemic. Recent research by the Institute for Security Studies showed that 8% of functional police already had HIV in 2000. Estimates are that this figure would rise to 14% by 2015. Age-specific prevalence projections indicate that HIV prevalence among 25- to 29-year olds and 30- to 34-year olds is expected to increase from 15% to 17% in 2000 and to approximately 35% and 45%, respectively by 2015 (SAPS Health Management 2000: 1–2).

In 2000, the SAPS* launched a 5-year strategic plan to eradicate HIV/AIDS within the police force. This plan has incorporated an aggressive educational campaign, proactive mechanism to decrease the high risk faced by its members, preventative measures, and after-hours counseling services. The participant in this program will have to be able to utilize the acquired knowledge in preventing the contraction and spreading of HIV/AIDS (SAPS Health Management 2000: 1–2). The basic learning objectives include

- Teach SAPS members about healthy lifestyles by necessary skills and relevant knowledge.
- Develop positive attitudes and values toward HIV/AIDS.
- Explain what HIV/AIDS is.

---

* It came into being in 1994 after the amalgamation of the 11 independent policing agencies that existed before the nation's transition to democracy. The key aims and programmes of the SAPS are based on the objectives provided for in Section 205 of the Constitution. The fundamental SAPS's responsibility is to create a safe and secure environment for all South Africans [Government Communication and Information System (GCIS) 2004: 452].

- Enable employees to discuss about HIV/AIDS.
- Understand how big the STD, HIV/AIDS problem is and what you can do about it.
- Understand the risk of infection.
- Identify ways of transmissions and differentiate between facts and unfounded myths surrounding transmission.
- Identify stages of the disease.
- Gain information regarding HIV testing and counseling.
- Ensure that every participant gets clear and accurate information.

The aim of the program is to reach all the personnel of SAPS on a continuous basis. The peer educators play a fundamental role in the enhancement of training, the distribution of condoms, and the maintenance of condom dispensers (Stutterheim and Khumalo 2000). It is necessary that this program be carried out urgently; the onslaught of AIDS will seriously compromise the police's ability to fulfill its obligations. With an increasing number of HIV-positive police officers falling ill and dying, impacting on the availability of experienced personnel, the capability of the police to prevent, investigate, and respond to crime could be substantially diminished. Within a few years, this could mean a heavy reduction in the levels of service provided for by the SAPS (Schönteich 2003: 1).

The mortality rate and dismissal from the police service because of poor health has already risen significantly (Brits 2003). The cost of each HIV infection is likely to be higher, as police officers make use of employer-based pension and medical assistance plans. Moreover, the potential rapid skills loss will place additional strains on the functioning of this sector. This means a frequent staff turnover, with a concomitant regression of professionalism within the police service. Higher recruitment and training costs can thereafter be expected (Schönteich 2003: 4–5).

During a poster discussion at the XVI International AIDS Conference in Toronto, Themba Masuku of the Centre for the Study of Violence and Reconciliation (CSVR) presented a preliminary report which documented in detail the experience of HIV-positive police officials to understand how they are coping within the police environment. The study further explored the general perceptions and attitudes of police officials toward HIV/AIDS and its impacts on the delivery of services. He found that the SAPS HIV/AIDS-prevention strategy has not been properly implemented because there is a lack of leadership at different levels since some police managers do not consider HIV/AIDS as their personal or primary issue. Masuku thoroughly interviewed some commanders at Johannesburg's police stations and found that half of them had never attended HIV/AIDS training. Fifty percent of police commanders indicated that HIV/AIDS was not their key responsibility and saw attendance at HIV/AIDS workshops as interfering with their duties. But, according to Senior Superintendent Magda Laubscher, head of the SAPS HIV section, the programs have been implemented as an effective strategy to create awareness among police. This strategy aimed at preventing new infections, building capacity at different levels, and mobilizing resources and support. A large number of social workers have been trained as training officers, and provincial coordinators of the HIV/AIDS program have also been deployed.

Senior Superintendent Laubscher agreed that prevention in the workplace is important, especially among police who are vital to the country's safety and security. For two successive years, the SAPS has allocated R10 million from its budget to the HIV/AIDS workplace in order to implement the program at all levels. The program uses voluntary counseling and testing (VCT), and while it promotes police officers knowing their status, they are not forced to get tested (Blandy 2006). Employees have the right to confidentiality regarding their HIV/AIDS status and cannot be compelled to disclose their HIV/AIDS status to the SAPS or any other employee. If an employee chooses to voluntarily disclose their status to any other employee, this information may not be disclosed to others without the employee's expressed written consent (Ngobeni 2005). One model of the first SAPS VCT program has been organized in the beautiful vineyard district of Stellenbosch in December 2003. This event highlighted the steps taken by the SAPS to inform and support the members of the organization regarding HIV/AIDS (De Beer 2004). Moreover, while Laubscher thinks that the SAPS program can mitigate the stigma and discrimination of the disease in an effective way, the CSVR report found—through case studies of police officials living with the disease—that stigma and discrimination are still a problem. Some police officials visit social workers for counseling late at night or early in the morning so they will not be seen openly entering offices (Blandy 2006).

Community Policing: A Strategy at Risk?

Public safety and crime prevention are still commonly viewed as security issues to be dealt with by the criminal justice system and particularly by the police. But these concepts need to be thought as "social health" issues. The lead responsibility for crime prevention is not the exclusive responsibility of the police, but it would be far more appropriate to involve the departments of the social services sector, which include the South African departments of social development, health, and education. The engagement of these departments can allow a wider understanding of crime as a "social health" issue rather than solely as a security issue. Most of this is already provided for in existing policy. What is needed is to refine the policy to take account of the peculiar South African context (Pelser and Louw 2002: 3–4).

The SAPS is the result of a reorganization process which has amalgamated all separated policing structures (the apartheid homeland police) into a single national police organization. The completion of this process saw approximately 30,000 police officers (most of whom were blacks) become part of the SAPS. The new rank structure of the SAPS starts with constables at the lowest level, followed by sergeants, and then inspectors. These ranks comprise the noncommissioned officers (NCOs). Commissioned officers, who make up the managerial ranks found at station level, start with captains, followed by superintendents and directors (Newham et al. 2006: 18). In the past, the internal demographics of the organization had been highly skewed. Four-fifths of black police officers occupied the lowest rank of constable, compared with less than half of white officers (Brogden and Shearing 1993: 77). Racial inequity became increasingly acute toward the upper echelons of the organization, with 95% of commissioned officers being white. In 1996, the new government and SAPS engaged to build a new and more representative police system and announced a goal of ensuring that middle and senior management levels comprised at least 50% black people and 30% women by 2000 (Rauch 2000). In August 1998, the Minister of Safety and Security established an independent committee of inquiry to investigate and report on racism in the SAPS as a whole. The findings of this committee are highly informative and can be summarized in the following points:

- The racial representation in the SAPS did not reflect the demographics of the country, nor the organisation. Whites were over-represented in the senior ranks of the organisation, while blacks were over-represented in the lower ranks;
- As the top echelons of the SAPS were almost exclusively white, decision-making and discipline remained an area of white control;
- Racism manifested itself in different localities (i.e., provinces, areas, etc.) and had different dynamics;
- Some of the training colleges were still not racially integrated;
- The professional tasks were assigned on race basis, with blacks performing tasks considered inferior and hazardous, while administrative and office jobs were given primarily to whites; and
- There were disparities in the allocation of resources along racial lines. (Zulu et al. 1999).

While there was scepticism that these targets could be achieved without fundamentally affecting capabilities of the organization, it appears that they had been largely attained by the intended date (Rauch 2000). If the ultimate ideal is that the SAPS should reflect the racial demographics of the population (i.e., affirmative action), the place to start would be with the overall population statistics. Table 12.1 presents recent estimates for the race demographic of the country (as of mid-2005).*

Table 12.2 shows the proportional racial demographics of the total SAPS personnel.

As can be seen from Tables 12.1 and 12.2, there is a marginal difference in terms of the racial proportion between South African population group and the total SAPS strength. Black people are underrepresented by 15.1% in the SAPS group, while all other race groups are overrepresented: coloureds (mixed race) by 2.4%, Indians by 0.8%, and whites by 11.9%.

Table 12.3 presents the racial composition of the SAPS at the commissioned and NCO level.

Since its establishment, the SAPS has made substantial strides toward improving racial representation at management levels. In 1995, approximately

Table 12.1   2005 Mid-Year Estimates for South Africa by Population Group

Race	Number	Percentage
Black	37,205.700	79.4
Coloured	4,148.000	8.8
Indian	1,153.900	2.5
White	4,379.800	9.3
Total	46,887.400	100

Source: Statistics South Africa, *Mid-Year Population Estimates: South Africa 2005*, Statistical Release P0302, StatsSA Pretoria, South Africa, 2005.

Table 12.2   Total Racial Profile of the SAPS

Race	Number	Percentage
Black	95.766	64.3
Coloured	16.621	11.2
Indian	4.993	3.3
White	31.590	21.2
Total	148.970	100

Source: Newham, G. et al., *Diversity and Transformation in the South African Police Service*, CSVR, Johannesburg, South Africa, 2006.

* The population estimates are based on the 2001 national census figures published by Statistics South Africa.

Table 12.3   SAPS Racial Profile by Commissioned Officer Level

Race	Number	Percentage
(a) Commissioned officers		
Black	7.002	43.5
Coloured	1.321	8.2
Indian	993	6.2
White	6.767	42.1
Total	16.083	100
(b) Noncommissioned officers		
Black	61.874	67.3
Coloured	9.766	10.6
Indian	2.838	4.2
White	17.230	18.8
Total	91.708	100

Source: Newham, G. et al., *Diversity and Transformation in the South African Police Service*, CSVR, Johannesburg, South Africa, 2006.

80% of commissioned officers were whites. Nevertheless, the SAPS organization still has to work to achieve the 2004 employment equity plan targets that were set for management levels. However, at the level of NCOs, the SAPS has managed to largely achieve the equity targets that it had set for management levels. The lowest ranks of the organization largely reflect the racial composition of the country. For example, at the level of constable, 70.6% are blacks, 1% are coloureds, 2.3% are Indians, and 9.1% are whites (Newham et al. 2006: 24).

Increasingly, the SAPS has started to focus on implementing a strategy called "sector policing," which calls for a more focused approach to policing at the local level including the establishment of "sector crime forums" (SCFs). They are grounded within the same elements that underpin community policing forums, that is:

- Service orientation: The provision of a professional policing service, responsive to community needs and accountably for addressing these needs.
- Partnership: The facilitation of a cooperative, consultative process of problem solving.
- Problem solving: Identification and analysis of the cause of crime and planning of innovative measures to address these.
- Empowerment: The creation of joint responsibility and capacity to address crime.

- Accountability: The creation of a culture of accountability in order to deal with the needs and the concerns of communities (Maroga 2004: 1–2).

The 1998 *White Paper on Safety and Security* represents the first official policy document with reference to the concept of sector policing, which must be

- Proactively, firmly, and fairly managed
- Based on precise orders from police commanders to patrol officers
- Focused on specific problems within any area
- Implemented on agreed time frames
- Developed in accordance with local police services and other relevant role players (Department of Safety and Security 1998: 18)

In the same year, the SAPS issued the first official guidelines on implementing sector police. These guidelines referred to three sources of ideas on sector policing—British, American, and the 1998 *White Paper on Safety and Security*—and defined sector policing as:

> [...] a method of policing in smaller manageable geographical areas within a police precinct, which involves all roleplayers in identifying particular policing needs in each sector and in addressing the root causes of crimes, as well as enabling and contributing factors, in order to ensure effective crime prevention (South African Police Service 1998: 3).

Sector policing is a UK-based policing model that can be traced back to the previous decade, initially known as neighborhood policy (Dixon 2000). This model adopts a decentralized approach to policing in order to address the root cause of crime at specific geographical locations in accordance with particular communities at the local level. Thus, sector policing can be seen as a community-oriented policing approach geared toward engaging local community in crime prevention. Thus, it is evident that the SAPS sector policing aims to give effect to a philosophy of community policing and to bring police and the people served closer together. And it sets out to do this dividing policing areas into small units and mobilizing other institutions to join with the police in identifying and resolving local crime issues. This sector approach is also ambitious because it seeks to engage underutilized resources outside the organization—primarily the mobilization of police reservists (volunteers) (Dixon and Rauch 2004: 55). Trojanowicz and Bucqueroux (1994) characterized community policing as a philosophy and an organizational strategy in which people work jointly with the police to redefine citizen community safety. They defined it as

> a philosophy of full service policing, where the same officer patrols and works in the same area on a permanent basis from a decentralised place, working in a proactive partnership with citizens to identify and solve problem (p. 3).

The philosophic approach to community policing encourages, aids, and abets community cooperation. Community policing empowers average citizens by enlisting them as partners with the police in order to make their community safer (Trojanowicz and Bucqueroux 1991). It means inviting citizens to participate in auxiliary policy activities: police-support volunteer units, community crisis-intervention teams, quality of life action groups, neighborhood councils, and town meetings. These activities are the result of the work of an entire department and each of its subdivisions in order to provide information previously not available on perpetrators of crime, gang members, and drug dealers. People have the chance to help to set local police priorities and to develop creative solutions to community problems. And it may well change the quality of life for both the police practitioner and the public (Gentile 1995).

Community policing takes a proactive approach to crime and disorder, while traditional policing is reactive. Community policing focuses on solving the problem, and arrest is obviously one of the most potent tools that community officers can use. While in line with the traditional approach, community policing advocates also see making arrests as a way to solve problems on the street (Trojanowicz and Bucqueroux 1991). This policing methodology provides training to defuse neighborhood situations before they become crises, mobilizing the "grass-roots" forces of the community and establishing community participation. The department should evaluate the model every 6 to 12 months for effectiveness. Indications of success include a decrease in the incidence of crime, better cooperation with the police, improved quality of life, and a more positive public image of the police. But no model is permanent and will change as a particular community's needs change (Gentile 1995).

South Africa has one police member for every 320 people. A ratio of one per every 400 is considered good, while one per every 600 is considered bad (Bayley 2000: 48). However, these ratios do not account for the high crime levels experienced in South Africa. But the police do not seem unduly burdened by international standards. There were approximately 4.6 violent crimes (defined for comparison as murder, rape, robbery, and aggravated assault) per police member in 2000. This is less than that in Canada (4.7) but more than that in the United States (2.8) (Bayley 2000: 37). Thus, current crime-to-cop ratios in South Africa do not seem to constitute an untenable situation, if all of these members were assigned to tasks directly involving crime. That this is not the case is demonstrated by the proportion of South African police personnel engaged in investigation duties. About 18% of total police personnel are detectives, which is more than that in Britain or the United States (15%), but less than that in Japan (20%) (Bayley 2000: 25). It is obvious that the ratio of crimes to detective varies quite a bit between crime types.

Since the coming of the new democracy in South Africa, there happened a restructuring process based on integration of members of the former home-land police departments. These members did not have the same level of train-ing and skill as the regular police, but they were transferred laterally when the 11 separate departments merged. The final result of restructuring was the hiring of thousands of undertrained and inexperienced police officers in the SAPS. A desire for parity, a quota-based affirmative action policy, and union pressures have caused this development. The problem has been also exacer-bated by the lack of new intake on the bottom end. As a result, there are pres-ently more than four times as many inspectors (the senior noncommissioned rank) than constables (the entry level rank). Constables, intended to be the primary street-level operatives, comprise 12% of the total SAPS personnel.

This development has resulted in an effective chaos of the rank structure. The rank of inspector is supposed to represent the senior field supervisory rank, the equivalent of "lieutenant" in many American departments. At pres-ent, however, inspectors have been placed in charge of whole teams of other inspectors, some of which have greater seniority in terms of years of service than their commanders. Without a sense of a clear chain of command, field supervision is at risk, highlighting the need for individual performance indi-cators. Once a member becomes a commissioned officer with the rank of captain, he is often effectively removed from field duty, and the SAPS has almost as many captains as it does constables. A huge share of total sworn personnel* (6600 members, or about 7%) are assigned to the head office func-tions in Pretoria. Despite these early infusions of personnel, total SAPS staff-ing has been in decline in recent years because the capacity of the police to train new members has become dubious. The instructors are few, and many of the infrastructures are old and unusable. In spite of that, the management is committed to train 6000–7000 members a year through this system; the consequence will be an expansion of raw numbers at the expense of qual-ity. Thus, the SAPS faces some serious challenges in redeploying resources to optimize performance. The Police Service is burdened with a range of responsibilities extraneous to its core functions and not tallied in the expec-tations of the South African citizens. There is an excess of management-level staff, and only a small fraction of members is engaged in visible patrol on the streets. Total personnel levels are in decline, and present training capabilities make countering this trend difficult (Leggett 2003).

As mentioned above, the capacity of the police to deliver an effective service is undermined by structural and organizational problems. But, the negative impact of HIV/AIDS on health of the police officers has made mat-ters worse. This illness will lead to a loss of skills and a break in the continuity

---

* It is composed of individuals who have successfully completed basic policing training and is granted certain policing powers by the SAPS Act, 1995 (Newham et al. 2006: 21).

of command, with likely negative implications on morale, discipline, and cohesion (Heinecken 2001: 110–113). Productivity will decline because of time off and the deteriorating health of HIV-positive employees. The average age and experience level among police employees will likely fall, with negative impacts for institutional memory and coherence. Police personnel numbers in rural areas and disadvantaged communities may be particularly vulnerable to absenteeism or death among staff (Schönteich 2003: 4). Moreover, the unconstitutionality to conduct HIV testing on the police forces and recruits makes difficult to determine how seriously the lower and higher ranks have been affected and infected.

Richard Ngidi, the provincial secretary of the South African Police Union (SAPU) in Kwazulu Natal,* said that the impact of the epidemic on the police service has been tremendous and the effect endless. He said that the union's records showed that more and more SAPS members were suffering from posttraumatic stress, often as a result of HIV and AIDS in the family.

> The problem is that they cannot break the silence because they don't know who they can talk to. [...] The time is ripe for SAPU to take initiative and break the ice with the establishment of crises centres, with the involvement of psychologists and psychiatrists to assist members. [...] If we do not act now service delivery to the community could be seriously affected (Leeman 2002).

Policing and investigation work demand practice and experience which are necessary to collect different forms of evidence in such manner that prosecution services can build up a convincing case in court. HIV/AIDS places additional strains on the shrinking number of experienced officers and detectives. A rapid loss of skills means fewer teachers for new recruits, and a concomitant increase in the burden placed on experienced police officers (Schönteich 2003: 4).

The high incidence of infection, illness, and death are particularly high among lower-ranking members of the police force which are in a high-risk age group for HIV infection—the sexually active 25- to 35-year age group (Brits 2003). Military culture tends to exaggerate male behavior inculcating in immature men a sense of risk-taking and invincibility, a promoting aggression, and toughness as the male ideal—attitudes that extend to sexual behavior (Fleshman 2001: 16). There is a marked preponderance of NCOs who are less educated and earn less than commissioned officers, and black people who make up a greater proportion of NCOs compared to commissioned officers. The consequence is that AIDS will disproportionately affect

---

* It appears to have the highest HIV prevalence in South Africa (South African Department of Health 2006).

the NCO ranks within police service, thereby exacerbating the already skewed rank structure within the organization (Schönteich 2003: 5).

A great deal of experience and skill could be lost because of staff with HIV/AIDS retiring from service or dying, and because these skills would take years to replace. The epidemic has also dramatically dropped the number of officers patrolling the streets. This, and a chaotic process of reorganization of the police sector, will have a negative effect on the investigation processes and crime prevention which are based on an efficient community policy model. The probable effect will be a growth of street crimes and gang activities which will endanger the safety of the populations of cities and townships (Leggett 2002).

Strategies for the Future

The tragic AIDS situation in South Africa is well documented, with thousands of deaths being reported. One of the most affected sectors is the police, with a rising number of members that are infected by HIV/AIDS. Most of them are young with an average age of 30. This 20- to 30-year old age group has the highest risk for contracting AIDS. Police morale has shown a significant decline in both medical and psychological directions. Under these circumstances, the danger is that the South African police will eventually become a completely ineffective institution, incapable of carrying out fully its duties. The fear is that criminals would then be able to freely move across the country without any form of social control. And, one must further consider the assumed connection between the potential of AIDS orphans engaging in increased juvenile delinquency and criminal activity.

The number of AIDS orphans is expected to rise dramatically over the next decade, releasing an uncontrolled youth population onto the streets. Growing up without education and/or any parental guidance and protection, this growing pool of orphans will be at greater than average risk of engaging in criminal activities. Many South African teens consider deviant behavior as a way to meet what they consider their needs. It clearly is an issue of great concern that must be dealt with immediately.

A renewed emphasis on HIV-prevention plans (sexual education, condom distribution, AIDS awareness campaigns, etc.) can mitigate the impact of AIDS on society, but it is believed that only antiretroviral treatment programs for all HIV-positive individuals who need treatment can cause a dramatic effect on the number of orphaned children. Such program may succeed in extending the lives of a large numbers of infected parents until their children can become self-sufficient. An increasing number of children orphaned by HIV/AIDS will seek foster care, and therefore the HIV/AIDS epidemic will continue to place enormous pressure on South Africa's child welfare system.

Social workers are grappling with heavy caseloads, while caregivers applying for foster care grants have sometimes been known to wait for as long as 2 years for their submissions to be processed. The application process for foster care grants is a lengthy, complex, and extremely labor-intensive process, despite the necessary documentation being in place. The long processing time has been attributed to an insufficient number of social workers who do not have more time to perform adequately most job tasks, such as counseling and community work.

The foster care system has lost its relevance when compared to other government agencies. The absence of a credible child welfare mechanism has moved the task of dealing with the growing juvenile population to the police. It is necessary for the South African government to organize a more equitable system that can meet the needs of a rising number of orphans. To accomplish this, the government needs to employ more social workers or create a separate financial grant pool dedicated to AIDS orphans (UN Integrated Regional Information Networks (IRIN) 2004).

HIV-prevention services and education must be targeted at vulnerable groups, including orphans, prisoners, and uniformed personnel. HIV/AIDS is a threat not only to uniformed personnel but also to their families and other social contacts, including sex workers. In this regard, HIV/AIDS interventions among police personnel are most effective if there is close collaboration between civilian health and education authorities (UNAIDS 2003). The government and the SAPS must now engage in the development of initiatives such as multiskill training courses for both new recruits and existing personnel; adoption of a code of conduct; voluntary, anonymous, and confidential testing of police personnel; counseling and the provision of generic medications to ill police officers; and social and economic assistance to the families and survivors of sick police personnel (Fleshman 2001: 17). Moreover, more can be done to destigmatize HIV/AIDS within the police and to create an environment in which police officers can feel safe to disclose their HIV status and utilize available support systems. Record-keeping is critical to acquiring better data for assessing the impact of this epidemic and the development of a legitimate strategy within the organization. It is necessary to increase the hiring of workers engaged in HIV/AIDS issues and to improve the resource allocation and budget management of the SAPS strategy and programs (Masuku 2006).

It is feasible to state that South Africa risks plunging into lawlessness unless the issue of lost generations—police, orphans, and teens—is properly addressed through medical, social, and political remedies. It is necessary to involve not only the three core government departments comprising the criminal justice system (i.e., Safety and Security, Justice, and Correctional Services), but also include the social welfare departments such as Health, Welfare, and Education and to gain the support of police executives in order to develop appropriate preventive strategies against juvenile crime.

References

Allen, J. 2003. HIV/AIDS sowing fertile ground for crime in South Africa. AEF201. April 3.

Bayley, D. 2000. *Police for the Future*. Oxford University Press: New York.

Blandy, F. 2006. How AIDS could threaten SA's security. *Mail & Guardian Online*. September 22.

Brits, E. 2003. HIV/AIDS shock for police. *Die Burger*. October 21.

Brogden, M. and C. Shearing 1993. *Policing For a New South Africa*. Routledge: London, U.K.

Clarke, L. 2003. Messengers of death take AIDS into society. *Cape Argus*. March 02.

Constitution of the Republic of South Africa. Act 108 of 1996. Section 205 (3).

De Beer, E. 2003. Voluntary counselling and testing launch, World AIDS day. SAPS Homepage Journal. SAPS, Pretoria. [On-line] Available at: http://www.saps.gov. za/docs_publs/publications/journal/vol3iss01/aids.htm

Department of Safety and Security 1998. *White Paper on Safety and Security*. South African Government: Pretoria, South Africa.

Dixon, B. 2000. *The Globalisation of Democratic Policing: Sector Policing and Zero Tolerance in the New South Africa*. University of Cape Town: Cape Town, South Africa.

Dixon, B. and J. Rauch 2004. Sector policing. Origins and prospects. *ISS Monograph* 97.

Fleshman, M. 2001. AIDS prevention in ranks. UN targets peacekeepers, combatants in war against disease. *Africa Recovery* 15(1–2): 16, UN Department of Public Information.

Foreman, M. 2002. *Combat AIDS: HIV and the World's Armed Service*. Healthlink Worldwide: London, U.K.

Gabel, S.M.D. 1992. Behavioural problems in sons of incarcerated or otherwise absent fathers: The issues of separation. *Family Process* 31(3): 302–314.

Gentile, J.R. 1995. Community policing: A philosophy, not a program. *Community Policing Exchange* (November/December). Article Four: www.ncjrs.gov/txtfiles/cpe1195.txt

Government Communication and Information System (GCIS) 2004. *South Africa Yearbook 2004/05*. South African Government: Pretoria, South Africa, p. 452.

Goyer, K.C. 2002. HIV/AIDS and the case for prison reform. *SA Crime Quarterly* 2: 23–26.

Goyer, K.C. 2003. HIV/AIDS prison. Problems, policies and potential. *ISS Monograph Series* 79.

Hartlej, W. 2005. South Africa: Call to address high AIDS-related deaths in prisons. *Business Day*. October 12.

Heinecken, L. 2001. Strategic implications of HIV/AIDS in South Africa. *Conflict, Security & Development* 1(1): 109–115.

Heuveline, P. 2004. Impact of the HIV epidemic on population and household structure: The dynamics and evidence to date. *AIDS* 18(Supplement 2): S45–S53.

Institute for Security Studies (ISS) and Malawi Institute for Management 2003. *HIV/AIDS and Attrition: Assessing the Impact on the Safety, Security and Access to Justice Sector in Malawi*. ISS: Pretoria.

Katz, R.S. 1999. Building for a side-by-side explanatory model: A general theory of crime, the age-graded life-course theory, and attachment theory. *Western Criminology Review* 1(2). http://wcr.sonoma.edu/v1n2/katz.html

Kinghorn, A. and M. Steinberg 2000. *HIV/AIDS in South Africa: The Impact and the Priorities*. Department of Health: Pretoria, South Africa.

Leeman, P. 2002. AIDS means less cops for KZN—Police union. *IOL*. August 05.

Leggett, T. 2002. Everyone's an inspector: The crisis of rank inflation and the decline of visible policing. *SA Crime Quarterly* (1): 23–26.

Leggett, T. 2003. What do the police do? Performance measurement and the SAPS. *ISS Occasional Paper* 66.

Makubalo, L., Netshidzivhani, P., Mahlasela, L. et al. 2003. *National HIV and Syphilis Antanatal Sero-Prevalence Survey in South Africa*. Department of Health: Pretoria, South Africa.

Maroga, M. 2004. *Sector Policing: What Are the Challenges?* CSVR: Johannesburg, South Africa.

Masuku, T. 2006. Time to deliver: HIV care and support in the workplace. Paper presented at *XVI International AIDS Conference*. Toronto, Ontario, Canada.

Mattes, R. 2003. Healthy democracies? The potential impact of AIDS on democracy in Southern Africa. *ISS Paper* 71.

Newham, G., Masuku, T., and J. Dlamini 2006. *Diversity and Transformation in the South African Police Service*. CSVR: Johannesburg, South Africa.

Ngobeni, M.J. 2005. HIV/AIDS can be controlled. *SAPS Journal* 4(8).

Pelser, E. and A. Louw 2002. Where did we go wrong? *SA Crime Quarterly* 2: 1–4.

Pharaoh, R. and M. Schönteich 2003. AIDS, security and governance in Southern Africa. *ISS Paper* 65.

Rauch, J. 2000. Police reform and South Africa's transition. Paper presented at the *South African Institute for International Affairs Conference on Crime and Policing in Transitional Societies*. Pretoria, South Africa.

SAPS Health Management and South African Police Service 2000. *The South African Police Service's Five-Year Strategic Plan to Combat HIV/AIDS: 2000–2005*. Pretoria, South Africa.

Schönteich, M. 1999. Age and AIDS: South Africa's time bomb? *Africa Security Review* 8(4): 34–43.

Schönteich, M. 2001. A generation at risk: AIDS orphans, vulnerable children and human security in Africa. Paper presented at the meeting on 'Orphans and Vulnerable Children in Africa' convened by the Nordic Africa Institute and the Danish Bilharziasis Laboratory. Uppsala, Sweden.

Schönteich, M. 2002. The coming crime wave? AIDS, orphans and crime in South Africa. *The Southern African Journal of HIV* 1: 30–33.

Schönteich, M. 2003. HIV/AIDS and the South African Police Service. *SA Crime Quarterly* 5: 1–6.

Sekhonyane, M. 2005. Prison reform in Africa: Recent trends. *CSPRI Newsletter* 10.

Shisana, O., Rehle, T., Simbayi, L.C. et al. 2005. *South African National HIV Prevalence, HIV Incidence, Behaviour and Communication Survey*. Human Sciences Research Council: Pretoria, South Africa.

South African Department of Health 2006. Report: *National HIV and Syphilis Antenatal Sero-Prevalence Survey in South Africa, 2005*. Government Printer: Pretoria, South Africa.

South African Police Service 1998. *Draft Guideline on Sector Policing*. SAPS: Pretoria, South Africa.

Statistics South Africa 2005. *Mid-Year Population Estimates: South Africa 2005.* Statistical Release P0302. StatsSA: Pretoria, South Africa.

Stutterheim, E. 2000. *The Peer Education Programme in the South African Police Service.* SAPS: Pretoria, South Africa.

Stutterheim, E. and C. Khumalo 2000. *The HIV/AIDS Programmes in the SA Police Services.* SAPS: Pretoria, South Africa.

Trojanowicz, R. and B. Bucqueroux 1991. *Community Policing and the Challenge of Diversity.* Michigan State University: Ann Arbor, MI.

Trojanowicz, R. and B. Bucqueroux 1994. *Community Policing: How to Get Started.* Anderson: Cincinnati, OH.

UN Integrated Regional Information Networks (IRIN) 2004. *South Africa: Child Welfare System Leaves many AIDS Orphans Stranded.* IRIN: New York.

UNAIDS 1998. AIDS and the military: UNAIDS point of view. *UNAIDS Best Practice Collection.* UNAIDS Press: Geneva, Switzerland.

UNAIDS 2000. *Consultation on STD Intervention for Preventing HIV: What is the Evidence?* UNAIDS Press: Geneva, Switzerland.

UNAIDS 2003. HIV/AIDS and Uniformed Services. *Fact Sheet* No. 1. UNAIDS Press: Geneva, Switzerland.

UNAIDS, UNICEF and USAID 2004. *Children on the Brink. A Joint Report of New Orphan Estimates and a Framework for Action.* UNICEF Press: New York.

UNAIDS/WHO 2005. *AIDS Epidemic Update: December 2005.* UNAIDS Press: Geneva, Switzerland.

UNICEF 2003. *Africa's Orphaned Generations.* UNICEF Press: New York.

Whiteside, A. and C. Sunter 2000. *AIDS: The Challenge for South Africa.* Human & Rosseau LTD: Cape Town, South Africa.

Whiteside, A. and G. Wood 1996. *AIDS in KwaZulu-Natal: An Emerging Threat.* Kwazulu-Natal Briefing. Helen Suzman Foundation: Johannesburg, South Africa.

WHO 1993. *Guidelines on HIV Infection and AIDS in Prisons.* WHO Press: Geneva, Switzerland.

Zulu, P., Gounden, V., Oakley-Smith, T., and M. Seleone 1999. *The Independent Committee of Inquiry into Racism in the South African Police Service Report.* South African Police Service: Pretoria, South Africa.

Improving Commitment and Productivity within the Nigerian Police

13

A. OYESOJI AREMU AND A.A. JONES

Contents

Introduction

Interest in organizational commitment has intensified in recent years (e.g., Babalola et al., 1996; Irving et al., 1997; Lee et al., 2001; Babalola, 2003). This has resulted in this concept being openly accepted as one of the indices through which employees' productivity could be measured. Mowday et al. (1982) have suggested that gaining a greater understanding of the processes related to organizational commitment has implications for employees, organizations, and society as a whole. It has therefore been suggested that research efforts on organizational commitment should be intensified.

Mottaz (1988) contended that commitment can take different forms and it is a complex construct. Becker (1990), however, suggested that there are different foci of commitment. That is, individuals can feel committed to the organization, top management, superiors, or the work group. This, somewhat, can be referred to as an attitudinal disposition of the employees. Brown (1996) defined attitudinal commitment as both a state of positive obligation to an organization and a state of obligation developed as a byproduct of past actions. These past actions, according to Brown (1996), comprised employee and employer deeds. Behavioral commitment, on the other hand, Brown (1996) again contended, is represented by what is termed attributional approaches to commitment and it results from the binding of individuals to behavioral acts.

Similarly, Meyer and Allen (1997) gave a three-component conceptualization of organizational commitment—affective, continuance, and normative commitment. Affective commitment refers to a psychological attachment to the organization (Meyer and Allen, 1997). This refers to a desire to maintain employment in an organization. In easiest terms, it is the employee's emotional attachment to the organization. Shore and Wayne (1993) affirmed this when they argued that employees who perceive a high level of support from the organization are more likely to feel an emotional attachment to the organization. Becker (1990) described continuance commitment as costs associated with leaving the organization, which results from investment in the agency as well as the perceived lack of alternative employment opportunities. The third component, normative commitment, Becker (1990) said, might develop as a result of organizational investments in the individual (e.g., training or tuition subsidies) or socialization experiences that stress the value of loyalty.

The foregoing is best summed up by Reichers (1985) in his contention that commitment has been significantly and negatively associated with turnover and to a lesser extent with other withdrawal behaviors such as decreasing performance and increased absenteeism and tardiness. In essence, commitment to the organization is expected to bring about higher productivity.

In the following review, the aim is to review relevant constructs that support organizational commitment. This will be exhibited by situating these constructs within the context of the Nigeria police and by examining how this would affect organizational commitment of its personnel.

Police Organizational Commitment

Literature has established that commitment within the police organization may be compromised by commitment outside the organization (Reichers, 1985). This implies that some police officers may be more committed to other things other than the police agency. Similarly, Beck and Wilson (1998) have suggested that the experience of police personnel would be the most important factor in the development of organizational commitment. According to Beck and Wilson (1998), these experiences could be placed into two categories, i.e., personal positive experiences and shared negative experiences. Personal positive experiences are those that indicate the organizational values and the support for the individual, confirm their expectations, and increase their investments in the organization. Conversely, shared negative experiences are those that indicate a lack of support or confirmed expectations. The explanation to this is that police personnel expect their organization to be all-supportive to their career. When this appears not to be attainable, they might look elsewhere. Beck (1999), however, contended that the provision of viable alternative should provide uncommitted police officers with an alternative to quit the organization, and leave the organization with a more strongly committed workforce. This perhaps accounts for the position of Beck and Wilson (2000) that police agencies may have unique organizational characteristics and managerial practices that highlight a lack of support, justice, and value as they build on an inventory of bad experiences.

As interesting as the foregoing may seem, research on organizational commitment among police personnel has received only limited attention (Beck and Wilson, 1997; Metcalfe and Dick, 2000). Metcalfe and Dick (2000) then submitted that the small number of studies undertaken suggests a relatively negative relationship between organizational management and employee job commitment. Harr (1997), e.g., contended that low levels of police personnel commitment reflect their bad experiences, some of which was in essence a function of the type of work they engage in. Metcalfe and Dick (2000) also conveyed that police commitment is significantly affected by an individual's identification and commitment to the organization's value. This, they contended further, included the extent to which police personnel are prepared to improve their performance. In a more succinct way, Metcalfe and Dick's (2000) findings suggested that job commitment is enhanced when police personnel are involved in decision-making, feel supported by superiors, and receive adequate levels of feedback about their job performance and job expectation.

James and Hendry (1991) reported that police officers around Australia have low level of commitment to their organizations and this is even lower than their overseas counterparts. This, James and Hendry (1991) further contended, may be detrimental to the effectiveness of the police organization. Beck (1999) concluded that a series of studies on police organization has shown that experienced police officers have low level of commitment to their organization. Similarly, Beck and Wilson (1997) stated that low levels of commitment of police officers might probably result from a culmination of diverse poor experiences with organizational management and other factors.

In Nigeria, there has not been much research on police organizational commitment as has been undertaken in Europe and America. The few studies available are therefore not enough to support the research contentions held by earlier studies in Europe and America. Other than this, the organizational setting is also not the same. Therefore, there could be variations in study results in Nigeria when compared with other international studies and findings. There is a need for any study examining the Nigeria police to not only bridge this apparent research gap, but also to advance the frontier of research in police organizational commitment as it is has been evaluated in Europe and America.

Agboola (2004) reported that police in Nigeria were not committed to their job. However, Babalola (2003) in another study discovered that job satisfaction, life satisfaction, and career commitment could predict the organizational commitment of police personnel. Of all these predictors, Babalola (2003) reported that career commitment has the most contribution to organizational commitment of police. Obviously, it is not empirically sufficient to conclude that police personnel are committed to their organization. There is still more to be analyzed. It is therefore first critical to have a look at the organizational structure of the Nigeria police (see Figure 13.1).

The Organizational Structure of the Nigerian Police

The Nigeria police organization is structured along three-tier framework: departments, zones, and commands. In all, there are six departments in the Nigeria police:

1. "A" Department: Finance and Administration
2. "B" Department: Operations
3. "C" Department: Logistics and Supplies
4. "D" Department: Investigation and Intelligence
5. "E" Department: Training and General Policy
6. "F" Department: Research and Planning

These departments are headed by police officials that are not less than a deputy inspector general of police (DIGP) in rank. And organizationally, the DIGP is the next rank to inspector general of police (IGP), which is the highest rank in the Nigeria police.

The Nigeria police also has 12 zones with each zone headed by an assistant inspector general of police (AIGP). These AIGPs have supervisory control over the commissioners of police (CPs) who are in charge of the 36 state police commands and federal capital territory police commands. A deputy commissioner of police (DCP) assists each of the state CPs. At the state level, there are divisional police commands headed by divisional police officers who are not below the rank of chief superintendent of police (CSP). Each police station is headed by an assistant superintendent of police (ASP). And last, there are police posts (see Figure 13.1).

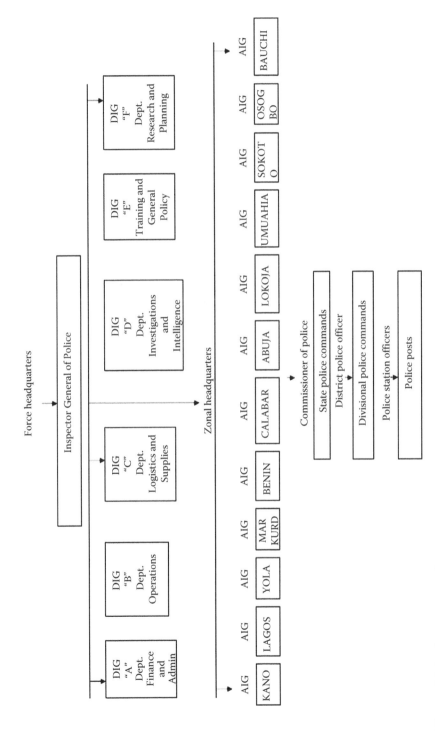

Figure 13.1 The Nigeria police organogram.

Perceived Organizational Support and
Organizational Commitment

Researchers have discovered that a positive relationship exists between perceived organizational support and organizational commitment (Mottaz, 1988; Reyes, 1992; Meyer and Allen, 1997). Eisenberger et al. (1990) defined perceived organizational support as the extent to which employees perceive the organizational values, their contribution, and care about their well-being. In a similar vein, Robinson et al. (1994) suggested that organizational commitment might be construed as an array of obligations performed as a result of inducements accepted from the organization.

Studies have shown that perceived organizational support is positively related to the performance of conventional job responsibilities, citizenship behavior, and commitment (Eisenberger et al., 1990; Shore and Wayne, 1993). Eisenberger et al. (1986) were of the opinion that high perceived organizational support would (a) meet needs for approval, esteem, and social identity; and (b) produce the expectation that superior conventional performance and extra role behavior carried out for the organization by the employee would increase productivity. This has a support in Wayne et al. (1997) contention that leader–member exchange may play a key role in affecting employees' perceptions of organizational support.

According to Jones et al. (1995) and Guzzo et al. (1994), work-related outcomes that have been found to be related to perceived organizational support include affective organizational commitment, evaluative and objective measures of in-role job performance, help given to coworkers, constructive suggestions for improving the operations of the organization, and influential tactics designed by employees to make supervisors aware of their dedication and accomplishment. Studies have also shown that perceived organizational support has been found to be negatively related to absenteeism and turnover intentions (Guzzo et al., 1994; Wayne et al., 1997). Similarly, it has also been found to serve as a socioemotional resource for employees just as perceived support from friends and relations may fulfill socioemotional needs in interpersonal relationships (Cohen and Wills, 1985). The foregoing perhaps made Armell (1998) conclude that perceived organizational support should be especially satisfying for police officers with high needs for esteem, affiliation, emotional support, and approval. Beck and Wilson's (1998) findings seem to support this when they report that police officers are more likely to become committed to the organization if they feel that the organization values and supports them as individuals. This latter report notwithstanding, efforts can still be made to further verify empirically, this contention.

Perceived Fairness and Other Contextual Factors of Organizational Support

Perceived fairness is all about the way in which employees are treated by the employer (McFarlin and Sweeney, 1992; Martin and Bernett, 1996; Meyer and Allen, 1997). Skarlicki and Folger (1997) were of the view that employees see fairness of organizational policies and system in terms of distributive procedural and interactional justice. This, Konovsky and Cropanzano (1991) contended, has shown robust relationships with work attitudes. In literature, procedural justice is the term used to refer to perceived fairness. This, in turn, determines the amount of reward or benefit given to employees. Leventhat et al. (1980) suggested that an organization's policies and systems are considered fair by employees if the decision-making process is consistent, unbiased, accurate, correctable, representative, and ethical. In the same vein, Folger and Konovshy (1989) reported that feedback (i.e., two-way communication), resource (i.e., opportunity discuss procedures), and planning (i.e., accurate and adequate information about how performance is evaluated) combine to give the employees a sense that they are respected and supported by the organization.

In relation to the police organization, Palmer (1994) believed that visionary police service organization should have a corporate plan that is developed after consultation with staff that may be affected by the organization's policies. This in essence means that the greater the involvement of staff in formulating the vision, the greater the chances of success in obtaining ownership and commitment to the vision. Convergence evidence has shown that if organizational decisions and managerial actions were deemed unfair and unjust, the affected employees would experience feelings of anger, outrage, and resentment (Folger, 1987, 1993; Sheppard et al., 1992). These could impact the tenure of the employees in the organization. Studies have shown that there is a positive correlation between organizational commitment and organizational tenure (Mathieu and Zajac, 1990; Kushman, 1992; Meyer and Allen, 1997). Similarly, Irving and Meyer (1994) submitted that some employees' relationship to the organization is based upon a strong continual organizational commitment. They advanced further that the employees remain with the organization because the cost of doing otherwise is too high. Citing the case of New South Wales and New Zealand police officers, Meyer and Allen (1984) discovered two distinct stages in the development of organizational commitment—a rapid and substantial decrease in commitment over a few years of employment. Advancing the same thought, Beck and Wilson (2000) reported that police commitment decreases as the time in the organization increases. Corroborating this, Babalola (2003) concluded that Nigerian police record low levels of organizational commitment due to the absence of job satisfaction and career commitment. Surprisingly, some police officers want to stay with their organization in spite of their low commitment. This low commitment more often than not affects the perceived autonomy of the police.

Colarelli et al. (1987) defined autonomy as a concept that permits employees to use fully their "talents and ingenuity"; and also one that causes employees to assume personnel responsibility for work. Colarelli et al. (1987) then argued that lack of autonomy and the use of close supervision in organizations might result in diminished performance and employee stress.

Breaugh (1985) identified three dimensions of autonomy: work scheduling autonomy, work method autonomy, and work criteria autonomy. All these are achievement-oriented. Thus, individuals with high achievement are more likely to enjoy the freedom and personal responsibility provided by a high task autonomy condition, to be more interested in their work, and to be more committed to the organization (Fisher, 1978). Beck (1997) in his study suggested that for police officers to increase organizational commitment, the management of that agency should trust and respect individual officers, ensure that the performance and needs of individual officers are recognized, allow officers to participate in decision making, and improve both pay and promotional opportunities.

Other than the variables reviewed above, other variables investigated in the study were: gender, job status, age, and marital status. These are reviewed alongside organizational commitment in spite of the little research carried out in this area (most especially, on the police). Irving et al. (1997) found that age is positively correlated with affective and normative occupational commitment. Similarly, Mathieu and Zajac's (1990) meta-analysis finding yielded a medium positive correlation between age and organizational commitment. Camilleri (2002) affirmed that older employees would have higher degree of organizational commitment based upon the promise that older employees view their past years of service to the organization as an investment; and have the perception that it would be more difficult for them to move to another job. This implies that they would likely be more committed to the organization.

Age has been associated with different forms of commitment, possibly for different reasons. Meyer and Allen (1984) argued that age might be correlated with affective commitment because it serves as a proxy for seniority that is associated with opportunities to better one's position in the organization over time. In another study, Meyer and Allen (1997) found that age is related to affective and normative occupational commitment, but is not found to be related to continuance commitment.

Research on gender and organizational commitment is inconclusive. For instance, Mowday et al. (1982) reported that women are more committed than men. However, Maier (1999) noted that men and women experience similar levels of organizational commitment. In their study, Mathieu and Zajak (1990) believed that there is a link between gender and commitment. Variations, however, across professional groups led them to conclude that there is no consistent relationship between gender and organizational commitment. In an attempt to give further justification on the ambiguity of research on gender and organizational commitment, Aven et al. (1993) concluded that similar commitment could be won from males and females when organizations treat all employees fairly. Similarly, Kushman (1992) reported that gender is not a factor that influences organizational commitment. Corroborating this, Powell (1999) submitted that there is inconsistent support that commitment levels between men and women may vary.

However, gender studies in police organization have somewhat largely tilted toward men. Martin (1996) was of the opinion that the study of women in criminal justice was virtually ignored until the rise of what is loosely called police feminist writings dating from the 1960s. Heindenshohn (1992) was also of the view that women are largely invisible in that much of crime and police management studies are focused on offenders and victims. These have grossly limited studies on gender and police organizational commitment. This notwithstanding, the police profession is seen more as a masculine job.

This study also investigated the prediction of job and marital status as variables of interest in police organizational commitment. It is therefore well directed to include these variables as predictors of police organizational commitment. Although, the variables appear salient to organizational commitment, researchers have not made efforts to investigate their predicting effect (most especially, on the police in Nigeria). There is ultimately reason to believe that job and marital status could be variables of interest in police organizational commitment.

The primary purpose of the study if police in Nigeria is to investigate the impact of these factors, both as they are organizationally related and contextually associated with organizational commitment of Nigerian law enforcement officials. The secondary purpose is to examine relations between some organizational and contextual factors as they affect the organizational commitment of police. It is assumed that, in view of the current challenges being faced by the Nigerian police, the study would be of immense benefit to the Nigerian police administrators and government officials.

As a result of this evaluation, two research questions will be examined. They are

1. What is the combined effect of the predictors on organizational commitment of the police?
2. What is the relative contribution of the predictors to the criterion (organizational commitment)?

Research Design

This study adopted a cross-sectional survey design in the collection of data. The target population of the study was made up of officers and men of the Nigerian police assigned to the Lagos State Police Command. Ranking officers in the Nigerian police are in the executive levels and include commissioned officials whose ranks are between ASP and IGP. Also included in the rank and file of officers in the Nigerian police are police inspectors. These representatives of the Nigerian police are low level (not commissioned), and include also new recruits. Their ranks are between constable and sergeant. The Lagos State Police Command is headed by a CP and assisted by a DCP. The command is divided into eight police area commands with 38 police divisional offices. Data collection was purposively done in four out of the eight area commands.

Research Participants

The participants were 349 personnel of the Nigerian police ranging from 19 to 53 years of age with a mean age of 28.6 years and standard deviation of 5.6. In terms of demographic characteristics, the sample included 252 (72.2%) males and 97 (27.8%) females; 99 (28.41%) were officers ranging from ASP to DSP, while 250 (71.6%) were junior cadre police officers ranging from constable to sergeant; on marital status, 127 (36.4%) were singles, while 222 (63.6%) were married. The participants' job experience ranged between 1 and 25 years.

Methodology

The participants were conveniently sampled using a nonrandomized technique. The administration of the questionnaire was done by the researchers at the Lagos State Police Command. This was facilitated with the assistance of the police public relation officer (PPRO) in Lagos. The Lagos State Police Command is one of the 36 state police commands in Nigeria, including federal capital police command, Abuja. The Lagos State Police Command includes approximately 6000 police personnel. It is considered the largest police complement within Nigeria. The main reason is that the state of Lagos is the official financial capital of and the most cosmopolitan state in Nigeria.

The administration of all the questionnaires covered a 2-week period. And from the 500 questionnaires administered, 437 questionnaires were returned, out of which 349 were properly filled and useful for data analysis. This gave the study a 69.8% success rate in terms of questionnaire administration.

Permission to conduct the study was granted by the police commissioner of the state of Lagos. The administration of the survey, which was conducted between October and November (5 weeks) in 2004 was mainly without major difficulty. However, some participants were uncooperative and even demanded gratifications as a condition for responding to the items of the questionnaire.

Instrumentation

The participants completed four subscales from the police organizational commitment scale (POCS). The POCS contained five sections. Section A of the instrument contained five variables designed to measure respondent's demographic variables (contextual factors). Those examined included: gender, marital status, job status, age, and job tenure.

Sections B, C, and D measured fairness, perceived organizational support, and autonomy, respectively, and contained five items each with a four-point response format—Strongly Agree = 4; Agree = 3; Disagree = 2; and Strongly Disagree = 1. The items in the three sections were presented to a group of selected police officers to further ascertain the reliability of the items. Using a split-half method, the following internal consistency coefficients were reported for sections B, C, and D, respectively: 0.73, 0.69, and 0.71. Examples of the items of the subscales are

Fairness:	• Superiors praise, recognize, and distribute awards for police officers in a fair manner.
	• Police command resources are allocated without favoritism.
Perceived organizational support:	• My organization values my accomplishments.
	• My command shows concern for the needs, which I express regarding the duty I perform.
Autonomy:	• I have reasonable freedom to direct police activities in the commanding, which I work.
	• Within the bounds of any applicable police policy and laws, I have sufficient freedom to act as a police.

Section E of the instrument contained eight items on organizational commitment. The items of the scale were adapted from the original instrument of Meyer and Allen (1984). This scale measures affective organizational commitment with response options varying from Strongly Agree (4), Agree (3), Disagree (2), and Strongly Disagree (1). According to Meyer and Allen (1997), the median reliability estimate for the scale from more than 16,000 employees from various employment groups was 0.85. In the current study, a split-half reliability estimate of 0.79 was obtained when administered to a group of police officers. Two examples of the items on the scale are

- I enjoy discussing police organization with people outside it.
- I would be happy to spend the rest of my career with the police.

The items for each subscale of the instrument were coded and averaged to create a score for each of the subscales. Multiple regression analyses were then conducted.

Data Analysis and Results

For purposes of analysis, answers were provided to the two research questions earlier raised in the paper. To answer the two questions, multivariate analysis was employed.

For the first research question, a composite analysis of the independent variables (fairness, organizational support, autonomy, gender, job status, age, job tenure, and marital status) was carried out and regressed against organizational commitment. Results from the hierarchical regression analyses done on the combinatorial effects of the independent variables on the dependent variable (organizational commitment) showed that jointly the predictors could not determine organizational commitment of Nigerian police officers. Thus, jointly the predicting effect as shown in Table 13.1 was not significant, $F = 1.839$, $p = 0.072$, adj. $R^2 = 0.033$. Similarly, the independent variables examined made only a joint contribution of 7.2% to the prediction of the organizational commitment of the sampled police officers.

In an attempt to lend a further statistical weight to the results in Table 13.1, intercorrelation of the predicting variables to organizational commitment was also computed. Results in Table 13.2 showed that despite the fact that the correlation coefficient is very low, there is strong statistical evidence to conclude that there is a strong positive relationships between

Table 13.1   Summary of Regression Analysis on Sample Data

Multiple $R = 0.268$
R-Square $R^2 = 0.072$
Adjusted R-square $= 0.0711$
Standard error $= 3.159$
Analysis of variance

Source of Variation	Sum of Square	Df	Means Square	F Value	Sig	Remark
Regression	146.863	8	18.358	3.29	>0.05	NS
Residual	1896.343	340				
Total	2043.206	348	5.58			

Table 13.2 Intercorrelation of the Predicting Variables to Organizational Commitment

	OC	F	OS	A	S	JS	A	WE	MS
Organizational commitment	1.000								
Fairness	0.222**	1.000							
Organizational support	0.149*	0.520**	1.000						
Autonomy	0.089	0.454**	0.675**	1.000					
Sex	-0.093	0.128	0.033	-016	1.000				
Job status	-0.059	-0.055	-0.080	-0.152*	0.065	1.000			
Age	0.042	0.031	0.052	0.137	-0.169*	-0.389**	1.000		
Work experience	0.022	0.036	0.018	0.124	-0.074	-0.482**	0.776**	1.000	
Marital status	-0.039	-0.109	-0.008	-0.023	-0.118	-0.100	0.309*	0.277**	1.000

Note: OC, organizational support; F, fairness; A, autonomy; S, sex; JS, job status; A, age; WE, work experience; MS, marital status.
* and ** Strongly correlated.

fairness and organizational commitment of the sampled police ($r = 0.222$, $p < 0.05$). Similarly, there were notable relationships between organizational support and organizational commitment, autonomy and organizational commitment, and marital status and organizational commitment ($r = 0.149$, $p < 0.05$, $r = 0.454$, $p < 0.05$, $r = 0.309$, $p < 0.05$). These were all strong positive relationships. However, the table also showed that strong negative relationships existed between job status and organizational commitment ($r = -0.152$, $p < 0.05$), age and organizational commitment ($r = -0.389$, $p < 0.05$), and work experience and organizational commitment ($r = -0.482$, $p < 0.05$). These findings lend statistical support to conclude the unsignificant joint effect of the combined variables on the organizational commitment of the police.

Discussion

The results obtained in this study have shown that a combination of fairness, perceived organizational support, autonomy, gender, job status, age, job tenure, and marital status are significantly ineffective in predicting organizational commitment of the sampled Nigerian police officers. The calculated F ratio of 1.839, which was found not to be significant at 0.05 alpha level, was a statistical evidence of the ineffectiveness of a combination of the independent variables in the prediction of organizational commitment of participants. This is further bolstered by the results that revealed a coefficient of multiple correlations of 0.268 and a multiple R-square of 0.072. The latter result is interpreted to mean that the investigated independent variables accounted for only 7.2% of the variance in organizational commitment among the police officers studied.

These results implied that 7.2% of the variance in police organizational commitment is unexplainable by looking at the combined effect of the eight variables investigated in this study. In simpler terms, the variables investigated could not influence police personnel organizational commitment. This finding has some far-reaching implications for the Nigerian police organization, its personnel, and for contemporary policing in general. In Nigeria, police personnel are not only poorly remunerated; salaries are even owed in arrears for 4–5 months. And in view of the nature of their job, police are not supposed to go on strike to express their displeasure toward their organization and the government. In addition, due to the poor indices of the Nigerian economy, which among others include high unemployment, police are not induced economically to quit their job. These would cumulatively translate to noncommitment to the police organization. This could be interpreted to mean that police personnel only want to keep their job for economic reasons. This finding is supported by the work of Beck and Wilson (1997), in which they contended that low levels of commitment of police officers might probably result from a culmination of diverse poor experiences with organizational management and other factors. Similarly, this finding confirms the assertion held by Metcalfe and Dick (2000), in which they contended that the small number of studies on police organizational commitment is as a result of relatively negative relationships between organizational management and the police job. In what appears to be a semblance to this finding, Aremu (1999) submitted that the negative perception of the police by the public does actually demoralize the former and subsequently affect the police organizational commitment. Another explanation for the negative relationship between police and organizational commitment might be as a result of the job frustration police perceive in terms of their personal welfare granted by the authorities. Thus, it might be difficult for police to be committed. Given these explanations, it sounds reasonable to conclude that the noted absence of influence or effect of the suspected predicting variables on organizational commitment on the sampled Nigerian police is worrisome in view of the serious organizational role expected of the Nigerian police in nation building. And more importantly, it leaves more to be desired internally for the police organization in Nigeria. Without commitment, effectiveness and likely efficiency would be negatively impacted. Truly, any expected paradigm shifts within a police agency would be effective if its personnel were well motivated.

However, in spite of the traditional negative experiences of police personnel, it is surprising that many still identify positively with their organization. What motivates this phenomenon cannot be strongly deciphered from Table 13.2. Nevertheless, it can still be extrapolated that the police are trained to be loyal no matter what the situation is. This can also be explained by the concept of esprit de corps within police organizations. No matter the situation, police have been trained to display loyalty. This is consistent with assertions of Leventhat et al. (1980) and Folger and Konovsky (1989). Certainly, this finding has shown that police employees cherish an organization that accommodates their feelings, understands that they too can contribute to the development of the organization, and ensures fairness and justice in the implementation of its policies.

From the foregoing, it is less surprising that the findings reported showed that the variables investigated could not predict the organizational commitment of Nigerian police. And more importantly, it is apparent that of all types of organizational commitment, organizational support seems to be the more crucial factor within the Nigerian police. A likely explanation is that the corporate and executive support of the police organization is what the police subordinates need to move their agency forward.

Counseling Implications for the Nigerian Police

The findings of this study have implications for counseling within police agencies, policing policy and practice, and for researchers. In the first place, it has been revealed that the Nigerian police need a better orientation that would endear the organization to its members. It becomes pertinent therefore that police administrators in Nigeria must reengineer the police organization in order for its personnel to be more proactive. This, if done, would enhance the commitment of police personnel. Presumably, police personnel need to be more committed to their organization for the desired result of good policing to be achieved. The Nigerian police authorities should therefore take all efforts to review all existing policies, to determine which are not in the interest of effective policing. In so doing, law enforcement executives and government leaders would attain the expected change within the Nigerian police.

Finally, the insignificant relationship between the participants and their commitment to the police organization showed that research efforts should be intensified in Nigeria and globally on research examining organizational commitment.

Survey Limitations

Caution is warranted in generalizing the findings of the above research. As noted earlier, most of the studies linking police efforts to organizational commitment have been conducted in Europe and America. This may have placed some limitations on the accuracy of the discussion of the findings reported in the Nigerian study. The findings reported may also be limited only to the sampled police in Lagos State Police Command. Second, the number of survey respondents was very small in comparison to the police population in Lagos and in Nigeria in general. That said, it could become improper to generalize the above findings to the entire police in Nigeria. The Nigerian study only investigated the outlined eight predicting variables on organizational commitment. While these appear to be far reaching, it must be stressed that there may be several other factors that could impact the organizational commitment of police personnel.

These limitations notwithstanding, the findings of the study have contributed significantly to existing, but limited, literature on law enforcement within Nigeria. Further related research is warranted.

Conclusions

From the findings reported above, one can clearly conclude that the police organization in Nigeria needs to be more sensitive to the welfare of its personnel. This becomes necessary if government officials expect the police to show more commitment, effectiveness, and efficiency. Globally, policing and the police practice are of critical importance to internal domestic security. Enhanced productivity would be best achieved by a police mechanism that provides appropriate support to its officers and front-line personnel. In so doing, agency employees would not only be proactive, efficient, and committed, but they would be ready to give their best efforts to their profession. Commitment to the police task is also expected by members of the public.

The lessons from these findings and recommendations underscore a challenge for police authorities in Nigeria. It would not be unreasonable to submit that successful policing can be realized when agency personnel are motivated and committed. The results could be measured by examining the productivity of agency personnel, both totally and individually and by evaluating job satisfaction and passion to perform. This expected change would be possible when police administrators place the welfare of their personnel on a high premium. And as Sutton (1996) concluded, if management and employees are unable to treat each other with mutual respect and fairness, how can members of the community "keep faith" within their police? Ultimately, a nation cannot rise above the quality of her police personnel.

References

Agboola, A.O. (2004). Correlates of job commitment motivation, self-esteem and work environment on HIV/AIDS attitude of Nigerian Police. Unpublished BEd Project, University of Ibadan, Ibadan, Nigeria.

Aremu, A.O. (1999). Public perception and work strain of Nigerian Police: Some psychological explanations. *Nigerian Journal of Applied Psychology*, 5(1), 45–51.

Armell, P. (1998). Perceived organizational support and police performance: The moderating influence of socioemotional needs. *Journal of Applied Psychology*, 83(2), 288–297.

Aven, F.F., Parker, B., and McEvoy, G.M. (1993). Gender and attitudinal commitment to organizations: A meta-analysis. *Journal of Business Research*, 26, 63–73.

Babalola, J.A. (2003). Job satisfaction, life satisfaction and career commitment as correlates of organizational commitment in the Nigeria Police. An unpublished MEd Project, University of Ibadan, Ibadan, Nigeria.

Babalola, S.S., Balogun, S.K., and Oriaku, C. (1996). The influence of leaders' behaviour and participative decision-making on organizational commitment. *African Journal for the Psychological Study of Social Issues*, 3(2), 176–144.

Beck, K. (1999). Measuring morale: A manager's guide to the job condition survey. Report No. 122.5. National Police Research Unit, Adelaide, South Australia.

Beck, K. and Wilson, C. (1997). Police officers' views on cultivating organizational commitment: Implications for police managers. *Policing: An International Journal of Police Strategies and Management*, 20, 175–195.

Beck, K. and Wilson, C. (1998). The development of organizational commitment: Recruitment, training and probation. Report No. 122.2. National Police Research Unit, Adelaide, South Australia.

Beck, K. and Wilson, C. (2000). Development of affective commitment: A cross functional sequence change with tenure. *Journal of Vocational Behaviour*, 12(5), 23–35.

Becker, T.E. (1990). Foci and bases of commitment: An empirical examination of proposed distinctions. An unpublished doctoral thesis. The Ohio State University, Columbus, OH.

Breaugh, J.A. (1985). The measurement of work autonomy. *Human Relations*, 38, 551–570.

Brown, R.B. (1996). Organizational commitment: Clarifying the concept and simplifying the existing construct topology. *Journal of Vocational Behaviour*, 49, 230–251.

Camilleri, E. (2002). Some antecedents of organizational commitment: Results from an information systems public sector organization. Retrieved from www.askjeeves.com on June 23, 2004.

Cohen, S. and Wills, T.A. (1985). Stress, social support and the buffering hypothesis. *Psychological Bulletin*, 98, 310–357.

Colarelli, S.M., Dean, R.A., and Konstants, C. (1987). Comparative effects of personal and situational influence on job outcomes of new professionals. *Journal of Applied Psychology*, 72, 558–566.

Eisenberger, S., Huntingdon, R., Hutchinson, S., and Sowa, D. (1986). Perceived organizational support. *Journal of Applied Psychology*, 71, 500–507.

Eisenberger, R., Fasolo, P., and Davis-LaMastro, V. (1990). Perceived organizational support and employee diligence, commitment, and innovation. *Journal of Applied Psychology*, 75, 51–59.

Fisher, C.D. (1978). The effects if personal control, competence, and extrinsic reward system on intrinsic motivation. *Organizational Behaviour and Human Performance*, 21, 273–288.

Folger, R. (1987). Distributive and procedural justice in the workplace. *Social Justice Research*, 9(2), 1143–1159.

Folger, R. (1993). Reactions to mistreatment at work. In J.K. Murnighan (Ed.), *Social Psychology in Organisations: Advances in Theory and Research* (pp. 161–183). Englewood Cliffs, NJ: Prentice Hall.

Folger, R. and Knovsky, M.A. (1989). Effects of procedural and distributive justice on reactions to pay rise decisions. *Academy of Management Journal*, 32(4), 115–130.

Guzzo, R.A., Noonan, K.A., and Elron, E. (1994). Expatriate managers and the psychological contract. *Journal of Applied Psychology*, 79(4), 617–626.

Harr, R. (1997). They're making a bad name for the department: Exploring the link between organizational commitment and police occupational deviance in a police patrol bureau. *Policing: An International Journal for Police Strategies and Management*, 20(4), 786–812.

Heindenshohn, F. (1992). *Women in Control: The Role of Women in Law Enforcement*. Oxford, England: Claredon Press.

Irving, P.G. and Meyer, J.P. (1994). Re examination of the meta-expectation hypothesis: A longitudinal analysis. *Journal of Applied Psychology*, 79(5), 937–949.

Irving, P.G., Coleman, D.F., and Cooper, C.L. (1997). Further assessment of a three-component model of occupational commitment: Generalizability and differences across occupations. *Journal of Applied Psychology*, 82(3), 444–452.

James, S. and Hendry, B. (1991). The money or the job: The decision to leave policing. *Australia and New Zealand Journal of Criminology*, 24(3), 169–189.

Jones, B., Flynn, D.M., and Kelloway, E.K. (1995). Perception of support from the organization in relation to work stress, satisfaction, and commitment. In S.L. Sauter and L.R. Murphy (Eds.), *Organisational Risk Factors for Job Stress* (pp. 41–52). Washington, DC: American Psychological Association.

Konovsky, M.A. and Cropanzano, R. (1991). Perceived fairness of employee drug testing as a predictor of employee attitudes and job performance. *Journal of Applied Psychology*, 76(2), 698–707.

Kushman, J.W. (1992). The organization dynamics of teacher schools. *Educational Administration Quarterly*, 28(3), 5–42.

Lee, K., Allen, N.J., Meyer, J.P., and Rhee, K. (2001). The three-component model of organizational commitment: An application to South Korea. *Applied Psychology: An International Review*, 50(4), 596–614.

Leventhat, G.S., Karuza, J., and Fry, W.R. (1980). Beyond fairness: A theory of allocation preferences. In G. Mikula (Ed.), *Justice and Social Interaction* (pp. 167–218). New York: Springer-Verlag.

Maier, M. (1999). On the gendered substructure of organization: Dimensions aid dilemmas of corporate masculinity. In G. Powell (Ed.), *Handbook of Gender and Work* (pp. 34–49). Thousand Oaks, CA: Sage.

Martin, C. (1996). The impact of equal opportunities policies on the experience of women police constables. *British Journal of Criminology*, 36(4), 528.

Martin, C.L. and Bennett, N. (1996). The role of justice judgments in explaining the relationships between job satisfaction and organizational commitment. *Group and Organization Management*, 21(5), 84–104.

Mathieu, J.E. and Zajac, D.M. (1990). A review of meta-analysis of the antecedents, correlates, and consequences of organizational commitment. *Psychological Bulletin*, 108, 171–194.

McFarlin, D.B. and Sweeney, P.D. (1992). Distributive and procedural justice as predictors of satisfaction with personal and organizational outcomes. *Academy of Management Journal*, 35(3), 626–637.

Metcalfe, B. and Dick, G. (2000). Is the force still with you? Measuring police commitment. *Journal of Managerial Psychology*, 15, 812–832.

Meyer, J.P. and Allen, N.J. (1984). Testing the side-bet of organizational commitment: Some methodological considerations. *Journal of Applied Psychology*, 69(4), 372–378.

Meyer, J.P. and Allen, N.J. (1997). *Commitment in the Workplace: Theory, Research, and Application*. Thousand Oaks, CA: Sage Publications, Inc.

Mottaz, C.J. (1988). Determinants of organizational commitment. *Human Relations*, 41(5), 467–482.

Mowday, R., Porter, L.W., and Steers, R.M. (1982). *Employee–Organization Linkages: The Psychology of Commitment, Absenteeism, and Turnover*. San Diego, CA: Academic Press.

Palmer, M. (1994). Managing a hierarchical para-military organization. In K. Bryett and C. Lewis (Eds.), *Un-Peeling Tradition Contemporary Policing*. Melbourne, Victoria, Australia: Macmillan.

Powell, G. (Ed.) (1999). *Handbook of Gender and Work*. Thousand Oaks, CA: Sage.

Reichers, A.E. (1985). A review and reconceptualisation of organisational commitment. *Academy of Management Review*, 10(1), 465–476.

Reyes, P. (1992). Preliminary models of teacher organizational commitment: Implications for restructuring the workplace. Report No. EA 024 290.

Robinson, S.L., Kraatz, M.S., and Rousseau, D.M. (1994). Changing obligations and the psychological contract: A longitudinal study. *Academy of Management Journal*, 37(3), 136–152.

Sheppard, B.H., Lewicki, R.J., and Minton, J.W. (1992). *Organisational Justice: The Search for Fairness in the Workplace*. New York: Lexington Books.

Shore, L.M. and Wayne, S.J. (1993). Commitment and employee behaviour: Comparison of affective commitment and continuance with perceived organizational support. *Journal of Applied Psychology*, 76(5), 637–643.

Skarlicki, D.P. and Folger, R. (1997). Retaliation in the workplace: The roles of distributive, procedural, and interactional justice. *Journal of Applied Psychology*, 82(3), 434–443.

Sutton, J. (1996). Keeping the faith: Women in policing a New South Wales perspective. Paper presented at the *Australia Institute of Criminology Conference: First Australasian Women Police Conference*, Sydney, Australia, July 29–31, 1996.

Wayne, S.J., Shore, L.M., and Liden, R.C. (1997). Perceived organizational support and leader–member exchange: A social exchange perspective. *Academy of Management Journal*, 40(1), 82–111.

Examining the Implications of Intelligence-Led Policing on Human Rights in South Africa

14

CHRISTIAAN BEZUIDENHOUT

Contents

Introduction

Police cannot operate without information from and about the community. This is why the concept of "intelligence-led policing" (ILP)* was so significant to the police. ILP is a concept that is widely used, but the full operational definition of this paradigm is still vague. ILP refers to a recent shift or change in crime control thinking and the related policing practices. Intelligence gathering by means of different tactics and the proactive strategies designed around the gathered information explains the basic meaning of ILP. This new era of proactive and ILP is also known as the "police revolution" within South Africa. Although "intelligence-led" policing can officially be traced back to the 1830s and evidence exists that the warranted tampering with mail in the name of intelligence gathering and safety was condoned, a clear

---

* For the purposes of this contribution "crime intelligence" and "crime information" will be used as parallel concepts.

demarcation of its boundaries and substance does not exist. It can be argued that ILP is important to monitor airports and ports and to infiltrate terrorist groups or syndicates for national security (e.g., to avoid a duplication of the September 11, 2001 terrorist attack in the United States).

From a contemporary law enforcement perspective, proactive policing involves community policing (CP) and voluntary community involvement with greater emphasis on crime prevention and problem solving. The main difference between CP and ILP is the typical absence of voluntary consent in the case of ILP. As noble as the idea of community policing may seem, CP or partnership policing are not doing well, especially in South Africa (SA), because the community still does not trust the police. The South African Police Service (SAPS) and other police agencies globally are therefore forced to use ILP and other technologically enhanced tactics to gather information on the population. This leads to a critical question that needs to be asked while recognizing the fact that police and community relations in the new millennium are in trouble. We must therefore ask: Is the intention of ILP political or in actuality a method to have law enforcement agencies police proactively?

Overview

Adoption of the Constitution of the Republic of South Africa (1996) has resulted in the previous police force becoming redundant and being replaced by a police service. In becoming a "service," the way was theoretically paved for law enforcement to provide excellence to all South African citizens. The SAPS is nonetheless finding it difficult to make any significant inroads into crime reduction and control endeavors. Furthermore, the population usually views members of the police in a negative light. One of the key elements of proactive policing and crime prevention is intelligence that is divulged by the community to the police to enable the police to react to a situation before a crime is committed. However, the SAPS is finding it arduous to get information from the community as the local residents still deem the SAPS as either corrupt or the pawns of the government. The majority of the population before 1994, when SA became a democracy, also shared this view (Stevens and Yach, 1995:76). It is therefore important that the police start using other tactics to gain information and intelligence to enable them to police SA effectively, as they are unable to obtain the necessary information from the community. The CP approach was introduced as a mainstream enforcement and service approach in SA after 1994 and is entrenched in the South African Constitution. It was thought that the community will embrace this new approach and that they will supply the SAPS with enough information to make proactive and problem-oriented policing a success. CP unfortunately does not live up to this expectation. The introduction of several complaints and oversight mechanisms also did not result in a sudden change in community and police relationships.

The negativism toward the SAPS and the nonembracement of CP by the population are indirectly contributing to the high crime rate in SA. If the community reacts and divulges all the information they have on criminal activities that is taking place in their neighborhoods, the police will be able to react proactively and prevent crimes before they are committed. At a 5-day workshop presented in June 2007 to 250 male and female nursing students, a general discussion was commenced to discuss violent crimes and the role of the criminal justice system (CJS). During these discussions the students indicated that they did not trust the police and that they believed that some police officers are involved in crime. One student made the following remark: "You cannot trust the police because they are in 'cahoots' with the serious criminals." Another student commented: "I know of a lot of criminals and what they do in my area but I won't say anything to the police. The criminals will kill me if I talk to the police. I don't think the police are doing their job." More students in the group reacted with similar observations. When interviewed further with the following question: "If you know of a person who is committing or are involved in crime will you inform the police?," only five students indicated that they would divulge this information to the police. The students were overwhelmingly adamant that the police will not do anything with the information and that they will put themselves and their families in danger if they were identified as police "impimpis"* (informants). The different responses ranged from "it is not worth the effort" to "you will be crazy if you do that."

Two important themes emerged during the discussions with the group, namely:

- A lack of trust in the SAPS
- The majority of the group will not divulge information to the police

If the police have difficulty in gathering crime intelligence from the community, the following questions arise:

- What are the SAPS doing to get information in their different areas of responsibility?
- Who are monitoring the techniques the SAPS are using in their intelligence gathering efforts?

---

* Before 1994 an impimpi was a person who compromised the struggle against apartheid by being a police spy—they were often killed either by necklacing (a burning tyre around the neck/body) or stoning.

Another example of lack of trust in the CP initiatives of the SAPS can be examined. During a community project at a school in the Tshwane Municipal District in Pretoria, South Africa, during September 2006, grade 8–10 pupils also aired their concern about the lack of trust in the police. The project was initiated to better community and police relations in the area. The aim was to inform the pupils about the different telephone help lines they could use to seek help if needed and to encourage them to share information with their local police station regarding drug-related problems in the area. However, the pupils found the initiative humorous and made audible gestures during the presentation. When the author asked them why they were reacting negatively toward this police outreach initiative, the pupils replied by declaring that the police were corrupt and dishonest. Some pupils reported that police officers were often seen drinking alcohol while they were on duty and did not care about the problems in the community. A few pupils said that they actually saw policemen that specific morning who were driving around in their area in a marked police vehicle while they were consuming beer. Adults supervising these students also reacted in a similar fashion as the student group above. They also believed that the police in their area are corrupt and did not really deem their jobs as serious and important. It was clear that the majority of the group also did not trust the police enough to divulge crime-related information to them.

To look at the issue more broadly, one should look at the historical position of ILP and problems that also contributed to the lack of trust between the police and the community. ILP in Britain and SA will be discussed in further detail and some of the techniques intelligence agencies and the police use to gather information, sometimes illegally, will be investigated.

Contextualizing Intelligence-Led Policing

British thinking has influenced policing in SA from the time when SA was a colony of Britain. Furthermore, consultants from Britain and other parts of Europe have spearheaded modern policing ideas in SA such as CP since the early 1990s (Stevens and Yach, 1995:xi). It is therefore appropriate that the British version of a complaints system and ILP are discussed, as British history will serve to highlight important lessons for the SA version (1994 to date).

The British Version

The issues between the community and the police that were highlighted above are not unique to SA. In Britain, similar problems were experienced since the introduction of formal policing in 1829. These problems are still part and parcel of British policing today. To understand the almost universal problem global police agencies experience, one must contextualize intelligence gathering, proactive policing, and the complaints that are documented against the police. The art of intelligence gathering aimed at deterring potential criminals can be traced back to the thinking of the classical deterrence theorist Jeremy Bentham and the police reforms of Sir Robert Peel in 1829. By creating an impression of omnipresence (e.g., regular foot patrols) it was believed that potential criminals would be deterred and information supplied by cooperative local communities for policing purposes. Despite these expectations the same antagonistic feelings that existed toward watchmen (guards before the introduction of formal policing) also existed toward the formal police. With regard to formal policing in Britain, Brown et al. (2007:184) postulate that

> Widespread resistance had to be overcome because English citizens had a marked distrust of centralized government. ... This profuse mistrust of police authority continued after Peel's new police, dubbed 'Bobbies' and 'Peelers' ... took the streets.

Primarily allowing them the freedom to act almost as they desired exacerbated the problem of the police not being accepted with the anticipated societal admiration. No significant system was in place to monitor police behavior and accountability. This is an issue that is still noteworthy in many policing and intelligence agencies in the world. Furthermore the police are still the only officials with the legal power of arrest.

In Britain, police accountability was for the first time addressed by the Royal Commission on Police during 1962. This led to the promulgation of the Police Act of 1964. The Police Act of 1964 did not protect citizens as such and most complaints against the police were dealt with internally (Maguire, 1991:177–178). It appears that the different complaints systems that were used in Britain since 1964 such as the Police Complaints Board (PCB)—(very similar to the Independent Complaints Directorate in SA) failed to protect citizens against police officials who abused their powers.

Gradually it became more evident to the population that police officers were abusing their powers (e.g., by obtaining forced statements and confessions or the way they gather criminal intelligence). The complaint system in Britain was inadequate to cope with public demand and this, amongst other factors, contributed to citizens' concerns about the abuse of power by the police. In the later era (1970s–1980s), relations between the police and the public reached an all time low in certain areas and overt hostility was growing daily. This led to a number of clashes between the British Police and the public (Governments on the www, 2004).

It is important to note that the civilian police complaint processes in Britain until recently did not include an independent oversight element. An investigation of police misconduct was therefore completed without an independent arbiter. These in-house actions paved the way for corruption and unethical behavior or cover-ups to safeguard the police image (Hall, 2002:225–234).

A clash that took place in Brixton between the police and the citizens served as the watershed for the revision of complaint structures in Britain against police abuse. After the rioting between April 10 and 12, 1981, the then Home Secretary, William Whitelaw, appointed Lord Scarman to conduct an inquiry into the riots. Scarman (1981:I–VII) recommended a change of the system for handling complaints against the police and to rekindle public and police relations. Lord Scarman emphasized that complaints against police who abused their powers on the street caused a "dangerous" (McLaughlin and Johansen, 2002:635–653) lack of confidence in police actions such as stop and search practices. It was also established that some population groups (e.g., young black males) are more likely to be stopped because they represent a significant group of the criminal and prison populations. In this regard, it was argued that the police use their powers "intelligently" to prevent crime proactively. Stop and search policing led to arrests in approximately 10% of the cases and many arrests were for public-order offences arising from antagonism to the group concerned (Waddington, 1999:50–51). Scarman reported that a breakdown between the community and the police existed and that these problems had to be addressed (Hall, 2002:225–234). He wrote his report in a time when the community was pleading for change in respect to fair and accountable police practices. Scarman pointed out that the police should take some responsibility for the disorder that occurred and for the lack of trust in their accountability. This made a significant inroad in the authoritative image of the police that was constructed over many years (Brake and Hale, 1992:38).

Major changes were evident and new stop and search legislation was developed taking into account the defects of the preexisting stop and search powers. The recommendations made by the Royal Commission on Criminal Procedure (1981) was that the new legislation included within the Police and Criminal Evidence Act (PACE) of 1984 should incorporate certain safeguards against abuse, stipulate the reasons for the specific police action, and mandated that a written record of any searches should be available on request (Brown, 1997). Although more effective scrutiny of the investigation conducted against a police officer was intended, it is important to note that senior police officers still conducted the enquiry internally after a citizen lodged a complaint against law enforcement personnel under their guidance (Maguire, 1991:177).

Another important outcome of PACE was the replacing of the PCB by the Police Complaints Authority (PCA) that was established and became fully operational in April 1985. The PCA gained the power to supervise investigations into serious cases of police who abuse their powers. It was anticipated that complaints against police who misuse their powers would be effectively regulated with PACE. An important aim of PACE was to reduce tough street policing or in other words to reduce overt brutal behavior. Furthermore, introducing the use of compulsory video recording of interviews in police interrogation rooms promised to reduce alleged sinister practices to obtain confessions. Comparison of statistical data (Cotton and Povey, 1998–1999:1–15) on complaints regarding police abuse of power show that the average number of cases reported stayed consistent during the mid 1980s and 1990s (20,000+ registered cases nationally per year). Less than 50% of the cases were formally investigated and less than 3% of the cases that were substantiated were handled by means of disciplinary charges. A reason for this is that the police were predominantly controlling the system, and it is believed that many complaints were not recorded. Police abuse victims were often labeled as complainants and are never given the morally validated status of victim. This supports that the civilian police complaint process is being used as an instrument of police management (Smith, 2001:372–392). Hearings take place behind closed doors and the chief officer concerned maintains all the documentation relevant to the cases. In these disciplinary cases, proof beyond reasonable doubt is usually the yardstick. Contrary to citizens not being allowed to have legal representation, police officers are permitted to have a lawyer present (McLaughlin and Johansen, 2002:635–638). The deduction that can be made is that the complaints process is being used to the advantage of the police administration to identify malpractice and to "prepare" for citizens who lodge complaints. Absolution of the police officer is given priority, while the victim's complaint and reparation is awarded a secondary position. Efforts have been made to have Crown Prosecuting Service personnel in police stations improve general legal advice to police officers (Dixon, 1997:278). The informal rule existing within the police culture, namely, the practice that police officials should back each other up, often referred to as the "police code of silence," is also complicating matters. The few citizens who are aware of a complaint structure therefore find it extremely difficult to lodge a complaint against the police in cases where human rights may have been breached.

The police reacted to PACE pressures and demands by developing their capacity to respond with a stronger intelligence capacity and by relying heavily on paramilitaristic covert techniques (Brake and Hale, 1992:38). The expected immobilizing effect of PACE therefore never reached its potential. To highlight this statement, one police officer responded as follows during an interview regarding the neutralizing effect of PACE: "… We've got enough authority now. There's not much we can't do now" (Dixon, 1997:277). The limitations of the altered complaint structure and the lack of "limitation" placed on police powers and freedom became more evident with the passing of time. Police, for example, adapted their interviewing strategies from a more physical approach (e.g., torturing a suspect) to a more psychological approach (e.g., using deception and untrue statements during interviews and interrogations). Police also increasingly started making use of paid informants to build up evidence for cases (Dunnighan and Norris, 1999:67–86). Some police officers even circumvent PACE to get to a favorable end result in a case. This implies that the police strategy (means) to get information had to be changed (e.g., informants) to prove that someone is guilty (end) of an offence.

At this point, it is safe to argue that PACE and PCA did not have the desired effect on citizens' concerns about unacceptable police actions in Britain. These concerns were highlighted and reached a pinnacle after the death of Stephen Lawrence* in April 1993 and the subsequent Macpherson Report that followed. Once again, the limitations of the existing structures highlighted the public's concern and placed full responsibility on the proactive style of policing. Macpherson accentuated that at that time the existing laws dealing with police misconduct were inadequate. He also made several recommendations (for which certain groups in the community have long campaigned) concerning police accountability (Bridges, 1999:298–322).

Although many uncertainties existed with respect to policing methods used at that time, significant changes in the criminal world (e.g., crime syndicates that operated globally using advanced technology) were taking place, thereby challenging global policing structures. These changes could not be ignored because crime trends were changing rapidly and threatened social stability in many countries. The British Police had to address a significant increase in crime rates from the 1980s as well as to respond to the new challenges in global crime patterns. Parallel to these crime issues, the nucleus of police longevity was challenged by local negativity from the citizenry. The police were therefore forced to adapt because externally they were losing public support and internally they were challenged by the private sector (e.g., private security companies that thrived on a new wave of security services) (Ratcliffe, 2003:1–6). They realized that they had to adapt because they became marginalized in certain areas of policing. During the 1980s and 1990s all these changes overlapped with the calls from the British Home Office for the police to be more effective and cost efficient.

The British Police were facing two major challenges: firstly, to address the changing patterns of crime, and secondly, to win back public support by being accountable for their actions. The second challenge implied that

---

* Stephen Lawrence was an 18-year-old sixth form student who was stabbed to death in Eltham, south London, on the night of April 22, 1993. The murder was motivated by racism. No one has been punished for the murder.

the police had to adhere to certain legal constraints regarding their strategic behavior. The police culture that usually did not welcome restrictions on its freedom opted to prioritize the changing patterns of crime and adapted its actions accordingly. This choice demanded a change in the policing style to cope with technological advances (e.g., methods of intelligence gathering that were already used by the military and private security companies) and computer crimes (e.g., computer fraud schemes) being committed by a "new" breed of criminals. In effect the hi-tech advances and the focus on ILP, favored the police as they now also had the means to police the community without the community knowing that they were being policed 24 h a day. This contributed to the police shifting their focus from reactive to proactive policing because they had the means and they could now break away from a problem that had been haunting them for a very long time, namely, accountability to citizens. Meanwhile, the British government was trying to find answers to the poor police–citizen relationship that existed in Britain.

In an attempt to answer the questions, why poor relations existed and whether the police complaints process enjoyed public support, four inquiries were given governmental approval during the 1990s to investigate these issues. These inquiries were: the Royal Commission on Criminal Justice inquiry, the Home Affairs Committee inquiry, the Stephen Lawrence inquiry, and the European Committee for the Prevention of Torture and Inhuman or Degrading Treatment or Punishment inquiry (Smith, 2001:372–392). The recommendations made by Macpherson following the Stephen Lawrence inquiry were the yardstick to implement new changes in the civilian police complaint system. Changes were, however, taking place too slowly and this led to legal firms encouraging complainants to take civil action against the police. Financial settlements were becoming the rule and not the exception with the provision that no publicity came out of the action and that the officer's identity would not be disclosed (McLaughlin and Johansen, 2002:635–638). In many cases, it is alleged that police officers were able to get and are still getting away with serious breaches of human rights. They do not have to take any responsibility for negative actions because a culture of nonaccountability has apparently become institutionalized in the present civilian complaints structure. Many claim that information is often gathered by the police illegally and by means of dubious methods. One can conclude that this reveals that the police culture is inflexible toward incursions of law and administrative policies (Ericson and Haggerty, 1997:33).

In view of the abovementioned, it can be concluded that the civilian complaints system in Britain is working in favor of the police and that citizens' concerns do not occupy a priority position within daily police operations. Instead, the police have prioritized their style of policing and how they were going to adapt to the policing of the risk society. The Home Office Minister, Lord Faulkner, stated in *The Guardian* of July 29, 2002, that "people really like to have closed-circuit television (CCTV) cameras because the police and the people ... believe it brings greater security" (Coleman, 2004:13). However, a dearth of research exists regarding the impact of CCTV monitoring and other intelligence gathering techniques (Brown, 1995). The population is also increasingly complaining about the invasion of their privacy. People are being watched in almost all aspects of their lives—in shopping malls, while they are driving, in the streets, in taxicabs and trains, as well as during social events (e.g., soccer matches, dance clubs, pubs, etc.). It seems that the more they are being watched the more difficult it is to complain about misuse of surveillance and intelligence gathering because most people did not know they were being watched. This makes it almost impossible to know in what way you are being scrutinized, watched, and discussed (e.g., a lady in a miniskirt). It is unclear how one can lodge a complaint against the "invisible" big brother? Bearing in mind that the United Kingdom is the "largest market for CCTV in Europe and accounts for one-fifth of all CCTV cameras worldwide" (Coleman, 2004), one could question the existing complaints and monitoring structures in Britain. The question also arises whether it is a political strategy to regain some form of sovereign governance over the whole populace?

The South African Perspective

After democratization, it was expected that the SA public would have changed their perception of the police. It was also envisioned that the people would start to trust the police and that they would divulge information to the police without any reluctance (Stevens and Yach, 1995:6). The actual nature of CP is the direct involvement of the community in law enforcement strategies. After democratization in South Africa, CP became the buzzword in policing (Kempen, 2006a:39). The South African Police (SAP) was changed to the South African Police Service (SAPS) and this new service was demilitarized. Furthermore, organizational decentralization, an expansive problem-oriented police mandate and a commitment to consultation with local residents in establishing police priorities, developing tactics, and coproducing safety, were some of the outcomes that were expected from CP (Dixon, 2004:252). It was thought that the community would get involved in policing matters and that the police would provide a service to the community. In doing this, it was hoped that the community would get involved with the police in problem solving in their different areas. However, it has become clearer that there are unmistakable implications of the rise of proactive (CP and sector policing) and ILP on the public's perception of police accountability. It has been reported in the police magazine *Servamus* that "the concept of community policing was never embraced by the community, or there were problems regarding the powers and responsibilities of community police forums" (Kempen, 2006a:39).

On the one hand, citizens have concerns about police competency and the police abusing their powers, but on the other hand, police complain that the community does not want to become partners in the efforts to reduce and combat crime. The forum for community participation in local policing is the Community Police Forum (CPF). However, a recurring issue noted is the unwillingness of the community to get involved in crime prevention and the reluctance to divulge information to the police officials in their area. Many of the CPF chairpersons have raised similar issues about the police and the police raised similar issues about the community. The CPF chairpersons usually blamed the police for their poor performance and lack of skills, and also insisted that the police did not really care about the problems that the local residents are experiencing. The SAPS members at the meetings usually blamed the community for a lack of dedication to crime prevention efforts. Furthermore, police officials were frustrated with the noninvolvement of the community. Police officials were of the opinion that the community had a lot of information on crime, criminals, and other problems in their area, but were not willing to divulge that information to the police. Private security initiatives were sometimes blamed for the lack of interest in public policing matters. Arguments such as: "We are paying double for security, namely our tax money for paying the police and then we have to hire private security as well" were usually vented. Kempen (2006a:39) states in this regard that "the community does not feel safe and often feel that police officials are not reliable and accountable in the fight against crime."

Although the SAPS has been demilitarized (e.g., change in rank structure, change in insignia, and the change in the powers to shoot at criminals who are fleeing a scene), recent media reports show that the opposite of demilitarization, namely, "tough policing" actions are once again in favor by police management. The National Commissioner of the SAPS, Jackie Selebi, made it known to the media that the police will use force to counter serious criminals in the country. He even declared that the SAPS would shoot back at the thugs in SA. Such declarations hardly reflect a service-oriented approach. The police are therefore in a paradoxical position. They were demilitarized and they were advised to involve the community in their policing initiatives. However, it appears that demilitarization has caused a lack of respect for management from subordinates. Several initiatives were put in place to accelerate promotion of previously disadvantaged police officers to mid and upper level management positions. As a result, an exodus of many skilled police officers, mainly whites, has taken place. They have either gone into early retirement or they have searched for greener pastures in the private security industry. The SAPS are therefore in a very difficult position at present. South Africa is experiencing the same problems as Britain, albeit different crime trends, namely, an increase in violent crime (e.g., crimes against the person, armed house robberies, farm killings, etc.) since 1994, and an onslaught of global crime syndicates (e.g., drugs trading, motor vehicle hijackings, illegal abalone fishing, fraud, etc.). Although the government has announced that more police officers will be trained, especially with the 2010 Soccer World Cup in mind, serious issues regarding trust, skills, and the collection of crime information, are limiting the effectiveness of the SAPS. Increasing numbers of police abuse complaints are being reported in the media (Lambrechts, 2005a:73), for example, criminal case files being sold or lost, reports of police officials who are being bribed, and cases being thrown out of court because of improper evidence collection. As a result, some motivated police officials are sometimes forced to use unethical tactics to generate crime intelligence. In addition, poorly trained SAPS officers have to face highly organized as well as well armed criminals on a daily basis (Kempen, 2006b:18–19).

The above problems, such as bribery and other forms of corruption, can only take place in a society that presents these opportunities to police officers. If the entire community was involved in their neighborhood policing efforts and if they developed a relationship of trust, then corruption and police abuse should decrease drastically. Ultimately, the community should assist the police in preventing crime to reclaim the streets.

Several mechanisms in SA are in place to monitor police accountability. The Department of Safety and Security is a government department with a police oversight responsibility. Furthermore, CP was introduced with the idea to ensure transparency and civilian involvement in policing practices. The Independent Complaints Directorate (ICD) is a government department that was established in April 1997 to investigate misconduct against members of SAPS and the Municipal Police Service (MPS). It operates independently from the SAPS and investigates any complaints from society regarding alleged misconduct and criminality by a police officer (see www.icd.gov.za).

Police officials are also inclined to act properly and professionally by abiding by internal regulations, namely, the South African Police Service Discipline Regulations, introduced in 2006. These regulations specifically address offences such as aiding an offender to escape, bribery, corruption, and extortion. These regulations also provide that an employee of the SAPS may be suspended by the National or Provincial Commissioner on reasonable grounds if the employee committed any misconduct. In addition, serious misconduct cases could result in criminal charges being lodged against police officers. However, in such serious cases, SAPS officers have been routinely suspended pending the outcome of their trial (Lambrechts, 2005b:70; Lambrechts, 2006:70–75).

Interestingly, research shows that the majority of people who filed a civilian complaint at the ICD have not been satisfied with the outcome of the investigation. Their dissatisfaction includes a variety of factors such as

Complainants view ICD investigations as biased in that they mainly favor the perpetrators (police), a similar problem that is encountered in Britain.

The ICD does not regularly communicate the progress of their investigation process to the complainants.

The ICD does not communicate the status of the case to the complainants, that is, the complainants are not informed whether their case have been finalized or not; they only discover about the status of their case during their own follow up about the case.

The investigation process takes so long that the complainant often forgets that they have lodged a complaint with ICD.

The ICD focuses mainly on high profile cases and puts little effort into investigating other complaints that are low key.

The statistics (number of complaints) regarding successes are also questioned by opposition political parties (see www.news24.com).

From the foregoing, one could expect that SAPS members who are guilty of misconduct will be dealt with harshly. They face criminal charges, possible disciplinary charges, and likely suspension. Still it seems that current mechanisms and initiatives have failed to restore the necessary trust in the citizenry of SA to partner with the SAPS in the fight against crime. In addition, the objectivity of the ICD is being questioned. In an article titled "Police watchdog overworked" (see www.news24.com), the committee chairman Mluleki George stated that "there had always been a general feeling that the ICD's independence was "questionable" and that it was too closely associated with the police." The proper functioning of the ICD is also in doubt. In the same article it was stated that the safety and security portfolio committee informed Parliament that "a mounting workload and lack of funds have compelled police watchdog Independent Complaints Directorate (ICD) to refer most of its cases back to the police for investigation."

Despite these monitoring initiatives in SA and potential complaints involving police misbehavior, the SAPS has been compelled to gather information to enable them to successfully execute their task as law enforcement officials. The SAPS cannot wait until relationships are positive between them and the community before they will police their areas of responsibility. Other intelligence agencies also face this challenge and are forced to gather information by means of questionable techniques. Recently, initiatives to generate and gather information about criminal activity, such as the joint Primedia/SAPS venture "Crime Line," has been hailed as a great success in the generation of criminal intelligence. After 7 weeks, 83 persons have been arrested and close to R1.5 million worth of stolen property, drugs, and other items have been seized and arrests have also been made for minor offences. These arrests were possible because of the anonymous information that was forthcoming from the community (file:///E|/CRIME LINE Your anonymous crime tip-off line.htm).

However, if one considers the magnitude of crime and its related problems in SA, this initiative hardly addresses the serious lack of communication between the police and the community. Furthermore, this initiative does not really address the current breakdown in police and community relations, as it is anonymous and faceless. The police cannot react proactively if they do not have the community to supply them with enough information to fulfill their policing responsibility, namely, ensuring a safe and secure SA. The question that one should address now is: What other means are available to gather crime intelligence?

Proactive Intelligence-Led Policing Using Technology

Proactive policing involves CP and voluntary community involvement with greater emphasis on crime prevention and problem solving. However noble it may seem, CP or partnership policing is not doing well because the community still does not trust the police. In a utopian society, the community will trust its police service, will work in a partnership with them, and will spontaneously divulge information that will enable the police to act proactively and prevent crimes. This "trust-relationship" between the police and citizens does not exist in most societies. Police cannot operate without information from and about the community. This is why the birth of ILP is so significant to law enforcement. Although the concept of ILP is widely used, its operational definition or full meaning is still vague. ILP refers to a recent shift in crime control thinking and the related policing practices. Intelligence gathering by means of different tactics and the proactive strategies designed around the information explains the basic meaning of ILP. This new era of proactive and ILP is also known as a "police revolution" in South Africa. Although "intelligence-led" policing can officially be traced back to the 1830s when according to existing evidence the Home Secretary in Britain warranted tampering with mail in the name of intelligence gathering and safety, a clear demarcation of its boundaries and substance does not exist (Manwaring-White, 1983:84). It can be argued that ILP is important to monitor airports and ports and to infiltrate terrorist groups or syndicates for national security (e.g., to avoid a duplication of the September 11, 2001 terrorist attack on the Twin Towers in the United States, the terrorist bombings of trains in Spain (2004) and the bus bombings in the United Kingdom (2005)). The main difference between CP and ILP is the typical absence of voluntary participation in the case of ILP.

Therefore, the question one needs to ask is: How far can the police go in breaching citizens' rights of privacy with ILP and still be accountable? It must be again highlighted that many have concluded that the civilian complaints systems and oversight bodies supervising the police are not yet functioning in favor of the community. Few community members have knowledge of the existing civilian police complaint structure and now new police practices that are even more difficult to detect or prove are being implemented and have been used at a rapid pace to control the community. Many of these practices, such as the use of CCTV in public places, breach all the rights citizens have to privacy. In this regard, Ashworth (1998:108–140) questioned the ethical grounds of deceptive practices in policing. These apparently improper actions include strategies such as the use of undercover police officers, paying informants for criminal intelligence, fabricating information to deceive suspects, spying, covert observation, the use of infrared and telescopic cameras, tapping mobile and landline telephones, face detection computer software, and CCTV in shopping malls and on roads. One could argue that practices such as these invade the ordinary citizens' living space and right to privacy. Norris and Armstrong (1999:205–230) refer to the intensified technological surveillance of the community as the "maximum surveillance society" or "total panopticanization." Citizens are being watched and monitored without their consent, all in an effort to prevent crime. This is in line with the government's request that the police should be more effective and creative. The positive side of ILP is that the police can conduct law enforcement operations under the provision that they are doing it for community safety and that they are monitoring streets and crime hot spots to prevent crime.

CCTV is one of the most well known forms of surveillance and information gathering in the world. Success stories with CCTV monitoring also enjoys widespread media coverage. In Britain, footage from CCTV cameras was used to identify Anthony Harding, a multiple murderer, as the person who dumped body parts in a dustbin. In addition, the international terrorists who murdered dozens in the London subways were all identified on CCTV monitors within the train system. Incidents like these may cause people to overreact regarding the effectiveness of ILP. Maguire (2000:315–336), however, warns against this and argues that there is a dearth of clear research evidence pertaining to the effectiveness of ILP techniques such as CCTV monitoring.

To support Maguire's argument, perspectives of some critics can also be noted. In the May 2006 *Servamus Safety and Security* magazine, it is reported that "opponents of CCTV point out the loss of privacy of the people under surveillance, and the negative impact of surveillance on civil liberties. Furthermore, they argue that CCTV displaces crime, rather than reducing it. Critics often dub CCTV as 'big brother surveillance'" (ONIKA, 2006:34).

Manwaring-White (1983:84) reported on cases where the police use ILP strategies such as telephone monitoring devices outside the guidelines provided by the British government. The Home Office's thinking on bugging and surveillance seems to be paradoxical. For example, the bugging of a post office phone requires ministerial backing, while this is not required in any other methods of bugging and surveillance. Tapping is approved when the person under surveillance is suspected of a crime that could carry a prison sentence of three or more years. The implication of this is that a network analysis can be initiated. This means that any individual the person under surveillance talks to over the telephone becomes part of the investigation. Furthermore, British Telecom (BT) developed a system, using the BT network, which can switch on telephones in all houses to listen to conversations in the vicinity of the telephone (Uglow, 1999:287–299). In some situations, video recordings are made or pictures are taken of specific actions or behaviors. Furthermore, individuals are sometimes bugged or informants are allowed to involve themselves in wrongdoing as long as they provide information that outweighs their own criminal actions. Although they usually decline from using the information in court, the police often use the information to understand the perpetrator and his or her actions better. Furthermore, the current legislation regulating wiretapping and bugging is confusing. The Regulation of Interception of Communications and Provision of Communication-related Information Act 70 of 2002 deals with tapping, bugging, interception of postal articles, and the monitoring of e-mails via the Internet—lawful as well as unlawful. According to the Government Gazette Number 28075 (September 30, 2005) this Act came into operation on September 30, 2005 except for certain sections. One section is of particular interest, namely, Section 62(1), which repeals the previous Interception and Monitoring Act 127 of 1992. Section 62(1) of Act 70 of 2002 is not yet in operation. This implies that Act 127 of 1992 and Act 70 of 2002 exist in conjunction with each other. Lambrechts (2005a:71) also feels that it is very confusing to use or interpret this legislation.

In addition to the difficulty in the interpretation of this legislation, new technological advancements have been progressively used in the fight against crime. Massive millimeter wave detectors can scan through walls and clothes to detect items such as firearms. Mobile telephones can be used as tracking devices and signals can be enhanced while individuals are working on their computers to extract information from it. A question that arises from this is: How much protection or privacy does a citizen have in these situations?

Is the right to privacy being violated? In the United States, courts have developed an exclusionary rule that prevents the prosecution from relying on evidence that has been obtained in violation of constitutional protection. Due process prioritizes the rights of the accused over the public interest during the hearing of a crime. However "in the United States there is no such data protection mechanisms, it has been questioned whether CCTV evidence is allowable under the Fourth Amendment which prohibits 'unreasonable searches and seizures.' The courts have generally not taken this view" (ONIKA, 2006:35).

Uglow (1999:287–299) has postulated that in Britain it will be difficult "to envisage that this dilemma would ever trouble the English courts." Traditionally, British courts have only asked whether the evidence is relevant to the case and reliable without questioning the source and whether any fundamental rights had been violated. With limited legal regulation, it is understandable why the police are increasingly changing their police practices and targeting sections of the community where police intrusion is less visible. It is clear that globally, legal loopholes exist in current legislation that leaves citizens vulnerable to the perceived negative aspects of ILP. The police can, for example, deny citizens access to their intelligence files and under the current British Data Protection Act 1998, the registrar has no statutory powers of review over the police (Maguire, 1998:232).

Some researchers (Dunnighan and Norris, 1999:85) observe that police are moving toward less visible intrusion in the United Kingdom because of the regulations that were put in place with PACE on the stop and search strategies and the difficulty in obtaining information from the community. Another issue that needs clarification is the cost effectiveness of certain practices such as the real costs in using informants (paid with tax payers' money). In Britain, the Audit Commission is supporting the use of informants and is encouraging the police to use them. Calculations made by Dunnighan and Norris (1999:69) show that the total costs involved in the day-to-day use of informants are high. Other issues that they raise are: the time officers spend to recruit informants; the disregarding of criminal offences some informants have committed in order to facilitate the flow of information; and that sometimes nonfinancial reinforcement is used to motivate individuals to become informants (e.g., the promise of nonprosecution). These activities breach citizens' rights as they are being misguided on the use of informants and the unlawful actions of some police officers to solve cases. Taking this view, it could be concluded that the use of informants is profitable and effective. Ashworth (2002:161–179) also refers to certain problems or "dilemmas" that should be taken into consideration when informants are used, such as guaranteeing their safety after they have divulged information, the use of children as informants and the impact on them, and accountability issues with regard to police corruption to support evidence in a case. When directly asked, most police officers assigned to criminal investigations often believed that the courts would not listen to a case if the correct procedures with the Director of Public Prosecutions (DPP) were not followed. In contrast to this they did declare that they sometimes "turn a blind eye" on informants' wrongdoing if they get worthwhile tip-offs and information.

In concluding the discussion on ILP, it is important to note that technology and new ways of obtaining information have definitely enhanced the capacity of the police to "… collect, retrieve and analyze information" (Chan, 2003:673). Policing and its reactive character have to its disposal a powerful resource to change policing forever provided it is used in acceptable ways within the boundaries of clear and uncompromising guidelines. The capacity of this new trend in policing has not been explored fully as technological progress is taking place too rapidly. Then again if the community is not willing to cooperate to divulge information freely, the police have no choice but to adapt their intelligence gathering in the community. A logical issue that neutralizes this argument is the privacy concern.

The moral issue of some citizens' fear that their every move is being spied on and their privacy jeopardized is a matter of concern. It can be argued that the utilization of ILP techniques are morally acceptable if substantial proof exists that the police will prevent serious crime from being committed or if considerable suspicion exists that a serious crime is to be committed and that ILP is the only means to prevent it. The motivation must be based on the argument of whether or not it will contribute to the greatest happiness of all citizens. In this regard, police integrity and professionalism play a fundamental role.

Although guidelines do exist, it is still unclear which forms of deception should be permitted and which not within an accountable policing structure.

Regaining Citizen Support for Community and Police Interaction

An effective transparent police oversight and civilian complaint system is fundamental in the guaranteeing of accountable policing and in ensuring public support for the police (Hill et al., 2003:1). Past undertakings by the British Government, specifically the Police Act 1964, the Police Complaints Board, the Police and Criminal Evidence Act 1984, The Police Complaints Authority, and the Data Protection Act 1998 did not succeed in guaranteeing citizens a fair opportunity to have those police officials who allegedly abuse their powers taken to task. The current structures in SA (e.g., ICD) are also finding it difficult to win back the trust of the community to cooperate with the police and divulge information freely. Although the British model is not very successful, the ICD has entered into partnerships with Scotland Yard to deliver training for their investigators with specific reference to capacity building and strengthening of investigative skills. The British High Commission is funding this project, which commenced in September 2002. Bearing in mind that only a few cases of police misconduct against the citizenry were reported in the beginning (1997), 2913 cases of police misconduct were reported in the seventh annual report of the Independent Complaints Directorate during 2002 and 2003 (Independent Complaints Directorate— Annual Report 2002/2003). This report is clear and shows the progress that has been made from 1997 through 2003. However, the latest Annual Report

2005–2006 is a 50-page explanation of the financial expenditure of the ICD. It does not give the reader any idea of the latest successes of the ICD and one gets the feeling that a lot of excuses are forthcoming in this document (see www.icd.gov.za).

For example, Xinwa, the Acting Executive Director of the ICD, had the following to say in the Annual Report about the ICD's performance during 2005–2006: "the capacity constraints experienced by the ICD necessitate the urgent intervention from the relevant decision-makers. The eventual shift away from the monitoring of certain complaints of police criminality and misconduct, to the active investigation of all these complaints, has not only negatively influenced the ICD's performance levels but the continued increase in the number of complaints received for investigation necessitate an urgent reconsideration of the active investigation of all complaints" (see www.icd.gov.za). No mention is made of the number of complaints involving police misconduct that they had received and the successes that they had achieved during the 2005–2006 timeframe. It is clear that the ICD is experiencing problems and that the way forward looks bleak for the one police oversight body that is strategic in building positive relations between the community and the police.

Since the inception of policing, citizens were faced with an isolated establishment that in many instances operated above the law. Policing was originally intended to protect the interests of the ordinary citizen. It has been proposed that a citizen who currently complains about police abuse is usually seen as troublesome and not as a victim. The civilian complaint system and oversight body in SA is not functioning properly after 10 years (1997–2007) in existence and could lead one to question future success and effectiveness.

In Britain, which is presently assisting and training SA ICD officials, complaints can only be lodged that involves alleged misconduct of an individual officer and not against the police department in general. In this regard, Maguire (1998:230) states that "... the UK lacks a general law ... for individual citizens." Demands from the community but also from the European Convention for the Protection of Human Rights and Fundamental Freedoms forced the British Government to comply with international trends to protect citizens against police misconduct. The Police Reform Act 2002 (Ormerod and Roberts, 2003:141) is the latest effort of the Government to address allegations of police abuse of power. A new addition in the complaint structure is the Independent Police Complaints Commission (IPCC). The IPCC replaced the PCA, and became operational in April 2004. The aim of the new IPCC is to recruit and train civilians that will investigate allegations of serious police misconduct. However, the primary responsibility of recording complaints is still in the hands of the police. IPCC is a Non-Departmental Public Body (NDPB), funded by the Home Office, but by law entirely independent of the police, interest groups, and political parties and whose decisions on cases are free from government involvement. It needs to be highlighted that the Secretary of State will exert powers over the appointments and dismissals of the civilians and that the police will still investigate most cases internally with the IPCC operating as the "watchdog" (McLaughlin and Johansen, 2002:635; Hill, Cooper, Hoyle and Young, 2003:iii; www.ipcc.gov.uk).

The IPCC has the specific task to ensure that cases are handled efficiently and effectively. More avenues to initiate complaints are envisaged thus making access more citizen-friendly. They must also "… establish and maintain public confidence" (Ormerod and Roberts, 2003:147).

While it seems as if governments are still grappling with their police–civilian complaint and oversight structures, restorative justice (RJ) techniques are being employed to address some citizen complaints. Informal approaches (e.g., a restorative conference between the complainant and the police officer involved) are being used more frequently. However Hill and coworkers found that police officers usually did not attend these conferences, as attendance was voluntary (Hill et al., 2003:28). This contributed to a large number of the citizens expressing their dissatisfaction with the RJ conference. In this regard, it was found that 72% of research participants felt that the entire British complaints structure and oversight body needed upgrading. Informal resolution in resolving complaints did not notably support the argument that this should be the way forward and the answer to an ineffective complaints structure in England. If SA is following the same trend as in Britain (bearing in mind that Scotland Yard officials train South African ICD officials), similar problems can be expected.

A possible solution may be found in the reorganization of future civilian complaint mechanisms and proper evaluation and monitoring thereof. Elements of RJ as well as rigorous formal processes need to be integrated to address police misconduct with more vigor as it undermines police legitimacy and increases citizens' concerns regarding the abusive image of the police (Mawby, 2002:53). This image is reinforced by every police act that has been found to be unacceptable and in violation of basic human rights (e.g., corruption or unnecessarily invading citizen privacy). With the dawn of ILP and the dearth of research regarding its impact, it can be hypothesized that the existing complaints and oversight structures in the United Kingdom, South Africa, and many other nations are not on par with current policing trends. The following aspects need to be addressed without delay: a police oversight structure that functions independently from any governmental or police influence; police diversity and sensitivity training across the board; an intensive marketing campaign to inform the community of the existence and functioning of the civilian complaint structure; and the promulgation of clear and understandable legislation that will stipulate the acceptable use of ILP within the community. An increase in poorly trained police officers that are not loyal to their oath and mission will only increase police misconduct. The current trend in SA is to put more unskilled and under trained police officials on the streets. This will only exacerbate the current disparity and misunderstanding between the community and the police. This indirectly favors criminals as the community increases their distrust for the police and the police view the community as negative and uncooperative. An ineffective civilian complaint and oversight structure ultimately also may contribute to the infringement of human rights. The government should refocus unnecessary energy that is being spent on lip service and empty promises and embark on relationship building between the police and the community. A significant number of police officials take their jobs seriously and would do anything in their power to stop crime. Citizens should support these officials unambiguously. If the citizens feel safe and if they see crime in general and corruption by CJS officials as being addressed vigorously by the government, they will probably change their negative perceptions of the police and contribute more wholeheartedly to the fight against crime by supplying more information and thereby improve the quality of life in their respective neighborhoods.

Conclusion

The lack of a proper civilian complaint mechanism, the absence of comprehensive legislation to protect citizens from infringement of their personal rights, and the tendency to treat complaints against police as hampering issues in the fulfillment of their policing duties need to be addressed comprehensively by government officials. The government should treat the right to safety that is a constitutional guarantee with more accountability. Uncertainty about the impact of ILP on crime and the resultant invasion of privacy beyond acceptable boundaries are intimidating to ordinary citizens. ILP is at present somewhat of a phantom phenomenon to the government and the population and needs to be formalized and examined thoroughly. Adequate legislation and effective police training could be utilized to reform existing questionable law enforcement practices. Any substantiated breaches of human rights should be punished severely. Citizens should be informed (e.g., rigorous marketing campaigns) of their rights, the existence of civilian complaint structures and oversight bodies, as well as the procedures to be followed if they believe that they have become victims of police exploitation. Transparency regarding the government's motivation for monitoring the population and the almost clandestine matter in which it takes place makes one wonder whether this is a brilliant ploy to regain a sense of governance (or control) over the general population. Regardless, allegations of police abuse will result in limited trust in the police and government officials must address this concern seriously.

References

Ashworth, A. (1998). Should the police be allowed to use deceptive practices?. *Law Quarterly Review*, 114, 108–140.

Ashworth, A. (2002). Re-drawing the boundaries of entrapment. *Criminal Law Review*, 161–179.

Brake, M. and Hale, C. (1992). *Public Order and Private Lives: The Politics of Law and Order*. London, U.K., Routledge.

Bridges, L. (1999). The Lawrence inquiry—Incompetence, corruption, and institutional racism, *Journal of Law and Society*, 26(3), 298–322.

Brown, B. (1995). CCTV in town centres: Three case studies. Crime Detection and Prevention Series Paper 68. London, U.K., Home Office Research Group.

Brown, D. (1997). PACE ten years on: A review of research. Research Study No. 155. London, U.K., Home Office.

Brown, S.E., Esbensen, F-A., and Geis, G. (2007). *Criminology: Explaining Crime and Its Context* (6th edn.). Cincinnati, OH, Anderson.

Chan, J.B.L. (2003). Police and new technologies, in T. Newburn (ed.), *Handbook of Policing*. Devon, U.K., Willan Publishing.

Coleman, R. (2004). *Reclaiming the Streets: Surveillance, Social Control and the City*. Portland, OR, Willan Publishing.

Cotton, J. and Povey, D. (1998–1999), Police complaints and discipline, *Home Office Statistical Bulletin*, 12(99), 1–15. London, U.K., Home Office.

Dixon, D. (1997). *Law in Policing*. Oxford, U.K., Oxford University Press.

Dixon, B. (2004). Community policing: Cherry pie or melktert? *Society in Transition*, 35(2), 251–272.

Dunnighan, C. and Norris, C. (1999). The detective, the snout, and the audit commission: The real costs in using informants. *The Howard Journal of Criminal Justice*, 38(1), 67–86.

Ericson, R.V. and Haggerty, K.D. (1997). *Policing the Risk Society*. Oxford, U.K., Clarendon Press.

Governments on the www: Great Britain and Northern Ireland, Government Website, http://www.gksoft.com/govt/en/gb.html (accessed November 24, 2004).

Hall, S. (2002). From Scarman to Stephen Lawrence, in Y. Jewkes and G. Letherby (eds.), *Criminology: A Reader*. London, U.K., Sage, pp. 225–234.

Hill, R., Cooper, K., Hoyle, C., and Young, R. (2003). Introducing restorative justice to the police complaints system: Close encounters of the rare kind. Occasional Paper No. 20. Centre for Criminological Research, Oxford, U.K.

Kempen, A. (2006a). Community police forums: An update. *Servamus*, 99(11), 39. Pretoria, South Africa, SARP Publishing.

Kempen, A. (2006b). Dealing with corruption and putting an end to the erosion of the trust between the police and the community. *Servamus*, 99(3), 18–21. Pretoria, South Africa, SARP Publishing.

Lambrechts, D. (2005a). Pollex legal column. *Servamus*, 98(11), 70–74. Pretoria, South Africa, SARP Publishing.

Lambrechts, D. (2005b). Pollex legal column. *Servamus*, 98(12), 70–74. Pretoria, South Africa, SARP Publishing.

Lambrechts, D. (2006). Pollex legal column. *Servamus*, 99(10), 70–75. Pretoria, South Africa, SARP Publishing.

Maguire, M. (1991). Complaints against the police: The British experience, in A. Goldsmith (ed.), *Complaints against the Police: The Trend to External Review*. Oxford, U.K., Clarendon Press.

Maguire, M. (1998). Restraining big brother?, The regulation of surveillance in England and Wales, in C. Norris, G. Armstrong, and J. Moran (eds.), *Surveillance, Closed Circuit Television and Social Control*. Hampshire, U.K., Ashgate.

Maguire, M. (2000). Policing by risks and targets: Some dimensions and implications of intelligence-led crime control. *Policing and Society*, 9, 315–336.

Manwaring-White, S. (1983). *The Policing Revolution: Police Technology, Democracy and Liberty in Britain*. Brighton, U.K., Harvester Press.

Mawby, R.C. (2002). *Policing Images: Policing, Communication and Legitimacy*. Devon, U.K., Willan Publishing.

McLaughlin, E. and Johansen, A. (2002). A force for change? The prospects for applying restorative justice to citizen complaints against the police in England and Wales. *British Journal of Criminology*, 42, 635–653.

Norris, C. and Armstrong, G. (1999). *The Maximum Surveillance Society: The Rise of CCTV*. Oxford, U.K., Berg.

ONIKA. (2006). Closed-circuit systems. *Servamus*, 99(5), 34–35. Pretoria, South Africa, SARP Publishing.

Ormerod, D. and Roberts, A. (2003). The police reform act 2002—Increasing centralisation, maintaining confidence and contracting out crime control. *Criminal Law Review*, 7, 141–164.

Ratcliffe, J.H. (2003). Intelligence-led policing. *Trends and Issues in Crime and Criminal Justice Series*, 248, 1–6.

Scarman, L. (1981). *The Scarman Report: The Brixton Disorders*, Parts I–VII. London, U.K., Penguin.

Smith, G. (2001). Police complaints and criminal prosecutions. *Modern Language Review*, 64(3), 372–392.

Stevens, P. and Yach, D.M. (1995). Community policing in action: A practitioners guide. Cape Town, South Africa, Juta.

Uglow, S. (1999). Covert surveillance and the European convention on human rights. *Criminal Law Review* 287–299.

Waddington, P.A.J. (1999). *Policing Citizens*. London, U.K., UCL.

Developing Democracy and the Rule of Law in the Republic of Cameroon

15

JEAN LOUIS MESSING

Contents

Introduction

If there is one area of public activity that is an integral part of the present-day social tissue, it is undoubtedly the maintenance of law and order. In an organized society, one cannot ignore the state of things that enables people to go about freely without disturbance, either to satisfy their personal needs or to preserve general interest. Numerous studies* have been carried out on this situation, but emphasis will be placed upon its acuteness and the problems it poses in the twenty-first century.

Generally speaking, it can be said that the development of a civilization is fundamentally based on the desire to establish peace and security, the substratum of the socio-political, economic, and cultural development of contemporary societies. Consequently, it is incumbent on governments to make national or international maintenance of law and order the cornerstone of their battle horse because without peace and stability, no sustainable social development can be planned. Peace and development are therefore interrelated and pursue the same goal: the development of the citizen.

The underlying causes of the maintenance of law and order† are the same both in developed countries and in the so-called developing countries, namely, an increasing quest for individual freedom, access to a more acceptable low cost standard of living, and a growing concern about the management of public affairs. Till recently, these situations were managed using standardized and classical methods, which essentially took into consideration internal factors. But with the fall of the Berlin Wall and the dislocation of the Soviet bloc, things suddenly changed.

Worse still, the swift and the precipitated democratization of young states, especially African States (following recommendations from the G7 and some former colonial powers), the destruction of the entirely state-owned economic tissue, and the conditions established by the IMF and the World Bank, have contributed to a large extent in impoverishing these states while plunging them into a pernicious cycle of widespread turmoil and disorder.

---

* The author of this chapter has three books to his credit including a *"Doctorat de troisième cycle"* on: The Problems of Maintenance of Law and Order in Black Francophone Africa: The Case of Cameroon, defended in 1994, at the University of Yaounde.
† In Cameroon, maintenance of law and order is governed by: Decree No. 68/DF/33 of January 22, 1968 outlining the missions of defence by regular forces, back up troops and auxiliaries taken in the application of Law No. 67/LF/9 of 12/06/1967 on National Defence; Decree No. 78/485 of 09/12 1978 laying down the functions of Heads of Administrative Constituencies and Law No. 90/054 of 19/12/1990.

Clearly overtaken by events and ill prepared, these states were shaken to their very foundations, and this was aggravated by the rebirth of old tribal quarrels and all sorts of derailment.

The necessary balance between social components, especially between individuals on the one hand, and between individuals and institutions on the other, brings about frictions, which, if not contained, may jeopardize social cohesion. Hence, the institution of the maintenance of law and order, which relies heavily on legal structures, encourages the freedom of speech and preserves society from excesses. It is therefore, incumbent on rulers to ensure in time and space, public tranquility, security, stability, and decency.

Before the 1990s, the aim of the maintenance of law and order was to ensure by all means state authority, with the resolute determination to condemn in strong terms the least disturbance of established order. The only security guarantee for the people was the scrupulous respect of the instruments in force, i.e., total respect for public authorities. With the complicity of existing legal devices,* numerous cases of violation of human rights, brutal repression of public demonstrations, and all forms of inhuman and degrading treatment were registered.

With the advent of human rights and freedoms, as well as the institution of the rule of law,† the physiognomy of the maintenance of law and order changed especially within the context of globalization, where nothing can be done in total secrecy. It is more and more a matter of preserving the dignity of the human person while maintaining public order.

The fundamental question that arises is how to reconcile the security imperative, which presupposes the eradication of insecurity and the protection of human rights needed for building any state that abides by the rule of law. In other words, at the start of the twenty-first century, what has developed as the philosophy of the maintenance of law and order within the context of new challenges that involve the security imperative, the emergence of new forms of disturbances of public order, and the taking into account of individual freedom? The answer to this question is of undeniable importance inasmuch as it entails updating knowledge and skills adapted to the new environment, and streamlining services and manpower for more citizen action.

State of Affairs in Cameroon

In Central Africa, under constant change due to the different socio-political crises, Cameroon remains a symbol of peace and stability that no prudent

---

* See especially the 1964 law on repression of subversion.
† The Head of State enacted into law on December 12, 1990 about 50 instruments liberalizing political life in Cameroon.

international political analyst can contest as we move on into the new millennium. In fact, if one excludes the case of the Republic of Gabon, the other countries have faced or are facing serious problems resulting from intertribal, religious conflicts or from civil war. These situations have led to the massive movement of people towards more hospitable lands including Cameroon.

These migrations have sometimes brought together within the same host territory, nationals of the same country with different political orientations.* This ultimately creates problems concerning security, all the more so as borders remain porous. It is not uncommon to note that some asylum seekers have been discovered in possession of functional arms and other weapons. One can then immediately understand the complexity of the security imperative at this juncture because, coupled with internal realities, there are factors linked to the pressing need to provide relief and assistance in accordance with International Humanitarian Law.

Democracy and the Permanent Nature of the Maintenance of Law and Order

The maintenance of law and order has from the time of the earliest civilizations been the major concern of rulers. This evolved into the main activity of administrative authorities and the facilitators of law and order carried it out with pleasure. But with the advent of democracy, the context evolved. The social freedom of speech set in and brought about a multitude of claims exacerbated by an acute economic crisis.

Increase in Socioeconomic Claims

With the dismal poverty of populations within many African states following the drastic fall in the prices of exports, one could expect nothing short of an increase and a persistence of these claims. As a matter of fact, in order to better understand the peculiar situation of Cameroon and quoting a few examples, one can mention the fall in the prices of cocoa and coffee, the main cash crops of the vast majority of the population of the Central, South, East, West and Littoral provinces (equatorial and semi-equatorial regions). The prices of these two crops fell respectively from 1200 CFAF a kilogram to 650 CFAF for cocoa and 850 CFAF to 250 CFAF for coffee for the 2004 and 2005 seasons. This in absolute terms involved more than half the income of

* Supporters of overthrown successive regimes in neighboring Chad stayed in the same refugee camps in the North of Cameroon, and this for about 10 years.

these populations, while at the same time the prices of staple consumer goods witnessed a 100% increase during the same period.

At another level, many state corporations have been closed down or have been restructured upon the recommendation of the IMF and the World Bank. The situation has lead to a dramatic reduction in the manpower previously assigned to public service, as all employees had been public employees. Social tensions have therefore reached the summit at all levels of society and the police have been compelled to be at the forefront of the strategy to deal with turbulent situations.

Financial Implications

The liquidation or restructuring of some state corporations undoubtedly resulted in serious and negative financial consequences. With the support given by some trade unions, staff representatives, employees, and former employees were encouraged to lay claim to their rights, with some excessively frustrated as they had accumulated 28 months of salary arrears or were unable to get back their savings from the competent services.* The most common locations to voice discontent were on public streets where barricades were set up or where a sit-in protest had been organized in front of public buildings, especially the Prime Minister's Office. In addition, it is worth mentioning the wage claims by teachers of primary education who had worked on temporary contracts, but who had never seen their financial situation regularized by the Ministry of Finance, even after 2 years of service. Unfortunately in both cases, the impact has not been enough to warrant a proper government response and the objective of the demonstrators turned to merely catching the attention of public authorities and getting the general public to side with them.

Student Unrest on Campuses

It is in university campuses in Cameroon that one has observed different responses that have alternated between peaceful demonstration and clear acts of violence. Out of the six state universities in Cameroon, only one has structures worthy of an internationally recognized academic institution. This is the University of Yaounde.† One major negative consequence involving education results from the reality that each university campus was built to accommodate around 1000 students, but is now dealing with more than

* Examples are workers of companies like MATGENIE, LABOGENIE, ANADEFOR, or CAMEROON POSTAL SERVICES.
† Examples: University of Yaounde II on the premises of the ENIET of Soa; Douala in those of the ENSET or Dschang on the premises of the ENSA, etc.

10,000 students at each site. To this dramatic overcrowding, one can add the absence of financial assistance, limited or no housing, and the lack of public transportation alternatives. It therefore takes a minor incident or misunderstanding for the situation to escalate into a demonstration, sometimes wild, disorganized, and often led by individuals with doubtful morals and tied to political parties known for their inclination to violence. One example of this short fuse occurred in 2001, when a simple traffic accident in Ngaoundere, in which a student was crushed to death by a truck from Chad while traveling within Cameroon, resulted in students erecting barricades and systematically looting oncoming vehicles. This unrest caused considerable damage that required the robust intervention of law enforcement personnel. Another example involved another simple traffic accident between two transport vehicles on the road going to the University of Yaounde in Soa, at the outskirts of the capital city, in which about 10 students died. This quickly provoked a violent strike leading to the suspension of classes and the arson of the office of the university director.

Even though relative calm has prevailed since then, a cyclical wave of demonstrations appeared at state universities in Cameroon in April and May 2005 with the aims of improving the living conditions of students and the suppression of university fees. At most campuses, law and order was reestablished rather promptly and with little violence in Yaounde and Douala, however in Buea there was confrontation involving students, who had been joined by members of the general population, and this led to the death of three persons and many more were injured and some police vehicles were completely burnt to ashes.

Discontentment among the Working Population

Following the drastic cuts in their purchasing power, the working population, especially small business owners, did not fail to seize an opportunity to express their discontentment with government leaders. Many claimed to be victims of injustice following the increase in taxes and charges, following the adoption of the Cameroon Finance Law in 2005.

Because of the specific nature of the landscape and history of Cameroon, some regions are destined for farming and others for livestock breeding. Farmers claim that their crops are being destroyed by cattle and other livestock, which has led to misunderstanding and disorder in some of the regions concerned. This has happened in the North-West province where a latent conflict has developed between the bororo breeders and the grass field farmers. Police authorities have had to regularly intervene to prevent the loss of human life. The same problem has appeared in the Far North province between the Arab Choas and Kotokos who have been perpetually fighting for grazing land for their livestock.

Religious Fundamentalism

The phenomenon of religious fundamentalism is not widespread in Cameroon because of the highly developed secular nature of the government and state regulation. Nevertheless, this issue arose in recent history when in 1992, two radical Islamic groups known as the Sunnites and the Tidjanites struggled to gain control of mosques, but public authorities reacted promptly by expelling the instigator, a Nigerian national, and this contributed in reassuring and pacifying the Muslim faithful.

Natural Disasters

Cameroon has been the victim of many disasters. Over the last 5 years, there has been the release of toxic gases, three volcanic eruptions of "Mount Cameroon," tornadoes, floods, landslides, fire accidents, invasion by migratory locusts, and damages caused by elephants. To these disasters, one can be added sizable outbreaks of cholera, meningitis, and red diarrhea epidemics (see Table 15.1).[*]

Such are the many areas that call for the attention of public authorities and the concerted action of the forces of law and order, especially with regard to prevention, giving relief to the population in difficulties, and the protection of the region and properties.

Street Robbery and Other Criminality

For the economies of developing countries to improve, the phenomena of street robbery and other criminality need to be overcome, or at least reduced. The population clearly wants to enjoy the fruit of its work without being deprived by criminals. But with widespread poverty, lack of jobs, and the allure of easy ways of getting rich, the recurrence of violent crime, theft, and street robbery complicate the efforts of public authorities who are concerned with ensuring the recovery of the economy and avoiding discontent exhibited by potential foreign investors.

In Cameroon in particular, even if the problem is not yet alarming, it has nevertheless raised concern among government and law enforcement leaders. In addition to traditional criminality, there has been the re-emergence of armed attacks on homes, on businesses, and those aimed at trucks, buses, and vehicle operators. There has been a dramatic increase in armed groups that can be commonly encountered on streets and highways and in the vicinity of border crossings. In everyday language, they are called highway

---

[*] Statistics are furnished by the Department of Civil Protection of the Ministry of Territorial Administration and Decentralization.

Table 15.1   Summary Table of Some Disasters in Cameroon

Type of Disaster	Place	Year
Gas release	Lake Monoum	1984
	Lake Nyos	1986
	Nsimalen	1996
Floods	Kribi	1998
	Lagdo	1998
	Maga	1998
	Diamare	1996, 1998, 1999
	Limbe	2001
Landslides	Bafaka Balue	1997, 2001, 2002
	Yaounde	
Serious fire accidents	Nsam-Yaounde: more than 200 dead	1998
	Bafoussam market	1999
	Mokolo market in Yaounde	1998
	Limbe market	2000
	Sangmelima market	1998
	Essos market in Yaounde and ammunition dump at army headquarters	2001
Damages by elephants	Diamare (Far North)	1996, 1998, 1999
Epidemics	Cholera	North and Far North 1996, 1997, 1998, 1999 Littoral 2000, 2005
	Meningitis	More than 1000 case in a year from 1998 to 2005
	Red diarrhea	Ngoyla, Messok (East) Mbalmayo
Hunger/drought/ invasion by locusts	Far North with losses of 140,000 ton of agricultural byproducts per year	Since 1998

robbers and bandits, but the reality is that they are heavily armed. Formerly, they operated mainly in the northern part of the country with the aim of stripping traders of their assets, but for some time now, they have extended their scope of action throughout the country, to the towns as well as to the countryside, to the west as well as to the east of the country, masked or with uncovered faces. While originally considered isolated events from a previous era, often related to the numerous civil wars fought in Chad, these present-day street and highway robberies, due to their insolence, the weapons used, and the modus operandi of the attackers who act in large groups using commando style tactics and often wearing military outfits, has become a societal phenomenon that many relate to terrorism.

The reaction of government authorities is intended to reassure the population and has involved the combined efforts of all aspects of the justice and the law and order mechanism, with force being exercised to ensure that these armed groups are eliminated.*

Demonstrations of a Political Nature

Political pluralism brought about in Cameroon, a proliferation of political parties[†] with national, regional, tribal, or family configurations. The numerous misunderstandings resulting from the way the country is being governed or on the manner elections are organized were at the origin of the often violent contentions. It is necessary to call to mind that after 15 years of democratic practice, some political leaders still promote demonstrations on the streets to express their views, trampling on the principles governing such demonstrations. Worse still, elected representatives of the people have spearheaded these demonstrations, coming into confrontation with the forces of law and order, with all the unpleasant occurrences that this may entail.

Thus, as can be pointed out easily, the domestic life of a country is packed with misunderstandings, and coercion may often be controlled for the good of the individual and for social cohesion. It is necessary however, to include some additional explanations to better clarify Table 15.1.

International Environment Impacting Law Enforcement Management

Certain international crimes committed within and outside the national territory of Cameroon require the attention of public authorities:

Terrorism

Since the attacks of September 11, 2001 in the United States, one can conscientiously appreciate the scope and the danger posed by this form of ideological threat, with the underlying goal to frighten large sections of people and to provoke repercussions on the internal and the external security of states across the globe. Often fuelled by national liberation, secessionist, or fundamentalist movements in some countries, the actions of terrorists can have global consequences.

The "war on terrorism" led by the NATO coalition against the terrorist organization Al-Quaida in Afghanistan or against member states of the

---

* Special operations of maintenance of law and order are organised here, sending into action third category forces—Military—together with restrictions to freedom of movement and widely seen administrative measures.
† The Cameroonian political landscape today has more than 160 political parties.

"axis of evil," such as Iraq, affects all countries across the globe regardless if directly involved or otherwise. The terrorism phenomenon concerns everybody because terrorists can strike anywhere, any time, and in any circumstance without distinction of objects, race, gender, or global location.

In Cameroon, even if the phenomenon is not yet widespread, it is nevertheless true that in the heat of the second Gulf war, there were alarming rumors that members of the Al-Quaida group had infiltrated Cameroon so as to carry out a series of attacks on diplomatic missions and interests of countries within the NATO coalition. The consequence of these rumors was the reinforcement and the adoption of special security measures around these missions.*

Transborder Criminality

Transnational crime is one of the major obstacles to the development of states, particularly developing democracies and countries. Transborder criminality is routinely carried out by organized crime networks, skillfully organized and targeting various sectors.

Drug Trafficking

Despite the ravages caused by drugs among populations, this area remains flourishing, the more so because the expected gain is proportional to the risks taken. Considered for a long time as a minor problem, drug trafficking has become a concern for the entire international society in general and that of Cameroon in particular. This is because many crimes committed in Cameroon are linked to the use of these illicit substances. Furthermore, Cameroon, although used predominantly as transit territory,[†] has been overwhelmed by the amount of drugs seized at airports, thereby giving the impression that the substances are used in the country. Undoubtedly, the use of drugs like cannabis, which is widely cultivated, "D10" tablets, and the inhalation of "gum"[‡] provide unlimited challenges to law enforcement officials in Cameroon. Criminal enterprises and cartels enhance this risk for the police.

Trafficking in Human Beings

Trafficking in human beings remains one of the most popular offences committed in Cameroon today, and it is carried out with or without the

---

* Like barricades in front of chancelleries and residences, physical presence of armed policemen, etc.
† Persons arrested at the Douala airport were on transit to Europe or Asia, but often coming from South America.
‡ These products are used mostly by street children and other pickpockets.

consent of the victim. Once again, the desire to make money in an easy way comes into play here. Under false pretense, victims are routinely recruited, especially from among the most vulnerable members of society, namely, women and children, who are then sold to procuring and to trafficking networks to work either in controlled (or coerced) houses or on plantations.

In Central Africa, and especially between the borders of Cameroon, Gabon, and Equatorial Guinea, hundreds of children between 8 and 12 years have routinely been discovered loaded in trucks transporting food items. Many were nationals of the Republics of Niger and Mali. After intensive negotiations, and with the support of the Cameroon Red Cross, their repatriation was ensured under close and coordinated security supervision.

There is also an exponential increase in prostitution within Cameroon, which for reasons linked especially to material poverty, questionable morals, and the environment, plunge women, with no explicit age limit, and young boys into this domain of tragic activity.

There is also the seemingly unusual practice involving the trafficking in the bones of human beings, which is more common in southern Africa and Asia. Exhumation of and thefts from tombs is often routine, but organ removal, particularly from young children, and trading are also not uncommon.

Smuggling

Smuggling in Cameroon is carried out by criminal networks and some legitimate businessmen who function routinely outside the law. This is a serious threat to the economic stability of many states given that items illegally imported do not obey safety standards and no custom revenues or taxes enter the public treasury. In Cameroon, there has been a dramatic increase in fuel, cement, and animal hide smuggling* along the borders with Nigeria. There is the additional problem of the fraudulent importation of food items (especially meat, fish, sugar, and rice).

White Collar Crime and Currency Counterfeiting

White collar crime and the counterfeiting of local and foreign currencies are closely linked, when considering that their modus operandi, actors, and actions are linked to specific criminal groups and to governmental corruption. These two phenomena were at their highest levels when young economies were in their darkest days and when there was shortage of cash in public treasuries and national banks, as had occurred in Cameroon in

---

* This smuggling often goes hand in hand with dubious products, not fit for consumption.

1988. As a result, structured networks of corrupt officials set up in different governmental administrative services clearly hampered the desired equality of citizens. Public servants had decided to "live for today" and line their own pockets at the expense of the general public. The new generation of fraudsters involves professional swindlers, who promise high profits in intricate scams and the distribution or sale of counterfeit currency.

In addition to the negative impact on the national economy, these criminals have tarnished the image of Cameroon in front of the rest of the international community.

The criminal phenomena within Cameroon, mentioned above, continue to challenge the maintenance of domestic law and order and negatively impact community development and social peace.

Community-Oriented Policing

The maintenance of law and order is dependent on the ability of the police to distinguish between actual and factual elements. In Cameroon, for a long time, the police was often viewed as an opponent of the people,* because of its apparent blind involvement in the maintenance of law and order under the colonial masters or the First Republic of Cameroon through 1982, the year in which the political regime changed hands. The image portrayed of the police officers during those time frames could be compared to that of a hangman called to execute without discernment of sentence. This sentiment led to the undermining of state authority. During those years, the presence of the police was synonymous with provocation. The democratization of Cameroon and the globalization movement has resulted in the need to revamp the justice mechanism.

Modern Policing in Cameroon

The constant desire for the positive adaptation of the police relies on the flexibility to respond to social evolution and unforeseen events. Police officials have to be free of political interference, but steps must be taken to move law enforcement officials properly into the new millennium. To achieve this, many actions must take place:

Appropriate Training

Efficient and effective action can be obtained through contemporary basic and in-service training that combines both theory and practice. Today's

---

* Through its very large set up, the police was used in operations to track down opponents since the colonial period or to provide information concerning them.

police officials must be acquainted with evolutionary notions that include the environment, human rights, political rights, psychology, and other issues that permit the smooth accomplishment of the police mission and the assimilation of newly developed or developing facts.

The revision of the curricula at the Cameroon police training centers and management colleges can supply new meaning to the police profession. Continuous in-service training enables a rapid improvement in the capacities of crime control and disorder intervention. Unfortunately, funding for such initiatives within Cameroon is limited.

Proper Resources and Staffing

After training, Cameroon has to address the rational human potential of its justice agencies. Management staff must be available, conscientious and properly trained, and educated for task accomplishment. Maintenance of law and order being very exhausting, only the supervisory staff could support these challenges for a relatively long time. One goal could be to limit police managerial staff to no more than 5 years in one position before being redeployed to other sectors within the police agency. In addition, new and workable equipment must be allocated and distributed to police personnel.

Improving Public Confidence in the Police

The police must regain lost public confidence. There is need to reorient police action toward some concrete areas that have been clearly forgotten. One area for improved police–public interaction is response to natural disasters. Planning could involve the joint involvement of police and local civil agencies. Meetings would involve the interaction of the police and the community they serve. The public must also understand that the fight against crime is an effort to fight poverty, if the government takes action to improve the social conditions of local residents.

Police and Democratic Change

The police agency in Cameroon has been placed under the authority of the President of the Republic.* In this capacity, the Cameroon lawmakers have granted full powers to the chief national executive to successfully carry out the maintenance of law and order and to provide security throughout the country. As such, all the actions carried out by the police have always been attributed to this high personality. An interesting question arises. How

* See Article 2, paragraph 1 of Decree No. 2002/003 of January 4, 2002 to organize the General Delegation for National Security.

should a police officer behave in a period of regime change? The answer to this question is impacted greatly by many factors, the most important of which is the fear of the future that is apparently uncertain, and the potential loss of certain advantages linked to police position or rank and, in many cases, the systematic political overhaul in government services. It is therefore, difficult to maintain a consistent personal ideology that involves the desire to serve one's country even in a period of change. It would be prudent for police officials in Cameroon to strongly consider the following principles:

- Every police official must not be afraid of a change of regime.
- Every police official should remain at the service of legally established institutions.
- Every police official is governed by instruments in force in the State.
- Whatever the regime, every police official should remain subject to the same ethical and deontological principles.
- Every police official must welcome the possibility of a change of regime.
- Every police official is entitled to be informed of planned changes in the agency.
- Every police official must be prepared to inform government officials on actions that will improve agency efficiency and effectiveness.
- Each police official must be capable of foreseeing some situations likely to disturb social order.
- Each police official shall refrain from engaging in political favoritism with government officials and with subordinates.

If the above conditions are not respected and adhered to, there will be a pollution of the work environment, a promotion of confusion, and a complication of the implementation of agency mandates. One truly has to consider the recommendation of a Cameroon elder who stated "that a good policeman must know how to adjust tokens of respect and dignity. He must give in neither to the temptation of bondage, nor to that of familiarity. The authorities we are talking about here have a permanent need of an efficient and competent police and not servants and handy men" [1].

One critical concern involves the role of the police during elections. Police officials must independently master the major aspects found in the electoral process, notably recurrent problems linked to registration in electoral lists, the setting up of polling stations, the counting and the proclamation of results, and electoral disputes. While remaining independent of political influence, the primary endeavor for the police should be to provide a secure environment at all stages.

In many countries of southern Africa, including Cameroon, there have been frequent allegations of voter intimidation and the masking of the true number of voters, and the reported seizure and disappearance of "manu militari" (hand) ballot boxes. One example of positive efforts is the seminar held at the National School of Administration and Magistracy in Yaounde at the end of September 2004, which dealt with the management of elections throughout Cameroon. One relevant point that this meeting concluded was that

- A professional police official must master the working tool put at his disposal, in common agreement with the principles of deontology, equity, and those relating to the respect of the human condition.

The police, being at the beginning and at the end of the process of social change, should strongly consider the above critical principles in order to avoid possible excesses and properly manage the security of citizens. However, these efforts would not be complete if international cooperation is not taken into account.

International Cooperation

The concept and era of socialist economic self-sufficiency have passed. Furthermore, the mobility of persons and goods coupled with access to the electronic media has created the need for international cooperation. It is therefore necessary, and timely, that frank and clear police cooperation be established among nations.

Exchange of Information

The success of any venture depends on the data that one has. The management of problems linked to the security of humanity and goods being traded, depends on the reliability of reports and information. Two concerns are involved:

- The fight against terrorism (e.g., formation, motivation, bases, possible targets, means, etc.)
- The prevention of disasters (e.g., warning mechanisms, frequency, and scope)

These data must absolutely be communicated to the countries concerned for them to take prompt and effective measures to prevent death, injury, and widespread damage.

International Police Cooperation

There already exists cooperation through INTERPOL, which indisputably furnishes useful information to different member countries. However, cooperation with other organizations is needed to properly address terrorism and cybercriminality. Cameroon has been greatly assisted by EUROPOL, which has assisted in the dismantling of networks promoting pedophilia, child pornography, and football hooliganism.

The situation in the central African region needs to be mentioned. Even with the formation of a regional committee of police chiefs and the enhanced transborder communication that has resulted, armed criminal gangs still easily carry out their activities in some states and escape to countries with questionable law enforcement practices. This is clearly disturbing as they commit serious violent crimes and are involved in abduction, hostage taking, and looting along their travel routes.

The absence of regional communication by many countries does not enable efficient action to be taken, often due to the lack of will by national and local leaders. Internal quarrels among and within some countries have brought about either civil wars, coups d'état, and the decentralization of political powers, often by criminally oriented "leaders." The negative effects of the lack of communication have been identified by the Economic Community of West African States (ECOWAS), among whom real cooperation exists, but the threat of coercion still persists.

Support for Professional Training

Training in cybercrime, transborder criminality, and effective strategies to combat them has to be provided throughout Africa. This training is often provided at the bilateral level by some countries like France (SCTIP), Belgium (SCB), the United States (ICITAP), and many others, but it would probably be more effective and consistent, if it were provided by internationally recognized agencies like INTERPOL, EUROPOL, or the United Nations that have the financial capability to ensure that these issues are addressed not only throughout the African continent, but across the globe.

One can plainly conclude that as the "world gets smaller," there is a strong need for international cooperation and support to fight criminal and terrorist groups globally. We are all in this fight together!

Reference

1. Paul, P., *The Police in Cameroon*, Editions CLE, Yaounde, Cameroon, 1988, pp. 217.

Traditional Ideologies Deter Progress in the Contemporary Justice Practices in Nigeria

16

ROBERT D. HANSER AND SCOTT MIRE

Contents

Introduction: The State of Affairs in Nigeria

The Federal Republic of Nigeria is the most populous nation in Africa. This country is very influential throughout the West African region and struggles to reform its internal infrastructure amidst military and economic chaos that reflects that area of the world. This nation is also one that has a very short official history and a disconnected sense of self-identity. Indeed, Nigeria is not yet even 50 years old as a nation, having achieved independence from British rule in 1960. Further, this nation's early history was plagued with a series of coups and unstable governmental developments, which ultimately resulted in 16 years of rigid and heavy-handed military rule.

In 1999, Nigeria constructed a new constitution with a corresponding shift toward a civil (as opposed to military) form of government. This shift has been considered fairly successful, though corruption of government officials is rampant throughout the nation. Nevertheless, in April of 2007, elections were held resulting in the first civilian-to-civilian transfer of power to take place throughout the nation's history (CIA, 2007). This is of course an important event for any nation, but this is particularly important for Nigeria and its people because of the widespread problems and internal conflicts that have plagued this nation. The lack of trust in the government, widely held by the populace of Nigeria, can only be overcome with time and a genuine commitment to civilian rule.

The criminal justice system of Nigeria is, quite naturally, an extension of the government and has a negative past image that it must contend with. The policing arm of the nation's criminal justice system has traditionally played a quasi-military role and has committed a number of serious abuses against the civilian population throughout the country's history. Much of this poor form of civilian policing was modeled after the methods that were employed by the British during Nigeria's occupation and subjugation to Great Britain. The judiciary is likewise corrupt and inefficient and is viewed as being a manipulative tool of the wealthy. As would be expected, the nation's prison system is similarly defunct and serves as a symbol of pestilence and squalor, reflecting an apathetic government and criminal justice system.

Amidst these difficulties, Nigeria must contend with a multitude of ethnic identities, multiple religions, and an array of spoken languages that fall within her borders. A variety of competing ideologies make civilian rule difficult to implement and also hinder modern progress in many arenas of government, including those related to criminal justice processes. Still, these ideologies are ironically a better basis of conflict resolution, crime prevention, and criminal processing than are the official institutions in place. Due to the graft and corruption that permeates Nigeria's criminal justice system and also due to the rampant criminality within the country, these competing ideologies and indigenous belief systems tend to have a more favorable view among the public and are therefore reinforced; making it even more difficult for sincere reforms on the part of the government. It is with this point in mind that this chapter will continue, demonstrating that contemporary justice practices in Nigeria may not only be deterred by traditional beliefs of the indigenous Nigerian population, but they may actually be out of synch with that nation's chances of achieving any sense of cultural harmony. We begin first by examining the policing function of the Nigerian criminal justice system, moving to the courts as well as the correctional components. This examination of Nigeria's system of justice is juxtaposed against the presentation of a multiethnic fabric that is similar to a patchwork quilt woven from a variety of randomly selected cultural groups, coming together as a product that is both complicated and difficult to examine in any singular or organized fashion.

Policing: Past and Present Issues

Policing in Nigeria has a relatively short history, for the most part. The earliest traces of a formalized police force can only be traced back to about 1861, when the acting governor of Lagos Colony established a small official police force, called the Hausa Constabulary, during that year. The term Hausa, refers to a specific indigenous African group in Northern Nigeria. The constabulary that was formed at this time was drawn from this ethnic group, hence the name. Onyeozili (2005, p. 35) notes that "this formation marked the beginning of the first modern police in the history of Lagos. It was also the first modern police force in the territories later designated Nigeria by the British." From this, it can be determined that the early origins of an official civil police were established through British influence, yet consisted of an indigenous composition.

However, it should not be presumed that such a development was for benevolent purposes. Rather, the institution of slavery was alive and well in Lagos during the 1860s (with the United States being a prime customer) and much of the work of the Hausa constabulary centered around maintaining order for the wealthy European aristocrats that held power in Lagos during this time. Further, the Hausa were not native to the area near to Lagos, the capital of Nigeria. Since Nigeria's initial colonial and postcolonial policing and court systems originated in Lagos, this means that the first origins of criminal justice in the capital of Nigeria consisted of English-based and imposed systems and/or enforcers from other distant areas of Nigeria. Add to this that the Hausa were traditionally Muslim, and it becomes clear that this early police force was distant from the population that it was tasked with protecting.

In fact, it is clear that the early colonial rulers of Nigeria specifically desired disharmony between their appointed native Nigerian police and the remaining citizenry in and around Lagos. Consider the following excerpt from a letter written by then Colonial Governor Denton in 1893:

> In our Hausa force we have a body of men dissociated from the countries immediately around Lagos both by birth and religion, and who are as a matter of fact the hereditary enemies of the Yorubas. This is such an enormous advantage in any interior complication [opposition to colonial rule] that I should be sorry to see it abandoned if it were possible to obtain a supply of recruits in any other way (Alemika and Chukwuma, 2004, p. 33).

It is clear that the British colonial rulers had an interest in ensuring that hostility remained between the police and the citizenry. The colonial government specifically created a policing instrument that would impair any likelihood of obtaining any rapport with community members. Rather, the members of the police force would squelch riots, oppose independent thought, and suppress those that might seek a better life. The rule of law, honoring human rights, and public service were all ignored. Further, the police were designed to ensure that the rich remained in power by keeping the masses of poor under tight control.

Onyeozili (2005) lends support to the notion that the early police forces were simply tools designed to further the colonial political agendas. This then means that the police were not much different than an invading force that held dominion over the public, creating an image and flavor of oppression rather than one of citizen protection. The fact that justice processes during this time served to further the interests of European conquerors is made clear by the court system structure that existed during the 1860s. During this time, four courts existed—the police court, the commercial court, the criminal court, and a slave court. The *police court* handled minor criminal cases while the *criminal court*, overseen by British merchant assessors, addressed more serious crimes. Another court, the *slave court*, heard issues related to slave and ownership and property, while the *commercial court* was overseen entirely by British merchants to process debt and breach-of-contract cases. The emphases of these courts were primarily centered on economic concerns that supported the wealthy British elite. Because of this, the tenor between government enforcement functions and the general population is one that smacks of oppression. The tension between Nigerian law enforcement and the citizenry has been a historical reality in Nigeria and continues to have an impact on justice practices today.

It was not until late 1895 and/or early 1896 that the police in Lagos would mirror the actual population of that region. On December 27, 1895, Police Ordinance No. 10 was passed establishing a civil police force called simply, the *Lagos Police*. This new police force was separated from the military and consisted of indigenous persons of Yoruba descent. The Yoruba were native to Lagos and this then represented a point in time where Nigeria (at least in Lagos) policed itself with an official and professionalized police force. Following this development, in 1906 the police forces of Lagos and Southern Nigeria were combined into the Southern Nigeria Police Force. It would not be until 1914 that both the northern and southern protectorates of Nigeria would merge. This was followed in 1930 with the police forces merging, marking an important point in Nigerian policing. This was the beginning of what is now known as the Nigerian Police Force. The Nigerian Police Force was and continues to be a central issue of attention in Nigeria, particularly during the decolonization periods of Nigeria when Britain relinquished control of the nation.

From the early 1900s to the late 1950s, the Nigerian Police Force was a symbol of oppression since it was viewed as a tool of a government that economically and politically exploited much of the population. The police during these decades were tasked with brutal assignments of suppression. Throughout these decades, the police maintained a very definite military perspective, concentrating more on riot control and methods of social order maintenance rather than genuine civilianized policing. Throughout this time, the police played a leading role in efforts to consolidate Nigeria and to repress a citizenry that had been "colonized" by other outside forces. Supporting these points, Onyeozili (2005) notes that

> Post-independence law in Nigeria is marked by entrenched colonial social-
> ization. Following freedom from the colonial masters, the political class in
> Nigeria perpetuated the inherited hegemonic policing policy. While adapting
> to the Western culture, the traditional values were compromised and this had
> adverse implication for the institution of law enforcement (p. 39).

On October 1, 1960, Nigeria became an independent nation that was formally separate from British rule. A formal legal framework, known as the Independence Constitution was drafted along with the Republican Constitution of 1963. These documents authorized local police forces and further cemented the role of the Nigeria Police Force (the national police force). However, the reign of the Republican government was short-lived, ending with a military coup that occurred in 1966. This military government eliminated all local or indigenous police forces as a means of centralizing control. Further cementing this approach are the intentions of the 1979 and 1999 constitutions that prohibit the establishment of other police bodies aside from the Nigeria Police Force.

During both the colonial periods and the turbulent periods of Nigerian independence, the police remained distant from the police and served more as government agents than civilian police. Naturally, this remained true during the reign of the military regime of the 1960s and 1970s. There are two key points to understand in regard to the police's role during these points in Nigerian history. First, the decade-long experiences grafted into the minds of Nigerians that the police were nothing more than agents of social control, being more politicized than anything else. Second, because the police were arms of the political groups that held power, this meant that little attention, training, or allocation of resources were devoted to genuine crime-fighting processes. These two points are critical because they form the foundation of everything else that follows in establishing any sense of justice in Nigeria. The politicized nature of the police force left it extremely vulnerable to corruption, both within and without the agency confines. In addition, the lack of genuine police training provided a force that was largely incompetent to fulfill a true policing function geared toward protection of the public. This then created a climate where the police were viewed as both corrupt and ineffectual by the general citizenry.

Throughout Nigeria's tumultuous history that has followed, the police have retained this image among the common public. This is so true that a number of informal policing groups have emerged throughout that country, despite the fact that the Nigerian constitution clearly forbids such actions. According to Alemika and Chukwuma (2004), at least 16 types of informal policing structures have been identified in various communities. The groups were established in various communities to deal with crime in a manner that is more reflective of the traditional practices used by indigenous groups and sources of authority. Interestingly, the term used most often for these groups is "vigilante," regardless of the specific language that is employed (Alemika and Chukwuma, 2004). The development of these informal police structures is an important element of the Nigerian social control system and represents the fact that the public has lost faith in its official police force.

The informal policing systems that currently exist use a number of very unorthodox techniques to carry out their mission. Among these methods of policing, traditional divining methods, protection methods, the use of praying and fasting, and even the use of mob-related actions have been noted (Alemika and Chukwuma, 2004). The use of traditional divining methods and/or protection methods points to the reliance on traditional indigenous folk remedies for enforcing social customs and laws. In a land of near lawlessness, it is not surprising the population would resort to such alternative forms of protection. This is particularly true when considering that the national police are viewed as corrupt and as enemies of the citizenry.

It was thought that more stability and economic prosperity would come to Nigeria after the shift from autocratic military rule to democratic rule in 1999. However, the new democratic government in Nigeria has only ushered in a sense of insecurity and lawlessness that pervades the entire country (Alemika and Chukwuma, 2004). Currently, the state of justice administration in Nigeria is chaotic and quite unjust. Numerous human rights issues are of consideration, the policing and court systems are corrupt, and tensions between differing ethnic and/or religious groups tend to magnify the problem. Traditional ideologies steeped in ethnic and religious differences create a tumultuous system that has never truly broken free of its colonial background. The wounds are deep and keep the Nigerian system of justice in a fragmented state of flux. Added to this is the widespread corruption that exists in this nation's justice system, which prevents any true reform from taking hold. The following four issues: (1) ethnic/religious ideologies, (2) disorganized institutional structures, (3) incompatibility of indigenous and European justice philosophies, and (4) corruption within the justice system, will serve as the basic framework of discussion throughout the remainder of this chapter. It will be demonstrated that these three areas of concern prevent Nigeria from combating the crime problem that is experienced and, therefore, exacerbate the dismal state of affairs in that country.

Ethnic and Religious Ideologies

Nigeria's 2007 population is estimated to be over 130,000,000 people within an area that is approximately 356,000 square miles. Thus, this country has a fairly dense population and it is the most populous nation in Africa. Nigeria is a multiethnic country that has over 250 ethnic groups. The national borders of this country are largely the work of British colonial rule, with the official area of the country evolving through subjugation and amalgamation of various peoples and regions between the years of 1861 and 1914. Literally hundreds of separate groups were forced under one banner and, once the area of Nigeria was established, the British divided the region into two protectorates: the Protectorate of Northern Nigeria and the Protectorate of Southern Nigeria. During this time, each successively subjugated region was given its own local police force or constabulary. As noted in the introductory section of this chapter, the North and South Protectorates were united in 1914 and in 1930, the Nigeria Police Force was officially established.

Of the many ethnic groups in Nigeria, three groups predominate. The first of these is the Hausa-Fulani, who dwell in the northern sections of Nigeria. The Hausa originated from the eastern region of Africa, somewhere in what is current day Sudan. The Fulani have origins that are unknown and speculative, but they have intermarried with the Hausa since their arrival in Nigeria during the thirteenth century. The Fulani have, for the most part, adopted the customs and language of the Hausa though many do deviate by maintaining their traditional nomadic lifestyle (the Hausa being city dwellers by origin). Important to mention is the fact that both the Hausa and the Fulani have been Muslim in religious faith. This places them distinctly apart from those sections of Nigeria that hold Judeo–Christian religious beliefs and/or other groups that practice their own localized and indigenous forms of spirituality or religion. As was mentioned earlier, this difference was one of the reasons that early European rulers in Lagos selected members of the Hausa-Fulani for policing in Nigeria during the colonial era.

The second major ethnic group is known as the Igbo. The Igbo are in actuality a group of many other smaller groups that voluntarily banded together. Examples include the Onitsha Igbo, the Southeastern Igbo, the Afikpo Igbo, and so forth. Collectively, they share obscure origins but have dwelled in the forested areas of Southeastern Nigeria along the Niger Valley. This location as home has important historical precedents, since the Igbo selected this area as a means of protection from the Fulani's slave raids during the 1700s and 1800s. The Fulani used cavalry as a means of making slave raids and the forested regions that the Igbo selected made it difficult for cavalry slave abductors. Naturally, no love is lost between the Igbo and the Fulani, and relations have traditionally remained a bit conflicted throughout the years since the slave-trading period. The Igbo are known for a truly decentralized social structure based on extended family. Indeed, few officials existed and, when they did, they had little power. Igbo villages were democratic in nature, reflecting further a strong difference in ideologies between themselves and the Hausa-Fulani.

The third major ethnic group, known as the Yoruba, also consists of numerous smaller groups of people. These groups, however, share very common lineages and histories with one another and the collection of groups is based on amicable relationships. Throughout centuries, they have coexisted in peace and share the common belief in the deity Oduduwa. The various groups belonging to the Yoruba also hold the town of *Ife* as their own respective place of origin. The town of *Ife* is considered to be a holy city by the various Yoruba groups. It is the belief in an indigenous deity and the common link to Ife that serves as the primary social glue for this group.

Despite their larger sizes, these first three groups only constitute roughly 60% of the entire Nigerian population. The remaining citizens are members of a variety of smaller groups. It should be mentioned that most of these groups, including the Igbo and, to a lesser extent, the Yoruba, were the equivalent of *stateless societies*, which rely on family lineages to govern day-to-day events rather than elected government or monarchs. This system worked well for many Nigerian groups until the British took control of the country. Rather than working with the lineages and relationships that had existed for centuries, the British drew national boundaries that were best suited for commercial interests, without consideration of the territorial claims established by indigenous people. Since this time, ethnic and religious tensions have greatly troubled this country.

Understanding the ethnic diversity that exists among tribes, the conflicts between them, and the effects that British border-setting has had on this country is important if one desires to understand the challenges to the Nigerian justice system. The conflicts that have occurred and that still occur are serious and prevent the oil-laden nation from achieving the same sense of stability that exists among other industrialized nations. Indeed, it is because of these ethnic conflicts, coupled with excessive corruption that Nigeria cannot seem to make the transition from a developing country to an industrialized and fully developed nation. These conflicts tend to be bloody and also tend to be over multiple problems and sources of anger. Relations between ethnic groups and between some family lines are quite caustic, including social, cultural, and economic dimensions. Naturally, control over life-providing resources such as water, fuel, and so forth are often a tangible component of these conflicts.

Tribal lineages and clannish allegiance have paralyzed most governmental efforts to create harmony in the country. One can define ethnicity as that which pertains to a people, especially those groups sharing a common language and distinctive cultural patterns, and who retain a consciousness based on such factors as language, legends, customs, and religion (p. 112). These ethnic differences exist on several dimensions, including language, religion, and traditions. The source of this ethnic conflict is no different than that found in Rwanda, Liberia, or Mozambique. Problems with religious conflict are world renowned as indigenous religions, the Christian faith, and Islam are practiced with regularity within Nigeria's borders, creating a religious confluence that has not mixed well.

Further, during some conflicts, the police have even taken the side of one group or another, depending on the particular ethnic identity of the responding police. This has further diminished the public view of the police since it is clear that bias runs deep within their ranks. This has historically been the case with the police, with the 1966 massacre where Nigerian police engaged in genocidal attacks against southeasterners. The memory of this time period is still in the minds of southeastern Nigerians and this has created a climate where it seems that police and citizen relations will be permanently scarred. Indeed, families teach their children to not trust the police and communities reinforce the sense of distrust. Thus, any improvement in relations will require significant community outreach and the ability to overcome barriers that seem quite permanent.

The economic conditions around Nigeria tend to be dependent upon the petroleum industry. Indeed, many foreign nations operate a variety of oil drilling operations in that country, both on land and especially off Nigeria's coast. So chaotic is the state of this nation that foreign companies have to provide bolstered security to guard against coastal pirates and potential kidnappers. Add to this the fact that crude oil, Nigeria's main economic export, routinely fluctuates in price, and it is clear that there is marked fluidity in economic conditions throughout the year. The economic conditions are intertwined with the politics and governmental running of the country. Perhaps Onyeozili (2005) describes the situation best by stating that

In the past 22 years beginning from the early 1980–81 when its economic crisis began to manifest on a serious scale, Nigeria has witnessed political instability, protracted military rule (involving four different regimes), widespread insecurity, ethnic and religious conflicts, annulment of a presidential election conducted in June 1993 followed by a gruesome specter of military dictatorship under General Sani Abacha. Although an elected government (under Olusegun Obasanjo who was the nation's military head of State from 1976 to 1979) came to power on May 29, 1999, however after four years no significant achievement has been recorded in the tackling of the nation's core economic, political and social problems (p. 41).

Last, amidst the ethnic differences, there also exists all of the difficulties associated with any multilinguistic society. In a plural and semi-illiterate society such as Nigeria, it is common for persons to resort to their own indigenous language during their daily routines. One example might be the Hausa speaking police who tend to experience difficulty performing their duties non-Hausa-speaking areas of the country. This is actually quite problematic because since the time when the British occupied and exploited Nigeria, a substantial segment of the Nigerian police force has been of Hausa origin. Despite Nigeria's attempt to provide practical training and knowledge of second languages among its police, the linguistic challenges remain a major hurdle in rectifying problems between police and the community.

It is clear that the ethnic tensions facing Nigeria are many and that these problems permeate the justice system of Nigeria. This is important to remember because it prevents the nation from simply implementing a standardized approach to resolving its justice issues. Indeed, for many with political power, such a standardized approach may not be desirable since the powerful stand to lose economic and political privilege if such a system ever were to be realized. Given the graft and corruption associated with the political process and the policing system, it is unlikely the justice system of Nigeria will be truly democratic and unbiased any time in the near future.

Traditional Indigenous Ideologies of Justice: Precolonial Periods

Prior to the arrival of British rule in 1849, Nigeria was a stateless region that was composed of multiple communities. These communities ranged from villages to city-states, with elders, chiefs, Emirs, and Kings that would provide judgment over disputes in the community (Ebbe, 2000). Offenses were viewed as abominations, taboos, or as offenses against the earth, deities, or ancestors (Ebbe, 2000). The person holding highest authority typically settled any questions regarding interpersonal victimization, but the notion of this being a *crime*, per se, did not exist among these indigenous groups. Rather, these behaviors were seen more as a deviation from the customs of the tribe or the community, and punishments tended to revolve around the notion of a communal form of resolution.

It was not until 1904 that a true criminal law was established throughout the whole of Nigeria. This law, the Nigerian Criminal Code of 1904, was of British origin and was drafted from prior codes used in other areas subjugated by the British such as Australia and Jamaica (Ebbe, 2000). The criminal code was based on British values and the English common law system, not the values or norms of the Nigerian population. Further, this code was drafted entirely by Englishmen, and was based solely on the standards and interests of British officials. In fact, the criminal code "provoked conflicts of norms among the citizens of Nigeria because it criminalized some customary practices and normative standards of the Nigerian people" (Ebbe, 2000, p. 186). One example provided by Ebbe (2000), is that of polygamy. In Nigerian culture, men who have two or three wives are given social prestige and respect and this has been a cultural norm among the various tribes and ethnic groups well before the arrival of the British. The criminal code forbade the practice of having more than one wife, demonstrating that this legal process completely lacked any congruence with the culture that existed throughout Nigeria. In the Islamic Maliki Law, under which nearly half of all Nigerians are subject, men are allowed up to four wives (Ebbe, 2000). Even still, despite decades of reform and a variety of amendments made to the British-based criminal code, inconsistencies between that law and the norms of the country's people still exist.

In 1959, the current Nigerian criminal code was essentially removed from the governmental operation of Northern Nigeria. Much of this was due to prior difficulties in effectively applying this law in the northern region where Emirs practiced Islamic (Maliki) Law. As a means of negotiation and as a matter of sheer practicality, the penal code was created and adopted to accommodate the values, traditions, and beliefs of the Muslim population (Ebbe, 2000). The penal code was drafted from the earlier Sudanese penal code due to the fact that the Muslim law in Sudan was very similar to those of the Maliki Code that prevailed throughout Northern Nigeria (Ebbe, 2000). The Maliki Code, following the criminal law tradition of Shari'a, hears most all civil case issues and does provide for the application of punitive sanctions (Reichel, 2002).

After the criminal code became applicable to the entire realm of Nigeria, most criminal cases were still overseen by the indigenous legal systems. This is often referred to as customary law because it is based on the customs of local tribes and ethnic groups in a given area. The British had tried to eliminate most of these legal systems because of the lack of consistency that existed from area to area. However, this was never completely successful and what eventually occurred was a series of modifications to various local systems. Since Nigerian independence, both the criminal code (based on English common law) and the penal code (based on Maliki law) have been amended on numerous occasions to accommodate the norms, values, and standards of the indigenous Nigerian population (Ebbe, 2000). In addition, certain Nigerian customs that were criminalized by prior English-based systems have been legalized, better reflecting the ethnic beliefs in a given area. The customary courts are especially popular in the southern areas of Nigeria, where cases are processed based on customs, beliefs, and values of ethnic groups in that region (Reichel, 2002).

Each of the prior court systems exist at the state level, demonstrating how much Nigerian law and legal philosophy changes from state to state. In addition, Nigeria's federal court system exists and provides an additional set of considerations when understanding underlying ideologies impacting the justice system of Nigeria. At the federal level, the highest court is the Supreme Court of Nigeria. The Supreme Court consists of the chief justice and a number of associate justices that are appointed by the president. The Federal Court of Appeals consists of a president and several other justices as prescribed by legislation, with at least three mandatory justices in Islamic law. While the federal court system, the state court systems, consisting of the criminal code (common law) and the penal code (Shari'a) may exist on paper, none of these systems are popular with much of the nation's population. In fact, the public often avoids utilizing the court system due to excessive delays that exist within the modern system. These delays have kept many people that are presumed innocent in a detained status in terrible, overcrowded, and unhealthy prison systems where they await trial. Reichel (2002) states that "whether the Nigerian's efforts to shun the modern court are a result of the delays in getting a complete judgment in a case or because the people have little confidence in modern courts" (p. 224).

The political system of Nigeria is ineffectual, open to corruption, and at best would be described as fragile. The Nigerian constitution is itself under-mined and given little credit due to the numerous transfers of power that have been experienced in that nation. This is further compounded by the fact that in most cases where the government has changed hands, the Nigerian Supreme Court has refused to make comment. Indeed, it is often the case that a similar social group exists where those affecting a coup and those in the upper judiciary stand to gain from tacit approval of one another's actions by simply ignoring obvious violations that might occur. On numerous occa-sions, the federal judiciary in Nigeria has been found to be complicit in cor-rupt actions by government officials (Okereafezeke, 2003).

This then means that the public in Nigeria tend to turn to customary courts or lay courts as a means of informally addressing problems that arise. This avoids excessive delay and also tends to circumvent much of the corrup-tion that exists within the formal court structures (Ebbe, 2000). Indeed, the use of lay judges, chiefs, or village council elders as mediators in criminal pro-ceedings occurs at very little cost to the victim, offender, or the community (Ebbe, 2000). Naturally, this type of system has some resemblance to restor-ative justice principles that are in vogue around the world. This is because, in actuality, traditional Western African methods of justice and correction are inherently restorative in nature. It is precisely because of this that the English methods of using adversarial forms of justice have been so incompat-ible with traditional tribal forms of justice administration in Nigeria. Aside from these fundamental philosophical differences in orientation, there is a tangible and measurable benefit in using customary courts; they also reduce the number of undecided cases filed with magistrates and higher-level courts (Ebbe, 2000).

It is important to understand how the use of customary courts has impacted Nigeria's progress to use more contemporary forms of justice administration. The customary courts, and those based on Shari'a, tend to be more grounded in the beliefs of persons in their respective jurisdictions. This alone breeds familiarity and also produces outcomes that have a bet-ter cultural fit than do those with an English common law basis or those at the federal level. Indeed, those at the federal level may have judges that are from a differing ethnic group than the parties that are involved in a given case. Thus, both the victim and the offending party are likely to prefer the use of customary courts where the context of a given social infraction is better understood. Because these processes, based on traditional ideologies, are simply more effective than many contemporary forms of justice, it is no wonder that Nigeria cannot modernize its system of justice delivery. Further, the contemporary court system is often co-opted with organized crime, political coups, and other forms of corruption. Likewise, the policing system tends to also be corrupt, acting as an arm of the wealthy and the political elite than as a genuine force designed to uphold and enforce the rule of law (Alemika and Chukwuma, 2004). There has been considerable research that has demonstrated the corruption of both the courts and the police in Nigeria (Alemika and Chukwuma, 2004; Elechi, 2006; Okereafezeke, 2003). The courts have been implicated in a number of cases where politically based crimes (including murder) are essentially unpunished (Onyeozili, 2005) and where the police simply fail to take certain persons into custody due to their relations with persons of wealth and power (Alemika and Chukwuma, 2004). Indeed, the police in Nigeria have been likened to a Marxist institution of social control where crime and crime control are simply tools for the rich to maintain the status quo and control over the poor (Alemika and Chukwuma, 2004). Thus, it is not so much that traditional ideologies are standing in the way of positive progress in the Nigerian administration of justice, but it is instead the case that customary forms of justice are less likely to be corrupt, tend to be more efficient, and are familiar to the local people. It is no wonder that the Nigerian public does not find incentive to utilize more contemporary justice administration processes.

Further, as previously noted, the indigenous groups in West Africa have a community-based and human-centered basis that employs restorative and transformative principles of conflict resolution (Elechi, 2006). Much of the reason for the development of this type of justice was due to the fact that unlike Europe and the United States, the use of prisons was never a widely adopted practice in much of rural Africa. Thus, methods were created whereby offenders that would not comply would be given sanctions where they were restricted from certain privileges, denied the right to marriage, and/or restricted from other benefits of the community. With appropriate effort, such offenders could work their way back into mainstream tribal belonging and participation. In short, most indigenous West African forms of customary justice were reintegrative out of mere necessity. In extreme cases, when the offender simply would not comply, death or banishment was the option utilized. Aside from those cases where reintegrative techniques simply did not work, traditional African thought on conflict resolution and justice administration are nearly identical to current restorative justice philosophies. Elechi (2006) provides a full explanation, stating that

Ideally, African indigenous justice systems provide opportunities for dialogue amongst the victim, the offender, their families and friends, and the community. Conflict provides opportunities for primary stake-holders to examine and bring about changes to the society's social, institutional and economic structure. African indigenous justice system is also victim-centered, with victims, offenders, their families and the general community involved in defining harm and repair. As an inclusive system, it seeks to address the interests of all parties to the conflict. The social solidarity and humane emphasis of the system is reflected in the treatment of offenders. Offenders are encouraged to understand and accept responsibility for their actions. Accountability may result in some discomfort to the offender, but not so harsh as to degenerate into further antagonism and animosity, thereby further alienating the offender. Strenuous efforts follow chastisement to reintegrate the offender back into the community (p. 2 and 3).

There are numerous other researchers and authors who have noted that Nigerian culture has used restorative justice principles throughout its history (Adeymi, 1994; Elechi, 2006; Udenta, 2004). Indeed, in Southeastern Nigeria, there is a well-known group, the Afikpo, who practice an alternative form of justice that emphasizes restorative and communitarian principles (Elechi, 2006). Named after this group, the city of Afikpo is the second most populous in the state of Ebonyi, one of the 36 states that exist in Nigeria. The Afikpo belong to the Igbo ethnic group that inhabits the southeastern area of Nigeria. The Afikpo use extra-legal means of justice that are perceived by the people as legitimate and effective. This is despite the fact that the Nigerian criminal justice system is considered the official authority on criminal issues.

Afikpo forms of indigenous justice administration includes family, patrilineal, and matrilineal groups that use methods similar to modern-day mediation when addressing social wrongs and/or disputes. As with any typical restorative justice process, the Afikpo indigenous system emphasizes solidarity and the restoration of harmony within the group. Indeed, Elechi (2006) states that "the traditional justice process is an exercise in counseling. The purpose of counseling is to bring about positive change in the offender and also to protect and restore group harmony. The process is participatory, negotiative and geared toward enhancing understanding, reconciliation, and the healing of the victim and the offender" (p. 11).

The Afikpo also utilize a system that is considered to be age-graded and "is built on a cohort principle that organizes people born within approximately 3 years intervals. It is a peer group that is very effective in dispute settlement and social control. It is also a major agent of "re-socialization" (Elechi, 2006, p. 12). This reformative process is sometimes augmented with the use of village courts or elder cohorts. When augmented in such a manner, the justice process is considered a bit more formal among the Afikpo. Even so, there is still a democratic tone to the process and consensus is still considered the primary means of deciding a case. As always, the maintenance of social harmony is the overarching goal of these forms of justice. "Further, since most of the indigenous institutions of social control are also institutions for social and economic activities, they are very effective in crime prevention" (Elechi, 2006, p. 12).

In a different vein, the Afikpo have recently started to utilize their own forms of police enforcement as well. While the use of informal mediation processes, tribal councils, village elders, and such can be seen as a quasi-judicial function, the actual means of physically protecting the community has become an issue in recent years. Indeed, Elechi (2006) notes that in recent years, there has been a spate of robberies throughout the entire southeastern region of Nigeria. The armed robberies occur both at night and in broad daylight and are conducted by roving bands of men, sometimes numbering 15–20 such criminals in composition. Often, these criminals have high-powered and sophisticated firearms that have been obtained from neighboring war-torn countries that surround Nigeria. These groups of robbers (being nothing less than groups of free-roaming bandits) go from urban area to urban area and roam the countryside, robbing people at gunpoint during robbing sprees that may last days. Indeed, these groups may even go up and down a given street in a town, robbing one house at a time until the entire street has been cleaned of any notable wealth (Elechi, 2006).

In fighting this type of crime, the official police have been found to be ineffectual. In fact, there are even reports that the police stations themselves are occasionally robbed of their own guns and ammunition, while the officers are on duty in the station itself. This demonstrates how truly beleaguered the police system is by the rampant crime in Nigeria. Further, organized crime groups are expected to operate with impunity since, in many cases, they operate through payoffs to major political figures in the area. The police are given clear orders to stand aside and to simply maintain security for the affluent and politically connected within Nigerian society.

In response to these chaotic and corrupt conditions, the Afikpo have developed their own vigilante forms of protection and informal law enforcement. These groups brandish their own firearms and act in a proactive manner, patrolling their own areas and communities with the intent to shoot and kill those that appear to criminal threats (Elechi, 2006). These groups are naturally similar to those discussed earlier in this manuscript but the situation in Southeastern Nigeria and among the Afikpo make the development of these groups all the more understandable. Simply put, the Afikpo have had no choice but to use their own form of traditional indigenous justice (both in judicial and enforcement terms) since the official system is incompetent, uncaring, and corrupt. Initially, these vigilante groups were found to be very successful in reducing the robbery problem. Much of this was due to the fact that these groups were simply killing the robbers when they were found and informally tried (Alemika and Chukwuma, 2004). In many cases, the robbers were burned alive, being forced to wear used tires around their body and set aflame after being doused with gasoline (Elechi, 2006). These horrid means of retaliation have drawn the attention of numerous international groups concerned with human rights issues (Alemika and Chukwuma, 2004; Elechi, 2006). Further, these forms of vigilante militia are not limited to the Afikpo but are actually common throughout the entire nation of Nigeria, the police and court systems being uniformly incompetent throughout the nation as a whole (Alemika and Chukwuma, 2004; Elechi, 2006). What is now of concern is that even the vigilante groups have become corrupted. Elechi (2006) provides a clear depiction of how serious the problem has become when stating the following:

> Vigilante groups in Nigeria are involved in extra-judicial killings. They have literally usurped the functions of law enforcement. They have set up illegal detention centers, tortured crime suspects and summarily executed some. Some of them have received the support and financial backing of some state governments. The vigilante operations were initially, hailed by the people who were obviously frustrated with soaring armed robbery and police ineffectiveness. Vigilante operations at the beginning recorded sharp declines in armed robbery in the cities with vigilante groups. Fear and disappointment soon followed as Nigerians discovered innocent people were also tortured and killed by vigilante groups. It was also discovered that some states and local governments, and powerful politicians have hijacked the vigilante outfit and used them to threaten, torture, and murder political opponents (p. 15).

Thus, it is clear that while well intended, the use of vigilante groups has not been a panacea to the crime problem in Nigeria and, as it turns out, now contributes to it just as do the other social conditions throughout the country. The fact that vigilante groups initially seemed successful and now contributes to the problems associated with Nigeria's unstable justice system is important, because this shows the pros and cons associated with indigenous responses to crime. However, Alemika and Chukwuma (2004) have conducted extensive survey research throughout Nigeria and have found that in many cases, communities are providing more support for these groups, given more status to such members, providing equipment (such as appropriate footwear, uniforms, flashlights, and radios), and developing standards and protocols of response. This does take on the tone of a formal policing function and seems to parallel the private policing and private security movement that seems to be taking place in other industrialized nations.

Given that there is a trend to provide better conditions for vigilante groups and that there is also a move to require accountability, it might well turn out that this form of indigenous response is ultimately an innovative solution to Nigeria's internal crime problem. On the other hand, the government has no control over such a function and is left to simply accept the fact that illegal and informal units of protection maintain the safety and security of its people. Further still, this may simply be an inevitable outcome when the government itself is not viewed as legitimate (particularly at the state level) due to the fact that fraud and other economic crimes are routinely committed by governmental figureheads and due to the fact that many government figures are found to be in league with organized crime syndicates. These syndicates often engage in a variety of electronic fraud schemes, forms of gun trafficking, and use Nigeria as a stopover point when transporting drugs from South America to Europe. This then means that the situation in Nigeria is complicated both in the breadth and depth of crime problems that face the country.

As noted earlier, in extreme criminal cases (particularly with repetitive violent offenders), many of the tribal and communal groups in Nigeria, and all of West Africa for that matter, find it necessary to resort to the penalty of death or banishment. Banishment, due to modern border circumstances, is not used with near the frequency as in the past, and it is the death penalty that tends to be exacted by these groups when restorative methods simply proved to be ineffective. The use of stoning and other forms of death are even more frequent among those states that adhere to Shari'a and this has drawn international attention as women have been sentenced to stoning for crimes of adultery and other such behaviors that are generally not criminalized in most modern countries. In addition, Shari'a courts deliver *hudud* sentences such as amputation for theft, caning for fornication, and public intoxication (U.S. Department of State, 2006). Because no applicable cases have been appealed to the federal judiciary, there has been on official ruling on the actual constitutionality of these forms of punishment (U.S. Department of State, 2006). Though stoning and amputation sentences have been overturned on procedural or substantive or evidentiary grounds, none have even been challenged on the basis of constitutionality (U.S. Department of State, 2006).

However, it should be pointed out that while Islamic law is practiced by nearly half of the Nigerian population and while it has not been overturned based on constitutionality, this form of law was not the original form of justice indigenous to Nigeria. Thus, Shari'a is also a system of justice that is transposed over the underlying indigenous African forms of restoration. Unlike the English common law system that exists in Lagos, there is no separation of church and state within such a legal orientation. While roughly a third of all Nigerians are of the Christian faith, this does not mean that they necessarily practice the English common law of justice administration. Indeed, many Nigerians of Christian origin may utilize customary forms of justice resolution, whereas this is not the case with the Islamic population of Nigeria who ardently adhere to the precepts of Shari'a. The competing ideologies of Islam and federal law based on the English system have created a number of conflicts that have gained international attention. This serves to complicate reform even further as this is an additional splinter section of the justice scheme in Nigeria that also has both formal and informal mechanisms.

From the discussion so far, it should be clear to the reader that the social fabric in Nigeria is quite complicated and that there is truly no sense of uniformity throughout the nation. The English system that is officially incorporated at the federal level incorporates Islamic representatives as well. This puts inherent conflict in the system from the top down to the bottom. Added to this is the political instability where justice is sold to the highest bidder, all the while criminal activity runs rampant. Meanwhile, across the landscape, local regions must take justice into their own hands or be victimized both by the widespread activity of the offender population and by the brutal and heavy-handed tactics of the corrupt policing system. This is the same policing system that fails to do anything at all when the criminal activity is in league with corrupt government officials.

While substantial attention has been given to the policing and the judicial segment of the Nigerian system and the challenges associated with progressive reform, little attention has been given to the correctional end of this country's system of justice. It is important to not overlook this segment of this nation's response because this also demonstrates further complexities that exist and also further demonstrates the ineffectual operation of Nigeria's overall justice system. It is with this in mind that we now turn our attention to prison operations within Nigeria, keeping in mind that the means by which a nation handles its prisons is reflective of the true level of civilized development that exists within its borders and among its people.

Prisons and Punishment in Nigerian and West African Regions

The British Imperial Government introduced the prison system in Lagos between 1861 and 1900 (Adeymi, 1994). By 1960, there was a prison in every provincial region of Nigeria (Adeymi, 1994). The previous two historical points are actually significant for two key reasons. First, the concept of the prison is not one that is indigenous to Nigeria or to the West African sense of justice or criminal punishment (Adeymi, 1994; Elechi, 2006; Udenta, 2004). Rather, this was yet another European convention that was brought to Nigeria and was essentially imposed upon its former means of meeting out sanctions and addressing punishment for criminal behavior (Elechi, 1999; Elechi, 2006; Onyeozili, 2005). Second, it is clear that it took over 60 years for this concept to take hold throughout the entire nation (Adeymi, 1994). This is because the loss of liberty as a sole and independent means of punishment is somewhat alien to the Nigerian cultural mindset.

Further, the costs involved with prison operations exceeded what most Nigerians would wish to pay so that an offender could simply remain in captivity (Adeymi, 1994; Elechi, 2006; Udenta, 2004). Rather, as noted earlier, it was more the tradition of Nigerian tribes and social groups to reintegrate the majority of offenders and/or to remove particularly stubborn recidivists from their respective communities. Therefore, prisons are an unnatural fit with traditional Nigerian culture. It is for this reason that prisons are perhaps hardly used in Nigeria when compared to other industrialized nations.

For instance, in 2005, the total prison population for the entire nation of Nigeria consisted of 39,438 inmates (International Centre for Prison Studies, 2007). At that time, the nation's population was approximately 136.1 million total (International Centre for Prison Studies, 2007). This placed the rate of incarceration in Nigeria at about *29 out of every 100,000* people (International Centre for Prison Studies, 2007). Compared to the United States, this is a very small population of inmates and a very low rate of incarceration (Walmsley, 2005). This is very important point for any person examining the Nigerian system. Indeed, during the same year, the United States had 2,245,189 persons in prison with an overall national population of 299.4 million people (International Centre for Prison Studies, 2007). This placed the rate of incarceration at *750 people out of every 100,000* (International Centre for Prison Studies, 2007). Thus, the rate of incarceration is 25.8 times greater in the United States than in the nation of Nigeria. It is clear that Nigeria does not use prison as its primary form of punishment, unlike the United States.

Further, the dynamics associated with Nigerian prison populations are totally different than those in the United States and other developing countries. For example, in Nigeria nearly 65% are pretrial detainees. Therefore, only one-third are actually in prison to serve a sentence due to conviction of a crime. In the United States, only about 21% are pretrial detainees. Close to four-fifth of all inmates in the United States are actually serving their sentence. This again demonstrates that Nigeria does not rely on prison as a form of sentencing, its rate of imprisonment being exponentially lower than that in the United States, and this also demonstrates that the Nigerian conception of incarceration is mainly one that is based on pretrial detention; making the Nigerian prison system primarily a jail system, for the most part. The large percentage of pretrial detainees within Nigerian prisons reflects the inept operation of the Nigerian judicial system, which as noted previously is viewed by the public as ineffectual and corrupt.

It is clear that the nation of Nigeria does not view its prison system as a primary mode of punishment. Though the official capacity of the Nigerian prison system is reported to operate at only 90% capacity (International Centre for Prison Studies, 2007), it is known that this is, in fact, untrue. The U.S. Department of State (2006) found that prison and detention facilities in Nigeria often operate at 200%–300% of maximum capacity. Further, conditions are harsh and life threatening, largely due to hygiene and overcrowding issues. Most prisons in Nigeria are over 70 years old, built of mud brick, with sewers, food, health care, education, and recreational facilities either being totally lacking or well below standard. To further illustrate the deplorable conditions in Nigerian prisons, consider that only inmates "with money or whose relatives brought food regularly had sufficient food; petty corruption among prison officials made it difficult for money provided for food to reach prisoners. Poor inmates often relied on handouts from others to survive. Beds or mattresses were not provided to many inmates, forcing them to sleep on concrete floors, often without a blanket" (U.S. Department of State, 2006, Section 1c). Reports have found that the denial of proper medical treatment contributed to the deaths of numerous prisoners, and dead inmates are often buried on prison compounds, usually without notification being given to the family (U.S. Department of State, 2006, Section 1c).

Tkachuk (2001), confirms these reports and demonstrates that West African countries have no intent to make prisons a central scheme of their punishment systems in the future. Tkachuk notes:

> Notwithstanding noticeable rapid growth rates in national populations over the past twenty years and increased crime rates leading to more individuals being sent to prisons, there is hardly evidence of new penal institutions being constructed in that period. The result of this is overcrowded prison populations affecting thirteen of the fifteen African countries mentioned in the study. This issue combined with inadequate resourcing results in non-observance of most international and regional standards. In many cases, prison overcrowding aggravates and precipitates the increasing indignities and suffering on the part of inmates. In some situations inmates not only lack adequate clothing, food and basic hygiene requirements, but worse, they are denied space to lie or even sit (2001, p. 3).

From the comments above, it is clear that Nigeria does not expect inmates to stay in prison for long periods of time, at least not in a manner where they can serve a long-term sentence. The fact that no new institutions are being built and that outdated facilities and living conditions continue to remain in operation belies the lack of commitment that Nigeria has for prison as a reformative sanction in general and its own prison population in particular. Simply put, prison facilities and those held within them are an afterthought to the government of Nigeria. It is no wonder that Nigerians seek to avoid the formal court system and its formal sanctions; the courts and the prison system is not only ineffectual but it is overly harsh when considering the nature of the day-to-day garden-variety crimes that tend to occur in most communities. From this, it is clear that the Nigerian public does not trust any segment of its criminal justice system, whether this be the police, the judiciary, or the correctional component.

Conclusion: Graft, Corruption, and Instability as Ideology

It might be argued that British colonialism was in itself a form of corruption that ultimately contaminated the Nigerian social system. Certainly, the indigenous population of Nigeria would have preferred self-rule as opposed to rule by England. Added to this is the fact that a number of institutions were imposed upon various ethnic groups in Nigeria, creating a system that was incompatible with what had existed for hundreds of years prior to the British invasion. This is where the breakdown in a stable region began, though on the face of things, it may have appeared that the British had actually tamed the region. If left to their own devices, it may well be that a number of smaller might exist but that these states might be more stable in internal governance. Such conjecture is merely speculation and history cannot be changed. Nevertheless, the British laid a groundwork that magnified conflict between ethnic groups and further fueled economic disparity between various social groups in the region.

Since this time, the nation of Nigeria has never known peace. This creates the illusion that European influence was beneficial, but such subjugation led to the exploitation of the country's resources and its people. The British created power imbalances that would not have existed otherwise and produced a series of regional borders that ignored traditional tribal lineage and loyalty. It is no wonder that Nigeria has struggled internally to maintain a stable form of government. Indeed, the nation has been independent for less than 50 years. It is only natural that growing pains would occur and that the mosaic blend of ethnicities would need time to morph into some semblance of a united body. The internal power structures, revolutions, coups, and governmental changes are all the result of these dynamics that were set into motion upon the departure of the British that had kept the region stable through brute force and economic exploitation.

Dire economic conditions have generated a desperate region where crime is rampant. Both individualized, gang-related, and organized crime plagues this nation. These challenges alone would be enough to besiege most modern police forces in industrialized nations. Considering the economic and technological challenges of the region, it is no wonder that Nigerian police forces are unable to effectively combat and control crime within its borders. Further, the internal corruption among governmental leaders ensures that police are given directives that allow the nation's resources to be plundered and its economy raped of all sustainability. Add to this that countries such as Liberia and Sierra Leone have had a number of bloody conflicts and civil wars, and it is clear that the instability does not simply fall upon Nigeria alone. This naturally impacts Nigeria's military and domestic security and also affects its economy. This also draws organized gun traffickers and a number of other unsavory sorts to the region, providing weapons for guerilla fighters and criminal groups alike.

The fact that corruption is known to be widespread within Nigeria makes it impossible for the public to have any confidence in its leadership. This has led to public embrace of traditional forms of administering justice and has deterred most from using the official justice system. In addition, communities take matters into their own hands out of necessity in order to protect their families and property. The incompetence of the police coupled with the brutality used against its own citizenry ensure that communities do not turn to legal resources, thereby further reinforcing the use of extra-legal options, such as vigilante groups.

Lastly, to say that Nigeria is diverse would be an understatement. The nation has a long list of ethnic groups that have differing languages, customs, and religions. Languages vary considerably within the country even though English is widely used and illiteracy rates are high. Witchcraft (there are even modern trials that prosecute persons for this activity), Christianity, nature worship, Islam, and a variety of local religious practices are all practiced with regularity in this country, resulting in further differences between groups and further grounds for conflict. All of this complicates the potential for harmonious existence within the country. Whether Nigeria will be able to resolve these internal dissimilarities has yet to be seen but will prove central to achieving any sense of positive and contemporary change within its current justice system.

References

Adeymi, A. A. (1994). Personal reparations in Africa: Nigeria and Gambia. In U. Zvekic (ed.). *Alternatives to Imprisonment in Comparative Perspective*. Chicago, IL: Nelson-Hall Publishers.

Alemika, E. E. O. and Chukwuma, I. C. (2004). The poor and informal policing in Nigeria. Lagos, Nigeria: Center for Law Enforcement Education.

Central Intelligence Agency (2007). *The World Factbook 2007*. Washington, DC: Central Intelligence Agency. Retrieved from: https://www.cia.gov/library/publications/the-world-factbook/geos/ni.html#Govt

Ebbe, O. N. I. (2000). The judiciary and criminal procedure in Nigeria. In O. N. I. Ebbe (ed.). *Comparative & International Criminal Justice Systems* (2nd edn.). Boston, MA: Butterworth-Heinemann.

Elechi, O. (1999). Doing justice without the state: The Afikpo (Ehugbo)—Nigeria model. PhD dissertation, Simon Fraser University, Ottawa, Canada.

Elechi, O. O. (2006). *Doing Justice without the State: The Afikpo (Ehugbo) Nigeria Model*. New York: Routledge.

International Centre for Prison Studies (2007). World prison brief. King's college, London, U.K.: International Centre for Prison Studies. Retrieved from: http://www.kcl.ac.uk/depsta/rel/icps/worldbrief/world_brief.html

Okereafezeke, N. (March 2003). Traditional social control in an ethnic society: Law enforcement in a Nigerian community. *Police Practice & Research: An International Journal*, 4(1): 21–33.

Onyeozili, E. C. (2005). Obstacles to effective policing in Nigeria. *African Journal of Criminology and Justice Studies*, 1(1): 32–54.

Reichel, P. L. (2002). *Comparative Criminal Justice Systems: A Topical Approach* (3rd edn.). Upper Saddle River, NJ: Prentice Hall.

Tkachuk, B. (2001). *World Prison Population: Facts, Trends, and Solutions*. Turin, Italy: United Nations Interregional Crime and Justice Research Institute.

Udenta, U. (2004). Emerging trends in the application of restorative justice principles in Nigeria: Key legislations and advocacy work. Paper presented at *New Frontiers in Restorative Justice: Advancing Theory and Practice*, Centre for Justice and Peace Development, Massey University at Albany, New Zealand, 2–5 December.

U.S. Department of State (2006). Nigeria: Country reports on human rights practices. Washington, DC: U.S. Department of State. Retrieved from: http://www.state.gov/g/drl/rls/hrrpt/2005/61586.htm.

Walmsley, R. (2005). *World Prison Population List* (6th edn.). London, U.K.: International Centre for Prison Studies. Found at: http://www.kcl.ac.uk/depsta/rel/icps/world-prison-population-list-2005.pdf

Revising Traditional Law Enforcement in Asia to Meet Contemporary Demands

IV

An Econometric Method of Allocating Police Resources in New Zealand

17

GARTH DEN HEYER, MARGARET MITCHELL,
SIVA GANESH, AND CHRISTOPHER DEVERY

Contents

Introduction

Traditionally, police agencies have allocated resources in response to their operational demands or requirements, with the majority of resources being distributed in response to political demands and public calls for service. The revised operational move toward the public service ethos of accountability and "do more with less" means that historical methods of allocating police officers may not meet an agency's strategic goals.

The relationship between social, economic, and demographic factors with the number of police officers is not well understood. However, a study examined this issue using the econometric method to analyze the New Zealand social data for the period 1997–2002 and explore the relationship with police deployment. As a result, a recommended resource allocation model for law enforcement, called police resource model (PRM), was developed to recommend a more appropriate resource allocation formula for the New Zealand Police. As will be articulated later, this study identified that the new econometric resource allocation model developed appears to be more effective than the allocation method that had been used by the New Zealand Police or by other police agencies which base allocation solely on population.

Policing in New Zealand

The increasing importance of proactive policing has highlighted the need to ensure that the police utilize their resources both efficiently and effectively. After unprecedented increases in the number of reported offenses in the late 1980s and early 1990s, crime reduction became a primary concern of the New Zealand Police, government, and the community they serve. In recent years, there has been a greater emphasis by police to deliver services proactively, to direct resources to specific geographic areas of high crime or to specific crimes, and to apply intelligence-led targeted policing initiatives.

A challenge facing local and national governments is balancing resources and service levels with budgetary constraints and community desires. Police salaries and associated costs account for over 75% of the total New Zealand Government expenditure on policing (New Zealand Police, 2003). Where public demand for police services is rising and increased expenditure on resources is not feasible, the issue of managing and allocating resources becomes crucial (Stockdale et al., 1999).

In the last two decades, the control of crime has benefited from increasing public interest and from nontraditional crime research skills. In fact, there is strong evidence to support the notion that important facets of crime have become amenable to economic and econometric analysis and solution. Eck and Maguire (2000) noted that most economists would argue that the problem of crime and its solution hinge in a very fundamental way on how society allocates its resources at the local and national levels.

Viewed from the perspective that resource allocation requires optimizing behavior (Becker, 1968), the fact that New Zealand has the control of crime mandated as a central government responsibility creates difficulties in efficiently allocating resources for the protection of persons and property. In this context, the New Zealand delivery of police services is different from many other countries in that there is one police organization responsible for all policing issues at both the local and national levels. As a result, this imposes organizational problems in allocating police staff at a police area (PA) level and with regard to the total number of police officers required to meet the social outcomes identified by government.

It is apparent that an improved police resource allocation methodology could be developed by New Zealand authorities. A study has been conducted that analyzed New Zealand social data for the period 1997–2002 utilizing the proposed PRM as a method to allocate police officers to the 50 PAs.

Examining Police Resource Allocation

Is the level of crime in a particular location affected by the number of police officers in that location (Bayley, 1998)? Many politicians and members of the community believe this is so. The primary resource of any police agency is its personnel, and it is for this reason that "more [police officers] are thought to be better, fewer are thought to be worse" (Bayley, 1998, p. 6).

The managers of police organizations and their political masters continually adjust the number of police officers, seeking the optimal ratio of police to population in order to make the smallest investment of resources to produce the greatest public satisfaction. The number of police officers in a geographical area is allocated by police managers according to formulas, institutional traditions, tacit understandings, and contract rules, all of which have little or nothing to do with the reduction of crime. Bayley (1994) proposes that police budgeting represents the triumph of organizational process over rational decision making.

According to Goldstein (1990), police resources are not used rationally to achieve public safety. For this reason, the Audit Commission of Local Authorities and The National Health Service (1991) in Britain concluded that public debate needs to move away from the assumption that more police officers and expenditure will necessarily result in higher quantity and quality of police outputs (Audit Commission of Local Authorities and The National Health Service, 1991, p. 12).

Previous studies of police resource allocation have been inconclusive as to whether or not an increase in the number of police officers in an area decreases or increases crime and have not established the relationship between socioeconomic and the sociodemographic variables and the number of police officers (or police agency budget or the number of hours produced by a police agency). As a result, debate on which variables are associated with police staffing levels and which are associated with the level of crime continues. (Table 17.1 summarizes the results of previous United Kingdom and United States studies.)

Of 55 studies examined, most concluded that variation in police strength over time does not affect crime rates (van Tulder, 1992; Niskanen, 1994;

Table 17.1   Results of Previous Studies of Police Resource Allocation

Many aspects of the economic theory of crime are supported by empirical data

The level of crime can be decreased by either increasing the probability of capture, conviction, or punishment or by increasing the severity of punishment

Increasing the number of police in an area can have a mixed result on the crime rate

Chamlin and Langworthy, 1996; Eck and Maguire, 2000). However, two studies using time-series analysis suggest that marginal increases in the number of police are related to decreases in crime rates (Marvell and Moody, 1996; Levitt, 1997).

Brandl et al. (1995) note that several studies of police strength have not taken the different functions of the police agency into consideration in their analyses. In addition, it is difficult to identify the effects of increased police numbers, especially over time, since organizations, methods (e.g., the use of Compstat-like approaches or intelligence-led policing), technology, and even core missions change.

There is an obvious relationship between the presence of police and crime. Case studies of the effect of sudden withdrawal of police, for example, during a police strike, show a resultant increase in crime (Sherman, 1997; Sherman and Eck, 2002). Brown and Haldane (1998) noted that during the Melbourne Police strike of 1923, members of the community resorted to opportunistic plundering, robbery, and vandalism; a similar effect was seen during the police strikes in Boston in 1919 (Russell, 1975) and in New York in 1978 (Lardner and Reppetto, 2000).

The mixed findings of previous research are largely attributable to matters such as variation in how police strength is defined across different studies, variation in the unit of analysis across studies, poor and/or inconsistent model specification, and complexities involved in interpreting the mutual effect variables such as the relationship that crime and police have on each other.

Further, prior studies have not clarified if increasing the number of police officers will produce greater public safety or reduce the level of crime. Not only has previous research found little connection between crime rates and the number of police, but some have oddly concluded that adding police may increase crime rates, at least in the short term due to increased observation or police on patrol and hence an increase in reported crime.

Variation in the number of police officers in an agency or geographical area can be explained through one of three theoretical economic frameworks: "rational public choice or consensus theory," "conflict theory," and "organizational stress theory." The first theory, "rational public choice or consensus theory" (Nalla et al., 1997), is from economic consumer theory and links variation in the number of police to the demands on police services, such as the level of crime and the size of the population. The second theory, "conflict theory" (Chamlin and Langworthy, 1996), holds that governments increase the number of police in response to a growth in subgroups deemed to be threatening by the dominant groups. Finally, the third theory, "organizational theory" (Nalla, 1992), stresses the influence of internal organizational factors on the size of police agencies and the number of police.

Among academics, there remains little consensus with respect to the social factors that are related to criminal activity, how to appropriately model criminal activity or police resources, and what public policies might serve to lessen criminal activity (Carr-Hill and Stern, 1973, 1979; Avio and Clark, 1978; Benson and Rasmussen, 1991; Benson et al., 1992; Becsi, 1999). In a symposium on the economics of crime, DiIulio (1996) argued that economists have not focused adequate attention on modeling crime or police resource allocation through the use of sophisticated quantitative and modeling skills that are part of the economist's toolkit. DiIulio laments the fact that much of the research in this area has remained the domain of sociologists and criminologists who tend to use less sophisticated empirical analyses.

The literature is often confusing and contradictory in regard to the effect of some social factors on the level of crime and the number of police officers in an area. For example, research has identified that some social factors can have a differential effect on the growth or decline in the number of officers in American police agencies (Nalla, 1992), and that an increase in crime results in an increase in police numbers, while a decline in crime has little or no effect in reducing police numbers. This phenomenon may be explained by organizational inertia or by the political difficulties posed by attempting to reduce the size of police agencies and that rising crime rates have more impact on police agencies than do declining crime rates.

Consequently, an examination of the relationship between crime and police numbers within an agency would be highly contingent on crime trends during the study period and assumptions about the functional relationship between the crime level and police numbers.

Estimating the demand for police can be treated in the economic literature in a simultaneous system of linear regression equations which are based on the premise that the demand for police services is partly determined by the crime rate which in turn is affected by the level of police resources (Carr-Hill and Stern, 1973, 1979). This is a simultaneity issue in that the number of police officers can affect the level of crime and the level of crime can affect the number of police officers.

The research study below has taken the deficiencies of previous research into account and uses a number of statistical methods to examine the socioeconomic and sociodemographic variables that may be associated with the number of police officers in a geographical area.

The Changing Operational Environment

Police salaries and associated costs can account for the majority of the total police expenditure of a police agency. Bayley (1994, p. 48) identified that in 1988 police officer salaries made up 80.7% of the costs of state and local law enforcement in the United States, 75% of the expenditures of police services in the United Kingdom and Wales, and 82% in Canadian police agencies. Given this, and that higher expenditure on police resources is not feasible, the issue of managing and allocating resources effectively becomes crucial. The new public service management environment raises the issues of fiscal and management accountability, with the measurement of police performance moving to the forefront of the political agenda. These evolving government requirements are especially important for police as a highly visible government agency. In addition, the demand by the community for government services is ever increasing, while fiscal policy constraints make it difficult or impossible for governments to fully meet these demands.

Historically, police agencies allocated resources in line with a perceived, rather than an empirically validated need, although this has changed mainly as a result of the introduction of the new public management philosophies of the mid-1980s. The new public management movement included the application of the theories of Keysianism and monetary economics to national, federal, state, and local governments. The implementation of these economic strands was based on the theory of agency and of choice, changing the relationship between ministers of the crown and heads or chief executives of departments and increasing management discretion within departments.

The basic thrust of the reforms was to improve the incentives for efficiency within the government sector. The distinction between the service outputs an agency produces and the outcomes the government seeks to achieve is central to these reforms. This approach arose from thinking about what is meant by the term performance and accountability. In this new environment, the performance of government agencies can be judged on whether they produce the agreed service outputs, and whether they do so effectively (Boston, 1999).

As a result of this changed operating environment, there is a requirement for the police to make resource allocation decisions more transparent, to be able to evaluate outputs and outcomes, and to be able to demonstrate that resources are being used to generate the best returns for specific communities and society as a whole.

Police Resource Allocation

There is limited information available on the methods used by police agencies in allocating resources. Most U.S. law enforcement agencies allocate resources based on the number of calls for service and the United Kingdom and Scottish forces allocate resources based on a combination of central and local government funding regimes. The steady increase in the number of police and the amount of police expenditure in Western democracies over the last few decades has been a concern for governments, policy makers, and researchers (Brandl et al., 1995; Craig, 1987; Grabosky, 1988; Chamlin and Langworthy, 1996; Stockdale et al., 1999). However, there is little information or agreement about the specific social or economic forces that affect the growth in police officer numbers or how police officers should be allocated to specific geographic areas. Brandl et al. (1995) noted that the number of police currently is most highly related to previous police numbers.

The New Zealand Police

The New Zealand Police is a national law enforcement body, comprising of approximately 7500 sworn officers and 2500 nonsworn staff and was formed by an 1886 Act of Parliament which saw the amalgamating of the national Armed Constabulary Force and the existing provincial police forces. The New Zealand Police was to be separate from the military and to be unarmed except in grave emergencies (Hill, 1986). In 1956, the word "Force" was dropped from the title and the police became officially known as the "New Zealand Police Service." The chief executive is the commissioner who is appointed by the governor general and is responsible for both the general administration and operations of the organization.

The police are responsible for the full range of law enforcement services and investigations from minor criminal offending to major crimes and are given enforcement powers under the majority of enacted legislation which enables specific government departments to investigate and prosecute breaches of legislation. For example, sworn police officers have the same enforcement powers as Fisheries Officers under the Fisheries Act (1996) or Customs Officers under the Customs and Exercise Act (1996). The New Zealand Police only investigates breaches of personal and company fraud under $500,000, while the Serious Fraud Office undertakes any investigations of offenses larger than this amount.

The police are also responsible for all traffic enforcement, including the checking and weighing of heavy motor vehicles. However, parking enforcement is the responsibility of city councils. The police are also accountable for disaster or emergency management, for national security, and for the security of major events and visiting dignitaries. The police undertake the majority of their own prosecutions. However, the crown solicitor undertakes the prosecution of serious offending which is heard in the High Court.

The police are organized into 12 operational districts, the Office of the Commissioner (OoC), which is responsible for the national management, finance and the development and implementation of policy, and the Royal New Zealand Police College (RNZPC), which is responsible for all organizational training. The 12 operational districts consist of 50 smaller geographical PAs.

Examining a New Resource Allocation Model

In developing their police resource allocation policy, Hsiao (1986) and Benson and Rasmussen (2000) recommend the use of either time series or panel data as the foundation of modeling based on regression analysis. Although official crime statistics, that is, those reported and recorded by police, do not reflect accurately the actual number of crimes committed, both cross-sectional and time-series analytic studies use this information as their basis. Inaccuracy, however, can stem from the definition of crime, its interpretation, and the administrative processes devised to record it.

Research Considerations

The research surrounding the proposed PRM incorporated regression analysis to examine the causal direction of observed relationships. As an example, it is likely that an increase in the number of crimes may result in a reduction of the rate with which the crimes are resolved, particularly if insufficient resources are available to deal with this increase. To overcome this issue in the below study, a two-way interaction was modeled simultaneously, using a system of regression equations based on the two-stage least squares (2SLS) regression analysis method. Each stage of the applied 2SLS process has taken account of the different characteristics associated with the panel data used. The first stage created new dependent variables which were substituted for the original variables, and during the second stage, an ordinary least squares regression was computed using the newly created variables.

TSLS was utilized in this study for the following four reasons:

1. It can be applied to an individual equation in a system of equations without directly taking into account any other equations in the system.
2. It provides only one estimate per variable.
3. It can be applied to recursive, underidentified, and overidentified equations.
4. The estimates obtained are consistent, meaning that as the sample size increases indefinitely, the estimates converge to their true population values.

The PRM study identified one dependent variable—the number of police officers—as a function of 25 different socioeconomic and sociodemographic variables believed to be relevant to allocating resources. The process of equation construction was undertaken through linear regression equation development and analysis, based on the general-to-specific approach. Developing an explanatory model through the construction of a regression equation will facilitate a better understanding of the situation under study and will allow experimentation with different combinations of inputs to study their effects on the dependent variable. In this way, the identified explanatory model can, by its basic formulation, be geared toward intervention, thereby influencing any future resource allocation through the identification of influencing variables.

Police Resource Model Study Variables

The 25 independent variables used in this study were selected on the basis of their hypothesized relationship to the number of police officers. The variable identifying PAs as urban or rural was included to examine the difference between urban and rural PAs. The census information included data that enabled the study to examine specific variables, such as the age groups of males, levels of income, and levels of education, and the five ethnicity variables included in the study are the major ethnic groups identified in the New Zealand census.

The deprivation variable used in the study pertains to 2001 Statistics New Zealand population information and was constructed by the New Zealand Health Services Research Center. The index combines nine census variables from the 2001 census which reflect aspects of material and social deprivation. The actual score applies to the PA rather than an individual or specific person.

Table 17.A.1 presents the definition of each of the 26 variables, one dependent variable and 25 independent variables, used in the study.

Examining the Study Data

To ascertain the distribution of the dependent and independent variables for use in the construction of linear regression models, the mean, standard deviation, and distribution of each variable were calculated. These are presented in Table 17.A.2.

The correlation matrix of the 26 variables indicated that a number of variables were significantly positively or negatively correlated. These results could present a problem for regression techniques, as according to Tabachnick and Fidell (1996), regression models work best when the independent variables are strongly correlated with the dependent variables, but uncorrelated with

Table 17.2   Summary of Significant Variable Correlations

Variable	Significantly Correlated With
Population	Males 20–29, one-parent families, full-time and part-time employment, the three income variables, and the four qualification variables
Males 15–19	Males 20–25
Males 20–24	Full-time and part-time employment, income less than $50,000, and high school, vocational, and tertiary qualifications
Males 25–29	Police budget, full-time and part-time employment, the three income variables, and high school, vocational, and tertiary qualifications
Number of police officers	Police productive hours, level of crime, resolution rate
Police budget	Males 25–29, police productive hours, level of crime
Police productive hours	Number of police officers, police budget, level of crime, resolution rate
Level of crime	Number of police officers, Police productive hours, resolution rate
Resolution rate	Number of police officers, police productive hours, level of crime
One-parent families	Population, full-time and part-time employment, income less than $50,000, and the four qualification variables
Income variables	Population, males 20–29, and one-parent families, high school, vocational, and tertiary qualifications
No qualifications	Population, one-parent families, income less than $20,000
High school, vocational, and tertiary qualifications	Population, males 20–29, one-parent families, and the three income variables
Full-time and part-time employment	Population, males 20–29, the three income variables, and high school, vocational, and tertiary qualifications

other independent variables. The significant correlations are summarized in Table 17.2.

To be certain that the model obtained from the raw data was statistically sound, the variables were converted to a number of different forms. The different forms of data were checked for normality, and a regression was estimated using the transformed data. Table 17.3 identifies the five different data forms examined for this study.

Each of the five methodological results was statistically similar, and the raw data model provided the statistically best model based on the coefficients of determination, the Durbin–Watson test, and tests of normality. As a result, the study utilized the findings and the results of the regression analysis based on the raw data.

Table 17.3   Five Different Data Forms Examined

1. Raw data
2. Police variable as a natural logarithm
3. All data as positive integers (without percentages)
4. All data converted to per 1000 population
5. Police variable converted to per 1000 population

Study Results

To establish which of the independent variables were associated with variation in police numbers, 25 variables have been included in a regression analysis (the all-inclusive equation). The results of this regression analysis are presented in Table 17.A.3.

The approach taken in the regression analysis was "general to specific." As a result, the final regression was comprised of a number of independent variables with the lowest levels of significance. These variables associated with the number of police officers are presented in Table 17.4 and form the basis of the PRM.

The results of the PRM show that for every increase of approximately 84 people of European descent in the population, there is an increase of one police officer, with other variables remaining constant. While for an increase of approximately 100 males between the ages 15 and 19 years, there is a decrease of one police officer, with other variables held constant. The remaining predicted values or coefficients have been interpreted in the same manner.

The points of interest are the variables which are included in the equation and the direction of the relationship with the outcome. The variables that are included in the equation are those which had a significant association with the number of police officers. From a policy perspective, these are the socioeconomic and sociodemographic variables associated with the number of police officers in a PA in New Zealand. The inclusion of the variables relating to the number of incidents, the level of crime, and the resolution rate appears to be appropriate as these variables would all have an effect on police workload.

However, why are two of the male age groups associated with the number of police officers and not the third? And why do the males between 15 and 19 years have a negative association and the males between 20 and 24 years have

Table 17.4   The PRM Results

	Variable	Coefficient	Standard Error	T-Ratio	Probability
1	European ethnicity	83.684	14.686	5.628	0.000
2	Other ethnicity	555.837	127.561	4.357	0.000
3	Males 15–19	−0.0093	0.0039	−2.382	0.018
4	Males 20–24	0.0164	0.0044	3.696	0.000
5	Incidents	0.0022	0.0003	7.886	0.000
6	Level of crime	0.0063	0.0012	5.236	0.000
7	Resolution rate	0.0081	0.0026	3.123	0.000
8	Full-time employment	−0.0029	0.0005	−6.032	0.000
9	Income greater than $50 k	0.0036	0.0009	3.787	0.000

a positive association? This situation may arise because this third category measured the age group of males between 25 and 29 years which is usually a traditional age where the involvement in minor crime drops off, especially street offending and lower scale burglary. However, a significant number of recidivists will move into less physical crime pursuits such as dealing in drugs or stolen property which, as it appears, is not associated with the number of police officers.

The results indicate that while the number of males aged between 20 and 24 years is positively associated with the number of officers, the number of males aged between 15 and 19 years has a negative effect. This result is at odds with the image of youth and the anecdotal evidence as to their involvement in crime. However, the explanation may lie in the fact that in New Zealand until 2000, it was illegal to purchase alcohol unless the person was 20 years old or older. In that year, the age limit was lowered to 18 years, and the majority of city councils introduced bylaws which made drinking in a public place a more easily resolvable offense. Instead of police officers arresting offenders for drinking in a public place, they are now able to confiscate the alcohol without any criminal action being taken.

The second reason as to the negative findings in regard to males aged between 15 and 19 years is possibly because this equation does not include any variables for road safety offenses or police officers assigned to traffic patrol. This would be the area where the majority of offenses would be committed for this age group. As a result, the noninclusion of traffic offending may be reflected in this finding.

The final finding of interest is in regard to the inclusion of the full-time employment variable and not the part-time variable, and the inclusion of only one of the three income variables. The predicated value for full-time employment has a negative relationship with the number of police officers. This means that as more people move into legitimate employment, their monetary needs would be met without the need to resort to crime and hence increasing the demand for an increase in the number of police officers. Further, if more people are employed, especially males in the age group 15–29, they are less likely to have time or the ability to commit offenses. This clearly is not surprising given similar conclusions in other countries.

The only income variable with a significant association with the number of police officers is that of people with an income of more than $50,000 per year. This might be explained by the fact that people who are the higher income earners in society also pay a larger percentage of taxes and so pay for more police officers. Greenberg et al. (1983, p. 385) noted that this result "suggests that where the tax base is stronger cities will hire more police independent of the crime rate." However, the fact that other income groups were not included as being associated with the number of police is at odds with the criminological literature. This literature identified that there is an association between the lower socioeconomic groups and the number of police officers as the group often commits crimes to subsidize their incomes.

The noninclusion of the percentage of Maori, Pacific Peoples, and Asian people in the equation is also possibly in conflict with the US literature. Liska et al. (1981) found that in the southern states of the United States, the percentage of nonwhites positively affected the change in police agency size, and Greenberg et al. (1985) and Chamlin (1989) found that the percentage of nonwhite population positively affects changes in police agency size elsewhere in the United States.

The inclusion of the variable for the percentage of European ethnicity is possibly a reflection that they are the majority population in all 50 PAs. On the other hand, the inclusion of the other ethnicity variable cannot be easily explained. The percentage of the other ethnicity variables in each PA population was the smallest of the five different ethnicity variables and represents an aggregate of minority ethnicities not identified by Statistics New Zealand. The result may possibly identify that the policing issues involving other ethnicities are occupying police time, especially in relation to immigration inquiries.

The fact that the equation identifies that there is no significant association between the percentage of Maori, Pacific peoples, and Asian people with the number of police officers in a PA may be as a result of their low percentage proportion in the population. Jackson and Carroll (1981, p. 294) suggest that when the proportion of a minority ethnicity in a population becomes large enough, minority group members may be able to convert their numerical resources to political power and in turn influence the increases in police agency size. They go on to identify that once a proportion of a minority ethnicity in a collectivity reaches some minimal level, subsequent increases in the percentage of this minority may result in increases in the police agency size at a decreasing rate or in an actual decline in police agency size. If this is the case in the PRM study, then the number of people from these different ethnic groups is insufficiently large to suggest the number of police.

Statistical Analysis

The result of the PRM study appears to be similar to the majority of English and American studies, though there were significant differences in regard to the youth and ethnicity variables in the model. This can also be said for the association and sign of some individual variables.

The PRM included 9 of the 25 variables used in the all-inclusive equation, and R^2 was approximately 80%. The PRM, while well explained, appears to be associated with variables that were not contained within the variables used in this study. This point is further identified within the statistical test results summarized in Table 17.5. In summary, while the PRM is explained to a level appropriate for further model construction and application, there is, however,

Table 17.5 Summary of Statistical Results

	PRM
R^2	0.80
$\beta_1 = 0$ (individual coefficients)	Yes
$\beta_1 = 0$ (all coefficients)	Yes
Durbin–Watson test	First-order serial correlation
Serial correlation	Rejected
Functional form	Correct (not rejected)
Normality	Rejected
Heteroscedasticity	Rejected

either a singular or a combination of socioeconomic and/or sociodemographic variables which are not identified and included in the original data that have a significant statistical relationship with the number of police officers.

Of the 25 variables included in the all-inclusive first equation for the number of police officers, 16 were not included. This result is interesting from the perspective that these variables were all initially included because they had been identified as having a relationship with police numbers in the literature of other countries. This is particularly relevant to the variable "rural." In the New Zealand context, it would have been presumed that the difference between the police numbers would be markedly large in a rural or urban setting. This result, however, could indicate that there is now very little difference between living in the country and living in a city. A further point could be that New Zealand cities are not as big as the larger cities of America or England and therefore do not have a significant statistical relationship.

The summary of statistical tests summarized in Table 17.5 indicates that the data were not normally distributed and that the equation is mis-specified. Autocorrelation and first-order serial correlation are present though the model's independent variables (individually or in total) influence the dependent variable in some way. Finally, the functional form test indicated that the PRM, as proposed, could be more effective in law enforcement personnel deployment.

As a result of the heteroscedasticity, the usual confidence intervals and hypothesis tests based on t and F distributions may be unreliable, and every possibility exists of drawing wrong conclusions if conventional hypothesis testing procedures are employed. Even though the data for the variables which make up the PRM were heteroscedastic and not normally distributed, the analysis of the linear relationships allows confidence in interpreting the regression results and for their practical application to the 50 PAs.

Applying the Police Resource Model

The results of the application of the PRM to each of the 50 PAs, by year and over the total period 1997–2002, are presented in Table 17.A.4. The table compares the actual number of police officers with that suggested by the application of the model and the difference between the two for each of the six individual years and for the total period. "Actual" relates to the annual PA data provided by the New Zealand Police for the number of police officers.

Table 17.A.4 shows the results of applying the PRM to the different PAs; a positive number indicates that a greater number of officers would be suggested by application of the model, while a negative number indicates a surfeit of officers compared with that suggested through the model. The national total number of sworn officers is allocated for the total period and for each of the six individual years. The unallocated figure of negative seven for the total period is the result of rounding and is disregarded in this discussion.

There are a number of differences in these figures, with some PAs having fewer officers than the model would suggest, while others have more. In some PAs, such as Auckland City, this difference is considerable. However, most PAs had a mixture of either requiring resources or having too many. In other PAs, such as Hornby, Rotorua, and Waikato West, resource requirements fluctuated widely from either having too many resources or having too few. On the other hand, a number of PAs, including Auckland West and Clutha South, are identified as requiring extra resources for the total period and for each of the six individual years.

In general, the PAs with the biggest discrepancies and the widest fluctuation were those from the Counties-Manukau and Canterbury Districts. These PAs included Hagley, Manurewa, Otahuhu, and Papakura. These fluctuations arose possibly as a result of the organizational restructuring and movement of staff within these districts which continued until late 1999. The Counties-Manukau District also moved from a reactive service delivery model to a mode called emergency response. This mode involved centralizing resources and differentiating between initial response to an incident/crime and investigation.

The results indicate that because of the large positive and negative fluctuations, any resource allocation decisions, particularly at the national level cannot be made or implemented on a yearly basis. This can be seen by the total period difference where a large number of both positive and negative discrepancies occur.

Policy Implications

The nine social variables that are associated with the number of police officers include six socioeconomic or sociodemographic and three "police"-relevant variables: the number of incidents, the level of crime, and the resolution rate. These determinants of the number of police officers suggest several policy implications, as the police are potentially able to influence the number of incidents, the level of reported crime, and resolution rate through their service delivery methods, deployment tactics, and practices. There are two further issues that need to be considered in any discussion on the policy implications of this study: whether the application of the PRM provides useful information and whether the PRM is an improvement on other methods of resource allocation. Table 17.A.5 presents a comparison of the differences between the actual number of police officers allocated to a PA and that suggested by the PRM for the period 1997–2002. There were a number of PAs where the difference was large and positive or negative between the study period years, while other PAs consistently had too many or too few police officers over the period.

For the New Zealand Police to be able to resolve the under- and overstaffing variations identified would mean that a large number of police officers would be needed to be transferred between PAs. One solution to the problems that this would cause is not to use the results of any individual year within the study period as the basis for transferring police staff, but rather to review the results of applying the model on the complete 6-year period, 1997–2002. Using the complete period rather than an annual basis substantiates the PRM approach to allocating resources as the organization is not responding to annual crises but would be strategically viewing resourcing requirements over a 6-year period. Finally, if a 3- to 5-year implementation cycle were to be introduced, the PRM's calculations can be updated annually using Statistics New Zealand demographic estimates. This process would allow for any demographic changes in a PA, and the number of police officers being allocated would still be correct according to the model.

The second issue pertains to whether the PRM is an improvement over other methods. The current resource allocation method used by the New Zealand Police is based on a mixture of historical numbers of officers and the size of the population at the district level and not at the PA level. Table 17.A.6 presents and compares two alternative allocation methods, with the actual current number of police officers in a PA in 2002. The two allocation methods compared are a method based solely on population and the PRM. The comparison produces a number of large differences between the number of police officers allocated by the population-based method and that suggested by the PRM. There are also a number of contradictions and differences between the two methods. Principally, in a number of PAs, the population-based method has recommended the opposite to that suggested by the PRM. The last three columns in the table present the difference between the numbers of police officers allocated by the two methods. There are a number of large differences even in central city areas with low populations, high levels of crime but large numbers of police officers such as Auckland and Hagley. Closer examination of the data reveals that application of the proposed model results in more officers being allocated to rural PAs than to city PAs, compared to the population-based method. This is because the PRM is not solely based on the level of population in a PA but is constructed from a number of socioeconomic and sociodemographic variables found to be associated with the number of police officers in a PA.

One can conclude that the PRM is the better of the two methods for two reasons. The PRM construction process included the variable that measured the population in a PA in the initial all-inclusive equation, but the variable was found not to be significantly associated with the number of police officers in a PA in the model.

Finally, in comparison to the allocation models proposed by the New Zealand Police in the 1990s, the PRM is not as complicated, and there are no exemptions of staff from the model who provide a national service function, for example, the meeting of international flights. For this reason and also because the PRM is based on a limited number of understandable social variables, the PRM would be more readily accepted by both police practitioners and policy makers. As a result, the PRM should be accepted as the preferred approach to allocating resources to a PA, and is an improvement on allocating officers solely on the basis of population.

Appendix A

Table 17.A.1   Variable Definition

Variable	Variable Definition[a]
Dependent variable	
1 Number of police officers	Number of sworn police officers assigned to criminal issues in a PA; excludes traffic officers
Independent variables	
1 Level of crime	Total number of recorded crimes in a PA
2 Resolution rate	Resolution rate measured by the actual number of reported crimes solved through arrest
3 Rural police area	Rural vs. urban PAs; rural is defined as a PA that does not include a major metropolitan center
4 Population	Population at December 31 each year in a PA
5 Unemployed	Percent of unemployed persons in a PA
6 Maori ethnicity	Percent of Maori persons in a PA
7 Pacific Peoples ethnicity	Percent of Pacific Islanders in a PA
8 European ethnicity	Percent of Europeans in a PA; defined as being of European descent
9 Asian ethnicity	Percent of Asian people in a PA; defined as being of Asian descent
10 Other ethnicity	Percentage of persons from other ethnic groups in a PA
11 Males 15–19	Number of males aged between 15 and 19 years in a PA

(continued)

Table 17.A.1 (continued)   Variable Definition

	Variable	Variable Definition[a]
12	Males 20–24	Number of males aged between 20 and 24 years in a PA
13	Males 25–29	Number of males aged between 25 and 29 years in a PA
14	Level of deprivation	Deprivation index rate is a measure of a PA deprivation level (1 = highest; 10 = lowest)
15	Number of incidents	Total number of incidents attended by police in a PA. Defined as calls for service attended by an officer
16	One-parent families	Number of one-parent families in a PA
17	Full-time employment	Number of full-time workers (including self-employed) in a PA
18	Part-time employment	Number of part-time workers (including self-employed) in a PA
19	Income less than $20 k	Number of people earning less than $20,000 per year in a PA
20	Income between $20 and $50 k	Number of people earning more than $20,000 but less than $50,000 per year in a PA
21	Income greater $50 k	Number of people earning more than $50,000 per year in a PA
22	No qualifications	Number of people with no formal or recognized qualifications in a PA
23	High school qualifications	Number of people with high school qualifications only, including fifth and sixth form certificate, higher school qualification, other New Zealand secondary school qualification, and overseas secondary school qualification in a PA
24	Vocational qualifications	Number of people with vocational qualifications only, including basic, skilled, intermediate, and advanced in a PA
25	Tertiary qualifications	Number of people with tertiary qualifications, including bachelor's and master's degrees and other recognized tertiary qualifications in a PA

[a] Variables are measured annually.

Table 17.A.2   Mean and Standard Deviation of Dependent and Independent Variables

Variable(s)	Rural	Pop	Unemp	Maori	Pacific	Euro
Maximum	1.0000	197294.0	0.13000	0.46000	0.52000	0.90000
Minimum	0.00	18153.0	0.020000	0.030000	0.010000	0.13000
Mean	0.50000	77113.7	0.064200	0.16350	0.052900	0.70537
Std. deviation	0.50084	40161.6	0.019432	0.10177	0.097620	0.16702

Variable(s)	Asian	Other	Male, 15	Male, 20	Male, 25	Depir
Maximum	0.16000	0.15000	10,435.0	8,669.0	16,000.0	9.0000
Minimum	0.010000	0.00	250.0000	400.0000	663.0000	3.0000
Mean	0.036567	0.041933	1,974.7	2,317.4	4,257.2	5.7800
Std. deviation	0.034784	0.021614	1,258.6	1,592.9	3,103.1	1.3630

Variable(s)	Police	Hours	Budget	Incidents	Crime	Resolve
Maximum	416.0000	692,384.7	2.13E+07	65,913.0	24,835.0	10,891.0

Table 17.A.2 (continued)   Mean and Standard Deviation of Dependent and Independent Variables

Variable(s)	Rural	Pop	Unemp	Maori	Pacific	Euro
Minimum	29.0000	91,992.6	3806303	4,324.0	1,950.0	330.0
Mean	129.4267	261,336.3	1.01E+07	20,097.4	8,890.6	3,531.0
Std. deviation	69.7244	115,146.5	3,836,345	11,076.5	4,587.1	1,785.8
Variable(s)	**Parent**	**FT**	**PT**	**IN20K**	**IN2050K**	**IN50K**
Maximum	8,384.0	71,319.0	20,898.0	60,090.0	50,121.0	25,905.0
Minimum	891.0000	5,904.0	1,737.0	6,009.0	3,796.0	818.0
Mean	3,445.3	24,915.8	7,745.6	26,036.1	17,793.3	5,701.4
Std. deviation	1,644.2	14,503.1	4,143.7	12,432.5	10,154.3	5,350.2
Variable(s)	**NOQUAL**	**HSQUAL**	**VOCQUAL**	**TERTQ**		
Maximum	28,734.0	61,005.0	28,296.0	38,994.0		
Minimum	2,549.0	3,725.0	1,985.0	1,731.0		
Mean	13,255.5	19,237.7	9,809.7	9,898.8		
Std. deviation	4,968.7	11,778.9	5,408.2	7,710.3		

Table 17.A.3   Number of Police Officers Equation (All Inclusive)

	Variable	Coefficient	Standard Error	T-Ratio	Probability
1	Rural	−3.107	6.518	0.48	0.634
2	Population	0.0011	0.0090	1.297	0.195
3	Unemployment	62.210	148.717	0.4183	0.676
4	European	617.030	828.60	0.7446	0.457
5	Maori	514.818	827.613	0.6220	0.534
6	Pacific	633.769	831.781	0.7619	0.447
7	Asian	595.975	835.888	0.7129	0.476
8	Other	1171.0	856.96	1.366	0.173
9	Male 15	0.0085	0.0059	−1.448	0.149
10	Male 20	0.0131	0.0070	1.869	0.063
11	Male 25	0.0084	0.0017	0.4823	0.630
12	Deprivation	−6.553	4.454	−1.471	0.142
13	Incident	0.0019	0.0003	5.415	0.000
14	Crime	0.0073	0.0016	4.519	0.000
15	Resolution	0.0076	0.0035	2.171	0.031
16	One parent	0.0071	0.0080	0.8817	0.379
17	Full time	−0.0032	0.0019	−1.670	0.096
18	Part time	0.0017	0.0066	0.2579	0.797
19	Income 20 k	0.0212	0.0125	1.691	0.092
20	Income 20–50 k	0.0189	0.0122	1.545	0.123
21	Income 50 k	0.0291	0.0131	2.218	0.027
22	No qualification	−0.0199	0.0121	−1.649	0.100
23	High school qualification	−0.0222	0.0120	−1.849	0.065
24	Vocational qualification	−0.0224	0.0124	−1.806	0.072
25	Tertiary qualification	−0.0247	0.0135	−1.824	0.069

Table 17.A.4   The Results of the Application of the PRM to the 50 PAs

Area	1997 Actual Number of Sworn Officers	1997 Number of Sworn Officers Suggested by PRM	1997 Difference	1998 Actual Number of Sworn Officers	1998 Number of Sworn Officers Suggested by PRM	1998 Difference	1999 Actual Number of Sworn Officers	1999 Number of Sworn Officers Suggested by PRM	1999 Difference	2000 Actual Number of Sworn Officers
Auck City	328	300	−28	347	334	−13	415	359	−57	411
Auck East	235	220	−15	235	225	−10	206	201	−5	176
Auck West	184	201	17	188	199	11	193	195	2	164
Clutha Sth	63	77	14	58	83	25	67	85	18	68
Dunedin	239	180	−59	230	230	0	226	206	−20	222
Far North	91	88	−3	75	97	22	71	86	15	92
Glsbome	127	98	−29	127	135	8	121	134	13	127
Hagley	272	240	−32	278	220	−58	416	317	−99	413
Hamlltn City	211	244	33	221	237	16	222	309	87	259
Hastings	125	115	−10	121	123	2	122	144	22	124
Homby	223	126	−97	116	112	−4	93	89	−4	97
Howick	67	79	12	59	50	−9	83	58	−25	88
Invercargill	135	106	−29	132	118	−14	135	145	10	129
K-Mana	169	167	−2	159	151	−8	155	132	−23	166
Lower Hutt	182	172	−10	165	166	1	157	165	8	169
Mangere	95	107	12	80	131	51	102	104	2	106
Manurewa	64	92	28	56	69	13	89	181	92	100
Marlborough	55	70	15	68	76	8	71	75	4	64
N Brighton	123	140	17	134	115	−19	114	94	−20	118
Napier	110	86	−24	108	106	−2	113	146	33	107
Nelson Bay	103	128	26	120	117	−3	129	119	−10	126
New Plyth	134	105	−29	145	124	−21	141	111	−30	133
Nth Shore	158	198	40	195	187	−8	198	171	−27	230
Otago	84	108	24	89	108	19	90	96	6	86
Otahuhu	82	109	27	113	57	−56	164	149	−15	164
Otara	74	72	−2	66	74	8	83	69	−14	87
Papakura	29	102	73	116	102	−14	153	119	−34	178
Papanui	95	118	23	116	91	−25	95	97	2	96
Pnth City	141	138	−3	132	123	−9	138	202	64	135
Pnth Rural	96	106	10	112	105	−7	116	124	8	123
Pukekohe	56	86	30	61	88	27	93	37	−56	90
Rodney	74	99	25	61	96	35	61	68	7	86
Rotorua	138	104	−32	143	141	−2	135	176	41	118
Ruapehu	45	48	3	53	47	−6	46	54	8	53
Sth Cant	124	108	−16	113	135	22	90	94	4	89
Sydenham	97	102	5	85	88	3	64	89	25	58
Taranakl	62	53	−9	60	48	−12	65	61	−4	60
Taupo	110	102	−8	102	109	7	102	128	26	116
Tauranga	109	85	−24	108	112	4	104	90	−14	102
Up Hutt	92	80	−12	73	74	1	73	49	−24	74
Waikato E	95	106	11	116	96	−20	112	105	−7	114
Waikato W	135	160	25	141	156	15	131	97	−34	139
Wairarapa	105	74	−31	88	84	−4	91	96	5	87

2000 Number of Sworn Officers Suggested by PRM	2000 Difference	2001 Actual Number of Sworn Officers	2001 Number of Sworn Officers Suggested by PRM	2001 Difference	2002 Actual Number of Sworn Officers	2002 Number of Sworn Officers Suggested by PRM	2002 Difference	1997–2002 Actual Number of Sworn Officers	1997–2002 Number of Sworn Officers Suggested by PRM	1997–2002 Difference
330	−81	342	227	−115	228	231	3	345	346	1
173	−3	201	229	28	188	200	12	207	221	14
165	1	158	222	64	180	191	11	178	189	11
86	18	65	81	16	71	86	17	65	86	21
205	−17	207	217	10	215	227	12	223	203	−20
102	10	92	99	7	102	105	3	87	94	6
131	4	113	129	16	116	122	6	122	136	14
214	−199	387	201	−186	406	194	−212	362	261	−101
252	−7	246	244	−2	227	236	9	231	268	37
155	31	122	128	6	129	119	−10	124	128	5
102	5	96	133	37	89	128	39	119	118	−1
63	−25	85	69	−16	87	68	−19	78	48	−30
107	−22	122	113	−9	113	111	−2	128	132	4
171	5	156	168	12	151	149	−2	159	152	−8
173	4	156	194	38	156	169	13	164	171	7
118	12	99	89	−10	101	95	−6	97	107	10
173	73	91	108	17	85	97	12	81	113	32
87	23	67	60	−7	79	74	−5	67	67	0
120	2	93	128	35	90	132	42	112	114	2
136	29	100	111	11	103	108	5	107	117	10
141	15	121	119	−2	129	140	11	121	114	−7
125	−8	122	117	−5	120	117	−3	133	121	−11
272	42	218	227	9	200	214	14	200	180	−20
101	15	86	102	16	100	115	15	89	108	17
116	−48	156	110	−46	90	104	14	128	106	−22
64	−23	86	71	−15	71	64	−7	78	76	−2
93	−85	173	117	−56	177	94	−83	138	120	−18
103	7	92	120	26	88	113	25	97	98	1
152	17	135	157	22	149	153	4	138	167	29
147	24	121	127	6	124	121	−3	115	111	−4
47	−43	89	84	−5	87	90	3	79	75	−4
90	4	100	107	7	105	109	4	81	80	−1
146	28	116	129	13	124	123	−1	129	149	20
53	0	51	45	−6	50	46	−4	50	49	0
95	6	87	120	33	85	116	31	98	118	20
68	10	61	91	30	55	86	31	70	84	14
63	3	58	52	−6	63	50	−13	61	52	−10
124	8	110	108	−2	116	107	−9	109	117	7
90	−12	93	81	−12	91	90	−1	101	100	−1
63	−11	71	73	2	75	66	−9	76	71	−6
130	16	119	91	−28	126	107	−19	114	90	−23
119	−20	132	154	22	158	164	6	139	137	−2
103	16	87	87	0	91	80	−11	92	94	2

(continued)

Table 17.A.4 (continued)   The Results of the Application of the PRM to the 50 PAs

Area	1997 Actual Number of Sworn Officers	1997 Number of Sworn Officers Suggested by PRM	1997 Difference	1998 Actual Number of Sworn Officers	1998 Number of Sworn Officers Suggested by PRM	1998 Difference	1999 Actual Number of Sworn Officers	1999 Number of Sworn Officers Suggested by PRM	1999 Difference	2000 Actual Number of Sworn Officers
Waitakere	158	204	46	186	203	17	248	204	−44	242
Wanganui	124	115	−9	119	114	−5	112	143	31	115
West BoP	68	69	1	74	58	−16	79	126	47	78
West Coast	59	68	9	64	70	6	63	52	−11	67
Wgtn	294	306	12	280	288	8	262	259	−3	288
Whakatane	63	68	5	76	80	2	89	93	4	87
Whangarel	155	125	−30	139	151	12	149	146	−3	153
Total	**6265**	**6266**	**0**	**6305**	**6303**	**−1**	**6647**	**6647**	**0**	**6774**

2000 Number of Sworn Officers Suggested by PRM	2000 Difference	2001 Actual Number of Sworn Officers	2001 Number of Sworn Officers Suggested by PRM	2001 Difference	2002 Actual Number of Sworn Officers	2002 Number of Sworn Officers Suggested by PRM	2002 Difference	1997–2002 Actual Number of Sworn Officers	1997–2002 Number of Sworn Officers Suggested by PRM	1997–2002 Difference
291	49	224	249	25	208	226	18	211	206	−5
127	12	110	117	7	107	145	38	115	124	9
131	53	87	99	12	96	99	3	80	83	2
50	−17	64	53	−11	74	65	−9	65	60	−6
303	15	279	296	17	264	273	9	278	272	−6
96	9	87	78	−9	67	82	15	78	86	7
204	51	156	159	3	152	153	1	151	149	−2
6774	**0**	**6489**	**6487**	**−2**	**6358**	**6358**	**0**	**6471**	**6464**	**−7**

Table 17.A.5 Comparison of Differences between the Actual Number of Police Officers Allocated to a Police Area and That Suggested by the PRM (1997–2002)

Area	1997 Number of Police Officers Difference	1998 Number of Police Officers Difference	1999 Number of Police Officers Difference	2000 Number of Police Officers Difference	2001 Number of Police Officers Difference	2002 Number of Police Officers Difference	1997– 2002 Number of Police Officers Difference
Auck City	−28	−13	−57	−81	−115	3	1
Auck East	−15	−10	−5	−3	28	12	14
Auck West	17	11	2	1	64	11	11
Clutha Sth	14	25	18	18	16	17	21
Dunedin	−59	0	−20	−17	10	12	−20
Far North	−3	22	15	10	7	3	6
Gisborne	−29	8	13	4	16	6	14
Hagley	−32	−58	−99	−199	−186	−212	−101
Hamiltn City	33	16	87	−7	−2	9	37
Hastings	−10	2	22	31	6	−10	5
Hornby	−97	−4	−4	5	37	39	−1
Howick	12	−9	−25	−25	−16	−19	−30
Invercargill	−29	−14	10	−22	−9	−2	4
K-Mana	−2	−8	−23	5	12	−2	−8
Lower Hutt	−10	1	8	4	38	13	7
Mangere	12	51	2	12	−10	−6	10
Manurewa	28	13	92	73	17	12	32
Marlborough	15	8	4	23	−7	−5	0
N Brighton	17	−19	−20	2	35	42	2
Napier	−24	−2	33	29	11	5	10
Nelson Bay	26	−3	−10	15	−2	11	−7
New Plyth	−29	−21	−30	−8	−5	−3	−11
Nth Shore	40	−8	−27	42	9	14	−20
Otago	24	19	6	15	16	15	17
Otahuhu	27	−56	−15	−48	−46	14	−22
Otara	−2	8	−14	−23	−15	−7	−2
Papakura	73	−14	−34	−85	−56	−83	−18
Papanui	23	−25	2	7	28	25	1
Pnth City	−3	−9	64	17	22	4	29
Pnth Rural	10	−7	8	24	6	−3	−4
Pukekohe	30	27	−56	−43	−5	3	−4
Rodney	25	35	7	4	7	4	−1
Rotorua	−32	−2	41	28	13	−1	20
Ruapehu	3	−6	8	0	−6	−4	0
Sth Cant	−16	22	4	6	33	31	20

Table 17.A.5 (continued)   Comparison of Differences between the Actual Number of Police Officers Allocated to a Police Area and that Suggested by the PRM (1997–2002)

Area	1997 Number of Police Officers Difference	1998 Number of Police Officers Difference	1999 Number of Police Officers Difference	2000 Number of Police Officers Difference	2001 Number of Police Officers Difference	2002 Number of Police Officers Difference	1997– 2002 Number of Police Officers Difference
Sydenham	5	3	25	10	30	31	14
Taranaki	−9	−12	−4	3	−6	−13	−10
Taupo	−8	7	26	8	−2	−9	7
Tauranga	−24	4	−14	−12	−12	−1	−1
Up Hutt	−12	1	−24	−11	2	−9	−6
Waikato E	11	−20	−7	16	−28	−19	−23
Waikato W	25	15	−34	−20	22	6	−2

Table 17.A.6   Comparison of the Allocation of Police Officers (in 2002) Based on Population and the PRM

Area	2002 Actual Number of Police Officers	2002 Number of Police Officers by Population	Difference between Actual and Population	2002 Actual Number of Police Officers	2002 Number of Police Officers Suggested by PRM	Difference between Actual and PRM	2002 Number of Police Officers by Population	2002 Number of Police Officers Suggested by PRM	Difference between Population Method and PRM
Auck City	**228**	**57**	**-171**	**228**	**231**	**3**	**57**	**231**	**-175**
Auck East	188	263	75	188	200	12	263	200	62
Auck West	180	289	109	180	191	11	289	191	98
Clutha Sth	71	82	11	71	88	17	82	88	-6
Dunedin	215	218	3	215	227	12	218	227	-9
Far North	**102**	**93**	**-9**	**102**	**105**	**3**	**93**	**105**	**-12**
Gisborne	**116**	**88**	**-28**	**116**	**122**	**6**	**88**	**122**	**-34**
Hagley	406	86	-320	406	194	-212	86	194	-109
Hamiltn City	**227**	**222**	**-5**	**227**	**236**	**9**	**222**	**236**	**-13**
Hastings	**129**	**129**	**0**	**129**	**119**	**-10**	**129**	**119**	**10**
Hornby	89	178	89	89	128	39	178	128	51
Howick	**87**	**160**	**73**	**87**	**68**	**-19**	**160**	**68**	**92**
Invercargill	113	86	-27	113	111	-2	86	111	-25
K-Mana	**151**	**162**	**11**	**151**	**149**	**-2**	**162**	**149**	**13**
Lower Hutt	156	161	5	156	169	13	161	169	-9
Mangere	101	79	-22	101	95	-6	79	95	-16
Manurewa	85	116	31	85	97	12	116	97	18
Marlborough	79	72	-7	79	74	-5	72	74	-1
N Brighton	90	172	82	90	132	42	172	132	41

Napier	103	95	-8	103	108	5	95	108	-14
Nelson Bay	129	140	11	129	140	11	140	140	0
New Plyth	120	112	-8	120	117	-3	112	117	-5
Nth Shore	200	320	120	200	214	14	320	214	106
Otage	100	86	-14	100	115	15	86	115	-29
Otahuhu	90	99	9	90	104	14	99	104	-5
Otara	71	62	-9	71	64	-7	62	64	-1
Papakura	177	74	-103	177	94	-83	74	94	-20
Papanui	88	177	89	88	113	25	177	113	64
Pnth City	149	129	-20	149	153	4	129	153	-24
Pnth Rural	124	136	12	124	121	-3	136	121	15
Pukekohe	87	88	1	87	90	3	88	90	-2
Rodney	105	133	28	105	109	4	133	109	24
Rotorua	124	113	-11	124	123	-1	113	123	-10
Ruapehu	50	29	-21	50	46	-4	29	46	-17
Sth Cant	85	87	2	85	116	31	87	116	-30
Sydenham	55	103	48	55	86	31	103	86	17
Taranaki	63	57	-6	63	50	-13	57	50	6
Taupo	116	92	-24	116	107	-9	92	107	-15
Tauranga	91	72	-19	91	90	-1	72	90	-19
Up Hutt	75	61	-14	75	66	-9	61	66	-5
Waikato E	126	124	-2	126	107	-19	124	107	17
Waikato W	158	140	-18	158	164	6	140	164	-23
Wairarapa	91	63	-28	91	80	-11	63	80	-17
Waitakere	208	291	83	208	226	18	291	226	64

(continued)

Table 17.A.6 (continued)   Comparison of the Allocation of Police Officers (in 2002) Based on Population and the PRM

Area	2002 Actual Number of Police Officers	2002 Number of Police Officers by Population	Difference between Actual and Population	2002 Actual Number of Police Officers	2002 Number of Police Officers Suggested by PRM	Difference between Actual and PRM	2002 Number of Police Officers by Population	2002 Number of Police Officers Suggested by PRM	Difference between Population Method and PRM
Wanganui	107	90	-17	107	145	38	90	145	-56
West BoP	96	144	48	96	99	3	144	99	46
West Coast	74	50	-24	74	65	-9	50	65	-16
Wgtn	264	258	-6	264	273	9	258	273	-14
Whakatane	67	77	10	67	82	15	77	82	-4
Whangarei	152	141	-11	152	153	1	141	153	-12
National	6358	6358	0	6358	6358	0	6358	6358	0

References

Audit Commission of Local Authorities and The National Health Service (1991) *Reviewing the Organisation of Provincial Police Forces*, London, England. February, No. 9.

Avio, K. and Clark, C. (1978) The supply of property offences in Ontario: Evidence on the deterrent effect of punishment, *Canadian Journal of Economics*, XI(1), 1–19.

Bayley, D. (1994) *Police for the Future*. Oxford University Press: New York.

Bayley, D. (1998) *What Works in Policing*. Oxford University Press: New York.

Becker, G. (1968) Crime and punishment: An economic approach, *Journal of Political Economy*, 76(2), 169–217.

Becsi, Z. (1999) Economics and crime in the States, *Economic Review*, Federal Reserve Bank of Atlanta, First Quarter.

Benson, B. and Rasmussen, D. (1991) Relation between illicit drug enforcement policy and property crimes, *Contemporary Policy Issues*, 9, 106–115.

Benson, B. and Rasmussen, D. (2000) Deterrence and public policy: Trade-offs in the allocation of police resources, *International Review of Law and Economics*, 18, 77–100.

Benson, B., Kim, I., Rasmussen, D., and Zuehlke, T. (1992) Is property crime caused by drug use or drug enforcement policy? *Applied Economics*, 24, 679–692.

Boston, J. (1999) The funding of tertiary education: Enduring issues and dilemmas, in *Redesigning the Welfare State in New Zealand: Problems, Policies, Prospects*, J. Boston, P. Dalziel, and S. St. John (eds.), Oxford University Press: Auckland, New Zealand.

Brandl, S., Chamlin, M., and Frank, J. (1995) Aggregation bias and the capacity for formal crime control: The determinants of total and disaggregated police force size in Milwaukee, 1934–1987, *Justice Quarterly*, 12, 543–562.

Brown, G. and Haldane, R. (1998) *Days of Violence: The 1923 Police Strike in Melbourne*. Hybrid Publishers: Victoria, Australia.

Carr-Hill, R. and Stern, N. (1973) An econometric model of supply and control of recorded offences in England and Wales, *Journal of Public Economics*, 2, 289–318.

Carr-Hill, R. and Stern, N. (1979) *Crime, the Police and Criminal Statistics: An Analysis of Official Statistics for England and Wales Using Econometric Methods*. Academic Press: London, U.K.

Chamlin, M. (1989) A macro social analysis of change in police force size, 1972–1982: Controlling for static and dynamic influences, *Sociological Quarterly*, 30, 615–624.

Chamlin, M. and Langworthy, R. (1996) The police, crime and economic theory: A replication and extension, *American Journal of Criminal Justice*, 20, 165–182.

Craig, S. (1987) The deterrent impact of police: An examination of locally provided public service, *Journal of Urban Economics*, 21, 298–311.

DiIulio, J. (1996) Help wanted: Economists, crime and public policy, *Journal of Economic Perspectives*, 10, 3–24.

Eck, J. and Maguire, E. (2000) Have changes in policing reduced violent crime? An assessment of the evidence, in *The Crime Drop in America*, A. Blumstein and J. Wallman (eds.). Cambridge University Press: New York.

Goldstein, H. (1990) *Problem-Oriented Policing*. McGraw-Hill Publishing: New York.

Grabosky, P. (1988) *Efficiency and Effectiveness in Australian Policing*. Trends and Issues in Crime and Criminal Justice, Number 16, Australian Institute of Criminology, Woden, Australia.

Greenberg, D., Kesseler, R., and Loftin, C. (1983) The effect of police employment on crime, *Criminology*, 21(3), 375–394.

Greenberg, D., Kessler, R., and Loftin, C. (1985) Social inequality and crime control, *Journal of Criminal Law and Criminology*, 76, 684–704.

Hill, R. (1986) *The History of Policing in New Zealand: Policing the Colonial Frontier (Part 1)*. Government Printer: Wellington, New Zealand.

Hsiao, C. (1986) *Analysis of Panel Data*. Cambridge University Press: New York.

Jackson, P. and Carroll, L. (1981) Race and the war on crime: The socio-political determinants of municipal police expenditures in 90 non-southern US cities, *American Sociological Review*, 46, 290–305.

Lardner, J. and Reppetto, T. (2000) *NYPD: A City and Its Police*. Henry Hott and Co.: New York.

Levitt, S. (1997) Using electoral cycles in police hiring to estimate the effect of police on crime, *The American Economic Review*, 87(3), 270–290.

Liska, A., Lawrence, J., and Benson, M. (1981) Perspectives on the legal order: The capacity for social control, *American Journal of Sociology*, 87, 413–426.

Marvell, T. and Moody, C. (1996) Specification problems, police levels and crime rates, *Criminology*, 32, 609–638.

Nalla, M. (1992) Perspectives on the growth of police bureaucracies, 1948–1984: An examination of three explanations, *Policing and Society*, 3, 51–61.

Nalla, M., Lynch, M., and Lieber, M. (1997) Determinants of police growth in phoenix, 1950–1988, *Justice Quarterly*, 14(1), 115–143.

New Zealand Police (2003) *New Zealand Police Strategic Intent: 2003/2004*. Wellington, New Zealand.

Niskanen, W. (1994) Crime, police and root causes. *Policy Analysis 218*. Cato Institute: Washington, DC.

Russell, F. (1975) *A City in Terror: 1919—The Boston Police Strike*. Viking Publishers: New York.

Sherman, L. (1997) Policing for prevention, in *Preventing Crime: What Works, What Doesn't, What's Promising, A Report to the Attorney General of the United States*, L. Sherman, D. Gottfredson, D. MacKenzie, J. Eck, P. Reuter, and S. Bushway (eds.), US Department of Justice, Office of Justice Programs: Washington, DC.

Sherman, L. and Eck, J. (2002) Policing for crime prevention, in *Evidence Based Crime Prevention*, L. Sherman, D. MacKenzie, and D. Farrington (eds.). Routledge: New York.

Stockdale, J., Whitehead, C., and Gresham, P. (1999) *Applying Economic Evaluation to Policing Activity*. Police Research Series Paper 103, Policing and Reducing Crime Unit, Home Office: London, U.K.

Tabachnick, B. and Fidell, L. (1996) *Using Multivariate Statistics* (3rd edn.). Harper Collins College Publishers: New York.

van Tulder, F. (1992) Crime, detection rate, and the police: A macro approach, *Journal of Quantitative Criminology*, 8(1), 113–131.

The Public Perception on the Quality of Policing in Indonesia

18

ADRIANUS MELIALA

Contents

Introduction

One way to investigate the quality of policing is through the perspective of the recipients of those law enforcement activities. Through the exploration of the opinions or judgments made by members of the public, the quality of service delivered by a public institution, such as the police, can be measured.

It is the public to whom the police should be accountable. Consequently, the police themselves could adjust their style and activities to the manner most preferred by the public. However, this view can be challenged by the police themselves who could put forward the question, "should we pay attention solely to what the public have said?" For some elements in the police, responding to the public's expectations would not be appropriate because some of the evaluation criteria used by the public are subjective and often rely on sensationalism, and ultimately many of the expectations can never be met.

At times, community input may not be the best method for improving police service, since there is always a certain level of bias in public perceptions of the police and their understanding of how they work. When the police perform their function of controlling people, there is always a section of the population that becomes reluctant or even rejects being totally controlled. They might believe that any action taken by the police is simply to prevent them from doing what they want. The complexities of the police role are such that the work of maintaining order has become somewhat of a very unpopular job. Furthermore, some elements of the public will cheerfully or even warmly welcome police inability to overcome public disorder, including the rare occasion when the police purposely decide not to react to a social disturbance.

Indonesia's Recent History

Policing within Indonesia, and even Indonesia itself, has not received adequate attention and has limited exposure in western literature. In comparison with the colorful history of its police organization, the political history of Indonesia, as highlighted by the changes in regime and presidents, seems much less complex.

Independence was granted to Indonesia in August 1945. The country's first president, Soekarno, was an engineer cum demagogue. He presided over the country for two decades before being ousted by the army in a military coup in 1967, because he was regarded as being too close to the Indonesian Communist Party (PKI) after having allied Indonesia politically to the Soviet Union. This move caused deep concern to the Indonesian military and to western democracies like the United States (Cribb and Brown 1995).

The soft coup's master mind, Army Major General Soeharto, became one of the longest serving presidents in the world. There was no doubt that an authoritarian style of leadership supported by the might of the military was needed to preserve his power over this long period of time (Singh 2000; pp. 1–11). During Soeharto's "New Order" regime, with the recognition of the armed forces as a functional group under the 1945 constitution, the Indonesian military continued to play an active role in politics (Kuppuswamy 2002). Soeharto was finally ousted in May 1998 primarily due to his inability to prevent the country from falling victim to severe economic recession, which began in 1997 (International Crisis Group 2000). Faced with a massive breakdown of law and order, the increased possibility of chaos and disorder, and through the pressure of protesting pro-democracy students, leaders of the Parliament began to call for the Indonesian president to step down. Rather than face impeachment, and unwilling to prolong the crisis by pitting the armed forces against the students, Soeharto ultimately resigned (Anwar 2001; pp. 3–16).

Soeharto's vice-president, Billy Joesoef Habibie, replaced him and became the first president in the so-called reform era. However, he was too closely connected with Soeharto and suffered by this association, and was perceived as being as corrupt as his predecessor (International Crisis Group 2000). He was a weak leader with little political influence and failed to be re-elected after less than a year in the palace. At the same time, the military, which was heavily criticized for prior human right abuses, proposed a new paradigm and suggested some fundamental changes in its organization, the most important being the separation of the police from the armed forces (Markas Besar ABRI 1998; pp. 17–19).

As a result, Abdurrahman Wahid, a noted Islamic cleric replaced Habibie in October 1999, immediately taking serious measures to exert civilian control over the military and rein in the army. He also made it clear that he supported reform of the police and its separation from the military (The Editors 2000). Because of this and other reasons, Wahid was regarded as being too outspoken, liberal, and erratic in managing the country. The parliament finally impeached him leading to his removal from the presidency in 2001.

It is worth noting that Wahid's successor, Megawati Soekarnoputri, is the eldest daughter of Indonesia's first president, Soekarno. The issues and challenges facing President Megawati's government, with respect to economic problems, originated from the previous governments. The financial shocks that struck Indonesia in July 1997, presented the administration with daunting challenges that seemingly overwhelmed efforts to bring the economy into a sustained recovery process (Djiwandono 2003; pp. 196–221).

History of the Indonesian Police

The most critical event for the Indonesian police occurred when a declaration was issued by the Temporary People's Consultative Assembly or MPRS (*Majelis Permusyawaratan Rakyat Sementara*) in 1960, stating that the police force had become a part of the armed forces or Abri (*Angkatan Bersenjata Republik Indonesia*). Further legislation followed that declaration, including Law No. 13/1961 on the Essentials of the National State Police (*Pokok-Pokok Kepolisian Negara*), which clearly defined the police's new position in the armed forces.

To understand the reason for this shift, it is necessary to recall the history of Indonesian politics around that period. According to one former police chief, the government at that time had become anxious about the possibility of police personnel being drawn into politics and having various political affiliations. This was regarded as dangerous, since it was considered necessary that the police remain clear of politics and remain neutral (Koenarto 1997; pp. 134–141).

Hence, there were mixed responses to the idea of incorporating the Indonesian Police Force or "Polri" into the armed forces. Not all parties in

Polri welcomed such efforts to eliminate the possibility of the elite layer of the organization using political power for themselves to leverage the authority of the organization and even advance their own positions. For example, previously, the position of police chief, clearly relevant and critical, was rather powerful as an appointed police chief might not agree to execute policies, even though they had been approved by the Indonesian president (Djamin 1999). In the new structure, the highest line of command was held by the Commander of the Armed Forces. It was hoped then, that the introduction of military values and command structures would reduce the tendency of police generals to indulge in politics.

This supposedly neutral organization was once again tested in relation to the rise of the Communist Party or PKI (*Partai Komunis Indonesia*) between 1963 and 1965. The party was successful in gaining influence, especially among Air Force personnel and even in an elite infantry battalion serving as the Presidential Guard, *Cakrabirawa*. According to Koenarto (1997; pp. 141–142), the Communist Party also had considerable influence within the police, often causing internal conflict in the organization, whereas the army was strongly anticommunist. Eventually, this political factionalism within the Armed Forces exploded in a coup attempt in September 1965, for which the army leadership blamed the PKI (Cribb and Brown 1995).

In response to that successful coup, a new government, headed by President Soeharto, issued a new policy to conduct a full-scale reintegration of the military. His policies were to dismiss the positions of the four commanders in chief/ministers and turn them back into mere chiefs of staff (for the Army, the Navy, and the Air Force), and also to introduce the position of police chief. There was also a centralized line of responsibility through the single command of Abri, the title of the position becoming Commander of the Armed Forces, or *Panglima Abri*, which went, above all, to the highest commander, the President himself. Lastly, a unification of uniform and preservice training/education became the foundation for consolidating the branches of the armed forces and preventing diversity and dissent.

By 1968, Polri was practically a new wing of Abri, without any autonomy of its own. A military-based management system had totally replaced Polri's original, more civilian orientation. Politically, there were some advantages. Polri enjoyed Abri's powerful position, as it could also utilize Abri's paramilitary facilities and take advantage of Abri's domination in Indonesian politics. However, the bad outweighed the good, as will be revealed later.

The history of Polri appears to have been not very well documented between 1968 and 1979. Available evidence suggests that during that time, there was a general perception among people that the reputation and work-ing performance of the Indonedian Police Force had declined to an intol-erable level. It was not easy to find even a single "clean" officer, since the working environment appears not to have provided incentives or support for uncorrupt officers. Even the fifth Chief of Police himself became a "victim" of this. In 1977, Police General Hoegeng Iman Santoso was sacked from his position by the President for arresting a noted Chinese businessman close to the President's family and having him prosecuted (Yusra and Ramadhan 1994; pp. 322–325).

Aware of the decline in quality of Polri and, while appointing Police General Awaloedin Djamin as the newly appointed Chief of Police (or *Kapolri*) in 1979, President Soeharto ordered both Djamin and the Commander of the Armed Forces/Minister of Security and Defenses to reorganize the police force back into its essential duties, to enforce the law and to maintain order, including all its related activities.

The police force made swift progress in Djamin's era (1978–1982). Under a general organizational policy called the *Pola Dasar Pembenahan Polri* ("The Basis of Polri's Reorganization"), the emphasis concentrated mainly on the internal reorganization of the force's structure and the enhancement of the value of *Tribrata* (The Three Ways of Life) and *Catur Prasetya* (The Four Missions) as the basic values of the police force. The policy he introduced was mostly based on a scientific approach to managing police work efficiently and with an emphasis on higher quality service.

However, there was another trend to revise police agency policies fol-lowing the replacement of the chief after the end of Djamin's era. Djamin's successor, Police General Anton Sudjarwo (1982–1986), introduced his overall re-organization program called the *Rekonfu* (Rehabilitation–Consolidation–Functionalization), which was eventually succeeded by the *Opdin* (Optimation and Dynamization) policies introduced by the next Police General Mohammad Sanoesi (1986–1991). Succeeding him was Police General Koenarto (1991–1993). He, in fact, avoided the so-called vision of the basic policies of his predecessor; on the contrary, he issued a kind of memo, "My Best Service for You" (*Untukmu Pengabdian Terbaik*), to remind all police officers throughout Indonesia of the high standard of services they should be providing. However, the memo has since been regarded as "just another policy" by his staff and subordinates (Koenarto 1997; p. 3) and was not widely implemented or accepted.

His successors, Police General Banurusman Atmosoemitro (1993–1996) and then Police General Dibyo Widodo (1996–1998), also continued this approach to policy. While Banurusman introduced the rather community-oriented motto, *Jati Diri Polri* ("The Inner Soul of Polri"), Dibyo's idea was to improve the three dimensions of police performance or what he referred to as the *Tiga Penampilan Polri* (the "Three Ps"), namely, field performance, agency performance, and individual performance.

Dibyo's successor, Roesmanhadi (1998–2000), produced a rather impressive managerial program called the *6Pro-3K* policies, which identified six principles of professionalism and three more to improve agency quality. Roesmanhadi's successor, Roesdihardjo, ran his office for only 8 months before being replaced by Surojo Bimantoro. During his short term of service, Roesdihardjo preferred to strengthen the core business of Polri by re-affirming what the focal point of Polri as a police organization should be.

Roesmanhadi and his successors found it difficult to fulfill the role of police chief in the era of civilian police in a democratic environment. The concept of civilian police is supposed to have an overemphasized meaning, since the police in essence ought to be civilians.

As outlined above, from April 1999, Polri was no longer a part of the military and police reform. The most negative impact arising from all these efforts at reform attempted by all these police chiefs was that it was difficult to find a single reorganizational program that had been fully implemented, sufficiently put into action, or properly evaluated. Since each chief of police had only 3 years or less in the position, no one initiative had enough time to be totally executed before being replaced by another reform policy introduced by another chief. The fact that each new successor, rather than continuing the ongoing program, commenced his own philosophical priorities, made matters much worse. This had the effect of rendering the vision of each specific Indonesian police chief virtually meaningless.

Analyzing the Indonesian Police

The historical path of the Indonesian police has made clear that what determines the dynamics of Polri is more external politics rather than internal demand to respond to public demands or desires. Even internal development within Polri, as at least indicated by strategies or programs established by each subsequent police chief, could be interpreted as emphasizing personal preference rather than incorporating a valid approach toward the identified problems of both the police and the public. As a result, there is apparent discrepancy between the practices of the Indonesian police and the expectations and opinions of the communities that they serve. It would be helpful to design and conduct surveys of the Indonesian public to better understand their perceptions of the Polri.

Previous Surveys of the Police

Over the period 1976–2000, a number of public perception surveys involving the Indonesian police were conducted and published, either in the form of rather unscientific surveys organized by the mass media, academic studies prepared by university researchers, or internal surveys instituted by the Indonesian police themselves. In addition to these surveys, other research projects analyzing the police have been conducted, using other methods, such as panel discussions or in-depth interviews. There were also surveys undertaken by one university nongovernmental organization dedicating itself specifically to monitoring police work in Indonesia (Indonesian Police Watch 2000), which incorporated secondary data (e.g., criminal statistics) maintained by the police.

The first studies worth commenting on were research projects conducted by the Indonesian police force. All of them were executed by the Police Research and Development Division, located at the Indonesian Police headquarters ("*Dislitbang Polri*"). The first major project in 1993 assessed the image of the police in the eyes of the residents of seven large cities in Indonesia (Jakarta, Banda Aceh, Pekanbaru, Banjarmasin, Bandung, Semarang, and Surabaya). This study involved 1261 respondents and, despite its weak validity, showed that the image of the Polri as an unbiased law enforcer was rather weak.

The second Polri survey, jointly undertaken by Dislitbang Polri and the Center of Security and Peace of The Gadjah Mada University in Yogyakarta (1999) was very impressive. This exploratory study was initiated in the midst of public pressure to remove Polri from the military and transition it to a civilian organization. The survey covered six regional police areas and used various data collection methods. The strategy of collaborating with an external partner, especially a university, was the Indonesian Police's way of increasing both the internal and external reliability of the data collected and of supporting the conclusions reached.

With respect to how the public evaluated police work, this study concluded that police personnel do not have enough discipline; they are not hard workers; they are plaqued by low morale; they have limited support for the "service" mentality; they are not diligent enough; they are easily convinced to give up on challenges and responsibilities; they are perceived as being arrogant; and they are not considered role models by the general public. Moreover, the respondents of this study also pointed to the low-adaptation capability and bureaucratic style of the police.

In addition, this study also covered the flow of off-budget funds within the police. The flow was called "the bottom-up finance flow," as it is clear that, even today, the lower level police units provide available funds to the higher levels, either by receiving a less operational budget than they are supposed to receive, or by providing money generated from the public. All in all, this practice prevents the Indonesian Police from being considered faithful to the communities they serve.

As one of the few academic centers with a large interest in police matters, the University of Indonesia (UI) has also conducted some research projects involving the police. The first was a survey evaluating the intention of members of the public to notify the police of criminal events. This was conducted by a research team from the UI in collaboration with a reputable weekly magazine, *Gatra*, in 1995. The focus of this survey was actually the fear of crime among the people in the Metropolitan Jakarta area while, at the same time, analyzing police actions undertaken to overcome that feeling of insecurity.

This survey found that when the respondents were asked for their reasons for not notifying the police about a crime that had occurred, the most frequent (67.5%) reason given was the respondent's perception that the police could or would do nothing to solve the problem or even to compensate them for their losses. A second reason stated was their doubt as to whether or not the police would do anything even if they reported these crimes (26.9%).

These findings are relatively similar to results uncovered elsewhere. Another result that is not less surprising is that about one-half of robberies and about two-thirds of assaults have never been reported.

Another intensive survey undertaken by UI's researchers was conducted in 2000 at the request of police headquarters administrators. This survey employed the Delphi technique and involved legal scholars, criminologists, and sociologists and concluded that the low level of professionalism exhibited by police personnel was to blame for many problems. Not only that, this survey also pointed out that the low level of perceived professionalism observed in the police was caused by several factors that had been highlighted in other surveys, namely, intensive interventions from external parties, low morale within the organization, and, lastly, the improper use of police authorities by police officers.

It can also be reported, that there are several other research projects, which while not focusing directly on law enforcement, have considered the public perception of the police as one of the many variables investigated. One example is the qualitative psychology survey on street kids as a prototype of urban neglected children, carried out by the University of Diponegoro in Semarang, Central Java (1997). This project concluded that the police were far from being seen as the protectors of those street kids. On the contrary, the police were regarded, by informants of this survey, as the enemy who were always chasing after and/or arresting street children as and when they pleased. Instead of being a protector, the police, in the eyes of these street kids, were the ones always creating trouble and anxiety.

Another investigation was conducted by students from the Universitas Negeri Malang (2001). They questioned 150 employed individuals using a telephone survey. As predicted, the responses given by the people of Malang were not altogether positive in the sense that they wanted the police to work harder. One illustration worth mentioning was the reaction toward the following question: "How responsive are the police in your area in responding to critiques and suggestions given by people?" Forty percent of the respondents indicated "police were less responsive."

It is also interesting to highlight the findings of the research carried out for the "National Survey on Corruption in Indonesia" by the UNDP Partnership for Governance Reform in Indonesia (2001). As this title suggests, this research did not relate to the police directly, however, it did describe public attitude toward the police. In relation to the latter, the results indicated that traffic police (together with customs officers and court-based officers) were regarded as the most corrupt. Almost half of the respondents of this survey (46.6%) also admitted that bribing a police officer is considered normal. Also, more than half (58.7%) indicated that they would pay a bribe if they were in a situation that required them to do so.

The mass media also focused considerable attention on police matters. One good example is the three series of surveys conducted by *Republika* (a daily circulated national Indonesian newspaper) in 1996, 1997, and 1999. The 1996 survey examined the dilemmas facing Polri, such as the low salary of its personnel, the low community involvement and support from the public, and the public's general comments on the police being unable to effectively deal with crimes and social disorder. The two later surveys were similar, in the sense that both investigated issues concerning the immediate shooting of street criminals, ordered by the chief of police. The aim of these surveys was to investigate that policy in relation to eradicating the excessive growth of street crimes occurring in the big cities, such as Metropolitan Jakarta, and the consequent fear of crime. This policy was regarded as controversial, since there are some elements among the Jakartanese who believe that this particular police directive was exaggerated and simplistic, and that the crime threat could actually be addressed by engaging in traditional policing.

The 1997 *Republika* survey resulted in a profile, which indicated that 82% of 500 Jakarta-based respondents believed that the policy of immediately shooting street criminals was "silently" ordered by the local chief of police. To a certain extent, one could interpret this as an indication of increasing fear of crime suffered by the residents of Jakarta due to the uncontrolled prevalence of violent street crime. However, only 22.2% of them were in agreement that the police should carry out these shootings without taking sufficient precautions or engaging in other options first.

In the 1999 *Republika* survey, which also included 500 Jakarta-based respondents, 74.2% indicated their agreement with the act of immediate shooting to stop criminals who were mugging people on the street. Nevertheless, even after having implemented such a stringent measure, only

31.3% of the respondents still believed that the police could ultimately control the crime situation in Jakarta.

The public support for this violent policy is clearly disturbing. To some, the preference for a shoot-on-sight policy can be regarded as an indication of frustration and narrow-minded decision making, rather than as responsible policy implementation. Another survey about the police was conducted by the weekly magazine, *Tempo*. This research project investigated public opinion following the separation of the Indonesian Police from the military in April 1999. For this survey, 507 persons who lived in Metropolitan Jakarta were interviewed. The majority agreed with the proposal to separate the police from the military. However, many felt that this action should be followed by major improvements and adjustments within Polri, particularly in terms of propensity toward bribery and other corruption.

The biggest and the most influential newspaper in the country, *Kompas*, also completed a survey under the title of "The feeling of safety of the inhabitants of Metropolitan Jakarta" (Anonymous, *Kompas*, January 29, 1996). This research concluded that only a small portion of its respondents (15%) had decided to inform the police when there were crime incidents involving themselves, either as victims or eyewitnesses. Another 16% of the respondents said they would rather choose their own way of dealing with the nuisance created by crimes, while the majority of the respondents (69%) chose to keep silent. Among the sample, only 27% of those who had ever been a victim of crime had eventually reported the incident to the police.

Two years later, *Kompas* initiated a series of surveys on the police to check the rates of public opinion toward the police. This was also extremely comprehensive and highly informative. The first survey was conducted in the middle of 1998 and was followed by another survey at the beginning of 1999, which was repeated in late 1999. Each of these surveys involved approximately 900 respondents.

The new *Kompas* results were compelling; whatever good the police may have done, either in exercising their powers proportionally or even when deciding to not take action, there was a very loose association with the optimum image of the police. *Kompas* recorded a stable pattern for public opinion of the police, but the newspaper also argued that the police actually deserved greater appreciation due to their achievements during the survey period. One explanation for the negative perceptions is that while a few people may have been directly affected by the improvements in actions exercised by individual officers, the majority of people in Indonesian society are still terribly cynical of the police as an organization and in relation to their contact with the community.

In relation to research by NGOs within Indonesia, there are two surveys worthy of discussion. First, there was a survey that was coordinated by the Indonesian Police Watch, an Indonesian-based NGO focusing on the police (2000). Collecting data from 1000 respondents in eight major cities, this survey concluded that its respondents had difficulty in finding even one good thing to say about the police. This data revealed a deeply rooted public perception of poor service by and poor dedication of the police. The second survey was conducted by the NGO Institut Studi Politik dan Pemerintahan in Yogyakarta. It undertook a survey in 2001 about the police and its service in relation to Polri's position within the autonomous local government. The new law on local autonomy (Indonesian Law No. 22/1999) stressed that the national police should provide more independence to local police stations, and that local governments should be permitted to provide funds for police operations within their localities, and in return exercise more control over them at the same time. This survey provided support to the assumption that respondents recognized no synergy between the police and their stakeholders in the local area.

Overview of Prior Research

So far, several points have emerged from the surveys discussed. First, it is clear that the means used by the public to observe the quality of policing is usually based on their own perceptions. The issue is that perceptions are often different from reality; the former is based on belief, while the latter is based on facts. However, a report by Redshaw (Redshaw et al. 1997; pp. 283–301) is one of many examples of research conducted on community policing in which the belief was held that it was alright to depend on subjective opinions as one way of evaluating the police.

It can be observed as well, that one problem regarding all the surveys discussed here is the difficulty respondents have to differentiate between the police and the general state apparatus. It is understood that in Indonesia, many parties take part in public order maintenance activities, whether they are the police, the military, the city council, or even teams of privately trained people recruited to help out the police. They are all seemingly part of the recognized state apparatus. The interpretation of the findings of the above research needs to keep this fact in mind.

Moreover, the police are, in fact, in a better situation than the other players in the criminal justice mechanism, owing to a more knowledgeable public and the media, which have a great interest in the police issue. Police leaders should view this as a source of valuable continuous feedback. One example relating to this is contemporary public policy that presupposes police officers should be racially representative of the areas in which they work in order to foster good police–community relations. When citizens were given an opportunity to speak about their preferences regarding the kind of officers they wanted assigned to their neighborhood, some studies found that what citizens wanted more was actually contradictory to conventional wisdom or beliefs. As Weitzer (2000; pp. 313–324) and Walker (1997; pp. 207–226) suggested, what citizens think of as the most desirable scenario may be opposite to what politicians had concluded (e.g., black people would prefer only black police officers working in their respective community).

Researchers and surveys have placed considerable emphasis on the police with little data collection evaluating how the Indonesian prosecutor's office works, how judges and courts operate, or how effective the prison institution is. In some ways, Polri should feel happy about the amount of attention given them by the members of the public. The deep involvement of the police in daily social life has enabled the public to have a broader opportunity to evaluate and comment on the police.

Recent Indonesian Police Research

A recent survey used a public perception questionnaire to analyze a variety of police functions and issues through the use of a 15-question survey that included closed, open-ended, or multiple-choice responses. The survey targeted respondents who were familiar with police operations, either because they had encountered the police in action or because the police had targeted them during their policing activities. With this in mind, the university student population has been identified as the most acceptable group of survey respondents in present day Indonesia. In addition, this survey data was collected when Indonesian society in general suffered major turmoil owing to political and economic instability and crisis. University students had played a very significant role in forcing President Soeharto to step down in 1998 and in demanding that reforms be introduced by the succeeding governments. In addition, public protests or potentially violent demonstrations were, sadly, quite often orchestrated by students. In dealing with these disturbances, the police exhibited a very clumsy performance. While they were acting as a loyal state apparatus in defending Soeharto, student protesters were prevented from getting out of their campuses, in order to prevent greater resistance given that other crowds were waiting outside the university areas for them. However, when Soeharto finally stepped down in May 1998, the police suddenly abandoned their previous position. The police, in general, did not regard students any longer as the enemy and were friendly to them instead, as they expected the students to help them in an effort to separate the police from the military. For example, a big seminar on the future of the police was held in UI in June 1998, which was sponsored by the Indonesian Police. It could well be imagined that this drastic reversal of the police could have been viewed as being unwelcome, but the students ultimately did give full support to police reforms.

A second reason why university students were deliberately chosen as survey respondents involved the fact that they have already had sufficient education in order to assess the past actions of the police. However, it is realized that university students are not totally homogeneous as a group. Variations within the student population may originate from the background of the educational institution, which consists of a blend of family and socio-economic backgrounds and personal orientations and preferences. What is more, students as a category do not belong to a specific region, but fall into another subgroup of "community" as they are people with similar interests and aims. As Correia (2001; pp. 1–11) explained, there are two conceptualizations of "community" recognized so far. The first pertains to the conveniently operationalized geographic notion of community and the second predominant conceptualization of community concerns the network of human interactions and social ties. However, Webb and Katz (1997; pp. 7–23) add that subjective awareness as a group or community may be even more important.

Bearing this in mind, the method of nonrandom and purposive respondent selection used in the survey of students was regarded as appropriate. In order to achieve the maximum inter- and intra-group variability, the study intentionally targeted diverse groups as respondents to serve as the basis for classifying the results gathered.

Police Survey Results

The survey consisted of a total of 201 respondents with a range in age between 18 and 35 years, with a distribution of 87 males and 114 females from nine Jakarta-based universities and 34 departments (ranging from religious studies and industrial engineering to postgraduate programs in politics). Most of the students were in either the second or the third year and were both at the undergraduate or the postgraduate levels.

The following tables delineate the results of the survey.

Not much discussion could be extracted from Table 18.1 due to the simplicity of both the question asked and likewise its response categories.

Table 18.1 Police Activities Most Admired

	Frequency	Percentage
Patrolling/guarding/maintaining safety	67	33.3
Searching/investigating/arresting	65	32.3
Others	25	12.4
Nothing	32	15.9
Irrelevant	6	3.0

Note: $N = 201$; giving no response permitted.

However, the one thing that can be learned from this is that the respondents seem to be similar to the greater public in being familiar with the two general categories of police activities routinely performed while undertaking conventional policing, i.e., public order policing and law enforcement duties (Redshaw et al. 1997; pp. 283–301).

One could perhaps interpret the results as being related to the "Stockholm syndrome." When this analogy is imposed on the police–public relationship, the public can be analogized to a kidnapped woman surrounded by the police performing conventional policing activities. The fact that the respondents of this survey were university students, the facilitators of Indonesian governmental reform who had been in serious confrontation against the police in the last days of President Soeharto's era, supports this interpretation (Table 18.2).

It would appear that the most dangerous enemies of the police are themselves, especially when dealing with money, guns, physical violence, and, lastly, emotions when challenged by a member of the public. Police could improve the impression they make on the public by implementing more active internal review procedures, or, as Walker (1997; pp. 207–226) suggested, by setting up a citizen review or public complaint institution, which could deal with allegations of police deviance.

Data provided in Table 18.3 were obtained from answers to the question, "Which police activities are highly recommended by members of

Table 18.2 Police Activities Most Hated

	Frequency	Percentage
Misusing police power	88	43.8
Accepting bribes	63	31.3
Controlling public protest	18	9.0
Excessive use of violence	13	6.5
All	7	3.5
Irrelevant	5	2.5

Note: $N = 201$; giving no response was permitted.

Table 18.3 Police Activities Highly Recommended

	Frequency	Percentage
Searching/investigating/arresting	82	40.8
Patrolling/guarding/maintaining safety	50	24.9
Public guidance/public service	22	10.9
Others	19	9.5
None	8	4.0
Not knowing	18	9.0

Note: $N = 201$; giving no response permitted.

the public?" Showing similar tendency with result displayed in Table 18.1, these confirmed that the image of the Indonesian Police is determined by conventional policing activities. By way of comparison, this is different to the perspectives noted by Redshaw and Sanders (1995; pp. 56–60) and Redshaw et al. (1997; pp. 283–301), whose list of core policing values has been recognized by police administrators. In both surveys, the police were given a strong public recommendation that delineated that police respond quickly to emergencies.

Modern policing styles, namely community policing, do not seem to be popular in the public's mind within Indonesia. This is shown by how seldom the respondents indicated that the public guidance/public service model should be implemented by the Indonesian Police. This would seem to indicate that the public has little desire in influencing policing decisions (recognized as one of the primary principles of community policing).

Another item worth noting concerns the possibility of bias included in the above responses. Conventional policing activities have long been the target of criticism and anger by some members of the public because of the prevalence of violence used against them and the traditional lack of accountability and corruption. Yet, what is of concern is the fact that since the police consistently emphasize law enforcement related activities and also public order management and, at the same time, treat the community policing-related concepts of public guidance/public service as marginal, the public has never developed its own ideas in terms of alternative policing styles. One could interpret the above results in another way. By performing law enforcement and order maintenance functions, the police are actually meeting the public needs, and are therefore sensitive to the demands of the community. Below are comments from an Indonesian Police general:

> We know, being the true believer of what we are now, that we have created a cost which sometimes we can not afford to pay. The problem is that there are too many crooks out there, too many vigilant people and too many violent demonstrations that need to be barricaded. Dealing with those, talking and smiling are no longer enough.

The pattern of responses given by the respondents regarding police practices that need to be eliminated (Table 18.4) revealed again that the public has a strong belief in and inclination toward the concept of the conventional policing style (Table 18.5). These bad practices can, presumably, be easily identified within a police organization that strongly executes a conventional policing style. As can be concluded, from an organizational standpoint, it is a strong police subculture that strengthens bad practices associated with conventional policing. Consequently, any efforts taken by police management anywhere to eliminate them would likely fail.

Table 18.4   Police Practices Recommended to Be Eliminated

	Frequency	Percentage
Being not disciplined/abusing police power	68	33.8
Bad activities involving public money	48	24.7
Bad activities involving excessive violence	31	15.4
Riot control	6	3.0
None	6	3.0
All	2	1.0
Not knowing	33	16.4

Note: N = 201; giving no response permitted.

Table 18.5   Type of Police Preferred

	Frequency	Percentage
Those being close to the community	101	50.2
Those emphasizing professionalism	78	38.8
Both	12	6.0
None of them	6	3.0
Not knowing	4 2	0

Note: N = 201; giving no response permitted.

As seen in Table 18.5, when questioned about the type of police preferred, the two most popular answers were, "the police who are close to the community" and "the police who emphasize professionalism." In reality, those two types are difficult to implement within the same time frame, since each has a different perspective concerning working procedures, parameters of success, steps of action, and also the issue of the rehabilitation of parties involved in cases having been drawn to the attention of the police. Another thing that should be taken into consideration is that the Indonesian Police and the public have different perspectives of the notion of "professionalism" as it is referred to by the police.

When asking the respondents about the type of policing preferred, for example, the respondents appear to prefer emphasizing police closeness to the community rather than just professionalism. While the former is a concept that is closer to a policing style that emphasizes quality, the latter is the favorite concept among the police who prefer more conventional methods.

Becoming professional on the one side and being close to the community on the other has, therefore, become a dilemma for the police. To be both, some believe, may be impossible or at least difficult to implement and achieve. While being close to the community seems to be preferred, it is not exactly desirable. However, due to the fact that "professional" police are admired

Table 18.6   Why Choose Police Who Emphasize Professionalism?

	Frequency	Percentage
The primary job of the police	36	17.9
Vital role being a public protector	28	13.9
The only way to eliminate crimes	16	8.0

Note: N = 201; giving no response permitted.

because of their correct attitude toward enforcement of the law, they may not be viewed as dependable as community policing officers with whom the public may be more familiar.

Basically, the pattern of responses given for this question, as outlined in Table 18.6, is simply inconsistent with the question posed in Table 18.5. Being professional would imply improved quality of police service. Given the past heritage of the Indonesian Police, which was full of corruption, brutality, and abuse, the Indonesian public has acknowledged the notion that being a professional cop is still better than nothing. When being professional, the police would likely be acting as a straightforward public protector, thus lending support to the second more popular response (13.9%).

There is a general assumption that if the police were close to the community, they might perform as indicated by the three top responses indicated in Table 18.7. Unfortunately, as the public would have to consent to what they actually want from the police, the policing style actually undertaken by the police may not fit the public's expectation. From the perspective of the police organization, the outcomes pointed out by the three top responses in Table 18.7 could be achieved by the availability of a rapid response unit, a high distribution of closed-circuit TVs in the surrounding neighborhood, or by taking immediate summary action against a suspect who disturbs public order.

Table 18.7   Why Choose Police Who Are Close to the Community?

	Frequency	Percentage
More effective in preventing crime	39	19.5
Encouraging public support/sympathy	38	18.9
More able to help people's need	32	15.9
Officer becoming more sensitive	3	1.5
Activity done after police working hours	16	8.0

Note: N = 201; giving no response permitted.

Discussion

One could conclude that a high-quality policing style would include three dimensions that involve the target of policing work, the role of police functions, and lastly, the quality of policing work.

Indonesian society, in general, has been the recipient of immature, unprogressive, and low professionalism exhibited by the policing styles of the Polri. As a consequence, only a small number of people (especially the ones who have been living abroad) have a rather different experience in terms of alternative police behavior and organizational policies. Therefore, one could then somewhat understand if the respondents, in reality, propose something they actually did not support.

As a result, both the public and the police are drawn into yet another paradoxical dimension of the police/public relationship. On the one hand, the public has never had the experience that would allow them to believe that the police could also be involved in initiatives that are new. On the other hand, when the police develop a program that is not only new, but also a high-quality one, they have first to determine whose justifications (the police's or the public's) they will use as the foundation for program development. However, a public mandate might be lacking.

Further implications regarding this are that the state itself and its apparatus should be the party or parties who initiate a new style, build up new fundamental understandings, or incorporate new ideas into the operational agenda. The role of the public in Indonesia seems negligible, and it apparently applies limited if any influence in pressuring the police to perform better.

Lastly, another conclusion that can be elicited is that policing is perhaps a rather elitist issue. The public, as reflected by the responses from the relatively well-educated participants in this survey, seem more familiar with current police policy and operations rather than acknowledging or accepting the concept that they could be the facilitators responsible for developing police strategy and action.

References

Anonymous (1996), The feeling of safety of the inhabitants of metropolitan Jakarta, *Kompas*, January 29, 1996.

Anwar, D.F. (2001), Indonesia's transition to democracy: Challenges and prospects, in Kingsburry, D. and Budiman, A. (eds.), *Indonesia: The Uncertain Transition*, Adelaide, Australia: Crawford House Publishing.

Correia, M.E. (2001), The conceptual ambiguity of community in community policing—Filtering the muddy waters, *Policing: An International Journal of Police Strategies and Management*, **23**(2), 218–233.

Cribb, R. and Brown, C. (1995), *Modern Indonesia: A History since 1945*, London, U.K.: Longman.

Djiwandono, J.S. (2003), Role of the IMF in Indonesia's financial crisis, in Soesastro, H., Smith, A.L., and Ling, H.M. (eds.), *Governance in Indonesia: Challenges Facing the Megawati Presidency*, Singapore: ISEAS.

Indonesian Police Watch (2000), Performance of the Metro Jaya Regional Police in solving criminal cases: Period of January–June 2000, unpublished brief report.

International Crisis Group (2000), Indonesia: Keeping the military under control, Asia Report no. 9, International Crisis Group, Jakarta, Indonesia/Brussels, Belgium, September 5, 2000.

Koenarto (1997), *Etika Kepolisian*, Jakarta, Indonesia: Cipta Manunggal.

Kuppuswamy, C.S. (2002), Indonesia: Armed forces and their diminishing political role, Paper no. 528, South Asia Analysis Group, Noida, India, www.saag.org/papers6/paper528.html

Markas Besar ABRI (1998), ABRI Abad XXI: Redefinisi, Reposisi dan Reaktualisasi Peran ABRI, Jakarta, Indonesia: Mabes ABRI.

Redshaw, J. and Sanders, F. (1995), What does the public want?, *Policing*, 11(1), 56–60.

Redshaw, J., Mawby, R.I., and Bunt, P. (1997), Evaluating core policing in Britain: The views of police and consumers, *International Journal of the Sociology of Law*, **25**, 283–301.

Singh, B. (2000), *Succession Politics in Indonesia: The 1998 Presidential Elections and the Fall of Suharto*, New York: St. Martin's Press Inc.

The Editors (October 2000), Changes in civil-military relations since the fall of Suharto, *Indonesia*, **70**, 125–138, Cornell University Press.

Walker, S. (1997), Complaints against the police: A focus group study of citizen perceptions, goals and expectations, *Criminal Justice Review*, **22**(2), 207–226, autumn.

Webb, V.J. and Katz, C.M. (1997), Citizen ratings of the importance of community policing activities, *Policing*, **20**(1), 7–23.

Weitzer, R. (2000), White, black, or blue cops? Race and citizen assessments of police officers, *Journal of Criminal Justice*, **28**, 313–324.

Yusra, A. and Ramadhan, K.H., 1993, *Hoegeng: Polisi Idaman dan Kenyataan*, Jakarta, Indonesia: Pustaka Sinar Harapan.

Policing Challenges in Turkey: Dealing with Honor Killings as Crime or as Culturally Accepted Norm

19

TÜLIN GÜNŞEN İÇLI

Contents

Introduction

Honor killing in Turkey is a form of violence that stems from the traditional value system of Turkey's sociocultural structure. This customary notion of "honor" in Asia and the Middle East must also be included when analyzing the concept of honor or "töre" killings. The notions of dignity and honor are among the basic values in determining behaviors and attitudes in female–male relationships, in the family structure and marriage, and in gender roles in Turkey, especially in rural and poor areas. These concepts not only reflect face-to-face, primary features of social relations in Turkey, but also mirror a social rather than an individual character. The killing of a female by a male relative in the name of protecting the family's honor and dignity has been in practice since a very long time. Suspicion of an extramarital sexual affair, infidelity to the husband, flirting with other men, eloping with a lover, and even being raped can all be reasons why killing women and girls has been justified in order to protect the family's honor and reputation.

The frequency of honor killings in Islamic societies is a contradiction. Although the people that commit these murders claim that their actions are justified, Islam strictly forbids killing as strongly as other notable religions. Particularly in rural communities, face-to-face relationships are dominant and misinterpretation of customs routinely facilitates these actions. In the sociocultural structure of Turkey, having a sexual affair before marriage and losing one's virginity dishonor the female's family and mean loss of her chastity (or purity). There are many in Turkey that believe that the honor and dignity of the family has to be absolved and this task is normally reserved for male members of the family (Sever and Gökçeçiçek, 1999).

In rural Turkey and in many traditional societies within the Middle East, a woman is often considered as the property of a man. This concept thus enables men in the family to protect a female family member's chastity and to decide about major issues occurring in her life. A woman's behaviors and attitudes are kept under control by her father and brother(s) before marriage. She is kept under pressure to behave acceptably and after marriage the husband takes over this control mechanism. A woman's sexual behavior is also under the guard of her male family members as well. Tradition and custom have dictated that in case of infidelity or premarital sexual behavior involving a woman, even with her consent, the father and older brothers understand that the honor and dignity of the family have to be absolved by making the woman and her lover pay for their actions, usually by killing. It is interesting to highlight that perpetrators of such killings in some Mediterranean and Middle Eastern countries are routinely not punished, particularly in rural areas or in those that accept traditional Islamic Sharia law as the norm. This would reveal society's tolerance and permission for such a significant and apparent civil right's abuse in this region of the world.

As a result, a woman's unjustified sexual actions, at least in the eyes of male members of her family, are used as justification for her murder by one or more males within her family, often involving her brothers. In Turkey and other traditional Islamic societies, the toleration or lack of sufficient punishment for these crimes often encourages these kinds of murders. In patriarchal societies, the male's dominance results in his accepted superiority within the family and his responsibility to protect the family's honor. In some cases, a female can also be punished for sexually related violence and rape that occurred without her consent. There have been many instances in which males of one family have forcefully gang raped a female in another family in order to retaliate against them for some prior misconduct, in line with another long standing tradition called the blood feud.

Changing the values within sociocultural structures apparent in Turkey and other regional countries has proven to be difficult. This is often compounded by poor educational standards in many rural neighborhoods. The prevention of honor killings is the primary task of the local police agency, but they can be assisted by other players within the government structure including social welfare and educational mechanisms. The presence of international nongovernmental organizations in areas of high incidence of töre killings could also enhance prevention efforts. It would also be beneficial for federal governments in this region to provide adequate training to law enforcement, prosecutorial, and judicial personnel to ensure that they fully comprehend that these honor murders are actually serious crimes that must be properly punished, rather than accepted as a local accepted practice.

Honor Killing within the Turkish Penal Code

The crime of murder is delineated within the former Turkish Penal Code (Turkish Law 765). In Article 448, the penalty for murder is outlined as 20–30 years of imprisonment. In Article 449, regarding the crime of qualified murder, the clause "…if murder is committed against wife, husband, brother, sister, father, stepmother, stepdaughter or stepson, father-in-law, mother-in-law, grooms, brides; the punishment will be the life imprisonment" has been defined. When the previous penal code was valid, honor killings were only addressed in these statutes and the punishments could also be increased from 20 years incarceration to life in prison. The former Turkish Penal Code contained no other article about honor killings.

The crime of murder is now described in the new Turkish Penal Code (Turkish Law 5237) within Articles 81 and 82. According to Article 81, "(t)he person who kills a person intentionally … will be punished with life imprisonment." Article 82 also delineates the types of qualified murder which would allow increases in punishment. According to Article 82, "if the crime is committed with the intention of honor, the person will be punished with qualified life imprisonment." The new Turkish Penal Code clearly emphasizes the concept of honor killing and thereby is attempting to prevent honor killings and has been designed to create a deterrent effect.

Within Article 38 of the new Turkish Penal Code, the acts of abetting, assisting, or supporting criminal activity are described. According to Article 38, "(t)he person who abets will be punished with the same punishment as the punishment of the main crime." Prior to implementation of the new law in Turkey, those who assisted in the honor killings were normally not punished and those who took responsibility for this crime were only minimally punished, if at all. Clearly the Turkish administration has taken credible action to deter honor killings. The true question is whether this legislation is enforced in practice. This will be examined later.

Of other note, according to Article 51 of former Turkish Penal Code, "(i)f a person commits a crime with the effect of the feelings of rage and anger generated by unjust provocation and if it is punished with death penalty, the punishment will be decreased." The statement of "unjust provocation" is unclear and subjective. In western terms, this would be similar to reductions in punishment when perpetrators of murder are given lighter sentences if emotional distress plays a role in the criminal action. As a result of this statute, honor killing were often previously handled taking this acception into consideration. For example, if a young girl went on a date to the movies with her boyfriend, then this could be considered as an "unjust provocation" which allowed a reduction in punishment. However, within Article 29 of the new Turkish Penal Code, the term "unjust act" is used, not "unjust provocation." As a result this has been interpreted to mean that only illegal acts will be considered in this context. Thus, a more legal and more objective assessment has been created.

Studies on Honor Crimes in Other Countries

Every year throughout the world, thousands of girls and women are killed by their husbands, fathers, or brothers. They are killed mainly based on the suspicion of their male relatives (Tripathi and Supriya, 2005).

In many societies, the meaning assigned to honor and dignity has often involved a distorted form of social values. Loftin and McDowal (2003) state that in some of the northern and western regions of the United States, honor related killings routinely occur and are accepted by the local population. As a clearer example, in some neighborhoods with lower socioeconomic development in large cities in America, residents often support the notion of killing someone who disrespected them in order to save face. While not legally acceptable, there is strong support that the community often does not perceive these murders as criminal actions, but rather as an expected norm. According to Loftin and McDowal (2003), cultural stability effects discussion-related killings positively, while they impact felony-related murders negatively.

Killings related to jealousy occurred also within Pakistan, Oman, Tunisia, the United Arab Emirates, Jordan, Kuwait, Egypt, Morocco, Iraq, and India (Women's International Network News, 2000). According to the results of research recently conducted in the country of Jordan (Kulwicki, 2002), 38 (42%) of 89 court files involved a murder in which a female was involved. Of those, 23 (61%) of these court cases were categorized as honor killings. When the age range of the victims was further analyzed, it was revealed that 38% of them were in the age group 17–20, followed by the age groups 21–25, and 31–35. Although the educational level and socioeconomical status of the majority of the group are not known, it was reported that illegitimate pregnancy, premarital sexual contact, adultery, and unapproved marriage were stated as the "causes" for these murders. In these cases, the most likely perpetrator was a brother of the victim. However, the most interesting point revealed by this research was that one-third of the offenders were sentenced to only 1 week to 1 year of imprisonment. The second most common punishment was 1 year in jail.

Adler (2003) has analyzed homicides within families committed between 1875 and 1920 in Chicago (United States) and has inferred that in that period murder rates had increased approximately 300%. While studying these domestic homicides, Adler has also mentioned the homicide of another male family member. Scholars have often treated family violence as a single category and have argued that domestic violence typically reflects conflict over gender roles. Such a focus has been well placed. But if data on domestic homicide in Chicago from 1875 to 1920 are separated by ethnicity and race, important patterns emerge. This analysis revealed that domestic homicide assumed culturally specific variations. German immigrants, Italian immigrants, and African Americans killed loved ones for different reasons, at different rates, and with different family members being involved. Although the violence revolved around challenges to gender identity and expectations, each group defined such challenges in distinct ways, reflecting a complex blend of cultural assumptions and material circumstances (Adler, 2003). Long standing cultural ideologies have traditionally been used to support violent acts, even serious crimes like murder.

Research on Honor Killings in Turkey

In order to better understand the concept of honor killings in Turkey, it is useful to reference studies on other violence targeting women. The study by İçli et al. (1995) was the first on this subject in Turkey. The research mainly sought to examine women who were victims of spousal violence in Turkey. In this respect, the social, cultural, and economic characteristics of abused (battered) women and their familial relations were studied in order to determine the possible reasons underlying the violence. This research also sought to highlight the cultural acceptability of physical aggression especially within the family. This research drew a sample from the married female population living in Ankara, İstanbul, and İzmir (the three largest cities in Turkey) by utilizing stratified cluster sampling. The sample included women from three different socioeconomic strata: the poor, the middle, and the upper classes. The sample consisted of 1070 married women. The incidence of violence against the married female sample in this study was found to be 21% and most of the women who were subject to violence at the hands of their husbands had low socioeconomic status. Economic problems were noted as the main reason for these females becoming subject to violence. Most of them were married at young ages and their husbands were chosen not by themselves but by their family. As a result, it could be interpreted that the main reason that these victims stay in an abusive relationship is economic dependence on the husband. Another important factor that inhibits the battered women from leaving their husbands may be the fear of disapproval from family and friends. According to the final conclusions of this study, the most determining factor was found to have a cultural context. In Turkish society, getting a divorce is a culturally disapproved event especially on the part of women. Traditionally, a married woman is expected to maintain the family unity, to be faithful to her husband, and not to raise her children without a father. Unfortunately, the common practice in many cases is to expose the female to brutal physical sanctions by her husband if he does not agree with her behavior (İçli, 1995).

In order to better determine the causal and regional range of crime and criminal profiles in Turkey, a survey was conducted involving 4000 convicted prisoners chosen by systematic sampling (İçli, 1993). Pursuant to this comprehensive research, the most relevant and common reasons for murders in rural villages are honor and jealousy, and the second important reason was the blood feud. Especially in rural country sides and despite the severity of the penalty, it could be interpreted that homicide was being used as a means for preventing conflict. This indicates how cultural ideologies and practices are influential in determining personal behaviors. Furthermore, the homicides committed because of a blood feud and for maintaining family honor in accordance with these accepted customs continues to gain social acceptance. This indicates a striking contradiction in that an action that is qualified as anomie in the social structure can actually be conceived as an expected and approved action within the cultural structure (İçli, 1993).

In another study about homicide, 7% of convicted prisoners have stated that they believed by absolving their honor and dignity, their reputation would be enhanced in the eyes of the community and within their own families (İçli, 1987). According to the results of later research made with the aim of examining the criminal profile within Turkey (İçli and Diğerleri, 2007), while 40% of convicted sex offenders thought that the blood feud should be discontinued, more than half of the same convicts (51%) stated that where honor is concerned, actions based on blood feud should be continued. Interestingly, nearly half of the respondents (48%) thought that offenders should face a more severe penalty if the crime is committed against themselves or if it involved one of their female relatives. Consequently, it is proposed that convicted prisoners are sensitive to the notion of "honor" (İçli and Diğerleri, 2007).

In general terms, within Turkey and other Middle Eastern countries, honor is a social value that generally determines sexual behaviors and attitudes within the cultural structure and honor has clearly been granted with particular importance. Being virtuous is an important obligation of women. As a result, a woman should avoid some behaviors and should obey the rules culturally determined in order not to tarnish her honor. The task of protecting a woman's honor is given to man. In other words, when honor is lost or tarnished, it is generally absolved by violence by a male relative.

In support of the above, the results of a field survey conducted in Turkey by Öğün (2005) involving 879 convicted prisoners between 1993 and 1995 revealed again that protecting honor was the preliminary reason for murder. Another significant finding was that homicides involving females occurred twice as often as murders of men. In honor killings, the most important factor was found to be spousal or parental conflict. In the event that a woman believed that she lost her respect and power because of a conflict with her partner, these females often believed that they could commit murder against him; therefore, honor murders could also be committed by a wife (Öğün, 2005).

While the meaning of honor differs from culture to culture, practices surrounding honor killings also vary. In Turkey, in order to put an end to an honor killing, a woman is sometimes married into another family even without being asked for her permission. This type of marriage is called "berdel" and is perceived as a peace offering between the two families.

The Turkish General Directorate of Security has analyzed the murder statistics that are related to the notion of töre (moral laws). They have been depicted in printed and mass media in recent years and are registered within 81 provincial security directorates; these reports examine various variables. These statistics are the first official data in Turkey on this subject. It should be noted that some of these deaths are often not reported to the Turkish police and are not counted in statistics, and some of the honor killings are recorded as accidents or suicidal deaths.

In order to better understand this phenomenon within Turkey, this comprehensive analysis was conducted. A total of 1091 töre cases have been revealed that involve murders that reportedly have been committed on the basis of a blood feud, marital or family disputes, sexual harassment or abuse, disapproved or forbidden relationships, rape or where the issue of honor played a role. These statistics are displayed more clearly in the tables and figures below.

Within the 1091 "töre" related files examined, it was revealed that 322 (or 30%) of them involve murder due to honor, while 318 (or 29%) were related to family conflict (Figure 19.1, Table 19.1).

When the regional distribution of "töre" cases are analyzed, it is disclosed that the Marmara region ranks first with 20% of the total cases and the Aegean region follows next with 209 incidents or 19% (Figure 19.2, Table 19.2).

When individual cities within the regions are examined, Figure 19.3 shows that Ankara ranks first with the rate of 10% and İstanbul and İzmir follow, respectively, with a rate of 9% (Figure 19.3).

Of the total "töre" cases, there were 1593 total suspects and 1413 of them were male and 180 were female (Figure 19.4, Table 19.3).

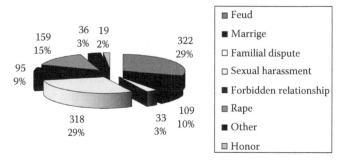

Figure 19.1 Causal distribution of 1091 cases that happened in police district between 2000 and 2005.

Table 19.1   Causal Distribution of 1091 "Töre" Cases

Cities	Blood Feud	Marriage	Family Dispute	Sexual Harassment	Forbidden Relationship	Rape	Other	Honor	Total
81 cities	109	33	318	95	159	36	19	322	1091

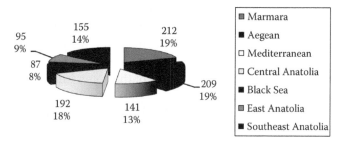

Figure 19.2 Regional distribution of 1091 cases that happened in police district between 2000 and 2005.

Table 19.2   Regional Distribution of the 1091 "Töre" Cases between 2000 and 2005

District	Marmara	Aegean	Mediterranean	Central Anatolia	Black Sea	Eastern Anatolia	Southeastern Anatolia	Total
Cases	212	209	141	192	87	95	155	1091

Within the "töre" cases the total number of murder victims was 1190 while 710 of them were male and 480 were female (Figure 19.5, Table 19.4).

When the age range of female suspects was analyzed, the age group 19–25 ranked first with 28% and the age group 26–30 ranked second with a rate of 23% (Figure 19.6, Table 19.5).

When the age range of male suspects was analyzed, it is seen that the age group 19–25 committed the most "töre" crimes with the rate of 22%

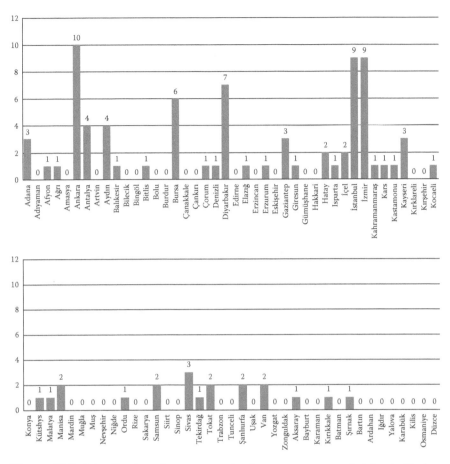

Figure 19.3 Distribution of cases examined as percentages of cities in Turkey (years 2000–2005)—the police district level.

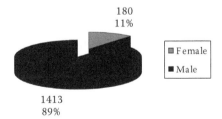

Figure 19.4 Gender of suspects who committed murder between 2000 and 2005.

and the age group 26–30 followed with 18%. One interesting note was the relatively high crime rates of juveniles under 18 (Figure 19.7, Table 19.6).

When female victims are analyzed, it was found that females in the age group 19–25 were

Table 19.3 Suspect's Gender

Female	180	Male	1,413

Figure 19.5 Gender of victims killed between 2000 and 2005.

killed most with the rate of 20% and females from the age group 26–30 followed with a rate of 19% (Figure 19.8, Table 19.7).

Table 19.4 Victim's Gender			
Female	480	Male	710

When male victims are analyzed, it is found that males in the age group 46 and over were killed most with the rate of 20%, and males from the age group of 31–35 followed this rank with 18% (Figure 19.9, Table 19.8).

When the suspects were analyzed with respect to birth place within the context of regions, it is seen that 24% of suspects were from the southeastern Anatolia region and 21% of them from the eastern Anatolia region. When offenders in western cities are analyzed, it is seen that most of them were originally from eastern regions (which tend to be more traditional ideologically) and the Marmara region was at the bottom of the ranking list (Figure 19.10, Table 19.9).

When the suspects are analyzed with respect to place of birth according to birth certificate, it was revealed that the southeastern Anatolia region ranked first with the rate of 24% and eastern Anatolia region followed with 21%. Interestingly, it was also disclosed that the place of birth of those convicted for crimes committed in western Turkish cities was predominantly in eastern Turkish regions. Also, while the western Marmara region ranked first according to the range of crime, the Marmara region ranked last with a rate of 8% according to birth place of suspects (Figure 19.11, Table 19.10).

When the birth place of victims was evaluated, it was shown that the eastern and central Anatolia regions tied for first place with matching rates of 19% and the southeastern Anatolia region followed them with a rate of 17% (Figure 19.12, Table 19.11).

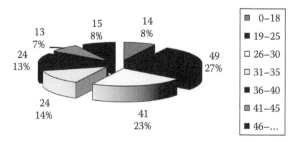

Figure 19.6 Age of female suspects.

In the analysis of the murder victim's place of birth according to birth certificate, it is discovered that while the eastern Anatolia region ranked first with 20%, the central Anatolia region followed with 19% and the southeastern Anatolia region with 17%. Of note, while the Marmara region ranked first in crime rate, it ranked last according to the victim's birth place based on birth certificate with a rate of 9% (Figure 19.13, Table 19.12).

It would have been believed that the eastern Anatolia region would lead in the incidence of honor and "töre" murders, but in fact, the Marmara and the Aegean regions ranked surprisingly first and second, respectively. When the honor murder rate was analyzed by city, the number one ranked city was the Turkish capital Ankara and not one of the cities to the east.

Table 19.5   Age Ranges of Female Suspects

Female Suspect's Age		
0–18	14	
19–25	49	
26–30	41	
31–35	24	180
36–40	47	
41–45	13	
46 and older	15	

While 89% of people involved in the honor and "töre" cases were male, 60% of people killed during 2000–2005 were male. When both genders were considered, the highest rate for the suspect by age belonged to the age group 19–25. Also the age groups 19–25 and 26–30 constitute the first two ranks in the age range of murdered women. As for males, the highest rates belong to the age groups 46 and older and 31–35. In clearer terms, young women and men were more likely to kill young women and middle aged men. Convicted suspects were mostly from eastern and southeastern Anatolia and they killed victims who are from eastern and central Anatolia. As it was stated previously, honor and töre killings are related to the more traditional culture of eastern and southeastern Anatolia. One could therefore conclude that the most important reason why honor and töre killings occurred in urban areas was the maintenance of customs and cultural ideology involving honor after their migration to city centers.

The author conducted research research on 144 files from the Turkish General Directorate of Security involving honor killings between 1995 and 2007.

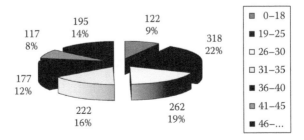

Figure 19.7 Age of male suspects.

When the correlation between the gender of the offender and the murder weapon was examined, it was found to be statistically significant (Table 19.13, $p > .05$).

When the place of murder, and the relationship between the offender and victim were analyzed utilizing cross tabulation, it was revealed that while relatives and couples are killed inside, foreigners are killed outside. There was no significant correlation between the offender–victim relationship and the place of the murder (Table 19.14).

When the correlation between the gender of offenders and murder weapon were evaluated using cross tabulation, it was disclosed that for both genders the most common murder weapon was a knife. Approximately 52% of males and 40% of females used a knife as the murder weapon. The chi-square test of the variables did not reveal a significant finding (Table 19.15).

The above analysis indicated that the attacks using a knife most often involved one stroke (Tables 19.16 and 19.17).

The age groups 16–30 and 31–45 were the most likely to use a knife as the murder weapon. The rate of strangulation was highest in the age group 31–45 followed by the age group 26–30. One explanation is that since murder by strangulation requires physical strength, it was more common in the younger age groups (Tables 19.18 and 19.19).

Table 19.6 Age Ranges of Male Suspects

	Male Suspect's Age	
0–18	122	
19–25	318	
26–30	262	
31–35	222	1413
36–40	177	
41–45	117	
46 and Older	195	

Related Correlation 1

		Offenders' Age	Victim's Age
Offender's age	Pearson correlation	1	0.182[a]
	Sig. (2-tailed)		0.029
	N	144	144
Victims' age	Pearson correlation	0.182[a]	1
	Sig. (2-tailed)	0.029	
	N	144	144

[a] Correlation is significant at the 0.05 level (2-tailed).

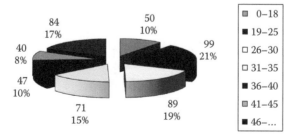

Figure 19.8 Age of female victims.

A significant correlation at the level of 0.05 was found between the age of the offender and the age of the victim. In accordance with this, one could easily conclude that young offenders kill or attack young victims.

Related Correlation 2

		Victim–Offender Relationship	Number of Strokes
Offender–victim relationship	Pearson correlation	1	−0.017
	Sig. (2-tailed)		0.871
	N	144	93
Number of strokes	Pearson correlation	−0.017	1
	Sig. (2-tailed)	0.871	
	N	93	93

In summary, the murder weapon mainly used in honor and töre killings by both genders was a knife. The correlation between the ages of the offender and the victim was found to be statistically significant. The examination also revealed that while acquaintances were killed inside, strangers were killed outside. This result is in line with normal findings involving crimes against persons.

In statistics supplied by the Turkish General Directorate of Security on honor and töre killings, the predominant reason for these murders was found to be familial dispute, while sexual misconduct ranked second. Forbidden relationships, blood feud, and disapproved marriages were found to be other reasons for these incidents (Table 19.20).

Table 19.21 evaluates the number of murders and offenders according to reported reason for murders between 2000 and 2006 as it relates to statistics supplied by the Turkish General Directorate of Security.

Table 19.7 Age Ranges of Female Victims

Female Victim's Age		
0–18	50	
19–25	99	
26–30	89	
31–35	71	480
36–40	47	
41–45	40	
46 and Older	84	

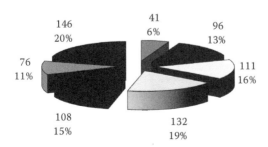 

Figure 19.9 Age of male victims.

According to a report by the Human Rights Directorate under the supervision of the Turkish Prime Minister, research on media reports in 71 Turkish cities indicated that in the last 5 years more than 1000 people were victims of honor killings. This analysis searched for the causes of murders committed for honor and the distribution of these murders according to cities and regions. According to the report, 948 honor killings were committed in between 2003 and 2008. If one adds the 117 related murder from 2008, the total count of the reported honor killings rises to 1065. The number of murders detected is given in the report as 150 in 2003, 175 in both 2004 and 2005, 216 in 2006, and 220 in 2007. Quite surprising is that despite the improvements in Turkish legislation on civil rights and women's rights in recent years, the fact that these types of murder continue reveal that the issue is multifaceted and involve economical, social, and cultural factors.

Table 19.8   Age Ranges of Male Victims

Male Victim's Age		
0–18	41	710
19–25	96	
26–30	111	
31–35	132	710
36–40	108	
41–45	76	
46 and older	146	

Furthermore, in this critical report, the final conclusion noted that the most important reasons for the "töre" killings involved the female victim's behaviors due to her traditional patriarchal gender role in association with the notion of honor. While the number of murders committed directly because of honor was determined to be over 300, this number constitutes 30% of the total number of reported murders. If the 94 people murdered due to disapproved relationships, another 71 due to premarital sexual contact, and 17 more due to allegations of rape are included, the rate where honor played a role exceeds 50%. Familial dispute, blood feud, and forbidden relationships were mentioned as the other reasons for these murders.

The report also analyzed the distribution of murders according to city location. This examination revealed that Istanbul ranked first with 167 murders, then Ankara with 144, İzmir with 121, Diyarbakır with 69, Bursa with 58, Antalya with 46, Aydın with 38, Kayseri with 34, Samsun with 32, and Sakarya with 30.

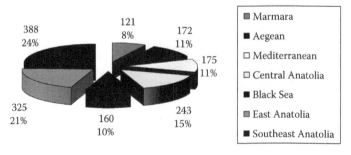

Figure 19.10 Regional distribution of suspects according to birth place.

Table 19.9   Distribution of Suspects according to the Place of Birth

Marmara	121
Aegean	172
Mediterranean	175
Central Anatolia	243
Black Sea	160
Eastern Anatolia	325
Southeastern Anatolia	388
Total	1584

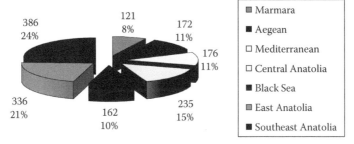

Figure 19.11 Regional distribution of suspects according to birth place certificate.

Table 19.10   Distribution of Suspects according to the Place of Birth Certificate

Marmara	121
Aegean	172
Mediterranean	176
Central Anatolia	223
Black Sea	141
Eastern Anatolia	336
Southeastern Anatolia	386
Total	1588

When examined by regional distribution, the Turkish regions that have the highest murder rates are: Marmara Region 294 (28%), Aegean Region 214 (20%), central Anatolia 213 (20%), southeastern Anotolia 130 (12%), eastern Anotolia 89 (8%), and Black Sea Region 62 (6%). While the rate of murders committed in eastern and southeastern Anatolia was found to be less than in Western Turkey, nearly half of the people who committed the murders were from eastern and southeastern Anatolia.

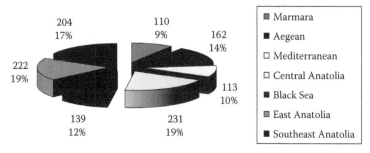

Figure 19.12 Regional distribution of victims according to birth place.

Table 19.11   Distribution of Victims according to the Place of Birth

Marmara	110
Aegean	162
Mediterranean	113
Central Anatolia	139
Black Sea	139
Eastern Anatolia	222
Southeastern Anatolia	204
Total	1181

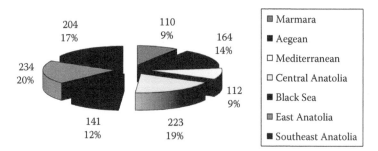

Figure 19.13 Regional distribution of victims according to birth place certificate.

Some of the other more notable findings in this report include

- as the educational level decreases, the number of offenders and victims increases;
- ...not only females but also males can be victims; even the number of men killed is more than the numbers of murdered females;
- Sometimes women were the offenders of these murders;

Table 19.12 Distribution of Victims according to the Place of Birth by Birth Certificate

Marmara	110
Aegean	164
Mediterranean	112
Central Anatolia	235
Black Sea	141
Eastern Anatolia	234
Southeastern Anatolia	204
Total	1188

Table 19.13 Cross Tabulation of Offender's Gender and Murder Weapon Relation

	Murder Weapon				
	Knife	Firearm	Battery	Strangulation	Total
Offenders' gender					
Male					
Count	60	47	11	10	128
Row percentage	46.9%	36.7%	8.6%	7.8%	100.0%
Column percentage	89.6%	88.7%	91.7%	83.3%	88.9%
Female					
Count	7	6	1	2	16
Row percentage	43.8%	37.5%	6.3%	12.5%	100.0%
Column percentage	10.4%	11.3%	8.3%	16.7%	11.1%
Total					
Count	67	53	12	12	144
Total row percentage	46.5%	36.8%	8.3%	8.3%	100.0%
Total column percentage	100.0%	100.0%	100.0%	100.0%	100.0%

Related chi-square tests

	Value	df	Asymp. Sig. (Two-Sided)
Pearson chi-square	0.501[a]	3	0.919
Likelihood ratio	0.465	3	0.926
Linear-by-linear association	0.174	1	0.676
No. of valid cases	144		

[a] 2 cells (25.0%) have expected count less than 5. The minimum expected count is 1.33.

Table 19.14   Cross Tabulation of the Place of Murder and the Offender–Victim Relationship

	Relatives	Couples	Acquaintances	Foreigners	Total
The place of murder					
House					
Count	29	29	2	11	71
Row percentage	40.8%	40.8%	2.8%	15.5%	100.0%
Column percentage	55.8%	70.7%	22.2%	26.2%	49.3%
Outside					
Count	20	9	6	27	62
Row percentage	32.3%	14.5%	9.7%	43.5%	100.0%
Column percentage	38.5%	22.0%	66.7%	64.3%	43.1%
Working place					
Count	3	3	1	4	11
Row percentage	27.3%	27.3%	9.1%	36.4%	100.0%
Column percentage	5.8%	7.3%	11.1%	9.5%	7.6%
Total					
Count	52	41	9	42	144
Total of row	36.1%	28.5%	6.3%	29.2%	100.0%
Total row percentage	100.0%	100.0%	100.0%	100.0%	100.0%

(Offender–Victim Relationship spanning Relatives, Couples, Acquaintances, Foreigners)

- The rate of juvenile suspects was quite low (9%); the most common age range of the suspects was between 19 and 35;
- The severity of the criminal penalties did not create a deterrent effect on others; it is believed that many suspects rarely regret these crimes;
- The development of women's shelters in number and in quality will become a more important instrument in producing more influential and embodiment solution to combat töre and honour killings, to prevent violence to woman.*

According to the results of a study conducted by Sır in 2003 that surveyed 430 people, most of the participants defined the notion of honor as involving "my wife, my sister, my mother;" "religious order;" and "chastity and sexuality of women." The notion of not being honorable was explained as involving adultery by a woman, loss of virginity, causing family rumor, dressing immodestly, inappropriately talking to men, disapproved marriages, and going out with a member of the opposite gender without permission. In cases involving a woman's adultery, around 37% of the participants stated that any woman who engaged in this conduct should be killed. Other

* http://www.hurriyet.com.tr/kadin/9224965.asp?gid=229&sz=16371 (date accessed: June 19, 2008).

Table 19.15   Cross Tabulation of Victims' Gender and Murder Weapon

	Murder Weapon				
	Knife	Firearm	Darp	Boðma	Total
Victims' gender					
Male					
Count	42	32	3	4	81
Row percentage	51.9%	39.5%	3.7%	4.9%	100.0%
Column percentage	62.7%	60.4%	25.0%	33.3%	56.3%
Female					
Count	25	21	9	8	63
Row percentage	39.7%	33.3%	14.3%	12.7%	100.0%
Column percentage	37.3%	39.6%	75.0%	66.7%	43.8%
Total					
Count	67	53	12	12	144
Total row percentage	46.5%	36.8%	8.3%	8.3%	100.0%
Total column Percentage	100.0%	100.0%	100.0%	100.0%	100.0%

Related chi-square tests

	Value	df	Asymp. Sig. (Two-Sided)
Pearson chi-square	8.818[a]	3	0.032
Likelihood ratio	8.903	3	0.031
Linear-by-linear association	6.169	1	0.013
No. of valid cases	144		

[a] 0 cells (0.0%) have expected count less than 5. The minimum expected count is 5.25.

Table 19.16   Case Processing Summary

	Cases					
	Valid		Missing		Total	
	N	Percent	N	Percent	N	Percent
Victim–offender * dar relationship strokes number	93	63.7%	53	36.3%	146	100.0%

penalties recommended by survey participants included cutting off the ears, nose, or hair of the woman. According to 64% of the participants, the person who was responsible for punishing these women was her husband. People choosing divorce as a solution constituted only 25% of the survey group (Sır, 2003).

Another interesting analysis was conducted by the United Nations Population Fund, Nüfus Bilim Derneği (the Turkish Population Science Association), and the United Nations Development Program (2007) and

Table 19.17   Victim–Offender Relationship * Number of Strokes' Cross Tabulation

	Number of Strokes				
	1.00	2.00	3.00	4.00+	Total
Offender–victim relationship					
Relatives					
Count	23	3	6	2	34
Row percentage	67.6%	8.8%	17.6%	5.9%	100.0%
Column percentage	41.8%	14.3%	42.9%	66.7%	36.6%
Couples					
Count	15	4	4	1	24
Total row percentage	62.5%	16.7%	16.7%	4.2%	100.0%
Total column percentage	27.3%	19.0%	28.6%	33.3%	25.8%
Acquaintances					
Count	1	5	0	0	6
Row percentage	16.7%	83.3%	0.0%	0.0%	100.0%
Column percentage	1.8%	23.8%	0.0%	0.0%	6.5%
Foreigners					
Count	16	9	4	0	29
Row percentage	55.2%	31.0%	13.8%	0.0%	100.0%
Column percentage	29.1%	42.9%	28.6%	0.0%	31.2%
Total					
Count	55	21	14	3	93
Row percentage	59.1%	22.6%	15.1%	3.2%	100.0%
Column percentage	100.0%	100.0%	100.0%	100.0%	100.0%

Related chi-square tests

	Value	df	Asymp. Sig. (Two-Sided)
Pearson chi-square	19.382[a]	9	0.022
Likelihood ratio	18.736	9	0.028
Linear-by-linear association	0.005	1	0.946
No. of valid cases	93		

[a] 9 cells (56.3%) have expected count less than 5. The minimum expected count is 0.19.

Table 19.18   Case Processing Summary

	Cases					
	Valid		Missing		Total	
	N	Percent	N	Percent	N	Percent
Offender's age–murder weapon	144	98.6%	2	1.4%	146	100.0%

Table 19.19 Offender's Age–Murder Weapon Cross Tabulation

Age Group	Knife	Firearm	Battery	Strangulation	Total
			Murder Weapon		
Offender's age					
0–15					
Count	1	0	0	0	1
Row percentage	100.0%	0.0%	0.0%	0.0%	100.0%
Column percentage	1.5%	0.0%	0.0%	0.0%	0.7%
16–30					
Count	30	20	4	5	59
Row percentage	50.8%	33.9%	6.8%	8.5%	100.0%
Column percentage	44.8%	37.7%	33.3%	41.7%	41.0%
31–45					
Count	27	25	8	6	66
Row percentage	40.9%	37.9%	12.1%	9.1%	100.0%
Column percentage	40.3%	47.2%	66.7%	50.0%	45.8%
46+					
Count	9	8	0	1	18
Row percentage	50.0%	44.4%	0.0%	5.6%	100.0%
Column percentage	13.4%	15.1%	0.0%	8.3%	12.5%
Total					
Count	67	53	12	12	144
Total row percentage	46.5%	36.8%	8.3%	8.3%	100.0%
Total column percentage	100.0%	100.0%	100.0%	100.0%	100.0%

Related chi-square tests

	Value	df	Asymp. Sig. (Two-Sided)
Pearson chi-square	5.343[a]	9	0.803
Likelihood ratio	7.112	9	0.625
Linear-by-linear association	0.053	1	0.818
No. of valid cases	144		

[a] 8 cells (50.0%) have expected count less than 5. The minimum expected count is 0.08.

involved interviewing 195 people in four cities (İstanbul, Şanlıurfa, Adana, and Batman) in 2005. This report, called "The Dynamics of Honour Killings in Turkey," revealed the following findings regarding how honor was perceived:

> Honor is everything for me … For example, if I was married, in that case the girl whom I married would be my honour. My sister is my honour too, so are my relatives, the daughter of my aunt and the daughter of my uncle are also my honour. That is, all of them is my honour (Batman, male, age 21).

Table 19.20   Statistics of Honor and Töre Killings between 2005 and 2006

Year	2005	2006
Blood feud	2	2
Marriage	1	1
Familial dispute	9	11
Premarital sex	3	6
Forbidden relationship	3	3
Rape	3	3
Honor	—	—
Total	22	26

In the end for a girl, I'm talking about for here honour is what's important for everything. Virginity. When virginity is lost, the girl has no meaning...A girl without virginity has no importance for me (Batman, male, age 26).

The research concluded that people who came from rural areas have strong family and tribal ties, keep in touch with their relatives in spite of migration to other towns, believe in a similar cultural environment and ideology, have a high status in the family and community they belong to, and perceive honor as a value that could support the murder of another. It was also observed that honor is related to the sexuality and control of a woman. This study revealed that the concept of honor involves a male's wife, sister, mother, and other females in his family.

Within the context of the notion of honor, while women are ascribed to a passive role, men are ascribed to an active one. This research also concluded that the predominant issues related to honor involved

- A woman having an extramarital relationship
- A married woman running away with a man
- A married woman getting separated or divorced
- A divorced woman having a relationship with another man
- A young unmarried girl having a relationship
- A young unmarried girl running away with a man
- A woman (married or unmarried) being kidnapped and/or raped

In this research, four sociocultural factors are also mentioned as causes of violence toward women and honor killings in Turkey:

- Patriarchal structure and sociocultural values
- Dominancy and reproduction of customs and culture that necessitate hierarchy and obedience

Table 19.21 The Statistics of Honor and Töre Killings between 2000 and 2006

Year	2000	2001	2002	2003	2004	2005	2006
Feud	Case count—1 Escape—1	Case count—6 Caught—6	—	Case count—4 Escape—1 Caught—3	Case count—2 Escape—1 Caught—1	Case count—2 Caught—2	Case count—2 Escape—1 Caught—1
Marriage	Case count—2 Caught—2	Case count—1 Caught—1	Case count—1 Caught—1	Case count—1 Caught—1	Case count—1 Caught—1	Case count—1 Caught—1	Case count—1 Caught—1
Familial dispute	Case count—12 Caught—12	Case count—6 Caught—6	Case count—5 Caught—5	Case count—7 Caught—7	Case count—10 Caught 10	Case count—9 Escape—1 Caught—8	Case count—11 Escape—1 Caught—10
Premarital sex	Case count—5 Caught—5	Case count—3 Caught—3	Case count—4 Caught—4	Case count—8 Caught—8	Case count—6 Caught—6	Case count—3 Caught—3	Case count—6 Caught—6
Forbidden relationship	Case count—7 Caught—7	Case count—7 Caught—7	Case count—6 Caught—6	Case count—5 Caught—5	Case count—5 Escape—1 Caught—4	Case count—3 Caught—3	Case count—3 Caught—3
Rape	Case count—2 Caught—2	Case count—2 Caught—2	Case count—2 Unknown—1 Caught—1	Case count—3 Unknown—1 Caught—2	Case count—1 Faili Meçhul—1	Case count—3 Caught—3	Case count—3 Caught—3
Family honor	Case count—1 Caught—1	Case count—2 Caught—2	—	—	Case count—2 Caught—2	—	—
Total	30	28	18	28	27	21	26

- Religious and cultural beliefs that recommend females and males not to share the same physical space
- High social pressure on individuals due to prevalence of large families, citizenship, and community relationships

As a result of the acceptance of these ideals, their perception of political and legal structures is confused by these traditional concepts (United Nations Development Program, United Nations Population Fund, and Nüfus Bilim Derneği, 2005).

In the research reported by the Human Rights Joint Platform in 2006, female suicides in eastern and southeastern regions of Turkey were determined to occur due to compulsion or where the result of reported suicides in which the evidence could be scrutinized. In some cities of eastern and southeastern Anatolia, the frequency of female suicide was found to be higher than for male suicide. Van and Batman, both in eastern Turkey, are two of the cities where the rate of female suicide was higher. The media and some NGOs believe that the enhanced penalty for honor killings is the main reason for a higher rate of suicide, but it is highly likely that these suicides are actually murders, but are reported as suicides due to cultural acceptance to honor killings.

In a further analysis, regional inequalities result in limitations in education and underemployment in the eastern and southeastern regions of Turkey. The economic and sociocultural inadequacies are visibly seen as one moved further away from western Turkey. This report further noted that the cities in the eastern and southeastern regions of Turkey have the lowest rate in terms of both Gender Development Index (GDI) and Gender Empowerment Measure (GEM). Among 79 cities, Batman ranks at 70 in GDI and 63 in GEM; Şanlıurfa ranks 72 in GDI and 65 in GEM, and Van ranks 74 in GDI and 65 in GEM. When viewed globally, Turkey ranks 70 in GDI and 76 in GEM within the UNDP Human Development Index (Human Rights Joint Platform, 2007, p. 7).

Regional difference is also noted in the educational level of females in Turkey. When the percentage of literacy is analyzed by gender, literacy for males stands at 19% and 6% for females. In addition, females have the highest educational level rates in primary school (37%) but lower educational level rates in higher education (4%). On the other hand, males have a 37% educational level in primary school and 7% in higher education. There were also notable differences in labor participation by gender in that 17% of females and 69% of males were working (Statistics for Women in Turkey, 2004).

In 1997, the legal term for compulsory primary education was increased to 8 years, but it was noted that one-third of female children in Şanlıurfa and Van did not attend primary school in 2003 (Human Rights Joint Platform, 2007, p. 7).

The Status of Women in Turkey

The majority of Turkish women are dramatically impacted by the male-dominated ideologies and institutions related to family, society, and the economy. As an Islamic country where religion and state are separate, the status of women in Turkey is clearly complex and multifaceted. In the urban areas, most of the women are highly educated and employed professionally. In the rural regions, females are caught between two different worlds. One is shaped by culture and tradition that largely restricts their activities to the family home environment. One could conclude that urban migration supports both traditional behavior and the enhanced position of women in Turkish society.

According to a recent national census, half of Turkish population is female and the other half is male. As has been reported above, around 19% of women and 6% of men are not literate. In every stage of educational level, the rate of males is higher than females. The higher education level is 4% for females and 7% for males. Especially in rural regions, there is a struggle between the problem of not schooling girls because of cultural obstacles and the lack of financial support provided by families to send their daughters to school. Labor force participation rates for women in rural area and in cities differ. According to recent data, at the ages of 15 years and older, labor force participation rates are 31% for females and 71% for males. In parallel with this finding, unemployment rates for females are higher than those for men. Women generally work as unpaid family workers at the family farm. Females that migrate from the countryside to the urban centers normally obtain positions only in the service industry. And those from the suburban settings with lower education levels who migrate to the city settings often prefer to settle down in the neighborhood where people from their regions have migrated and have been living. Therefore, even those who move to the more modern settings continue to live and maintain their traditional customs. In addition, the representation rate of women in the political arena is low. Even though Turkish women acquired suffrage rights much earlier than women from many other countries, the rate of elected women in the last elections was only 9%. This finding also holds true for women in executive positions in the corporate world.

Due to these concerns, the Turkish Ministry of National Education and UNICEF have organized an agency centered in eastern and southeastern Anatolia called "Haydi Kızlar Okula" and as a result, over 177,000 girls and 87,000 boys have started to receive an improved education.

Conclusion

The above has revealed that in murders committed in the name of honor or family dignity, the main objective was to protect familial social prestige.

However, from a social perspective, particularly in eastern and southern regions in Turkey, upholding the honor of a family is culturally acceptable, even at the cost of murdering a family member.

In Turkey, the person who transfers social values to the next generation is the mother. Female children are taught to imitate the mother. As a result, one could conclude that if the mother is well-improved socially, is self-sustained economically, and has a higher educational level, she is more likely to bring up healthy and self-confident children. One could also support that if the mother is self-conscious and wise, this would promote younger members of the family to grow up and live in more healthy conditions. To support this hypothesis, Turkish statistics show that the rate of deaths at early ages are lower when highly educated and conscious mothers pay attention to their children's necessary health and nutrition requirements.

In Turkey, even though marriages at early age are less common than in previous times, they still exist. The responsibilities of most of these women who marry at an early age, and who commonly have low educational level and no qualified job, are very heavy. Having many children at an early age will further increase the woman's responsibilities. Unfortunately, tradition also mandates that these women can no longer return to their own families, even after a divorce. If these females are exposed to domestic violence at the hands of her husband, her parents no longer get involved. As a result, her only options are to remain in the abusive relationship or suffer economically after obtaining a divorce. The reality that she is susceptible to becoming a victim of an honor killing if she acts in a perceived unacceptable fashion further complicates a woman's plight. This exists even with the legal reform that highlighted the criminal nature of these "töre" killings.

One improvement has been the involvement of NGOs and government agencies in vulnerable regions in Turkey making strong efforts to improve educational opportunities for both girls and boys.

As is very well known, change in customs is very difficult and tardive. Enhancing women's social status could quicken this period of change. Resisting to and being up against customs by herself alone is very difficult for women and clearly men have also to change. Firstly, females have to teach their sons that violence is an undesirable behavior, problems cannot be solved by violence, and how violence aimed at women is wrong. Violence is a learned behavior and the child who learns violence as a behavior pattern of his or her father against the mother will likely inflict violence later to their own family. The building of quality women's shelters for those subjected to violence or threatened with töre killing will also provide credible options. These women have also to be assisted economically in order to live independently. Turkish social agencies and NGOs must strive to make these possibilities into reality.

Eliminating serious crimes such as the blood feud and honor killings is not possible only by increasing the criminal sanctions, but rather other measures have to be taken. It is the responsibility of mass media and government leaders to enlighten society and raise awareness. Gaining the support of notable and recognizable figures such as television and sport stars to promote these agendas will bring the issues to the forefront. More efforts have to be made to increase educational opportunities for females (and males) in the eastern and southern regions of Turkey in order to provide reasonable opportunities for independent survival. Ultimately, government, media, and international agencies and local social welfare institutions must act in unison to avoid the continuation of violence within and between families. Clearly, the police and the justice system within Turkey are not solely responsible for eliminating this phenomenon, but these actors must be trained to enforce the laws that address honor killing as a crime, even if it may go against their own cultural and traditional ideologies.

Acknowledgment

The author wants to thank Aylin Arslan and Neval Karanfil for their assistance in translating this paper from Turkish to English.

References

Adler, J.S. (2003). "We've got a right to fight; We're married:" Domestic homicide in Chicago, 1875–1920, *Journal of Interdisciplinary History*, 34(1), 27–48.

Anonymous (2000). Honor crimes, *Women's International Network News*.

İçli, T.G. (1993). Türkiye'de Suçlular: Sosyal, Kültürel ve Ekonomik Özellikleri, *Atatürk Kültür Dil ve Tarih Yüksek Kurumu, Atatürk Kültür Merkezi Yay*, p. 71.

İçli, T.G. (1995). Ailede Kadına Karşı şiddet ve Kadın Suçluluğu, *Bizim Büro*.

İçli, T.G. and Diğerleri (2007). Türkiye'de Hükümlü Profili (unpublished research report), Ankara, Turkey.

İçli, T.G. (1987). *Adam Öldürme Olayında Sosyo-Ekonomik ve Kültürel Faktörlerin Önemi*, published by Hacettepe Üniversitesi, Edebiyat Fakültesi Dergisi, 48(2), 21–45.

Kulwicki, A.D. (2002). The practice of honor crimes: A glimpse of domestic violence in the Arab world, *Mental Health Nursing*, 23, 77–87.

Loftin, C. and McDowal, D. (2003). Regional cultures and pattern of homicides, *Homicide Studies*, 7, 353–367.

Öğün, A. Kadının Suç İşlemesinde and Suç Kurbanı olmasında Geleneklerin Önemi (2005). Namus Cinayetleri, V.Türk Kültürü Kongresi, *Cumhuriyetten Günümüze Türk Kültürünün Dünü,Bugünü ve Geleceği Gelenek–Görenek, Örf-Adet,Giyim-Kuşam*, Cilt XV, Atatürk Kültür Merkezi Başkanlığı Yay, pp. 39–48.

Sever, A. and Gökçeçiçek, Y. (1999). Culture of honor, culture of change: A feminist analysis of honor killings in rural Turkey, *Violence against Women: An International and Interdisciplinary Journal*, 7(9), 964–999.

Sır, A. (2003). Namus Cinayetleri Anketi, *Voice of America*.

Tripathi, A. and Supriya, Y. (2005). For the sake of honour: But whose honour?:—Honour crimes against women, *Asia Pacific Journal of Human Rights and Law*, 2, 63–78.

United Nations Development Program (2004). *Statistics for Women in Turkey*, Ankara, Turkey.

United Nations Development Program (2007). *The Dynamics of Honor Killing in Turkey*, Ankara, Turkey.

Law Enforcement in the Kingdom of Thailand: Addressing Ethical Dilemmas, Extremist Terrorism, and the Government Coup

20

ATTAPOL KUANLIANG AND ROBERT D. HANSER

Contents

Introduction

In order to understand Thailand and the historical factors associated with that country, one must understand that first and foremost Thailand is officially recognized as a kingdom. The King of Thailand, King Bhumibol Adulyadej, is a constitutional monarch who largely acts as a figurehead for the nation (Baker and Phongpaichit, 2005; Warren et al. 2006). Though his formal authority does not carry the same weight as that of the Prime Minister, he has still been very instrumental in resolving several political stalemates and has interceded during prior crises, thereby adding to the government's stability. Further, King Bhumibol Adulyadej is credited with facilitating the transfer to democracy during the 1930s. King Adulyadej is the longest reigning monarch in Thai history (he was born in 1927 and assumed the throne in 1946) and, most importantly, he is well loved and highly respected by the people of Thailand (Warren et al. 2006; Wyatt, 2003). Though it is the Prime Minister of Thailand that makes the primary decisions and carries the weight of authority during day-to-day operations of the country, the king is adored by the public for his philanthropic work and for a variety of domestic duties that he performs within the nation (Warren et al. 2006).

Despite the fact that Thailand's king is the world's longest-serving head of state, the current state of political affairs in Thailand is one that is best described as being in "flux." The year 2006 witnessed a military coup against former Prime Minister Thaksin Shinawatra and since that time the nation's interim government, essentially steered by a military junta, has operated under a temporary constitution with the permanent constitution only recently being passed in July 2007 (BBC, 2007a,b; McGeown, 2006). To understand the political flavor that now exists in Thailand, it might be considered that this junta has made it illegal to criticize the drafting of the new constitution. The junta has maintained strict control over much of the crafting of various legislative pieces, particularly the constitution and other important documents. Surprisingly, King Bhumibol Adulyadej did support the coup during its early takeover and this has served to add some credibility to the actions taken in modern-day Thailand and also provides some support for the current Prime Minister, Surayud Chulanont, who was appointed by the junta chief Sonthi Boonyaratglin, the military leader who was largely behind the coup staged against Thaksin Shinawatra (BBC, 2007a,b; McGeown, 2006).

Needless to say, the historical developments during the past 2 years have been rapid and unpredictable. This has affected police operations since leadership among the police has been lacking. Upper administrative figures in the police system of Thailand were accustomed to having a prime minister who was a former police officer and administrator. This meant that a strong bond existed between Prime Minister Shinawatra and the police, with the prime minister incorporating many innovative reforms within that area of government (Shinawatra and Pongcharoen, 2006). The actual role and expectations of the police under the new government is yet to be clearly understood, meaning that the police operate more on a day-to-day routine level without broad- or national-based planning as had occurred during the Thai War on Drugs and other comprehensive crime fighting strategies.

Further, it will be demonstrated that several ironies exist within Thailand as a result of the events that have transpired. Indeed, the former prime minister has a doctoral education in criminal justice and is noted as being the first prime minister to have been a former police officer and he is also known for his passion for police training, improvement, and ethical behavior (Shinawatra and Pongcharoen, 2006; Singhsilarak and Cheurprakobkit, 2007). What is ironic is that this same man, well known for his improvements in police professionalism and ethics in Thailand, was himself ousted by his own countrymen due to alleged ethical lapses in financial dealings and leadership, resulting in a successful and quite peaceful coup that occurred in the later quarter of 2006 (BBC, 2007a,b).

Another irony, further demonstrating the surreal qualities of this set of events, is that Thailand, a traditionally peaceful nation where Buddhist beliefs are widespread, continued to have difficulty gaining any sort of peaceful resolution with the Muslim community in the south that desires autonomy. Indeed, the new Prime Minister Surayud Chulanont, himself a Muslim who replaced Thaksin Shinawatra shortly after the 2006 coup took place, has contended that the situation continues to escalate. Ironically, this is despite the fact that Chulanont reversed the former administration's use of martial law, implementing instead a policy of conciliation. Chulanont offered an apology to Muslims in southern Thailand for past violence and vowed to use peaceful approaches toward conflict resolution (Mydans, 2007). But this has only been met with increased violence among extremist separatists in the south (Mydans, 2007). Thus, even the current Thai government, with its leadership being Muslim, have concluded that the wounds have been so deep throughout the Muslim south that nothing may work to assuage the anger and rage that exists among the area's extremist population for quite some time to come.

In regard to ironies and contradictions inherent to the Thai policing system and its operations, it is important to note that while strides in ethical understanding have been made, the Thai police are paid very poorly (Royal Thai Police, 2004). This has led to a system where Thai police are expected (at least informally) to supplement their incomes with "fees" that are charged to various businesses by the police. This is actually an elaborate system that is not necessarily considered corrupt but is considered a simple reality among police personnel and community members. Often, the fees are for allowances to stay open beyond traditional business hours (such as with nightclubs and/or other nightlife businesses), to avoid enforcement of various ordinances, or perhaps the payment of a citation to the officer on-the-spot and to that officer in lieu of an official charge. Much of these occurrences are fairly common throughout Thailand and in Bangkok in particular.

Naturally, this type of culture in policing makes it very difficult for progress toward ethical policing behavior, particularly when these types of activities are not necessarily viewed as corrupt by the community itself (Singhsilarak and Cheurprakobkit, 2007). Indeed, Thai culture is the key denominator to understanding some of the seeming contradictions that have occurred and provides insight for Western readers that wish to understand developments within Thailand during the past decade. It may well be that what would seem to be a dilemma in western thought and culture is simply a commonplace dichotomy of no consequence to Thai culture (Sandhu et al. 2003; Sue and Sue, 1990). This actually makes sense to some extent since it is commonly known that western cultures tend to polarize options and solutions, having more "yes" or "no" and/or "black" or "white" outlooks than do most eastern cultures. Thus, ethical dilemmas in Thailand may be different than most westerners might expect and in some cases, there may be no dilemma at all (Sandhu et al. 2003; Sue and Sue, 1990).

Thailand is a nation that is well admired for its beauty, tranquility, and its serenity. Yet, along with this is the fact that Thailand also serves as a primary juncture from which wealthy Japanese and United States businessmen fuel an internationally known sex industry (Poulin, 2004). This sex industry, consisting of any variety of services imaginable (for a price), draws a customer base that has money as well as women and children who come from impoverished backgrounds (Poulin, 2004). Though prostitution is illegal in Thailand, one must seriously question the enforcement of this restriction if conditions are such that scholars and laypersons routinely write and talk about this sex industry that is enabled within Thailand's borders. Though rural Thai culture does not overtly condone or encourage prostitution, there are still strong structural pushes and pulls that result in many young girls and women from rural Thailand being smuggled into the sex industry in and around Bangkok (Poulin, 2004). This is an important point because it again demonstrates that though such activity is not approved of culturally, the reality is that many rural Thai families consider this option an inevitable outcome and have even found means of resolving the ethical and cultural dilemmas that emerge.

In addition, Thailand falls within the region commonly dubbed the *Golden Triangle*, where drug trafficking abounds. It is Southeast Asia, along with the Middle East's Golden Crescent, which serves as a primary source of most of the world's opium trade (Hanser et al. 2008). On the international market, opium is distributed from this region to the United States (the primary demand source) and Europe in huge volumes. An astute observer would again realize that the primary demand sources that fuel this activity are those nations that are industrialized and wealthy (Hanser et al. 2008). This is important because these nations often are those that seek to impose ethical behavior on military and policing elements within developing nations. Yet, these nations provide much of the incentive for developing nations to compromise their own internal operations, particularly when governmental figures are among those that stand to gain from illicit activity or activity that falls within the "grey areas" of international law.

On a cultural level, readers should consider that Thailand is a nation where thousands of Buddhist monks routinely practice. Indeed, they are readily visible all over Bangkok; one cannot visit that city without seeing such monks within plain view. Yet at the same time, vice such as prostitution and drug usage is common. Every country has its problems and Thailand by no means has a monopoly on the profession of prostitution or the drug trade. Yet, it would seem that this country cannot rid itself of an image that automatically draws to mind sex and drugs among persons around the world. Most criminal justice writings in regard to Thailand focus on these aspects of the country. Thus, these images are fairly pervasive despite any improvements that might have been made within the Thai policing system. This is an important aspect of this chapter because it is against this background that Thai police must work and operate. Naturally, this has an impact on any effort to improve policing within Thailand, in addition to other social factors.

While former Prime Minister Shinawatra and the Royal Thai Police Academy have worked to improve ethics and professionalism among the Thai police, there still exists a surrounding environment that is not necessarily conducive to such operations. To be clear, this is not meant to imply that Thai police are unethical; this is simply not the case. In fact, Thai police tend to be very professional and present a very positive public image. They tend to know their communities and do very well in keeping the peace. However, it is clear that the sense of ethics common to Western thinking, as imported by Dr. Shinawatra and by the Police Commissioner, Dr. Pongsapat Pongcharoen of the Royal Thai Police Cadet Academy, has faced and will continue to face challenges within the country. Given the peaceful nature of the Thai people and given the top-notch training and guidance delivered to Thai police cadets at the Royal Thai Police Cadet Academy, the shift toward professionalism and ethical operations has seen great successes. Nevertheless, any true picture of the Thai policing system and its routine operation must include at least a minimal discussion of the Thai cultural, religious, and economic variables that impact ethical and professional behavior among its police.

Buddhist Social Ethics in Thailand

Roughly 95% of the Thai population practice Buddhism (Warren et al. 2006). This is an astounding source of homogeneity in the Thai population. Indeed, general awareness of the Buddhist way of life of the sangha (the Buddhist clergy) is common for almost all Thais, providing a common social fabric within Thai culture (Warren et al. 2006). Furthermore, roughly half of the entire male population has gone through at least some period of monk ordination and service in their lifetime. This routinely occurs during the early stages of a man's life and is always before he marries; the ordination may be as short as 3 months or may last much longer. It should be noted that monks in Thailand are highly revered and in most Thai towns the *wat* (temple) is the primary source of social and religious life (Warren et al. 2006).

Historically speaking, Buddhism had its origins in the nation of India and made its way to Southeast Asia over time, eventually being fully adopted by the Thais (DeVoss, 1994; Tavivat, 1998; Warren et al. 2006). The main tenet or principle of Buddhism is the notion of personal liberation from human suffering that occurs throughout the life cycle. Although Buddha did teach ethical principles regarding social, economic, and political conduct, the primary concern for the individual Buddhist was, and still is, the personal liberation from psychological suffering (Tavivat, 1998). It is important to understand that this belief system is etched into the minds of the common Thai person. Buddhism de-emphasizes materialism and emphasizes mindfulness and the beauty of simplicity, with Buddhists seeking enlightenment through asceticism.

It is important for any person unfamiliar with Thai culture to understand how pervasive and important Buddhism is in Thailand. The Thai population predominantly practice a certain form of Buddhism known as Theravada Buddhism, which places particular emphasis on meditation and philosophical approaches to life. Throughout Thailand, one will find that *wats* abound, with the populace regularly engaged in meditation, providing donations, and basically keeping the tenets of the Buddha in their minds and hearts (DeVoss, 1994; Warren et al. 2006). The impact of Buddhism is clear to any visitor in Thailand and it is also clear that the tenets affect the daily routine and outlook of the Thai population, with peacefulness, calm, and serenity being key values. In addition, a genuine sense of humility and respect for others is common among the Thai. Though this is actually common to many countries in East Asia, the tendency toward a humble self-identity and serenity is particularly pronounced among the Thais (DeVoss, 1994; Warren et al. 2006).

While these characteristics are common among individuals, the macro picture of Thailand is one that stands in sharp contrast. Indeed, Tavivat (1998) makes it clear that many of the individual Buddhist teachings have not actually translated to sociological, political, or economic realities. It would seem that Buddhism's emphasis on individual escape from human suffering, desires, and wants has failed to have any impact on the structural realities within Thailand. This is particularly evident in urban areas of Thailand, such as Bangkok, where there is a very clear class distinction, with that distinction creating an ever increasing gap between the rich and the poor. This is not really any different from many of the economic realities in many other areas of the world and this is, in part, the point that Tavivat (1998) makes when noting that Buddhism has failed to impact the macro levels and structural components of Thailand.

In many countries across the world, the effects of globalization have resulted in further outsourcing of labor and production to countries where labor costs are cheap and easy to obtain (Friedman, 1999). This has created a worldwide class system of laborers that are inexpensive and, over time, has lowered the overall wage that the commoner is able to obtain. In developed countries, this has been a source of angst among the common population but in less developed countries this has allowed the extremely poor to obtain a wage that is considerably better than that which they would obtain otherwise, even if their standard of living is still well under that of truly industrialized nations. Correspondingly, the wealthy in these countries gain great profits from western businesses since they are coopted into the economic, governmental, and social circles that grant companies the ability to operate within their borders. The entire process leads to a system that many perceive as exploitative of the lower classes in underdeveloped countries since it ensures that they will remain within the lower strata of material ascension (Friedman, 1999). However, in countries like Thailand, where the general mindset is not based on materialism, it would not seem that this would be problematic.

Yet Thailand has modernized and has sought to become increasingly industrialized out of necessity so that the country is able to compete within the world market. In today's globalized system, a failure to maintain interaction with the global community and to seek competitiveness will only set that country behind developmentally, at least in relation to the remainder of the world. Today's international community truly emphasizes a "go along to get along" mentality, and Friedman (1999) confirms this with his own theoretical perspective that he dubs the "Golden Arches Theory of Conflict Prevention." This theory notes that countries must not only have successful interrelations within the global arena if they are to survive, but it also contends that it is now much more economically and politically adaptable for countries to specifically avoid international conflict, if at all possible. The payoffs are seldom worth the effort and the use of conflict now carries such great risk and social costs as to make such a choice nothing less than poor governance and leadership. Friedman's theory contends that globalization significantly raises the costs for countries that choose to use warfare as a means of advancing their interests. The level of economic integration along with the widespread proliferation of capitalistic values provides strong international constraints on foreign policy and discourages nations that are members of the international economy from choosing warfare as a potential option (Friedman, 1999). In other words, warfare costs much more than it is worth and does not provide an adequate return on the investment that it entails. While this does not ensure wars and conflicts will be fully eliminated around the world, it does mean that those countries that routinely resort to this option will find that they are less competitive in the world market (Friedman, 1999).

Though Friedman's points may seem unrelated to the situation in Thailand, nothing could be further from the truth. The external international economic forces are quite significant when considering developments within Thailand. The impact that these forces have had upon the Thai economy helps to explain many of the contradictions that were previously noted. Indeed, the economic pushes and pulls on countries like Thailand are the central reason for many of the problems denoted within Thai policing and the ability of its government to ensure that adequate law enforcement occurs throughout the nation. Specific examples of how these influences have provided challenges to improvements in law enforcement operations will be discussed later, but for now it is sufficient to simply note that external market conditions have led to circumstances that have created a desire for material goods and better standards of living while, at the same time, creating further separation between the rich and the poor in Thailand. This undoubtedly impacts criminal activity related to the sex trade in Thailand (particularly in Bangkok) as well as the opium trade that occurs in the north.

Tavivat's (1998) own points regarding Thailand's economic development and the undermining of Buddhist ideals simply provide further evidence of the assertions made by Friedman (1999). Tavivat (1998) notes that prior to the nation's modernization, Siam (the original name of Thailand) was a society where Buddhism predominated. Tavivat notes that the Thai government, under the leadership of Prime Minister Phibun Songkhram, changed the name of the nation in December 1938 as a means of demonstrating a shift to westernization of the country. Tavivat goes on to add that

> The contrast between yesterday's Siam and today's Thailand, [sic] developed over time as a consequence of basic economic and social changes, themselves the product of government efforts to modernize the country. This modernization has shattered the self-sufficient economy of local communities and centralized the relatively self-sustained polity of the provinces. Ultimately, this process has tied the country economically to the global market economy, and politically to the new international order. These economic and structural changes have had a great impact on all social and cultural aspects of Thai society, and consequently have affected the social values and well-being of the Thai people (1998, p. 2).

This is actually profound because it clearly and succinctly demonstrates that law, order, and social mores in Thailand are quite different from those just two or three generations past. While it is true that the world has changed considerably over the past few decades, it is Tavivat's contention that the internal sense of culture, ethics, and informal social control has been gutted in many respects. Tavivat also implies that Buddhism has failed to provide Thailand with a strong sense of ethical guidance throughout these global changes, itself being devalued and undermined due to an emphasis on economic pursuits.

Naturally, any criminological theoretician will notice that this may actually sound familiar to the work of criminologists who claim that the capitalist system in the United States has undermined and devalued informal and formal socializing institutions that do not primarily revolve around economic pursuits. This is an important point because it demonstrates that the spread of capitalism, while opening doors for many nations and their populations, has served to devalue noneconomically driven socializing institutions in a variety of countries. This also explains much of the crime that occurs in Thailand, particularly in relation to gang activity, illicit drug trafficking, and the sex industry.

Modern pressures in Thailand are very powerful. Even though developmental projects have brought numerous modern-day conveniences (i.e., roads, television, etc.), many Thai people are simply not happy or content with older lifestyles. Traditional values continue to be threatened by poverty and the desires associated with consumerism (Tavivat, 1998). Now, most rural Thai family systems are torn apart by these forces, and under such circumstances, it is hard for the young to stay in rural villages. In many cases, young Thai girls and women find the life of a prostitute to be much more agreeable than the back-breaking work that is often encountered in rural and agriculturally based Thai villages.

As a result, the macro-level factors as influenced by globalized demands, have led to a sex industry that is reported to generate around 500 billion bahts annually, the equivalent to about $124 million (Poulin, 2004). Indeed, it has been estimated that prostitution represented anywhere from 2% to 14% of the total economic activities in Thailand (Poulin, 2004). Further, studies have concluded that when taking all peripheral businesses into account (i.e., hotels, restaurants, and other affiliate businesses) the tourist industry as a whole draws roughly $4 billion a year to the Thai economy, with a very substantial portion of those tourists being men simultaneously interested in sex industry services (Bishop and Robinson, 1998; Poulin, 2004). This has led to a common Thai notion that the only fruit more delicious than the Thai durian (a tasty local fruit) is the young Thai woman (Poulin, 2004).

Going further, it is important to understand that the sex industry has been part of a broader development strategy in Thailand. Given extensive obligations of debt repayment, Thailand and other developing countries have been "encouraged by international organizations such as the International Monetary Fund (IMF) and the World Bank to develop their tourism and entertainment industries" (Poulin, 2004, p. 40). The development of these sectors of business then work to further augment the sex trade in Thailand, creating local, regional, and international markets for the sex trade industry within the country. The point to this is that such market forces obviously have huge economic benefits for Thailand and it is then less likely that Thai policing elements would be encouraged to truly enforce laws against prostitution. When considering this point, it is interesting to note that Thailand repaid its debts to the IMF in advance of projected timelines, with foreign exchange reserves doubling from $30 billion in 2001 to over $60 billion in 2006. To presume that this success was tied to the sex industry is purely speculative, but authors like Poulin (2004) would seem to indicate that this might be so.

Thus, Thai scholars bemoan the fact that Thai, on an individual level, adhere to Buddhist beliefs but that this seems to breed a sense of docility among the population. In other words, the tenets against materialism and other Buddhist precepts do not seem to translate into broadbased social order change. Rather, a contradiction exists within Thai society that has resulted from alien pressures foreign to the indigenous Thai traditional culture. This and other difficulties facing the Thai social structure create a very unique environment for police operations and also breed a sense of ethics that is very foreign to western thinking. It is against this background of competing and cross-purposed emphases that the Thai police have developed. Add to this the fact that politics in Thailand have experienced several coups and power transfers since 1932, and it becomes clear that Thai police are expected to "keep the peace" amidst an unstable and/or very dubious set of social conditions, whether this be due to moral, economic, or political considerations (Fearon and Laitin, 2005). Attention will now be turned to Thai police behavior, ethics, and professionalism within a society that has been affected by external pressures and a weakening of much of the social glue that has kept the country together throughout centuries past.

Thai Policing and Ethical Dilemmas

The Royal Thai Police have a history that spans several 100 years, going back to 1375 A.D. to the reign of King Borom Tri Lokanart (Shinawatra and Pongcharoen, 2006). This king issued a royal decree that called for the establishment of a police division. Because the establishment of the police force occurred at the direction of the king, a certain spiritual value was attributed to the work of the police in Thailand during the early years of their formation (Shinawatra and Pongcharoen, 2006). However, the spiritual aspects of this type of profession have been lost upon the contemporary police force. This is of course most unfortunate and this runs completely counter to much of Thailand's broader social fabric. This also reflects the points made by Tavivat regarding Buddhist influence in Thai culture; the Thai, by tradition have been a spiritual and harmonious people. This is so true that the traditional role of the police was given a sense of higher-order purpose, weaving a sense of social, philosophical, moral, and ethical commitment into the profession (Shinawatra and Pongcharoen, 2006). The reforms implemented by Shinawatra and Pongcharoen (at the Royal Thai Police Cadet Academy) sought to reshape the policing role into one that adopts those same intrinsically motivating traditional views.

However, market forces as they are, it is important to understand that the Thai police are not paid well, their official salaries often hovering around 6000 baht (roughly $125) per month (Royal Thai Police, 2004). The low income, along with a variety of cultural nuances, has led to some innovations that are not necessarily unethical in Thai culture, but would be questioned by most western standards. This again shows that it is important to understand the entire cultural context surrounding a police force since many of the behaviors and actions may seem, on the exterior, to be aberrant but are actually perceived as normal (or even expected) within that society. In Bangkok, police officers tend to get much of their support from their community, which often comes in the way of protection activities for certain businesses (i.e., gold and jewelry shops), traffic violations and other fines based on personal behavior that are paid at the point of detection (without a formal citation being recorded), unofficial commissions from brothels and nightclubs, or money from nightlife entertainment businesses to stay open later than the legal restrictions allow. These and other alternative forms of income greatly supplement the income of police in Bangkok and other urban areas.

It is unclear as to exactly how routine these practices are among Thai police, but many Thai readily acknowledge these realities as a means of simply doing business. Foreigners living in Thailand often quickly learn that processes can be expedited when economic incentives are provided, such as with the clearance of different types of paperwork and/or permissions. While the total amount of external revenue may vary, and depending upon the area of Thailand that an officer may be stationed, it has been noted that a portion of this income is actually given to the agency so that it can be passed along the chain of command and used to augment the salaries of personnel restricted to desk activities. It is important to note that all of this is carried out in a discreet manner, with no official recognition of this system existing. This has been a common problem among Thai policing elements for decades and, despite many efforts to reform ethics within the policing arm of the government, this system is nearly impossible to eradicate. Indeed, the police personnel have learned that by cultivating "grey" areas where behaviors and activities would be technically illegal, they maintain a sense of discretion and power that they might not have otherwise. Naturally, this increases the range of power and response by Thai police while simultaneously enhancing their otherwise dismal income.

In most cases, these activities are commonly accepted by the local Thai as common practice. In fact, most of the "fees" that may be given to Thai police are viewed as being similar to the customary gratuity that one might provide a waiter or waitress. In many cases, there is no actual penalty for not paying such fees to police, but businesses will then be expected to maintain their activities within the confines of the law. Thus, it is not that businesses and persons with specialized interests are extorted or forced to pay such money but it is more that such businesses or persons should not expect any additional benefits or leniency other than what the law may allow. In other words, this bribe system is a win-win for both parties and is addressed in such a manner. Some may even liken this to a realistic means of doing business.

Even with this being said, there are constant news and media reports that allege widespread graft and corruption. One prime example would be the notoriety associated with Mr. Chuwit Kamolvisit of Bangkok. This man is a notorious sex industry broker and owner of numerous massage parlors, men's clubs, and general places of ill repute. Kamolvisit is referred to as Thailand's foremost sex tycoon, with thousands of women reportedly in his employment, working in labyrinth-like massage parlors and servicing a wide variety of political figures, police administrators, and general police personnel. During 2003 and 2004, Thai newspapers provided stories that unveiled a far-reaching and long-lived plot that included a look into a system of police graft and corruption where under-age prostitution, kidnapping, and illegal business deals have been alleged to be common practice. Examples of detectives having sex with masseuses during "investigations" of potential prostitution rings and other such illicit activity were graphically portrayed during this period.

In fact, Kamolvisit developed a sort of hero status among Thais that, on the one hand did not condone his sex empire, but on the other hand grew weary of a corrupt and decadent political system. It was among these circumstances that Kamolvisit made a spectacle of Thai politics by creating his own political party (he had the financial resources to do so) known as the Trakun Thai Party (Thai Ancestry Party), of which he was the declared leader. Accordingly, this party's agenda was to correct practices that for years Kamolvisit himself supported, call these practices "evil injustice" and denouncing the corruption that, according to Kamolvisit, extends across a large section of the political establishment all the way up to the Prime Minister at that time. Amidst this political fray, nearly 100 police officers were suspended, transferred, or investigated but none were reported to be prosecuted. Kamolvisit himself was charged with employing under-age masseuses and other more minor offenses.

Kamolvisit ran for governor of Bangkok and came in third. Later, in the 2005 legislative elections, he merged his party with the Chart Thai Party, a more conservatively branded political group, and by doing so was able to become a member of parliament. Such odd twists of events and the obviously ludicrous events such as these, stand as testament to what many refer to when they say "*This is Thailand*," referring to the unique and outlandish events that pass as normal within Thai governmental operations. Just as odd as was his ascension into politics, Kamolvisit was later removed from his position by the Thai Constitutional Court in 2006 due to the fact that he did not meet the specific qualifications to be a member of parliament. But this story serves to demonstrate how the economic factors affect police operations, police corruption, and the types of criminal activity that are nearly commonplace in Thailand. What is even more interesting is the fact that police operations, police corruption, and criminal activity are thoroughly intertwined with one another in a seemingly symbiotic relationship; all against a political and economic backdrop that enables a convoluted form of justice enforcement to exist despite any training reforms that might be implemented.

To further highlight this point, consider also the means by which the Thai police and paramilitary forces have dealt with the drug trade. This aspect of Thai policing demonstrates a true dilemma where, on the one hand, the Thai have been criticized for being lax and thereby enabling the opium trade, while on the other hand, being criticized for reacting too harshly during the Thai War on Drugs that occurred. Though the Royal Thai Police Academy has made great strides in training its police, it would appear that the commitment to human rights has been compromised when fighting the drug trade within Thailand. Indeed, the Asian Legal Resource Center (ALRC) issued 40 statements regarding serious alleged violations to the 61st Session of the UN Commission on Human Rights in Geneva that occurred in April 2005. According to the ALRC, the 2003 War on Drugs declared by the government of Thailand, resulted in the deaths of hundreds of people, most of which the ALRC contends are wrongful deaths. These complaints led to the UN's Office of the Secretary General scheduling visits to Thailand, the first of which were delayed by the Thai government.

Well-known criticism has been leveled at the government of Thailand by the United Nations for the use of extrajudicial killings, where the Thai police have reportedly killed drug runners by "cutting the red tape," thereby denying any systematic sense of procedural integrity. While Thai police routinely contend that these deaths are the result of vendettas between drug runners and also the result of self-defense among it police, the general public and the international community remains extremely skeptical. Further violence was reported to continue into 2004, demonstrating that such practices were a deliberate and long-term strategy. The negative fall-out from these extrajudicial killings should not be underestimated. Indeed, they put Prime Minister Shinawatra on an opposite polarity from the UN's peacekeeping and human rights enforcement efforts.

Though the UN's Office on Crime and Drugs supported the efforts of the Thai government, this still did not dissuade other agencies from contending that the efforts were riddled with foul play. Even the United States Department of State provided the following synopsis within its 2005 report:

> There were approximately 1,300 extrajudicial killings of suspected drug traffickers during the government's "War on Drugs" campaign in 2003, and more than one thousand investigations into these cases. By year's end most were closed, due to "a lack of evidence." Many cases were settled out of court, with officers paying compensation to the family of the deceased. The government maintained that the deaths resulted from disputes between those involved in the drug trade. Local and international human rights groups, including the National Human Rights Commission (NHRC), disputed this claim. Procedures for investigating suspicious deaths, including deaths occurring in police custody, required among other things that the prosecutor, a forensic pathologist, and a local administrator participate in the investigation and

that family members have legal representation at the inquests. However, these procedures often were not followed (p. 1).

There is an additional irony that exists within the Thai response to the international drug trade. This lies in the fact that while Thailand does not support the drug trade, there is undoubtedly a great deal of money that changes hands and some of that money must eventually pour into the legitimate Thai economy. Thus, the Thai economy is hurt, at least indirectly, by any crack in the opium trade. While this is not to imply that the Thai deliberately encouraged drug trafficking to benefit their economy, the obvious fact of the matter is that poor Hmong hills people in northern Thailand can and do make a much better living from this type of activity than they could managing their other agricultural operations. Equally interesting is the fact that this "War on Drugs" tended to focus on methamphetamine production more than opium production. As it turns out, Thailand is one of the leading consumers of methamphetamine pills, which are reportedly smuggled into Thailand by the hundreds of millions annually from factories operated by the united Wa State Army in the nation of Burma (Hanser et al. 2008; United Nations Office on Drugs and Crime, 2003). In fact, the abuse of stimulants has dramatically increased in Thailand, where methamphetamine, referred to as *ya baa* meaning "crazy medicine," reportedly accounts for nearly 70% of all addictions (United Nations Office on Drugs and Crime, 2003; Zickler, 2001). This increase in methamphetamine addiction in Thailand represented a dramatic shift when considering that just 5 years ago, 70% of addicts in Thailand were using opiates (Zickler, 2001). While the opiate trade still exists as an export from Thailand to the rest of the world, the methamphetamine trade has been plaguing the Thai home front for a number of years. Thus, the Thai war on drugs has tended to focus on the drugs that were a danger to the Thai people yet did not lavish the same concern for the opiate trade.

Though reports note that opium production in and around Thailand is down, there is still a substantive opium transportation network that is lucrative for drug traffickers. The international demand for opium is certainly great enough to produce sizable profits for drug dealers and exporters in Thailand. With this in mind, some scholars and researchers contend that the reasons for the singular focus on methamphetamines in the Thai War on Drugs is twofold; first to eliminate debilitating drug-of-choice used by the Thai people (i.e., methamphetamine) and, second, to avoid any negative impact upon the booming Thai economic market as might occur if the opiate export system—generated by the pull of external international customer demand rather than internal local Thai consumption—were severely curtailed.

To be sure, Thaksin Shinawatra was an avid reformer of the police in Thailand and he took a very firm stance against the drug trade. In addition, he made a point to allocate good funding for the police and he took an active and direct interest in cultivating a truly professional force. However, as has already been noted, there were a number of competing factors that did not work in tandem with his desires for police reform. Primary among these were those that were economic in nature. Shinawatra was aware of this and in his text entitled *Reforming the Police in Thailand*, he provides the following offset inserted statement:

> The majority of those who run afoul of the criminal justice system are the poor and the disadvantaged. Great care must be taken to ensure that they are treated fairly, in an even-handed manner. No longer should there be any distortion of the law because of poverty or lack of opportunity (p. 176).

It is clear that Prime Minister Shinawatra was deeply aware of the economic disparity that existed in his country and it was also clear that he understood the often cited link between poverty and crime. Further, Shinawatra's government had designed many policies to be of benefit to the rural majority throughout the country. For instance, Shinawatra's government initiated village-managed microcredit developmental funds, low-interest agricultural loans, deposits and donations of cash into a variety of infrastructure development funds, as well funds for the development of entrepreneurial enterprises among the poor. What is interesting is that Shinawatra oversaw this generosity during all points in the year and throughout his tenure, and not just during politically crucial times; he also made a point to have the money village-managed, meaning that the villages had a wide degree of autonomy in the use of these funds. These acts of kindness, along with his trust in village-level leaders, did well for the general economy and also encouraged a positive rapport between the government in Bangkok and the outlying rural regions of the country.

Even more interesting, Shinawatra was very concerned with the virtues and moral decision-making of the police in Thailand. Shinawatra (2006) and King Bhumibol of Thailand, both shared similar sentiments regarding the role of the police, noting that the Royal Thai Police Cadet Academy was obligated to instill a set of virtues in Thai police officers that would encourage honesty, ward against unwholesome desires, persevere in the face of hardship, and "abstain from wrongdoing, including corruption, and to sacrifice personal benefits for the greater good of the country as a whole" (p. 131). Going further, the Prime Minister provided a set of additional moral guidelines that seemed to almost speak directly to the points made by Tavivat (1998). Shinawatra spoke directly on Buddhism's impact on Thailand and the need to insert that belief system more prominently within the macrostructure of the Thai governmental and economic decision-making processes. In particular, points 4 and 5 of his short list speak directly to Tavivat's contentions. Shinawatra and Pongcharoen (2006, p. 131) noted that these moral values should be classified as

1. Self-reliance and industriousness
2. Thrift
3. Self-discipline and compliance with the law
4. Behaving in accordance with the moral precepts of the Buddhist religion
5. Love of the nation, Buddhism, and the monarchy

While all of the above moral points are good and prosocial character-istics, it is noteworthy that Shinawatra chose to infuse Buddhism into his points since this was sure to appeal to a large majority of the police and public and since this is particularly what has been undermined by Thai modern-ization. It is clear that Shinawatra was of course aware of the graft and corrup-tion that infiltrated Thai politics and Thai policing. An appeal to police to safeguard their integrity and to keep their passions in check is simply typical of any police agency's emphasis on ethical service, but to coopt this with Buddhist principles was to speak to the very fiber and soul of the public and the nation itself. This is identical in point and purpose to what Tavivat (1998) noted as necessary and demonstrates the depth to which Shinawatra under-stood the challenges to developing a modern and ethical policing system.

In addition, King Bhumibol was (and still is) greatly loved and respected by the people of Thailand, particularly those of the poor sectors of the coun-try. The king is known for philanthropic activities and for providing public services to help the people and it was a very important move on the part of Shinawatra to include loyalty to the monarch within this set of moral values. This increased cohesion but it again emphasized a sense of selfless service that the king embodied within the public eye. Though all of this was laud-able and indeed necessary, it is not clear how well these attempts at ethi-cal empowerment have been in effecting change within the policing system. While Thai police have a reputation of being reasonable, balanced, and good willed in service, their integration into a system structured around bribery and vice seems to be a cultural norm that is so pervasive as to completely counter any initial recruit training that cadets may receive. In other words, it may simply be that this *is* what policing is expected to be by the public and that anything else is largely beyond comprehension among the public and the police themselves. To generate a change in values that are so broadly reinforced is likely to be very difficult and require years, perhaps generations. This was the goal that Tahksin Shinawatra chose (a truly higher-order goal) with the knowledge that such reforms would only come within due time.

Even after the coup against Shinawatra, it is clear that police ethics and moral development is a concern and a problem within Thailand. During

2007, the interim Prime Minister, Surayud Chulanont, called for extensive reform of the police system in Thailand. Measures have been set in place to amend the 2004 Police Act and to allow for an independent complaints procedure for citizens. Chulanont's implementation of this procedure emanated from a recommendation made to Shinawatra by the United Nations Human Rights Committee in 2005. One key change that is expected through these amendments would be the decentralization of policing command, providing increased discretion for regional commanders, while providing better salaries and career incentives for policing personnel (Asian Human Rights Commission, 2007).

There is widespread skepticism among the public in regard to these reforms. Indeed, the job of reforming an entire police force, particularly a national police force, is truly onerous and within Thailand this is likely to be even more true due to entrenched power bases that are often intertwined with corruption and self-financing. Further, it would stand to reason that the police will at least subversively resist the reforms, particularly if their jobs are made more difficult, they are expected to have more public accountability, or if they are subject to forms of outside control (Asian Human Rights Commission, 2007). However, if the interim government is able to generate public support, then police resistance to reform is much more difficult. Then again, it may well be that graft and corruption is so entrenched into Thai culture that reforms may not emerge as an important public agenda. The Asian Human Rights Commission (AHRC) also notes that decentralization, albeit a well intended move toward police integrity in an open society, may have negative effects that are far reaching in consequence. The AHRC noted that

> Decentralisation of policing may be a good idea in principle but in Thailand it may prove to be highly regressive. The police in Thailand had their origins as a decentralised force. Local governors organised and used units as their personal security and paramilitary forces. Over time power became concentrated in Bangkok in order to diminish the control of governors, local politicians and others over the police. Thus, the capacity of national-level politicians, including the former prime minister–himself once a police officer–to influence and control the police increased, without really rubbing out the influence of local authorities. The current proposal may well end in a reversion to the earlier model of locally politicised police, rather than nationally politicised ones, and no change in the overall level of influence and corruption (2007, p. 2).

At this point, it is unclear what the future of policing in Thailand will hold. It is even less clear if the various ethical dilemmas will ever be truly addressed so that the policing system can operate as an open learning organization. As long as the hands of power keep changing in Thailand (keeping in mind that numerous coups have occurred throughout the country since 1932) and as long as there continues to be widespread corruption, extreme disparity between the affluent and the impoverished, and a criminal industry that is fueled by an international market, it is unlikely that any true reforms will take hold for the average Thai police officer.

Extremism in the South

Extremist groups in Thailand are not a new threat to that country and reflect a movement that actually has been active throughout a number of nations in the area. For Thailand, the threat is largely due to Muslim extremists that seek to have an autonomous Muslim state. These Islamic extremists are located in the southernmost provinces of Thailand and include the provinces of Narathiwat, Yalla, and Pattani. These three provinces were once part of an independent Muslim sultanate that had been named Pattani. This region bordered Malaysia and in addition to being predominantly Muslim, it was also composed primarily of persons of Malaysian ethnic origins. In 1902, Thailand annexed Pattani and then divided the sultanate into three separate provinces (Fearon and Laitin, 2005; Neuman, 2005). Naturally, this was not a popular occurrence with the persons living in the region and resentment has been harbored against the Thai government for decades to come.

During the 1960s, the National Liberation Front of Pattani and the Barisan Revolusi Nasional emerged as guerilla factions causing problems for the Thai government (Neuman, 2005). Indeed, the Thai government was still viewed as an occupying and alien force in many respects since the Thai had afterall annexed the region years before. In fact, it is a bit surprising that extremist groups such as these had not surfaced long before the 1960s. If they did previously exist, their activity was unorganized and not under the banner of identifiable groups or organizations. The key emphasis of these groups was to promote the region as Malaysian in ethnic background and Muslim in religion (Neuman, 2005). These two distinctions were considered sufficient grounds by these extremists to reinstate Pattani as an independent Islamic nation.

Though this region has always been at odds with the Thai government, it was not until the 1990s that this Islamic push in the south would be considered a true threat to overall Thai national security. This is because it was during this time that the Muslims in the area began to identify with other Muslims in the region and throughout the world. The very conservative and rigid Wahhabi teachings of Islam were increasingly adopted by the people in this area and this made the population even further removed from the Thai nation and also detracted from the likelihood of a peaceful coexistence (Neuman, 2005). In addition, many Thai mercenaries were returning from the conflict between Afghanistan and the former Soviet Union and were bringing back the teachings and beliefs of the Mujahidin that had existed in that region. This also led to tighter bonds between Pattani Muslims and those in the Middle East. In essence, the Pattani were no longer alone in their struggle; they had friends and supporters throughout the Muslim world. This also meant that the goal of Muslims in southern Thailand went from an independent sultanate to a separate united Islamic nation that would span Indonesia, Malaysia, Singapore, and Brunei (Neuman, 2005).

Throughout the past decade and during Thaksin Shinawatra's entire reign, the problems with Islamic unrest in these southern provinces continued to escalate. Violence resurged in 2001, but unlike the past decades, attacks after 2001 tended to concentrate on police officers, military personnel, and schools (Mydans, 2007; Neuman, 2005; Smith, 2004). It was during this time that the first mention of discontent with Thaksin's methods of combating these problems was voiced among the Thai public. The public image of the Prime Minister was at stake while the violence continued to become progressively worse. In 2004, an incident occurred where Islamic youth attacked Thai police with machetes and killed five members of the police security forces in the region. During the fighting, 107 of the Islamic attackers were killed. According to the Thai government, the identification of those organizing the attacks as well as determining the causes for the unrest were very difficult (Mydans, 2007; Neuman, 2005; Smith, 2004). In many cases, local community leaders pointed toward the rough and abusive treatment that security forces used with the Muslim population. Interestingly, the Thai government's Human Rights Commission confirmed that abusive treatment often did occur and that many Muslim protestors cited this as a reason for their violent actions. Further, the Thai government often faulted politicians and security officials that reportedly resisted efforts to end government corruption and to professionalize the police forces by either adding problems to the conflict or turning a blind eye when violence would take place. Indeed, one of the key challenges cited was the rampant corruption that existed among the security forces, many of whom were involved in illicit activities such as drug smuggling and gun trafficking. As an example, in 2004, over 300 weapons were stolen from a governmental army base in southern Thailand. As odd as it may be, the police reported to Shinawatra that members of the Thai army had stolen the weapons and then sold them in Indonesia, after which the soldiers blamed the raid on separatist Muslims in southern Thailand (Neuman, 2005; Smith, 2004).

In late 2004, another incident occurred in which 84 Muslim human rights protestors were killed in Tak Bai when the Thai military attacked members of a peaceful protest by people that simply wished to protest the mistreatment of civilians by the Thai military. It was at this point that Prime Minister Shinawatra further escalated the level of military and police activity in the Muslim populated regions. As small conflicts continued, July 2005 saw the enactment of an emergency decree to help maintain control over the

Muslim provinces. During this same year, Shinawatra established what was called the National Reconciliation Commission to oversee the processes to establish peace in southern Thailand. This commission's ultimate report was released in June 2006 with the recommendation that Islamic Law be officially recognized in the region and that Pattani-Malay be adopted as an official language of the region. The Thai government considered these options but was not able to resolve the issues before the coup against Prime Minister Shinawatra occurred in 2006.

Events Leading to the Coup d'État

In 2006, General Sonthi Boonyaratglin was the Commander-in-Chief of the Royal Thai Army. He was rather unique since he was the first Muslim military commander-in-chief in Thai history (BBC, 2007a). This was quite an accomplishment when one considers, as mentioned before, that roughly 95% of the Thai population are Buddhists. The Royal Thai Army is then naturally one that has predominantly Buddhist soldiers. General Boonyaratglin had engaged in a number of political maneuvers in 2006, removing and/or transferring many key military personnel loyal to former Prime Minister Shinawatra from their posts while consolidating the positions of other officers who were primarily loyal to his own cause. Further, Boonyaratglin was known to have had several public disagreements with Shinawatra, the most notable involving General Boonyaratglin's desire to attempt talks with militants in the Muslim south as a means of avoiding further bloodshed. Shinawatra disagreed and remained firm on militant methods of addressing the unrest in the Muslim regions of Thailand. Among these disagreements was the apparent public knowledge that Boonyaratglin was close to King Bhumibol and that he occasionally played the role of unofficial spokesman for the Thai king (BBC, 2007a).

During this same year, another circumstance arose that, while unrelated to the general's complaints about Prime Minster Shinawatra, did serve to weaken Shinawatra's hold on the country. These circumstances involved a decision by the Thai Prime Minister's family to sell its shares of Shin Corporation, an important Thai company, which placed the control of the company in the hands of investors from Singapore, not Thailand. The sale of this stock netted the Shinawatra family roughly $1.9 billion and it was alleged that the family had somehow avoided paying taxes on the monetary exchange (BBC, 2007b). This and other circumstances where it was discovered that Shinawatra had not fully disclosed all of his family's financial holdings led to numerous public protests involving Thai citizens. The street protests, alleging numerous forms of fraud and abuse of government power, continued and over several months the political instability had degenerated to a state of political gridlock and crisis.

According to the BBC (2007a), it was these and other political crises that led to General Boonyaratglin's ever bolder statements of his dissatisfaction with the prime minister. In many cases, the general would imply that his own concerns were also those of the king. Interestingly, King Bhumibol never challenged the general's claims nor did he ever contradict the very public statements of General Boonyaratglin. During this time, the general continued to deliver public statements indicating King Bhumibol's displeasure with decisions of the prime minister and the general went on record noting that since he was ultimately a soldier of the king, his duty would be to adhere strictly to whatever advice the King of Thailand might provide. The political unrest culminated with General Boonyaratglin's successful coup d'état in September 2006. Shortly after the coup took place, King Bhumibol provided his own public support of the takeover, thereby adding legitimacy to the change in government and garnering public support for the drastic actions that took place. Later in 2007, General Boonyaratglin stepped down from military service to become the Deputy Prime Minister of national security, while Surayud Chulanont (a former military supporter) became Prime Minister of the country.

Since this time, the new government has drafted a constitution that limits the powers of the prime minister and also limits service to two terms in office. Further, the new constitution makes it easier to impeach a prime minister while also eliminating many loopholes that were reported to exist; loopholes that provided prime ministers with mechanisms to abuse their power, according to the post-coup government. In addition, the new constitution apparently contains more concern for minority rights throughout the country, reflecting concerns over fundamental fairness in relation to the Muslim population. Beyond these changes, the post-coup government's Thai Election Commission has claimed that roughly 60% of the voter population participated in the process of legitimizing the new constitution, with a strong majority voting in its favor.

Lastly, the new government charged the Thai Rak Thai party (Thaksin Shinawatra's political party when he was in power) with electoral fraud and with failure to obey the rule of law. Interestingly, this followed with King Bhumibol publicly noting that political discomfort would follow regardless of the decisions made by the new government to punish or exonerate the former prime minister's party. Throughout his reign, King Bhumibol has seen 24 prime ministers come to power, witnessed 18 coups take place, and has observed the drafting of 17 constitutions in Thailand (Baker and Phongpaichit, 2005; BBC, 2007a). The political tensions of 2006 were nothing new to the King of Thailand and he made it known that with any divisive issue, there would always be at least minimal resistance and unrest. Shortly thereafter, the Thai Rak Thai party was completely disbanded in Thailand and was barred from practicing politics for 5 years (BBC, 2007a). In addition, the new government had publicly called for the formal arrest of Thaksin

Shinawatra while pursuing further investigation of other alleged financial crimes and violations.

Many Thai scholars have commented on the coup and have indicated that while the King of Thailand may not have necessarily initiated the change in government, he did not act to prevent it (BBC, 2007b). As a result, the contention is that the King of Thailand tacitly supported the events. Furthermore, many political scholars and analysts from Thai universities in and around Bangkok have expressed staunch support that such a coup simply could not take place if King Bhumibol had been in opposition. The king's role would have been critical in any such crisis and given his public popularity, no party would consider such a move without knowing that they had at least the tacit support of the monarchy. Rather, these analysts, noting prior problems between the king and Shinawatra, have concluded that the scenario was one that culminated in a showdown between the two. The king, revered as a near divinity by the people, had spent decades winning the minds and hearts of the people through public works and acts of selfless kindness. Thaksin Shinawatra having a strong political base among the northern rural poor due to his economic incentives overvalued his emphasis on materialist consumerism to motivate the nation. Ultimately, it would seem that the Buddhist characteristics of kindness, peace, harmony, and serenity, all attributes widely equated with King Bhumibol, had reached the hearts and minds of the individual Thai, translating (afterall) into macro-level change in the governmental structure. In addition, the fact that the King of Thailand remained firmly in power despite any political or military turmoil that may have befallen the nation serves to further demonstrate that Thailand is, first and foremost, a kingdom. Nevertheless, as befitting the ironic nature of the Thai social landscape, the work involved in such a macro-level change occurred at the hands of a Muslim general, not a Buddhist, all with the tacit support of a Buddhist king. Further demonstrating the unique nature of this interesting country where one can still see and hear citizens and visiting foreigners shake their heads smiling, noting that *"This is Thailand."*

References

Asian Human Rights Commission (2007). Thailand: Police reforms without public or constitutional law are meaningless. Honking, China: Asian Human Rights Commission. Retrieved from: http://www.ahrchk.net/statements/mainfile.php/2007statements/1112/

Baker, C. J. and Phongpaichit, P. (2005). *A History of Thailand.* New York: Cambridge University Press.

BBC (2007a). Profile: Thai coup leader. London, U.K.: BBC. Retrieved from: http://news.bbc.co.uk/2/hi/asia-pacific/5361932.stm

BBC (2007b). Profile: Thaksin Shinawatra. London, U.K.: BBC. Retrieved from: http://news.bbc.co.uk/2/hi/asia-pacific/1108114.stm

Bishop, R. and Robinson, L. (1998). *Night Market. Sexual Cultures and the Thai Economic Miracle.* New York: Routledge.

DeVoss, D. (1994). *A Portrait of Thailand.* New York: Todtri Productions Limited.

Fearon, J. D. and Laitin, D. D. (2005). Thailand. Retrieved December 5, 2007, from Stanford University Web site: http://www.stanford.edu/group/ethnic/Random%20Narratives/ThailandRN1.3.pdf

Friedman, T. L. (1999). *The Lexus and the Olive Tree: Understanding Globalization.* New York: Anchor Books.

Hanser, R. D., Wallace, W., and Jones, K. (2008). The global opium trade: Cultivation, production, and distribution. In F. G. Shanty and P. P. Mishra (eds.), *Organized Crime: From Trafficking to Terrorism.* Santa Barbara, CA: ABC-CLIO.

McGeown, K. (2006). Thai king remains center stage. London, U.K.: BBC News. Retrieved from: http://news.bbc.co.uk/2/hi/asia-pacific/5367936.stm

Mydans, S. (2007). Muslim insurgency stokes fear in Southern Thailand. Paris, France: International Herald Tribune. Retrieved from: http://www.iht.com/articles/2007/02/25/news/thailand.php?page=1

Neuman, Z. (2005). Thailand's south embroiled in sectarian conflict. Washington, DC: The Jewish Institute for National Security Affairs. http://www.jinsa.org/articles/articles.html/function/view/categoryid/1701/documentid/2802/history/3,2360,655,1701,2802

Poulin, R. (2004). Globalization and the sex trade: Trafficking and the commodification of women and children. *Women Studies/Les Cahiers de la femme,* 22(3), 38–43.

Royal Thai Police, Human Resources Bureau (2004). *The Royal Thai Police.* Bangkok, Thailand: The Royal Thai Police's Publisher.

Sandhu, D. S., Leung, S. A., and Tang, M. (2003). Counseling approaches with Asian Americans and Pacific Islander Americans. In F. D. Harper and J. McFadden (eds.), *Culture and Counseling: New Approaches.* New York: Allyn & Bacon.

Shinawatra, T. and Pongcharoen, P. (2006). *Reforming the Police in Thailand.* Bangkok, Thailand: Royal Police Cadet Academy Association.

Singhsilarak, J. and Cheurprakobkit, S. (2007). Police education and training in Thailand. In P. C. Kratcoski and D. K. Das (eds.), *Police Education and Training in a Global Society* (pp. 57–70). Lanham, MD: Lexington Books.

Smith, A. L. (2004). Trouble in Thailand's Muslim south: Separatism, not global terrorism. *Asia–Pacific Security Studies,* 3(10), 1–5.

Sue, D. W. and Sue, D. (1990). *Counseling the Culturally Different* (2nd edn.). New York: John Wiley & Sons.

Tavivat, P. (1998). Toward a Buddhist social ethics: The case of Thailand. *Cross Currents,* 48(3), 347–365. Retrieved from: http://www.crosscurrents.org/buddhistethics.htm

United Nations Office on Drugs and Crime (2003). Ecstasy and amphetamines: Global survey 2003. New York: United Nations. Retrieved from: http://www.unodc.org/pdf/publications/report_ats_2003-09-23_1.pdf

Warren, W., Stone, D., and Tettoni, L. (2006). *Thailand: A Traveller's Companion.* Bangkok, Thailand: Asia Books.

Wyatt, D. K. (2003). *Thailand: A Short Story* (2nd edn.). New Haven, CT: Yale University Press.

Zickler, P. (2001). Thailand conference focuses on methamphetamine research. Washington, DC: National Institute on Drug Abuse. Retrieved from: http://www.nida.nih.gov/NIDA_Notes/NNVol16N1/Thailand.html

The Positive Influence of Unionization on Police Professionalism

V

American Policing at a Crossroads: Are Police Unions Taking on the Challenge or Impeding Change?

21

RONALD G. DELORD

Contents

Introduction

The diverse profusion of American police unions and their agenda, the extent of their networking, and the strategies that they employ to optimize union impact on law enforcement policy and practice in the United States must be examined more closely. American police unions have been self-centered and elitist in their quest for higher wages and benefits, and police unions have not elected to participate in the social reform of the police profession. Insight must be gained into dilemmas facing the law enforcement profession in the United States: police unions have no unified national voice with the federal government; the criminal justice system is decentralized; there is no uniform national labor law; and there is no uniform national standard for professional ethics, training, policies, or practices. This decentralization, fragmentation, and disorganization reduce the opportunities for change or reform. This is because there is no shared vision for the future of the police profession by police management organizations, police labor unions, academics, community activists, and elected officials. There are many challenges facing American police management organizations and police labor unions, particularly if they wish to promote the ideals of justice and effectiveness when policing communities.

Terminology

Except for the United States, most countries use the term *police* for all civilian law enforcement. In the decentralized American system, there are municipal police officers, county police officers, county sheriff's deputies, county constables, state police, state and county highway patrol, state troopers, and special agents at every level of government. In order to simplify terminology utilized below, the terms *police, police officer, police department,* or *law enforcement agency* will include municipal, county, special district, and state or federal law enforcement officers and agencies. The term *police chief* will include police chiefs, sheriffs, constables, or the head of a law enforcement agency.

The term *union* is the common denominator in the name of most labor organizations worldwide. There is no one common denominator when it comes to organizational names or affiliations for police labor organizations in the United States and most other countries. One theory is that since labor unions are identified by the general public and media as representing blue collar workers, police labor organizations overwhelmingly use the term *association*, *federation*, or *lodge* instead of *union* in an effort to be identified more closely with professional organizations such as those representing doctors and lawyers. A reason for this reluctance to use the term *union* is rooted in their belief that police work is a profession and not a blue-collar job or a "craft." Since the most common international term to describe a labor organization is *union*, the term *police union* will be inclusive of all police and law enforcement labor organizations regardless of their name, agency, or organizational affiliation.

As we continue into the twenty-first century where there is a global questioning about democracy and equality, it makes sense to question whether police unions are willing to mobilize to promote the ideals of justice and effectiveness when policing communities. The evidence so far indicates that the trend is going in a negative direction. The reasons for this are complex, as are the solutions.

The first analysis below will examine the fragmented local, state, and national police labor movement and the lack of a unified voice from police unions on issues, including those pertaining to the democratization and improvement of policing in the United States. There is at present no coordinated strategy or networking by the various local, state, or national police unions. This is somewhat worrying given that police unions have a major impact on the implementation or the rejection of new police policies and practices, especially at the local government level. The loudest and most unified voice coming from the various police unions is that they all oppose any control by the general public over police policies and practices through civilian review boards.

A further examination will provide some insight into dilemmas created in the United States due to a decentralized criminal justice system. Yet, while this is taking place, simultaneously American policing is also changing from a civilian "community" police model to a more "national" militaristic police model. In addition, the cost of policing is increasing, and agencies have had to examine the value of non-sworn civilians and private contractors doing jobs that were traditionally done by sworn police officers. Technology has displaced police jobs with the introduction of red light, speed, and surveillance cameras. These changes, coupled with decentralization, greatly reduce the cooperation and interactions among police officers, police unions, and law enforcement agencies at each level of government, and thus reduce the opportunities for change or reform. The rivalry between law enforcement agencies for funding, status, and control at the local, state, and federal level is well known and creates an atmosphere of distrust and a lack of cooperation.

Another aspect to consider is the federal legislation being pursued by national police unions and the impact on law enforcement officers caused by the lack of uniform national labor laws. The federal government has not adopted a national collective bargaining law, a Police Officers' Bill of Rights, or any uniform policies pertaining to wages, benefits, pensions, or working conditions other than the Fair Labor Standards Act. Despite this unfriendly terrain, there is no real networking between the various national police unions. Inter-union rivalries have hamstrung the national police unions and prevented the unions from achieving a greater success on labor legislation at the federal level. The national police unions have similar political agendas, and compete to get a seat at the table with the political party in power.

Finally, the central challenges facing American police management and police labor unions will be outlined, namely, how to create a forum to develop a shared vision of the police profession; make recommendations to improve the effectiveness and efficiency of the police service nationwide; seek ways to balance the need for domestic policing and the new duties caused by international criminal activities; and outline how police agencies can get ahead of the curve on the global changes impacting the police profession and local communities.

Disorganized Labor

Police Unions Collapse: 50 Years since the 1919 Boston Police Strike

The late 1800s and early 1900s were a time of social unrest, political strife, and labor violence. After witnessing the economic gains made by trade unions, firefighters, and other public workers, the American Federation of Labor (AFL) started getting requests for charters from local police benevolent associations who were clamoring to join organized labor.

The unionization of the police caused a firestorm of protest. Private corporations had traditionally called upon elected officials to use the police as strikebreakers. The use of police officers as strikebreakers caused bitter feelings toward police officers by trade union members and their leaders. Police chiefs saw the police service as an arm of the government like the military, and the chiefs did not want police officers forming unions and alliances with political, labor, and social activists. Politicians and police chiefs saw trade labor unions as a threat to the national security and felt they needed the police force to be independent of organized labor.

However, wages, benefits, and working conditions for police officers were dismal and harsh, even for that period. After Boston firefighters formed a union and threatened a strike, the city increased wages and improved working conditions somewhat for firefighters and police officers. In 1919, the Boston Police Social Club requested recognition by the new police commissioner. The police commissioner refused to recognize the union.

The policemen appealed to the AFL for a charter and were accepted. When the union requested bargaining rights, the commissioner terminated the appointments of 19 union leaders. On September 9, 1919, a four-day strike started with 1117 of the city's 1544 policemen walking off the job. Widespread looting, hundreds of injuries, and seven deaths occurred before the National Guard restored order. All the striking policemen were fired and never rehired.

The distrust and hatred of the police as strikebreakers caused the AFL unions to balk at calling a general strike to support the Boston policemen. It was a defining moment for the AFL and the fledgling police labor movement. The decisions made during this strike forever changed the police labor movement. Police unionism practically ceased to exist until the 1960s, when police organizations started becoming more militant.

In 1969, 50 years after the Boston police strike, the American Federation of Labor-Congress of Industrial Organizations (AFL-CIO) received a request to charter a national police union. The AFL-CIO rejected the request, because the same old hard feelings against the police still lingered. It was not until 1979 that the AFL-CIO chartered the International Union of Police Associations (IUPA) as a national police union. What caused the change of heart by organized labor toward police officers? The AFL and CIO peaked in membership when they merged in 1955, and without the competition between the two unions the AFL-CIO's membership began a decline that exists to this day. By 1979, the AFL-CIO could not ignore the vast numbers of potential new police union members, and put finances ahead of old grievances.

The Police Labor Movement after 1979

The police labor movement is a maze of different union affiliations. One would need a playbook to determine which associations, lodges, and unions are affiliated with which state or national police unions. In addition, many police unions have dual affiliations. The Boston Police Patrolmen's Association and the Los Angeles Police Protective League are affiliated with the AFL-CIO chartered IUPA and the independent National Association of Police Organizations (NAPO). The AFL-CIO chartered International Brotherhood of Police Officers (IBPO) has also affiliated with NAPO for federal legislative purposes.

There seems to be some confusion about what *unionization, collective bargaining,* and *meet and confer* mean in American police labor relations. There is a false assumption that the police force is unionized only if the officers have collective bargaining rights with a binding impasse procedure and the officers belong to a national union affiliated with the AFL-CIO. In reality, when police officers form a local association, lodge, or union for the purposes of improving their wages, benefits, and conditions of employment, with or without the ability to collectively bargain or meet and confer with the public employer, the officers are unionized. There is no substantive difference between the police unions affiliated with the AFL-CIO and the independent lodges and police associations. The terms *collective bargaining* and *meet and confer* are basically interchangeable terms in the United States, and have no relationship to whether the officers have an impasse procedure or not.

The police labor movement is divided into two camps: the independent police labor organizations and the police labor organizations affiliated with organized labor through the AFL-CIO. Approximately 80%–85% of all police labor organizations would be classified as independent, and have no affiliation with the AFL-CIO. There are no accurate reports on how many of the 800,000 sworn officers are members of a police union. The best estimate would be 75%–80%, which would rank police officers with firefighters as having the highest unionization rates in the United States. As stated earlier, it is often confusing, because a local police union may have an AFL-CIO charter and also be affiliated with an independent labor group. Fundamentally, all local police unions are independent bodies with very similar constitutions, governance structures, ideologies, missions, and strategies regardless of national affiliations.

The Fraternal Order of Police (FOP) was the only national police organization to survive the 1919 Boston police strike. FOP was founded in Pittsburgh in 1915 as a social, benevolent, and fraternal organization. While FOP has evolved since the 1960s into a labor organization, the FOP constitution still prohibits its lodges from being affiliated with organized labor. FOP reports a membership of 310,000 and is unquestionably the nation's largest police labor organization. FOP has built its membership by appealing to police officers on two levels: the fraternal nature of policing as an extended family, and brotherhood combined with supporting primarily conservative political candidates. To emphasize their conservative political leanings, FOP's advertisements in *American Police Beat* newspaper show their National President seated next to U.S. President Bush. There is a question about how many of the reported members are actually retired officers. FOP reports that they have a state lodge in all 50 states. Some states have a separate fraternal state lodge and a FOP Labor Council which handles labor relations for the lodges (http://www.grandlodgefop.org/).

The second largest national police organization is NAPO, which reports 236,000 members in 2,000 local police associations. NAPO, which is a federation of labor unions and not a labor union per se, is composed primarily of independent police unions who did not want to be affiliated with FOP.

Since NAPO is not a labor union, FOP lodges can join without violating the National FOP Constitution that prohibits affiliations with organized labor, and AFL-CIO police unions can join NAPO without violating the prohibition against dual unionism in their constitution (http://www.napo.org/).

The remaining 15%–20% of unionized police officers are members of associations and unions affiliated with organized labor through the AFL-CIO. The AFL-CIO is an umbrella federation of 57 unions with a reported membership of 13 million members. No records are kept on how many police officers are represented, but the best estimate on the number of police officers in AFL-CIO affiliated unions is probably between 100,000 and 150,000.

The largest AFL-CIO union with a substantial police membership is the International Union of Police Associations. IUPA is the only chartered AFL-CIO police union. IUPA reports a membership of 100,000, and recently gained the affiliation of formerly independent police unions in Los Angeles, Boston, and Cleveland (http://www.iupa.org/).

It would seem that just about every AFL-CIO national union has police officers as members. The American Federation of State, County, and Municipal Employees (AFSCME) reports approximately 10,000–15,000 police members. The IBPO reports 10,000 members. IBPO is a division of the National Association of Government Employees, which is a sector of the Service Employees International Union (SEIU). SEIU has police locals outside of IBPO. The International Brotherhood of Teamsters reports to have 15,000 police members. Recently, the Communications Workers of America created a sector called the National Coalition of Public Safety Officers (NCPSO) for the national union's reported 26,000 police and corrections officers.

Surprisingly, even more AFL-CIO national unions report some police membership. Some examples of AFL-CIO unions with affiliated police unions include Paper, Allied-Industrial, Chemical, and Energy Workers' International Union; Marine Engineers' Beneficial Association; United Steelworkers' Union of America; United Automobile Workers Union; United Food and Commercial Workers' International Union; Operating Engineers International Union; American Federation of Government Employees; and International Longshoremen's Association.

It is immediately evident the number of police officers alleged to be members of unions exceeds the actual number of police officers in the United States. There are two primary reasons. First, dual unionism is a common and accepted practice. In the private sector, it is a violation of the union constitution to belong to more than one union with the same jurisdiction. To join another competing union is ground for expulsion from the union. Police officers in the same agency can, and do, belong to more than one union. The overlapping memberships allow national unions to each rightfully claim the same member.

Second, on the national, state, and regional level, membership inflation is not only common, but also accepted. All unions, but especially national police unions, puff up their membership numbers without the least bit of guilt. The national police unions all include retired members to make their membership numbers appear to be higher than they are. All police union membership figures must be viewed with some skepticism. More accurate membership numbers are only found when the union is representing a designated department where the authorized strength is publicly and officially known.

The Competitive Nature of the Police Labor Movement

The organizing and unionization environment of the police has always been turbulent, hostile, volatile, disruptive, and virtually void of any national, state, or local union support. It has become even worse in the twenty-first century. Every state except Hawaii has multiple police organizations competing for members within each law enforcement agency. But even in Hawaii, the police officers that are represented in one bargaining unit by the State of Hawaii Organization of Police Officers (SHOPO) affiliated for a short time with the AFSCME (AFL-CIO) before disaffiliating and returning to independent status.

Switching national unions or returning to independent status is common. There is very little long-term loyalty among American police unions, either to the local, state, or national union. Unions poaching other unions for members, disaffiliations, re-affiliations, de-certifications, and splinter groups within a law enforcement agency are the rule and not the exception. For example, the independent San Francisco Police Officers Association affiliated with IUPA (AFL-CIO), disaffiliated and returned to independent status, and now is affiliated with SEIU (AFL-CIO). The Police Association of New Orleans (PANO) affiliated with the Teamsters Union, but after the disastrous 1979 police strike, disaffiliated and affiliated with SEIU (AFL-CIO). PANO later disaffiliated from SEIU and is now affiliated with the independent NAPO.

More Fragmentation: Different Ranks, Different Unions, and Multiple Affiliations

In the private sector in the United States, federal law excludes supervisors from the right to form a union and collectively bargain. While some state laws exclude police supervisors from collective bargaining, there are generally nonsupervisors and supervisors in joint or separate police unions in the public sector. In many police agencies, different unions represent the rank-and-file officers and supervisors. Oftentimes, these local unions have different state and national affiliations. For example, the Association for Los Angeles Deputy Sheriffs represents rank-and-file deputy sheriffs, and is affiliated with MEBA (AFL-CIO). The Los Angeles County Professional Peace Officers Association represents sergeants and lieutenants, and is affiliated with IUPA (AFL-CIO). New York City Police Department patrol officers are members of the Patrolmen's Benevolent Association (PBA). Detectives, sergeants, lieutenants, and captains all have their own separate unions and bargaining rights.

Even in law enforcement agencies with one bargaining agent, other police unions exist with members from the same agency, which would be dual unionism in the private sector. In some agencies, one union is the bargaining agent and the second union is perceived as the fraternal organization. For example, the Los Angeles Police Protective League is affiliated with NAPO and IUPA, but has an FOP lodge with elected leaders representing its members on state and national labor issues on behalf of FOP. The Omaha Police Union (IUPA affiliated) and Seattle Police Officers Guild (CWA affiliated) have advertisements for the local FOP lodge in their union newspapers.

This dual unionism is not always as compatible as it would appear in Los Angeles, Omaha, and Seattle. The minority union, which may appear as benign or fraternal to the majority union, can be a vehicle for dissident members to use to unseat the bargaining agent. Even where the members have ousted one union, that union may continue to exist and wait in the shadows for the majority union to make a mistake. Even if the minority union never achieves majority status again, the minority union strives to trip up the majority union's leaders, in particular during contract negotiations. Police management, the media, and elected officials like to see a divided membership.

Union hopping and dual unionism by members creates an unhealthy atmosphere for police union leaders, who fear that one misstep in dealing with the employer or management will result in dissident officers starting a drive to oust the union, not just the union president. The competition among the various police unions and the poaching of each other's membership does more damage to the stability of the local union than management could ever do. One need only look at the achievements of the Australian and Canadian police unions to recognize that, in the United States, the police unions and police officers themselves are to blame for the chaos and lack of a national collective bargaining bill.

What Does the Future Hold for Police Unity in the United States?

NAPO, FOP, and IUPA have participated in various conferences of the International Law Enforcement Council (ILEC). ILEC was formed by the

Canadian Professional Police Association to bring together the leaders of national police unions from democratic nations every even-numbered year, to discuss the future of the police profession. At the 2004 conference in Edinburgh, Scotland, ILEC adopted a set of in principle agreements that included: Assaults on Police, Risk of Contracting Infectious Diseases, and Legislative Protection; Equipment Standards; Independence and Integrity of Investigations of Police; Government Obligation to provide for Public Safety; Police Mobility and Professionalism; and Freedom of Association (http://www.cppa-acpp.ca/index-english.htm).

The U.S. national police unions need to seek a forum similar to ILEC to allow for a free and open debate about the role of police unions in shaping the future of policing and the police profession. A national police union forum should seek to adopt a set of in principle agreements similar to the international ones adopted by ILEC. The U.S. national police unions need to seek closer ties to the budding police union movement in less industrialized countries, and offer to assist them in improving their wages, benefits, and conditions of employment.

A civil war cannot end without someone defeating the other side or the parties deciding to reunite. Poaching at the state and local level breeds animosity and creates a national union leadership afraid to even communicate with another national police union. All of the national police unions have decentralized governance structures and are without any power or authority to force change on state and local bodies. The strife and turmoil will continue unless one or more of the national unions can set aside personal ego and historic grievances to unite one or more of the competing unions into a federation. The AFL and CIO decided that the financial and emotional cost of the fighting over workers was self-defeating, and merged as the AFL-CIO in 1955. There is no substantive difference in services on the national level between FOP, NAPO, IUPA, IBPO, and NCPSO. They all profess to be focused on federal legislation and assistance to their state and local affiliates. So why has there not been an effort at merging the national police unions into one powerful police labor union? Sergeant Harold Melnik, who was the president of the Sergeant's Benevolent Association of the New York City Police Department, has tried to answer this question. He shared his observations at the National Symposium on Police Labor Relations sponsored by the Police Foundation in 1974:

> There is no single individual who has openly come forth with the ability, acceptability and platform to rally all or most police organizations for merger into a national police union...It can be said that while the police association leaders of the major cities recognize the awesome power that could be obtained through a national body properly led, a fear of assimilation with a loss of identity still exists in the minds of many of these leaders. Until the day comes when police officers readily identify themselves as a part of labor, only local and statewide groups will suffice and prosper.

The American Policing Model

Decentralized, Disorganized, and Disconnected

The United States is a country founded by immigrants. These immigrants were often fearful of the military and national police forces in their homelands. This fear of a centralized national police force led elected officials in the United States to oppose the creation of a national police force or allowing the military to act as a domestic police force. Federal law enforcement officers represent only about 10% of all sworn law enforcement officers.

The United States has approximately 18,000 law enforcement agencies employing 940,275 sworn and civilian employees. Virtually every political jurisdiction in the United States has at least one law enforcement agency, and the vast majority of law enforcement agencies have less than 10 officers. The U.S. Department of Justice, Office of Justice Programs, Bureau of Justice Statistics, 2000, reported:

Type of Agency	Number of Agencies	Number of Full-Time Sworn Officers
Total		796,518
All state and local	17,784	708,022
Local police	12,666	440,920
Sheriff	3,070	164,711
Primary State	49	56,348
Special jurisdiction	1,376	43,413
Texas constable	623	2,630
Federal[a]		88,496

Note: The special jurisdiction category includes both state-level and local-level agencies. Consolidated police-sheriffs are included under local police category. Agency counts exclude those operating on a part-time basis.

[a] Nonmilitary federal officers authorized to carry firearms and make arrests.

There is no unified command structure for the 800,000 law enforcement officers and no shared communications between the 18,000 law enforcement agencies. No common mission, strategy, or philosophy is in place or proposed by the federal government or advocated by police unions. There does not appear to be a significant level of trust between federal, state, and local law enforcement agencies. This lack of trust was clearly demonstrated by the color-coded terrorist alerts issued by the Department of Homeland Security that gave local and state law enforcement agencies no greater information than was given to the general public and media. The public and law enforcement agencies quickly lost confidence in the alerts, and little media attention is given to the color-coded alerts today.

The ability to implement change in American law enforcement agencies is complicated, because so many different law enforcement agencies with concurrent and overlapping jurisdictions exist. It is impossible for the average citizen or visitor to differentiate between the multitudes of law enforcement agencies in a community. Many states, counties, and municipalities have law enforcement agencies within the same jurisdiction that are not a part of the primary law enforcement agency. These states, counties, and municipalities have separate law enforcement agencies with separate command structures to deal with the airport, parks, building code enforcement, fire marshals, school district, sanitation, corrections, courts, lifeguards, water authority, lakes, public housing, health department, and virtually every conceivable state, county, and municipal department.

This makes the United States different from countries that have a more centralized policing system. For example, Ireland, Northern Ireland, South Africa, and Scotland each have a single national police force. While there is a separate transport police and some island police forces in England and Wales, 43 police forces have been consolidated into one national bargaining unit for constables below the rank of superintendent. Australia has only nine law enforcement agencies: six states organizations, two territories organizations, and one Federal Police organization. Canada has a national police force which the federal government contracts to 8 of the 10 provinces to provide provincial police services, the 3 northern territories, and 200 individual municipalities. There are 3 provincial services, and only 200 municipal and 17 regional police forces in all of Canada.

The federal government in America has taken a step toward consolidating many of its law enforcement agencies. Congress recently created the Department of Homeland Security. However, many federal non-law enforcement agencies still maintain their own uniformed police forces. For example Congress, Supreme Court, State Department, FBI, Secret Service, Library of Congress, Parks Service, Interior Department, Labor Department, Veterans Administration, Government Printing Office, and virtually all federal agencies maintain and control a uniformed police force.

In May 2003, The International Association of Chiefs of Police (IACP) conducted a study entitled "Consolidating Police Services: An IACP Planning Approach." The study reviewed the pros and cons of consolidating law enforcement services. Despite some consolidation of law enforcement services since the 1950s, very few of the 18,000 law enforcement agencies are seriously considering consolidating services (http://www.theiacp.org/).

The Impact of Global Events on Domestic Policing in the United States

There are many challenges to policing in the twenty-first century. Maintaining law and order on the domestic front oftentimes means a balancing test between the need for societal security and the desire for individual freedom and rights. Prior to September 11, 2001, it appeared to be the general consensus of politicians and the public that the policies and practices of law enforcement agencies should balance the desire for individual freedom and rights at least as importantly as the need for societal security. But this seems to be changing with the threat of terror dominating security concerns in the United States, and indeed worldwide. The move away from localized and community oriented policing is most evident in the recent diminishing of the Community Oriented Police Services (COPS) program. President Bill Clinton created the COPS Program at the U.S. Department of Justice in 1994 to create 100,000 new police positions, and issued millions of dollars in federal grants to state and local police agencies to hire more officers and use those officers to improve community policing at the grassroots level. The COPS program expired in 2000, but was extended year to year by Congress. In 2005, the president and Congress have virtually depleted funding for the COPS program, and shifted that money to training and equipping state and local police for a battle against terrorists (Blau, 2005).

The global crisis created by international terrorism has caused the majority of federal law enforcement agencies to shift their focus to combating terrorism both domestically and abroad. With the support of President Bush, Congress created the Department of Homeland Security—the most comprehensive reorganization of the Federal government in a half-century. The Department of Homeland Security consolidates 22 agencies and 180,000 employees, unifying once-fragmented Federal functions in a single agency dedicated to protecting America from terrorism. A comprehensive national strategy for Homeland Security was developed, focused on six key areas: intelligence and warning; border and transportation security; domestic counterterrorism; protecting critical infrastructure; defending against catastrophic threats; and emergency preparedness and response. President Bush won overwhelming support for the USA Patriot Act, a law that the administration believes gives intelligence and law enforcement officials important new tools to fight terrorists. This legislation is viewed by others as evidence of the shift away from individual freedoms and more toward societal security (http://www.whitehouse.gov/homeland/).

The federal government then shifted traditionally domestic law enforcement tasks that were being handled by federal law enforcement agencies and the military to state and local police forces. The overwhelming majority of American law enforcement agencies—federal, state, and local—were not prepared for the shift in policies and practices to realistically handle international terrorism on a domestic and international level. A report published by IACP stated that the nation's homeland security strategy is "handicapped by a fundamental flaw—it was developed without sufficiently seeking or incorporating the advice, expertise, or consent of public safety organizations at the state, tribal, or local level." The IACP report also criticized the Bush administration for cutting grants to local police forces, which has hampered state, local, and county police from meeting with community groups in their day-to-day work (Mark, 2005).

The Price of Policing a Community

In addition to the rising costs of police wages and benefits, police agencies also face rising costs to recruit, train, and equip police officers. Elected officials and police management are being forced to evaluate what traditional police jobs can be sufficiently undertaken by civilian employees, private contractors, and technology.

California Governor Arnold Schwarzenegger has pledged to privatize, reduce, and even eliminate pension benefits for state employees, despite ongoing public disapproval from public employee and police unions. Governors in Massachusetts, Rhode Island, Alaska, and Illinois are all reviewing the high costs to the taxpayers to maintain public employee pension systems.

Public policing, with all that this promises, is now under threat. How to balance the cost of each police officer and define what constitutes police work is the global question impacting all police agencies. American anti-unionism is driving down wages for all workers at the same time that the cost of putting a fully trained and equipped police officer on the street is soaring. And the police unions, in advocating for higher wages, may unintentionally have made the future of public police officers more insecure. Despite the problems caused by poorly trained private security employees, police authorities and employers are likely to look for cheaper avenues to policing than the highly unionized public police employees, despite the risks.

Given the global quest for cost cutting in the public sector, it is hardly surprising that the number of civilian non-sworn employees of police agencies has been rising. In many agencies, former police jobs—background investigations of applicants, crime scene investigations, evidence technicians, property rooms, parking violations, nonemergency calls, building security, courts security, prisoner transport, and detention—are now done by civilian employees. This has not occurred without a fight from police unions. Two recent examples illustrate the battle over the civilianization of police agencies. In Chicago, the police union won an arbitration overturning a city ordinance that allowed civilian employees to work traffic details formerly handled by uniformed officers. In Pennsylvania, the Governor and the State Troopers Association have clashed over whether to hire 270 more troopers or replace troopers in the central dispatch center with civilian employees (*American Police Beat*, 2005). In another case, the union for San Diego police officers was approached to consider allowing the city to rehire retired police officers on a part-time basis for supervisor and nonsupervisor positions to fill vacancies. If this had occurred, the police union would not be able to negotiate for these retired members and the jobs would be lost to active members. The city already has 1,000 mostly retired citizens in the Volunteers in Policing (VIP) program. The city furnishes vehicles and police radios to citizen volunteers to call in suspicious persons and report crimes.

Technology has also dramatically changed the police environment, and its ongoing incorporation into police agencies has led to the displacement of police officers. Speed and red light cameras generate tremendous amounts of revenue for governments without the cost of a police officer. Surveillance cameras in high crime cameras have allowed police agencies to reduce the number of officers needed to patrol these areas.

The privatization of policing in the United States continues to grow. At present the estimated number of private security guards exceeds 4 million—four times the number of police officers. The debate over private contracting of police work is not whether police jobs will be displaced by private contractors, but how many police jobs will be lost. While the privatization of prisons has been the most public issue, private contractors are seeking to bid on just about every aspect of policing, including patrolling the streets. This issue is not peculiar to the United States, but characterizes the policing landscape throughout the world.

Where are police unions in reference to these global changes to the profession? With few exceptions, police unions have fought tooth and nail against civilianization, privatization, and technology. It is much like the trench warfare in World War I. Despite the introduction of machine guns, tanks, and aircraft, the leaders on both sides refused to change their tactics and fought back and forth over a few feet of ground. Technology had changed the landscape, and no amount of insistence on the traditional methods could overcome these changes to the environment. Police unions are losing ground to civilianization, privatization, and technology, and they know it intellectually. However, it seems each police union leader wants to delay the inevitable until they leave office.

The Uniqueness of "Political" Policing in the United States

The police forces in Canada, Australia, New Zealand, and the United Kingdom are unionized, but are generally restrained or prohibited from being involved in election campaigns of individual candidates or political parties. Police unions in these countries have opted to focus on using public platforms and the media to shape public debate on policing issues such as the allocation of police resources for fighting crime and staffing levels. While in each of these countries there have been times when police unionists have openly endorsed particular political candidates and parties, this is the exception rather than the norm, and is frowned upon by the public and by politicians.

By contrast, the overwhelming majority of American police unions are politically active in the campaigns of those persons elected to control the police themselves. The direct involvement of American police unions in the political campaigns of the elected officials who control them is diametrically opposite to the national political views of most democratic countries. The vast majority of American police unions have a distinct political advantage over appointed police chiefs and law enforcement agency heads in openly campaigning for individual political candidates. Traditionally, appointed police chiefs cannot endorse candidates for political office, work in political campaigns, or make political contributions. That distinct demarcation between a police chief and politicians has started to fade. Appointed police chiefs are starting to appear more and more in the political *photo ops* of their elected bosses. Any time the U.S. president, the governor of a state, or a city mayor conducts a press conference involving crime or police-related issues, one can expect to see the police chief and uniform officers standing as a backdrop for the press conference.

What separates the police union from the police chief in the world of politics is that the police union has the ability to endorse a candidate and work in the candidate's political campaign. However, the greatest advantage for the police union is its ability to contribute money to the candidate. In many parts of the United States, the police union's Political Action Committee (PAC) is the largest campaign contributor to a candidate. Despite protests from the editorial boards of newspapers about the perceived political power of many police unions, candidates for public office continue to seek the endorsement and resources of the police union. The real political power of the police union is its ability to deal directly with the elected officials, the media, and the public, and to bypass the police chief and government administrators. The ability of the police union to make a political end run frustrates police chiefs and government administrators wanting to change or reform police polices and practices.

As a result, police unions have become major players in the "Court of Public Opinion." The political power game in the United States revolves around money. The police union brings money to the game, but more importantly it brings the name and reputation of the police (not the police union) to the candidate. This power game is institutionalized into the American political culture, and police unions can either play the game or have the game played for them—but it will be played regardless. With few exceptions, police unions for the most part have not taken this political power and used it to improve the efficiency and effectiveness of the department, to promote social reforms of the profession, or sought to bring community activists into the decision-making of the police force. Having political power and then using it for the greater good of the profession and community does not seem to be happening among U.S. police union leaders.

Decentralized Labor Laws

Incoherent Labor Laws

After decades of strikes and labor violence, the U.S. Congress passed the *National Labor Relations Act* (*NLRA*) to extend the right to form a union and collectively bargain to certain private sector employees. The National Labor Relations Board (NLRB) was created to enforce this right, and prohibited employers from committing unfair labor practices that might discourage organizing or prevent workers from negotiating a union contract. In reality, the NLRB has failed to protect employees who try to unionize, as witnessed by the steady decline of private sector unionization. The Bureau of Labor Statistics reported that union membership as a percent of the total workforce in 2002 was 13.2%. Union density was 8.5% in the private sector and 37.5% in the public sector (www.psrf.org/info/unions.jsp). Today, just one in 13 workers in the private sector is in a union, down from one in three a half-century ago (Greenhouse, 2005).

The failed Boston police strike in 1919, which led to the subsequent passage of draconian anti-union laws for police officers, basically ended police unionization until the 1960s. While private sector workers were fighting for protections to unionize and collectively bargain, police officers were not organized and their union rights fell to the wayside.

Today, the police labor relations system in the United States is very complex. Congress has not seen the need to extend any federal protections and rights to state and local police officers. The United States is one of the few highly industrialized democratic countries that do not have uniform national labor laws for police officers. The decentralized American police model allows each state to determine its own labor laws and policies as regards the police. If a given state does not regulate police labor relations, the local government is free to adopt its own policies and practices. To date, 39 states have some form of collective bargaining for public employees; however, many states prohibit police officers from having bargaining rights (http://www.afscme.org/). Twenty-two states have enacted right-to-work provisions that prohibit union membership being mandatory and prohibit unions from charging nonmembers a fee for the costs of bargaining. Most of the Southern states prohibit public employees and police officers from being recognized as a labor union and collectively bargaining (http://www.nrtw.org/).

The one substantive federal law impacting police officers is the *Fair Labor Standards Act* (FLSA), which was passed by Congress and did not cover public employees. In 1985, the U.S. Supreme Court in a 5–4 vote extended the *FLSA* to cover all public employees. *FLSA* requires all employers to pay covered employees who are not otherwise exempt at least the federal minimum wage, and to pay additional "overtime" compensation after 40 h of work in

1 week. The U.S. Department of Labor promulgated the rules and regulations, and decided to set special overtime standards for police officers and firefighters separate from nonuniform public employees. The law does allow officers covered by a collective bargaining contract to supersede *FLSA* provisions if the contract creates a better benefit (http://www.dol.gov/esa/whd/flsa/).

Where Are the Police Unions on Federal Legislation?

There is no question that collectively American police unions on the local, state, and national levels are major players in the political game, and significantly contribute to both the success and failure of change and reform in the police profession. Police unions have been successful in raising professional standards, increasing wages and benefits, and improving the overall living conditions of officers, but this change has been city-by-city and state-by-state and not a product of any coordinated federal legislative strategy by the national police unions. But the wins that have been achieved by the police unions are limited due to the fragmented and competitive nature of the police union movement in the United States. There is no national strategy around issues such as professionalism and reform, nor any comprehensive approach to respond to the changes taking place in policing more generally. This is not to say that there is a total lack of a shared vision in the police union movement. An examination of the Web sites of the independent FOP and NAPO, and the AFL-CIO affiliated IUPA and IBPO reveal that all have similar postings for the same federal legislation. All national police unions support a federal collective bargaining bill and a Police Officers' Bill of Rights, despite the fact the Bush administration and a Republican controlled Congress do not support either bill. There are two common federal legislative successes touted by all national police unions: the passage of HR 218: *The Law Enforcement Officers' Safety Act*, and the Bush administration's removing police officers from amendments to the *FLSA*.

The rights of police unionists are extremely limited in a number of states where police members have no right to collectively bargain or even rights to due process. That has not stopped national police unions from claiming legislative victories. The federal legislation supported by all national police unions and hailed as a major police union success was HR 218: *The Law Enforcement Officers' Safety Act*. The bill exempts qualified active and retired law enforcement officers from local and state prohibitions on carrying of concealed weapons. HR 218 was hugely popular with many rank-and-file police officers and retired police officers. Since the national police unions have had zero success with police labor bills, many police unions felt this bill was close enough to declare a labor victory.

The second common theme among national police unions is their proclaimed labor victory at convincing President Bush to rescind his amendments to the *FLSA* effecting police officers to make more American workers exempt from getting paid overtime. The national police unions, except FOP, joined an informal coalition of labor unions primarily inside the AFL-CIO to fight the amendments. FOP and International Association of Fire Fighters took an independent path and took a "just save the police and fire" plea to the president.

Politically, strategic alliances have been forged between the various police union groupings. The 2004 national elections were looming as HR 218 and the *FLSA* amendments were being debated. FOP, the nation's largest national police union with 310,000 members, endorsed President George W. Bush for re-election based upon his signing of the "Right to Carry Bill" and for not excluding police supervisors from the protections of the *FLSA*. NAPO with 236,000 members endorsed Democrat John Kerry, but many of its affiliated local and state police unions broke ranks and endorsed President Bush. The dissenting NAPO affiliated police unions used the same arguments as FOP as a reason for a police labor union to endorse President Bush. Ignored in these endorsements was the president's decision to merge 170,000 federal law enforcement officers into the Department of Homeland Security to abrogate their collective bargaining contracts and civil service rights and to gut the COPS program that had put thousands of new police officers on the street.

The Greatest Challenge Facing American Policing

Forging Shared Common Visions between Unions and Management

To date, the national police unions have lacked the foresight to campaign jointly for a national collective bargaining bill, despite the fact that they would view this to be a very positive achievement. Any quest for national bills governing the labor rights of police workers would, however, be contested by police management organizations despite the real contribution that collective bargaining arrangements have had for the morale and professionalization of police officers.

Even around seemingly shared policies, unions and police management have trodden separate paths. To some extent, this is due to the exclusion of police unions from major decision-making forums. For example, in 1979 the International Association of Chiefs of Police, National Organization of Black Law Enforcement Executives, National Sheriff's Association, and Police Executive Research Forum established the Commission on Accreditation for Law Enforcement Agencies (CALEA) as an independent accrediting authority. The Commission has 21 members; 11 members are law enforcement practitioners, and the remaining 10 are selected from the public and private sector. None of the commission members is a rank-and-file police officer or a police union leader (http://www.calea.org/). Accreditation of a law enforcement agency is voluntary, time consuming, and expensive. Many police unions do not support the accreditation program because they do not see any benefit to the rank-and-file officers. CALEA does not have any rank-and-file education program directed at police officers or police unions to gain their input or endorsement.

But, attaining national rights to collective bargaining would not necessarily impact directly on the union's positive contribution to police reform and democratization. First, local agreements and agency accreditation would only generate change in one community at a time, and do not address the larger racial and social problems dividing the police and some members of the community. Second, collective bargaining agreements and national accreditation do not address such issues as decentralized police services, candidate recruitment, lateral movement of officers, and diversity in hiring and promoting minorities and women. Third, the unequal distribution of wealth that oftentimes determines the quality of policing in a community is not addressed by a local collective bargaining agreement or agency accreditation.

There is no current forum for national police unions and national police management organizations to pursue the development of a shared vision of the police profession. A review of the agendas of the national police unions and national police management organizations reveals that none of these groups routinely invite the other side to address issues of mutual concern. In fact, it would appear that neither side sees any issues of mutual concern. To make matters worse, national police unions do not come together to form a network with the capacity to lobby and effect changes. As a result, there is no police union network capacity to network with national police management organizations. In an age of networked communication and action, the policing profession in the United States has been left behind.

The Absence of a Uniform National Professional Police Standard Framework

The United States has almost one million people employed as sworn police officers and police support personnel, and no uniform national professional police standards. The standard of conduct, recruitment, training, policies, and practices of 90% of all law enforcement officers is left to each state and local government.

The International Association of Directors of Law Enforcement Standards and Training (IADLEST) is an international organization of training managers and executives dedicated to the improvement of public safety personnel. The mission of IADLEST is to research, develop, and share information, ideas, and innovations that assist states in establishing effective and defensible standards for employment and training law enforcement officers.

IADLEST has developed model minimum state standards to "set a floor" on officer professionalism. The association has a reciprocity handbook with the employment criteria in all 50 states. IADLEST is not a government agency and does not have any authority to mandate professional police standards on a national basis. The association is composed of standards and training managers and leaders, and none of their board members represent police unions or police management organizations (http://www.iadlest.org/index.htm).

Nationwide, the quality of policing in each community varies greatly, depending on whether the state has mandatory training standards, the capacity of local government to provide competitive wages and benefits to attract qualified applicants and retain veteran officers, and the local financial resources available to fund a modern police agency. In virtually every metropolitan area, suburban police forces will be better staffed, equipped, and paid than the urban police force. Urban and suburban police agencies are generally better funded and trained than rural police forces. The majority of states that have a Police Officer Standards and Training (POST) board issue only voluntary guidelines, and have no ability to regulate individual police officers, training academies, or law enforcement agencies.

Three problems result from the lack of national uniform professional police standards. First, citizens, residents, and visitors to the United States have no basis for evaluating the conduct of police officers from one jurisdiction to the next. The effectiveness and efficiency of the police is largely dependent on the resources available in any given local community. Second, it is very difficult for police officers to move laterally to another agency at the city, state, or federal level. Union contracts, civil service laws, varying state training laws, multiple pension systems, and different promotional schemes are prohibitive in regard to professional police mobility. Third, in a country with 18,000 separate and distinct law enforcement agencies, it is virtually impossible to effectively change or reform the police profession without uniform national professional police standards in which to judge law enforcement agencies and officers. Community activists and elected officials who desire change and reform have had to fight the battle at every local level. As a result, the world is changing much faster than the police profession, and there is no time to fight 18,000 separate battles to improve the quality of policing in the United States.

A New Model: A National Police Labor-Management Council

A potential solution would be the creation of a national police labor-management council. In order for this to occur, national police management organizations and national police unions would need to initiate informal discussions with one another. This process could be facilitated by a panel of academicians who have links with police management and with labor and criminal justice reform. In coming together in a joint forum, the parties would have to agree that they have a vested interest in communication and the exchange of ideas, with the ultimate goal of confronting the challenges presented to the policing profession locally, nationally, and globally.*

It is hoped the parties would agree on a more structured national police labor-management council composed of representatives of police management and police unions at the federal, state, and local levels of government. The council should also include academicians, researchers, criminal justice reformers, and community activists, either on the board or in ex-officio positions. One option would be to gain the support for an American Police Labor-Management Council from the U.S. Congress in either legislation or funding to an existing federal agency such as the U.S. Department of Justice. Such a council could provide a forum for debate and a conduit for all of the stakeholders concerned about the changing police environment and profession. The APLMC's primary agenda should be to seek to develop a shared vision of the police profession; make recommendations to improve the effectiveness and efficiency of the police service nationwide; seek ways to balance the need for domestic policing and the new duties caused by international criminal activities; and outline how police agencies can get ahead of the curve on the global changes impacting the police profession and local communities. The APLMC would be the only national voice of the police that is inclusive of police management and labor, which would make its recommendations to the U.S. Congress and the president more meaningful.

There are apparently eight issues that an American police labor-management council should focus on.

Uniform National Police Professional Standards

There is a need for mandatory uniform standards of professional ethics, training, policies, and practices for every law enforcement agency and law enforcement officer in the United States. The diversity in hiring standards, training, wages, and benefits causes some law enforcement officers to see other officers as less qualified.

Build a Network for Communicating

One task for the Council would be to establish centralized communications tools for rank-and-file officers, police union officials, police mangers, community activists, and the media. Local, state, and national police unions,

---

* The Australasian Police Professional Standards Council (APPSC) is composed of the police commissioners of each state, territory, and the federal government and representatives of the Police Federation of Australia and the New Zealand Police Association. The APPSC is one existing model for cooperation and communication between police labor and management.

national police management organizations, and law enforcement agencies all have Web sites and internal forums, but there is no linkage between these Web sites and forums. The Council could act as a conduit for bringing these diverse networks together, such as bulletin boards for information exchange.

Lateral Movement within the Police Profession

After the adoption, funding, and implementation of a uniform professional standard for all law enforcement officers in the United States, the Council should seek to develop avenues for lateral movement at all ranks. Federal legislation should be proposed to address pension portability, seniority, civil service rules, and collective bargaining contract conflicts. A business model could be adopted that allows for the free market enterprise system to work. True professionals have the ability to market their talents and skills to various employers. Law enforcement agencies would be able to compete for the most skilled and experienced officers. Officers could be identified and offered employment where their skills are most needed.

Defining the Core Components of Public Police Work

The costs in wages, benefits, training, and equipment to put a police officer on the street are soaring. Competition between agencies for the best candidates and police unions bargaining better contracts is driving the cost even higher. Both police management and labor have failed to take heed of the rapidly changing policing environment. Civilians, volunteers, retired officers, and private contractors have already begun to take over many of the roles traditionally undertaken by sworn officers. A Council could advocate for the rights and integrity of the public police if they had a shared understanding of what the core roles and functions of the public police are. Related to this would be a determination regarding the kinds of education, training, and supervision that the public police require.

Modernize Police Recruitment Processes

Virtually every law enforcement agency in the United States is facing a problem recruiting qualified applicants. In most jurisdictions, a person desiring to become a police officer must untangle a myriad of civil service rules and regulations and apply at each separate police agency. The business and military recruitment models need to be examined and adopted. Young people today use monster.com and other Internet search vehicles to post their resumes. A national law enforcement job data bank created and managed by the Council would assist candidates and agencies meeting each other's needs.

Diversify the Police Profession

If the Council wishes to promote community policing, then what is required is a police agency that reflects the community. While every agency claims to be interested in hiring more minorities and women, very few agencies have made the changes necessary to make the police profession more appealing to minorities and women. Police unions, shortsightedly, have resisted changes and reforms to civil service and collective bargaining contracts that would make promotional schemes, seniority, special assignments, and leave provisions more minority- and female-friendly. The Council needs to conduct research and develop models that reflect modern work rules that would attract minorities and women to law enforcement. For example 1,600 recruits recently graduated from the New York City Police Department academy where the class was majority-minority. (*New York Times*, 2005). New Zealand police are actively recruiting gays and lesbians, females, and people from different ethnic backgrounds (Keith, 2005).

Bring Community Groups to the Table

The lack of trust and respect for the police in many communities, especially by minorities, gays, and poor people, cannot be overcome if these stakeholders do not have a seat at the table. The police world (both management and labor) has an "Us vs. Them" attitude. Police officers worldwide believe that no outsider can really understand how hard it is to be a police officer in a democratic society. Police officers see themselves caught in a continuing no-win situation of being called racist by minorities regardless of the facts, second-guessed by police management who are afraid to support officers even when they are right, abandoned by politicians when the media circus begins, and used by the media to increase ratings. The "circle the wagons" approach by U.S. police unions has only caused more anger and resentment toward police officers. The Council should encourage a free and open debate about how communities and social justice oriented organizations can be a part of the solution. Police unions need to accept the profession, warts and all, and acknowledge that there is a need for change and reform on a constant basis.

Advocate for an International Role for U.S. Police Officers and Police Unions

Police forces in Australia, Canada, New Zealand, and many other countries see international police service as way to provide less advantaged countries with much needed training and guidance in developing a professional police service. These police officers return after their foreign assignments with experiences and knowledge that cannot be gained from working only in their home countries. Because the United States does not have one federal law enforcement agency like the Australian Federal Police to act as a conduit for federal and state officers to serve on international police missions, the United States contracts with private companies to recruit former U.S. police officers to serve in these assignments. State and local police comprise 90% of U.S. police forces, and unless they retire or resign, the opportunity to serve on an international police force is not available. State and local police officers of all ranks are losing out on this experience and knowledge, and in turn U.S. police are not exposed to the global police networks. The Council should advocate for the Department of Homeland Security to provide officers for international police duties, and not just hot spots like Iraq and Kosovo, and allow state and local police officers to serve and return without penalty to their hometown agencies. Using active federal, state, and local police officers instead of for-profit corporate security guards would accomplish several goals: enhance the image of U.S. police officers internationally; expand the global police networks to include rank-and-file police officers; and U.S. police representatives would be accountable to the public, and not the shareholders of a private corporation.

Conclusion

Despite decentralization, fragmentation, and the disorganized nature of American police agencies and police unions, the fundamentals are in place for progress to be possible. Elected officials, police management, and police unions have started to recognize the changing nature of police work, global forces impacting on domestic policing, the need for new costing arrangements for policing, and the need for qualified professional police officers. Each group is aware of the detrimental effect of a failure to network and communicate effectively.

While the police unions have been very successful in winning improved conditions of service for the police, this success has proven to be a double-edged sword. The high cost of policing has forced the general public, media, elected officials, and police management to reconsider what constitutes public police work and what jobs are better done with a cheaper nonpolice substitute, and has resulted in increasing civilianization and privatization of policing.

At present, police management and labor in the United States seem to be operating in parallel universes that occasionally cooperate or collide. Networking is not taking place either between police agencies or between police union representatives. This has resulted in a lack of a shared vision among policing professionals and representative bodies. Police unions are not networking with each other, much less with community organizations and police management. What is required, given the competitive arena of police agencies and unions, is a safe haven where all of the stakeholders in the police profession can gather and exchange information and ideas and develop common strategies. But to date, none of the national police unions or national police management organizations has made any effort to host symposiums on the future of the police profession and included the other organizations.

Those that represent the police profession need to think more nationally and globally. They need to think critically about the shifts that are taking place in policing, and what policing arrangements would benefit both communities and police officers. Police unions (and management) should think beyond their own narrow self-interest, and engage more meaningfully with minority and community organizations. The future of the policing profession needs to be reviewed, with some recognition that not all police work needs to be done by a sworn police officer.

Police unions and management need to keep their membership abreast of the changes that are taking place in the policing environment. This will allow police organizations to move ahead with police reform, with the support of individual police officers. A knowledgeable social base will promote the effectiveness of the unions and police management to directly shape the debate and the shifts that are already underway in policing.

Sadly, to date, police unions in the United States have focused on achieving economic gains for their members, and they have expressed little or no interest in the advocacy for justice and effectiveness of policing communities. The big question is: Will police unions take on the challenge, or will they throw up roadblocks to the evolving policies and practices of the police?

References

Blau, R., Bush slashes program: Weiner hits mayor on COPS funding, *The Chief-Leader*, June 17, 2005.

Fraternal Order of Police (FOP) wins battle on details: But city will appeal Labor Board's ruling, "Numbers," *American Police Beat*, 12(7), July 2005.

Greenhouse, S., Five unions to create a coalition on growth, *New York Times*, June 13, 2005.

Keith, L., Police to seek more gay, lesbian recruits, *New Zealand Daily News*, July 9, 2005.

Lee, J., In New York's most diverse police class, blue comes in many colors, *New York Times*, July 8, 2005, p. A22.

Mark, N., Chiefs say expertise ignored, *American Police Beat*, 12(7), July 2005, pp. 1–28.

The Canadian Professional Police Association: Promoting Accountability, Democracy, Justice, and Equality in Twenty-First Century Policing

22

DAVID GRIFFIN

Contents

Introduction

A new equilibrium for effective twenty-first century policing can be proposed: in order to sustain a police culture that respects and protects the fundamental human rights and dignity of citizens, the citizenry must respect the fundamental human rights and dignity of police members.

In Canada, increasing social, cultural, political, and economic pressures are being brought to bear on policing. These forces shape the way in which Canadian police services respond to and accommodate the needs of citizens. While demands for police accountability and respect for the rights of citizens under the Canadian Charter of Rights and Freedoms were prevalent in the last decades of the twentieth century, members of Canadian police services are increasingly aware of, and exercising, their individual rights as citizens of a democratic state.

In order for modern police associations and unions to effectively impact policing policies and practices, it is recommended that police association and union leaders strategically position their organizations as influential and respected advocates for their members. As a result, Canadian police associations can play an integral role in promoting accountability, democracy, justice, and equality in twenty-first century policing.

The following critical issues need to be examined:

1. The underlying rationale for a new equilibrium.
2. The evolving role of Canadian police associations.
3. The growth of advocacy as a strategic police association priority.
4. The networks employed and strategies at play in advancing the fundamental rights of police members.
5. The opportunities that exist to expand strategies and networks beyond the traditional realm to achieve a new equilibrium.

Overview of Policing in Canada

Approximately 59,906 police officers and 22,187 civilian members provide police services to Canada's population of nearly 32 million people. At 187.5 police officers per 100,000 population, Canada is well below England and Wales (241), the United States (230), and Australia (212).*

Policing in Canada is the responsibility of all three levels of government: federal, provincial/territorial, and municipal. In addition, many

---

* Per. Shankarraman (2003, 2004), data for Australia and England and Wales is based on 1996–2000 reports.

First Nations (Aboriginal) communities also administer their own police services.

The federal government, through the Royal Canadian Mounted Police (RCMP), is responsible for the enforcement of federal statutes in each province and territory, and for providing National Police Services such as forensic laboratories, identification services, the Canadian Police Information Centre (CPIC), and the Canadian Police College.

Each province/territory assumes responsibility for its own provincial/territorial and municipal policing. Provincial policing involves enforcement of the Criminal Code and provincial statutes within areas of a province not served by a municipal police service, such as rural areas and small towns. In some communities, provincial police perform traffic duties on major provincial thoroughfares that pass through municipal jurisdictions.

Municipal policing consists of enforcement of the Criminal Code, provincial statutes, and municipal by-laws within the boundaries of a municipality or several adjoining municipalities that comprise a region (e.g., Durham Regional Police in Ontario) or a metropolitan area (e.g., Montréal Urban Community). Municipal governments essentially have three options when providing municipal policing services:

1. Form their own municipal police service.
2. Join an existing municipal police service.
3. Enter into an agreement with a provincial police service or the RCMP.

Newfoundland and Labrador, Yukon, the Northwest Territories, and Nunavut are the only provinces and territories in Canada without municipal police services. In Newfoundland and Labrador, the Royal Newfoundland Constabulary, which is a provincial police service, provides policing to the province's three largest municipalities (St. John's, Corner Brook, and Labrador City) as well as in Churchill Falls. Newfoundland and Labrador contract the RCMP to provide policing to the remaining municipalities and the rural areas on the southeastern oceanfront.

The RCMP provides provincial/territorial policing in all provinces and territories except Quebec and Ontario, which maintain their own provincial police services: the Sûreté du Québec and the Ontario Provincial Police, respectively. In Ontario and Quebec, the RCMP only provides policing at the federal level as it relates to federal law.

In addition to federal, provincial, and municipal policing, there are also various types of First Nations policing agreements for Aboriginal communities in place across Canada. These may also include the development and administration of the community's own police service, or an agreement with the RCMP or provincial police service.

One of the most significant changes in the delivery of police services over the past three decades has been the consolidation of police service delivery through the amalgamation of municipal police services, or the disbandment of local police services in favor of contract policing with provincial police or with the RCMP. The number of police services has decreased by over 50% during this time (Kinnear, 2005) to approximately 220 in 2004.

Police Labor Relations in Canada

Canadian labor relations are divided into provincial and federal jurisdiction. The Canada Labour Code (CLC) governs federal works, undertakings or businesses, and their employees. This code also applies to all aspects of labor relations in undertakings of First Nations on reserves, as well as other key industries and certain Crown corporations. The CLC does not, however, apply to federal government employees, who are subject to the Public Service Staff Relations Act (PSSRA). Members of the RCMP and the military are excluded from the CLC and PSSRA. In recent years, First Nations police personnel have successfully gained union and collective bargaining rights under the CLC. RCMP members remain prohibited, however, from forming a union and do not have collective bargaining rights.

The balance of labor relations in Canada is subject to provincial jurisdiction under their respective labor codes and trade union or labor relations acts. While there are many consistencies within police labor relations, there remain exceptions in some jurisdictions:

- Most jurisdictions restrict representation of police officers to associations formed by the members. Only the provinces of New Brunswick, Nova Scotia, and Prince Edward Island allow representation of police officers by external, non-police bargaining agents. Although bargaining units in these three provinces are not restricted to public sector union representation, the Canadian Union of Public Employees (CUPE) and the Nova Scotia Government Employees Union are currently the only outside agents representing police officers.
- Several jurisdictions have separate statutes to address police labor relations, while others have included labor relations in their policing statute.
- Several jurisdictions define the bargaining authority in the provincial Code or Act that governs all workers and employers, and members are afforded all the protections therein. Those who are not may be restricted from unfair practice protection and other labor law tenets.

- Essential service designations, prohibitions on affiliation with outside labor groups, and restrictions on political activity are common clauses in statutes governing policing.
- Saskatchewan allows police the right to strike, albeit fettered, by advance notice to the employer, the ability of government to order conciliation or arbitration, and the authority to send in the RCMP to provide policing services during a labor dispute. The right to strike is still on the books in a couple of other provincial jurisdictions, but essential service designations and other legislative arrangements negate the option. The province of Nova Scotia recently replaced the right to strike with binding third party arbitration—a move that was supported and advocated by police associations in the province.
- In some provinces, such as Ontario, civilian employees of police services may be represented by the same police association that represents police officers; in other jurisdictions, these employees may be represented by public service employee unions.

Labor–Management Relationships

The labor relations structure of police services in Canada has been compared to a three-legged stool; three distinct components discharging equally important responsibilities:

1. Governance—A Police Services Board, like the Board of Directors of a Private Sector Corporation, oversees the management of the police service, provides strategic governance through its policy-setting role, and represents the interests of its shareholders, in this case the community.
2. Management—Responsible for managing the operations of the police service and achieving the corporate vision established by the governors.
3. Labor—The association representing the interests of the front-line employees, as the collective bargaining agent.

For the system to function properly, there needs to be a balance and equality between these three legs in discharging their respective roles and responsibilities. If any of these legs is weak, the other two carry a disproportionate share of the load. If any of the legs pushes up too far, the stool loses its balance.

It is important that the parties understand and respect each other's roles and responsibilities. There must be an environment of trust and mutual respect that permits each to carry out its responsibility with confidence and dignity. Today's leaders must focus on problem solving and dispute resolution, which begins with the process of identifying common ground. The three must work together wherever possible to find mutually agreeable solutions to complex issues and problems.

Quality of Police Labor Relations in Canada

The Police Futures Group (Biro et al., 2000) reported the results of a survey they conducted with senior executives of police services. Participants were asked to describe the relations with police labor organizations:

Police Executives' Relations with Police Labor Organizations			
Good	Sometimes difficult	Poor	Other
72%	24%	3%	2%

The authors asked respondents to identify potential sources of conflict with labor organizations:

- Flexibility, in terms of staff deployment, shifts, promotion, part-time staff, and sick benefits.
- Clarity, regarding the terms of the collective agreement.
- Control, with respect to deployment, overtime, shifts, promotion, and benefits.

Police Association leaders were also surveyed as part of the Police Futures Group study. These respondents identified the following shortcomings for police executives:

- Lack of communication and human resources skills
- Inadequate management and leadership abilities
- Insufficient training and preparation for the job of police executive
- Lack of knowledge and understanding of labor matters

Police Association respondents identified the following factors as critical to improved police labor relations:

- Trust
- Respect
- Representation
- Meaningful consultation
- Access to independent and impartial resolution

Fundamental Principles of Police Employment

With origins in British Common Law, the role and legal status of police constables and police officers has evolved in Canada over the past two centuries. Canadian police officers and Chiefs of Police (Chief Constables) are generally expected to exercise their duties with a high degree of independence from political interference. Police officers cannot be ordered to lay a charge (or to not lay a charge); however, they remain under the control and direction of the chief and police management. Police chiefs are afforded considerable autonomy in operational policing decisions, including the conduct of investigations. Police boards or governing authorities may, however, establish the budgets, objectives, and priorities for the police service, and monitor the performance of the chief of police.

Policing is one of the most highly regulated professions in Canada. As enumerated by Ceyssens (2002), Canadian police officers are subject to a variety of oversight mechanisms:

1. Supervision of police services by ministers of the crown, municipal councils, or municipal police boards.
2. Failure to comply with the *Canadian Charter of Rights and Freedoms* may jeopardize prosecutions or expose police officers to civil proceedings.
3. The civil law process.
4. Police discipline processes.
5. Public complaints processes.
6. Human rights law processes. Allegations may be adjudicated before a tribunal under human rights law, police discipline processes, civil law processes, criminal law processes, and public inquiries.
7. The criminal law process.
8. Coronial law and fatality inquiries.
9. Provincial police commissions and ministry policy.
10. Public inquiries.
11. Ombudsman legislation.

In terms of appointment, police officers in Canada are generally considered to be "office holders," as opposed to employees or agents of the state. As such, most police officers are subject to comprehensive procedural schemes and codes of discipline offences in statutes and regulations. In most instances, employers cannot opt out of the disciplinary process or resort to other legal mechanisms to discipline or remove a police officer from office.

Accordingly, a set of basic principles applies to ensure that police officers are afforded procedural fairness and natural justice in the disciplinary process:

1. A formal notice must be served, advising of the proposed action.
2. Explanations for the disciplinary charges must be provided.
3. A meaningful opportunity must be provided to make representation before the decision is made. For probationary constables, this may be limited to an opportunity to respond, orally or in writing. Otherwise, most police officers are afforded a formal administrative hearing with the right to be represented by legal counsel or an agent.
4. The decision must be made in good faith.

These distinctions, which separate police officers from other professionals and workers, have recognized the importance of independence and impartiality in the exercise of police duties. There remain, however, significant variances between jurisdictions with respect to the rights and protections afforded to police officers. In addition, as will be discussed further in this paper, there has been a tremendous push on the part of some police managers, governing authorities, and oversight agencies in recent years to curtail the employment status or rights of police officers.

Police Associations in Canada

At the local and provincial level, there is considerable consistency in Canada in terms of collective bargaining rights and responsibilities. Most, but not all, of our member associations in Canada enjoy statutorily designated bargaining units, the legislated ability to negotiate with their employers, and binding, independent, and impartial third-party dispute resolution.

Police associations have been required to expand their activities from the traditional focus on collective bargaining and internal discipline issues to broader representation on issues that are increasingly the subject of public scrutiny and debate. This is not something police associations have sought to do, but rather it is something they have been required to do in order to represent the legitimate interests of their members. While this was very much a reactive approach a decade ago, police associations have become much more proactive in their approaches in recent years.

Like their counterparts in the United States, United Kingdom, New Zealand, and Australia, many police officers and their police association leaders consider themselves different from, and independent of, trade unions. This may be attributed to several factors, including

1. As previously noted, several provincial jurisdictions prohibit police members from affiliating with trade unions. Police labor laws in

some jurisdictions also create distinctions for police personnel, which exclude them from certain standards or rights afforded to other workers.

2. A culture of conservatism, which tends to separate police personnel from the social justice objectives of the trade union movement.

3. Perceived professional status and a preference toward a professional association as compared to blue-collar trade union.

4. Historical conflicts and animosity arising in situations where police have been called upon to keep the peace or quell disturbances at public demonstrations and picket lines involving organized labor. While police services have, in recent decades, become more sophisticated in their responses to these types of situations, there remain those within organized labor and police labor who consider the organizations at odds, despite their many common activities and interests.

One strength of police associations, driven perhaps by the traditional bond of the "thin blue line" that exists within the profession, is the solidarity that exists within and between police associations in Canada. As the jurisdiction for municipal and provincial policing rests solely with provincial governments, Canadian police associations affiliate within provincial associations and federations. These provincial organizations assume a leadership role within their provinces on legislative and regulatory issues affecting policing within the province. These associations provide representation with governments, and influence policy and legislation governing the ability to bargain for fair wages, benefits, and to improve working conditions. These provincial associations and federations also provide a significant network for association leaders to engage and consult with their peers on common issues and concerns.

Canadian Professional Police Association

Like their provincial counterparts, the Canadian Professional Police Association (CPPA) is the national voice for more than 200 police associations representing 54,000 police personnel across Canada. Membership includes police personnel serving in Canada's smallest towns and villages, as well as those working in our largest municipal and provincial police services, more than 2,000 members of the RCMP, railway police, and first nations (tribal) police personnel.

As the national center for police labor relations, the role of the CPPA is to

- Promote the interests of police personnel and the public they serve, in the national legislative and policy fields.
- Provide a collective support network for member associations to successfully improve representation and conditions for their

own members in collective bargaining, education and training, equipment, health and safety, and protecting members' rights.

- Advocate for adequate and equitable resources for policing.
- Identify key national issues which impact on Member Associations and facilitate the resolution of these issues.
- React and respond, upon request, to local policing issues that may have national ramifications.
- Liaise with the international policing community on issues affecting Canadian police personnel.

As the national voice for front-line police personnel across Canada, the CPPA brings a unique perspective on progressive justice reform. The CPPA has contributed to the deliberations on such issues as youth criminal justice; child pornography; impaired driving; sentencing, corrections and parole reform; national sex offender registry; criminal pursuits; organized crime; drug enforcement; and technological innovation in policing, such as DNA testing.

The CPPA was formed in August of 2003, with the merger of the Canadian Police Association (CPA) and National Association of Professional Police (NAPP). The leaders of these two predecessor organizations entered into merger discussions in 2002, with the common goal of establishing one national association representing all police association members across Canada. The strength of one national organization was seen as critical in advancing the rights and collective objectives of Canada's police personnel (Canadian Professional Police Association, 2002, 2005).

The Evolving Role of Canadian Police Associations

Over the past two decades, there have been a series of changes in the police sector, which have introduced new challenges in the workplace and affected the evolution of police labor-management relations. In some cases, these issues have dramatically affected the manner in which police services are delivered.

Over the past two decades, the police profession has been confronted with extraordinary challenges and reforms that have dominated the agenda for profession. These include

- Reform of Police Discipline and Public Complaints processes.
- Increased use of criminal consequences for police conduct (e.g., Special Investigations Unit).
- Impact of the *Canadian Charter of Rights and Freedoms*.
- Increased civil litigation.

- The impact of Human Rights legislation on external and internal police practices, including Workplace Harassment.
- Increased Occupational Health and Safety requirements, including prosecutions against police services.
- Downsizing, fiscal constraints, and budget cuts, including government-imposed wage restrictions.
- Political influence on police services.

These issues have required all parties to introduce new approaches to labor-management relations, and have dramatically affected the way in which police associations conduct their business. Police associations have been compelled to expand the scope of services and representation afforded to members, including a significant increase the in the use of legal representation.

Emerging Challenges in Police Labor Relations

Canada's police officers expect to be treated fairly, and are increasingly aware of and exercising their individual rights as citizens of a democratic state. Many have high expectations for advancement and recognition, and will seek and expect career opportunities within or outside the organization or profession. Unfulfilled expectations will lead to discontent.

They are increasingly more demanding of their employers and the bargaining unit with regards to working conditions, wages, benefits, and their rights, as provided for under the Charter and Humans Rights legislation. They are more likely to challenge or question, in a constructive way, authority or direction. They will not be blind followers, as they have been raised as masters of their own destinies. They value their personal time and leisure pursuits, and are highly mobile.

They are increasingly more likely to seek remedy by invoking labor law rights and all forms of due process, such as the Occupational Health and Safety Act. This is consistent with the trends in all aspects of society.

These factors do not sit well in a quasi-military structure. Police management must be prepared to lead and guide, and to move completely away from the command and control model. The democratization of police services, including employment rights for police members, increases the accountability of police managers and those responsible for the governance of police services.

Police associations have to meet the higher expectations of their members, who no longer accept the role of their association on blind faith or fraternal loyalty. Police associations will have to be problem solvers on behalf of their members, and will aggressively compete for their member's time, attention, loyalty, and interest. Police associations will be compelled to constantly demonstrate their value, relevance, and effectiveness. To meet this challenge, advocacy continues to grow as a strategic priority for police associations.

Police labor–management relations will continue to be impacted by external forces and issues, such as

- Human rights advancements, including external enforcement liability (i.e., racial profiling), and internal liabilities, such as harassment, accommodation, and substance abuse
- Accountability and oversight
- Labor law decisions
- Economic and compensation pressures
- Privacy law
- Competition between police services for resources and territory
- Private competition for public policing functions
- Public competition between public policing organizations
- Technological advances, both in crime and law enforcement
- The "talent war" to attract, retain, and motivate skilled workers
- Succession planning, to manage the anticipated exodus of an aging police workforce
- The demand for increased police training
- Adequacy and effectiveness standards for police services
- Globalization

Success will be achieved through collaborative resolution of issues in a fair and equitable manner. Police officers will expect their leaders to produce results that satisfy their needs and expectations. Failure will be marked by increased confrontation and acrimony.

Competing Demands in Domestic Policing

Twenty-first century policing in Canada is faced with competing demands and interests that present enormous challenges for the effective delivery of public police services. When police officers fail to meet the expectations of the community, the response is often disciplinary, rather than remedial or policy related. As a consequence, police officers are faced with increasing liability for the attempted good faith performance of their duties. Police associations are confronted with an increasing liability in the representation of their members.

Conflicts between Public Insecurity and Individual Human Rights

Like many countries, Canada is at a crossroads in the challenge to provide domestic security in the post-9/11 era. While Canada has been relatively immune from these acts to date, the concern for domestic security has been sustained by terrorist bombings of public transportation systems in London and Madrid. While there is a heightened sense of insecurity in the wake of these terrorist events and demands for increased public security, there remains a debate concerning the conflict between increased security measures and individual human rights. A public inquiry continues to unfold concerning the arrest and deportation of a Canadian who had been suspected of terrorist links, who was allegedly the subject of Human Rights violations when deported to a foreign country.

While the public policy debates occur in the pristine environment of legislative chambers and courtrooms, police officers are the front-line instruments of domestic policy, situated at risk of criticism, complaints, discipline, and even criminal prosecution for their efforts to fulfill their domestic security activities.

The evolution of the Canadian Military is a similar example. As peacekeepers abroad, members of military forces were sent abroad into hostile situations to preserve the peace. Having been trained as soldiers to battle a foreign enemy, some members of the military suffered from a phenomenon described as *role confusion*. According to some analysts, the training and traditional expectations for military personnel was not in keeping with their new mandate and responsibilities.

A similar conflict may develop for public police agencies engaged in "homeland security" and the "war on terrorism." It is critically important that police organizations sustain a culture that respects individual rights and freedoms. This begins by respecting the individual rights and freedoms of those within the organization.

Unfortunately, governments do not necessarily consider the link between internal employment practices and external policing expectations. In Canada, the RCMP are prohibited from basic collective bargaining rights and the right to be represented by an association, which are rights afforded to most other Canadian police officers.

This is inconsistent with the expectations of a twenty-first century democracy. According to Marks and Fleming (2006), "… in countries where democratic governance has not taken hold and where police organizations are still conceived of as militaristic agencies in defence of government, police employees are likely to be denied rights to freedom of association and collective bargaining."

The Underlying Rationale for a New Equilibrium

Police employment issues are increasingly matters of public attention, not confined to traditional labor-management forums. Given the very public role of policing, the sometimes intrusive or invasive aspects of police duties and powers, and the potential consequences of police actions, it is not uncommon for police issues or actions to be the subject of intense public scrutiny, commentary, and debate. In the extreme, this places enormous pressure on decision makers that fuel disciplinary actions, as decision makers struggle to ensure that "justice is seen to be done."

In order to promote the highest standards within our profession, and foster a culture that is respectful of the rights of our citizens, a new equilibrium is required:

1. It must be recognized that fundamental rights afforded to all citizens are not negotiable. By treating police officers differently than other Canadians, placing limits or exceptions on the rights afforded police officers, we suggest that it is permissible to have limits or exceptions on the rights enjoyed by all citizens.
2. Our practices relative to police conduct must be consistent with the fundamental human rights afforded to our citizens, including procedural fairness, natural justice, and access to independent and impartial adjudication.
3. The democratization of policing for the public requires police to be afforded basic democratic freedoms. Marks (2004) observed that "Democratic policing is discussed with reference to accountability structures and processes; civilianization; policing outcomes and performance measurement; and community participation and partnerships. However, there is almost no mention (of) the labour and social rights of police employees in regard to the democratisation of police organizations." Democratic structures within police organization increase the accountability of police managers and those responsible for the governance of police services.
4. We must preserve the fundamental principles that preserve police independence and impartiality from further erosion. Police officers cannot feel threatened that their good faith efforts to uphold the law can result in punitive consequences. They should not believe that they may become scapegoats to a politically expedient resolution.
5. As Fisher (2003) observed, police officers are exposed to a unique combination of risks and stressors not normally associated with most other occupations. These include systemic workplace stresses such as role ambiguity and role conflict and frustration with the courts, corrections and parole systems, and the justice system in general. Inequality in the treatment of police officers only serves to exacerbate these stresses and the resulting cynicism and distrust.
6. Inequality breeds discontent. Sunahara (2004a,b,c) reported that alienation and disenchantment of police officers and the sense of self

sacrifice can be the seeds of a corruption, through a distorted sense of entitlement or perceived justification in the pursuit of a noble cause.

7. Contemporary Canadian policing encourages police officers to be innovators and problem solvers. This is not without risk of failure. Policing needs to shift from a reactive disciplinary culture to a pro-active learning environment. Police officers require the confidence that is fostered by fairness and equality.

8. We need to embrace one standard nationally, and eliminate discrepancies and inequalities between jurisdictions.

In Pursuit of a New Equilibrium: The CPPA Bill of Rights

Canadians have a tendency to consider themselves as an example for others when it comes to democratic freedoms and fundamental human rights. Police officers and members of police services play an important role in respecting the rights of their fellow citizens, and in ensuring that the fundamental values we embrace as a nation are not compromised. The CPPA contends that "in order to promote such high standards in policing, it is paramount that police personnel are treated with the same dignity and respect for their human rights as is expected of them in dealing with others."

The CPPA cites the following as a few of the countless examples of violations of police officers' rights that support a new equilibrium:

- Several First Nations police officers formed a police association in their community and were rewarded for their efforts by being dismissed. Their only crime was to stand up for their lawful rights.
- Many RCMP members have fought vigilantly to have their right to form an association and bargain collectively recognized by the federal government and RCMP Commissioner, without success. The CPPA observed that "police officers in South Africa have this right, why not in Canada?"
- The Toronto Police Services Board is actively seeking to limit the rights of the police association executive to be politically active. The Board wants to prevent the association from its practice of endorsing candidates in local, provincial, and federal elections, based on the performance of the elected officials. The CPPA notes that "school teachers, fire fighters, nurses, and doctors all enjoy the right to participate in these democratic processes; Why should police officers be any different?"
- During his tenure, the former Chief of the Toronto Police Service, Julian Fantino, commissioned a report by Justice George Ferguson (2003a,b), which recommends that police officers be required to

submit to drug testing and financial background checks before applying for promotion or special assignments. The police service has since introduced policies to require drug tests and financial background checks, regardless of whether or not any grounds exist to warrant such intrusions. The CPPA contends that the solutions is not to compromise the fundamental human rights of police personnel, but rather to ensure there are adequate and effective supervision and management practices that identify employees at risk.

- Police officers in several Atlantic provinces have lost their jobs because their community decided to contract local police services with the RCMP, and the RCMP decided that some of these officers did not meet RCMP recruiting "standards." Surely a police officer who has been policing a community for 15 years is good enough to police that community in an RCMP uniform?

- The President of a first nations police association is injured while off duty. He is able to return to work on modified duties; however, the employer refused to accept its duty to accommodate the officer in a court position.

- The nature of police work will generate a number of public complaints and allegations of misconduct, which are later proven to be malicious. Despite this, many police officers in Canada can be suspended without pay prior to a trial, formal hearing, or appeal concerning the allegations.

- Although two Saskatoon City Police Constables have never been charged with a disciplinary or criminal offence, they now find themselves fighting for their livelihood. Bowing to immense political pressure, the Chief of the Saskatoon Police Service suspended and then dismissed the two officers not long after a flawed report was released by a public inquiry into the death of an aboriginal youth. The Chief ignored the pleas of the officers, their families, their lawyers, their police association, and the CPPA to give them the opportunity to defend themselves before a proper hearing. The officers have filed appeals under the Saskatchewan Police Act, and the onus now falls upon the Chief to prove his allegations. Despite contemporary principles of police independence from political interference, these officers have been sacrificed for purely political reasons.

Police work requires members of police services to accept risks in order to preserve public safety, and police officers are often called upon to intervene in situations when the safety of others may be at risk. Police officers accept this risk, with the expectation that they will be properly supported by their employers, lawmakers, and the justice system when they are the subject of malicious attacks, including malicious allegations with respect to conduct.

This is a fundamental covenant between police officers and the state. Police officers protect us from harm, and we will protect police officers from being targeted for doing their jobs.

Unfortunately, the above examples point to a disturbing trend that is undermining this covenant and the independence of police officers. The CPPA is therefore promoting a "Police Officers' Bill of Rights," with the intention that this be adopted by federal, provincial, and municipal governments, as a basic and consistent set of principles governing the standards applied to our members. A goal of the CPPA Bill of Rights is to extend these protections into the workplace, particularly with respect to internal and public complaint allegations and prosecutions.

Proposed CPPA Police Officers' Bill of Rights

1. The right to form and participate in a labor association.
   a. The right to bargain collectively.
   b. The right to access binding third-party arbitration.
   c. The right to be represented publicly by this association without fear of discipline.
2. The fundamental principles guaranteed to all Canadian citizens under the charter should be afforded to all police officers in relation to their duties as public officials:
   a. The right to be presumed innocent until proven guilty, including the right to retain office without loss of pay, seniority, compensation, benefits or status until proven guilty in a court or tribunal of competent jurisdiction and the conclusion of all legal appeals and processes.
   b. The right to be protected from unlawful search and seizure, including the protection of personal information such as photographs and DNA.
   c. The right to a disciplinary framework that fully complies with the rules of procedural fairness and natural justice.
3. The right to retain employment, with no loss of seniority, compensation, benefits or status, when the method of policing the community changes as a result of restructuring, amalgamation, or contract policing.
4. The right to retire with dignity on an unreduced pension after 25 years of service.
5. The right to privacy.
   a. The right to a private life as a private citizen.
   b. The right to privacy and protection of personal information, including personnel and employment records. Police officers

should be afforded protection from the misuse of personal information or misinformation on Web sites.

6. The right to be protected by the employer from bodily harm arising from their duties, including

   a. The right to a healthy and safe workplace, including the right to be provided protective equipment for known and identifiable risks.
   b. The right to refuse unsafe work unless such work arises from an emergency situation where the lives of innocent persons are at risk and the risks cannot be mitigated.
   c. The right to be protected from communicable disease.
   d. The right to be provided proper training and supervision to carry out required duties.

7. The right to be afforded reasonable protection from harm, including mandatory minimum sentences for those who commit infractions against members of police services (e.g., assaults, false accusations).

8. The right to be politically active and engage, without reprisal, in Canada's democratic system.

9. The right to be properly and fully accommodated in the workplace, consistent with the fundamental principles of contemporary Human Rights legislation, including the right to retain office without loss of seniority, compensation, benefits, or status.

Networks and Strategies

Police officers have a legitimate interest in ensuring that their views are also factored into the decision-making process. Few government officials have a working knowledge of the issues affecting the association's members, and thus the association can take the role of providing accurate, timely information about issues and concerns.

Advocacy as a Strategic Police Association Priority

In order for twenty-first century police associations to be effective, they must engage in strategic activities that position the organization as an influential and respected stakeholder on issues concerning the safe and effective delivery of police services in their communities (Griffin, 2001, 2004a,b). Police associations have a bona fide, legitimate role to play in ensuring the legitimate interests of their members are considered in the decision-making process.

This role is not unique to police associations. Advocacy is often the single most important function for a wide range of associations, grass root organizations, professional lobbyists, and special interest groups. Groups representing a vast variety of interests—such as chicken farmers, drug companies, victims of crime, and competitive sports—all seek to influence public policy within their sectors through their advocacy efforts.

Typically, associations will deal with government for the following reasons (CSAE, 2001):

1. To seek relief from government measures such as sales taxes or customs duties.
2. To influence public policy and the administration of government programs.
3. To lobby the government for changes to legislation and laws affecting the membership.

Forms of proactive advocacy implemented by Canadian police associations to raise awareness include

- Organized *non-partisan lobbying/advocacy* efforts, such as the CPPA Lobby Day, where association representatives meet with their local Member of Parliament to discuss policing and public safety issues. Similar events are organized by our provincial affiliates, coordinating meetings between police association representatives and their members of provincial legislative assemblies.
- Non-partisan *candidate endorsement* at the local, provincial, and federal levels. Through the endorsement process, the association supports champions in the political arena who have been supportive of policing issues.
- Attendance at *political party events*, such as party policy forums. This ensures police have a voice in the process of setting political policy that may ultimately influence policing direction.
- *Building relationships* with decision-makers. Developing strategic alliances to create a broader understanding of the association's issues.
- Participation in *consultation* processes, such as government roundtables, community forums, and regular meetings with police management.
- *Public opinion polling* to gauge public support on an issue. This provides essential data that can be used to support the association's position, identify gaps, develop messages, and promote resolution.
- *Raising awareness* of the association's issues by implementing effective communication and media relations programs to inform members, decision-makers, and leaders, and by promoting the association's position and activities.
- Forming *strategic alliances* with organizations that share common objectives on a given issue of concern. This may include
  - Other police organizations, such as the Canadian Association of Chiefs of Police and Canadian Association of Police Boards.

- Victims groups, such as the CPPA sponsored Canadian Resource Centre for Victims of Crime, Victims of Violence, and Mothers Against Drunk Driving (MADD).
- Local business associations, chambers of commerce, and community groups.
- *Collective bargaining*, through which police associations have made advancements in the compensation and working conditions of their members, including such features as
  - Parental leave
  - Education leave and subsidies for tuition costs
  - Family leave
  - Experience pay or retention pay
  - Workplace Harassment protocols
- *Coordination of effort* through established networks and forums of police associations, including
  - Provincial and national conferences
  - Meetings of the "Big 10" police associations held across Canada
  - Major associations meetings (Ontario)
  - Interprovincial conferences, such as the Western Wage Conference (Manitoba, Saskatchewan, Alberta, and British Columbia) and similar meetings between eastern police association representatives
  - Coordinated bargaining (Quebec and British Columbia)
  - Pattern bargaining (Saskatchewan)
- *Education*—The Police Association of Ontario hosts an annual Police Labour Relations Conference, which is open to all police stakeholders and government representatives. The agenda features speakers from all levels of policing, government and academia on current issues and challenges within the sector.
- *International Affiliation*—The CPA hosted the inaugural meeting of the International Law Enforcement Council (ILEC) in 1996 and the second meeting in 1998, to bring international police associations together to share information and strategies. The Police Federation of England and Wales hosted ILEC in 2000, the Police Federation of Australia in 2002, and the Scottish Police Federation in 2004. The 2006 ILEC conference will be hosted by the Combined Law Enforcement Associations of Texas (CLEAT). In 2004 ILEC delegates agreed that a Secretariat was required to coordinate communication between conferences, and Dale Kinnear of the CPPA has been appointed to fulfill this role.
- *Protecting* the interests of police members and ensuring accountability of police *managers* by challenging unfavorable decisions or policies, including *litigation* where necessary.

Challenging the Status Quo

Police Associations have been prepared to take their grievances to the public when other approaches fail. Reflecting on this evolution, Kinnear (2005) observed,

> Although cautious, we have not been bashful since police unions and collective bargaining was established. In the last 25 years we've had our share of protest in the form of mass marches, non-confidence votes, picketing, job actions, media campaigns (radio, television and print: paid and unpaid), billboards, election handbills and just about anything else in practice, including strikes in the two provincial jurisdiction where the right to strike still exists. Unions have taken to these tactics in staffing campaigns, over legislative change and to garner public support over fundamental bargaining issues. Canadian (police) unions have toppled a few Chiefs of Police, helped defeat at least one provincial government, several mayors and lots of municipal councillors.

Police associations are more likely to apply external pressure to resolve concerns when

1. There is no recourse to independent and impartial third-party resolution.
2. The systems or processes are not working in terms of addressing the legitimate interests of the association and its members.
3. The association is not being afforded an appropriate role or consideration in the decision-making process.

This can lead to public airing of internal problems or concerns, as a means of exerting pressure on the other parties to change their practices (Kinnear, 2002).

If the relationship is healthy and the dispute resolution systems are working, many issues can be resolved without taking more aggressive forms of action. Public airing of internal issues should be viewed as a symptom or manifestation of systemic problems, and provide a wake up call and catalyst for change.

In the 1980s and 1990s, police services in Canada have been influenced by political pressures from all levels. Police officers have seen special interests brought to bear to influence political decisions concerning police officers and the services they provide. Too often police officers and their associations have been excluded or marginalized in the decision-making process, and have found it necessary to take their issues public as a means of addressing their concerns.

Police are not unique in Canada in terms of this approach. Public sector employees and professionals across Canada, including physicians, teachers, firefighters, and nurses, have found it necessary to be more politically active in recent times than they would have found themselves 20 years ago. Governments have become much more aggressive in their dealings with public sector employment issues, compelling organizations representing those employees to adopt more adversarial tactics.

Not all public awareness activities initiated by police associations have been confrontational. The Royal Newfoundland Constabulary Association (2003) commissioned a professional study of their staffing levels, equipment, and working conditions. A comprehensive brief was presented to the provincial government, which became the catalyst for major reforms within the police service, including the hiring of additional personnel and equipment upgrades.

In the province of Alberta, the Edmonton Police Association retained an advertising agency to assist them in developing a public awareness program to inform citizens about staffing shortages within the police service.

Opportunities to Achieve a New Equilibrium

In many respects, dialogue between police associations and those who take a more critical view of police activities has been limited. Often, the parties view the situation as an "us versus them" adversarial relationship. The agendas are often competitive, and the rights of individuals may be in conflict with those of individual police officers.

Police associations have become more proactive in the past decade in terms of developing relationships with police oversight agencies, and by providing "the other side of the story," where possible, to opinion leaders.

There remain, however, opportunities to expand these strategies and networks to develop relationships beyond the traditional realm to pursue common issues and achieve a new equilibrium.

As Marks (2004) observed, police labor organizations should be challenged to meet the demands of newly configuring social, political, and economic environments, and to contribute positively to debates on the future of policing and such issues as privatization, citizenship, and emerging security threats.

While it could be argued that the evolving role of police associations is taking up such challenges, new networks and strategies are arguably required to gain prominence in these forums. While many police associations in Canada have maintained a distance from traditional labor organizations, there may be a need to re-evaluate this approach. Police associations share many common interests and concerns with public and private sector unions. In addition to traditional collective bargaining issues, police associations are increasingly concerned about the privatization of core police activities and the threat of two-tier policing. We can learn from our counterparts in the medical, education, and local government sectors, which have been battling privatization and two-tier public services for many years, such as defending public Medicare in Canada. In fact, it could be argued that medical professionals have been far more successful in raising public awareness regarding the privatization of medical services in Canada than police professionals have been in preserving public policing from privatization.

For police associations to realize success in the pursuit of a new equilibrium that respects the fundamental individual rights and freedoms of police officers, we must engage proactively in the debate concerning democratic governance, human rights, and social justice. As Fleming et al. (2004) suggest, police associations may want to promote rights "beyond the shop floor" and invest in "community unionism" activities that build links and develop agendas with a wider community. Advancing the agenda to develop a rights-based culture and equilibrium within policing may involve reaching out to community advocacy and human rights groups.

This is not without risk. Internally, association members may feel dubious of alliances being formed between their representative association and those who have traditionally been considered critics of the police. There are also those representing community interest groups who have historically argued to curtail the rights and protections afforded to police officers in order to advance their agendas. These representatives may not share the view that a new equilibrium is the solution to their grievances, and may be cynical of its purpose or intent.

The debate begins, however, by educating internal and external audiences of the overarching principles that should guide the debate; that, fundamentally, rights are not negotiable, nor can rights be restricted or limited in a discriminatory manner. Democracy and equality are the cornerstones of a new equilibrium, and are fundamental to justice and accountability.

While the debate starts within our traditional networks and constituencies, opportunities exist to expand into new networks and constituencies where social justice and human rights are of concern.

Conclusion

In order to sustain a police culture that respects and protects the fundamental human rights and dignity of citizens, the citizenry must respect the fundamental human rights and dignity of police members.

In Canada, increasing social, cultural, political, and economic pressures are being brought to bear on policing. These forces shape the way in which Canadian police services respond to and accommodate the needs of citizens. While there is a heightened sense of insecurity in the wake of terrorist events in New York, Madrid, and London, and corresponding demands for increased public security, there remains a debate concerning the conflict between increased security measures and individual human rights. Police officers are the front-line instruments of domestic policy, situated at risk of criticism, complaints, discipline, and even criminal prosecution for their efforts to fulfill their domestic security activities.

Given the very public role of policing, the sometimes intrusive or invasive aspects of police duties and powers, and the potential consequences of police actions, it is not uncommon for police issues or actions to be the subject of intense public scrutiny, commentary, and debate. In the extreme, this places enormous pressure on decision makers that fuel disciplinary actions, as decision makers struggle to ensure that "justice is seen to be done."

While demands for police accountability and respect for the rights of citizens under the Canadian Charter of Rights and Freedoms were prevalent in the last decades of the twentieth century, twenty-first century Canadian police officers expect to be treated fairly and are increasingly aware of and exercising their individual rights as citizens of a democratic state.

The democratization of police services, including employment rights for police members, increases the accountability of police managers and those responsible for the governance of police services. In order for modern police associations to effectively impact policing policies and practices, police association leaders will strategically position their organizations as influential and respected advocates for their members.

In order to promote the highest standards within our profession, and foster a culture that is respectful of the rights of our citizens, a new equilibrium is required. Opportunities exist for police associations to advance this agenda into new networks and constituencies where social justice and human rights are of concern. Through the pursuit of a new equilibrium, Canadian police associations will play an integral role in promoting accountability, democracy, justice, and equality in twenty-first century policing.

References

Biro, F., Campbell, P., McKenna, P., and Murray, T. (2000). Police executives under pressure: A study and discussion of the issues. Police Futures Group Study Series No. 3. Canadian Association of Chiefs of Police. Ottawa, Ontario, Canada. <http://www.policefutures.org/docs/PoliceUnderPressure.pdf>.

Canadian Professional Police Association. (2005). Police officers' bill of rights. CPPA Express Magazine, (63), 6. Canadian Professional Police Association. Ottawa, Ontario, Canada. <http://www.cppa-acpp.ca/publication/publications-english.htm>.

Canadian Professional Police Association and Canadian Association of Chiefs of Police. (2002). Strategic human resources analysis of public policing in Canada. Human Resources Development Canada, Ottawa, Ontario, Canada.

Canadian Society of Association Executives (CSAE). (2001). Advocacy primer for associations. <www.csae.com>.

Ceyssens, P. (February 2002). *Legal Aspects of Policing*. Earlscourt Legal Press Inc. Salt Spring Island, British Columbia, Canada.

Ferguson, G. (January 2003a). Review and recommendations concerning various aspects of police misconduct, Vol. 1. Report Commissioned By: J. Fantino, Chief of Police, Toronto Police Service, Toronto, Ontario, Canada.

Ferguson, G. (January 2003b). Review and recommendations concerning various aspects of police misconduct, Vol. 2. Report Commissioned By: J. Fantino, Chief of Police, Toronto Police Service, Toronto, Ontario, Canada.

Fisher, P. (2003). Workplace stress and trauma in policing: Sources, outcomes and implications: A review document prepared for the Canadian Police Association. Victoria, Canada, March 28, 2003.

Fleming, J., Marks, M., and Wood, J. (2006). 'Standing on the inside looking out': The significance of police unions in networks of police governance. *Australian and New Zealand Journal of Criminology*, 39(1): 71–89.

Griffin, D. (2001). Police association advocacy—A strategic priority: Police associations, political activism and public opinion. Paper presented at the *Police Employment in 2001 Conference*. Toronto, Ontario, Canada, February 27, 2001.

Griffin, D. (2004a). Political expedience. *CPPA Express Magazine*, (62), 2. Canadian Professional Police Association. Ottawa, Ontario, Canada. <http://www.cppa-acpp.ca/publication/publications-english.htm>.

Griffin, D. (2004b). Your rights must be protected. *CPPA Express Magazine*, (60), 8. Canadian Professional Police Association. Ottawa, Ontario, Canada. <http://www.cppa-acpp.ca/publication/publications-english.htm>.

Kinnear, D. (2002). Overview of policing in Canada. Canadian Police Association. Ottawa, Ontario, Canada.

Kinnear, D. (2005). Policing and police labour relations in Canada: Similarities and contrast with the United States of America. Canadian Professional Police Association. Ottawa, Ontario, Canada.

Marks, M. and Fleming, J. (September 2006). The untold story: The regulation of police labour rights and the quest for police democratisation. *Police Practice and Research*, 7(4), 309–322.

Royal Newfoundland Constabulary Association. (2003). Securing our community: Strengthening our commitment, Final Report. St. John's, Newfoundland, Canada, April 24, 2003.

Shankarraman, G. (2003). Police resources in Canada, 2003. Canadian centre for justice statistics. Statistics Canada. Ottawa, Ontario, Canada, December 2003, p. 5.

Shankarraman, G. (2004). Police resources in Canada, 2004. Canadian Centre for Justice Statistics. Statistics Canada. Ottawa, Ontario, Canada, December, p. 6. <http://www.statcan.ca:8096/bsolc/english/bsolc?catno=85-225-X>.

Shankarraman, G. (2003). Police resources in Canada, 2003. Canadian Centre for Justice Statistics. Statistics Canada. Ottawa, Ontario, Canada, December, p. 5.

Sunahara, D. (2004a). Organization-induced stress and financial corruption. Canadian Police College. Ottawa, Ontario, Canada. <http://www.cpc.gc.ca/research/induced_e.htm>.

Sunahara, D. (2004b). Searching for causes: Entitlement and alienation as precursors of unethical police behaviour. Canadian Police College. Ottawa, Ontario, Canada. <http://www.cpc.gc.ca/research/causes_e.htm>.

Sunahara, D. (2004c). Task orientation and the alienation of police officers from their police service: When motivation and rules collide. Canadian Police College. Ottawa, Ontario, Canada. <http://www.cpc.gc.ca/research/report_e.htm>.

Developing Internal Democracy and Civil Rights within the South African Police Service: Police Labor Association Implementation

23

ABBEY WITBOOI

Contents

Brief Historical Background of Police Labor Rights in South Africa

South Africa is a country that has its history rooted in the apartheid system, which was formerly used by the white European minority regime to oppress and segregate people based on race. The racial prejudices affected many racial groups in the country (e.g., Indians, mixed race "coloreds," blacks, and others); however, the black people were the most affected by the racially biased laws. These groups, the black people in particular, did not have basic rights. The values of human dignity, equality, and freedom of movement and association were practically nonexistent. And, of course, prior to 1994, black people in South Africa were denied the right to vote and to shape the governance of the country. Conditions of employment for black people (including the police) were appalling, with most salaries being below the poverty line.

The police under the control of the apartheid regime in South Africa were the key government agency used to enforce apartheid policy and to repress

503

any instances of resistance on the part of subjugated populations. Police were routinely expected to implement and maintain laws that were atrocious and inhuman to their fellow citizens. It is this duty of taking orders, implementing laws, and maintaining them, which made not only the white police officers but the entire police force very unpopular with the black communities. Black police officers were viewed by their fellow brothers and sisters in their communities as tools in the hands of the apartheid regime. This led to serious conflicts in 1985 between black police personnel and their communities, and the rate of police killings during this period was very high. Black police officers, in particular, were targeted because they were perceived as "enemies." The ultimate end result saw black police officers being expelled from their own communities. The state responded to this black police community "exile" by organizing makeshift tents outside of the black townships to accommodate black police personnel.

Many black police officers felt extremely compromised by their role during apartheid governance. They felt dislocated from their communities and felt uncomfortable with the role they were expected to play. They were also extremely unhappy about their terrible working conditions, particularly when they compared these to their white peers. Black police were denied access to medical aid and housing subsidies, and their salaries were unacceptably lower than their white colleagues. This situation came to a head in September 1989, when a group of black police officers decided to take a stand against the role they were expected to play. On September 5, 1989, a handful of black police officers embarked on an act of remarkable conscience and bravery that would shape the face of South African policing forever. Black police personnel defied commands from law enforcement superiors directing them to use force against protesting crowds.

After this event, a few police officials and prison warders met and decided they would form an organization whose key goals and values would be creating parity and job satisfaction within the police force and prison service, while respecting the civil rights of the community. The organization was called the Police and Prisons Civil Rights Union (POPCRU). Its slogan was "Justice for All," and it identified itself as both an industrial union and a civil rights organization. This was an extremely brave stand to take given that police unions and associations were prohibited at the time. POPCRU adopted an unusual position for a police union, namely, the issues they would focus on would include not only salary and benefits, but would also encompass the broader political spectrum.

The Formation of POPCRU

POPCRU was finally formed in November 1989, with the clear purpose of promoting stability, unity, and impartiality, and furthermore to recognize, promote, and protect the civil and basic human rights of all South Africans. Among other founding aims and objectives of POPCRU was the fight against various forms of discrimination, such as racism, sexism, and tribalism. These objectives included the fight for the improvement of working conditions of police, prison, and traffic enforcement personnel. These battles encompassed negotiations on collective bargaining issues, which included but were not limited to issues such as equal rights for all at the workplace, freedom of association, recognition agreement, etc. POPCRU settled a recognition agreement with police management in 1995. Ironically, at the same time, a rival union was formed by police management members. The membership of this union was predominantly white, organized into a union precisely to counteract POPCRU and to perpetuate the interests of those who were opposed to change or transformation of the country. This union was called the South African Police Union (SAPU).

Following its establishment in 1989, POPCRU experienced an adversarial relationship with law enforcement management, which at that stage was seen to be resistant to change, often resulting in the dismissal and suspension of members belonging to POPCRU. However, the relationship improved over time, as management realized that this progressive gain was irreversible and that change was inevitable, especially toward the demise of apartheid in 1994.

In 1997, POPCRU decided to affiliate with the broad trade union federation in South Africa, the Congress of South African Trade Unions (COSATU). In so doing, POPCRU clearly identified itself with other workers in the public and private sector, and made very clear its political affiliation with the anti-apartheid movement in South Africa. Today, POPCRU maintains its union identity and strives to pursue a progressive agenda underscored by the values of democracy, social justice, and equality. POPCRU is also affiliated to Public Service International, which is the international public service representative organization.

Today, POPCRU has 90,000 members in three South African federal agencies involving the correctional services, the traffic department, and agencies involved in safety and security. POPCRU is continuously growing, in large part because staff in the above-mentioned agencies are realizing the difference that the union is making in terms of improving the working conditions and benefits in this sector.

Promoting Sound Labor Relations in South Africa and Southern Africa

South Africa

The formation of POPCRU in South Africa in 1989, coupled with the achievement of multiracial democracy in 1994, has contributed immensely in laying the necessary framework conducive for improving the working conditions and benefits for staff members in that sector. Up until 1993, the police labor relations framework was extremely autocratic, and police members were not awarded any basic labor or social benefits or rights. But, largely as a result of the struggles waged by POPCRU, the current police labor legislation, which was promulgated in 1993, allows for the recognition of police unions within South Africa. Police now have the right to bargain collectively and to associate freely. These are basic labor rights that the police would not have even dreamt of in years past. The police are now included in the new 1995 Labour Relations Act. In accordance with this legislation, the police have the same rights as other employees in the public and private sectors, including the right to freedom of association and the right to collective bargaining. Police employee representative organizations are now included in all key policy planning decision-making forums conducted by the South African Police Service or South African government. Codetermination and consultation processes established so far promote a cooperative atmosphere and support stronger relations between police officers, management, and civilian personnel. POPCRU is actively involved in shaping the institutions established for mediating labor management relations. POPCRU is committed to dismantling any unnecessary hierarchical arrangements within the police service and promotes social dialogue between rank-and-file police and police managers at all levels.

Southern Africa

In 2000, POPCRU decided to embark on a new project aimed at networking with police managers and employees in the southern African region to discover what options existed, and are available, for coordinated police labor–management relations in the region. The project began when POPCRU commissioned researchers from the Trade Union Research Project and the Sociology Department at the University of Natal to conduct preliminary research into the state of police labor relations in the sub-Saharan region. Why did POPCRU decide to embark on this project?

When POPCRU was formed in 1989, it had two main objectives. Its first objective was to represent and speak for those police officers who felt compromised by having to enforce "law and order" in an extremely unjust society. Doing this job often meant employing highly repressive means against the most disempowered and impoverished members of the South African communities. Most early supporters of POPCRU came from these same disadvantaged neighborhoods. With this objective in mind, POPCRU viewed itself as an organization promoting civil rights and social justice.

POPCRU's secondary objective at that time was to collectively represent police and prison officials in regards to industrial and workplace related matters. This was desperately needed as police and prison officials had no collective or individual labor or civil rights. They had no recourse to challenge management and employer directives, no access to bargaining processes or structures, and no mechanisms for input into policy and planning. Added to this, black police officers were those at the sharp end of apartheid policing, expected to enforce unjust laws in the black townships and to legitimatize apartheid policing practices.

In November 1989, police and prison officers came together, declaring collectively for the first time that they would no longer accept their indefensible role, nor would they continue to acquiesce to poor and discriminatory working conditions. These were dramatic statements and actions, and were not well received by government officials and employers. Government officials and police managers refused to recognize POPCRU, and POPCRU supporters were imprisoned, suspended, and dismissed from service. Undeterred, POPCRU supporters continued to mobilize and organize in solidarity with the broader defiance movement that was organizing in South Africa at that time.

The intrepidness and the staying power of the early POPCRU members proved to be extremely worthwhile and judicious. While it would take four years for the police union to be recognized in 1993, police labor legislation was promulgated, which had allowed for the recognition of police unions in South Africa for the first time. This legislation also provided a framework for collective bargaining in the police. The labor rights of the police were further guaranteed when the police were included in the new 1995 Labour Relations Act. In accordance with this act, the police received the same rights as other employees in the public and private sector, including the right to freedom of association and the right to collective bargaining. However, the police still do not have the right to strike as they are considered an essential service, which compares to other democracies across the globe. Today, in South Africa, police employees have the same rights as other employees in the public service (aside from the right to strike) and are able to directly influence decision-making processes within the police service. Over the years, both POPCRU and the police management union have come to realize that there have been tremendous benefits to police employees and to the police organization itself resulting from a liberalized labor relations framework.

These benefits include

- Police employee representative organizations are now included in all key policy and planning decision-making forums in the police. This means that police members have an active say in what happens in their own organization.
- The fact that police representative organizations are able to engage in collective bargaining on key issues of mutual concern has meant

that the traditionally hierarchical nature of the police organizations has been challenged. Police members are now less vulnerable to the unilateral dictates of high-ranking police officers than they were previously.

- Police members are now able to bargain for fairer and more compassionate practices in the police service. For example, police managers are no longer able to unilaterally transfer police members from one location to another without the consent of the particular police officer.
- Codetermination and consultation processes as well as established forums for negotiation has fostered cooperative relations between police workers, police managers, and police employers.
- The opportunity for police employees to participate in determining the conditions of their daily working lives builds morale and commitment to the service.

In addition to industrial benefits, police employees now share the same social and labor rights as other South Africans. This has resulted in important impacts on broad democratization processes. As police officers in South Africa have come to value these awarded rights, they are better able to appreciate (and protect) the rights of other citizens, particularly the rights to freedom of association and freedom of expression. What this means is that the rights of police officers are inextricably linked to broader social and political rights, and the democratization of South African society has directly benefited police employees.

Recently, POPCRU has recognized that the attainment of social and political rights for police employees is not only important in South Africa, but should be achieved in the rest of the sub-Saharan African region as well. There are two reasons for this commitment to facilitating the rights of police employees throughout this region. First, POPCRU is committed to the democratization of the entire southern African region and maintains that civil and political rights for police employees is an integral part of broader societal democratization projects. Second, and perhaps somewhat more instrumental, POPCRU is concerned that South African police unions will be increasingly isolated if nowhere else in the sub-Saharan African region do police have the right to associate freely or to collectively bargain.

POPCRU has therefore committed itself to coordinating a network whose objective is to open up alternatives for improved labor–management relations within public police organizations throughout this area. It has therefore embarked on a long-term project aimed at facilitating deliberations among police managers, employers, and employees about the different options available in the arena of police labor–management relations; assisting with developing representative structures (whether these be unions, associations, federations, or lodges) in public police organizations in the region; as well as formulating mechanisms and frameworks for more social dialogue within these organizations.

A few general observations can be made about police labor relations in the sub-Saharan region:

- Police labor relations and police labor rights are not considered a key area for discussion or consideration by authorities in most southern African countries.
- The only two countries that had collective bargaining arrangements and structures for police were South Africa and Lesotho. In both Lesotho and South Africa, police are viewed as both workers and professionals by the government and the union movement.
- The prospect for creating independent police employee representative organizations with collective bargaining rights was poor. In most countries in the region, police were not viewed as "workers."
- Despite past and recent moves toward democratization in each of the countries under consideration, the police remained extremely acquiescent and were unwilling to "rock the boat." In part, this was because the police felt that there were more important issues of public order and social control that needed to be dealt with, particularly in those countries where there is currently political instability and uncertainty, such as in Zimbabwe.
- Police management (and even rank and file) seemed not to support the move toward increased social and labor rights for police. There appeared to be two reasons for this. First, given the high levels of unemployment in each of these countries, police members viewed themselves as a high status grouping, and were unwilling to jeopardize this status or their job security. Second, police members indicated a poor understanding of unionization. In their view, unions inevitably engage in strike activities, and this is perceived as unacceptable and inappropriate. However, police officials in Namibia did indicate a curiosity about police unions, and exhibited a desire to learn more about alternative models for structuring police labor relations. They expressed a concern about their marginalization from the rest of the population with regard to such issues.
- Police officials and union representatives (except for in Lesotho) did not feel that the progress in police labor relations in South Africa had had any impact on police agencies in the rest of the sub-Saharan region. For the most part, there was no real understanding of the current arrangements and legislation regarding police labor relations in South Africa. Police officials, even those who were sympathetic to the need for more democratized labor relations practices

in the police, indicated that the existence of POPCRU (and SAPU) had not inspired a move toward police unionization. To the contrary, POPCRU had initially been viewed as being militant and troublesome.

- While each of the countries under consideration are designated as democracies, many governmental administrations and ministries had clearly stated that there will be no tolerance for the collective organization of police members. The national police had been excluded from existing labor law legislation, and thus did not have the same rights and freedoms as other workers in the public service.
- A labor law review process has been commenced throughout the sub-Saharan African region. While the public sector is part of this review, there has been no discussion within police agencies as to how they could benefit from this effort.

POPCRU also discovered that there were a number of problems regarding the current International Labor Organization (ILO) conventions as regards to police labor rights. While police are not excluded from these rights in any definitive way, the ILO conventions stipulate that national governments have the right to determine the labor and social rights of police employees.

POPCRU has therefore resolved to embark on an ongoing engagement with the ILO. In the short and medium term, the ILO should assist police organizations in the region in creating an environment and processes for social dialogue. In the longer term, the ILO could consider reassessing the current status of police employees in existing key conventions, with the aim of facilitating the liberalization of police labor rights internationally.

To date, POPCRU has initiated a number of forums with police employers, managers, and employees throughout Southern Africa. Processes are underway where POPCRU is facilitating dialogue between police managers and employees about the prospects for developing new labor relations frameworks. POPCRU is working together with the ILO in forging this program, and makes every effort to link the rights of police employees to the quest for democratic policing.

In promoting police democratization, POPCRU has hosted an international symposium on the democratization of policing in 2006. The symposium explored labor relations as one important consideration, among others, in enhancing the democratization of policing. POPCRU intends to use the African base to make an impact in the international police arena, particularly in regards to promoting fair labor relation practices globally.

At the local level, POPCRU has embarked on a Youth Leadership Program. The program is intended to bring young people together to discuss and share ideas. While POPCRU promotes formal learning, the program aims to instill a sense of democratic citizenship within young people by encouraging them to participate in community projects involving environmental protection, HIV/AIDS awareness, and neighborhood support programs. POPCRU is concerned with black communities adversely affected by apartheid. The program thus continues to aim to build links and positive relations between the police and the communities that they serve. The aim is to develop exchange programs between local South African youth and adolescents across the globe in an effort to better understand their respective national issues and to exchange ideas about how to deal with them.

Challenges Facing Law Enforcement and the Role of Police Unions

POPCRU sees a number of important challenges for the future. Some of these challenges are internal to the union, and others involve a better understanding of how to make South Africa a more safe and secure country to live in.

Internally, POPCRU wishes to build a more active and informed support base. They continue the program for member capacity building through educational and training programs. This training is targeted at organizational development, leadership negotiation, and communication skills.

POPCRU has confronted the South African government with its own two-pronged strategy for dealing with crime. First, POPCRU believes that the underlying social causes of crime, such as poverty and inequality, need to be dealt with. Second, the police need to develop trusting and reciprocal partnerships with communities and community groupings. Since its inception, POPCRU has embraced (and indeed forwarded) the concept of "community policing," which has been recognized as strengthening police–community relations. As a direct result, POPCRU's engagement in this regard has promoted and improved relations between the police and the neighborhoods in which they serve. And POPCRU is adamant that police officer working conditions must be viewed as a priority if they are to be central to the fight against crime and insecurity. Consequently, it has embarked on a number of protest actions calling for increases in pay and improved working conditions for the police. But POPCRU is also concerned that police employees deserve improved working conditions, and this means increasing the professional conduct and service of the police. POPCRU has therefore come out strongly against police corruption, arguing that it lowers the morale of the police and tarnishes the reputation of the entire police service. In addition, POPCRU wishes to see a police service that is free of racism and inequity. At the 2001 and future POPCRU congresses, the union has committed itself to eradicating racism in the service and to promoting the transformation of the SAPS.

POPCRU is well aware of the privatization of public services occurring globally. POPCRU is opposed to the privatization of policing, believing that the state should be responsible for providing for the social needs of the majority of poor South Africans. In this regard, POPCRU strongly identifies with its umbrella trade union federation, COSATU. In 2001, POPCRU joined COSATU in an anti-privatization strike. POPCRU's involvement in anti-privatization activities is just one way of demonstrating our commitment to the promotion of peace and justice of all in the face of the growing impact of globalization.

In order for POPCRU to have an impact on and to shape policing agendas in ways that benefit the poor and most vulnerable members of society, it is important for the union to form part of national and international networks. As an affiliate of COSATU, POPCRU is in close association with the trade union movement, both in South Africa and internationally. POPCRU maintains its commitment to fighting for social justice and representing the voices of the less powerful in society. They align themselves with community groupings, and have long called for the democratization of policing and for the deepening of community policing practices in South Africa. As a police union, POPCRU is constantly seeking allegiances with other groupings whose objective is to maximize safety and security for all peoples. POPCRU is open to learning about new policing practices and new policing philosophies, and in joining new policing networks.

POPCRU is aware of its many internal problems. One has been the complete neglect on behalf of POPCRU's leadership to record its history, achievements, and failures, and to critically examine these matters. POPCRU should creatively examine lobbying and campaign strategies so that they are assured that they have strong influential capacity within policing debates and forums. Unfortunately, some claim that the POPCRU leadership has at times become distanced from its membership.

Conclusion

POPCRU has achieved many substantial gains for the police in its 20 years of existence. Prior to 1989, when POPCRU was formed, front-line police personnel had experienced adversarial relations with agency management. Over the years, POPCRU has now developed a constructive relationship with police management. Police unions are now recognized and play a central role in all police planning and policy making. The South African Police Service is now almost entirely unionized and consists of modern labor relations institutions. The police, via the police unions, are able to engage in collective bargaining on key issues of mutual concern, which has meant that the traditionally hierarchical nature of the South African Police Service has been challenged, making union members less vulnerable to unilateral dictates of high-ranking officers. These efforts have enhanced morale and commitment to the South African Police Service.

There are a number of other important results from these efforts to extend social and labor rights to the police. As POPCRU members have come to value their newly awarded benefits, they are better able to appreciate and protect the rights of other citizens, particularly the rights of freedom of association and freedom of expression, which are clear and basic democratic rights. The rights of police members are inextricably linked to broader social and political rights of society. POPCRU, as both a civil rights and industrial union, is acutely aware of the mutually beneficial outcomes of institutional benefits and of the broader social and political rights.

The advantages and rights that POPCRU has secured over the past two decades have been hard fought. POPCRU is well aware that these rights can only be safeguarded if the union is strong, has a vision, and is in touch with contemporary developments in law enforcement, both at home and abroad. POPCRU must continue its quest to be a part of international police union networks and has committed itself to building police unionism in those parts of the world where police rights have been curtailed and where the democratization of policing has been restricted.

Finally, it is extremely important that police unions like POPCRU participate in international conferences so as to keep abreast of new policing trends around the world, to participate in current debates, and to network with other actors who share similar policing visions. By remaining current, both police unions and their related agencies can continue to progress and ensure effectiveness and efficiency.

Reference

This chapter is the text from a verbal presentation made by the author at the International Police Executive Symposium conference in the Czech Republic in 2005.

The Influence of the New Zealand Police Association on the Evolution of the Police, Policing, and the Law and Order Paradigm

24

GREG O'CONNOR

Contents

Introduction

New Zealand is a democratic country that occupies a land area approximately the same size as Great Britain but with an elongated shape that is divided into two main islands. This geography greatly influences how business is conducted, how the population there is dispersed, and our weather variations. It also means the police are required to carry out a wide variety of roles that vary from district to district, often dependent on the topography and climate. An obvious example of this would be search and rescue requirements in a mountainous, bush-clad country, as compared to a similar operation in a seaside region.

New Zealand was colonized by the English in the early 1800s. The indigenous people, the Maori, were colonized and largely deprived of their land and fishing ownership despite the signing of a treaty with the British Crown—the Treaty of Waitangi—in 1840. Grievances emanating from the crown's failure to honor the treaty play a large part in the political and policing environment today. The Maori renaissance, backed by favorable legal decisions passed down from the English Privy Council (until recently, the highest court governing New Zealand) paved the way for the Maori to seek compensation and redress in the New Zealand courts.

The Maori currently comprise approximately 20% of the New Zealand population (Statistics New Zealand, 2005). Although Maori and European have integrated comparatively better than the colonizer and colonized have in most colonial situations, underlying divisions still exist. The Maori are heavily represented in the lower socioeconomic groups, and individuals of Maori descent comprise 50% of the New Zealand prison population (Department of Corrections, 2004).

In 2009, approximately 10.5% of police officers in New Zealand were of Maori descent. Over the last 10 years, police have actively encouraged the adoption of Taha Maori (Maori protocols and culture). Senior police are expected to open formal addresses with a Mihi (greeting) in Maori, and the same officers are routinely welcomed to a new posting with a Powhiri (traditional welcome) hosted by the local Iwi (tribe).

The New Zealand Police Association continues to mirror this practice. However, the union membership has been cynical of this requirement, and the organization has been slow to implement this fully in order not to alienate its membership.

The New Zealand Police

The New Zealand Police was established in 1886. It evolved from the Armed Constabulary, which was a quasi-military force very active during the Maori Land Wars of the mid- to late-1800s. The Armed Constabulary had absorbed the provincial police forces in the 1860s against the wishes of the provincial governments (Hill, 1989). That decision was to be an extremely important one, resulting in the situation that exists today where New Zealand has one police force. Although there was a 10-year period when both the Armed Constabulary and provincial police forces existed, New Zealand Police developed as a disarmed constabulary, a situation that exists today. At the same time, New Zealand developed one criminal code, and provincial governments were abolished in 1876 (Hill, 1989).

Local councils took up the enforcement of traffic regulations as the motor vehicle became more prevalent. Councils operated their own traffic police until the 1970s and 1980s, when they were integrated with the Ministry of Transport. The Ministry of Transport was a completely separate police force, which solely policed the roads and undertook related activities such as driver and vehicle licensing. Traffic officers were separately recruited and trained, and only had limited coercive powers. They were not regarded or referred to as "police" by New Zealanders, and wore different uniforms. They were separately funded and their activities were not governed by the Minister of Police but by the Transport Ministry.

New Zealand Police, for their part, although enjoying the same authority and powers of traffic officers, only occasionally policed the roads. This meant that the New Zealand Police enjoyed a unique relationship with their public, in that they were only required to police crime and disorder in addition to public duties like search and rescue, water policing, and public events. These are functions that generally do not bring police into conflict with the average New Zealander.

In 1992, a political decision was made to integrate the Ministry of Transport with its 1300 traffic officers with the New Zealand Police, with its then 4500 sworn officers. This integration was made at a time when New Zealand was undergoing considerable economic reform and restructuring, so this event went relatively unnoticed by a change- and reform-weary New Zealand public. New Zealand underwent considerable economic reform and restructuring following the election of a Labor Government in 1984 when, in a very short time, it went from one of the most heavily regulated economies in the world to one of the most deregulated.

The then police association leadership supported the integration, seeing it as an instant membership increase. Previously, the Public Service Association had covered traffic officers industrially. Subsequently, all traffic officers joined the police association. Association members generally did not support the integration, and the association leadership was subsequently heavily criticized for not consulting or reflecting its membership. However, there was no loss of existing membership.

Since its implementation, this integration has resulted in a change in the relationship between police officers and the New Zealand public, who in the past have not been acclimated to the police carrying out the unpopular traffic enforcement duties. It also brought the police under the overall control of one cabinet minister, the Minister of Police, although funding still comes from the Ministry of Transport for road policing activities. This dual policing role—and, importantly, dual funding role—has politicized the police, in that there is competition within the police sub-departments for funding and prioritization demands from two ministries.

The New Zealand Police are funded by the central government as part of the justice sector. This means that they must compete for funding with the Department of Corrections who run the prisons, the Justice Ministry itself (which now includes the former Department for Courts), and two smaller departments that are also funded by the Justice budget. This is highly significant for the New Zealand Police Association, which must target its lobbying for more funding for police, including funding for salary increases, in a manner which could ultimately bring it into conflict with unions representing the prison guards, court staff, and other public servants.

The New Zealand Police now has 7500 sworn members and 2500 non-sworn or public servant employees. It is run by a Commissioner and two deputies, who comprise the Board of Commissioners at the Office of the Commissioner situated in Wellington, the capital city.

New Zealand is divided into 13 policing districts, of which 12 are geographic and 1 functional. Many policing responsibilities in the districts, such as the prosecutor's office and training, report centrally to the Office of the Commissioner, and not through their local district commands.

The New Zealand Police Association

The New Zealand Police Association represents 98% of all sworn police officers and approximately 92% of the civilian staff. The decision to represent non-sworn employees, which was made in late 1998, was a reaction to the increased civilianization of police and a desire to ensure that the police association represented all police employees. This has created some complications and challenges for the police association, especially when the association wants to argue for the retention of sworn positions when non-sworn members are demanding better career prospects within the police.

The major difference is in bargaining. The contract for sworn police personnel is negotiated under the parameters laid out in the Police Act of 1958, and includes a binding compulsory arbitration facility for wages. This is in lieu of any ability to take industrial action defined as any deviation from normal duty. Non-sworn employees must bargain under the universal provisions of the Employment Relations Act of 2001, which covers every non-exempted employee in New Zealand and has its underlying philosophy in "good faith" bargaining.

In representing both groups, one aspect that has become obvious to the police association is that the leverage available for sworn officers in galvanizing public and political support during any dispute or campaign is considerably greater than that for non-sworn members. This became obvious in 1998, when the acting national government ordered a review of police financing with the stated intention of cutting $50 million from the police baseline budget. The police association galvanized public opposition to the proposal, and established an audit group composed of New Zealand's wealthiest businessman, including an economist, a constitutional lawyer, and a management consultant.

The impact of the assessment of New Zealand Police organization was mitigated considerably, and proposed reductions in sworn staff numbers were limited to a small number of senior ranking police officials who opted for an early retirement package. On the other hand, non-sworn police positions were lost, as the government decided that attrition of these civilian positions would be of negligible political consequence.

There has been a reorganization in the membership within the New Zealand Public Service Association, which now only represents a very small number of non-sworn public servants (approximately 60). Another union developed, the Police Managers Guild, which represents about 150 commissioned officers, above and including the rank of Inspector, and senior non-sworn management employees. The police association represents a similar number of higher-ranking police officials as the Police Managers Guild. The majority of these management officials in the police association are involved in operational policing activities and other executive roles.

The relationship between these two organizations is cordial, and they do join together for salary bargaining. However, it has been the opinion of the police association that two groups representing police in the public and political environment create the potential for the government and police administration to split the essential unity that police must portray to best represent police employees.

The New Zealand Police Association was formed in 1936, and like many police unions it has had to fight for the constitutional right to associate (McGill, 1992). From the time of this union's inception, the role of association's leader, the national secretary, has always been held by a civilian recruited from outside of the policing environment, generally a person with professional qualifications, and usually an attorney. The first full time president was appointed in 1984 and, since that time, the New Zealand Police Association has had three full time presidents, all operational Senior Sergeants at the time of their election. The police association presidents are on paid leave from their agency for the duration of their tenure. Of the entire police association staff of 35, which includes four geographically dispersed field officers, the president is the only police officer employed full time at the police association national office. Most of the union staff are nonpolice employees.

An interesting point is that the New Zealand Police Association operates a fully owned subsidiary, the New Zealand Police Welfare Fund, which owns and operates a health insurance provider that currently covers more than 27,000 active members, retirees, and their family members. Other benefits include options for life, fire, travel, and mortgage insurance. In addition, the Police Welfare Fund owns and operates 50 vacation properties throughout New Zealand, which are available to members at reasonably priced or discounted rates.

In addition to industrial and legal assistance in case of disciplinary charges, the police association continues to respond to national events and allegations made against law enforcement personnel. One example of the police association responding to the political environment occurred after the introduction of the mixed-member proportional (MMP) voting system implemented into government in New Zealand in 1996. Up to the end of the last millennium, one of the two political parties—the Conservative National Party or the Social Democratic Labour Party—governed the nation exclusively for most of the twentieth century. Since the advent of MMP, neither of the two major parties has enjoyed a majority and, as a result, they have been required to govern either in a formal coalition with smaller political parties from the conservative or liberal sides. The lack of an absolute ability to govern without compromise has strengthened the position of groups like the New Zealand Police Association in the lobbying arena. Gaining the support of a coalition partner or a party pledging to support the government on confidence and supply is of considerable advantage when negotiating with the government.

The Mandate of the New Zealand Police Association

Up until the 1970s in New Zealand, policing was a relatively benign profession. An examination of the annual crime and incident logs in police stations throughout the country in the 1970s reveals that public calls for police service were infrequent by today's standards. During the 1950s and 1960s, New Zealand transitioned from a rural-based economy, with the vast majority of wealth located in provincial areas, to a more urbanized, industrialized model. This was accompanied by a move to the cities by rural Maori and Pakeha (non-Polynesian New Zealanders) and by immigration from the Pacific Islands, primarily Western Samoa. The New Zealand Police were not well equipped for this rapid urbanization, accompanied by the inevitable social upheaval and increases in crime and calls for service to the police. This urbanization and the mixing of three previously distinct cultures, combined with the general social disturbances of the 1960s throughout the western world, the introduction of illicit drugs such as heroin, and the arrival of television in New Zealand, changed the previously conservative, benign, and relatively isolated New Zealand society considerably. A consequence of the exposure to these new influences, combined with real increases in criminal offending, was an increased fear of crime among the general population.

Police, for their part, were slow to respond to these changes. They centralized operations in order to react to increased demands, but did little proactive work internally or externally to ensure that they were prepared for the evolving community situations they were facing, most especially the increase in crime and the expansion of the suburban population and residential areas. As crime and the fear of crime among communities grew, demands for reassurance and safety grew accordingly. However, the New Zealand Police continued to adopt a very reactive model.

As fear of crime began to increase through the 1970s and 1980s, opposition parties began to use the increasing crime rates as a tool to criticize acting government officials, citing inadequate budgetary investment and policy oversight into the problem. Police had limited, if any, research capability at that time. Academic study had never been encouraged in policing, and tertiary study in sociology and criminology, in particular, was not seen as adding value to policing. The predominant training emphasis on education highlighted management and the legal field. The New Zealand Police were relatively effective at detecting and prosecuting serious crime such as homicide, aggravated robbery, and reported rapes, but prevention and detection of high-incidence crimes, such as burglary and car theft, were very low. The issue of the "street kid"—which involved large numbers of mainly Polynesian teenagers who gathered around city centers, committing visible disorder offences such as graffiti vandalism, and who graduated onto more serious assaults, robberies, and drug offences—became especially prevalent in the 1980s.

Since the government and police mechanisms were not concerned with research or innovative programs, it was left to the educational institutions to take the lead in these endeavors. The Victoria University of Wellington Institute of Criminology became influential within the upper management levels of the New Zealand Police, and was the lead partner in the introduction of the community policing concept, which was initially implemented in Wellington's Kapiti-Mana district in the late 1980s and 1990s. Kapiti-Mana district included Porirua City, a large government-subsidized housing area near Wellington, with high incidences of poverty, low socio-economic status, and high violent crime rates.

The community policing model introduced there involved the decentralization of existing resources. Although field police personnel generally regarded this initiative as unsuccessful and ineffective, it became the standard model for policing adopted throughout New Zealand, particularly the decentralization aspect.

In late 1993, in order to address rising crime rates, a Crime Prevention Unit was established in the Department of Prime Minister and Cabinet. Interestingly, only police officers (i.e., the lowest ranking "Inspectors") were involved in the Crime Prevention Unit. In 2001, the Crime Prevention Unit moved from the Prime Minister's Department to the Ministry of Justice. The police association has had very little direct input into the Crime Prevention Unit, since they were often viewed by government officials as being obstructive and interfering, emphasizing police benefits rather than productive law enforcement.

In the 1980s, the New Zealand Police began sponsoring officers through university study. In the late 1980s and early 1990s, the government created a generous tertiary funding program that allowed police officers to subsidize their university study. However, many officers utilized this opportunity to enhance their secondary skills and study topics outside of the police profession rather than enhancing their law enforcement and justice skills. Those who did embark on relevant criminology and legal studies, particularly at the undergraduate level, were heavily influenced by the ideas of the academic institutions in which they studied. As police agencies are hierarchal bodies, the middle and upper level managers who had availed themselves of these educational opportunities began to implement some of the ideas that they were exposed to through their studies. Accordingly, the academic influence on the police environment became more pronounced in the late 1980s and 1990s era.

Another significant development in the 1990s, which was to greatly impact the relevance of and opportunities for the police association, was the appointment of the John Banks as the New Zealand Police Minister. Banks took an extremely active interest in his position, and publicly described himself as the "Minister for Police" as opposed to the Minister of Police. He had a reputation as an old-style dictatorial politician, with little respect for the previous separation of power between the Commissioner and the Minister. Banks was the minister responsible for the merging of Police with the Ministry of Transport. He was also responsible for appointing Police Commissioner Richard MacDonald, who provided little resistance to the ideas initiated by Minister Banks. Minister Banks appointed the next Police Commissioner, Peter Doone. Commissioner Doone had obtained a Masters Degree while working in the New Zealand Police, and had received post-graduate training in the United States. He had a vision to take the New Zealand Police forward to become the most technologically advanced police agency in the world, and he invested heavily in a computer system known as INCIS (Integrated National Criminal Intelligence System), which would see New Zealand Police operating off one database in a fully integrated electronic environment.

The police had partnered with the corporation IBM in the project. Ultimately, the project was regarded as an extremely expensive failure. The New Zealand Police had invested $160 million, and IBM had invested considerably more. While a significant proportion of the police funding was on top of the operating budget, the New Zealand government had expected a return of investment by way of a more efficient and less costly law enforcement mechanism. In fact, the original agency proposal was to result in the eventual reduction of 540 positions in police once the project was completed. Surprisingly, the police association leadership had signed off on the agency plan, even though job losses were to result.

The business partner of the New Zealand Police, IBM, withdrew support from the project in 1999. From 1993 to 1999, during what became known as the "INCIS period," investment in policing in New Zealand suffered considerably. Due to dramatic budgetary overruns, the Labor Party government in 2000 removed Police Commissioner Doone from office and replaced him with Deputy Commissioner Rob Robinson. Because of the cavalier way in which the New Zealand Police had dealt with budgetary costs during the INCIS period, strict controls were placed on the police agency funding. Government officials from all political parties and their advisors from the Ministries of Treasury and State Services (the predominant employer of New Zealand public servants) had for some time been frustrated at the New Zealand Police inability to operate within the state sector spending and accounting rules, citing operational reasons, not least crime increases, as the reasons for their budget overruns. Government administrators actually threatened to close some police stations and reassign staff, even though this was not well received by the public and could be considered to be politically damaging, as crime rates had continued to increase. Many politicians believed that the New Zealand Police Association had colluded with police managers to avoid budgetary reductions. While government leaders called for staff reductions, the police association was successful in campaigning for the hiring of 900 more police. Reducing police budgets at a time when crime rates escalated was clearly not a popular maneuver.

In 1999, the new ruling administration, headed by the Labor party, was determined to exert control over the police bureaucracy. A strategic plan was created, implemented, and overseen by a committee comprised of representatives from the New Zealand Treasury, from State Services, and from the Department of Prime Ministers and Cabinet. The police representative on the committee was the newly appointed Civilian Deputy Commissioner, a public servant appointed from the Department of Archives in New Zealand.

The police association sat on the oversight body in a consultative role, and was able to have limited input. Most importantly, however, control was imposed over police by the imposition of a tagged funding model, whereby the budget appropriations allocated to police in the annual funding round were tagged to specific areas of policing. In the 2004–2005 budget document, policing activities were funded into seven areas.* The model was provided by the Ministry of Transport's road policing model, whereby outputs were purchased from police by government. Using this traffic model, the government purchases hours of policing from the police, one of 14 output classes, which must be contractually met by the financial year end. A management regime was imposed throughout the organization to the front-line unit level, requiring delivery of a set number of traffic hours or Safety Administration Programme (SAP) hours. This was audited by each police officer, who is required to account for each half hour period of his or her working day by

---

* These are policy advice and ministerial servicing, general crime prevention services, specific crime prevention services and maintenance of public order, police primary response management, investigations, case resolution and support to judicial process, and road safety program (New Zealand Treasury, 2005).

a coded output class. The traffic funders strictly audit this. The same output class has been extended to other parts of police and, subsequently, any additional funding to police is specifically tagged to be delivered in a specified area of policing (i.e., output class). This model provides the opportunity for the providers of the funding (i.e., the government) to ensure funding is channeled into the area they believe most appropriate.

Unsurprisingly, the temptation to direct funding to the areas based on political influence has proved to be too much for the local and federal governments. Aligning the output funding with public demand for service and the long-term policing strategy with political need has, to date, proved beyond the providers (i.e., the government). Underlying this is the increased contract and performance management regime in the police, which sees remuneration aligned with performance. Performance is increasingly measured against output delivery, and crime reduction efforts often require creative accounting by district administrations in an attempt to align the funding requirements with policing needs. This has generally been accomplished to date as a robust economy with full employment, and a changing social demographic has impacted positively on all crime classes with the exception of serious violent crime.

The increasing politicization of policing strategies and direction has therefore created an opportunity for the New Zealand Police Association. As police administrators have increasingly had their power usurped through funding and increased political influence, a vacuum had been created whereby senior police officials were contractually disempowered in both negotiation and advocacy. A combination of an ever-increasing fear of crime and demand for policing service, combined with a disempowerment of the police commissioner by politicians and the ruling government of the day, has meant that the New Zealand Police Association has been able to establish itself as a influential factor on a wide range of issues beyond wages and conditions of its members.

The New Zealand Police Association has been assisted in this by the fact that it is a national police organization able to comment on both national and local issues. A very good example has been the increase in the manufacture, distribution, and use of what are described as party drugs, in particular methamphetamine. As an island country, New Zealand has been relatively free of white powder drugs since a major drug ring, the New Zealand-based "Mister Asia" syndicate, collapsed in 1980. However, since then, the predominantly white motorcycle gangs have built capability and capacity through the 1990s and the start of the new millennium, and have become major manufacturers, distributors, and subsequently importers of methamphetamine and related drugs.

New Zealand had been relatively free from organized crime groups until the methamphetamine trend and associated industries hit this nation.

The New Zealand Police Association, acting on warnings from front-line members, began actively warning the public and government through the media that local gangs were evolving into organized criminals and that methamphetamine would very soon become easily available. Consequently, the same problems that have been experienced overseas would soon be witnessed with New Zealand as a result of excess methamphetamine use.

The police administration not only did not attempt to take action to discourage or prevent the gangs from becoming powerful and entrenched on the back of the methamphetamine industry, but actively denied—publicly and to the government—that this was a problem. One of the main reasons for this was because of the funding regime—there was actually no funding directed toward policing organized crime and the drug trade, and therefore any policing that did take place was done figuratively out of petty cash. It was only when the inevitable high-profile methamphetamine-related crimes began appearing on front pages of the papers, other media, and in New Zealand courts that the government and funding agencies became involved and specific tagged funding was made available to counter the problem.

The New Zealand Police Association has been given full credit by the government and the media for alerting New Zealand to what was going to happen and what subsequently happened. As a consequence, the police union's credibility as advisors and commentators on law enforcement matters increased considerably. The police association conducted a special conference, and invited speakers from overseas to talk about methamphetamine and the consequences of failing to adequately control or deter it. They also brought speakers to New Zealand to talk about the problems with organized crime, particularly outlaw motorcycle gangs. These conferences were well publicized and they proved to be prophetic.

The New Zealand Police Association also conducted a series of surveys on, and publicly warned about, inadequacies in the New Zealand National Communication System, which had been designed during the 1990s as part of the previously mentioned INCIS computer project. Again, because of the way in which police are funded, each new project with its tagged funding failed to take into account the additional resource required for infrastructure. This failure particularly impacted the National Communications System in which three centers handle all calls for service, both emergency and nonemergency, throughout New Zealand.

The New Zealand Police Association predicted that the system would fail spectacularly, which it subsequently did. Unfortunately it was the loss of a life, young female Iraena Asher, that became the premiere example of the failure of the Police Communications System. Again the subsequent media commentary highlighted the fact that the police association had been warning and advocating for more resourcing of the communication centers. Once again the inability of police to sufficiently invest in this mission-critical area, due to inflexibility in the manner in which they are funded, impacted negatively on public satisfaction with the police. Internal and external surveys continue to highlight reduced trust and confidence in the police and that fear of crime has not diminished despite reductions in reported crime in all categories (other than violent crime) since the late 1990s.

As the power and decision-making ability of New Zealand police executives diminished and has been usurped by government, the New Zealand Police Association continues their endeavors to act as the voice of the police in the public and political arena. In an atmosphere where significant decisions are being made by government officials without significant police official input, the police association can serve as a conduit to ensure the opinions of police officers are heard and considered.

A very good example of this was the introduction of DNA enabling legislation, which proposed that trained police officers be permitted to obtain buccal swabs from suspects without the need for a trained medical professional. The formal police request had been opposed by Justice Ministry officials, and was not to be considered before the parliamentary select committee considering the legislation. A presentation by the association to the select committee included a demonstration of the swabbing of a suspect, a simple, noninvasive procedure that positively influenced the outcome in favor of the police.

The police association has also prepared submissions on a range of legislation that has impacted law enforcement in New Zealand, including the Evidence Bill, which codifies common law and statutory provisions relating to evidence, and the Criminal Proceeds and Instruments Bill, which amended criminal asset seizure legislation. In both cases, the police association's submissions closely mirrored the submissions of the police hierarchy, which had been rejected by government officials or politicians in the drafting of the legislation.

There were and will continue to be occasions, however, when the police association position will be markedly different than that of police administrators, particularly in areas impacting front-line policy and conditions. A good example was the Police Amendment Bill (No. 2 of 2001), which proposed an amendment to the Police Act of 1958. The negotiating framework for sworn police is contained in the 1958 Police Act, which contained a provision for final offer binding arbitration on wage settlements. The legislation, proposed by the Police Minister and supported by the Commissioner, inserted a clause to add to the criteria to be considered by the arbitrator. The clause proposed that the arbitrator must consider police ability to fund and pay settlement with existing police budget. With no ability to take any type of industrial action, this would have placed police association negotiators entirely in the hands of the government funders in determining an appropriate level of settlement. The association lobbied successfully to have the legislation overturned, and was also successful in broadening the criteria to retain the status quo.

The police association strongly believes that it must be credible and well informed in using its resources to influence the broader law and order environment beyond industrial issues. To maintain and enhance its credibility in this area, it has a robust research capability and continues to employ a policy analyst/advisor with a PhD in criminology.

There continues to be a major challenge for the New Zealand Police Association. Like all police associations, they exist primarily to enhance the wellbeing of their members and their families. As a member-based organization, the police association must be cognizant of the need to retain the support of its membership, most of whom are primarily concerned in the ability of the union to enhance their wages and conditions.

However, the association is acutely aware of the need to respond to changes taking place in the law enforcement arena. One of the challenges facing them is the issue that the New Zealand Police senior administration is increasingly comprised of professional bureaucrats with no police background. A series of highly publicized scandals have brought considerable pressure to bear on police to change what is considered a macho, misogynist culture. As an example, the task of changing the police subculture is now spearheaded by the Deputy Commissioner of Resources and Management, who is a career bureaucrat.

The police association has no interest in retaining deviant or incompetent police officers in the New Zealand Police. It does, however, have an interest in ensuring that changes that are made to the New Zealand Police come from an informed public and government administration with the ultimate goals of improving the police organization. Because of the extreme public pressure on police administrators to be seen as making changes to satisfy media and political demands for measurable changes to the police subculture, the association is taking an active part in all forums related to this issue. One of these forums is the "commission of inquiry" into the way in which the New Zealand Police investigate complaints of sexual misconduct involving police officers, their family members, and their acquaintances. The police association has employed an attorney full time to attend all proceedings to ensure that the interests of not only those being accused but of the police organization, in general, are not subverted by the need to be seen to be acting against the police. The police association is also conducting a marketing campaign in order to improve government funding for an increase of more than 500 front-line sworn police officers as soon as possible.

The New Zealand Police has been very successful, and is often regarded as one of the world's best practitioners in traffic enforcement and road policing. The incidences of road deaths have reduced by nearly 30% since 1996. Population adjusted volume crime has also reduced since 1996, which includes a burglary reduction of more than 35%, a decrease in car theft by 40%, and the decline in general theft by more than 25%. These are areas where funding had been directed through the tagged funding regime. However, the directed (or more aptly, redirected) funding in these areas has meant that the front-line emergency and public response branch has had its capacity reduced to put resources into these other more politically vulnerable areas. The result has been a fall in public confidence in police, as failures in the emergency response area have become more prevalent and more highly publicized.

Again, the challenge for the police association is to build its profile as improving police professionalism and service delivery, and not to be narrowly interested in only employee benefits. Credibility earned in involvement in broader policing matters becomes important during such campaigns when political opponents attempt to label the police association as a self-serving union. The seeming inability of police administrators to be more critical of government policing initiatives provides the police association with the opportunity to be a key influential factor in matters affecting police with the full backing of its membership.

The challenge for the police association will come when the vacuum of power at the top of police is filled either by a police commissioner able to free himself or herself from the shackles of political oversight, and this will essentially only be done by a commissioner prepared to leverage on the opportunities the public fear of crime presents; or the power will be diminished by a significant reduction in the fear of crime itself. In either of these scenarios, the leadership of the police association must build a résumé of credibility, capability, and relevance in the law and order environment to ensure that it remains a significant participant in the law enforcement environment when it comes to lawmakers, the public, and, most importantly, its membership. Failure to understand where the association's true power comes from will consign it to future irrelevance. The police association must be able to foresee changes to the criminal justice environment and be prepared to adapt to those events. A likely future development in the New Zealand Police will be the introduction of a second tier of front-line police personnel, similar to the Community Support Officers in the United Kingdom. Tiering of police organizations, with both armed and unarmed uniformed personnel, is now viewed as a more economical option to increasing the number of sworn police officers.

The current cost of training and resourcing a police officer to the required standards, combined with the difficulties in recruiting people who are suitably qualified and interested in a law enforcement career, has meant that initial personnel costs will continue to rise. As more compliance demands are made on officers, particularly in the way they conduct themselves professionally and in private, the pool of suitable candidates will diminish. Already, the New Zealand Police has been forced to recruit British police officers directly into the New Zealand Police, and to reinstitute a cadet training scheme recruiting school students. As has been found in other jurisdictions, police officers so well qualified and, consequently, so well paid, will be increasingly reluctant to perform the process-oriented and menial tasks that are the basis of front-line police work. A good analogy has been witnessed in the nursing profession, where lesser trained, less qualified, and lower paid nurse aids increasingly carry out the nursing functions at the more physical end of patient care previously performed by fully trained nurses.

The New Zealand Police Association needs to recognize that there will be an increasing gap between what is routine police work and what is policing. In New Zealand, many tasks previously carried out by sworn police officers are now performed by lesser trained and lower paid private security staff, and even by local council–funded staff. These tasks include beat patrolling in the city center, prisoner transport, courtroom security, security at sportings events, and attending to burglar alarms.

New Zealand has one tier of national government and has no upper house. Legislative change can be introduced and implemented quickly and efficiently with no constitutional forum in which to challenge these legislative revisions. As a result, New Zealand has often been at the forefront of social change in the western world. New Zealand was the first country in the world to grant universal suffrage and has recently legalized prostitution and same sex civil unions. More significantly, there is little opportunity for organizations like the police association to challenge legislation affecting its members outside the realm of public and, more importantly, published opinion. Being seen as credible and effective in this forum is now (and will remain) important to the future relevance of police unions.

New Zealand has a proven record of responding actively and innovatively to changes in the way the world does business. As a national organization representing one unified law enforcement agency, the New Zealand Police Association has the advantage of being able to look internationally to see where the policing environment is changing, and to be able to constantly monitor and evaluate the impact of such changes within New Zealand and, indeed, throughout the world.

Police Association Participation in International Forums

The New Zealand Police Association actively pursues relationships with similar organizations globally, particularly in the English speaking countries. Although relatively unique as a national organization representing all law enforcement officials, the New Zealand Police Association understands that associations and unions representing state, provincial, and even city police unions are generally well informed about trends in their own forces and services. Thus, it is extremely valuable to take part in symposiums where not only union matters, but also standard law enforcement matters are being discussed.

Policing strategies being tested or piloted in different parts of the criminal justice arena often attract the interest of policy makers in New Zealand, and result in politicians and policy advisers making fact-finding visits to these locations. The "Broken Windows" crime reduction strategies implemented in New York City in the mid-1990s was a good example, and a number of New Zealand politicians and officials visited there over the last decade.

The New Zealand Police Association, through contacts with the New York City Police Benevolent Association (the union for police officers), was able to spend time with NYPD colleagues, and invited former NYPD Deputy Commissioner John Timoney to New Zealand to explain the strategy. In establishing relationships with police unions and associations internationally, attempts to locate the most relevant areas of interest to the New Zealand Police Association have been somewhat arbitrary. The association maintains a close relationship with The Police Federation of Australia and its affiliates, and although not eligible to be a member of the PFA, has a standing invitation to sit at the executive table, which it routinely does.

The growth of the International Law Enforcement Conference (ILEC) organization, a group that welcomes national police association and federation bodies, provides for an exchange of information and ideas on police union best practice and on effective law enforcement trends. An ILEC conference takes place every 2 years. ILEC met in Edinburgh in November 2004, and a series of motions or confirmations were signed off by representatives at the conference, which outlined the principles of the organization. The predominant principle agreements were:

Assaults on police, risk of contracting infectious diseases, and legislative protection: The International Law Enforcement Council views attacks on a police officer acting in the lawful execution of their duty as an attack on society itself. They call on governments to take seriously the question of prevention, prosecution, penalty, and post-incident support for officers subject to such attacks.

Equipment standards: The International Law Enforcement Council calls upon all police governing bodies to provide equipment that meets or exceeds minimum safety standards to provide officers with a safe work environment.

Independence and integrity of investigations of police: The ILEC argues that the public deserves a police force that is free from improper prosecutions or sanctions borne out of undue political influence and special interest group pressure.

Government obligation to provide for public safety: The ILEC argues that public safety, the core obligation of government, is being compromised when governments choose to utilize the services of inadequately trained and qualified persons as an inappropriate substitute for properly trained law enforcement professionals in public law enforcement responsibilities.

Police mobility and professionalism: The ILEC seeks an internationally accepted accreditation system for law enforcement professionals that allows for the increased mobility of police through initiatives such as mutual recognition of the equivalency of qualifications from other jurisdictions, comparable to doctors, nurses, and other like professionals.

Freedom of association: The ILEC, through structures such as the International Labour Organization, calls upon all governments to recognize the right of police officers to freedom of association and the right to bargain collectively.

As a result of these stated standards, the New Zealand Police Association believes that ILEC has the potential to become a significant contributor to law enforcement and to police unionism globally.

Conclusion

The New Zealand Police, due to the loss of control of the law enforcement agenda, particularly through having a strictly audited tagged funding regime placed over its administration, and through government and bureaucratic determination to bring the police within public service boundaries of operation, have lost much of their traditional power to determine their own direction and structure. As a result, a vacuum of influence has been created, which has provided the New Zealand Police Association with an opportunity to represent the views and interests of its members in external forums, including the media, both politically and in formal policy areas. These opportunities have not been available at times when the New Zealand police commissioner was not as contractually bound to the bureaucracy as he currently is. The future challenge for the police association will be to use the opportunities the current regime presents to participate credibly and relevantly in setting the direction of policing in the future, and at the same time, ensure that its members' wages and conditions of service are enhanced to their satisfaction.

The police association is determined to improve its research capability to ensure it is well equipped to foresee and to react accordingly to the inevitable changes in policing in New Zealand and internationally. Furthermore, the association is determined to be regarded by police administrators, government officials, and the bureaucracy as a responsible participant in the development of effective law enforcement. To this end, the association endeavors to provide a conduit for the ideas and opinions of police officers, to ensure that their concerns are taken into consideration when statutory and policy decisions affecting policing are made at every level.

Finally, the association recognizes that there will be inevitable changes to the way the government administers and devolves the coercive powers that are the core business of the police, particularly given the heightened fear of crime that accompanies the militant Islamic terrorist threat in the western world today. The New Zealand Police Association will ensure that as the range of organizations that acquire coercive powers expands, it will need to constantly reassess who it represents to remain relevant as a commentator on law enforcement and criminal justice issues.

References

Department of Corrections (2004). *Census of Prison Inmates and Home Detainees 2003*. Wellington, New Zealand: Department of Corrections.

Hill, R. (1989). *The Colonial Frontier Tamed: New Zealand Policing in Transition, 1867–1886*, Vol. 2: *The History of Policing in New* Zealand. Wellington, New Zealand: Government Printer.

McGill, D. (1992). *No Right to Strike—The History of the New Zealand Police Service Organisations*. Wellington, New Zealand: New Zealand Police Service Organisation.

New Zealand Treasury (2005). *Budget 2005, The Supplementary Estimates of Appropriations for the Government of New Zealand*. Wellington, New Zealand: New Zealand Treasury.

Statistics New Zealand (2005). *Key Statistics*. Wellington, New Zealand: Statistics New Zealand.

Significant Issues Facing Twenty-First Century Law Enforcement VI

From Border Control to Transnational Responsibility: An Example of Management Decision-Making in Explaining Police Practices

25

LARRY KARSON

Contents

Introduction

Decision-making is deemed a principal responsibility of police management and yet, as obvious and trite as that may sound, the literature dealing with decision-making in police management is quite limited (Swanson et al. 2001). Nonetheless, an understanding of the *process* of decision-making is essential

535

in determining the reason for the *product* or outcome of any given decision. How a decision is made can determine why one possible alternative or outcome is chosen over another. Process determines product (Bennett and Hess, 2006; Corder et al. 2004; Drucker, 1973). An understanding of the manner of decision-making can assist in explaining why a police department or other criminal justice organization may pursue a policy that, from an outside perspective, may not have been determined to be the most optimal. Examples include the Branch Davidian standoff at Waco, Texas; the MOVE confrontation in Philadelphia; and the Black Panther raid and killing of Mark Clark and Fred Hampton by the Chicago Police Department (Osterburg and Ward, 2004; Swanson et al. 2001).

Swanson et al. (2001) identify numerous models of decision-making acknowledged in management theory that are used in law enforcement organizations, including rational, incremental, heuristic, as well as other alternative models developed from systems theory. These alternatives are identified as "elaborations" of the rational model and tend to be of use in quantitative problem solving (p. 529).

As mentioned earlier, though the literature of police administration and decision-making is limited, in the fields of political science, public administration, and management science it is quite extensive with numerous journals devoted fully or partially to the subject (JSTOR identifies over 80 scholarly journals in its archival database in the disciplines of business, economics, and political science). One theory discussed and cited during the past three decades but rarely mentioned in criminal justice literature is Allison and Zelikow's (1999) decision-making models that were originally presented through a case study of the decision process utilized during the Cuban Missile Crisis by the Kennedy administration. Cited over 1100 times within 20 years of publication, *Essence of Decision* "helped shape interpretations in disciplines interested in decision-making and provoked many methodological and conceptual critiques" (Bernstein, 2000, p. 134). Yet, with few exceptions, this perspective is overlooked by writers in criminal justice.* Vaughan (2002), one of the exceptions, recognized that alternative decision models such as Allison's theories may affirm the "influence of the social context on individual choice" (p. 122). Allison's theories would influence public administration, diplomatic studies, and political science for the next 30 years.

Whenever government or agency officials identify a major problem, the choices offered in resolving the issue are often constrained by the available options within each organization's bureaucracy. Allison argued in 1971 (the second edition of his work being coauthored with Zelikow in 1999) that leaders have a choice of which governmental programs to use and to what

---

* See Vaughan et al. (2004) for a listing of the limited journals pertinent to police management, decision-making, and organizational theory.

extent, what procedures or practices can be used in a different manner, or whether to use multiple strategies in reacting to the nation's interests.

It is Allison's position that not all decisions are necessarily rational, rational meaning that a decision finally made is calculated to be most advantageous in fulfilling the original goals. He suggested alternative models of decision-making that have applicability to understanding historic policing decisions and in explaining current organizational choices.

The choices made, or not made, as described by Allison, can be viewed using three different models:

- Rational actor model (Model I)
- Organizational model (Model II)
- Governmental politics model (Model III)

The first, and normally believed by the uninitiated as the predominate model, is the belief that all available alternatives have been studied and the best of them is purposely selected to address a crisis. The difficulty is that this rational actor (or unitary rational actor) model (Model I) is not necessarily the model followed when decisions are made, though it is often exploited to justify a decision to others outside the decision-making cadre.

A second identified model, the organizational behavior (or process) model (Model II), where an organization's processes and procedures determine the options chosen, may be a better model in determining why a specific decision predominated. An example would be the differences in responses from an investigative unit and that of a patrol division in deciding to address an increase in crime within a specified geographical area. The investigative unit would, in all probability, choose to work the area utilizing undercover officers and/or investigative techniques more suited to its nonuniformed expertise while a patrol division may be more apt to use saturation patrols and/or other focused uniform patrol techniques to address the problem.

Finally, a third model, identified as the governmental (or bureaucratic) politics model (Model III) is one that many will conceal by attempting to justify a final decision as being rational but in reality, the ultimate decision is determined by governmental politics. It is not an example of organizational outputs but of "bargaining games"; no single actor but "many players who act... according to various conceptions of national, organizational, and personal goals"; decisions "not (as) a single, rational choice but by the pulling and hauling that is politics" (p. 255). An example would be a police aviation unit designed to support patrol operations being placed under an administrative support officer instead of the patrol commander because the administrative officer has the "ear" of the chief of police and he or she was able to influence his or her decision to increase his or her duties and responsibilities so as to assist him toward a future promotion while at the same time assuming that the new structure would serve the police organizational goals more effectively.

It is Allison's position that "for many purposes, there is powerful evidence that (the Rational Actor Model) must be supplemented by frames of reference that focus on the government machine—the organizations and political actors involved in the policy process" (p. 5).

The relevance of Allison's models to policing organizations can be seen, as an example, in the 200-year history of the United States Customs and Border Protection.

With the creation of the Department of Homeland Security (DHS), the U.S. government was continuing a process of decision-making that it has utilized since the birth of the republic. Historically, one agency, Customs—now known as Customs and Border Protection (CBP), has been an example of a readily available organization that could, and would, be tasked with addressing both national border and maritime issues, whether or not they possessed the capability, or were the most rational choice, to effectively address the concerns of any administration. Traditionally thought of as a revenue organization (having been under the treasury department prior to being included in the creation of DHS) or a narcotic enforcement agency (having numerous agents overseas investigating narcotics smuggling prior to the creation of Drug Enforcement Administration), it has continually been tasked with the responsibility of addressing other non-fiscal national and, in some cases, international crises. From the nation's first military confrontations to the current Iraq conflict, Customs has consistently been charged with reaching beyond the U.S. borders to serve as a transnational organization in the fulfillment of the nation's missions. In so doing, all three of Allison's models of decision-making, rational actor, organizational, and governmental (bureaucratic) politics, would be employed.

Nineteenth Century: The Embargo Acts

As the war between England and France was unwillingly pulling the newly formed United States into European affairs, various nonintercourse and embargo acts were passed by Congress to minimize U.S. involvement in the conflicts. Enforcement was delegated to Customs prior to and during the War of 1812. The enforcement of these acts was assigned to the officers of the Customs, as they were principally responsible for maritime issues within the central government (Schmeckebier, 1924). These laws, along with the federal revenue statutes, contributed to the employment of the first detectives by the federal government in the early days of the new nation (Reppetto, 1978).

When, on Christmas Day, 1807, the owners of almost 300 ships at anchor in New York harbor received news of the passage of the first act placing an embargo on trade, many immediately sent word to their vessels to depart post haste. Scores of ships sailed half-manned, with or without cargo. In an attempt to prevent their sailing in violation of the law, Customs sent naval gunboats and revenue cutters to prevent their departure reacting in what can only be considered an organizational procedure or process using the tools at hand (Model II) for timely action instead of addressing the departure via the courts. Not until the end of the war would the attempts at illicit trade disappear. The challenge of enforcing the embargo acts became a prologue to Customs serving as an implement of presidential policy (Rubin, 1961; Prince and Keller, 1989).

The "Revenue Cutters"

The revenue cutters mentioned by Rubin (1961) were an attempt by the first Secretary of the Treasury, Alexander Hamilton, to protect the revenue needed by the new nation to survive. King (1978) described the extent of the problem: "By 1789 smuggling was not only a well established national custom; it had acquired recognition as a meritorious enterprise" (p. 10). Years of avoiding the payment of tariffs to the British Crown had bred a contempt of customs laws in American seamen.

In 1790, Hamilton presented to Congress a bill requesting the establishment of the United States Revenue Marine composed of 10 small cutters to protect the revenue. This logical choice (Model I) for securing the revenue followed the British maritime precedent for the enforcement of the customs. The operational control of these cutters and crew would eventually be placed under the local collector of customs due to the "inexcusable conduct" of some of the officers aboard one of the cutters and Hamilton's personal belief that the collectors were more financially prudent (King, 1978, p. 84).

Hamilton's personal conviction and decision to place the cutters under the collectors illustrates an early example of the governmental politics model (Model III) in the nation's decision-making for officers achieved their positions by presidential commissions, each officer having some level of patronage within the government thanks to previous service in the war of independence (Evans, 1949). Hamilton would have to have overcome that influence to succeed in placing them under another government appointee. The cutters would, in later years, be used to address both piracy and illegal slave running as an adjunct to the U.S. Navy, exemplifying Model II decision-making.

The Mexican Border

In the mid-1800s, as the personnel of Customs continued to follow the borders of the United States as it expanded westward, it became obvious that the government would have to address various borderland issues along the U.S.-Mexican frontier, foremost of them being smuggling. Illegal trade had "long been a way of life in the region" (Hall and Coerver, 1988, p. 142). But this traditional mission would, in turn, lead it to the responsibility for the enforcement of immigration laws and to the pursuit of illegal aliens, Customs being the primary border regulatory agency on scene. In 1854, the first "mounted inspectors," employed to search for items imported illegally, were authorized, and though few would be employed, they formed the first border patrol in the United States (Prassel, 1972). This force, developed from a Model I decision, was an attempt to address enforcement issues along the Rio Grande River (U.S. Customs Service, 1988, p. 30) though by 1887 only 25 officers, 11 of them mounted inspectors, covered over 900 miles of border from Presidio, Texas, to the Gulf of California (Haley, 1948).

In 1882, the Chinese Exclusion Act was passed and Customs, already on the border, became responsible for the enforcement of the act and eventually appointed "Chinese inspectors" along the border to address its mandated requirements. El Paso became the largest smuggling center on the land border with Chinese migrants being smuggled from Mexico through El Paso and on to cities such as New York, Chicago, and San Francisco (Farrer, 1972; Prassel, 1972). Customs agents would operate throughout northern Mexico in an attempt to develop intelligence to identify various smuggling endeavors (Benhan, 1898; Nadelmann, 1993). Their success would depend on the relationships (Model III) they would have to eventually develop with the commercial and governmental interests within Mexico.

San Francisco, a hub of Asian intercourse, had various steamship companies that controlled Chinese emigration to the United States. Because of the profit made from smuggling human contraband, all the shipping companies were involved (Prince and Keller, 1989). In attempting to address these companies and their illegal conspiracies through the historical method of personal inspection (Model II), Customs, once again, was fulfilling the requirements of national policy with limited resources, attempting to enforce a poorly written law that, as drafted, created an illegal economic incentive for the unscrupulous to profit from.

Ultimately, the responsibility for the enforcement of these early transnational crimes passed to a newly created Bureau of Immigration (arguably a Model I choice but, as with any congressionally derived organizational structure, in reality a Model III decision with numerous stakeholders influencing the final hierarchy), but in the interim, Customs carried the burden while eastern politicians determined future immigration policy and how the bureaucracy would be structured to effectively address it.

The Filibusteros

As early as 1812, Spanish insurrectionists and American adventurers or *filibusteros* would attempt to overthrow the local Spanish representation in Florida and in the future state of Texas (Weber, 1992). During the late 1800s, Cuban nationalists, in seeking to obtain independence from Spain, attempted numerous revolutions and uprisings, all to no avail. To assist in these uprisings, exiled Cubans would endeavor to smuggle arms and other munitions into Cuba and other Western Hemisphere countries. These filibustering expeditions, initiated from the United States, were deemed to be violations of U.S. neutrality laws. Key West, Florida, less than 100 miles from Cuba, was one port continually active in thwarting filibustering expeditions just before the outbreak of the Spanish-American War. Customs agents would gather intelligence about ongoing attempts to smuggle arms and munitions from numerous sources, including representatives of the Spanish government utilizing Pinkerton private detectives (Linck, 1897), and then coordinate an enforcement action to intercept the expeditions, utilizing available revenue cutters, navy ships, and various treasury and justice department officials. The continued utilization of Customs was an organizational choice of Washington (Model II) for they were the tools that the nation already had available and the administration chose to employ without looking for a better solution.

Twentieth Century: Mexican Border Wars

In the early 1900s, when Mexico was under the dictatorship of Porfirio Diaz, the Partido Liberal Mexicano (PLM) called for the overthrow of Diaz, and PLM attempts to do so brought them into direct conflict with Customs.

The working relationship developed between Luther T. Ellsworth, the American consul at Ciudad Porfirio (now known as Piedas Negras), and Robert Dowe, the collector of customs for the district of Saluria, became critical for any success in enforcement of the neutrality laws. Ellsworth was appointed by the attorney general to "coordinate enforcement of the neutrality laws" (Carmen, 1976, pp. 13, 14) and with Dowe as collector (and Dowe's brother Luke as deputy collector at Del Rio, Texas), the political relationship between them exemplified Allison's governmental politics model.

Some Mexican leaders were eventually jailed for violating U.S. neutrality laws by organizing military expeditions from the United States against a friendly foreign power (Carmen, 1976). Munition shipments to revolutionaries were being investigated as early as 1909 with Customs officers instructed to "investigate everything and every Mexican not above suspicion" (Carmen, 1976, p. 15). Yet, faced with a lack of local experience, manpower, and legal muscle needed to be effective, Customs had little impact on the exports of weapons to Mexico. Carmen (1976) believed that in Francisco Madero's ongoing battle with Diaz, the United States' use of the neutrality laws to address gun smuggling was a solution that addressed the United States' apprehension for American interests in Mexico by presenting apparent support to Diaz, while more effective action against Madero was precluded for fear of retaliation by the latter's supporters (p. 74).

With Huerta eventually replacing Diaz and Wilson replacing Taft, both in 1913, the embargo was rescinded by President Wilson with the objective of overthrowing Huerta. The use of the embargo would vary over the next 10 years in an attempt to influence Mexican politics (Hall and Coerver, 1988). With such an ill-defined governmental politics model swaying policy, little support could be expected from Washington to strengthen the neutrality laws to assist the agents in preventing further violations.

World War I

Customs workload increased with its continuing responsibility for violations of the neutrality laws. Customs also served as agents for the Bureau of War Risk Insurance, responsible for insuring vessels, cargoes, and seamen against risks at sea due to a state of war. With the outbreak of war in April 1917, Customs officers were directed to seize 65 German and 14 Austrian ships lying in American ports. Cargo inspections for imports and exports under the War Trade Board were performed by Customs officers as were the issuance of certificates of citizenship and identification, approximately 200,000 being issued between February and July of 1918 (Schmeckebier, 1924).

Again, being the agency in contact with the beneficiaries of these services and with the Federal Bureau of Investigation busy with the investigation of neutrality, selective service, enemy alien, and espionage issues (Millspaugh, 1937), Customs ultimately received the responsibility for their administration from Washington. In New York, the major port of the United States, Customs would create a "Customs Intelligence Bureau" to address many of these new responsibilities. This force of almost 300 permanent and another 300 temporary men hired just for this mission would, at least in New York, inspect foreign crews, search and guard shipping, as well as providing port security through surveillance of port working vessels to prevent sabotage (Saba, 2001). These administrative techniques were a continuation of Customs port procedures expanded for a wartime mission, and illustrate a Model II choice by the agency.

Sky Marshals

When hijackings struck the airline industry in 1970, the government, once again, needed an immediate response. Utilizing the organizational capabilities of Customs, it created a sky marshal program, placing armed "customs security officers" onboard U.S. international flights. In responding to this crisis, Customs utilized its inspectional abilities and enforcement techniques and approximately 1200 individuals were hired to inspect outbound baggage and to fly undercover on U.S. carriers on most foreign flights over the next 3 years (Seidel, 1989). These duties were standard organizational outputs of the agency and by the nation's leaders deciding to use Customs, they had decided to use the outputs of border inspection (a traditional Customs function) combined with undercover enforcement (a second organizational tool used by its own narcotics investigators), employing the organizational behavior (Model II) of Customs for mission achievement. The responsibility for air security would eventually be passed over to the Department of Transportation, only to have them come under the same organizational umbrella of DHS at the start of the twenty-first century.

The Mariel Boatlift

In 1980, more than 100,000 Cubans departed Castro's dictatorship for the apparent freedom of the United States. What started as a trickle being welcomed to U.S. shores turned into a torrent with the United States ill prepared to address this sudden influx of Cuban immigrants. Larzelere (1988) stated that Customs went from granting clearances to U.S.-registered vessels for overseas trips assisting the first Cuban refugees at the start of the boatlift to ultimately enforcing U.S. policy in an unsuccessful attempt to stop further immigrant traffic as that policy changed in an effort to get a handle on what would eventually be declared a national state of emergency. Yet though treasury law amendments had been passed to strengthen enforcement efforts, the local regional commissioner for Customs would state that "only 6 arrests (for violation of Treasury laws) were authorized by Justice Department attorneys" (pp. 289–290).

Once again, Customs would be thrown into the breech to address an international crisis with little administrative support for formal enforcement action. The Customs Service was used to maintain a perception of sovereignty over the nation's borders while attempting to placate a south Florida Cuban population by allowing the boatlift to continue, a Model III example of decision-making. The White House, in an election year, recognized that violence in the Cuban American community was a possibility if the boatlift were prevented. Failing to take decisive action at the beginning to prevent the emigration from Cuba by not prosecuting violators operating the vessels transporting the refugees sent a message that Washington was supportive of the refugees bid for freedom. By the time the extent of the exodus was realized, it would be too late to prevent the 125,000 refugees who arrived in over 1,800 vessels over the next 5 months (Larzelere, 1988).

Nicaragua

In addressing the use of small aircraft being employed to smuggle narcotics into the United States, the Customs Service acquired Cessna Citation 550 business jets to find and pursue the airborne smugglers. The jets were distinctive in that they were equipped with night-vision viewing equipment and air-to-air intercept radars of the type used by F-16 fighters. These aircraft, the only ones of their type in the world at the time, allowed Customs to locate, at night, smuggling aircraft not otherwise detected by traditional means. They existed thanks to the political maneuvering (Model III of Allison and Zelikow's argument) of various members and associates of the House and Senate with the first acquired Citation jet being assigned to Tucson, Arizona, "the home district of Senator DeConcini, a strong proponent of the Customs air program" (Holden 2000, p. 36). Being designed for a highly specific mission, the detecting and tracking of covertly operated, slow-moving aircraft, the Reagan administration found them particularly useful in detecting gun-running planes making moonlight deliveries from the "Contras" in Nicaragua. Flying over Central America at night, a Customs Citation would "troll" for unauthorized aircraft flying from Nicaragua (Holden, 2000, p. 51). Once again, an administration was using assets designed for a domestic mission for an international tasking in response to a "national security" concern, in this case assisting the State Department and CIA. Customs would use its internal procedures and techniques developed in pursuing airborne smugglers in fulfilling the mission—a Model II solution. Eventually, the CIA would acquire its own radar aircraft.

The Balkan Embargo

In 1992, the United States, in support of the United Nations, imposed embargo against Serbian aggression in the Balkans and dispatched Customs agents to monitor compliance of the sanctions against Belgrade. The objective was to "pepper former Yugoslavia with monitoring groups doing all kinds of different things, monitoring sanctions, monitoring detention facilities, monitoring human rights, monitoring in areas where we're afraid there might be a spillover of the conflict like Macedonia" (U.S. Department of State, 1992).

Teams eventually were deployed to Romania, Bulgaria, Hungary, Macedonia, and Ukraine to monitor cross-border traffic and to control shipping along the Danube River, providing training and direction to local authorities in their efforts to monitor the embargo applied to Serbia and its ally Montenegro (BBC, 1993; Europe Information Service, 1992). With over two dozen agents assigned at any one time, the teams used the techniques and skills they had developed while serving with Customs in the United

States, again not necessarily the best practice but one that was effective in its original organizational context—another example of Model II decision-making (Oxman, 1993).

Mexico Support

Since at least the early 1990s, the United States has stationed Customs Citation aircraft in the Republic of Mexico in an attempt to prevent trafficking aircraft from Colombia from using Mexico as a landing site for narcotics in transit to the United States. Operating out of various locations in southern and central Mexico and flying with at least one Mexican national on board in an attempt to address local concerns for Mexican national sovereignty, the Customs jets would track trafficking aircraft to a landing while guiding Mexican law enforcement planes in to make an apprehension. Customs P-3s, again with Mexican nationals on board, have also transited Mexico while searching for smugglers (U.S. Department of State, 1991).

These missions were allowed, in spite of the sensitive internal issue of sovereignty, because of the personal rapport developed at numerous levels between the Mexican government and the United States—a classic Model III process. Besides the political issue of allowing representatives of a former military invader, the United States, to operate within its borders, the potential problem of greater exposure of Mexican domestic corruption had to be a consideration. In one case, Customs aircraft guided a planeload of Mexican federal agents into an airfield after a trafficker had landed, only to see the agents murdered by Mexican army soldiers protecting the narcotic load. The Customs Citation actually filmed the execution of the agents by the Mexican military with an on-board night-vision camera system (Golden, 1991).

Narcotic Source Country Support

In 1989, the administration directed the Customs Service to initiate aviation interdiction support to the U.S. Southern Command, Howard Air Force Base, Panama. Again, the administrators decided to utilize the aviation expertise of Customs in South American interdiction operations even though the responsibility of support for narcotic interdiction was a military and State Department task. With the immediate goal of detecting and tracking aircraft being operated by narcotic traffickers in South America, under a Presidential Directive (PDD 14), the service's aircraft would eventually be deployed further south, flying missions on a regular basis over the countries of Colombia, Peru, and Ecuador. By 2001, approximately 90% of all detection and monitoring flights over the narcotic source countries of South America were flown by U.S. Customs aircraft. These aircraft included, along with radar-equipped Cessna Citations, former Navy P-3 Orion four-engine anti-submarine aircraft that had been heavily modified by Customs with airborne radar systems (Winwood, 2001).

In 1994, after much discussion and with government attorneys questioning the tactical concept, the Clinton administration authorized the use of Customs aircraft to support the efforts of South American countries in shooting down narcotics-trafficking aircraft (Risen and Marquis, 2001). By 1995, Customs was operating four Citation interceptors as well as P-3 Orions for the Southern Command. From 1995 to 2001, these aircraft assisted in the shooting or forcing down of some of the approximately 50 suspect trafficking aircraft by the Peruvian or Colombian military aircraft (Weiss, 1995; Winwood, 2001).

Aircraft would also be operated out of Aruba, Netherlands Antilles, in an extended program of interception and tracking of suspected traffickers flying into the eastern Caribbean from Colombia (Salazar, 2000). The methods of operation were again a continuation of operational procedures previously used and further demonstrate the choice of Model II decision-making.

The Tragic 9/11 Events

In the immediate aftermath of the destruction of the World Trade Center on September 11, 2001, Customs aviation units were focused on protection from a repeat of the air-initiated disaster by the deployment of P-3 Orion surveillance aircraft to help the Defense Department identify suspicious aircraft (McQueen, 2001). Congress, and the administration, realizing that an attitude of "business as usual" would have far-reaching negative political ramifications, determined that a reorganization of federal law enforcement would be one response that would have an immediate positive public acceptance; thus, the creation of the Department of Homeland Security. Legislation was signed by the president, which brought about the movement of 180,000 persons and numerous agencies from their former organizations to the new umbrella DHS, the reorganization that, on the surface, promised "a painless way of making big changes" being that programs that supposedly "once worked at cross purposes now will work in happy unison" (Wilson, 1989, p. 265; Stevenson, 2002). Yet, history has tended to show the opposite. In previous federal reorganizations, the various individual bureaus, "each with its distinctive culture, professional outlook, and congressional supporters, continued for the most part to operate independently of each other" (Wilson, 1989, p. 268). While the U.S. Coast Guard and the U.S. Secret Service moved *in bloc* under DHS and while the FBI and Alcohol, Tobacco, Firearms and Explosives (formerly known as ATF) continued to stay independent of the department (ATF moving to the Department of Justice from the Department of the Treasury), one could only expect a continuation of the uncoordinated past. "No agency head is willing to subordinate his or her organization to a procedure that allows other agencies to define its tasks or allocate its resources" (Wilson, 1989, p. 269). Each of these agencies had the political clout (Model III) or the support of someone with the clout to prevent their merger with another agency, having the potential to weaken their responsibilities to the specific missions their own management had previously determined was primary.

Yet, during the time that these political responses were being developed, Customs was still dealing with misperceptions of its core missions and capabilities. Andrew H. Card, Jr., the president's chief of staff and reportedly the lead architect of the development of the DHS, was quoted as saying that "Customs probably sees its top priority as collecting tariffs when it should really be stopping that bomb from coming into a harbor. That's how times have changed" (Sanger, 2002). That, in spite of the fact that it was Customs aircraft flying air surveillance missions to prevent a repeat of 9/11, that Customs had sent numerous agents to Bosnia to enforce trade sanctions, including weapons smuggling, and that Customs was a lead agency involved in investigating money laundering committed in support of various terrorist organizations.

But, even with a key politician's ignorance of its contemporary duties, Customs was, once again, being called on to fulfill a transnational responsibility. Within 5 weeks of the fall of Saddam Hussein, teams of officers from the newly formed Customs and Border Protection (created by a merger of immigration inspectors and customs inspectors within the DHS organization) had been deployed to Iraq to help in the development of a new immigration and customs establishment (CBP Team, 2003). Agents were still serving in the Balkans a decade later (The Balkans, 2002) and former Customs aviation assets have been patrolling above major national special events such as the Super Bowl of the National Football League (MVP, 2002) and the 2002 Olympics (Mason and Jameson, 2002) to prevent airborne terrorist attacks (having previously completed the same national security assignment during the 1996 Olympics in Atlanta 5 years prior to the World Trade Center attack). Aviation assets were also permanently deployed to Washington to assist in the prevention of another air assault on the nation's capitol. All are current examples of Model II decision-making—all are using the policies, procedures, and processes in their new taskings as they had done in their former assignments, and they were all chosen for the missions to do exactly that.

Yet 2 years after the creation of DHS, internal politics continues to influence its organizational structure. As recently as November of 2004, the Customs aviation assets currently assigned to Customs and Border Protection had only recently been transferred from Immigration and Customs Enforcement, their original bureau upon the birth of DHS. With the assets operating under two different chains of command, one now under the Border Patrol management for those in the western United States and one under internal aviation management for those units in the eastern United

States having no international land border, one can only assume that the internal reassignment and reorganization is the most recent example of a Model III decision.

Substantiating Allison's identification of an administration's available alternative choices in a crisis, the nation's leaders have continually used the Customs agency's programs, in some cases in a unique way, with and without simultaneous action from other national organizations. With limited funding, manpower, and support, and in spite of attitudes as exemplified by the presidential chief of staff's comments, Customs has been continually employed as an expeditious instrument of national policy by Washington's decision-makers. As Prince and Keller (1989) acknowledged, "(Customs) has always tried to do the best it could with what it had, and for the most part successfully, bad law, bad politics and public friction notwithstanding" (pp. ii, iii).

In reviewing the decisions made both in initiating and in implementing governmental policy, the history of Customs and of various administrations supports Allison's proposition that a governmental politics model and an organizational behavior model are as likely a reason for a given governmental action as is the rational actor model. It also is as applicable to other police organizations, whether local, state, or federal, as it is to Customs.

References

Allison, J. and Zelikow, P. (1999). *The Essence of Decision: Explaining the Cuban Missile Crisis* (2nd edn.). Boston, MA: Little, Brown.

The Balkans (2002, December). The Balkans 10 years later: Rebuilding a secure border regime. *U.S. Customs Today*. Washington, DC.

BBC (1993, February 1). BBC summary of world broadcasts. Eastern Europe: Ukraine denies breaking sanctions against former Yugoslavia. London, U.K.: BBC. Retrieved on June 28, 2004 from the LexisNexis database.

Benhan, G. (1898). Correspondence of special employee George Benhan. National Archives, Record Group 36.

Bennett, W. and Hess, K. (2006). *Management and Supervision in Law Enforcement* (5th edn.). Belmont, CA: Wadsworth.

Bernstein, B. (2000). Understanding decisionmaking, U.S. foreign policy, and the Cuban missile crisis: A review essay. *International Security*, 25(1): 134 [Review of the book *The Essence of Decision*].

Carmen, M. (1976). *The United States Customs and the Madero Revolution*. El Paso, TX: The University of Texas at El Paso/Texas Western Press.

CBP Team (2003, September). CBP team in Iraq: Building new customs, immigration, and border systems. Washington, DC: Customs and Border Protection Today.

Corder, G., Scarborough, K., and Sheehan, R. (2004). *Police Administration* (5th edn.). Cincinnati, OH: Anderson.

Drucker, P. (1973). *Management: Tasks, Responsibilities, Practices*. New York: Harper & Row.

Europe Information Service (1992, October 10). EC/Yugoslavia: Tightening up sanction controls. Dublin, Ireland: Europe Information Service. Retrieved on June 28, 2004 from LexisNexis database.

Evans, S. (1949). *The United States Coast Guard, 1790–1915: A Definitive History.* Annapolis, MD: United States Naval Institute.

Farrer, N. (1972). *The Chinese in El Paso.* El Paso, TX: The University of Texas at El Paso/Texas Western Press.

Golden, T. (1991, November 29). Drug shootings in Mexico draw scrutiny to joint efforts with U.S. *New York Times*, p. A1.

Haley, J. (1948). *Jeff Milton: A Good Man with a Gun.* Norman, OK: University of Oklahoma.

Hall, L. and Coerver, D. (1988). *Revolution on the Border: The United States and Mexico, 1910–1920*, Albuquerque, NM: University of New Mexico.

Holden, H. (2000). *Aerial Drug Wars: The Story of U.S. Customs Aviation*, Niceville, FL: Wind Canyon.

King, I. (1978). *George Washington's Coast Guard: The Origins of the U.S. Revenue Cutter Service*, Annapolis, MD: Naval Institute Press.

Larzelere, A. (1988). *The 1980 Cuban Boatlift: Castro's Ploy—America's Dilemma*, Washington, DC: National Defense University Press.

Linck, J. (1897, September 20). Correspondence from special agent John Linck to the secretary of the treasury. National Archives, Record Group 36.

Mason, N. and Jameson, J. (2002, April). Light the fire within: Customs secures the 19th Winter Olympics. *U.S. Customs Today.* Washington, DC: U.S. Customs Service.

McQueen, A. (2001, September 15). Tight security keeps Washington residents, visitors in limbo. New York: Associated Press. Retrieved July 28, 2004 from LexisNexis database.

Millspaugh, A. (1937). *Crime Control by the National Government.* Washington, DC: Brookings Institute.

MVP (2002, March). MVP of the super bowl XXXVII. *Customs and Border Protection Today.* Washington, DC: Customs and Border Protection.

Nadelmann, E. (1993). *Cops across Borders: The Internationalization of U.S. Criminal Law Enforcement.* University Park, PN: Pennsylvania State University.

Osterburg, J. and Ward, R. (2004). *Criminal Investigation: A Method for Reconstructing the Past* (4th edn.). Cincinnati, OH: Anderson.

Prassel, F. (1972). *The Western Peace Officer: A Legacy of Law and Order.* Norman, OK: University of Oklahoma.

Prince, C. and Keller, M. (1989). U.S. customs service: A bicentennial history. Washington, DC: U.S. Customs Service.

Reppetto, T. (1978). *The Blue Parade*, New York: Free Press.

Risen, J. and Marquis, C. (2001, May 22). Officials long debated risks of anti-drug patrol in Peru. *New York Times*, p. A1.

Rubin, I. (1961). New York State and the long embargo. Doctorial Dissertation, New York University, New York, 1990.

Saba, A. (2001, February/March/April). True heroes in the customs tradition: The port of New York & the Customs Intelligence Bureau in World War I. *U.S. Customs Today.* Washington, DC: U.S. Customs Service.

Salazar, A. (2000, June 9). Prepared testimony, counter-drug implications of the U.S. leaving Panama, House Committee on Government Reform Subcommittee on Criminal Justice, Drug Policy and Human Resources. Retrieved on June 28, 2004 from the LexisNexis database.

Sanger, D. (2002, June 9). Traces of terror: The reorganization plan; in big shuffle, Bush considered putting F.B.I. in his new department. *New York Times*, Sec. 1, p. 35.

Schmeckebier, L. (1924). *The Customs Service: Its History, Activities and Organization.* Baltimore, MD: Johns Hopkins Press.

Seidel, S. (1989). Epilogue. In C. Prince and M. Keller (eds.), *The U.S. Customs Service: A Bicentennial History* (pp. 299–303). Washington, DC: U.S. Customs Service.

Stevenson, R. (2002, November 26). Threats and responses: The President; signing the homeland security bill, Bush appoints Ridge as secretary. *New York Times*, p. A1.

Swanson, C., Territo, L., and Taylor, R. (2001). *Police Administration: Structures, Processes and Behavior* (5th edn.). Upper Saddle River, NJ: Prentice Hall.

U.S. Customs Service (1988). *History of Enforcement in the United States Customs Service: 1789–1875.* Washington, DC: U.S. Customs Service. [Unnamed author is Michael N. Ingrisano].

U.S. Department of State Background Briefing Concerning Yugoslavia (1992, September 10). [(Richard Boucher) Federal Information Systems Corporation, Federal News Service]. Retrieved on June 28, 2004 from the LexisNexis database.

U.S. Department of State Dispatch (1991, April 15). Fact sheet: Mexican initiatives and cooperation with the United States. *U.S. Department of State Dispatch*, 2(15), Retrieved on June 28, 2004 from the LexisNexis database.

U.S. Department of State Dispatch (1993, August 9). Containment of the Bosnian conflict, [Stephen A. Oxman].

Vaughan, D. (2002). Crime and the sociology of organizations, *Crime, Law and Social Change*. 37(2): 117.

Vaughan, M., Del Carmen, R., Perfecto, M., and Charand, K. (2004). Journals in criminal justice and criminology: An updated and expanded guide for authors. *Journal of Criminal Justice Education*, 15(1): 61–192.

Weber, D. (1992). *The Spanish Frontier in North America.* New Haven, CT: Yale University.

Weiss, G. (1995, October 31). Testimony. Hearing of the House International Relations Committee. Washington, DC. Retrieved on June 28, 2004 from the LexisNexis database.

Wilson, J. (1989). *Bureaucracy: What Government Agencies Do and Why They Do It.* New York: Basic Books.

Winwood, C. (2001, May 1). Testimony. Hearing of the Senate Caucus on International Narcotics Control. Washington, DC. Retrieved on June 28, 2004 from the LexisNexis database.

Child Abuse and Sex Crimes: Examining Police Officer Interview Techniques Involving Juvenile Victims*

26

BELINDA L. GUADAGNO AND MARTINE B. POWELL

Contents

* This chapter was originally presented at the IPES Conference in Prague in 2005, then published in similar form within *Police Practice and Research*: Guadagno, B.L. and Powell, M.B. (2009) A qualitative examination of police officers' questioning of children about repeated events. *Police Practice and Research, 10*(1), 61–73.

Introduction

Police officers throughout the world are unfortunately often faced with an uncomfortable criminal event, the sexual abuse or violation of children. Not only have these juveniles been the victims of traumatic experiences, but the police investigators must understand that they are likely to face difficulties when interviewing young children who may not fully comprehend the extent of the criminal conduct. Clearly specific training is needed and the following research study will reveal critical issues that law enforcement officials and social workers must properly understand in order to better deal with these unfortunate incidents.

Interviewing Children about Victimization

For an offender to be charged and convicted in relation to child abuse, a statement from the victim is usually needed. This is especially the case when there is no strong corroborative evidence (e.g., physical evidence, other witnesses) to support the allegation of abuse. In cases where several different acts of child abuse were allegedly perpetrated, or a particular act was perpetrated on multiple occasions over an extended period of time, successful prosecution (in most jurisdictions) requires that individual offenses be "particularized." Specifically, each separate act for which the suspect is charged must be identified with reasonable precision with reference to time, place, or some other unique contextual detail (S v. R, 1989).

Although some jurisdictions allow prosecution to proceed with a general account of the alleged abuse, most require detailed information about individual incidents that are specific to place and time, e.g., details about when the abuse occurred, who was there, where it occurred, and the specific acts performed (Podirsky v. R, 1990; S v. R, 1989). Without this requirement, the ability of the accused person to respond to the allegations is potentially eroded.

The prior research has led researchers to propose several broad recommendations regarding how investigative interviewers *should* interview children about repeated abuse. One of the main recommendations is that children (irrespective of their age) be initially allowed to report what happened in each occurrence of the repeated event in their own words (i.e., in response to broad open-ended questions) and without interruption (Orbach et al., 2000; Powell and McMeeken, 1998; Roberts and Powell, 2001). Overall, there are several distinct benefits of using open-ended questions as opposed to more focused questions. First, responses to open-ended questions are usually more accurate than responses to specific or closed questions (Lipton, 1977). The greater accuracy of open-ended questions may occur because the resulting free narrative format allows the witness to use a more stringent metacognitive level of control or because the retrieval process is less influenced by external contamination, namely, the interviewer. Second, open-ended questions where responses generally require more words compared to specific questions lead interviewers to better estimates of the child's cognitive or language limitations (Powell and Snow, 2007). Third, open-ended questioning, which is conducted at the interviewee's own pace, allows the interviewee time to collect his or her thoughts and consequently promotes elaborate (more detailed) memory retrieval. Excessive questioning—as opposed to asking fewer, but open-ended questions—is distracting for witnesses because the questions redirect the witness' attention from searching internally through memory to focusing externally on the interviewer's questions (Broadbent, 1958; Kahneman, 1973).

In addition to the use of open-ended questions where possible, interviewers are instructed to be cautious to minimize confusion and misunderstandings when phrasing questions. Questions need to be appropriate for the child's developmental level and they should not raise or suggest details that have not already been mentioned by the child. Overall, these are important recommendations for any interview, irrespective of whether it is about a single (onetime) or repeated event.

Aims and Rationale of the Current Research

So how well do investigative interviewers of children adhere to the guidelines offered by experts? We know that the underuse of open-ended questions is a global limitation of police officers (see Powell et al., 2005, for review). However, apart from documenting the form of the questions used, no prior research has indicated the precise way in which police officers try to assist children to *identify* occurrences and to describe the way in which particular occurrences of abuse *differ* from other occurrences. For example, do police officers consider it important to find out how many times the event occurred? How early in the interview process (if at all) do officers try to establish whether the event was repeated? Once they have established that the event was repeated, how do they decide which occurrence or occurrences the child should recall? How do they label the occurrences? The current research aims to provide a detailed description of the nature of details (particulars) sought by police officers when questioning about an occurrence of a repeated event and the way in which police officers attempt to identify and distinguish between occurrences of a repeated event. Both field interviews about abuse, as well as mock interviews (about a repeated innocuous event that was staged in the children's schools) were examined in this research. The main reason for including a mock interview paradigm is that a record of the event (and its structure) was available, which allowed us to identify when false inferences were drawn from the children's evidence and the potential problems associated with certain questions.

It is important to note that this research is purely descriptive in nature. It is not designed to test the effectiveness of various questions; such research requires larger samples where age and question type are controlled. Nonetheless this work makes two potential contributions. First, by allowing officers to *perceive* firsthand any limitations in their own questioning style, this research provides a potentially important incentive for adopting a more open-ended interview technique in the initial stages of the interview. Prior evaluation research indicates that open-ended questions are rarely used in the field (see Powell et al., 2005, for review) and one of the major contributing factors is interviewers' overestimation of the value and importance of using specific questions to elicit specific event details (Guadagno et al., 2006; Wright and Powell, 2006, 2007). Unless interviewers can see (in black and white) a high level of specific questions that they use, as well as limitations in these questions, it is easy to deny or underestimate the need for a more open-ended approach.

The second rationale for the current research is that it may provide incentive, and help to generate ideas, for further research on the effectiveness of various interview techniques when questioning children about a repeated event. There is a paucity of prior research in this area, due in part to the high cost of such research (participant drop out rates of more than 50% are not uncommon). An understanding of what police officers do in practice and an analysis of the potential limitations in the current questioning approach provide an important framework for recruiting funds and for designing research and training programs that address issues of direct relevance and meaning to interviewers.

Methodology

Field Interviews

The field interviews constituted investigative interviews of 51 children (37 girls and 14 boys) aged 3–16 years (M age = 103.82 months, SD = 34.21 months). The interviews (which were transcribed and de-identified prior to their inclusion in this study) were conducted by police officers located in child abuse investigation units across three states of Australia. All of the police officers had completed specialized training in how to conduct investigative interviews with children, which included practice and critical feedback in the adherence of an open-ended nonleading interview approach.

The 51 interview transcripts included disclosures of a range of abusive events: 9 cases involved physical assault, 3 of sexual exposure, 22 of sexual touching or fondling, and 17 of sexual penetration. All of the interviews constitute the first recorded interview with the child about the alleged offense. In addition, the police officers' profiles indicated that the sample of interviewers was heterogeneous. It consisted of 29 female and 22 male police officers from diverse areas including metropolitan units ($N = 45$) and rural centers ($N = 6$).

The participants' level of experience in the field of child abuse investigation ranged from 6 months to 10 years. The ranks of the officers ranged from constable to detective sergeant.

The Mock Interview Paradigm: The Participants

Thirty-eight children (24 males and 14 females) participated in the mock interviews, which were administered specifically for the purpose of this research (M age = 119.37 months; SD = 12.4 months; age range = 7 years, 3 months to 11 years, 9 months). A "maximum variation" sampling framework was used to ensure that the child sample recruited was heterogeneous. This technique involved intentionally recruiting children of various ages (i.e., school grades), socioeconomic areas, and cognitive abilities. All children were located in the metropolitan region of a major eastern city in Australia and were recruited through letters to their caregivers that outlined the nature of the project and sought consent for the children's participation.

Thirty-eight police officers (14 males and 24 females) were recruited to conduct the mock interviews; one for each child who had attended the staged event. All officers were working exclusively in the area of sexual assault and child abuse investigation and had successfully completed training, which authorized them to conduct videotaped investigative interviews with children and other vulnerable witnesses. The officers were recruited via letters distributed by a senior member of their unit, inviting them to partake in the interviews so that they could practice their interview technique in an innocuous environment (the interviews were independently viewed by a police trainer who subsequently gave the officers verbal feedback regarding his/her interview performance). As with the children, a maximum variation sampling procedure was used: the officers were recruited from a range of areas (11 police stations in total) and were of various ranks. Their participation was completely voluntary. All of the police officers who were approached consented to, and completed, the interview for this study.

Staged Event

A 30 min staged event, referred to as the "Deakin Activities," was scheduled for the mock interviews because it is suitable for children of varying developmental levels and has been successfully used in many prior studies on children's memory of repeated events (e.g., Powell et al., 1999; Powell and Thomson,

1996, 1997). The event was administered on four separate occasions (twice a week for 2 weeks) in each child's regular classroom. Each occurrence of the event was administered using a standard script and consisted of 17 main "memory items." These items were administered in the same temporal order and centered around six main activities: meeting a koala, listening to a story, doing a puzzle, having a rest, getting refreshed, and receiving a surprise. The items represented various kinds of information (e.g., verbalizations, actions, objects, persons) and were repeated in different ways across the occurrences. While all occurrences of the event adhered to the same structure as that outlined above, many of the specific items had different instantiations across the occurrences. For example, the story that the confederate read to the children changed in every occurrence of the event and therefore had four different instantiations across the series. The story was about *Easter* on the first occurrence, about *Supercat* on the second occurrence, about a *sea creature* on the third occurrence, and about an *elephant* on the final occurrence. Items that included a new instantiation in each occurrence of the event were referred to as "high variability" items.

Not all of the target items, however, had a unique instantiation in every occurrence. For some items, the instantiation was identical across all four occurrences. For the remaining items there were two instantiations across the four occurrences (i.e., one instantiation occurred during one occurrence and the other instantiation occurred during the remaining three occurrences). Table 26.1 provides a list of the main items that made up the event.

Table 26.1   Questionnaire

1. Children sat on _____.
2. Leader wore a _____ cloak.
3. The koala puppet's name was _____.
4. The _____ kept the koala puppet awake.
5. Children had to _____ to warm-up.
6. The story came from the _____.
7. The story was about _____.
8. _____ held up the pictures for the story.
9. The helper's name was recorded with _____.
10. The jigsaw puzzle was of a clown _____.
11. Children heard _____ when they rested.
12. Children had to rest their _____.
13. Children got refreshed with _____.
14. The leader gave children _____ sticker.
15. The leader kept the stickers in _____.
16. After the event the leader was visiting _____.
17. Children had to wear a _____ badge.

Only the children's teacher and the research assistant who staged the event were present in the classroom when the children participated in the event. All teachers were instructed not to talk with the children about the event or to inform them that the research assistant would return to administer subsequent occurrences of the event. The teachers were also instructed not to inform the children that they were to be interviewed by a police officer about the event until the morning of the interview.

Procedure

Each police participant individually interviewed one child within 2 weeks of the final occurrence of the event. Approximately 1 week prior to the interview, each of the police officers was mailed a set of instructions regarding the interview procedure (outlined below), and was reminded of these instructions on the day of the interview as well. Specifically, the officers were told that a lady called Sarah attended the child's school to administer an event called the "Deakin Activities" and that their job was to elicit as accurate and detailed an account of this event, "in a manner they would normally do when interviewing a child in the field." Although the officers were not told any specific details about the event, they were informed that the event may have been repeated.

Interviews were conducted in an isolated room at the child's school (not the room where occurrences of the event had taken place). The officers were allocated a maximum of 17 min to conduct each interview; 15 min to elicit information about the event with an additional 2 min for rapport building at the commencement of the interview. However, they were informed that they could terminate the interview earlier at the request of the child interviewee or if the officers felt they had exhausted the child's account (only three of the interviewers did not use the full 17 min). To ensure that the maximum time allocated was used to elicit an account of the event (as opposed to eliciting an initial disclosure), all officers were instructed to commence the interview with the question: "I heard that a lady called Sarah came to your school to do the 'Deakin Activities' event. Tell me everything you can remember about that."

Finally, a number of steps were taken to limit the likelihood that the police officers obtained information about the event (apart from that provided by the researcher) before conducting the interview. First, the interviewers were instructed not to discuss the details of their interviews with other colleagues. Second, police participants located in the same police station were scheduled to conduct their interviews consecutively on the same day and a research assistant stayed with them at all times while they were waiting for their interview to take place. Finally, the researcher, rather than the interviewing police officer, escorted the child to and from the interview room to ensure that the interviewing officer did not receive any information from the child prior to commencing the interview.

All of the children were briefed both prior and subsequent to the interviews. The researcher conducted each briefing in front of the full class (in the teachers' presence) and included a clear comment that the children were not in any trouble. The children were told that the purpose of the interview was merely to give police officers an opportunity to *practice* talking to children. The purpose of the debriefing after the interviews was to allow the children to share their experiences and to thank them for their participation.

Data Management and Analysis

All of the interviews (both field and mock) were transcribed verbatim. Qualitative analyses were used to identify the structure of the interviews (i.e., themes, categories from within the data set) and to summarize the questioning style used to assist the children in identifying and distinguishing occurrences of the events. Content analysis was used, which involved counting occurrences of major themes revealed in the two data sets (field and mock interviews). For each data set, an objective measure of each officer's use of open-ended questions was calculated using criteria defined by Powell and Snow (2007).

Open-ended questions referred to questions that were designed to elicit an elaborate response, but did not dictate the information that the child needed to report (e.g., "You mentioned you saw a koala. Tell me everything that happened"). All other questions were classified as specific questions. Inter-rater reliability, calculated as agreements/(agreements = disagreements) on 20% of the transcripts, was 98% for the field interviews and 96% for the mock interviews.

Study Results

The analysis revealed that the pattern of questioning was highly similar for the field and mock interviews. For ease of presentation, therefore, the results have been reported for both interviews combined and a qualification is offered where differences in the pattern of findings were revealed across each event type (innocuous staged event or actual abuse).

Many of the officers (65% for the field interviews and 68% for the mock paradigm) sought to establish at some point in the interview that the event was repeated, and attempted to distinguish one or more occurrences of the event from others in the series. Not all of the officers who established that the event was repeated explicitly sought acknowledgment from the child that this was the case. Several merely assumed that the event was repeated, possibly (in the case of the field interviews) based on prior information obtained about the case not known to us, or because the children provided cues to suggest that the event was repeated (e.g., speaking in present tense, or use of phrases such as "She *always* ..." or "The *first* time we ..." [such cues were often evident in the interviews]).

The types of details sought at different stages throughout the interviews varied considerably among the interviewers within each of the two data sets. However, irrespective of the interviewee/interviewer samples or the nature of the event (innocuous or otherwise), questioning about a particular occurrence of the event usually happened in the early stages (i.e., within the first third) of the interview and within two or three questions after eliciting an acknowledgment from the child that the event was repeated. Further, accounts of one or more occurrences were not usually exhausted before attempting to elicit specific contextual and temporal details related to the occurrence and details related to other occurrences. The following transcript (taken from a field interview with a nine-year-old male child) provides a typical example of how the focus and nature of the questions used by the officers rapidly changed throughout the interview.

Sample Interview 1

Interviewer: Do you know [alleged offender's] full name? *[Eliciting specific details about the offender]*

Child: [Alleged offender's name]

Interviewer: And how many times has [alleged offender] kicked you? *[Establishing whether the event was repeated]*

Child: Heaps of times. He always kicks and hits me.

Interviewer: Can you remember the last time he hit you? *[Eliciting account of the last occurrence]*

Child: Yeah.

Interviewer: Tell me what happened that time.

Child: Well, he just got really mad because I was home late because I um I didn't get um there on time and he just started yelling and all that and then he picked me up and threw me.

Interviewer: Can you remember what day this happened? *[Eliciting time of last occurrence]*

Child: Um ... not sure but I think it was Thursday.

Interviewer: Was that Thursday just gone, or a different Thursday?

Child: No, ages ago.

Interviewer: Ages ago. How do you know it was a Thursday?

Child: Um ... not sure.

Interviewer: Can you remember who was there? *[Eliciting persons present during last occurrence]*

Child: When?

Interviewer: This last time it happened?

Child: Oh, um, I don't know.

Interviewer: Has there ever been a time when someone saw [alleged offender] hit you? *[Establishing whether there's been a witness to any occurrence]*

Child: Yeah, Mum saw it heaps of times but she just yells, she just yells at him and stuff but he doesn't stop.

Interviewer: Mmm. Can you tell me about a time when mum saw it happen? *[Eliciting account of an occurrence witnessed by the mother]*

Child: It's always the same. She just yells and all that but he doesn't care. He just says it's not her business.

Interviewer: Okay. So going back to this last time, you said [alleged offender] threw you and kicked you. Did this happen during the day or during the night? *[Eliciting time of last occurrence]*

Child: At night.

Consistent with the above transcript, the majority of questions asked by the interviewers were specific in nature. The proportion of open-ended questions was relatively low (M field interview = 0.17, SD = 0.07; M mock interview = 0.22, SD = 0.13—the desired amount is approximately 0.75; Powell et al., 2005). Further, the child's free narrative account of the event or an occurrence of the event was rarely exhausted prior to introducing specific questions.

For instance, a mean number of only 1.61 (SD = 1.46) open-ended questions for the mock interviews and 1.86 for the field interviews (SD = 1.27) were asked before the first specific question. When considering the nature of the open-ended questions that were asked, these were quite limited in terms of their ability to elicit detailed responses. The majority of open-ended questions (86% for the mock interviews and 90% for the field interviews) tended to be broad in nature (e.g., "Tell me everything about the [activity or event]") as opposed to questions that asked for further detail about aspects mentioned earlier (e.g., "Earlier you said that you.... Tell me more about the part where you ...").

The remainder of the "results" section presents a more detailed description of the questioning style used by most of the police officers when attempting to understand the structure of the event, the specific contextual or temporal details, and the way in which the occurrences differed. The questioning style is discussed under three separate themes, which were clearly evident in both the field and the mock interviews. These themes include: (i) establishing whether the event was repeated, (ii) eliciting details of one or more occurrences as distinct from other occurrences in the series, and (iii) establishing distinctions across the series of occurrences in the event. The nature of any confusions or misunderstanding (if any) that arose from certain questions is also discussed.

Establishing Whether the Event Was Repeated

Approximately half of the interviewers (58% in the mock and 55% in the field paradigm) attempted to determine whether the event was repeated. Four techniques were used to achieve this aim: (a) asking whether a previously mentioned abusive act occurred on one or more occasions, (b) establishing whether certain previously mentioned abusive acts (e.g., being burnt; being hit) occurred on the same or different occasion, (c) asking whether an occurrence of abuse ever occurred *before* or *since* the occasion described (this technique was only evident in the field interviews), and (d) asking *how many* times the abuse occurred. Interestingly, despite limitations in children's ability to estimate the number of occurrences of the event (of the 13 times that this question was asked for the mock interviews, a correct answer was elicited on only one occasion), this seemed important to the police officers in its own right, not merely as a technique for establishing whether the event was repeated. Many officers (74% in the mock interviews and 65% in the field interviews) asked at some point in the interview how many times the Deakin Activities event/abuse took place even though most had had already established that the child had experienced repeated occurrences of the event/abuse. Further, several interviewers asked this question repeatedly, even when the child indicated that she or he did not know the answer.

The problem with raising previously mentioned items or details in a question (as in techniques (a) and (b) above) is that because the interviewer was naive regarding the event structure, it was not uncommon (in the mock interviews) for the interviewer to ask questions that made false presumptions about the way in which items or details co-occurred. This problem is well illustrated in the following section of dialogue taken from an interview with an 11-year-old male child.

Sample Interview 2

Child: There was a puzzle of a clown eating some cakes and um we sat on this thingy too.

Interviewer Q1: What did you sit on?

Child: Oh, um, like one of those black rubbish bags.

Interviewer Q2: And did you sit on the rubbish bag on the same day that you did the clown puzzle, or did you sit on the bags one time and then do the clown puzzle on a different day?

Child: Um, the same, um no different days. Or um, I think … I don't know.

When considering the structure of the events described in the questionnaire, neither of the options provided by the interviewer in Question 2 provided an accurate depiction of how these items co-occurred. In fact, the children had a clown puzzle in each occurrence *and* they sat on a mat in each occurrence of the event too. However, the *nature* of the clown puzzle varied across occurrences of the event. Thus, when considering clown puzzles per se, the first response option provided by the interviewer in Question 2 is correct. When considering the *specific* clown puzzle that was referred to by the child immediately prior to Question 1 (the clown eating cakes), both response options would be correct.

Rather than explaining why the second question was inappropriate (this was probably too difficult for the child to articulate), the child instead expressed confusion and said he did not know the response. This confusion, which was possibly related to the inappropriate nature of the question, could easily have been misinterpreted by the interviewer as a difficulty remembering the event.

False presumptions about the event structure (such as that described above) were not limited to questions about how items co-occurred. They also occurred when the child was asked to indicate *how many* times the Deakin Activities event occurred. For example, two officers asked, "How many times did *Sarah* [the leader] come to your school?" This question is inappropriate because it inaccurately presumes that Sarah only ever attended the children's classroom to stage the event, or does not make it clear whether Sarah's visits prior to staging the event should be included. In fact, Sarah *had* visited the children's classroom several times prior to the first occurrence of the event (to collect parent consent forms). Thus whatever response the child gives to this question, the response is ambiguous.

Eliciting Details of One or More Occurrences of the Event

All except one of the officers who established or assumed that the staged or abusive event was repeated attempted to elicit details from the child about one or more occurrences as distinct from other occurrences in the series. On average, these officers attempted to elicit details of multiple occurrences (M mock interviews = 2.04, SD = 1.10, range = 1–5 occurrences; M field interviews = 2.90, SD = 0.97, range = 2–5 occurrences). Before questioning about a particular occurrence, the police officers needed to first *identify* the to-be-recalled occurrence. Three distinct techniques were used by the officers to achieve this aim, one of which was to use temporal terms (e.g., "first" and "last"). Another technique involved using details previously provided by the child as a label for an occurrence. For example, "You said there was a time when [alleged offender] kissed your rude spot. Tell me about the time he kissed your rude spot." One problem with this technique that was evident in the mock interviews was that because the officers did not know the structure of the event, the labels they generated were not necessarily unique to an occurrence or effective in discriminating the occurrence from others in the series. None of the officers first clarified with the child whether a detail was unique before using it to label an occurrence.

The third technique used by the police officers was to use the term "another time" or the time they "remembered the best." Unlike the previous two approaches, this technique allowed the child to choose the to-be-recalled occurrence. In these cases, the children *did* identify a new (not previously discussed) occurrence by referring to a temporal or contextual detail related to the occurrence (e.g., "There was one day when Sue [a class mate] wasn't in the activities. She went to flute," "There was one time when [alleged offender] did it when we were in the garage at his house"). However, in the case of the mock interviews, the identifying detail provided by the child was not always unique to only one occurrence (e.g., Sue missed two of the occurrences).

When eliciting details of particular occurrences, it was not uncommon for interviewers to repeatedly swap focus between occurrences without providing appropriate verbal cues to indicate that they had done so. As a result, the interviewers sometimes *inadvertently* linked one or more particular details to the *wrong* occurrence because of a lack of clarity about which occurrence was being referred to. In some cases, interviewers rapidly shifted focus from one occurrence to the next and then back again within as few as five turns of dialogue.

This problem is well illustrated in the following dialogue taken from an interview with an 11-year-old female child in the mock interview paradigm.

Sample Interview 3

Interviewer: Tell me everything you can remember about the *last time* you did the Deakin Activities.

Child: The lady told us this story about animals and then um we had to lie down and um hear kids playing in the park.

Interviewer: So the last time you did the Deakin Activities you heard a story about animals and you heard kids playing in the park?

Child: Yeah.

Interviewer: And what about the *first time* you did the Deakin Activities, what happened that time?

Child: The first time Sarah came she gave us this thing to wear on our jumpers, um, this thing like a sticker. Yeah, and mine was green and it had bark and mud on it but it just fell off all the time.

Interviewer: You didn't tell me about getting a sticker the *last time* you did the Deakin Activities. Did you get a sticker that time?

Child: Yeah we always got one.

Interviewer: What else happened the *last time* you did the activities?

The proportion of open-ended questions when eliciting details of specific occurrences was generally low (M mock interview = 0.15, SD = 0.12; M field interview = 0.16, SD = 0.09). The questions tended to focus on eliciting specific information in three areas: (a) acts or descriptions, (b) contextual details (e.g., location of persons, event, etc.), and (c) temporal details (e.g., timing, frequency, duration, etc.). A wide range of temporal and contextual details was sought. These included: when and how long ago the occurrence took place; the day, time, date, and location of the occurrence; the length of time between two or more occurrences; the duration of the occurrence; who was present. Officers tended to ask questions that increased in their level of specificity as the interview progressed. This pattern is well illustrated in the following dialogue taken from a field interview with a 10-year-old female child.

Sample Interview 4

Interviewer: What happened on the second day you were there?
Child: He just started putting his hands down my pants.
Interviewer: And whereabouts did that happen?
Child: At his house.
Interviewer: Yeah that's right, but which part of his house was it?
Child: The lounge room.
Interviewer: And who was at home when that happened?
Child: No-one, just [alleged offender] and me.
Interviewer: And where was [alleged offender's wife]?
Child: At work.
Interviewer: Okay. And what day was it?
Child: The second day.
Interviewer: Do you know what day of the week?
Child: I think a weekend because we only go there when Mum works.
Interviewer: A weekend. And what time of the day did this happen?
Child: Um probably early.
Interviewer: Would it have been before lunch or after lunch do you think?
Child: Um … before lunch.

Questions That Focused on Distinctions between Occurrences

As indicated earlier, many officers who established or assumed that the Deakin Activities event was repeated, attempted to establish distinctions across the series of occurrences. Three distinct approaches were used inter-changeably throughout the interviews: (a) questioning whether the content of the occurrences differed across the series, (b) asking whether a *specific* act (e.g., kissing, reading a story) or detail was the same or different across two or more of the occurrences, and (c) questioning about where in the series of occurrences a previously mentioned item occurred.

Errors sometimes directly resulted from these questions. In some cases when children were asked to establish distinctions between occurrences of the Deakin Activities, they replied that there were no differences when there were (e.g., "It was always the same. We always did the same stuff every time we did it"). Children sometimes identified *false* differences between the occurrences (e.g., one child said "We listened to different music each time" when in reality the children heard bird sounds on the first three occurrences and heard sounds of children playing in a park on the final occurrence). Finally, children sometimes erred by linking a specific item to the wrong occurrence (e.g., by saying the fluffy badge was received the last time they did the Deakin Activities event when it was included in the third occurrence only). All children made at least one of the above-mentioned errors when trying to establish distinctions across the series of occurrences of the event.

Discussion

Helping the children to "particularize" one or more occurrences of the event/offense was an important aim for all the officers who partook in this research. Indeed, many of the questions during the field and mock interviews focused exclusively on establishing how the occurrences were distinguished from one another, as well as establishing precise temporal and contextual details related to one or more occurrences.

As expected, the *types* of questions used to particularize one or more occurrences of the event were predominantly specific, as opposed to open-ended, questions (this is a robust finding in the training literature). The innovative aspect of this work is that it isolated the precise way in which specific questions were being used by police to assist children in particularizing an offense.

Further, the research highlighted potential limitations in the questioning used by the officers to generate labels for occurrences and to determine the way in which details varied across the series of occurrences. Overall, three common deficiencies in the interviews were observed. First, a high proportion of the questions focused on eliciting highly specific contextual and temporal details such as the *number of times* the event occurred, *when* and *where* the occurrences took place, *the time and duration* of each occurrence, *who was present*, and *where* specific items occurred within the series.

Second, interviewers frequently shifted the focus between occurrences of the events, sometimes confusing the child. Third, the interviewers sometimes used ineffective labels to identify occurrences of the Deakin Activities event. Although many interviewers did invite the children to identify to-be-recalled occurrences, they did not always attempt to establish that labels they utilized were unique. Further, ineffective labels sometimes arose when the officer swapped focus between occurrences without providing appropriate verbal cues to indicate that they had done so.

So how can these limitations in questioning be overcome? We know from the prior training research that a free narrative style of questioning is dependent on the adoption of training programs that include *ongoing* regular practice and feedback in the use of open-ended questions (see Powell et al., 2005). The officers who took part in this research (like most in the field) attended isolated block-training programs where ongoing training was not offered within the workplace after the training ceased. However, apart from demonstrating the value of open-ended questions, the prior research has not yet defined the best way to assist children in distinguishing between specific occurrences with various age groups and within various interview contexts (see Roberts and Powell, 2001, for review). One phenomenon of remembering repeated experiences is that a generic representation of the event is established whereby features that are common across the occurrences are well remembered and distinctive features are less likely to be reported (Roberts and Powell, 2001). While the findings highlighted the inadequacy of the specific questioning techniques used, it did not identify more effective ways of eliciting specific contextual or temporal details when attempts to elicit these using open-ended questions were initially unsuccessful. Further, it did not identify effective techniques for assisting children to identify and label occurrences.

Large-scale research (controlling for age and question types) is clearly needed to identify more effective questioning strategies. Although costly, the financial detriment of such research is not likely to outweigh the many benefits gained by improving the competency of investigative interviewers. Child abuse investigation has one of the lowest reporting and prosecution rates of all offenses and there is evidence to suggest that conviction rates involving these offenses are actually dropping in some countries (Victorian Law Reform Commission, 2004). Indeed, inadequacies in the nature of the questions, and ambiguity regarding which occurrence is under discussion, are key reasons cited by judicial officers for not proceeding with certain child abuse charges (Guadagno et al., 2006).

So what type of research is most needed at this time? Two particular areas warrant further investigation. These include: (i) exploring the effectiveness of different types of nonleading questions in eliciting "particulars" and (ii) establishing ways to improve children's generation of labels for occurrences. In the absence of effective labels, interviewers will obviously continue to struggle to accommodate the needs of child witnesses while eliciting highly specific evidence that is required by law to prove a case of abuse that occurred on more than one occasion.

References

Broadbent, D.E. (1958). *Perceptions and Communication*. London, U.K.: Pergamon Press.

Guadagno, B., Powell, M.B., and Wright, R. (2006). Police officers' and legal professionals' perceptions regarding how children are, and should be, questioned about repeated abuse. *Psychiatry, Psychology and Law, 13*(2), 251–260.

Kahneman, D. (1973). *Attention and Effort*. Englewood Cliffs, NJ: Prentice Hall.

Lipton, J.P. (1977). On the psychology of eyewitness testimony. *Journal of Applied Psychology, 62*, 90–93.

Orbach, Y., Hershkowitz, I., Lamb, M.E., Sternberg, K.J., Esplin, P.W., and Horowitz, D. (2000). Assessing the value of structured protocols for forensic interviews of alleged child abuse victims. *Child Abuse & Neglect, 24*, 733–752.

Podirsky v. R. (1990). 3 WAR 128.

Powell, M.B. and McMeeken, L. (1998). 'Tell me about the time when …': 9 golden rules for interviewing a child about a multiple offence. *Australian Police Journal, 52*(2), 104–108.

Powell, M.B. and Snow, P.C. (2007). Guide to questioning children during the free-narrative phase of an investigative interview. *Australian Psychologist, 42*(1), 57–65.

Powell, M.B. and Thomson, D.M. (1996). Children's memory of an occurrence of a repeated event: Effects of age, repetition and retention interval across three question types. *Child Development, 67*, 1988–2004.

Powell, M.B. and Thomson, D.M. (1997). Contrasting memory for temporal-source and memory for content in children's discrimination of repeated events. *Applied Cognitive Psychology, 11*, 339–360.

Powell, M.B., Roberts, K.P., Ceci, S.J., and Hembrooke, H.H. (1999). The effects of repeated experience on children's suggestibility. *Developmental Psychology, 35*, 1462–1477.

Powell, M.B., Fisher, R.P., and Wright, R. (2005). Investigative interviewing. In N. Brewer and K. Williams (Eds.), *Psychology and Law: An Empirical Perspective* (pp. 11–42). New York: Guilford Press.

Roberts, K.P. and Powell, M.B. (2001). Describing individual incidents of sexual abuse: A review of research on the effects of multiple sources of information on children's reports. *Child Abuse & Neglect, 25*, 1643–1659.

S v. R. (1989). 168 CLR 266.

Victorian Law Reform Commission. (2004). *Sexual Offences: Law and Procedure Final Report*. Melbourne, Australia: Victorian Law Reform Commission.

Wright, R. and Powell, M.B. (2006). Investigative interviewers' perceptions of their difficulty in adhering to open-ended questions with child witnesses. *International Journal of Police Science and Management, 8*(4), 316–325.

Wright, R. and Powell, M.B. (2007). What makes a good investigative interviewer of children? A comparison of police officers' and experts' perceptions. *Policing: An International Journal of Police Strategies and Management, 30*(1), 21–31.

Public Perception of Police Effectiveness and Its Relationship with Crime and Fear of Crime: An International Study

27

SEONG MIN PARK AND WILLARD M. OLIVER

Contents

Introduction

Since the 1980s, with the advent of community-oriented policing (COP), many studies have been conducted to clarify what are the core determinants of the public perception of the police. Few studies, however, have been conducted to reveal the relationship between the public perception of the police and the crime rates, a key concern of the role of the police in society. Moreover, there exists little research designed to analyze this relationship from an international viewpoint. This is most likely because (1) it is very difficult to exclude other variables that affect the public perception of the police in each country, (2) there are so many differences in the way of calculating the crime rate from country to country, and (3) it is not easy to obtain standardized data due to different languages and cultures. However, in spite of these difficulties, the study of this relationship from an international viewpoint has a merit of its own. The cross-national studies of crime and criminal justice issues play an important role in building theory and guiding public policy (Bennett and Lynch, 1990) and, therefore, they can help in focusing the effort of the police in increasing the confidence level that the public have in them. One of the primary goals of this study is to examine the long-lasting assumption in the field of criminal justice that the police can increase the confidence level that the public have in them by focusing on a reduction of the recorded crime rate.

Fear of crime also emerges as one of the most important factors in the COP strategy (Oliver, 2004; Rosenbaum, 1994, 2000). In contrast to the crime rate, fear of crime has been studied for its relationship with the public perception of the police. Some studies (Cao et al., 1996; Dowler, 2003; Roh and Oliver, 2005) reveal a positive correlation between the two. This study also attempts to examine this relationship from an international viewpoint.

The Emergence of "Public Perception of Police"

Even though the history of scholarly attention to the public perception of police effectiveness can be traced back to the time of Sir Robert Peel (Haung and Vaughn, 1996) and the Metropolitan Police Act of 1829 (see Uchida, 1997), it was not until the turbulent and riotous 1960s that this perception became a main consideration of criminal justice scholars and police executives. During this period, a series of summer riots in urban ghettos initiated several studies on the public perception of police (Jesilow et al., 1995), most of which were conducted at the request of the President's Commission on Law Enforcement and Administration of Justice.

The President's Commission report, released in 1967, recommended many changes in policing. A number of these recommendations focused on the amelioration of the relationship between the police and the community. The traditional model of policing, often called the "reform era" that stressed police professionalism (Kelling and More, 1986), had been under serious attack, and the role of the police was being reconsidered by leading police scholars (see Rosenbaum, 2000). The intimate relationship between the community and the police became the basis for identifying, prioritizing, and resolving crime problems, and community–police partnership became the central idea in the policing stage.

As Zamble and Annesley (1987) insist, "public support is essential for police work because citizens contribute significantly to the success of crime control measures." Public support of the police has become the core idea of community policing and it is the prevalent philosophy in present-day policing.

The Concept of "Public Perception of Police Effectiveness"

Public perception of police effectiveness can be defined as people's insight or knowledge about whether the police achieve their goal or play their role appropriately. Besides public perception, "public attitude" and "public evaluation" have also been used with the same meaning by other studies (Brandl et al., 1994; Dowler, 2003; Jesilow et al., 1995; Reisig and Correia, 1997; Zamble and Annesley, 1987). Some scholars have also used "confidence level" as having the same meaning (Cao et al., 1996).

There are also some confusing terms that should be clarified at this point. According to Worrall (1999), "police image" has dominated the literature on public perceptions of the police. However, police image relates to whether police officers "treat all citizens equally," "are courteous," or "provide quality service" (e.g., Reisig and Correia, 1997:315). Public perception of police effectiveness, on the other hand, relates more to whether the police accomplish their role and purpose such as fighting against crime and reducing disorder.

"Police efficiency" is often used in the same context as police effectiveness (e.g., Hall, 1998). But police efficiency is more related to whether the police use their inputs, such as budget, officers, and equipment, with greater output. As Rosenbaum (2000) mentioned, police efficiency reflects "to make every effort to see that these equitable and effective (police) services are provided at minimal cost to society" (p. 49). However, police effectiveness relates more to how successfully the police achieve their goals and how appropriately they carry out their roles.

Most of all, the difference between police effectiveness and public perception of police effectiveness is very important to this research. As Bayley (1985, 1994) said, "police effectiveness is judged in terms of whether police are achieving the objectives for which they were formed, and the criterion of police effectiveness requires a reduction in crime" (Bayley, 1985:79). That is to say, police effectiveness is an objective actuality, and the use of crime statistics and crime clearance figures by the police has traditionally been identified as an indicator of police effectiveness (Loveday, 2000). However, public perception of police effectiveness is the people's subjective understanding of the police effectiveness and can therefore be affected by many other personal and environmental factors.

Previous Research

Studies on "public perception of police effectiveness" in the late 1960s indicated widespread satisfaction and positive views of the police. More recent studies have reached similar conclusions (Albrecht and Green, 1977; Bayley and Mendelsohn, 1969; Campbell and Schuman, 1972; Correia et al., 1996; Peak et al., 1992:35; Zhao et al., 2002). However, these sentiments are not equally distributed across all levels of American society (Worrall, 1999). Many minorities tend to display contempt for police officers (Dean, 1980; Erez, 1984). Other studies on an individual level have revealed that the elderly are more inclined to view the police favorably (Hadar and Snortum, 1975; Ren et al., 2005). Some experiential variables, such as police–citizen contacts, victimization, and fear of crime, have also been examined (Carter, 1985; Mastrofski, 1981), and the number and nature of contacts are revealed to be statistically related to the public perception of the police (Worrall, 1999).

Ironically, there has been little research on the relationship between crime rates and public perception of police effectiveness. This is because it is generally accepted that crime rates are highly related to public perception of police effectiveness. For example, many police experts have claimed that the police in Japan enjoy much wider support from the public than do the police in the United States because of the much lower crime rate in Japan (Ames, 1981; Bayley, 1994; Hoffman, 1982; Kim, 1987; Parker, 2001; Thornton, 1992). However, Cao et al. (1998) found in their quantitative research that Japanese people have significantly lower levels of confidence in their police than do Americans.

Another important point when studying public perception of police effectiveness is the changing role of the police under COP (Oliver, 2004). Based on the COP model, disorder, which can be defined as various behaviors and physical conditions that violate the social norms of the local community, stimulates fear of crime (Arnold, 1991; Ferraro, 1995; Ferraro and LaGrange, 1998; Lewis and Salem, 1986). The fear of crime causes the community to use the local environment less frequently and to withdraw behind locked doors (Bennet and Flavin, 1994; Covington and Taylor, 1991; Lavrakas et al., 1980; Skogan and Maxfield, 1981). The avoidance of public areas reduces a neighborhood's capacity to regulate social behavior, thus providing additional opportunities for potential offenders to engage in antisocial and criminal conduct without sanction (Rosenbaum, 2000:51). Therefore, reducing the fear of crime, another subjective consideration in policing, has become one of the most important factors of police effectiveness in community policing, and some research have demonstrated that perceived police effectiveness is statistically related to fear of crime (Dowler, 2003; Zhao et al., 2002).

There has been little research on the global trends of public perception of police effectiveness. Most of the previous studies were conducted with regional data. According to Zamble and Annesley (1987), the vast majority of the research had been carried out in large cities. Even though there was some research on public perception of the police at the national level (Cao et al., 1998, Nilson and Oliver, 2006), it compared only between two and four countries and tried to find the differences between them. The current research, however, is attempting to reveal the global trends of public perception of the police and its relationship with fear of crime and crime rate by using international data from the International Crime Victim Survey (ICVS) in 1989, 1992, 1996, and 2000, and the International Comparisons of Criminal Justice Statistics 2001. Therefore, this study intends to test the following two hypotheses from an international viewpoint: Hypothesis 1: The lower the crime rate is, the more positive the public perception of police effectiveness will be.

Generally, it can be said that the police are more effective in a country or region when the crime rate in that place is lower than others (see Bayley, 1985); and it is surmised that the people's insight about police effectiveness will be more positive if the crime rate is lower than other surrounding areas (Ames, 1981; Bayley, 1994; Hoffman, 1982; Kim, 1987; Parker, 2001; Thornton, 1992). Therefore, the second hypothesis, formally stated, is as follows: Hypothesis 2: The lower the fear of crime is, the more positive the public perception of police effectiveness will be.

There are common traits between "fear of crime" and "public perception of police effectiveness." Both are subjective reactions to the criminal environment and decided mainly based on individual experience and preconception. Dowler (2003) insisted that fear of crime is weakly related to actual crime but it is rather more related to perceived police effectiveness. This hypothesis would be more reliable than the first one. In support of this hypothesis, Cao et al. (1996) revealed that fear of crime exerted a larger effect on confidence in the police than did any of the demographic variables (p. 12).

Methodology

Research Samples

This study employs the data of "the public perception of police effectiveness" and "fear of crime" from the ICVS. The ICVS is a far-reaching program of standardized sample surveys that investigates householders' experiences with crime, policing, crime prevention, and perceptions of safety.

This survey was conducted in 1989, 1992, 1996, and 2000; parts of each survey included national samples while other parts were restricted to a main city in the surveyed countries. In this research, to obtain standardization in the data and monitor the global trends, only the former parts—the national-level data—have been used for analysis (see Table 27.1).

Table 27.1   Country Sample Sizes in the National-Level ICVS by Year

Country	1989 n (%)	1992 n (%)	1996 n (%)	2000 n (%)
England and Wales	2,006 (6.6)	2,001 (9.2)	2,171 (12.5)	1,947 (5.7)
Scotland	2,007 (6.6)	—	2,194 (12.6)	2,055 (6.0)
Northern Ireland	2,000 (6.6)	—	1,042 (6.0)	1,511 (4.4)
Netherlands	2,000 (6.6)	2,000 (9.2)	2,008 (11.6)	2,000 (5.8)
New Zealand	—	2,048 (9.4)		—
(West) Germany	5,274 (17.3)	—	—	—
Switzerland	1,000 (3.3)	—	1,000 (5.8)	4,234 (12.3)
Belgium	2,060 (6.8)	1,485 (6.8)	—	2,501 (7.3)
France	1,502 (4.9)	—	1,003 (5.8)	1,000 (2.9)
Finland	1,025 (3.4)	1,655 (7.6)	3,830 (22.0)	1,782 (5.2)
Italy	—	2,024 (9.3)	—	—
Spain	2,041 (6.7)	3,139 (14.5)	—	—
Norway	1,009 (3.3)	—	—	—
United States	1,996 (6.6)	1,501 (6.9)	1,003 (5.8)	1,000 (2.9)
Canada	2,074 (6.8)	2,152 (9.9)	2,134 (12.3)	2,078 (6.0)
Australia	2,012 (6.6)	2,006 (9.2)	—	2,005 (5.8)
Japan	2,411 (7.9)	—	—	—
Sweden	—	1,707 (7.9)	1,000 (5.8)	2,001 (5.8)
Portugal	—	—	—	2,000 (5.8)
Denmark	—	—	—	3,007 (8.7)
Poland	—	—	—	5,276 (15.3)
Total	30,417	21,718	17,385	34,397

There were 16 countries selected for the national-level ICVS in 1989, and 11 countries in 1992 and 1996. In 2000, the ICVS was conducted in 47 countries*; 16 of them consisting of national-level data and 31 of them with only city-level data. Among them, the samples from Indonesia in 1989, Malta in 1996, and Catalonia in 2000 were excluded from this analysis as the standardized crime rate data of those countries were unavailable.

The Dependent Variable

The dependent variable "public perception of police effectiveness" is measured by the survey questions, "Taking everything into account, how good do you think the police are in your area in controlling crime? Do you think

---

* England and Wales, Scotland, Northern Ireland, Netherlands, Switzerland, Belgium, France, Finland, Sweden, Portugal, Denmark, Catalonia, the United States, Canada, Australia, Poland, Estonia, Czech Republic, Russia, Georgia, Slovenia, Latvia, Romania, Hungary, Albania, Croatia, Ukraine, Belarus, Bulgaria, Lithuania, Philippines, Mongolia, Azerbaijan, Cambodia, Republic of Korea, Uganda, South Africa, Botswana, Namibia, Swaziland, Lesotho, Nigeria, Zambia, Mozambique, Argentina, Colombia, and Panama.

Table 27.2   Values of Public Perception of Police Effectiveness from the ICVS by Year

Country	*n* (%) of Those Responding Police Doing a Good Job by Year			
	1989	1992	1996	2000
England and Wales	1,398 (81)	1,319 (76)	1,474 (77)	1,404 (81)
Scotland	1,418 (81)	—	1,523 (77)	1,580 (82)
Northern Ireland	1,260 (75)	—	655 (76)	1,016 (76)
Netherlands	1,163 (74)	993 (68)	900 (63)	1,030 (69)
New Zealand	—	1,611 (88)	—	—
(West) Germany	3,547 (74)	—	—	—
Switzerland	501 (82)	—	548 (72)	2,857 (82)
Belgium	1,098 (71)	705 (65)	—	1,603 (71)
France	928 (75)	—	560 (76)	646 (80)
Finland	653 (78)	—	2,096 (70)	1,244 (76)
Italy	—	1,003 (55)	—	—
Spain	1,088 (65)	1,230 (50)	—	—
Norway	709 (85)	—	—	—
United States	1,606 (82)	—	771 (81)	887 (93)
Canada	1,851 (89)	1,764 (88)	1,707 (89)	1,818 (92)
Australia	1,474 (85)	1,447 (84)	—	1,528 (85)
Japan	1,416 (62)	—	—	—
Sweden	—	997 (75)	615 (82)	1,220 (74)
Portugal	—	—	—	908 (49)
Denmark	—	—	—	2,130 (86)
Poland	—	—	—	2,403 (47)
Total	20,110	11,953	10,849	22,274

they do a good job or not?" Respondents can choose from the following responses: 1 = "good job," 2 = "not good job," 3 = "don't know."

In order to operationalize the responses into a variable representing each country's "public perception of police effectiveness," the number of people who answered "good job" is divided by the total number of people whose answer is meaningful in each country (see Table 27.2). The value of "public perception of police effectiveness" of each country is the percentage of the people who think their police are doing a good job in controlling crime. As the response "don't know" provides no informed opinion, they are excluded from this study.

The Independent Variable

There are two independent variables in this research: "crime rate" and "fear of crime." The variable "crime rate" consists of the number of total crimes recorded by the police in each country divided by the total population for each corresponding year. The number of total crimes is extracted from the International Comparisons of Criminal Justice Statistics 2001 (Barclay and Tavares, 2003). These data bring together statistical information on criminal justice collected by the Home Office and the Council of Europe, and includes all European Union members,[*] the EU accession countries,[†] as well as other select countries.[‡]

Many factors affect recorded crime rates, such as (1) different legal and criminal justice systems, (2) rates at which crimes are reported to the police and recorded by them, (3) differences in the point at which crime is measured for some countries—this is the time at which the offence is reported to the police while for others recording does not take place until a suspect is identified and the papers are forwarded to the prosecutor, (4) differences in the rules by which multiple offences are counted, (5) differences in the list of offences that are included in the overall crime figures, and (6) data quality (Barclay and Tavares, 2003). Therefore, absolute comparison of crime rates is impossible. This research, however, tries to reduce these risks by using standardized data extracted from a recognized and reliable source. The number of crimes is divided by each country's population to derive the standardized crime rate (see Table 27.3).

The second independent variable, fear of crime, is measured by the survey questions, "Now I would like to ask some questions about your area and about your opinion of crime in your area: How safe do you feel walking alone in your area after dark?; Do you feel very safe, fairly safe, a bit unsafe, or very unsafe?" The questions were first used by the ICVS in their 1992 survey. As a result, there is no data for "fear of crime" in the 1989 survey. Therefore, this study analyzes the data of the surveys conducted in 1992, 1996, and 2000 to research the relationship between public perception of police effectiveness and fear of crime (see Table 27.4).

To modify these sample values into the variable fear of crime, the total number of people who answered "bit unsafe" and "very unsafe" is divided by the total number of people who answered this question in each country. Thus, in this research, the value of fear of crime of each country is operationalized as the percentage of people who think it is unsafe to walk alone after dark because of crime. The responses "unknown" were excluded from this study as they provide no meaningful value to the analysis.

---

[*] Austria, Belgium, Denmark, Finland, France, Germany, Greece, Ireland, Italy, Luxembourg, the Netherlands, Portugal, Spain, Sweden, and the United Kingdom (England and Wales, Northern Ireland, Scotland).
[†] Cyprus, Czech Republic, Estonia, Hungary, Latvia, Lithuania, Malta, Poland, Slovakia, and Slovenia.
[‡] Australia, Canada, Japan, New Zealand, South Africa, and the United States.

Table 27.3   Crime Rate by Country[a]

Country	Year			
	1989	1992	1996	2000
England and Wales	77.49	109.96	94.80	97.67
Scotland	94.17	—	88.13	82.74
Northern Ireland	34.83	—	41.21	70.63
Netherlands	71.75	77.11	69.21	73.83
New Zealand	—	134.35	—	—
(West) Germany	55.11	—	—	—
Switzerland	48.99	—	49.94	37.74
Belgium	33.82	38.51	—	82.79
France	57.87	—	60.98	63.61
Finland	78.27	77.38	73.56	74.52
Italy	—	41.98	—	—
Spain	26.34	23.61	—	—
Norway	56.17	—	—	—
United States	56.27	55.23	49.44	40.73
Canada	88.63	100.41	89.24	76.47
Australia	63.86	66.04	—	74.63
Japan	13.60	—	—	—
Sweden	—	137.90	133.06	137.19
Portugal	—	—	—	36.27
Denmark	—	—	—	94.74
Poland	—	—	—	32.76

[a] Population: World Population Prospects (UN, 2003), http://www.statistics.gov.uk

Research Analysis

This study employs four types of analysis designs to test the hypotheses. Two of them are conducted for testing Hypothesis 1, while the other two are adapted for Hypothesis 2.

Analysis 1: Simple test of Hypothesis 1. As the first test of Hypothesis 1, this study examines the zero-order bivariate relationship between the crime rate and the public perception of police effectiveness. The unit of analysis for this study is "each country in each year." Thus, the first test of this study analyzes the data not only country to country, but also year to year. A total of 50 country samples have been used for the first analysis of this study.

Analysis 2: Variation test of Hypothesis 1. The most serious problem of any international study is the existence of numerous confounding variables (see Zvekic, 1996). People's insight about the police in each country may be affected by historical, cultural, social, and political backgrounds. Clearly, there are other intrinsic variables in each country that influence the public's

Table 27.4 Values of "Fear of Crime" by Year

Country	Year 1992	1996	2000
England and Wales	33.05	33.25	27.76
Scotland	—	26.93	20.15
Northern Ireland	—	22.36	22.72
Netherlands	21.70	20.41	18.40
New Zealand	38.18	—	—
(West) Germany	—	—	—
Switzerland	—	17.65	22.19
Belgium	19.66	—	21.27
France	17.47	20.22	21.81
Finland	—	17.45	18.58
Italy	35.05	—	—
Spain	—	—	—
Norway	—	—	—
United States	—	24.83	15.03
Canada	20.49	25.96	16.33
Australia	31.21	—	35.15
Japan	—	—	—
Sweden	13.53	11.07	14.73
Portugal	—	—	27.21
Denmark	—	—	17.24
Poland	—	—	34.83

perception of the police. This problem cannot be solved even by sophisticated statistical methods—it is difficult to determine which variables are more influential.

This study, therefore, uses "variation analysis," which tests the relationship between variation values of each variable year to year. This analysis is based on the assumption that other contextual variables make a change over a long period of time and, therefore, their effect on public perception of police will not change rapidly. This study attempted to exclude the effects from these variables by examining bivariate relationship between the variation of crime rate and the variation of public perception of police effectiveness across time.

This study employs the three-round differences of each country's value between the 1989 and 1992 surveys, the 1992 and 1996 surveys, and the 1996 and 2000 surveys. For some countries* that were not selected for the next

* Using the differences between 1989 and 1996 data: Scotland, Northern Ireland, Switzerland, France. Using the differences between 1992 and 2000 data: Belgium and Australia.

survey, the differences from the closest data were adapted for the analysis, and the data of some countries* in which the ICVS was conducted just once were excluded from this analysis. In the end, a total of 29 variation samples are adapted.

Analysis 3: Simple test of Hypothesis 2. The third analysis tests the zero-order bivariate relationship between fear of crime and public perception of police effectiveness. The unit of analysis is also "each country in each year," similar to the first analysis. However, in contrast to the first analysis, there were no ICVS data of "fear of crime" in 1989, so a total of 34 country samples were employed.

Analysis 4: Variation test of Hypothesis 2. The fourth analysis employs the same "variation analysis" as the second one. The bivariate relationship between the variation of the fear of crime and the variation of public perception of police effectiveness is examined. As there were no ICVS data of 1989 fear of crime rate, this study employs the two-round differences of each country's value between the 1992 and 1996 surveys and the 1996 and 2000 surveys. For some countries† that were selected in 1992 but not in 1996, the differences between the 1992 and 2000 data were adapted for the analysis, and the data of other countries‡ in which the ICVS was conducted just once were excluded from this analysis. A total of 17 variation samples were employed.

Research Findings

Analysis 1. Contrary to the hypothesis of this study, the result of the first analysis shows that the crime rate is positively correlated with the public perception of police effectiveness and it was statistically meaningful (see Table 27.5). Even though the use of crime statistics and crime clearance figures has traditionally been identified as an indicator of police effectiveness

Table 27.5 Bivariate Regression Tests

Value	Analysis			
	Test 1	Test 2	Test 3	Test 4
y intercept	64.58	0.02	82.05	2.84
Regression coefficient	0.16***	−0.04	−0.27	−0.39
t	3.452	−0.487	−1.007	−1.545
R^2	0.200	0.009	0.031	0.137
n	50	29	34	17

$p < .01$

* Japan, (West) Germany, New Zealand, Poland, Norway, Italy, Portugal, and Denmark.
† Belgium and Australia.
‡ New Zealand, Poland, Norway, Italy, Portugal, and Denmark.

(Loveday, 2000), people living in a country with a higher crime rate have relatively more positive perception of police effectiveness.

Analysis 2. The second analysis, which examines the relationship between the variations of crime rate and public perception of police effectiveness, reveals that there is a slight negative correlation between them, but it is not statistically significant. Thus, the value of public perception of police effectiveness demonstrated little correlation with the crime rate. Some countries show declining rates of public perception of police effectiveness in spite of decrease in the crime rates and vice versa.

Analysis 3. The third analysis of this study, which examines the correlation between each country's fear of crime and public perception of police effectiveness, shows that there is little correlation between them. As the outcome of slight negative correlation is severely affected by three outliers, it cannot be said that there is any correlation between fear of crime and public perception of police effectiveness.

Analysis 4. The last analysis of this study, which examines the correlation between the variation values of fear of crime and public perception of police effectiveness, shows a negative correlation between them, as predicted. The variation values of public perception of police effectiveness are scattered in relation to that of fear of crime, for, the more the fear of crime decreases, the more positive the public perception of police effectiveness becomes. However, this was not found to be statistically significant.

Discussion

This study tests two widespread assumptions in the policing field: (1) the fewer the crimes, the more positive the public perception of police effectiveness and (2) the less the fear of crime, the more positive the public perception of the police will be.

The results of this study, however, suggest that these assumptions may not hold true nor present the findings that people in those countries with higher crime rates claim their police to be more effective. This may suggest that when crime rates are high, people are aware of the crime problem, and they turn to the police to help them deal with these problems. As a result, they have a high opinion of the police and believe, out of necessity, that they are effective. Conversely, when crime rates are low, the public has no need for the police; hence the police are not at the forefront of their concern. Thus, perceptions of police effectiveness remain low. Even though there are some limitations in this study, these outcomes bring up possible considerations for present-day policing strategies, since police activities focusing on crime prevention may have little effect on their evaluation from the people.

Crime Rate and Public Perception of Police Effectiveness

The most eccentric outcome of this study is that of the first analysis because it produces exactly the opposite result of the stated hypothesis, which has been made on the basis of the common presumption. Contrary to the hypothesis of this study, the findings show that people who live in a country with a higher crime rate consider their police to be more effective. Furthermore, it is the only outcome that is statistically meaningful in this study.

The second analysis of this study fails to prove any relationship between the variation values of crime rate and the public perception of police effectiveness. The variation of the crime rate does not affect the variation of the public perception of police effectiveness. Even in a country with the highest increment in crime rate, the public's perception of the police effectiveness increases.

It is very clear that there are many limitations to this study. First, as crime rate is mainly related to the occurrence of the crimes, this outcome reflects only one side of police activities—the role of crime prevention—and does not reflect the effect of arresting activities of the police. If the number of crimes increases, it is only natural to assume that the number of criminals arrested will also increase, and the police can be thought of as being more active by the public. Moreover, even though it is the primary responsibility of the police to prevent future crimes, it will not be evident to the people that lower crime rates are due to police activities.

Second, the more prevalent the crime rates become in a country, the more the police activities come to the forefront, which, in turn, draws increasing attention from the public. In addition, people do rely on the police for their safety and security, and when crime rates rise, they look to the police for help. The mass media also tends to focus on criminal matters rather than on other societal problems. If police attention and reliance are mixed with active and visible police activities, the public perception of police effectiveness will surge, and the public will believe more in the police, even though the crime rate is higher than in other nations.

Based on this finding, one suggestion about police efforts to get higher evaluation from the public can be extracted. To raise the confidence level that the public has on them, the police should publicize their activities. As the public perception can be positively influenced by activities, such as arresting criminals, it will be more effective to inform the public of their activities. For example, periodical reporting of police activities through local newspapers and local TV news channels will help the people know what the police work on and thereby raise their credibility.

Fear of Crime and Public Perception of Police Effectiveness

Contrary to the hypothesis of this study, this study did not find any statistically significant correlation between fear of crime and public perception of police effectiveness. In the fourth analysis, however, most values of public perception of police effectiveness increase in the country where those of the fear of crime decreases. And in countries where the fear of crime increases, the public perception of police effectiveness does not increase as much as those in the countries where the fear of crime decreases, except for one outlier. It shows the possibility that the variation of fear of crime, not status of fear of crime, may affect the people's insight about the police. This possibility could mean that decreasing the fear of crime, the main goal of community policing, is useful not only for preventing crimes, but also for increasing the confidence level of the public in the police.

Conclusion

Despite the study's failure to find support for the hypotheses, some interesting points can be extracted from the outcomes. First, contrary to commonly held assumptions, the increase or decrease of crime rates appears to have little effect on the public's insight about the police; moreover, people in countries with higher crime rates have a more positive image of their police. Therefore, it can be surmised that visible and active policing, when the need for such policing arises, has more effect on the public's evaluation of the police. Police executives should consider these aspects when they try to ameliorate their relationship with the community.

Second, this study finds the possibility that the change in fear of crime may result in the change of public perception of police effectiveness. Contemporary law enforcement leaders across the globe should pay credence to the lessons learned from this study. Highlighting the successes of the police agency even in a perceived high-crime environment could have a positive impact on the public and lower their fear of crime.

References

Albrecht, S. and Green, M. (1977). Attitudes toward the police and the larger attitude complex implications for police–community relationships. *Criminology*, 15, 67–87.

Ames, W. (1981). *Police and Community in Japan*. Berkeley, CA: University of California Press.

Arnold, H. (1991). Fear of crime and its relationship to directly and indirectly experienced victimization. In K. Sessar, and H.-J. Kerner (Eds.), *Developments in Crime and Crime Control Research: German Studies on Victims, Offenders and the Public* (pp. 87–125). New York: Springer-Verlag.

Barclay, G., Tavares, C., Kenny, S., Siddique, A., and Wilby, E. (2003). International comparisons of criminal justice statistics 2001. Home Office Bulletin, issue 12/03. URL: http://www.homeoffice.gov.uk/rds/publf.htm

Bayley, D. (1985). *Patterns of Policing: A Comparative International Analysis*. New Brunswick, NJ: Rutgers University Press.

Bayley, D. (1994). *Police for the Future*. New York: Oxford University Press.

Bayley, D. and Mendelsohn, H. (1969). *Minorities and the Police: Confrontation in America*. New York: Free Press.

Bennett, R. R. and Flavin, J. M. (1994). Determinants of fear of crime: The effect of cultural setting. *Justice Quarterly, 11*, 357–381.

Bennett, R. R. and Lynch, J. P. (1990). Does a difference make a difference? Comparing cross-national crime indicators. *Criminology, 28*(1), 153–182.

Brandl, S., Frank, J., Worden, R., and Bynum, T. (1994). Global and specific attitudes toward the police: Disentangling the relationship. *Justice Quarterly, 11*, 119–134.

Campbell, A. and Schuman, H. (1972). A comparison of black and white attitudes and experiences in the city. In C. Haar (Ed.), *The End of Innocence: A Suburban Reader* (pp. 97–110). Glenview, IL: Scott Foresman.

Cao, L., Frank, J., and Cullen, F. (1996). Race, community context and confidence in the police. *American Journal of Police, 15*, 3–22.

Cao, L., Steven S., and Sun, Y. (1998). Public attitudes toward the police: A comparative study between Japan and America. *Journal of Criminal Justice, 26*(4), 279–289.

Carter, D. L. (1985). Hispanic perception of police performance: An empirical assessment. *Journal of Criminal Justice, 13*(6), 487–500.

Correia, M., Reisig, M., and Lovrich, N. (1996). Public perceptions of state police: An analysis of individual-level and contextual variables. *Journal of Criminal Justice, 24*, 17–28.

Covington, J. and Taylor, R. B. (1991). Fear of crime in urban residential neighborhoods: Implications of between- and within-neighborhood sources for current models. *Sociological Quarterly, 32*(2), 231–249.

Dean, D. (1980). Citizen ratings of the police: The difference contact makes. *Law and Politics Quarterly, 2*, 445–471.

Dowler, K. (2003). Media consumption and public attitudes toward crime and justice: The relationship between fear of crime, punitive attitudes, and perceived police effectiveness. *Journal of Criminal Justice and Popular Culture, 10*(2), 109–126.

Erez, E. (1984). Self-defined "desert" and citizen's assessment of the police. *Journal of Criminal Law and Criminology, 75*(4), 1276–1299.

Ferraro, K. F. (1995). *Fear of Crime: Interpreting Victimization Risk*. Albany, NY: State University of New York Press.

Ferraro, K. F. and LaGrange, R. L. (1988). Are older people more afraid of crime? *Journal of Aging Studies, 10*, 277–287.

Hadar, I. and Snortum, J. (1975). The eye of the beholder: Differential perceptions of police and the public. *Criminal Justice and Behavior, 2*, 37–54.

Hall, T. P. (1998). Policing order: Assessments of effectiveness and efficiency. *Policing and Society, 8*, 3–17.

Haung, W. and Vaughn, M. (1996). Support and confidence: Public attitudes toward the police. In T. J. Flanagan and D. R. Longmire (Eds.), *Americans View Crime: A National Public Opinion Survey* (pp. 31–45). Thousand Oaks, CA: Sage.

Hoffman, V. J. (1982). The development of modern police agencies in the Republic of Korea and Japan: A paradox. *Police Science, 5*, 3–6.

Jesilow, P., Meyer, J., and Namazzi, N. (1995). Public attitudes toward the police. *American Journal of Police, 14*, 67–88.

Kelling, G. and Moore, M. (1986). From political to reform to community: The evolving strategy of police. In J. Greene and S. Mastrofski (Eds.), *Community Policing: Rhetoric or Reality* (pp. 3–27). Belmont, CA: Wadsworth-Thompson Learning.

Kim, Y. (1987). Work: The key to the success of Japanese law enforcement. *Police studies*, *10*, 109–117.

Lavrakas, P. J., Lewis, D. A., and Skogan, W. G. (1980). Fear of crime and the Figgie report: America misrepresented. *Criminal Justice Newsletter* (Hackensack NJ), *11*(22), 3–7.

Lewis, D. and Salem, G. (1986). *Fear of Crime: Incivility and Production of a Social Problem*. New Brunswick, NJ: Transaction Book.

Loveday, B. (2000). Managing crime: Police use of crime data as an indicator of effectiveness. *International Journal of the Sociology of Law*, *28*, 215–237.

Mastrofski, S. (1981). Surveying clients to assess police performance: Focusing on the police–citizen encounter. *Evaluation Review*, *5*(3), 397–408.

Nilson, C. and Oliver, W. M. (2006). Changing latitude, changes in attitude: A comparative study of police officer perceptions of police effectiveness in Canada, Venezuela, and the United States. *Police Practice and Research: An International Journal*, *7*(3), 231–247.

Oliver, W. M. (2004). *Community-Oriented Policing: A Systemic Approach to Policing*. 3rd edn., Upper Saddle River, NJ: Prentice Hall.

Parker, L. C. (2001). *The Japanese Police System Today: A Comparative Study*. Armonk, NY: M. E. Sharpe, Inc.

Peak, K., Bradshaw, R., and Glensor, R. (1992). Improving citizen perceptions of the police: 'Back to the basics' with a community policing strategy. *Journal of Criminal Justice*, *20*, 25–40.

Reisig, M. D. and Correia, M. E. (1997). Public evaluation of police performance: An analysis across three levels of policing. *Policing*, *20*(2), 311–331.

Ren, L., Cao, L., Lovrich, N., and Gaffney, M. (2005). Linking confidence in the police with the performance of the police: Community policing can make a difference. *Journal of Criminal Justice*, *33*(1): 55–66.

Roh, S. and Oliver, W. (2005). Effects of community policing upon fear of crime: Understanding the causal linkage. *Policing: An International Journal of Police Strategies & Management*, *28*(4): 670–683.

Rosenbaum, D. P. (1994). *The Challenge of Community Policing: Testing the Promises*. Thousand Oaks, CA: Sage.

Rosenbaum, D. P. (2000). The changing role of the police: Assessing the current transition to community policing. In R. W. Glensor, M. E. Correia, and K. J. Peak (Eds.), *Policing Communities: Understanding Crime and Solving Problems* (pp. 3–29). Los Angeles, CA: Roxbury

Skogan, W. and Maxfield, M. (1981). *Coping with Crime*. Beverly Hills, CA: Sage Publications.

Thornton, R. Y. (1992). *Preventing in America and Japan: A Comparative Study*. New York: M. E. Sharpe, Inc.

Uchida, C. D. (1997). The development of the American police: An historic overview. In G. Alpert and A. Piquero (Eds.), *Community Policing: Contemporary Readings* (pp. 18–35). Prospect Heights, IL: Waveland.

Worrall, J. L. (1999). Public perceptions of police efficacy and image: The "fuzziness" of support for the police. *American Journal of Criminal Justice: AJCJ*, *24*(1), 47.

Zamble, E. and Annesley, P. (1987). Some determinants of public attitudes toward the police. *Journal of Police Science and Administration, 15,* 285–290.

Zhao, J. S., Scheider, M., and Thurman, Q. (2002). The effect of police presence on public fear reduction and satisfaction: A review of the literature. *The Justice Professional, 15*(3), 273–299.

Zvekic, U. (1996). The international crime (victim) survey: Issues of comparative advantages and disadvantages. *International Criminal Justice Review,* 6(1), 1–21.

Organizational Culture within the Norwegian Counterterrorism Unit: Heightened Responsibility and Stress Following Recent International Terrorist Attacks

28

RUNE GLOMSETH AND PETTER GOTTSHALK

Contents

The Norwegian Counterterrorism Unit—Tasks, Responsibilities, and Organization

While the terrorism threat within Norway remains relatively low, the Norwegian police have an independent counterterrorism unit (CTU), which is located within Oslo and is led by a police chief. It constitutes a separate police division in which all members are involved in operative activities. Administered and organized into staff elements responsible for planning, equipment and operation, training, and exercise, the CTU is comprised of four divisions, which are subdivided into eight special teams.

The Norwegian CTU has two main functions: one nationally and one locally oriented. The former implies that it is the Norwegian police's special unit to combat sabotage and terrorism, and to deal with hostage situations, complex armed assignments, as well as organized crime across the country. Its local function consists of reactive, uniformed policing such as around-the-clock vehicle patrol within the Oslo police district. Moreover, the CTU is responsible to provide assistance to other police districts whenever it is necessary. This means that the CTU accepts responsibility in highly demanding situations. Its members also take on a variety of assignments that uniformed police routinely are in charge of. The overall competence level within the unit is impressively high at the individual level, group level, and organizational level.

Organizational Culture: Focus on the Element Values

A number of very different definitions of the concept of "organizational culture" exist. One of the definitions describes organizational culture as "A set of shared norms, values, and perceptions of the world, which develop when the members of an organization interact with each other and the surroundings" (Bang, 1997). According to Alvesson (2002), the organizational culture is decisive for how the organization thinks, feels, and acts. The concept of organizational culture clearly is important in order to understand the nature of organizations and the behavior of its members. Organizational culture has also been used as an important factor in explaining the effectiveness, success, and growth of enterprises.

One emphasis of the following study will be on the core element values as they relate to organizational culture. Hofstede (1993), e.g., argues that values compose the core of any culture. Being relatively lasting, values are emotional perceptions of what is appreciated and preferred in an organization. In other words, values are essential for an organization's fundamental perception of what is right and what is wrong, and what is desirable and valuable within a work situation. Consequently, it is possible to claim that an organization's values dictate its behavior.

An Evaluation of Organizational Culture with the Norwegian CTU

An interesting and comprehensive research analysis was conducted that involved observations, questionnaires, interviews, and examination of documents involving the CTU, all of which were conducted in the period between July 2001 and April 2002. The response rate in this values survey was an impressive 100%. No distinction was made between managers and other employees, nor was information about the officers' length of service in the CTU taken into consideration. The main argument for this decision was that the purpose of this study was to unveil the shared values that give the CTU its distinctive feature.

As a result, the evaluation revealed that there were no significant differences between managers and the other CTU personnel. However, the preliminary analysis apparently indicated that minor variation, albeit insignificant, did exist between different age groups. Here are the more relevant revelations. Police officers in the CTU value conscious use of *time* and punctuality. Time is regarded as an important factor, both in relation to ordinary policing and training, and especially when they are faced with aggravated and dangerous crime. The time factor is particularly decisive in armed responses. The tendency is confirmed clearly by the fact that more than 90% of the respondents choose the three lowest values on a scale ranging from 1 to 7, with the average score being 1.83 (see the variables measured later in further detail).

Time is also an important factor as service lists and job rotation lists are employed. Occasionally, changes are made to these lists to accommodate special tasks. Moreover, respondents perceive of time as part of a uniform system. This is in accordance with the findings from personal interviews, which showed that structure and clear objectives are considered important. It is notable to highlight that clocks were installed both in the offices and in the lunchroom to remind everyone that efficient use of time is vital. Consequently, a conscious, purposeful, and structured use of time has been revealed as a highly prominent value within the Norwegian CTU.

Members of the CTU expressed "change" as a significant factor. However, they seem to find that change must be balanced with tradition and continuity. The tendency is clear here with more than 90% of the responses leaning toward change. The average value was 3.33. On the one hand, the police officers are almost continually preoccupied with self-development, team development, and with developing their division. The management encourages them to frequently test new equipment, enhance their competences, and further develop police methodology. During the interviews, the police officers confirmed that they are allowed room to develop and take part in the development of various aspects of policing. On the other hand, they also value experience and support thoroughly tested and proven routines and systems. Most organizations, in particular police agencies, view tradition and history as important issues. Fielding (1984, p. 574) also noted that police officers, to a great extent, tend to trust their previous experiences and arrangements, which have proven to work in the past.

The principles of seniority and experience, which are important in a police context, may have influenced the officers' responses. The fact that the police are clearly governed by rules is also indicative of a preference for tradition and continuity. Nevertheless, this research has revealed that change and development still constitute a clear and relevant value to Norwegian CTU members.

As for the question of "individual versus group orientation," there is a clear tendency toward the latter. More than 80% of the respondents emphasized group orientation. A typical feature of policing is team cooperation or cooperation between two partners. This is a particularly developed feature of the Norwegian CTU where regular partners go on vehicle patrols together. Partnerships of this kind tend to last for several years. In addition, each individual member of the unit belongs to a special team. At the same time, they feel a strong sense of identity toward the unit. From the interviews, it was revealed that the ability to cooperate is highly respected by the members of the CTU. These findings confirm the tendency of favoring group orientation in special police units.

On the other hand, police officers are often described as being strong individuals with distinct leadership qualities. Even more so, it is promoted within the Norwegian police that the individual members of the CTU are responsible for their own actions. These contrasting values have been examined further within a select number of CTU members. It should also be emphasized that individual qualities form the basis for enabling the CTU to solve complicated missions. What has, therefore, been revealed is a healthy combination of strong individuals who stress on cooperation and group orientation. This is a natural tendency that correlates well with other international police research where collectivism is clearly emphasized (van Maanen, 1978; Bailey et al., 1995).

The responses from examining the "freedom–control" dimensions show a clear inclination toward the value "freedom," with slightly over 86% of the responses leaning in this direction, with an average score of 3.19. On the one hand, the interviews and the description of the conditions in the CTU bear witness to a strong emphasis on structure, routine, and thorough planning.

From the research results, it was possible to discern that the emphasis on the above-mentioned aspects was necessary in order for the CTU to succeed with its responsibilities, in particular in connection with response to armed confrontations. The members of the CTU have emphasized that comprehensive planning and training exercises, personnel certifications, and work routines are prominent features and are thus viewed as highly important. On the other hand, the research findings also revealed that the chief of the CTU also stresses the importance of giving the individual team member room to act within certain frameworks.

The perspective on human life seems to be characterized by an underlying trust in the individual (see McGregor's "x and y theories"). Moreover, police research has shown that operative police work is to a great extent distinguished by autonomy (Ekman, 1999; Granér, 2004). This perspective explains that in spite of the need for and an extensive use of structure and systems, the value of freedom is held in great esteem by police officers in special units.

The dimensions "privacy–public/openness" were designed to capture how officers put into practice or value the social conditions within the CTU.

The intent was to reveal which topics are being discussed, and to what extent police officers feel that the CTU is characterized by openness and intimacy. The responses left little doubt; openness within the CTU is greatly appreciated by unit members. The average value is 5.31 and approximately 75% of the responses favor the openness value. Also, supporting these findings are the statements made by the respondents in the interviews concerning openness and social interaction. These values are found to be more respected in the CTU than in other workplaces that the respondents had worked in. It is a characteristic feature of the CTU that its members also socialize outside work. This would support that openness among colleagues is highly treasured among the CTU officers.

The responses made by the officers in relation to the dimensions "formal tone–informal environment" show a clear preference for the latter, illustrated by an average value of 2.33. More than 80% of the CTU members prefer an informal environment. However, this research did note that some variation does exist. For example, the interviews confirm that extensive banter occur frequently in the unit and dominate the language used by its members. Both Finstad (2000) and Ekman (1999) had also previously confirmed that this is also a general tendency within the Norwegian police as such. Finstad (2000) elaborated this point by reporting that she had rarely experienced a more friendly work environment dominated by an informal and joking atmosphere. Moreover, it is common knowledge that the span of supervision and control between the various management levels within the CTU is very small. The variation found in the responses along this dimension may be explained by a notion of seriousness which, among others, manifests itself in management structures that are clear to all members of the CTU.

This study also revealed that cooperation is a highly appreciated value by police officers in the CTU. Just over 80% of the responses show a clear tendency toward cooperation, with an average score of 4.81. Nevertheless, the responses seem to cluster around the extreme limits of the scale. This dimension must be viewed in relation to the dimensions "individualism–group orientation," which showed a similar tendency. The high value attributed to cooperation can also be explained by the way in which practical CTU work in ordinary and emergency service in pairs and teams is organized. Likewise is the attitude of CTU personnel toward cooperation regarded as crucial when recruitment to the unit takes place, and in the socializing process for newcomers to the unit.

Nevertheless, one must bear in mind that members of the CTU are highly competitive individuals with leadership abilities and a desire for achievement. These are all factors that encourage individual competition and competition between teams and divisions. On the whole, however, this research did emphasize the main impression that cooperation is appreciated and notable.

A clear tendency has also been identified along the dimension "equality and codetermination versus hierarchy and authority." More than 80% of the respondents were found to be oriented toward equality, with an average value of 2.38. Very few responses clustered around the middle of the scale, or around the values, authority and hierarchy. It is clear to Norwegian police officials that equality and codetermination work in routine police response; however, response to an armed crisis requires a clear hierarchy and commando structure in order to ensure an efficient and secure handling of the tasks. It should be noted that the Norwegian police do not carry firearms while on normal street patrol and are only permitted to remove their firearm from a locked container within their patrol vehicle under extremely exigent circumstances and normally with the permission of a supervisor.

The appreciation of equality is also found in the work environment of the CTU, which is characterized by equality, small distances within the layers of organization, few or no informal differences in status, a relatively tight social environment, and a welcome reception provided to new members. On the other hand, the age and experience factors appear to pull in the opposite direction. On the whole, however, the main impression left by this study is that equality and codetermination is held in great esteem by the members of the CTU.

In regards to the dimension meant to capture the focus on time management, the responses by CTU members are distributed across the entire scale with a main tendency toward the middle section. The average value is 4.38, with more than 60% of the responses showing a preference for long-term job focus and planning. However, Finstad (2000, p. 62) describes police work as guided by incidents and fragmented. This could indicate that extensive planning in police work may not be necessary or fruitful and that the focus on the issue of time would emphasize the short-term perspective. This would, therefore, appear to indicate a preference for short-term focus, fast solutions, and quick results. However, members of the CTU prefer, on the other hand, a more long-term focus, which means that they value thorough analyses when this is possible, as well as decision-making processes characterized by a well-planned and long-term perspective. To give an example, it takes 3 years to complete the training leading up to approval or certification of a specialist function such as in the Norwegian police scuba diving team. Likewise, CTU members have a long-term perspective on collaborative relations. From another view, this dimension is situational, as evidenced by the variation in the responses. An alternative explanation to this is that the variation is an expression of individual differences. That said, there may be a correlation between the preference for a long-term perspective and the tendency to favor a well-structured organization.

Schein (1994, p. 78) divided the time dimension differently. He talks about assumptions about time and points to the question whether organizations have a fundamental organizational direction emphasizing the past, the present, or the future. This is a very interesting perspective that can be conveyed to the CTU. On the one hand, lessons learned from past CTU incidents carry great significance, e.g., the Torp case. Likewise, members of the CTU have to focus on the present when dealing with tasks. At the same time, they are preoccupied with preparing for a potentially challenging armed response in the near future. The variation in the responses on the time dimension and Schein's understanding of this dimension can be interpreted as a confirmation that the CTU should have both a short-term and a long-term perspective, but with the main focus on the latter.

The responses in relation to the dimensions "work is more important" against "balance between work and spare time" give an average value of 4.32. The main impression is that the majority of responses cluster around the middle of the scale. However, there is great variation with a weak tendency toward a preference for balancing work and spare time. The results indicate that the officers are very enthusiastic about their jobs, their special field, and their work environment. One could infer from this that the members of the CTU show great involvement, and that in return they are given a sense of work satisfaction and identity.

The identity factor may be of particular importance in organizations such as the CTU. The average age of its members at the time the study was undertaken was approximately 34 years. With a few exceptions, this means the police officers are relatively early in their careers (since most Norwegian police officials work until at least 60 years of age). Possible explanations for this are that they wish to give priority to their personal career and that, to a certain extent, their assignment develops into a lifestyle. Both factors suggest that work is considered very important.

A prominent feature of the organizational culture within the Norwegian police is to regard police work as more than just an ordinary job. According to Granér and Knutsson (2000, p. 112), entering the police means adopting a new lifestyle. On the one hand, many police officers are also parents of small children, often many children, which is a factor that works contrary to the notion of police work as a distinct lifestyle. In addition, a great number of police officers are actively taking part in sports, outdoor life, and other organizational activities, as well as taking on their specific work duties.

"Task orientation" and "relation orientation" are dimensions that are frequently subjected to a variety of analyses as it relates to organizational culture. Members of the Norwegian police CTU express a clear preference for task orientation. Although more than 80% favor task orientation, the responses spread out across the scale. This tendency can be understood in light of the officers' strong interest in professional matters and the room that they are given for self-development. The emphasis on action and result orientation are likely to reinforce this tendency. One has to highlight the mortal danger that the members of the CTU occasionally must expect to face. This prospect underlines the need to focus on tasks, training, and preparations. CTU officers go to work in order to train, build competence, and carry out assignments. All of these factors point in the same direction; so too, the fact that the officers regard themselves as true public servants. The vision of the CTU is very clear in this respect. A preference for task orientation may also be reinforced by the unit's focus on routines, planning, and procedures, as well as considerations for the efficient and the productive use of time.

The relaxed and informal atmosphere within the CTU, the good social environment, and the necessity to cooperate with each other may seem to work in the opposite direction, toward the "relation orientation." The general impression from research on police underlines also team spirit and professional loyalty as clear features of the organizational culture. These are the factors that support the relation orientation. One could interpret the variation in the responses as an indication that both orientations are prevalent, but with task orientation as the more esteemed one.

The responses concerning "style of communication" are unambiguous. A direct style is preferred, and a clear tendency emerges, which has to be seen in relation to a context involving an open and relaxed tone between the officers and the absence of conflicts. In terms of subject matter and form, the unit's regular discussions encourage a direct style. Further, the members of the unit learn to know each other very well, which makes them trust each other through training and work. This feature also points in the direction of a direct style of communication, which is always a matter of discussion among the members of the unit. We infer from this that conveying one's opinion is appreciated by the members of the CTU.

Also interesting are the dimensions "action orientation" and "planning orientation." These are the only dimensions where it is possible to identify certain differences of some significance between managers and nonmanagers. This is a contra intuitive result as Johannessen and Olaisen (1995, p. 152) also raised. One could expect that managers were less oriented toward operative action than young and operative police officers on the beat. Reuss-Iannis (1993) distinguished between managers and police officers on patrol, and Ekman (1999) pointed out the widely different cultures within the two groups. Police officers who do not hold managerial positions display a general feeling of disdain for managers because they feel that management has "lost touch" with everyday practical policing.

To be fair, it should be noted that managers in the CTU are likely to possess the same qualities as their subordinates. Moreover, they have undergone the same selection process, education, and training. As a direct result, managers and non-managers within the CTU share the same experiences. However, as experienced officers and managers, their focus may be somewhat different. The main tendency for managers is toward great variation at the same time as the majority of the responses show an inclination toward action orientation. These results may be interpreted as a confirmation that both planning and action orientation are important. The control groups stressed also here that the responses would depend on the situation. This may indicate that the managers are somewhat more oriented toward action than their subordinates within their respective unit. These findings may be accounted for by extensive delegating of responsibility, so that the individual officer or partners in the same patrol vehicle place importance on obtaining useful information about situations and individuals, and through good planning ensure that their tasks are carried out in accordance with routines and regulations. In other words, a thorough analysis of the situation is conducted before making a decision concerning which measures are to be taken and put into effect.

The results show that the members of the CTU have a clear tendency toward a "practical and pragmatic orientation." The average value on this dimension is 2.14, and more than 90% rate a practical and pragmatic orientation higher than a philosophical and theoretical orientation. Respondents commented that there are a great deal of equipment and devices to be operated and mastered. The police officers reported that they are working continuously with the purpose of finding simple and practical solutions. Nevertheless, they admitted that theoretical knowledge played an important factor in this work, such as the handling of explosives, giving first aid, testing new equipment, and developing new plans. Granér (2004, p. 206) points to a possible distinction between an intellectually reflecting attitude in opposition to an intuitive, practical, and action-oriented attitude among police officers. Both attitudes appear to be present in the CTU.

The practical/pragmatic attitude displays a pattern that is entirely in accordance with findings in international research on police officers. This literature calls attention to, among others, a here-and-now attitude that is descriptive of the situational character of law enforcement. In addition, Fielding (1984) emphasized personal experiences as a source to understanding situations and solving problems. There is an evident anti-intellectualism within the police subculture, as argued by reference Granér and Knutsson (2001, p. 105). To the extent that it is possible to compare research findings found in British or American social conditions of the 1960s and 1970s with Norwegian society today, there may be a possible explanatory factor. One can assume that the nature of the CTU's tasks and technologies, as well as the emphasis on developing skills are factors that, to a greater extent, explain the importance attached to a practical and pragmatic orientation. Explosive blasts, shoot-outs, and fast response driving are examples of activities that contribute to reinforce this orientation.

The control group perceived of the dimensions "security and safety" and "challenges and suspense" as two-sided. On the one hand, it is a general feature of police officers in the CTU that they are drawn to suspense and seek challenges to test their ability to master difficult situations. During the interviews, it transpired that police officers who choose to apply for the CTU were motivated by factors related to professional and personal challenges. These findings are thoroughly described in other literature conducted in this field.

On the other hand, importance in the CTU is given to planning, structure, situation analyses, and training. The significance of security is underlined by the priority given to health, environment and safety regulations, as well as the emphasis placed on personal safety in connection with different assignments. All the above-mentioned factors point in the direction of security and safety. The same factors can also be said to be important for victims of serious crimes. In regards to victims of crime, these factors must be prioritized so that a good solution can be found. Finally, this can additionally be seen in relation to humbleness and professionalism where these factors are central.

"Legal protection and democracy" and "efficiency and productivity" are important and interesting dimensions for the entire public sector (Klaussen, 2001; Lundquist, 1998). Granér and Knutsson (2001, p. 17) link Lundquist's (1998, p. 53) concept of public ethos to the question about the role of the police as an institution in society with the right to use coercive force, and the question who the police should serve. This dimension, which is again discussed by Granér (2004), is of particular interest to the law enforcement profession, which acts as society's machinery of power. Consequently, the police priorities in connection with the execution of power have great impact on our democracy. This dimension is also important because the police are action and task oriented, which becomes particularly evident in the demanding operative work of the type that the CTU deals with.

It is not surprising that the central tendency of the CTU is that the value "legal protection and democracy" is valued highly. The average value is 1.71 and more than 80% of respondents chose the two most unambiguous scores (1 and 2). No other question asked in this survey has received a clearer response, which proves that democracy and legal protection are regarded as extraordinarily important by the members of the CTU. This is in accordance with the professional attitude routinely displayed by members of the CTU throughout all of their missions and is outlined in the unit's vision. In the interviews, respondents made it very clear that they looked at illegal and unnecessary use of force as a very negative factor, which should not occur in their division. The interviews left an unambiguous and clear impression in this respect.

These sentiments are in line with observations made in CTU meetings and during training. To underline this further, the CTU policy disapproves of illegal and unnecessary use of force. Finally, it may be worth mentioning that the trust in the CTU and legitimacy require both a clear attitude and consistent behavior in relation to questions that this dimension affects. The attention that the CTU naturally attracts implies that any errors committed by the unit in connection with this dimension will have a tendency to produce negative consequences.

Operative work and operative disposition may indicate that the wish to achieve results has priority over values such as legal protection and democracy in practical police work. International research shows that operative cultures rate results higher than legal protection. Certain reservations must be made, however, when the Norwegian or Nordic police forces are concerned. The value democracy and legal protection are viewed as important more often than not. In the annual survey undertaken by the Norwegian Market and Media Institute, the police are consistently the highest-scoring government service. Consequently, the survey gives a general impression of Norwegians as trusting the police.

Ekman (1999) noted that police activities are firmly regulated though a large number of laws, instructions, policies, plans, and routines. The Police Instructions (regulations) and the Criminal Procedure Act in Norway are central tools that are being used in order to ensure legal protection and democracy. These factors contribute to reinforce the "legal protection and democracy" values.

The dimensions "service and public services" and "crime prevention" are central to the police, and the responses vary considerably. About 13.5% of the respondents preferred service, whereas about 40% favored crime prevention. The average value is 4.73, with about 35% of the respondents choosing the value 4. The main tendency appears to be that the respondents consider prevention to be more important than providing service. Here too, it is important to make a distinction between ordinary policing and armed response to a terrorist threat when examining the figures. The great spectre in the responses may indicate that the CTU as a whole finds both considerations important. The main tendency can be explained by the unit's character and tasks. However, this goes contrary to the vision of the unit. Granér and Knutsson (2000, p. 56) show that the police tend to give priority to crime prevention over service, although the latter is frequently debated. In everyday policing, police officers demonstrate a healthy attitude toward providing service, and a willingness to accept that they are there to serve the public or protect citizens against criminal acts. Granér and Knutsson (2000) use the metaphor "I am a guardian too" to illustrate how police officers perceive of what their core tasks are.

The research also evaluated the distinction between preventive and problem-oriented or proactive policing as opposed to the more action-led and reactive perspective of policing. Although it may look like service is a value, which has received more acclaim in recent years, crime prevention is still very central to all police work.

According to this research, the members of the CTU appear to be concerned about both their service function and crime prevention, and that the issue of prioritizing one over the other may be situational. Also, they, in general, value crime prevention higher than providing service, which is not overly surprising, given the specific nature of their work responsibilities.

As for the respondents' attitude toward the dimensions "strong and firm management" and "freedom, trust and individual initiative," there are also great differences. The main tendency is that just below 80% of the police officers in the CTU prefer strong management. This is supported by the findings in the interviews and contributes to strengthen the support for this type of management.

This research survey closed with the dimensions "openness and transparency" and "professional loyalty and team spirit." Once again, the tendency is clear with more than 80% of the respondents preferring openness and transparency. This is a propensity that goes contrary to words commonly used to characterize police cultures, such as the esprit de corps, closure, secrecy, and the "us-versus-them" attitudes (e.g., Reuss-Iannis Cops Code, 1993).

In summary, the points highlighted and discussed above reveal that professional loyalty is highly valued in the Norwegian police CTU. This is also confirmed by the information obtained in related interviews of CTU personnel. The same goes for the way that work is organized. Transparency has its limitations in relation to resources, competence, and work methodologies. This is obvious when noting the unit's tasks and responsibilities. The clear distinction between the CTU and other police units is also evident. The intimate work environment, the extraordinarily strong identity, and the relatively great stability among the unit's members may also be indicative of a tendency to prefer professional loyalty and esprit de corps.

These factors are in line with elements that describe features of the police culture internationally. Structural factors can be identified, which point in the direction of closure and esprit de corps. On the other hand, one may assume that self-confidence, a firm identity, and consciousness about one's own role may counteract this tendency. An important factor in this connection is the manager's priorities and behavior as a role model. This factor shows clearly that both openness and transparency are desired and practiced to the extent this is possible. This applies also in relation to other police units, the Police Directorate, and the Ministry of Justice and the Police. And, so likely does the fact that the CTU is a specialized unit that easily can find itself subjected to criticism, which may have consequences for both individual members and the unit as a whole. Here, we recognize Schein's dimension of external adjustment (1994).

In conclusion, some of the clearest points assessed on the basis of the average responses in this survey should be highlighted. This research revealed that the police officers in the Norwegian police CTU gave the clearest answers in relation to the values, legal protection and democracy (1.71). Moreover, they stress that time consciousness is perceived of as fixed factor (1.83). This is one of the most unambiguous answers in the survey. What is more, it may be mentioned that the police officers attach great value to the informal culture and the value of equality and codetermination. Likewise, they value a practical and pragmatic attitude to their work. Finally, openness and good relations among colleagues were also strongly appreciated.

Both interviews and questionnaires were employed in order to study the organizational culture within the Norwegian police CTU. With the assistance of questionnaires, an additional attempt was made to survey the dominating values in the CTU. The members of the unit were asked to rate what they thought were the most prevalent values in the CTU along a total of 19 dimensions. The dimensions were designed as opposing pairs of concepts, as shown in Table 28.1. In this table, you will also find the average figure

Table 28.1   Average Cultural Values in the Norwegian CTU on a Scale Ranging from 1 to 7

No	Dimension	Answer
1	Time is fixed—Time is floating	1.83
2	Change—Tradition and continuity	3.33
3	Individualism—Group orientation	5.44
4	Freedom—Control	3.19
5	Privacy—Public/openness	5.31
6	Informal—Formal	2.33
7	Individual competition—Cooperation	4.81
8	Equality and codetermination—Hierarchy and authority	2.83
9	Short-term focus—Long-term focus	4.38
10	Work most important—Balance work/spare time	4.35
11	Task orientation—Relation orientation	3.31
12	Direct/explicit communication style—Indirect/implicit communication style	2.54
13	Action orientation—Planning orientation	3.85
14	Practical and pragmatic orientation—Philosophical and theoretical orientation	2.14
15	Security and safety—Challenges and suspense	2.40
16	Legal protection and democracy—Efficiency and productivity	1.71
17	Service, visibility, safety and public services—Combating crime and enforcement of law and order	4.73
18	Strong and clear management—Freedom, trust, personal initiative, and creativity	3.73
19	Openness, transparency—Professional loyalty, corps/team spirit	2.52

for each dimension. The scale goes from 1 to 7. The first dimension, time is fixed versus floating, gives an average score of 1.83, which means that the respondents are more likely to perceive of time as fixed than floating.

Here is the list of the competing values as they were surveyed:

Time is fixed	Time is floating
Change	Tradition and continuity
Individualism	Group-orientation
Freedom	Control
Privacy	Public/openness
Informal	Formal
Individual competition	Cooperation
Equality and codetermination	Hierarchy and authority
Short-term focus	Long-term focus
Work most important	Balance work/spare time
Task-orientation	Relation-orientation
Direct/explicit communication style	Indirect/implicit communication style
Action-oriented	Planning-oriented
Practical and pragmatic-oriented	Philosophical and theoretical-oriented
Security and safety	Challenges and suspense/excitement
Legal protection and democracy	Efficiency and productivity
Service, visibility, safety and public services	Combating crime and enforcement of law and order
Strong and clear management	Freedom, trust, personal initiative, and creativity
Openness, transparency	Professional loyalty, corps/team spirit

Through analyses of statistics, it was shown that the respondents had given very similar answers on a variety of dimensions. This means that these variables form one sole factor that can be called involvement. This new factor encompasses the following dimensions: 7 (competition versus cooperation), 10 (work versus balance), 11 (task-orientation versus relation-orientation), and 19 (closed versus open, i.e., inversed dimension).

The variation in the factor referred to as involvement is a consequence of the variation found in the dimensions involved. We identified three significant correlations as shown in Figure 28.1.

Therefore, three hypotheses* proposed were all supported:

- Hypothesis 1: The longer time perspective a police officer has, the higher degree of personal involvement.

---

* The research model above explained 28.5% of the variation occurring in the dependent variable. Statistical ANOVA showed that this model is significant. All the coefficients of the independent variables have been measured to have a significance, which is stronger than .05.

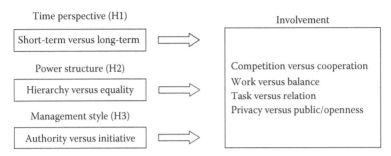

Figure 28.1 Research model to identify predicators of involvement.

- Hypothesis 2: The lower degree of hierarchy a police officer experiences, the higher degree of personal involvement.
- Hypothesis 3: The lower degree of authority a police officer experiences, the higher degree of personal involvement.

It is worth emphasizing that data from this survey reflects the values typical to the Norwegian police CTU, which was also the objective of the analysis. The analysis may not, however, give an accurate answer to the question of the extent to which the desired values and the values lived by correlate. Nevertheless, it is assumed that there is a relatively high degree of correlation.

Consequently, it is possible to describe the following values characteristic of the organizational culture within the Norwegian police CTU:

Competence- and development orientation. The unit emphasizes this value through a great deal of systemization, planning, and routines, as well as extensive training, socialization, certifications, and competence-building activities.

Safety under the law orientation. Unnecessary use of force is not tolerated in the CTU. This is a value that is linked to routines, training, and the providing of service.

Structure orientation. The unit is characterized by relatively many efficient and well-developed routines, which express themselves through the unit's activity plans, plans for building competence, training programmes, and certifications. Moreover, this emphasis also expresses itself through the importance attached to operative routines, rather than frequent meetings and reporting routines.

Performance orientation. The members of the CTU are individuals who seek vast professional as well as personal challenges. These challenges can be seen in light of a distinct quest for excitement.

Task orientation. Police tasks occupy a central place in the unit's activities, and police officers are constantly looking for new and better ways of solving tasks.

Action orientation. The ability to act is emphasized through training as well as through solving practical tasks. The police officers want to get things done, and there is an inner and collective drive to act and arrive at solutions for the challenges that they face.

Cooperation orientation. Throughout the selection process, education, training, and practical work, the ability to cooperate is being stressed. Cooperation implies putting together complementary competence and is exploited when tasks are being dealt with. Moreover, cooperation enhances the ability to solve tasks. Finally, cooperation also provides safety for the individual team member.

Humbleness orientation. Humbleness seems to be geared toward the tasks, competence, colleagues, and good connections. A sense of humbleness when confronted with the risks characterizing many of the unit's assignments was noted. Moreover, it is directed toward themselves in the role as representatives of the CTU.

In conclusion, those working in the Norwegian police CTU have revealed that esprit de corps, time consciousness, democracy, as well as other critical factors describe the personal and organizational ideologies of the unit members. These findings have been supported by other surveys conducted at the same time. Clearly, those seeking membership in this prestigious police unit routinely exhibit common characteristics. It is likely that these values may be found in other specialized police divisions.

References

Alvesson, M. 2002. *Organisasjonskultur og ledelse.* Oslo, Norway: Abstrakt forlag.

Bang, H. 1997. *Organisasjonskultur,* 3. Utgave. 2. Opplag. Oslo, Norway: Tano forlag.

Bailey, W. G., Strecher, V. G., Hoover, L. T., and Dowling, J. L. 1995. Occupational culture, In W. G. Bailey (ed.) *The Encyclopedia of Police Science,* 2nd edn. New York/London, U.K.: Garland Publishing, Inc.

Ekman, G. 1999. *Från text till batong—om poliser, busar och svenner, dr.gradsavhandling.* Stockholm, Sweden: EFI, Ekonomiska Forskningsinstituttet vid Handelshøgskolan.

Fielding, N. 1984. Police socialization and police competence. *The British Journal of Sociology,* 35(4): 568–590, London.

Finstad, L. 2000. *Politiblikket.* Oslo, Norway: Pax Forlag.

Granér, R. 2004. Patruljerande polisers yrkeskultur. Lund, Sweden: Lund Dissertations in Social Work 18.

Hofstede, G. 1993. *Kulturer og organisasjoner.* Oslo, Norway: Bedriftsøkonomenes Forlag.

Klausen, K. K. 2001. *Skulle det være noget særligt? Organisation og ledelse i det offentlige.* København. Børsen forlag.

Lundquist, L. 1998. *Demokratins Väktare.* Lund, Norway: Studentlitteratur.

Reuss-Iannis, E. 1993. *Two Cultures of Policing*. Piscataway, NJ: Transaction books.
Schein, E. H. 1994. *Organisasjonskultur og ledelse, er kulturendring mulig?* Oslo, Norway: Libro Forlag.
van Maanen, J. 1978. The Asshold, in P.K. Manning and J. van Maanen (eds.), *Policing: A View from the Street*. Santa Monica, California: Goodyear Publishing Company, Inc.

Conclusion

Striving for Improvements in Law Enforcement at the End of the First Decade of the New Millennium

The first 5 years of the new millennium witnessed the emergence of international terrorist threats in major cities across the world. Unfortunately, funding for law enforcement endeavors has been impacted dramatically by this new emphasis on emergency response and preparedness, and the gathering of international intelligence. In addition, the successes of proactive intelligence-led policing witnessed in the late 1990s and early 2000s have been negatively impacted by the political pressure to "do more with less." Decreased spending on community policing efforts have often moved the street patrol officers further away from the neighborhoods that they serve. Fortunately, technological advancements fueled by enhanced DNA analysis, biometric scanning, and automated video and audio surveillance have assisted law enforcement agencies in bringing more suspects to justice.

From an international perspective, the financial strain on the world's economic powers in the last 3 years of the decade have hampered the assistance that had been supplied to developing countries. The newest post-conflict democracies, Iraq and Afghanistan, continue to struggle, even as the improvement of rule of law in that corner of the globe has become an international priority. Other developing countries like Haiti, Nigeria, South Africa, and Kosovo continue to be plagued by corruption and political nepotism at a time when the developed world is shifting civilian police trainers to the Middle East. This has allowed these countries to continue to act as organized crime hubs for smuggling and the illegal trade of drugs, humans, and weapons. One has to hope that America and her European allies will recognize the need to more closely control and deter these criminal groups in order to quell the taint of drugs, trafficking in human beings, and the weapons market in their own countries. Investing in technology and personnel development in developing countries will clearly and positively affect crime rates and crime control endeavors across the globe.

While organized crime continues to thrive, street crime continues its surprising decline in many Western urban settings. The move from reactive to proactive policing and technology-enhanced, intelligence-led law enforcement has assisted policing agencies in North America, Australia, Europe, and other regions in deterring crime and apprehending criminals. This has often been accomplished with reductions in police manpower, which may reveal that technology may be the key in reducing criminality.

As the above chapters have revealed, law enforcement across the globe is a complex phenomenon. Cultural factors, both within and external to the police agency, have impacted organizational success, motivation, and dedication. Additionally, while many governments view unionization, particularly of the police, in a negative light, this book has revealed that the formation of police associations and unions can enhance morale, productivity, and cooperation between law enforcement managers and field personnel. Police administrators must also acknowledge that public perception of agency success and fear of crime are as important factors as actual crime rate and resource investment. Finally, it has become increasingly clear that transborder and international law enforcement and prosecutorial cooperation are elements that must be improved in order to eradicate crime and deter terrorism across the globe. Therefore, it has been the goal of this textbook to provide exposure to issues and concepts that will guide police leaders in enhancing law enforcement professionalism, effectiveness, and management efficiency through the new millennium. Clearly, new challenges will arise and law enforcement leaders must be properly prepared and educated to deal with them. Ultimately, it is the responsibility of the International Police Executive Symposium and related organizations to bring law enforcement administrators and criminal justice and criminology academics and researchers together in order to enhance efficacy and success within the challenging field of policing.

Index

A

Aircraft trafficking, 545–546
American Federation of Labor-Congress of Industrial Organizations (AFL-CIO), 455–459
American Federation of State, County, and Municipal Employees (AFSCME), 457
American police unions
  civilianization and privatization, 475
  decentralized, disorganized, and disconnected model, 461–462
  decentralized labor laws
    federal legislation, 468–469
    incoherent labor laws, 467–468
    forging shared common visions, 469–470
    fragmentation, 458–459
    global events, domestic policing, 462–464
  national police labor-management council
    advocate, international role, 474–475
    APLMC, 472
    communication network, 472–473
    community groups, 474
    core components, public police work, 473
    police profession diversification, 473–474
    police recruitment process, 473
  police labor movement
    AFL-CIO affiliated police labor organizations, 456
    collective bargaining, 455–456
    competitive nature, 458
    dual affiliations, 455
    dual unionism, 457
    FOP, 456–457
    IBPO, 457
    independent police labor organizations, 456
    meet and confer, 455–456
    NAPO, 456–457
    national, state, and regional level, membership inflation, 458
    police unions, collapse, 454–455
    police unity, 459–460
    political policing, 465–466
    price of policing, 464–465
  terminology
    definition of union, 453
    Fair Labor Standards Act, 454
    inter-union rivalries, 454
    national militaristic police, 453
    police chief, 452
  uniform national professional police standard framework, 470–472
Asian Human Rights Commission (AHRC), 441
Asian Legal Resource Center (ALRC), 437

B

Border patrol management, 547
British Common Law, 483
British Telecom (BT) network, 296
Buenos Aires city, 186–187

C

CALEA, *see* Commission on Accreditation for Law Enforcement Agencies
Canada Labour Code (CLC), 480
Canadian Police Association (CPA), 486
Canadian professional police association (CPPA)
  advocacy, strategic police association priority
    awareness, 495–496
    deal with government, 495
    decision-making process, 494
  competing demands, domestic policing, 488–489
  critical issues, 478

607

International Police Executive Symposium (IPES)
www.ipes.info

The International Police Executive Symposium (IPES) was founded in 1994. The aims and objectives of the IPES are to provide a forum to foster closer relationships among police researchers and practitioners globally, to facilitate cross-cultural, international, and interdisciplinary exchanges for the enrichment of the law-enforcement profession, and to encourage discussion and published research on challenging and contemporary topics related to the profession.

One of the most important activities of the IPES is the organization of an annual meeting under the auspices of a police or educational institution. To date, meetings have been hosted by the Canton Police of Geneva, Switzerland (Police Challenges and Strategies, 1994), the International Institute of the Sociology of Law in Onati, Spain (Challenges of Policing Democracies, 1995), Kanagawa University in Yokohama, Japan (Organized Crime, 1996), the Federal Police in Vienna, Austria (International Police Cooperation, 1997), the Dutch Police and Europol in The Hague, The Netherlands (Crime Prevention, 1998), and Andhra Pradesh Police in Hyderabad, India (Policing of Public Order, 1999), and the Center for Public Safety, Northwestern University, Evanston, Illinois, USA (Traffic Policing, 2000). A special meeting was cohosted by the Bavarian Police Academy of Continuing Education in Ainring, Germany, University of Passau, Germany, and State University of New York, Plattsburgh, USA, to discuss the issues endorsed by the IPES in April 2000. The Police of Poland hosted the next meeting in May 2001 (Corruption: A Threat to World Order), and thereafter the annual meeting was hosted by the Police of Turkey in May 2002 (Police Education and Training). The Kingdom of Bahrain hosted the annual meeting in October 2003 (Police and the Community).

The 2004 meeting in May of that year (Criminal Exploitation of Women and Children) took place in Chilliwack, British Columbia, Canada, and it was cohosted by the University College of the Fraser Valley, Abbotsford Police Department, Royal Canadian Mounted Police, the Vancouver Police Department, the Justice Institute of British Columbia, Canadian Police College, and the International Centre for Criminal Law Reform and Criminal Justice Policy. The next meeting (Challenges of Policing in the

21st Century) took place in September 2005 in Prague, The Czech Republic. The Turkish National Police hosted the meeting in 2006 (Local Linkages to Global Security and Crime). The 14th IPES was held in Dubai on April 8–12, 2007 (Urbanization and Security). The 15th annual meeting (Police without Borders: The Fading Distinction between Local and Global) was hosted on May 12–16.in Cincinnati, Ohio by the City of Cincinnati Police and the Ohio Association of Chiefs of Police in Cincinnati. The Republic of Macedonia hosted the 2009 meeting (Tourism, Strategic Locations, and Major Events: Policing in an Age of Mobility, Mass Movement and Migration) in Ohrid, Macedonia on June 9–14. There will be a Special Meeting of IPES in 2010 (November 2–6) on the theme of Community Policing. In the following year 2011 (June 26–July 1) the City of Buenos Aires, Argentina, will host the 18th (20th with two Special Meetings included) Annual Meeting on the topic of Mass Action, Violence, and Crime: Policing Disorder and Discontent.

The majority of participants of the annual meetings are usually directly involved in the police profession. In addition, scholars and researchers in the field also participate. The meetings comprise both structured and informal sessions to maximize dialog and exchange of views and information. The executive summary of each meeting is distributed to participants as well as to a wide range of other interested police professionals and scholars. In addition, a book of selected papers from each annual meeting is published through CRC Press/Taylor & Francis Group, Prentice Hall, Lexington Books and other reputed publishers.

The IPES fulfills its mission with the cooperation of a global network of Institutional Supporters.

IPES Institutional Supporters

Fayetteville State University, College of Basic and Applied Sciences (Dr. David E. Barlow, Professor and Dean), 130 Chick Building, 1200 Murchison Road, Fayetteville, NC 28301 USA. Tel: 910-672-1659; Fax: 910-672-1083. E-mail: dbarlow@uncfsu.edu

The University of Northumbria at Newcastle, Department of Social Sciences (Dr. Bankole Cole, Reader in Criminology), 226 Lipman Building, Newcastle-upon-Tyne, NE1 8ST, UK. Tel: +44 (0)191 227 3457. E-mail: bankole.cole@northumbria.ac.uk

National Institute of Criminology and Forensic Science (Mr. Kamalendra Prasad, Inspector General of Police), MHA, Outer Ring Road, Sector 3, Rohini, Delhi 110085, India. Tel: 91 11 275 2 5095; Fax: 91 11 275 1 0586. E-mail: director.nicfs@nic.in

Defendology Center for Security, Sociology and Criminology Research (Valibor Lalic), Srpska Street 63,78000 Banja Luka, Bosnia and Herzegovina. Tel and Fax: 387 51 308 914. Email: lalicv@teol.net

University of Maribor, Faculty of Criminal Justice and Security (Dr. Gorazd Mesko), Kotnikova 8, 1000 Ljubljana, Slovenia. Tel: 386 1 300 83 39; Fax: 386 1 2302 687. E-mail: gorazd.mesko@fpvv.uni-mb.si

Abbotsford Police Department (Bob Rich, Chief Constable), 2838 Justice Way, Abbotsford, British Columbia V2 T3 P5, Canada. Tel: 604-864-4809; Fax: 604-864-4725. E-mail: bobrich@abbypd.ca, swillms@abbypd.ca

North Carolina Central University, Department of Criminal Justice (Dr. Harvey L. McMurray, Chair), 301 Whiting Criminal Justice Bldg., Durham, NC 27707, USA. Tel: 919-530-5204, 919 530 7909; Fax: 919-530-5195. E-mail: hmcmurray@nccu.edu

University of the Fraser Valley Department of Criminology & Criminal Justice, (Dr. Darryl Plecas), 33844 King Road, Abbotsford, British Columbia V2 S7 M9, Canada. Tel: 604-853-7441; Fax: 604-853-9990. E-mail: Darryl. plecas@ufv.ca

National Police Academy, Japan Police Policy Research Center, (Suzuki Kunio, Assistant Director), Zip 183-8558: 3-12- 1 Asahi-cho Fuchu-city, Tokyo, Japan. Tel: 81 42 354 3550; Fax: 81 42 330 1308. E-mail: PPRC@npa.go.jp

Royal Canadian Mounted Police (Gary Bass, Deputy Commissioner, Pacific Region), 657 West 37th Avenue, Vancouver, BC V5Z 1K6, Canada. Tel: 604 264 2003; Fax: 604 264 3547. E-mail: gary.bass@rcmp-grc.gc.ca

Eastern Kentucky University (Dr. Robin Haarr), Stratton Building 412A, Stratton Building, 521 Lancaster Avenue, Richmond, KY 40475, USA. Tel: 859-622-8152. E-mail: robin.haarr@eku.edu

University of Kragujevac, Faculty of Law, (Prof. Branislav Simonovic), Str. Jovanba Cvijica 1, Kragujevac, 34000 Serbia. Tel: 381 34 306 580; Fax: 381 34 306 546. E-mail: simonov@EUnet.rs

Cyber Defense & Research Initiatives (James Lewis), LLC, P.O. Box 86, Leslie, MI 49251, USA. Tel: 517 2426730. E-mail: lewisja@cyberdefenseresearch.com

Audiolex (Kate J. Storey-Whyte, PhD), 9-10 Old Police Station, Kington, Hereford, Herefordshire, HR53DP, UK. Tel: 44 7833 378 379 (mobile). Fax: 44 154 423 1965. E-mail: cj@audiolex.co.uk

Molloy College, Department of Criminal Justice (Dr. John A. Eterno, NYPD Captain, ret.), 1000 Hempstead Avenue, P.O. Box 5002, Rockville Center, NY 11571-5002, USA. Tel: 516 678 5000, Ext. 6135; Fax: 516 256 2289. E-mail: jeterno@molloy.edu

The Senlis Council, Center of Excellence on Public Safety (George Howell), Rua Maria Queteria, 121/305, Ipanema, Rio de Janeiro, RJ 22410040, Brazil. Tel: 55 21 3903 9495; Cell: 55 21 8156 6485. E-mail: howell@senliscouncil.net

The Department of Applied Social Studies, City University of Hong Kong (Li, Chi-mei, Jessica, PhD, Lecturer), Tat Chee Avenue, Kowloon Tong, Hong Kong. Tel: 2788 8839; Fax: 2788 8960. E-mail: jessica@cityu.edu.hk

University of Maine at Augusta, College of Natural and Social Sciences (Prof. Richard Mears), 46 University Drive, Augusta, ME 04330-9410, USA. E-mail: Rmears@maine.edu

South Australia Police (Commissioner Mal Hyde), Office of the Commissioner, South Australia Police, 30 Flinders Street, Adelaide, SA 5000, Australia. E-mail: mal.hyde@police.sa.gov.au

University of New Haven (Dr. Richard Ward, Criminal Justice), 300 Boston Post Road, West Haven, CT 06516, USA. Tel: 203 932 7260. E-mail: rward@newhaven.edu

International Police Association, Illinois (Kevin Gordon), 505 N. 10th Street, Mascoutah, IL 62258, USA. E-mail: Treasurer@ipa-usa.org

UNISA, Department of Police Practice (Setlhomamaru Dintwe), Florida Campus, Cnr Christiaan De Wet and Pioneer Avenues, Private Bag X6, Florida, 1710 South Africa. Tel: 011 471 2116; Cell: 083 581 6102; Fax: 011 471 2255. E-mail: Dintwsi@unisa.ac.za

Justice Studies Department, San José State University (Mark E. Correia, PhD, Chair and Associate Professor), 1 Washington Square, San José, CA 95192-0050, USA. Tel: 408 924 1350. E-mail: mcorreia@casa.sjsu.edu

Australasian Institute of Policing (Ian Lanyon), P.O. Box 99, Pascoe Vale South, Victoria, 3044, Australia. Tel: 61-3-986-58208; Fax: 61-3-986-68325; Cell: 61-9-144-6614. E-mail: ian.lanyon@aipol.org

Mount Saint Vincent University, Department of Psychology (Stephen Perrott), 166 Bedford Highway, Halifax, Nova Scotia, Canada. E-mail: Stephen.perrott@mvsu.ca

For Product Safety Concerns and Information please contact our
EU representative GPSR@taylorandfrancis.com Taylor & Francis
Verlag GmbH, Kaufingerstraße 24, 80331 München, Germany